C000140197

NOT DROWNING BUT WAVING

This copy is for
Elsbeth
not to be given away
lend away
thrown away

with
love
P.

For Peter from David Hollywood oct 1980

Drawing by David Hockney

PETER ADAM

Not Drowning but Waving

AN AUTOBIOGRAPHY

ANDRE DEUTSCH

This is a book made up of memories and friendships.
It would not have been possible to mention all the many friends
who worked with me, taught me, entertained me, put up with
me – in short, made my life richer and less lonely. For their
patience, generosity and affection I like to thank them here.

Memories are often deceptive; the errors of judgement are
entirely mine.

Special thanks go to all who, during the long time of gestation,
took time to look at my manuscript, gave council,
encouragement and ironed out many inconsistencies and
self-indulgences: Richard Bates, Mary Blume, Prunella Clough,
Steve Cox, Nigel Crewe, Paul Duncan, Paul Golding,
Salina Hastings, Andreas Landshoff, Hendrik Scheepmaker,
René Staelenberg and Hanna and Rudolf Strauss.

I like to thank Dimitri Papadimos for the use of the
Lawrence Durrell photographs. Although every effort has been
made to trace present copyright holders of the other
photographs, I apologise for any unintentional omissions.

First published in Great Britain in 1995 by
André Deutsch Limited
106 Great Russell Street
London WC1B 3LJ

Copyright © 1995 by Peter Adam
All rights reserved

CIP date for this title is available from the British Library
ISBN 0 233 98912 9
Designed by René Staelenberg
Printed and bound in Belgium
An Andreas Landshoff Production

To my friends

Les poètes eux-mêmes ne pourraient écrire leur propre vie. Il y a trop de mystères, trop de vrais mensonges, trop d'enchevêtrements. Les dates se chevauchent, les années s'embrouillent.

Even poets cannot write their own life story. There are too many mysteries, too many true lies, too many tangles. Dates blur, years grow muddled.

JEAN COCTEAU, *Opium*

I was much too far out all my life
And not waving but drowning.

STEVIE SMITH, *The Past*

Contents

Prologue
Bowing Out

'Peter Adam's departure marks the end of an era of a particular kind of documentary film-making, of a genuine sense of vocation and innovation. Peter believed that television has something to do with education, and intellectual stimulation. We will miss him, but he's not the sort of chap to worry about or to feel sorry for. Peter leaves us in order to make a new life in Paris and to live with his friend of long standing, Facundo.' These were the concluding words of a speech by Alan Yentob, controller of BBC2, in 1989, at a dinner to mark my retirement. I felt sad, elated and moved as I listened, for I was bidding farewell not only to some extraordinary, exhilarating years of work, but also to London.

One hundred and forty-seven programmes had carried the end credit 'written and directed by Peter Adam'. I was nervously clutching the statutory album, a little green leather-bound volume with the BBC crest, and beneath it, in gold letters: 'Peter Adam BBC 1968–1989'. The pages bore loving and generous messages from the many people I had worked with. Many spoke of friendship and fun. I know that it is difficult not to say something complimentary on such occasions, but to be judged by one's peers is the greatest joy for any professional, and it was here that I most wanted to have my achievements read. The 136 people who were gathered to celebrate me out were a mixture of friends and colleagues: film-makers, editors, cameramen, writers, actors, publishers, painters, the tea lady and the mailman. At the end of the meal, after the many speeches which usually mark such occasions, the lights were dimmed. On the small screens scattered around the room appeared the title: *Peter Adam, The Story So Far*. For forty minutes I watched a potted history of my professional life, a witty, warm *laudatio* which my colleagues had made as a goodbye present.

It was the most formidable and touching gift that I have ever received, a film with a cast of thousands, or 237 to be precise, among them Jeanne Moreau, Lillian Hellman, Luchino Visconti, Willy Brandt, Charles de Gaulle, Lartigue, Peter Stein, Charles Aznavour, Vera Stravinsky, Lawrence Durrell, Lotte Lenya, Hildegard Behrens, David Hockney, Hans Werner Henze, Leonard Bernstein. An intimidating array of artists I worked with. While everybody around me fell about laughing, I thought about the ambiguity of success and its ephemeral pleasure. I was suddenly woken from my reverie by a bawdy cabaret singer whom I had once filmed. She was belting out: 'Ja, das ist die Berliner Luft, Luft, Luft!' ('Yes, this is the air of Berlin'), and I joined in the general merriment. For Berlin is where my story began.

1

Adams and Cucumbers

My earliest memory harks back to when I was about three: my twin sister Renate and I sitting in a large Russian sleigh-pram, wrapped in huge blankets to shield us from the bitter Berlin winter. My mother, dressed in a long fur coat and a cloche hat, was pushing us through the smart Berlin suburb of Dahlem, walking my father to the Underground.

I also recall my sister and me sitting in the kitchen on a wooden box, being fed our favourite breakfast, *Griessbrei* – semolina pudding, on which our *Kinderfräulein*, the good Dada, had painted a colourful pattern of raspberry syrup. After breakfast we would be allowed to see our mother. She would lie on her bed, propped up by lace cushions, still weary from the previous evening's social engagement, and we would hurl ourselves at her. Mother slept in what was known as a French bed, or *matrimonial*, a misnomer in our parents' case. Although very much in love, they kept separate rooms, each with its own *matrimonial*, which was considered very modern. Of course, we children had no idea about the marital etiquette of German society, and for a long time assumed that all parents slept in separate rooms.

This was around 1932. My father worked in the Ministry of Finance, in the centre of town. He was a government councillor and legal adviser to the German Chancellor, Heinrich Brüning.

My other recollections are of rooms filled with dark antique furniture, paintings and books. One entered our apartment through a hall, furnished only with a Récamier sofa and an eighteenth-century tapestry of Diana at the Hunt. Two glass doors led to a large drawing-room, its walls covered in red damask to match the curtains. The sofas and chairs were upholstered in dark velvet or brocade. The dining-room, with its formal array of neatly spaced chairs, had a terribly intimidating effect upon us children; only when filled with people in long gowns and black tie did it seem to come to life.

My father's realm was called the *Herrenzimmer*, a dark and austere library which always smelt of cigar smoke. There he would sit writing on the same French bureau-plat his father and grandfather had used. I sometimes watched him reading, sitting upright in a large armchair, as if he considered the reclining position my mother favoured not suitable for the serious pursuit of literature. On the second floor were my parents' bedrooms and our nursery. Somewhere there must have been rooms for the three servants, but I do not recall ever having seen them.

The flat was in the Thiel Allee, a street of detached villas with well-tended gardens. My parents were what was called *gutbürgerlich* or even *grossbürgerlich*, a word that was often employed to distinguish one from the rest of the populace. We were an affluent, respectable family and lived in a style which was certainly beyond the salary of a senior councillor, my father's official title, for my father, Walter Adam, came from a wealthy Jewish family.

The Adams originally hailed from Chodescia, a small town near Schneidemühl in West Prussia. My great-great-grandfather, Jacob Adam, was born in 1789. His family traded in wool and clothes since the beginning of the eighteenth century and their commerce took them as far as Lithuania and Poland. Jacob also travelled to Berlin, in order to pay his respects, or so he claims in his journal, at the grave of one of his ancestors, Rabbi Hatzel Piller. His memoirs were written in a mixture of German and Yiddish, and are preserved in the Leo Baeck Institute in New York.

If Jacob's memoirs are to be trusted, the earliest members of my family must have been living in Berlin in 1675. What is certain is that Jacob, who spoke some French, began to trade with the French military stationed there under Napoleon. Jacob prospered from these dealings but, as a Jew, was not free to settle in Berlin. So he returned to Chodescia, where he married.

When, in 1812, the law was changed and Jews were allowed to move freely within Prussia, he and his wife made their home in Berlin. Ten years later they had one daughter, Johanna, who around 1840 was to wed her cousin, Moses Adam. In 1849 my grandfather Otto was born.

Not much is known about my grandfather's upbringing except that, by the time he was thirty, he had made 35 million goldmark. He belonged to an emerging class of businessmen fuelled by the prospect of making money in a city which was fast becoming the largest commercial centre in Europe. Many fortunes were made during those years in Berlin. The industrialist August Borsig built his first locomotive in a converted dance hall, and Werner Siemens opened a small workshop.

Otto Adam had successfully speculated in property during the so-called *Gründerjahre*, the foundation years, a period of enormous building activity during which Berlin rose to become a formidable Prussian capital. The

My grandmother Ida Adam

My grandfather Otto Adam

rapid growth was short-lived, but it changed the face of the city. The centre of the town was the old quarter around the River Spree and its handsome bridges. This was the Berlin of Kaiser Wilhelm. Its heart was the avenue Unter den Linden, which ended at the Brandenburg Gate. The avenue was flanked by the museums, the Schloss, the Cathedral, the Opera House and the war monuments. The squares in this imperial Berlin bore names like Belle Alliance or Pariser Platz. Now whole quarters were built in the neoclassical style. The famous boulevard, the Kurfürstendamm, once a simple thoroughfare to the large forest, the Grunewald, became the place where the rich chose to live. In order to avoid the wind blowing chimney smoke into their homes, the affluent colonised the west of the city while the poor made do with the east. This remains the case to this day.

By 1880 Otto Adam had risen within Jewish society by marrying Ida Seelig, a ravishing Jewess with dark features. In German society, to be painted in oils was considered the *non plus ultra*, for it broadcast respectability and good taste. The Adams sat for a fashionable portrait painter, and the full-length oil of my grandmother reveals a striking woman with a gold snake bracelet coiled up her arm. Her dark hair is piled high as if not to mask her fiery eyes. She is dressed in a splendid evening gown of white lace, which emphasises her slim waist, and a long sable coat is draped over a chair. My grandfather's portrait shows a patrician with a short, trimmed beard and moustache, standing very erect in a long morning coat.

His parents also had their portraits done in oil, but not full-length, which I presume relates to the fact that the wealth of the Adam family had grown from one generation to the next. These paintings survived three generations, with the exception of that of my great-grandmother, who, alas, had not been blessed with great looks. So her likeness was banished to the attic, where it must have perished.

The Adams had a large town house in the smart Tiergarten section of Berlin. Their street, the Matthei-Kirch-Strasse, named after the church of St Matthew, which had been built in 1844, was small and exclusive. The banker Wassermann and the industrialist Hugo Stinnes also owned houses here. The Adams' home, a rather pompous villa in the neoclassical style, was built around 1850. It was crammed with 'antique' furniture, much of it, in fact, reproductions of eighteenth-century pieces, which was meant to denote that one could afford to have one's own furniture made rather than suffer the indignity of living with second-hand objects. Some of these copies prominently displayed the family's monogram, an intertwined I, O and A: Ida and Otto Adam.

Family portraits were not the only outward sign of wealth. Dutch paintings were in vogue and the Adams owned Steen's *Farmers' Wedding* and a landscape by van Ruysdael – Salomon, not Jacob, for the Adams always seemed to fall a trifle short.

Otto and Ida Adam had given birth to two children: Alice, and my father, Walter, born on 16 November 1886. The Adams did not quite belong to the top bourgeois Jewish circles – they were never like the Oppenheimers or the Mendelssohns, whose social gatherings were the envy of the Prussian capital. Nevertheless they tried to emulate the lifestyle of the aristocracy. Each birthday was marked by a specially made cup of silver or precious porcelain, bearing an inscription such as 'To Commemorate Walter's Fifth Birthday'. Some of these trophies displayed hand-painted portraits of the children who were photographed by the Prussian or Bavarian court photographers either in rococo costumes or before painted backdrops, carrying tennis rackets and wearing boaters. Alice inherited her mother's outgoing temperament and beauty, but Walter was timid, physically unremarkable, and wore spectacles from an early age.

From all accounts the Adams were urbane and, although not religious, fiercely conscious of belonging to the ever-confident Jewish upper class. They were also patriotic, German to the core. They cheered Kaiser Wilhelm and later applauded the democracy of the Weimar Republic. My father later served in the army during the Great War – 'For the Kaiser and the Reich' – and supported the Deutsch Nationale, the centre-right party. Like most Jews, he was, and would remain, a staunch liberal, 'national-liberal' as it was known.

The Adams also owned a villa in Wannsee, a green suburb of Berlin which boasted a beautiful lake. Wannsee was not yet linked to the city centre by the S-Bahn, so on weekends the family would board the train, pulled by a steam locomotive, to travel the ten kilometres to their 'country place'. The house was a rather ugly Wilhelminian specimen, but it had a fine garden with birch trees and a large wooden terrace, the perfect setting for a Chekhov play. There were many rooms and a separate house for the numerous staff.

I never saw my grandparents' town house, but their house in Wannsee survived the war, although not in its original condition. For when the Adams lived there it had boasted a mirrored dining-room aping Versailles. Their life was circumscribed within the boundaries of decent society, with the routine of receiving and paying calls, visits to the opera or the theatre, a cultural and, most of all, a social occasion.

In the summer Mrs Adam liked to travel to Wiesbaden, 'for the waters'. While the society columns of the day announced 'the arrival of Mrs Ida

Walter

Alice

Ida Adam with her children

Adam from Berlin with two children, nineteen pieces of luggage and two maids', my grandfather would, in her absence, rush to the cabarets 'to peep at the legs of the dancing girls'. Sometimes Mrs Adam's name even made it into the very social *Morgenpost*, which eulogised her celebrated wasp-waist. My father, modest and unassuming by nature, found the behaviour of both his parents unnecessary, even distasteful.

My other grandparents, the Gurkes (*Gurke*, believe it or not, means cucumber), were the total opposite – poor, Christian, and of peasant stock. For generations they had been farmers living in and around Stendal, a small town in the Altmark, made famous by Winckelmann. The size of their farms had varied with the tide of their fortune, and at the time that my mother was born, both the farms and the fortune were at a low ebb.

My maternal great-grandparents, the Leppins, lived on a little farm in Rohrbeck. In the attic of their small farmhouse stood two empty coffins which my great-grandfather had ordered to ensure that he would be properly buried. Great-grandmother Leppin still spoke in the traditional Plattdeutsch, the patois of the northern region. She was supposed to have had miraculous healing powers, and no wedding, christening or funeral was complete without her blessing. There were many tales of her gypsy blood. Given her temperament and dark eyes, it is easy to see why. Once, when a cow knocked her off the milking stool, she cut the poor animal's tail off in a fit of rage. But my favourite anecdote relates to my grandfather's new Confirmation suit. Unknown to my great-grandmother, the local tailor had made a tailcoat for the fourteen-year-old boy; according to him, this was all the rage in France. When my great-grandmother, on the morning of the Confirmation, saw the tailcoat, she dragged the hapless boy into the woodshed and, with the same axe that had so fiercely docked the cow, hacked off the offending jacket-tails.

Around 1880 her daughter Hermine had married Gustav Gurke, my maternal grandfather. My grandmother was an industrious, simple woman who had given birth to three girls and two boys: Friedl, Emmy, Walter, Fritz, and Luise, my mother, who was born on 3 May 1892. Gustav had many professions, from farming to running a small brewery, but he had never made any money, or at least none that ever reached the family. He preferred to take out the cart and horses and roam the locality, for he fancied himself a sort of lay lawyer and would spend whole days sitting in the courts listening to cases. He later sold his experience and knowledge by travelling from village to village 'peacemaking' in marital or neighbourly disputes. His wit and theatricality at these frequent court appearances were famous throughout the region.

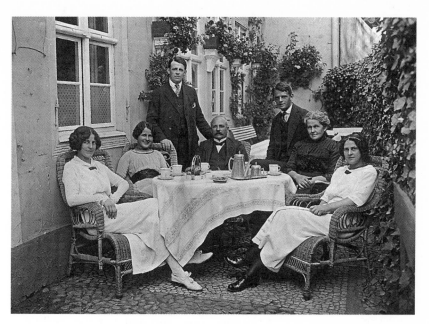

The 'Cucumbers' (Louise on the right)

My mother's childhood was spent on a small farm in Brunau. The children had a turbulent childhood. The story goes that Emmy and Luise, aged eight and ten, ran away with a travelling circus and had to be fetched home by force. The Gurke household was filled with laughter, for the three girls were always ready to clown around, Luise usually eclipsing her siblings. There was no shortage of suitors for the pretty girls, but Luise often reduced the others to tears simply by smirking as her sisters dressed for local balls. She knew that she was the prettiest and was not about to let the others forget it.

Of course there were no family portraits in oil in the Gurke household. But the few surviving sepia photographs show my grandmother as a kind-looking lady in a very correct black satin dress with a white lace collar. She sits in a country garden, flanked by a strikingly handsome gentleman with a moustache, and surrounded by their five pretty children.

The Gurke children did not see much of their father, for not only was he dashing but he was also a consummate womaniser, and my gentle, loving grandmother did not have a happy life. Hardship and pain pursued her: one son, Walter, died in the war; the other, Fritz, suffered the loss of a leg. Both she and her husband died young, my grandmother aged fifty-seven and her husband aged fifty-eight.

Although I have never seen the Gurkes' house, I am certain that they did not have silver or monogrammed furniture. In fact I never met any of my four grandparents: all had died by the time I was born.

On the third of August 1929, in a clinic in Berlin Charlottenburg, I was beaten into this world, for a quarter of an hour, by an unexpected creature, my sister Renate.

Neither of my parents was young when we were born. My mother was thirty-six and my father forty-four. They had met and married the year before our birth. The Adams had almost given up hope of seeing their son wedded. He was simply not the marrying kind, they used to say, not a ladies' man, with his bald head, glasses and slightly chubby figure. But his kind face and discreet, shy manner appealed to my mother.

My mother had previously been engaged to a painter whom she had met in the Harz, where she and her sisters earned a meagre wage as waitresses in a hotel. During a walk in the mountains, her rather pompous fiancé lost his carefully pepared road maps and, realising this, turned to my mother to confess his blunder. Luise burst into laughter and replied: 'Oh, those maps, I saw them drop out of your pocket an hour ago.' So at 2,000 feet, with the words 'Fräulein Gurke, I do not think we are suited for each other', he broke off the engagement. My mother could not have agreed more.

The three girls wanted better and more exciting things from life than jobs as waitresses and preferred the euphemism *Saaltöchter*, or 'daughters of the dining-room'. Emmy flirted with a career in films and changed her name from Gurke to Gurko, in an attempt to erase the 'cucumber' connotation. She ended up working in the canteen of the UFA studios in Berlin Babelsberg.

Friedl, who was a confirmed snob, added a *w* to the end of Gurko, which lent her surname an added Eastern flavour. She went to Heidelberg to study, she claimed, and attended Friedrich Gundolf's lectures. She considered herself an intellectual, and was unable to listen to music other than with her eyes closed in contemplation. In the end, she married the father of her child, a Dr Lauk, who soon after was killed in action in the Great War. But Friedl, like all the Gurkes, was a survivor: she began by making hats, then took a job in Berlin's labour exchange and even became mayor of a town.

Luise decided to remain a Cucumber, but inserted an *o* into her first name, to give it a French flavour. She became Louise to the world and even to her children, for she regarded being addressed as *Mutti* as far too conventional.

After the Great War, she became a nurse in a Berlin hospital. Her ebullient disposition and tireless energy earned her great popularity among patients and colleagues, but this ebullience got her into scrapes. There were stories about adjoining doors between doctors' and nurses' canteens having to be locked, because the doctors were invariably to be found at Louise's table. And then there was the scandal of the doctor who, after a midnight swim, had to sneak back to his quarters without any clothes on because nurse Louise had made off with them. There were parties and celebrations, and on one occasion Louise danced naked on a table, clad only in a black necklace which naturally matched the colour of her hair.

One never quite knew with Louise how much truth lay in her anecdotes, for she was a great *raconteuse* and could, for the sake of heightened effect, even portray herself as absurd. I, being of a similar disposition, have always wanted to believe them, but I can hardly imagine that the Adam family would have viewed such exploits with approval, never mind amusement.

For a long time my sister and I were told that our parents met at a respectable five o'clock tea. The truth was far more intriguing. On one of her days off from the hospital, my mother had gone to Kempinski, the fashionable Berlin restaurant. On her way out, she slipped on the stairs, but was caught just in time by a passing gentleman. Louise, struck either by fate or inspiration, agreed not only to be driven home in a cab, but further to a rendezvous the next weekend.

Dr Walter Adam and Fräulein Louise Gurke met for the second time at the Krumme Lanke, one of Berlin's many lakes. My mother was later to claim that they had dinner by moonlight. Louise invited her shy and distinguished suitor for a little swimming competition. There have always been doubts in the family as to the wearing of bathing costumes, but one thing is certain: when the couple reached the far side, they were engaged.

The Adams were not amused by my father's chosen bride, and referred to her as a *goyische Schickse*. Beauty hardly compensated for her poverty and lack of what they deemed breeding, or 'good stable'.

My Aunt Alice loved her brother, but she also loved the considerable collection of jewels his mother had left him. Meeting Louise, she was casually to mention the bride's 'working-class hands'. Alice spoke in French (Alice would): 'Les mains d'une ouvrière,' she remarked. My mother, though unable to understand French, was later informed of the aside, and was never to forget this wounding incident.

For their honeymoon, my parents went to fashionable St Moritz. Walter, wishing gradually to acclimatise his new bride to the height, had booked the first night in a hotel further down the slopes, a delicate gesture typical of their relationship. My mother was both touched and amused in equal doses. The next day they moved to the smart Kulm Hotel, where Louise excelled on the dance floor and Walter basked in the admiring glances that his wife received. Walter's fascination with his young, vivacious, outgoing wife, who never stopped laughing and talking, never diminished. Only once, during a sleigh ride, when her temper boiled over, did he calmly say: 'Not so wild, my dearest Louise,' a comment which might have been applied as a motto to her whole life.

Returning to Berlin, they sold my grandmother's jewels and used the proceeds towards the purchase of their new home. Soon after, Grandfather Adam died, leaving his son only a fraction of his fortune, which in any case had shrunk considerably due to speculation and maybe even the allure of the dancing girls.

'The stable always shines through' was a popular saying in those days. My mother's stable was not one to be broadcast, so my father lovingly became a Pygmalion. He took his new wife to lectures on modern art at the Galerie Friedländer on Unter den Linden, taught her to distinguish between baroque and Gothic, and instructed her in French. Louise wrote everything down like a diligent schoolgirl. Although much of this was new and exciting to her there were areas in which she needed no tuition. She

My parents

loved to dance, so she enrolled herself and her husband in a modern dance class. Walter, at the age of forty-five, was appalled by this prospect, but was incapable of refusing his wife anything, so he swore her to secrecy and consented. Alas, secrecy was not Louise's forte: one day, Chancellor Brüning walked into my father's office in the Ministry and announced: 'Your charming wife is downstairs, to fetch you for your dance lesson.'

Like all well-off people, the Adams travelled. The *Bildungsreise* (educational journey) was one of the favourite pastimes of the middle classes. Hordes of people armed with the essential Baedeker and phrasebooks boarded trains (preferably *wagons-lits*), boats and limousines to view the treasures of Europe. Walking sticks for mountain travel, and mosquito nets or pith helmets for the South, were *de rigueur*, and heavy solid leather luggage completed the ensemble.

My father had always loved to travel. A photograph shows him as a young man with his parents, mounted on a camel in front of the pyramids. But now he discovered the pleasure of travelling with an all-round enthusiast who had never been abroad and was eager to learn. There were the traditional trips of course: the Norwegian fjords, Florence, Venice and Rome. Their clutch of leather suitcases boasted colourful labels; we, the children, would decipher Hotel Baur au Lac, Zürich; Gritti Palace, Venice; the names of the glittering ships of the Hapag Lloyd line.

They recorded their travels in black and white photographs stuck into large green leather albums, each one labelled in white ink on black paper in my father's neat handwriting. There were shots of gleaming cars on the Corniche above Nice; Louise on skis wearing big bright Norwegian sweaters with knickerbocker trousers, Walter looking on; endless pictures of passengers on deckchairs, wrapped in tartan rugs or dancing on board ship. Everybody always looked so happy and relaxed, not least Louise, brown as a berry, naked as God intended, up on the beaches of the Baltic Sea.

Everyday life was very different then. At home, members of the household had their own quarters. My parents' realm was the drawing-room and library. We children ate and played in the nursery, and the servants lived in the kitchen. Children and servants were expected to knock before entering a room. We were never allowed to attend dinner parties, where bourgeois intellectuals cultivated their favourite pursuit: conversation. On Sundays, my sister and I were allowed in the dining-room for lunch. At the table one only spoke when spoken to. Conversation was about society or daily happenings. My mother's attempt to gossip was usually interrupted by my father's friendly 'Pas devant les enfants'. Money or business was never mentioned. Like most women, my mother had no income of her own: she did not work, and what she needed she received from my father. She knew nothing about bank accounts or cheque-books. The money needed was brought to the house by a special postman, the *Geldbriefträger*. In shops people paid in cash, and most purchases were delivered: food, wine, clothes.

In this regulated way of life parental authority and social customs removed a lot of agonising choices. My parents, our Dada and the two of us lived in a small world of stability, love and protection. It had an inbuilt, accepted and tested order that created an armour for the difficult times to come.

Europe was the cradle of culture, while America was still considered the Wild West. And nowhere was culture more central to society than in Berlin. Its open, liberal attitude to the new and unusual drew artists from all over the world. The 1920s were a time of experiments in all fields, social, cultural and political. Established forms and rules were broken everywhere, creating a feeling of euphoria which at times verged on despair. Fanaticism, corruption, decadence, idealism all lived side by side.

My parents' respectable bourgeois family life entailed society balls and dinners, but the centre of Berlin's social life was the theatre and the opera house. The Deutsches Theater drew *le tout* Berlin to the productions under Max Reinhardt, or to the Schauspielhaus under Leopold Jessner, with new plays by Ibsen, Hauptmann, Schnitzler, Kaiser and Wedekind. The society met in and dressed for the Premieren, opening nights. Louise's lifelong love for the theatre was forged in the first year of her marriage, and she never tired of telling us about evenings with the great stars of the German theatre like Joseph Kainz, Alexander Moissi, Tilla Durieux, Hélène Thimig, Maria Orska and, one of my mother's favourites, the chanteuse Fritzi Massary, whose blend of lasciviousness and elegance she admired along with a million other Berliners.

Like thousands of others, Louise claimed that she and my father attended the opening night of Brecht and Weill's *Dreigroschenoper* at the Schiffbauerdamm theatre in 1928. Later she was to describe how, when the curtain came down, the audience booed and whistled while others supposedly hurled their pearl necklaces onto the stage because someone had shouted: 'Bread for the poor!'

Like all cultured Germans my parents held subscriptions to concerts of the Berlin Philharmonic, where a young Wilhelm Furtwängler had taken over from Artur Nikisch as chief conductor. They also went regularly to the opera. Richard Strauss conducted at the Königliche Oper, the Opera in Charlottenburg played under Bruno Walter, and Otto Klemperer was musical director of the Kroll Oper. Louise knew nothing about music, but loved it, and to the end of her life attended concerts. Questioned once as to what she thought of a Karajan concert, she replied: 'Ein bisschen zu viel Musik.'[1]

Berlin also had a lively literary life: 175 newspapers and 150 magazines were printed here, and the city played host to some of the most influential publishing houses of the time, like Ullstein and Fischer, the first to publish the works of Gerhart Hauptmann, Thomas Mann and Hugo von Hofmannsthal and the German translations of Henrik Ibsen, August Strindberg and Leo Tolstoy.

My parents were not especially intellectual or daring in their cultural pursuits. Although they attended lectures on modern art at the Galerie Friedländer, they did not really like or understand it. Modern art to them was the Impressionists, Liebermann and Corinth, certainly not Picasso and Braque, never mind Paul Klee or Kandinsky, who were considered too avant-garde. At home, we subscribed to Avenarius' *Kunstwart*, a conservative arts magazine, rather than Herwarth Walden's *Der Sturm*, which from 1919 to 1932 represented the truly modern.

Like all respectable Germans, my father had a considerable library. It too reflected his conventional taste, for there were the standard classics, German, English, French and Latin, rows and rows of them, bound in leather – Herder, Hebbel, Shakespeare, Tolstoy, Racine, Socrates and, of course, Goethe and Schiller, Kant, Schopenhauer and Nietzsche. They had Wedekind and Freud, but no Kafka or Thomas Mann, nor any of the other contemporary authors. On the whole the library epitomised the reading fashion of a conservative society; most of its contents was reassuring, devoid of existential *Angst* – except for a sprinkling of Scandinavian literature in translation, Ibsen and Strindberg. All of Walter Scott's novels were there, in English, all of Maupassant, in French, yet neither Proust nor James Joyce.

Life was rosy bliss, or so it seemed. Few people could have imagined, in 1927 or 1928, a world economic crisis, much less that the small and noisy National Socialist Party would ever gain power. Hitler was mostly viewed as a rowdy upstart who could not really harm them. But then the crash happened and threw everybody, particularly the rich, into disarray. The famous Golden Twenties were not all that golden, for beneath the glittering surface the foundations were beginning to shake. The trauma of an inflation which pushed the cost of an egg up to 30 million marks, the

1 'A little bit too much music.'

humiliation following the treaty of Versailles, which had stripped Germany of all its colonies, and the millions of unemployed all reinforced the call for a new order. The Weimar Republic was seen by many as a time of chaos, corruption and decadence. In September 1930 the NSDAP, Hitler's party, suddenly had a big gain. To many, tired of the prevailing chaos, the National Socialists appeared strong and orderly and their dynamic leader seemed to bear a kind of mission, the promise of a brighter, better future. Yet with five million people out of work, many carried on with their businesses as if nothing had happened. My father reported that he had seen people in uniform, with a swastika on their armband, walking right in front of the Ministry in the Wilhelmstrasse while people just looked out of their office windows and laughed.

My parents, oblivious to the rise of Hitler and his followers, hardly ever talked about politics. They lived their cosy bourgeois existence and hoped that everything would blow over. The Nazis, who frequently quoted Goethe and Schiller, the Nibelungen and Luther, and revered Holbein and Dürer – the same cultural luggage my father had been brought up on – could not be altogether barbaric.

The first inkling of the future was gleaned when during a Brecht-Weill première, Brownshirts marched through the theatre and broke up the performance. My parents left feeling rather pale. Anti-Semitic slogans appeared on walls and many right-wing papers began openly to denounce the Jews.

It has always been assumed that hundreds of thousands of Jews lived in Berlin. This was not the case. A third of all German Jews lived in Berlin, but that amounted only to 6 per cent of the capital's population. Yet, for many, Berlin felt like a city run by Jews, for almost half of all doctors and lawyers were Jewish, and a third of all university professors. Jews seemed to hold all the prestigious posts in the world of theatre, music and film. Jews ran half of the banks and owned most of the big department stores. They were rich, and, as my mother remarked, the occasional ostentatious displays of jewellery at the Red White Tennis Club annual ball could be seen as evidence to support this prevailing myth. Anti-Semitism was most rife in the more conservative circles, as in Julius Streicher's obscene tirades on the Jews that appeared in the magazine *Der Stürmer* as early as 1923.

Socially, Jews only received Jews but they had to be the right type of Jews; from the liberal, urban, professional class. Jewish tradesmen from the East were looked down on. 'Don't talk with your hands,' my father would reprimand us, 'this is Jewish.' We were also told to sit up straight in order to avoid a 'Jewish hunch'. To read Hebrew was all right, but Yiddish most certainly not. My father, like most Jews of his acquaintance, did not regard himself primarily as a Jew, for he was not orthodox. He was above all German, and accordingly fully integrated into the fabric of the nation. Generations like him had been raised on the traditional values of German culture, married into other religions and attended mixed schools.

Yet many of my parents' Jewish friends prepared to leave: the Adler-Oppenheimers, who had leather factories in Luxemburg, the Lazaruses, the Freudenheims. My Aunt Alice, who had married a prominent lawyer, shrugged it all off. 'They won't do anything to us,' she said. 'We are too well known, they would not dare.' She, like many others who had never bothered to read Hitler's *Mein Kampf*, which spelled out his whole pro-gramme, mocked his ranting about blood and soil and the purity of the German race.

The National Socialists had soared in strength, and in January 1933 Hitler took power. A few days later, a letter arrived in our home informing my father that, on account of his race, his services at the Ministry were no longer required. It came as quite a shock, as he was only forty-eight. With-in a year the Communist party had been banned and the trade union movement dismantled. Nor did the Nazis lose much time in purging the German arts of 'Jewish impurities', and the cultural landscape of Berlin was changed forever. Every day my father would come home with news of yet more people leaving Germany, many of them famous household names, admired and applauded. The list of those who were deprived of their jobs and forced out of their homeland grew and grew. A few names stand for many: the musicians Arnold Schoenberg, Hans Eisler, Kurt Weill, Bruno Walter, Otto Klemperer, Fritz Busch, Arthur Schnabel; the writers Thomas Mann, Bertolt Brecht, Stefan Zweig and Franz Werfel. The theatre lost Leopold Jessner, Max Reinhardt, Erwin Piscator, Elisabeth Bergner, Lotte Lenya and Peter Lorre; the cinema, Billy Wilder and Fritz Lang. Pictures by Max Beckmann, Paul Klee, Otto Dix, Max Ernst and Wassily Kandinsky were removed from museums.

The impoverishment of Germany's cultural life was staggering. News-papers and magazines folded or were closed overnight. Every cultural ac-tivity was now controlled by the Reich's Cultural Chambers under Dr Joseph Goebbels, who took the absurd title of Minister of Enlightenment and Propaganda. After Hitler he became the second most important man in the land. Many artists, however, seemed not to mind, and within a short time these Cultural Chambers boasted 100,000 members, among them 15,000 architects, 17,000 painters and sculptors, 2,000 publishers and art dealers, and thousands upon thousands of writers, film-makers, actors and musicians. All had decided to toe the party line, trading the pioneer's spirit, the daring artistic exploration, for which Berlin was renowned, for the most trivial, narrow-minded ideas.

My parents looked on in disbelief at this frightening sell-out of artistic and intellectual integrity. For some artists it was a blend of cowardice, opportunism and political blindness. Some were simply taken in by the regime, and when they awoke it was often too late.

Many of our Jewish friends had by now left the country, and my parents sat about with those who remained and endlessly wondered where to go and what to do. England and America were considered the best options, but my parents spoke no English and for my father to start a new career on the brink of fifty seemed an impossibility.

Every time another family left we inherited more toys, which suited us fine. Our nursery began to fill up: there were the teddy bears of the Lazarus children and the dolls of Moishe Adler. There were some children we were quite glad to see no longer: Moishe Adler was a terrible little snob, who had asked for caviar at a children's party.

There was no longer any question of holding on to our expensive apartment, and in 1934 we moved to Cologne, where my father found a job as legal adviser to a large department store, Schloss und Levi. A new chapter of our life began.

2

Disorder and Early Sufferings

1933–1939

Life was suddenly less glamorous and without much lustre. Gone was the excitement we had experienced watching mother and father dress for the theatre or for soirées. Gone too was the ritual of elegant dinner guests coming up to the nursery to wish us good-night, which had always been the highlight of the evening for us. My parents' frequent journeys abroad were a thing of the past.

I missed most of all the balmy months spent on the small island of Hiddensee in the Baltic Sea. Hiddensee was a small and narrow island. If you stood on the dunes, you could see the sea all around you. From the white sandy beaches, the fishermen set out at night. We would find large pieces of amber thrown up by the rough sea. On either end stood a tall lighthouse, and there were no roads. The only means of transport between the three fishing villages was by horse-drawn cart, or on foot through miles and miles of heather. It was a blissful haven for artists. The great German writer Gerhart Hauptmann lived here, as did many painters and actors. The dark figure of the silent-film star Asta Nielsen, whose real name was Apolonia Chalupiec, and the maker of the famous Käthe Kruse dolls owned houses here. There was only one very small hotel. My mother, Aunt Emmy, a nanny and the two of us went to occupy a little thatched cottage with no running water. At weekends my father would join us, having travelled by train from Berlin to the city of Stralsund, from where, once a day, an old ship linked the mainland with Hiddensee. The boat's arrival was the sole event among glorious monotonous days of wind, sun and sand. My father, a pale and dignified figure in golfing trousers, looked somehow out of place, especially in the company of the two 'blackamoor' ladies my mother and her sister had become.

In Cologne my parents rented a large comfortable house with a garden in the suburb of Lindental. To make a new life in a city with hardly any friends was almost impossible. As a Jew my father had to maintain a low profile, so my parents kept mostly to themselves. Whenever they entertained, the conversation centred on the subject of emigration, where to and how. Grown-ups studied the atlas like schoolchildren. In South Amer-

The family on Hiddensee

ica doctors were needed, they were told; in South Africa, lawyers. Visas were not easy to come by. Most countries seemed to conspire to make immigration for German Jewish families as difficult as possible. 'You need to have money to be allowed out, and affidavits,' my father would explain. 'Some professions, intellectual ones, have it easier than others.' Those with no connections were condemned to remain.

With thoughts of emigrating to Spain, my parents began to learn Spanish, which in view of the imminent civil war was a further reflection of their political naïvety. Everywhere people were packing and repacking. What to take, what to leave, people spoke of nothing else. My parents constantly debated whether to take money or any of their paintings. We children did not notice much of their anguish. On the surface, our life appeared as normal as that of our friends, 'Aryans' and Jews alike.

Renate and I were not baptised or confirmed, despite having a Protestant mother and a Jewish father. There was no mesuza or menorah in our household. We were told nothing about the Jewish religion or its history. The meaning of life instead manifested itself in a proper education and a love for the arts. Of course we had to pray, for evening prayers were an important ritual in all German families, whatever your religion. With clasped hands and humbly we prayed: 'Lieber Gott mach mich fromm, dass ich in den Himmel komm.'[1] This was followed by a long list of people for God to protect: Mummy, Daddy, Aunt Emmy, Dada, Renate. I dragged the list out, adding more and more names in order not to have to go to sleep. Louise usually interrupted my litany with a kiss. 'That's enough dear, we'll pray tomorrow for the others.' But before she could leave the room I would burst into yet another prayer: 'My heart is pure, I am your...' Switching off the light put an end to my unsolicited pious outburst.

We were first-degree *Mischlinge,* as the Nazis called all people of mixed Jewish and Christian blood – a hideous word which used to haunt us. By way of protection for his children my father decided to have us baptised. Cologne was Catholic, and the Catholics seemed to be more powerful at protecting *Mischlinge* than the Protestants.

In the ruling of the Church, a little bit of water over the forehead and the words 'I baptise you in the name of Christ' would have been quite sufficient, at least in an emergency such as this. Yet the Adam snobbery surfaced at this point, and we were dragged into Cologne Cathedral. Nothing less would suffice. So it came to pass that Renate and Klaus-Peter were, at the age of five, admitted into the Roman Catholic Church. Like my parents' Spanish lessons, the Catholic baptism turned out to be a total

1 'Dear God make me pious, so that I may enter your kingdom.'

miscalculation, for Hitler did not care if you were baptised or not. Only race counted, and to him we were indelibly Jewish.

Renate and I were also sent to the local school. The first day was traumatic. We all arrived with a *Schultüte*, a large and colourful cone-shaped bag filled to the brim with sweets (dental care was not such a priority in those days). I was wearing a sailor's tunic with short trousers, and Renate a blue dress. Her long pigtails ended in a large white bow. Many children, my sister included, spontaneously burst into tears at the sight of the teacher in his dark suit and the orderly rows of wooden desks. Accompanying mothers, trying to console their offspring, forced yet more sweets upon them, and my lasting memory of this first day at school is of many children sobbing and several being sick.

School began at 8.00 with loud and military shouting of 'Heil Hitler!' We would spend hours copying row upon row of Gothic characters on little slates. The screech of chalk on the teacher's blackboard gives me goose pimples to this day. Our schoolbooks were crammed with the blond, beautiful Aryan heroes of German folklore, and children building sandcastles on the beach decorated with the ubiquitous swastika formed out of seashells. We were too young and too scared to question any of this, and the teacher's authority was absolute.

Some of our classmates had a book called *Trust no Fox and no Jew*, which featured a blond youth with a spade and beneath him the following rhyme:

> Der Deutsche ist ein starker Mann,
> Der arbeiten und kämpfen kann.
> Weil er schön ist und voll Mut,
> Hasst ihn von jeher schon der Jud.[1]

On another page was the drawing of a monstrous-looking creature with a crooked nose, carrying an attaché case, and under him the ditty:

> Das ist der Jud, das sieht man gleich.
> Der grösste Schuft im ganzen Reich.
> Er meint dass er der Schönste sei
> Und ist so hässlich doch dabei.[2]

---

1 'The German is a strong man, / Work and fight he can. / He is beautiful, brave and true, / So he's hated by the Jew.'
2 'This is the Jew as one can see, / The greatest villain in the land. / He thinks that he's the handsomest. / And so he's hated by the rest.'

It was shameful for us to read such verses and we vowed to tell nobody that we belonged to this 'ugly' race.

One day, on the way home from school, my sister and I unwittingly made our first political protest. A row of posters adorned a nearby wall depicting the man most hated by us, the man who was responsible for us having to leave our beloved Dada in Berlin. We began to tear the poster of Hitler off the wall, but were stopped by a young man who marched us home. My mother turned pale after she learned what we had done, and mumbled something like 'Stupid children'. Fortunately for us the unknown man took the matter no further.

That evening, my father gave us a lesson in politics. He told us about the Jews and the Nazis and about the difficulties awaiting those who, like us, had Jewish blood. This was the first time that we were made to feel outcasts. Children of five have only one desire, to be liked by everyone else. Their allegiance is to their home, to their school, perhaps even to their forest and their street. They have no inkling about fatherland or nations. That night, as we listened to my father's grave voice, the seeds of hatred towards Germany and my countrymen were sown. Everything changed. We became secretive, cautious and mistrustful in school and in play. We had grown up a little bit.

In the meantime my parents continued to debate the subject of emigration. It was such an enormous decision more than halfway through your life, to leave the country where you grew up, the language and culture you loved and the landscapes and customs you were used to. News came from France, America and England, about the difficulties and troubles which people had to face there; stories of wives earning a pittance as charwomen, whole families huddled into crowded lodgings. These were not people used to poverty and scrimping. Most of them came from spoiled, comfortable middle-class backgrounds and had spent many protected years in interesting, lucrative and respected professions. Now they sat in a country they knew little of, with a language they did not understand, grieving for their friends, their gardens, their books and their orderly existence, endured rather than invited.

'Maybe it will all blow over soon,' my mother sometimes said with feeble conviction. 'Why change a comfortable life for the unknown?' This was in 1935. The horrors of Hitler's Germany had not reached everybody, not even those most concerned.

We were spared the decision whether to leave or to stay when my father fell terminally ill with lung cancer. My mother resumed her role as nurse and stayed with him in hospital. She nursed him for eight months and shared his room. Walter Adam died on 11 November 1935, at the age of fifty. To my mother it was the end of nine years of laughter and happiness with the kindest and most considerate human being she had ever known. She now had to face a future in Germany with two small, half-Jewish children and no one to turn to.

We hardly recognised the darkly veiled woman who took us in her arms, mustered her strength and announced: 'Your father is dead, the three of us are now alone, we must love each other very much.' We children were spared the funeral and the conventions which accompany death.

Death means little to a child of six. Our inexperience protected us from total grief. In the weeks that followed I slowly began to realise that the man whom I had so often watched shaving would never again appear in my life, and for the first time I experienced a feeling of numb hollowness.

My mother proved courageous. Defeat was not in her vocabulary. Since there was no reason for us to remain in Cologne, she decided to return to Berlin, and make a new life for herself and her children. She had been left a comfortable income, and the Nazis, strangely enough, agreed to pay her a widow's pension. Furthermore, as the three of us were Christians, what could Hitler possibly do to us?

In Berlin my mother began to look for land to build a house on. The suburb of Dahlem was out of the question, not only because it was far too expensive but also because the National Socialist clique all owned houses there. Nothing would induce my mother to rub shoulders with one of them, even at the butcher's.

Louise found a small plot right next to an idyllic pine forest in the Berlin suburb of Nikolassee. She engaged an architect and commissioned what was then known as an *englisches Landhaus*, an English country house, an architectural style which had been in vogue ever since Hermann Muthesius, founder of the German Werkbund, had built in Nikolassee after working with Mackintosh in Glasgow.

Ours was a very much reduced version of Muthesius's rather grand red brick villas, but it was an attractive house nevertheless – the house where my mother was to die, and my sister was to marry and raise her children, and which, fifty-five years later, still belongs to my family. It was always known as the 'Waldhaus', the forest house. I lived there until I left home.

I never understood what it was that was so 'English' about this house, apart from an open fireplace, which was considered very Anglo-Saxon. Very few people had one in Germany, as my mother frequently pointed out. It was certainly very different from the surrounding villas, with their modernised look and straight lines. The most prominent feature, apart from the large low hanging tiled roof, was a pergola with a large thatched roof, like an outdoor living-room. Ironically, with its gaily painted wooden shutters, it was a Nazi dream of a house, in line with their love for quaint vernacular styles and their hatred for flat roofs.

We kept the old furniture, even if some of it was too grand for the size of the new house, notably my grandfather's Louis XV bureau with ormolu handles. The colour of the wood of a baroque armoire and the rich leather bindings of my father's books along the walls lent a feeling of warmth and bourgeois respectability which Louise was determined to preserve at all costs. There was no space for the large Brussels tapestry of Diana at the Hunt, but Ruysdael's *Forest Scene* took up the pride of place.

Renate and I had our own bedrooms with an adjoining door – no conventional children's rooms with toys and a bed, more like small sitting-rooms, with a desk, sofa bed and washbasin. For Louise had very precise ideas about independence, even for six-year-old children.

The bathroom was no ordinary bathroom. It had a bath and separate shower cubicle and was entirely black. At a time when even in middle-class families the bathing ritual was restricted to one bath per week – usually on Fridays – the presence of a bathtub and separate shower smacked of extravagance. A black bathroom was considered *louche*. In 1936 no one had a black bathroom, certainly not in Nikolassee. A further reason for Louise to have one.

Renate and I still had to go to school, so the Adam twins joined the local primary school, the West Volksschule. Our slate boards had been replaced by notebooks and the Gothic characters had become Roman, for Hitler associated Gothic writing with Jewishness. But, unsurprisingly, the academic day still kicked off with a rousing 'Heil Hitler!' We sat in pairs on hard wooden benches, which were stained with the ink of previous generations. It was a soulless learning of facts and figures with very little room for personal exploration.

By the time we returned to Berlin in 1935 the city had changed a lot, but even the Nazis had not yet managed to completely throttle its spirit. Germany did not yet feel like one big prison. For most people, the first few years of the regime represented a return to normality. People again had work and money. They could travel abroad.

Berlin was less National Socialist than other major cities and fewer people greeted each other with 'Heil Hitler!' Those who craned their necks to see their Führer mostly came from the provinces. Hitler had always mistrusted Berlin's liberalism, preferring the cosiness of Munich. The Prussian capital's cosmopolitanism had been a thorn in his flesh; he linked the big city with capitalism, decadence, modern art, homosexuality and Bolshevism. Until he eliminated them, all of these things were there in abundance.

The 1936 Olympic Games made Berlin appear both international and open-minded. Gone were the anti-Semitic slogans which had defaced the walls. Even the hateful newspaper *Der Stürmer* disappeared temporarily from the newsstands. Millions of foreign tourists flocked to the city to see the new stadium Hitler had built as a showpiece of the new Reich with its emphasis on health and a new monumental art.

Hitler's propaganda machine ran at full speed. There were brand-new cars everywhere, the open Mercedes and the Volkswagen. People were elegantly dressed and looked content. It all seemed so exciting. The venerable Richard Strauss wrote and conducted the Olympic anthem. It was all so very civilised that many were taken in. Everybody, even my mother, attended the Games, regardless of the fact that Hitler himself had inaugurated them. He had simply used the sports festival to seduce people into believing that a great future lay ahead. Germany took many of the gold medals, and with them it had finally removed the shame of the treaty of Versailles, responsible – as it was repeatedly drummed into us at school – both for the loss of all our colonies and for our deep national humiliation. Even we were fooled by the jamboree. We went to watch the Americans and the Blacks, the Chinese and the Indians in their saris. I remember seeing my first painted toenail peeping out of a pair of sandals belonging to an Indian lady.

The next year brought another great feast: the whole town was decked like a stage set for Mussolini's state visit, and Hitler once more wanted to give the impression of open-mindedness. There was a Marlene Dietrich week in the Kurbel, with *Shanghai Express,* and at the Marmorhaus people queued to see *On the Avenue,* the musical film based on the songs of Irving Berlin. Hitler had forbidden swing, but people danced in the Femina Bar to the music of Louis Armstrong, and records of Duke Ellington were sold in thousands. Meanwhile to the opera house came the ballet *Le Baiser de la Fée* by the 'cultural Bolshevik' Stravinsky, one of the many contradictions of the time. But this euphoria was short-lived. The minute the last tourist had left, Hitler tightened the reins.

To accommodate some of the 8,000 Jews who had worked in the theatre, the Nazis had allowed them a Jewish theatre and concert hall. This was part of their attempt to keep them in a ghetto-like existence. 'Aryans' were forbidden to attend. It was the only place where one could still hear the music of Mahler and Mendelssohn. Jewish actors performed in plays by Schnitzler, Zweig and Pirandello, all authors banned from the German stage, the former for being Jewish, the latter for being too avant-garde. Plays by Goethe and music by Mozart were prohibited in the Jewish theatre, for fear of seeing these German icons soiled in the hands of Jews.

Sixty-five Jewish newspapers were still published in Germany, most of them busily informing the Jewish population about possibilities to emigrate. A few Jewish schools and libraries remained open. Jews still had their doctors: 3,000 were still practising, as were a small number of lawyers. But all this would suddenly change. By the end of 1938, Jewish doctors, lawyers, chemists and veterinarians· were no longer allowed to exercise their profession. This was only the beginning of the myriad inhuman or petty laws which were to weigh down the lives of those too poor to leave the country.

For us children Berlin meant, most of all, old friends – our lovely Aunt Emmy, whose laughter would fill the house, and Annemarie, Friedl's 'love-child', who had become a journalist. Aunt Alice and her husband Job Sieskind were still in Berlin. My uncle was no longer allowed to practise, but he and his wife continued to live in their grand apartment. They still spoke French at table, and hid among the seventeenth-century tapestries as if nothing were happening.

This was in 1937, two years before the outbreak of war. Job was in the kitchen, learning from his cook how to make pancakes, hoping as a last resort at least to make a living by working in some restaurant. Aunt Alice, immaculately dressed, sat at a little easel painting a watercolour, just as she had done for the last thirty years. The fact that they were soon to become penniless refugees hardly crossed their minds. The next day they were gone, chased away, both aged sixty. They caught the last train to Sweden, taking with them only one painting: Steen's *Farmers' Wedding*, which they soon had to sell in order to survive. The Nazis were quick to occupy their apartment with the damask wall coverings, the Meissen porcelain figures and the antique furniture.

At least they were spared the terrible experience of the Kristallnacht, the night of the shattered glass. On 10 November 1938, Louise was suddenly called by friends, and we rushed into town. Smoke billowed from the synagogue at the corner of the Fasanenstrasse. The Kurfürstendamm was covered in broken glass. The stores belonging to Jews, which for years had borne horrid signs like 'Boycott Jewish shops', 'Don't buy from Jews', had had their windows smashed. People looked on silently, some even seemed embarrassed. One man said loudly: 'Damned shame', but then he too shut up. In the same night 25,000 Jews were arrested and taken to concentration camps.

With the departure of the Sieskinds, the last link with the Adam family was broken. From now on the Gurkes were to take over, armed with their energy and their love of life. *Nicht unterkriegen lassen*, 'Don't give in', was their motto. This attitude has also been mine.

One day I was amazed to see a girl arrive at school in a cart drawn by two white ponies. She even carried a food box with bananas, a luxury not affordable to everybody. She was Goebbels's daughter, Helga. I remember this because we were told that all of Goebbels's children bore names starting with *H* in honour of Hitler: Helga, Hildegard, Helmut, Holde, Hedda and Heidi. They seemed to live a charmed life, for the Goebbelses lived on an island, Schwanenwerder, in one of the nearby lakes.

When she heard that the child of one of the top ringleaders of the regime was in the same school, Louise prepared to move us, but when she found out that Helga was not in the same class, she simply told us to ignore her. Our mother's moment came at a school meeting. She always wore fetching hats, larger and more spectacular than most other mothers, a fact that made Renate and myself cringe. On this particular occasion, she found herself seated next to a lady in an even more grandiose confection than her own. This was Mrs Goebbels, a friendly lady who politely introduced herself. Louise coolly replied: 'I am Mrs Adam', a name which, though borne by many Christian families, held a strong Jewish connotation. Louise then proceeded to sit somewhere else.

My mother's resistance could often assume a childish form. Holidaying in South Germany, we were woken in the middle of the night by Louise, who handed us a box of drawing-pins. 'This place is full of Nazis,' she declared. 'Let's teach them a lesson!' Stumbling half-asleep along the deserted corridors of the hotel, we dropped drawing-pins into the rows of shoes which awaited polishing outside the rooms. But, alas, our mother decided to leave the hotel before we could hear the wails of the injured Nazis. Ineffectual as this ruse was, it left us in no doubt as to which side of the fence we were on.

Not that we had much chance of meeting real Nazis. Most people we knew – our neighbours, the teachers in our school – were docile and tried to remain as apolitical as possible. Some were privately opposed to Hitler, but they held their peace and showed no outward sign of rebellion.

We went to the Catholic church on Sundays, and at Christmas we attended the Protestant service with our mother. We were brought up not to see much difference between the two religions. On the whole my sister and I were still sheltered from political reality. We went to school, played cowboys and Indians in the forest, doctors and nurses in our cellar. Cops and robbers was my favourite game. Hide and seek I always found silly, as it gave no opportunity for role-playing.

Renate and I were avid readers. At first we had delighted in the fairy-tale world of *Hänschen im Blaubeerwald* and shuddered at the cruelty of Struwwelpeter. Now we advanced to *Dr Kleinermacher,* the story of a man who made children so small that they could crawl inside plants. My favourite was *Carlos und Nicholas*, which had a Chinese cook who rolled out pastry on his stomach. We also read Hugh Lofting's *Dr Dolittle*, A. A. Milne's *Winnie der Bär* and the fairy-tales of Selma Lagerlöf.

Louise loved us, but she did not concern herself much with child psychology. Healthy eating had to do not with vitamins, but with 'drinking fresh milk and eating butter'. But for depression, a word which nobody used, our mother prescribed fresh air. When we were good we were given sweets, when we were bad we were in for a hiding. The choice of sweets was small. Sometimes we got some caramels or bought a pennyworth of licorice. It came with a pretty ring for girls and a death's head for boys. It tasted horrible, and turned our mouths into a black hole. There was no Fanta, or cola. Children drank milk or water and sometimes *Brause*, a carbonated drink made by mixing water with little sachets of green or red powder. One of the great pleasures was to forgo the water and to put a bit of the powder in your hand and spit onto it: within seconds the powder would begin to rise with a sizzling noise and transform into a green, gooey substance that we would lick off our palms with great gusto.

We had few toys. As I grew older I was given a toy train with electric rails and a puppet theatre which I loved. I would invite the whole family to watch me perform: I took the whole matter most seriously and one day, when Aunt Emmy burst into uncontrollable giggles during one of my performances, I was so deeply offended and angered that I hurled the entire theatre to the ground. Touchiness and rage remain two of my less endearing characteristics.

Parents used to organise children's tea parties where we drank hot chocolate and ate home-made cakes. Guests would arrive smartly dressed and leave covered in chocolate. Louise would string up lanterns and we would play *Topfschlagen*, a version of treasure hunt, which entailed running blindfold through the garden with a wooden spoon until one struck the pot in which a present was hidden. This could also account for the occasional black eye.

Faced with the political situation, how could we have led such ordinary lives? Why did we never discuss what had happened to Aunt Alice and Uncle Job or what had become of all the children whose toys we still owned? Was it self-protection or Louise's dislike of her in-laws that made her silent? All those disagreeable truths had somehow been pushed aside from our lives. But from time to time reality disrupted our cosy existence and on each occasion it left a scar.

Our beloved Dada returned to look after us, not full-time, but whenever there was a gap between our many maids. She would sometimes take me to the small flat which she shared with her sister and brother-in-law in Moabit, the east end of Berlin, where the working classes lived. Moabit, Wedding, Kreuzberg and the area around the Alexanderplatz were a different Berlin from the one we normally saw. This was the real Berlin, the Berlin of the milieu, or *Milljöh*, as Berliners called it. 'Det is mein Milljöh' ('this is my Milljöh') sang Claire Waldorf, Berlin's most beloved chanteuse. People spoke with a broad Berlin accent. ('Icke, dette, kieke mal, Oogen, Flesch und Beene, nein mein Kind so heest det nich Augen, Fleisch und Beine' was a famous saying.)

The typical Berlin apartment block consisted of a house at the front facing the street, and a house at the back separated by an inner courtyard. Property speculators like my Grandfather Adam had made fortunes by building rented barracks, sometimes three to four blocks deep with small courtyards between.

Wealth and misery existed side by side; the first behind elaborate stuccoed façades in the front, the second behind the plain and soot-stained brick walls at the back. The buildings in the front were light, had sanitation, carpets on the stairs and sometimes even a lift; those in the back, the *Hinterhäuser*, had none of these amenities. The staircase in front smelled of furniture wax, the one out back smelled of cats and boiled cabbage. Dada lived in the back. To reach her flat you had to cross the inner courtyard with its row of outside lavatories. This was Dada's *Milljöh*. Every time she took me to her home, I was filled with excitement. I was served hot chocolate and gargantuan pieces of cake with whipped cream. Through the open window came the sounds of the courtyard; the chatter of women, with a cigarette dangling from the corner of their mouth, leaning on their windowsills to exchange some gossip. Occasionally the tunes of a barrel organ would be interrupted by the clank of pennies dropping into the beggar's tin plate. Children played hopscotch among cats and dogs. The maids would beat the Persian carpets, which were suspended from iron bars, and clouds of dust would rise to the third floor and into Dada's flat.

Here I spent some of my favourite afternoons. I found it more exciting than going to the zoo or to the Museum of Natural History. This was theatre. Dada's courtyard may have been dark and dingy but it was also where the real heart of Berlin beat.

Dada's brother-in-law, Wilhelm, sold coal from a barrel. He and his wife had a boy called Muckel, who was the apple of their eye. They also had an allotment by the tracks of the railway line. These too were part of the *Milljöh*. Thousands of Berliners had an allotment with a tiny hut on it.

They had no running water or electricity, but they displayed lace curtains on the windows and a small gravel path with two garden gnomes. One of Wilhelm's gnomes proudly displayed the golden Party medal (ordinary Party members had a simple medal, more 'trusted' members got a gold one) – a disrespectful addition painted by Wilhelm with Muckel's help.

The working class was not so enamoured of Hitler as was the lower middle class. Until the Nazis came to power, the central districts of Berlin were 'red'. In 1932 the Communists had been the strongest party in the city. Wilhelm had never been a member of the Communist party, but he had attended the May Day demonstration when the Nazis had opened fire. And ever since that day, he had hated the Brownshirts.

Hitler did his best to seduce the working classes. Not that he had much luck with the likes of Wilhelm, but many fell for the Nazi propaganda machine. Travel, which hitherto had been the preserve of the rich, was now for everybody. The organisation KdF – *Kraft durch Freude* (Strength through Joy) – was in charge of organising party-sponsored mass tourism, which was the Party's way of controlling people's spare time. Workers travelled for a fraction of the normal fare and stayed in hotels at reduced rates. There were museum visits, dances and theatre. Everything was shrewdly underpinned with racial and political indoctrination.

Every year 100,000 people sailed on the ships of the KdF Flotilla. Gone were class distinctions, as everybody travelled *Einheitsklasse* (One Class Only). A trip from Bremen to Norway, with seven days on board, cost only 42 marks. This was the life that until now most people only knew from the cinema. Everywhere we heard rapturous tales about a fortnight on Corfu or Madeira, and all for under 50 marks – the equivalent of one week's salary.

Wilhelm, his wife and their son Muckel had once joined an excursion to the island of Rügen. It was the first time they had seen the sea and sat on a beach. But Wilhelm found the speeches and the chanting of party songs disgusting. Later he commented: 'We are better off at home, and in any case Muckel got sunburn. This is not for the likes of us.'

There were other perks. Most households owned a radio by now – Hitler had seen to this. It was called the *Volksempfänger* (People's radio). Giant posters claimed: 'Das ganze Volk hört den Führer.'[1] It was one of the Nazis' most powerful weapons of propaganda. For 990 marks you could even buy a Volkswagen – quite a lot of money, but you could buy saving stamps towards the purchase. There was no question of Wilhelm being able to afford a car, but of course he had a radio.

Before selling coal from a barrel, Wilhelm had worked in a factory, and

1 'The whole nation listens to the Führer.'

the Nazis had modernised it. They had installed proper showers and in the canteen a bust of Hitler. Workers were offered milk and hot food instead of the sandwiches their wives had made for them at home, but Wilhelm was not fooled. He saw the ulterior motive of these campaigns for better light and better working conditions, so he left and began to sell coal. He took refuge on his small allotment by the railway, where he grew cabbages and potatoes, and when trains passed practically in front of his nose the apples shook in the tree.

The world around us fell into two parts: friends and enemies. The friends were few, the others multitudinous, but for some still inexplicable reason we were not unhappy. There was laughter and affection in abundance – Louise saw to that with a terrific show of spirit. I added a little prayer to my nightly ritual. I asked Jesus to kill Hitler. My belief in the power of God was confirmed a few weeks later, when we heard about a bomb attack on Hitler in the Bürgerbräukeller, the famous beer cellar in Munich. Unfortunately he escaped. People were beginning to talk about the *göttliche Vorsehung* (divine protection), a kind of special guardian angel for the Führer. The Catholic Cardinal Faulhaber ordered the singing of a Te Deum in the Frauenkirche of Munich to thank God for Hitler's salvation. So much for my father's foresight when he made us join the Catholic Church, which, even when the Jewish synagogues went up in flames, did not speak out in protest.

3

Hitler's War
1939–1943

I was a terrible pupil, and remained so throughout my scholastic career, always just scraping by. My behaviour, attention and diligence were only 'adequate', as were religion, drawing and calligraphy. Mention was made of what was to become one of my more notable traits: 'Klaus-Peter disturbs the class because he is too forward.' The marks for my handwriting and my less than dashing performance on the sports field oscillated between 'failure' and 'inadequate'. Only in music, languages and art was I always considered 'good', although never 'very good'.

On 20 April 1939 we had been given the day off from school. It was Hitler's fiftieth birthday. Most of my classmates had gone to town laden with banners, stepladders and chairs to see the Führer. Of course I was dead keen to see the huge parade, but Louise had made sure to organise a little personal excursion to the Blockhaus, one of our favourite cafés, on the Wannsee. As soon as we had ordered an ice-cream the noise of the shouting masses, who lined the East–West axis to celebrate the day, came over the loudspeaker. Louise quickly asked for the bill and we left. The next day the school was buzzing with vivid accounts of the festive parade of the 'glorious' display of tanks and goose-stepping soldiers. The Adam twins stood aside, listening with envy.

Nobody wanted war, but many people wanted to see the Sudetenland and Austria in German hands. The Austrians were so excited about it that, according to Louise, on the day of the *Anschluss* some shops even put a photo of Hitler's grandmother in the window display. For many it served as a further proof of Hitler's strength and mission. Even the American *Time* magazine selected Hitler as its Man of the Year. It became more and more difficult to be against Hitler; even the staunchest anti-Nazis sometimes began to doubt their belief.

Unification with Austria and Prague had long been a German dream. At school, after the annexation of Austria and the Saar, there was now an awful lot of talk about the Sudetenland, and German women being raped by Czech men, for Hitler was preparing the mood to justify an attack on Czechoslovakia, bringing German countries 'home to the Reich'. My fellow pupils had picked up horror stories at home. Louise would dismiss them as nonsense, but I was more inclined to believe my friends.

Hitler had signed a pact with Russia and suddenly everybody talked about the miserable life of the Germans in Poland. Grown-ups had for months been discussing the possibility of war. Few doubted the bellicose nature of the man who had claimed that 'the thought of striking up a war is always in me'. Chamberlain had been widely photographed in Munich, carrying an umbrella, which many Germans considered a very unmanly sight. At school the jokes about the Russians were suddenly replaced by jibes about 'cissy Englishmen'.

On 1 September 1939 Hitler attacked Poland to prevent, as most people believed, a Polish invasion. The war had begun. To this day I remember coming home and seeing my mother in tears. 'Another war,' she said. 'It's only twenty years since we fought the last one. I thought all that senseless killing would never happen again.' I was ten years old and did not know what war meant, but for my mother and for many of her generation, the horrors of the Great War, with its terrific loss of human life, had never been forgotten. I saw many people weeping during those first few days of a new war.

Within a few weeks most families had a father, son or lover at the front. At first the news was all good. It took Hitler nine days to overrun and crush Poland. The speed of this victory made people believe in the justice of the war and the possibility of a quick peace plan with the Western nations. But the joy was dampened by news of the first German casualties. The black-edged death notices with the iron cross began to appear in the papers, announcing the passing of the men 'in proud mourning' – some even added 'for Führer, Volk und Vaterland'.

As the war progressed the pride of this mourning began to fade into numbness. Soon everybody would know a family which had lost one, two or even three sons, but for the time being almost the entire nation was swept by fervent belief in Hitler and his cause.

Radio and newspapers were the only source of information, for although television had begun as early as 1935, during the Olympic Games almost nobody had a set at home. Listening to foreign stations was an offence punished by imprisonment. Nevertheless we began to listen to the German-language broadcast from Moscow, and to the BBC from London or to Beromünster. Louise would be sitting under a blanket to muffle the sound.

We had to black out. Everybody tried to find some dark curtains or wrapping paper with which to mask their windows, and Louise tore up an old black velvet evening dress. The streets too were almost dark, which gave everything an eerie feeling.

Rationing, strangely enough, had been introduced four days before the outbreak of war, and soon almost nothing was available except with ration cards: washing powder, coal, cigarettes, milk, clothes, petrol and, most of all, bread and sugar. At first there was no real hardship. In the first year of the war the meat ration was cut but we still had meat three times a week. There were still plenty of potatoes and we were allowed three loaves of bread, but there was scarcely any butter. The black market flourished, even though racketeering too was an imprisonable offence. A whole new secret language was invented. People would ask for 'a first class ticket', when they meant butter. A time of great bartering began. Louise was in her element: tobacco in exchange for margarine, silk stockings for sugar. Cigarettes were a great black-market currency. Louise did not smoke, so we were able to trade them for the most precious commodity of all: coffee, not the standard fare of *Malzkaffee*, a substance which contained chicory, but real coffee.

Unlike many, we were never really short of food during the war, for Louise always knew how to get things, *hintenrum*, or 'the back way'. The Christian of the family proved to be a genius at what was known as *organisieren*. Her chutzpah contradicted all the clichés about only the Jews being commercially enterprising. It was my father who had been shy and incapable of fending for himself, but Louise over the years would turn *organisieren* into a fine art. She always managed to get in front of the queue, always knew someone in the right place and would use her contacts shamelessly. As *Mischlinge* we were supposed to have special ration cards and were barred from *Sonderzuteilungen*, special bonuses. I never found out how she managed to acquire the normal ration cards for us. One did not ask too many questions those days.

Sometimes Louise took us in to town to try to find a restaurant where one still could eat without a ration card. Most would be fully booked, but she managed to get a table at Mampe's wine bar. People used to order two or three meat courses. I watched a family of four progressing from steak to half a goose.

On 31 March 1940 my sister and I went to our First Holy Communion. We were given scrolls declaring: 'Today you have become soldiers of Christ. Continue!' and despite my many lapses into paganism, I have vaguely tried to follow this advice.

Renate wore a white dress for the occasion, and I my first pair of long trousers. In church, Louise displayed one of her flamboyant hats and wept copiously. I had chosen the name of Michael as a confirmation name. I thought Klaus-Peter Michael had a ring to it. Despite my choice, Dada, who had also sobbed throughout the service, continued to address me as *Schniefke*, 'Sniffles', for I didn't like to use handkerchiefs. Although sometimes she would call me *Stern* (Star). Renate had chosen Maria as her confirmation name, but to Dada she was always *Puschel*, 'Curly top'.

All was going according to plan on this great day. I had remembered not to eat or drink, since Holy Communion could only be received after fasting. I had fervently confessed my sins, though at ten I hardly knew anything about the sixth commandment, the one concerning chastity. My sister had whispered something about birds and bees while we were playing doctors and nurses but my confession was limited to disobedience and white lies. For the first time I tasted the Host. It made me feel good, and for once not an outcast.

The entire family attended the reception which was held in our house, not least the three now inseparable sisters Louise, Friedl and Emmy. There were endless cakes served on the very best Meissen, and, of course, bubbly Sekt; even we children were given one glass. The three sisters entertained the guests with outrageous anecdotes of their youth, entirely inappropriate to the holiness of the day, upstaging each other in recounting scandals for the sake of the loudest laugh. Yet the peace of this seemingly perfect day was clouded. I realised painfully, not for the first time, that such a day could only ever lead to disappointment. Christmas or Easter, birthdays or holidays never quite lived up to my expectation and my dreams. This was a special day; it was meant to embody everything that was good and just, or so I thought. The first cloud had surfaced after church, as we were receiving our presents; a beautiful Biedermeier writing desk for Renate. Where was mine? I felt cheated. I was given a lot of books, mostly by Karl May because, like all German boys, I loved this bizarre writer, who had never left his native Radebeul but had written endless volumes about a Red Indian, Winnetou, and a white man, Old Shatterhand. Books, however welcome, hardly compensated for Biedermeier desks. Although I was promised one of my own it seemed like too little too late. The injury was done.

In the afternoon Renate was showing off her bureau, opening and closing the drawers in the most provocative way. Another of her presents was a manicure set, the importance of which I would have doubtless forgotten except that one of the sharp instruments, intended for pairing nails, ended up in my thigh. The ensuing fight produced pandemonium, blood and tears. The holy day had been desecrated, and our crime, my mother predicted, would haunt us for the rest of our lives. She was right. My sister still has the desk, I have the scar on my right leg, and injustice still sends me into a frenzy. For a long time my mind festered on revenge.

Renate and I fought a lot, and Louise often joined in the brawl. It was sometimes difficult for her to cope with two such temperamental children. The household lacked the authority of a father; her behaviour lacked logic, she was all emotion. It was a good thing that Renate and I had to separate, at least as far as school was concerned. Renate was enrolled at a local girls' school, the Henrietta von Meisendorf, and I was registered at the Französisches Gymnasium, the Lycée of Berlin. It was founded under Frederick the Great, an avid Francophile. Its main purpose was to provide the large and important Huguenot population of Berlin with its own school. It was considered one of Berlin's most distinguished schools, the place where diplomats and the upper crust sent their children. The Französisches Gymnasium was basically a boys' school and stood in the Dorotheenstrasse, a district of embassies, banks and ministries.

On the first day, we all stood, somehow lost, in the forbidding classroom. Our mothers, who had brought us here, displayed an exaggerated joviality, and showed off their sons while fathers looked on bored and embarrassed. As the parents were ushered out, we were left with the blackboard, the rows of hard benches and a teacher who began by asking us to spell our names. I eyed the eighteen boys destined to become my classmates with suspicion. Loneliness gripped me. The fear of being recognised as a *Judenjunge* (Jew boy) hung like a menace in the room. Above all I wanted to be like everybody else, and up to this day a sense of difference invariably grips me when confronted with new people. My desire to be alone and my desire to belong can never be totally reconciled.

Going to school involved a forty-minute train ride. The S-Bahn – with first- and second-class compartments – was the pride of Berlin's transport system. In the morning special trains would circulate, linking the four suburbs, Wannsee, Nikolassee, Schlachtensee and Zehlendorf, to the centre. They had only first-class compartments and would rush past the other twenty stations to their destination: Potsdamer Platz and Unter den Linden. They were nicknamed *Bankierzüge*, Bankers' Trains, for most of the passengers belonged to the smart business set who lived in Berlin's Villenviertel, the villa district, and worked in the city.

Being one of the few children who took the Banker's Train to school I felt frightfully superior. The school too was considered superior, for many of the boys had fathers who worked in embassies (although some of them only as drivers). My contemporaries included the grandson of the famous painter Käthe Kollwitz, both sons of the theatre director Walter Felsenstein, and the son of General Rommel.

The Lycée was a *humanistisches Gymnasium*, a high school which laid emphasis upon the classics and humanities rather than on mathematics.

Forms went by names like Untersekunda, Obersekunda and Tertia; I was in Unterprima.

The teachers were impeccably dressed in dark suits and had a tendency towards seriousness. We were brought up with Prussian tradition and French liberalism, a mixture which I have always found fruitful. The best of the Prussian tradition was never reconcilable with Hitler's primitive ideology. The school was, as its name implied, run very much along the line of a French establishment. English, compulsory in most German high schools, was replaced here by French as the official language. We spent two or three hours each day learning it and this routine continued for our first two years. When we had grasped the language we were taught biology, history and chemistry in French. Latin and Greek were translated into French rather than into German. Some of us already possessed a basic knowledge of the language, since we had spoken it at home. My father had been fluent in French and had always insisted that, in a restaurant, children had to be able to translate the menu before ordering. I had a flair for languages, and I won the praise of my teachers for speaking French to my friends even during the breaks, ensuring, of course, that it did not go unnoticed.

The school was different in many ways. Classes did not commence with 'Heil Hitler!' but with a French prayer, despite the fact that Dr Nix, the headmaster, could be seen sometimes in jack boots and sA uniform. On the whole we suffered very little political indoctrination, although this too would soon change. In the mornings, we were spared tedious questions about current political events, questions which had regularly put my sister and me on the spot while at primary school, as we seemed to be the only ones not to know about Hitler's birthday or the day of his taking power; my mother saw to that. Her information resulted mostly from listening to the BBC World Service, but we were never allowed to listen to the news in case we divulged our source of information.

My mother had engaged a new au pair, Anita, a lively young girl from the country, with blazing red hair and a contagious laugh. She was meant to stay only one year but remained with us for over twenty. Anita was young and pretty. She was not in favour of the war, but she forever loved soldiers and the soldiers forever loved Anita, often late into the night. In the morning I had to get up at 6.30 and on most days would run half asleep to the station in Nikolassee. But on countless mornings Anita would rush into my room, screeching in horror that it was already eight o'clock. The last bankers' train had left and I had to travel on the ordinary line. My mishap gave me the chance to see a different face of Berlin, that of ordinary people, of women in headscarves, often weary and sad.

Sometimes the train smelt of dirt and sweat, sometimes of a sharpish soap, for the special compartments reserved for people with luggage were used to transport prisoners of war and one could always tell by the smell whether those prisoners had been Russian or French.

To escape the war and the hazards of urban life, Louise sometimes took us to the mountains or to the Black Forest. We always stayed in small villages in bed and breakfasts, simple rooms with jugs of cold water and porcelain basins. The shelves of the wardrobe were lined with newspaper, and the standard price for a night was one mark per bed. Days were spent roaming the forest picking mushrooms or blueberries, which, eaten with sugar and cold milk, turned our tongues and teeth deep purple.

Despite the war, we continued to celebrate Christmas, like millions, in the same traditional way. Louise and Emmy would decorate the tree, with masses of gold angel-hair and red glass balls behind closed doors. On Christmas Eve, we would go to the little Protestant church in Nikolassee, where the vicar prayed for the soldiers and the homeless. There were also veiled prayers for those who had been imprisoned, leaving it open to speculation if he was referring to the German prisoners of war or to those Hitler had put behind bars. Churchgoing had become a kind of personal resistance. Finally Louise, in evening dress, would unlock the drawing-room door. There, beneath the glow of the candlelit tree, we would intone (for the tenth time): 'Silent night, holy night', aided by the hoarse sound of our old gramophone. In these early years she would have been able to 'organise' weeks before Christmas the traditional goose, to be served with apple stuffing and red cabbage.

Once, during the Christmas holidays, I was allowed to visit Aunt Emmy, who no longer worked at the canteen of the UFA film studios, but ran a large holiday home in a village in the Erzgebirge mountains. The hostel belonged to the Vitztum Gymnasium in Dresden and students could spend their holidays here. Emmy, still unmarried but very motherly, was in her element. The pupils had become her sons. Most were fourteen to eighteen years old and I felt enormously proud to be allowed into such a 'grown-up' circle. This seemed to be, at last, the real world, the world of boys who smoked and bragged about girls. My own innocence caused much hilarity as I was told the facts of life several times over.

Some of the boys were proud Nazis, but Aunt Emmy made sure that no one appeared at table in the Hitler Youth uniform for dinner. She thought it unseemly. She also advised me not to refer to my Jewish background.

This is where I experienced my first crush. The object of my affections was a much older pupil – almost eighteen, I think. He was the son of Axel

Munthe, the Swedish writer and scientist, author of the bestselling *Story of San Michele*. The young Munthe seemed very exotic to me; he was kind, took me seriously, and taught me how to ski.

Back home I decided to join the junior division of the Hitler Youth, the *Pimpfe*. Most of my schoolmates had already joined and the uniforms looked fantastic. I asked a friend to let me try on his, and was thrilled by the sight of myself in the brown shirt, black shorts, and black leather belt with the gleaming buckle. What did I care about the underlying philosophy of the movement? All I wanted was to join up, to be one of them. So when I was introduced to Volker, a Hitler Youth leader, I asked him to enrol me. He listened to me quietly, but then inquired: 'Aren't you a *Mischling*?' 'Yes,' I replied. 'All right, I'll see what I can do.' To my amazement, that same afternoon he came to our house and asked to see my mother. They talked for half an hour, and on leaving he gave me a smile. My mother took me in her arms. 'You can't join,' she said. 'Volker didn't have the courage to tell you but he is very sorry.' Volker was only sixteen, a decent German – they did exist.

I felt rejected, and the more I felt rejected the harder I pushed myself forward. I learned early the art of bribing affection or buying off hostilities, and I hid the shame of being Jewish behind a proud, overbearing façade. Not that I actually liked myself very much, but I managed to be popular. Boisterous pupils always are: it is the quiet, nice ones, the class always seem to turn against. Dr Nessler summed up my character and performance during the first year at the Lycée: 'If Klaus-Peter manages to use his inclinations and interests properly, he might eventually become an excellent pupil, but he is pushy, undisciplined and disorderly. His ability in sports is abysmal.' Sport consisted mainly of exercises on the horizontal and parallel bars, leapfrogging over a buck horse and racing. I was not convinced by the dictum *Mens sana in corpore sano* and hated the mindless running around the schoolyard in a herd of sweating and singing boys clad in black gym shorts and mud-brown shirts. Swimming was only marginally more fun; as I was a coward when it came to jumping from the diving board, I could not understand why we had to dive from a three-metre board when there was a perfectly good ladder to get into the water.

In class we did what generations of Germans had done before us: we struggled through Caesar's *De Bello Gallico* and learned endless lines such as: 'Words with the ending "is" are feminini generis.' We spent hours on *analyse de texte*, a page of Flaubert or Jean Giono dissected for its meaning or its *genitivus possessivus*. We were supposed to know our classics – Goethe, Schiller and Shakespeare (who was considered a German, and whose translation by Tieck and Schlegel was deemed far superior to the original). Poetry reciting also figured high on the school's agenda. We learned Schiller's 'Glocke' by heart until even in our dreams we could hear the verses: 'Festgemauert in der Erde.'

We were forever writing essays: about the greatness of our nation, about Kleist's *Michael Kohlhaas* ('Was Michael Kohlhaas a hero?'), or on the meaning of Schiller's *Die Räuber*. We also had to memorise the dates relating to Germany's glorious past. We crammed them into our poor heads by chanting *ad nauseam*: 'Charlemagne 742 to 814, Martin Luther 1483 to 1546, the Führer's birth date 1889.' To this last date in the ditty I would always secretly add 'to 1940' or whatever year we happened to be. If we forgot any of these dates we had to stay behind and write it down thirty times.

One of our favourite books was *Kampf um Rom* (Battle for Rome) by Felix Dahn, who traced the Germans back to Rome. The Greeks and Romans were considered Nordic precursors of the Great Germans. The myth of our Great German past was constantly stressed. It had been part of German education, long before Hitler came to power. Like generations before us we read the German sagas, and books by Gustav Freytag about an idyllic rural past – books that formed the base for the Nazis' ideas about blood and soil. The Nibelungen, the fortresses of the Rhine, the old folk customs, everything was dragged out in the rewriting of German history. In the teaching Germany was always victorious, noble and, of course, racially pure.

We were taken to museums, not the art museums but those which displayed the legacy of our victorious past, the Zeughaus with Prussian uniforms and decorations, or the Hohenzollern Museum which housed the relics of German generals and kings in wax.

Sometimes after school some of us would sneak into what we called a 'proper' museum, the Kaiser Wilhelm, Germany's National Gallery, which was only a few minutes away. Much of my understanding of the female anatomy stems from my visits to rooms where paintings by Rubens and Botticelli were hung. I would step forward and scrutinise each canvas as I had observed grown-ups doing it, examining the relevant parts with a knowledgeable expression on my face, at close quarters. Alas, my displays of sophistication and artistic sensibility were quickly marred by my friends erupting into loud laughter.

From the third year on, English became optional, but most students chose Greek, for English was regarded as the language of trade. I chose English, and my first lesson began with the sentence: 'This is Mr Raffke's new villa', Raffke being the nickname for a grabber and a parvenu.

I enjoyed reading but resented the regimental cramming. I wanted to make my own discoveries, not just to be spoon-fed. Basically I was lazy, always lagging behind in my homework, and spending my time reading rather than learning my irregular verbs. The world of Bulwer-Lytton's *The Last Days of Pompeii* was to me so much more wonderful than that of Tacitus. My mind tended to wander off, sometimes in the middle of a geography lesson. I would suddenly find myself elsewhere, immersed in the most extravagant daydream, only to be loudly interrupted: 'Adam! La capitale de l'Hongrie?'

My second infatuation involved a beautiful dark-haired boy, Alexander Schulte. Sacha was the son of a successful surgeon and a Russian mother. I admired his calm and self-possession, which was so much at odds with my own flamboyant and uncontrolled behaviour. Not that any of us looked especially glamorous. Most of us had only one suit and we wore the same outfit every day. This was not only on account of the war and rationing. Young people at that time never thought about fashion; all the pocket money we had went on books, cinema or theatre. Sacha and I swore loyalty and everlasting love and sealed this pact with blood. I also shared with him my greatest secret, the fact that I was half Jewish, which did not impress him. 'There are three others like you in our class,' he told me, and pointed at the Felsenstein twins and at Kurz, the son of a Protestant vicar. So, at least since we were four half-Jewish boys in the class, I was not the only outcast.

As the war continued, on the radio again and again Liszt's *Prelude* was followed by yet another special newsflash ('Sondermeldung. Sondermeldung'). The Germans had taken Brussels, and the troops were heading towards Paris. Holland too capitulated, Denmark was already occupied and there was bitter fighting in Norway. For us any news of Hitler's advances was disheartening. What would happen to Sweden, where Aunt Alice and Uncle Job had taken refuge? We had no news from them. Almost everybody around rejoiced in the reports of the victorious army, and at school people became intoxicated with the *Sondermeldungen* reporting another victory for them, another defeat for us.

The invasion of France in 1940 created a lot of upheavals in the Lycée. The motto in our textbook, *Liberté, Egalité, Fraternité*, began to sound hollow. It was difficult to reconcile the daily absorption of French culture and civilisation with the condemnation of that country as our enemy. Some of us began to discuss the issue secretly during breaks, and the first criticisms of the regime could be heard. Many of the boys hoped that Paris would soon be taken, simply so that they could go and visit the city.

On 14 June, Paris capitulated. Ten days later, Pétain would sign two-thirds of his country over to German control. This came as a shock to many of our teachers, since only a few were Nazis, but for the rest of the country the fall of France was further proof of Hitler's infallibility. A sense of victory gripped almost the entire nation. The invasion of the Balkans followed almost immediately. People seemed to lose all normal judgement. Many volunteered to go to the Front, since for them – mostly small civil servants, teachers – being made an officer meant a rise in class and a higher living standard. Everybody wanted to be part of Hitler's victory; even foreign countries seemed impressed.

On my way to school I often passed the new Reichskanzlei (chancellery), which Albert Speer had built. A few hundred people always gathered in front of the great pillared portals to catch yet another glimpse of their beloved Führer. They usually whispered, a curious look of expectation on their faces. From the Zietenplatz you could look right up onto Hitler's balcony. I never saw him standing there, but from newsreels we were all familiar with the sacred moment when white-gloved officers would pull the curtain aside and open the door for Hitler to step out to greet his people. He always was in uniform, one hand poised on his belt buckle, the other lifted to give the salute. At that point the crowd invariably went berserk. I once watched a row of shiny limousines drive into the vast courtyard and caught a glimpse of some foreign diplomats in top hats walking up the stairs, passing the huge doors guarded by Arno Breker's two nude statues, *The Party* and *The Army,* which I knew so well from postcards and reproductions in our schoolbooks. Hitler was obviously hosting a reception, and I wondered why so many people had come to drink with a man they knew to be a butcher.

The war also began to affect us in a more direct way. In September 1940 Hitler kept his promise to drop 40,000 tons of bombs on England. The word *Blitz* was coined and while the radio wallowed in celebration of London's destruction, the Adams worried about our many friends who had fled there. Then came the retaliation. Night after night we were awoken by air-raid sirens. Most people had made a makeshift shelter in the cellar of their homes. We slept, half-dressed, with our most precious belongings in a small bag, and every night, almost to the hour, we would stagger, half-asleep, into our shelter, where we remained for three or four hours, huddled together in fear, until the siren sounded the all-clear.

The next day children would roam about the streets in search of pieces of metal, and at school a lively trade in bomb splinters began.

Despite its horror, there was also a kind of beauty in watching an air-raid, for death came in such a spectacular way. Sometimes we were allowed to watch the fireworks of destruction from our garden. It was a fantastic sight. While the city was all in darkness except for the light of the burning houses, the sky was lit up by huge spotlights and the flares of Göring's anti-aircraft guns.

The air-raids intensified. The deadly planes returned night after night. For four years there was hardly a night without interruptions. We moved beds and mattresses to the cellar, and the four of us – Louise, Anita, Renate and I – spent our nights among the heating boiler, the coal, and rack upon rack of apples. There was no question of much sleep, for the anticipation of the deafening noise of guns and bombs, plus the constant fear of being hit, kept us awake. Sometimes the whole house would shake and the front door burst open. Occasionally one could hear the sound of shattering glass, of windows blown out by the pressure of falling missiles. There was a saying that the bomb you hear flying through the air will not hit you, a small consolation, for it did not make the noise any less frightening. Still to this day, if I close my eyes, I can hear the whistling of air mines as they shrieked over our heads. Suddenly all went silent, as if the attackers were catching their breath, and then the fear returned, stronger than before. We knew somewhere people were dying.

The nightly raids and their aftermath became the daily table conversations. Little else mattered, as more and more people were 'bombed out'. Within seconds all your belongings could be gone, all your life's gatherings turned to rubble. That was, if you were lucky. Others were buried alive or drowned in their cellars when the pipes burst. At last I had something in common with my friends, something I could share – the nightly fear of being killed.

Families began to evacuate their children to the country, away from the cities. The Lycée decided to open a camp and the school was sent to a mountain resort in Silesia. I don't remember much about this time, except weeks of annihilating homesickness which filled my nights. For many of us this was the first time away from our family.

Another incident clouded my stay. The school had organised a skiing competition and I had come first. The prizes, three sports medals, were presented by one of the Hitler Youth, and many parents had travelled to join their sons in this event. Louise unfortunately could not. I would have liked to share this victory with her. At the prize-giving I stepped forward. There was a sudden muttering among the teachers, and the sports master, a young man in his twenties, uttered the chilling words: 'This prize is not for a Judenjunge.' Embarrassment all around. I was so shaken that I noticed little of the noise in the gallery, and prayed for the ground to open up beneath me. I felt so ashamed, so humiliated. *Judenjunge*, yes, that is what I was, a Jew-boy. There might have been a few sympathetic glances, but no one spoke up for me. This medal had meant so much to me, I didn't care that it was a Nazi medal. I remember nothing else about this day, yet I know I cried bitterly. I have forgotten if friends came to console me. When I returned to Berlin, I was a changed person.

The signs in bars and restaurants too reminded us of our outcast state. 'Die Juden sind unser Unglück.'[1] Other more absurd ones proclaimed 'Für Juden und Hunde verboten'[2] or 'Der Deutsche grüsst mit Heil Hitler!'[3]

The adoration of Hitler seemed never to abate. Wherever he appeared, opening the Bayreuth Festival or inaugurating a new stretch of motorway, a sea of hands reached out for him. The photos of those raised hands in the newspaper and on the newsreels haunted me, hands lifted up for the Hitler salute, hands that shouted: 'Thank you, my Führer', hands that prayed for his health and survival.

One day, 12 May 1941, Louise woke us up in a state of excitement. The BBC had announced that Rudolf Hess had landed in Scotland. Maybe this was the end of the war. The next few days at school we talked about nothing else. Our history teacher had difficulties explaining the facts. Hess, a much praised politician, had to be seen as a traitor, a man who had lost his mind. When, one month later, Hitler began his invasion of Russia, Stalin, only yesterday regarded as a friend, had suddenly become Germany's enemy. On the radio, Hitler had spoken for over an hour about the treacherous Russians. But our history teacher was an intelligent man, and one could see how embarrassed he was about all our questions. We swiftly switched to the Thirty Years War.

Until 1939 Jews had been allowed to leave the country, provided someone abroad vouched for them financially, or they had enough money to pay a surety. Those who were too poor had to stay behind. From 1 September 1941 all Jews above the age of six had to wear the yellow star of David on the left side of their clothes with the word *Jude* written in black across. On their ID cards all women were called Sara. The name for a Jewish man was Israel. Their apartments had to be marked by a black star on a white ground. No one was allowed to speak to Jews. My mother always did. As soon as she spotted one of them in the street, she would rush up to them

1 'The Jews are our misfortune.'
2 'Jews and dogs not allowed.'
3 'A German says hello with *Heil Hitler*.'

and ask for the time or for a direction. A grateful look was usually the only answer. She got away with it: nobody ever stopped her.

If only more people had had her conviction and civil courage. You did not have to climb the barricades, only behave like a decent human being. Jews were not allowed to sit on public benches. Soon they were no longer admitted to cinemas, theatres and concert halls and were barred from the streets after dark. Eventually their milk and meat rations were withdrawn. At the beginning of the war they had to surrender all their personal jewellery and gold, their fur coats and woollen clothing; now they were refused ration cards for clothes. General shopping for them was only between 4.00 and 5.00 in the afternoon. Later they were deprived of their typewriters, bicycles, records and radios, a decree which was announced on Jewish New Year.

And yet 55,000 of them still lived in Berlin. I saw some of them daily on the streets, in the train, where they were not allowed to sit down, cold and miserably dressed, diverting their eyes when you looked at them. I sometimes tried to smile at them, wanting to convey some complicity with their plight, but hardly anybody ever acknowledged the smile of a boy. They were too frightened and I might have been a provocateur. Eventually they would even disappear from the trains, for they were no longer allowed to travel on public transport.

The deportations of Jews intensified, and rumours began to seep through, although the Nazis took great care to hide these ignominious preparations towards the 'Final Solution' from the public at large.

One day my cousin Annemarie took me on a trip to Dresden, to visit Aunt Friedl. The train left from one of Berlin's main stations. On the opposite platform stood a goods train. Neatly dressed nurses and helpers paraded up and down, while hundreds of Jews with their yellow stars boarded the train like cattle. No one protested. It all looked so orderly. This scene took place in front of ordinary passengers like ourselves. Nobody screamed or cried out, neither those who boarded the train, nor those on the other platform, nor us, but Annemarie turned ashen and whispered: 'They are being taken to a concentration camp.' This was the first time I had heard the expression 'concentration camp', and I thought of it as a kind of prison. I was only a child yet I asked myself, 'Why?'

Annemarie and I travelled to Dresden, in silence, but we travelled nevertheless. We were met by Aunt Friedl, who lived in a beautiful old farmhouse in Radebeul, a small town on the outskirts of the Saxon town. I played with my two cousins, Jochen and Krischan, as if nothing had happened that day. But at night as I lay in my bed I could hear my aunt weeping. She was a fierce anti-Nazi and had helped many Jews to emigrate. She knew the truth because she wanted to know. Most other people did not and closed their eyes.

We never found out what really happened to all those people. When in 1942 a commission worked out the plans for the 'Final Solution', most Germans knew nothing of these meetings, during which Germany shed the last vestiges of human decency. But many must have seen, as I did, men and women being loaded on trucks, their names written on placards hanging around their necks. Most Germans continued to do all the things the Jews were not allowed to do, and while the persecution of the Jews would continue, with more transports – relocations they were called – people would still think that this was all they were. The very idea that hundreds of thousands of people were being sent to their deaths was inconceivable. Our neighbour, who was chief of police, had mentioned some camps without giving any details. No one pressed him any further.

Not all Germans looked the other way, however. When neighbours started disappearing, certain brave people resisted, secretly giving food and clothes to Jews. Many persecuted people in hiding would not have survived without their sacrifices and assistance. Once Louise took some sleeping pills to the old mother of our banker, before she was taken to Theresienstadt, to help her to die.

In later life people have asked me again and again if Germans knew the truth about the concentration camps. My answer has always been no, we – us included – did not. Only after the war would I eventually learn the full horror. Had we known at that time, could we have lived with that knowledge? How much self-protection can an individual develop in order to avoid facing the truth?

Life for many became more difficult, yet people behaved as if victory were just around the corner. Louise always loved to shop and she sometimes took us to the big department stores, the Wertheim, Karstadt, and most of all the KadeWe, 'the Department Store of the West'. There wasn't much to be had. Everybody had a *Spinnstoffkarte*, or clothes ration card. Two coupons bought a pair of socks, for a skirt one had to part at least with six. A blouse or a pair of shoes set you back by nine. Mercifully for Louise, hats were not rationed, and I used to watch her among gaggles of other women trying on baroque confections of feathers and veils. For those with relatives at the Front it was a bit easier. Soldiers came home on leave with coffee, chocolate and butter from Holland. From Norway they brought fox furs and even astrakhan coats, so that, despite rationing, people managed to look well dressed, even elegant. Tailored suits, or *Kostüme,* were obligatory for that time, and hat and gloves remained *de rigueur* for a lady, at least in the smart areas of the town. Louise had an

In 1944   Louise during the war

innate sense of elegance, and although by now she possessed like most only a few pairs of shoes and a couple of dresses, she had hats. Luxury items like silk stockings had to be obtained on the black market or arrived as gifts from soldiers stationed in Paris.

Holidays were also a great diversion. The most important were the *Grosse Ferien*, the long vacation during July and August. Berlin's railway stations, marvellous neo-classical buildings, dated from the late nineteenth century. They had names like Stettiner Bahnhof and Görlitzer Bahnhof, which evoked Germany's eastern provinces, and were termini. Travellers did not pass through Berlin, they went there to stay, to visit friends, to shop, to go to the theatre, the museums or merely to breathe in the life of a big metropolis. Even the Nazis could not change that. Every summer the platforms were packed with families heaving rucksacks and suitcases. No longer able to travel abroad, they were on their way to the traditional holiday resorts on the Baltic Sea or in the Austrian mountains. People travelled to Königsberg, Danzig or to Upper Silesia. The Great German Reich spread far in those days.

We no longer went to the sea but to the mountains. One departed for Bavaria from the Anhalter Bahnhof. The main means of transport was still the train. And what trains! They were just as trains ought to be, like the toy ones we grew up with, drawn by a puffing locomotive, sooty smoke clouding the windows. There were three classes: third, with wooden benches; second, *Polsterklasse* (Upholstered class), with soft seats; and first, in red plush with little lace doilies and mahogany-panelled walls. People did not travel in large impersonal Pullman carriages but in small individual compartments, eight passengers in third class and six in second and first. We used second class, and we were allowed to open the window which bore multilingual warnings, such as *E pericoloso sporgersi* (It is dangerous to lean out) and *Défendu de cracher* (Spitting forbidden). There was an old-fashioned dining-car but most people took their own food on board – loaves of bread, sausages and large flasks of coffee. Despite the rationing, passengers always seemed to have plenty of provisions, and it was considered polite to share them with fellow travellers. Louise also liked to share her political views, and when we kicked her as a warning to desist, she would simply say: 'Stop kicking me! You will get wise in due course!'

Our first stop was always Munich, a day's journey from Berlin. It was a sleepy, slightly provincial town with picture-postcard buildings, castles and baroque churches. We normally stayed at the Bayerischer Hof, a smart hotel with waiters and waitresses decked out in Bavarian costumes.

There was a disagreeable side to all this picturesque beauty, as Munich was the 'Town of the Movement', the Nazi movement, and it did not let you forget it. Hitler fancied himself as successor to the Bavarian kings, Ludwig II and Ludwig III, who had turned Munich into an artistic capital. Not to be outdone he had erected here his pompous edifices, a new art gallery, the Führerbau (Führer building) and the Party Administration Building with two Temples of Honour. He claimed that they were 'built for eternity', and strangely enough they survived the war all but intact.

On one of Munich's splendid avenues, with neo-classical buildings by the nineteenth-century architect Leo von Klenze, stood the Feldherrn-halle, which the Nazis had chosen to commemorate their abortive Putsch of November 1923, a shrine to the 'blood victims', a name I found particu-larly distasteful. Every time you passed this building you were supposed to raise your arm in a Hitler salute. Louise of course would not yield to such 'nonsense', and could scarcely be prevented from turning this issue yet into another of her resolute anti-fascist demonstrations. Fortunately, however, there was a passage, a small alley behind the Feldherrnhalle, which the Bavarians had christened the *Drückebergergasse*, the dodger's passage. Many people took it rather than pass in front of the objectionable official monument.

Hitler had commissioned his favourite architect, Ludwig Troost, to build the new House of German Art. It resembled a Greek temple, which was precisely what Hitler had in mind. He himself had laid the foundation stone, in the presence of the entire art establishment. Unfortunately the hammer broke, not a good omen for the new German art. From 1937 onwards every summer the Great German Art Exhibition was held here, displaying the art sanctioned by Hitler and his party. 'All' German artists were invited to participate – all who were racially and politically suitable.

The Führer, who regarded himself as an artist, intervened in the selec-tion of the pictures to make sure that nothing 'unfinished' graced the walls of his new gallery. That same year, Hitler and his ringleader, Joseph Goeb-bels, had staged a particularly nasty exhibition of the so-called *Entartete Kunst*, degenerate art, by 'Jewish and Communist scribblers' such as Paul Klee, Wassily Kandinsky, Max Beckmann, and many others.

Our trips to Munich invariably included visits to art exhibitions. I did not see the exhibition of Degenerate Art; children were not allowed to see it for fear that the 'diseased minds of those parasites' could infect their pure German mind. Someone even suggested standing the artists next to their works, so that outraged citizens could spit at them.

We would however go to the official Great German Art Exhibition. Almost everybody I knew did. Thousands of people filed daily past the endless rows of German landscapes, country scenes, family groups, mostly farmers sitting in orderly fashion around their table, blond and healthy individuals, apparently happy and carefree. The stereotyped paintings which replaced genuine artistic expression appealed to popular taste. The majority of the visitors seemed to like what they saw. These were pictures they could live with, except for the size - most things the Nazis did were monumental. I must admit the neatly drawn pretty pictures appealed to me too. I was especially intrigued by the many nudes, women well-scrubbed as if emerging from a bath, standing upright and offering their bodies to the onlooker. Arno Breker's and Joseph Thorak's hunky athletes flexed their muscles and displayed their manhood totally unashamed.

There was also an avalanche of hideous 'party portraits', mostly of the Führer: Hitler as Statesman, Hitler as Architect, Hitler as Leader, always standing erect, gazing into the horizon, for a seated portrait would have been too intimate. Louise hurried us past these. 'Come along,' she urged us. 'There are prettier pictures in the next room', ensuring that other visitors heard.

We were too young and ill-educated, and Louise's taste was too conservative, to realise that these banal paintings were the artistic expression of a barbaric system, art to manipulate dreams and desires. Despite my visits to Berlin's National Gallery, I did not know much about art. Apart from drawing classes, most of our teachers were confused about what was and what was not allowed, so they avoided any reference to modern art. All agreed that Dürer, Holbein, Rembrandt and the painters of the nineteenth century were safer grounds for discussions.

From Munich we would travel to the castle of Elmau, an elegant hotel with eccentric guests, among them many writers, painters and actors. People went there to dance, to look smart and to forget the war. Louise was a regular guest at the Elmau, she liked to mingle with *Prominente*, the famous, especially when their prominence lay with arts. *Prominente*, she claimed, 'lead more interesting and less conventional lives, they are just more fun.' But there was another reason why she loved the Elmau: most guests shared her hatred for Hitler and some openly admitted as much.

Given its anthroposophic lectures and Bohemian atmosphere, the castle was not a place for children. But attached to it was a farm which took in paying guests, so we took rooms in this lovely Bavarian farmhouse with cheerful shutters. The balconies were bursting with geraniums and cows grazed right under our windows. There was milk and butter and we swam daily in the ice-cold lakes. From the instant when the horse-drawn cart collected us at the little station of Klais to take us on our hour-long ride into the mountains, our holiday was bliss.

Once a week we were allowed to accompany Louise to the castle, to learn to dance the quadrille, the dance which opened the weekly balls. After joining the flawless formations, prompted by French commands such as 'Changez vos partenaires', we would be sent back to bed, while Louise danced the night away.

In Berlin too there were lighthearted moments. Going into town was always a source of great excitement. *Kaffeetrinken*, or going for a coffee, even if the coffee was ersatz and the cake tasted of what Berliners call *toter Frisör* or 'dead hairdresser', remained a favourite pastime. In the Café Kranzler the waitresses wore tiny lace caps. In the Sarotti a turbaned Moor poured hot chocolate. Sometimes we stopped at Aschinger, another Berlin institution, where only *Erbsensuppe*, thick yellow pea soup with a sausage, was served. There were no tables or chairs and everybody had to eat standing up. One of the main attractions of Aschinger's were the free bread rolls. During the war one had to forgo the sausage, but everybody was still given a free roll, one with every bowl of piping hot soup.

On our birthdays, however, or on other special occasions, Louise would take us to lunch at the smart restaurant of the Hotel Adlon or even to Horcher. My favourite *Künstlerlokal*, or artist's restaurant, was *Das schwarze Ferkel* (The Black Pig), much to Louise's taste (Strindberg and the painter Munch had been frequent guests). Many of the old guests had left the country and the place had become rather grand, but there were still enough artistic-looking people around for Louise to feel in her element.

On Sundays we went to Potsdam, usually on bicycles, to visit Sans Souci, Frederick the Great's rococo castle, or to Berlin's many lakes. The biggest one, the Wannsee, had a proper Lido with sandy beaches on a seafront with umbrellas and canopied wickerwork deckchairs. Steamships with music and sailing boats cruised the lakes. Louise swam every day in the little Schlachtensee, summer and winter, but nothing could entice her to join the multitudes of suntan-oiled Berliners, who in hundreds of thousands packed, like sardines, the beach on the Wannsee. There were always many young people and Anita never needed much persuasion to take us there.

In literature I had progressed from Karl May to Dostoevsky, and Louise thought it was time for us to start going to the theatre and to concerts. We were sometimes allowed to go to special school matinées at reduced prices, and at school we performed scenes from plays. I excelled as Ferdinand in Schiller's *Kabale und Liebe*; my voice reached a crescendo at the line 'Deine Seele ist so matt wie Deine Limonade' (Your soul is as weary as your lemonade), which, although Schiller had intended that to be a tragic moment, provoked a hysterical laughter in my audience. I became convinced that one day I would end up in the theatre, and never stopped acting, which helped me to make friends. I was popular, worked hard at being liked, always clowned around and showed off.

It was not unusual for a twelve-year-old to be taken to the theatre. Theatre and concert visits were considered salutary, a favourite pastime of the educated classes, who went to the theatre primarily to be elevated, to learn something, not to be entertained. A German play is a play with a message. Louise was an avid theatre-goer and she held, like all good Germans, subscriptions to several theatres (an *Abonnement*). One subscribed to several performances per year, always going on a fixed day of the week and always in the same seat. She had a desirable subscription; a *Premieren Abonnement*, which enabled her to attend opening nights.

Despite the war, and the exodus of thousands of actors and directors, Berlin still had a fine theatre. The most famous actors at that time were Gustaf Gründgens, Käthe Dorsch, Heinrich George and Käthe Gold, who had been the cream of the theatre of the Weimar Republic; and Marianne Hoppe, Horst Caspar, Will Quadflieg, Victor de Kowa, Aribert Wäscher, Albert Florath and Paul Bildt.

Film and theatre were among the few enclaves not contaminated by the Nazis. Horst Caspar, though one-quarter Jewish, would nevertheless rise to become one of the young stars of Goebbels's films. Goebbels and Hitler often overlooked what was known as a *kleiner Webfehler*, a small slub in the weave. A famous contemporary adage claimed: 'Eine fesche jüdische Schauspielerin ist noch lang kein Jud'[1] and Goebbels himself is supposed to have stated: 'Wer Jude ist bestimme ich.'[2] The better known one was, the easier it was to put up some form of resistance. Some actors privately helped colleagues troubled by the Nazis. Many theatre people had never completely said yes to Hitler, although few had loudly said no either, or seemed not to mind pocketing the large sums of money which Hitler made available to them. Even those who did not sympathise with the Nazis had difficulties in resisting an invitation from the Führer or even being seen with him in public. This too was part of the Janus face of the entire time.

Concert life too flourished, although political thinking determined the

---

1 'A pretty Jewish actress is not necessarily a Jew.'

2 '*I* decide who is a Jew.' A singer like Margarete Slezak, though one-quarter Jewish, was nevertheless allowed to sing, and many famous actors had Jewish wives: Theo Lingen, Heinz Rühmann, Ottokar Wernicke. This might have affected their attitude to the regime, but not their career – one of the many contradictions of the times.

repertoire. After the occupation of France, French composers disappeared from the concerts, with the exception of Bizet, as he was too popular. With the invasion of Poland and Russia, Polish and Russian music was banned, exept for Chopin. Music had a sustaining power in the hardship of war. Culture provided a convenient camouflage, the acceptable face of a tyrannical system. Classical music stood high on the agenda of their propaganda effort, especially concerts with Beethoven, Brahms and Bruckner. Modern music was of course banned, as was the music of Jewish composers. One verse of a popular children's ditty about the fate of ten little negroes went like this: 'Fünf kleine Negerlein die setzten sich ans Klavier, der eine spielte Mendelssohn, da waren es nur noch vier.'[1]

I listened a lot to music at home and I knew the singers from the Staatsoper from the old 78s which I played on my ancient phonograph: Margarethe Klose, Tiana Lemnitz, Erna Berger, Maria Cebotari, Helge Roswänge. Our record player looked exactly like the one on His Master's Voice record labels, with the dog and the big horn. When Heinrich Schlusnus sang 'Stell auf den Herd die goldenen Reseden', I joined in as loud as I could manage.

As there was no television everybody listened a lot to the radio. It was a powerful weapon in Hitler's propaganda machine with its cunning mixture of light entertainment, political speeches and classical music. The *Wunschkonzert*, or request concert, was one of the most popular broadcasts of the war. Even though Louise disapproved of it, we tried not to miss it. Every Sunday at three o'clock the soldiers at the Front and the families at home were reunited on the airwaves. 'The Front greets the Heimat, the Heimat greets the Front,' the announcer would say. We would be informed of the birth of twins to Sergeant Müller, to the sound of a crying baby in the background. Soldiers and wives would request their favourite songs, which were often interrupted by news about a contribution to the war effort. A card requesting the song 'Good night mother' had been discovered, we were told, on a dead soldier, and while the whole of Germany wept the song was played. Many only heard about the deaths of their beloved through the *Wunschkonzert*. It must have been quite sickening in its sentimentality and blatant propaganda, yet millions listened to it, Sunday after Sunday.

By 1940 Hitler had stopped all foreign songs, in order to protect German culture from alien influence, but he allowed popular singers from abroad. They replaced the ones who left. Instead of Marlene Dietrich and

---

1 'Five little negroes sat at the piano. One of them played Mendelssohn, and then there were only four.'

American songsters we had Marika Rökk from Hungary (she was actually born in Cairo), or the guttural accent of Rosita Serrano from Chile. Jazz was forbidden too, it was 'nigger music'. Orchestras who played hot or let instruments howl were reprimanded. Loud drumrolls were OK in German marches, not in dance music. Pop music had to be orderly. The rumba too was banned, as un-German; tango and English waltzes were all right. Best, of course, were the old German dances, polka, waltzes and something called the Rhineländer.

Lale Anderson sang the most popular German song: Norbert Schultze's, 'Lili Marleen', which every night at nine o'clock was broadcast by a military station from Belgrade. Renate and I were always allowed to stay up until that point. After the fall of Stalingrad the Nazis even forbade that song; with its sentimental account of a girl waiting for her lover, it no longer fitted into the war effort.

Anita knew all of the popular songs, which originated mostly in the movies, the songs of Ilse Werner (her speciality was whistling) and of the Dutch Johannes Heesters. My favourite pop star was Zarah Leander, the Swedish nightingale. Anita and I would stand in the kitchen and loudly intone her great consolation hits 'Ich weiss es wird einmal ein Wunder geschehen' (One day a miracle will happen) and 'Davon geht die Welt nicht unter' (That won't be the end of the world). They were meant to demonstrate how to thrive in adversity, to encourage the public to hold their heads high. Another favourite in our kitchen and in the rest of the country was Heinz Rühmann, especially his appeal to virility 'Das kann doch einen Seemann nicht erschüttern' (This can't faze a marine). Of course we were not aware that these songs were part of Hitler's morale-boosters, meant to broadcast to the world that Germany was invincible, to lull people into believing that everything was civilised and cosmopolitan. For us they were just songs.

Many songs were pure propaganda, mostly in march tempo. At school we sang 'Es zittern die morschen Knochen' (The brittle bones tremble), which ended with the refrain:

> Wir werden weiter marschieren,
> Bis alles in Scherben fällt.
> Denn heute gehört uns Deutschland
> Und morgen die ganze Welt.[1]

---

1 'We will go on marching / until everything is smashed / Today we own Germany / And tomorrow we shall own the whole world.'

Other songs, like 'Wir fahren gegen Engeland' (We are flying towards England), I sang heartily with my class in the school yard, but I refused to join in the song called 'Die Stukas', on account of the refrain, which my mates belted out: 'We will not rest until England is entirely destroyed, entirely destroyed, the Stukas the Stukas the Stukas.' I was not that dumb.

Hatred of England was widespread, and there was no end to the stupidity it produced. When someone sneezed it no longer sufficed to say: 'God save Hitler', now they said instead: 'God punish England'.

The cinema too was a potent means of propaganda, and many films were particularly aimed at the young. Some of my friends at school had seen films like *SA Mann Brandt* or *Hans Westmark*, which celebrated the rise of the Party before 1933.

Louise had forbidden us to see these films, and my pocket money was restricted. I had no desire to see *Die Rothschilds* or *Jud Süss* with Werner Krauss, or the even more repugnant *Der ewige Jude* (The Eternal Jew), which displayed such open anti-Semitism that only the most fervent Nazis were taken in by them, but the one film I was dying to see was *Hitlerjunge Quex* (Hitler Youth Quex), which showed the heroic death of a Hitler Youth at the hands of the Communists, before Hitler's rise. All the boys were talking about this film and I borrowed money from a friend in order to go. Quex was a blond, rather neat-looking Aryan. When his father, a fat and unappetising Communist, played by Germany's great actor Heinrich George, caught his son singing a Nazi song, the audience sat up. Worse followed as the Communist bully began to thrash his young son, forcing him to sing the 'Internationale', until tears welled up in his true blue eyes. Naturally we all sided up with the victim; such was the power of propaganda. But I never dared mention this film at home.

Despite all these diversions the war rolled on relentlessly. The Germans had taken Yugoslavia and Greece and reached the gates of Moscow and Leningrad. Most of my schoolmates were in ecstasies. I secretly hoped that the joy of the class would soon be tainted, for Louise had told us that the Russians had broken through the Front and that the British were advancing in Africa. In December 1941 the battle outside Moscow had finally began to turn against the German army. The public's faith in Hitler's invincibility had received its first knock. Goebbels whipped up patriotic feeling by calling on civilians to collect for the troops. Everyone was always collecting something for someone – scrap metal or newspapers for the war effort or money for the *Winterhilfe*, the Winter's Help. Our class took some afternoons off to collect in the streets. Louise did not approve. She called it propaganda rubbish, which of course it was.

The army published miniature books, the so-called *Feldpostausgaben*, special Front editions, which were small enough for soldiers to carry in their pockets. I used to bind the tiny five-inch booklets, Hölderlin's poems, Kleist's *Marionettentheater* and Rilke's *Cornet*, in leather and send them to the Front, thinking that no soldier reading such literature could be my enemy. Louise approved of that. She was also not opposed to our collecting woollen clothing for the soldiers freezing to death in the savage cold winter of Russia.

The news from the Front was disheartening. Letters which had passed the censor undetected spoke of terrible hardships. Yet worse was to come. By the end of the winter people were talking about a quarter of a million dead, and a million wounded. Those who had so ardently predicted victory began to shut up, only the propaganda machine reeled on relentlessly. On the newsreels victorious canons continued to fire, and they showed pictures of tanks and airplanes in balletic scenes to rabble-rousing marches. The Nazis learned their best tricks from old music-hall numbers. There were pictures of German soldiers dying in the snow, but they had been defeated by the elements, not by enemy hands.

The Nazis had declared one Sunday per month to be the *Eintopf Sonntag* ('One-Pot Sunday'). This was meant to foster community spirit and unite the whole nation. Rich and poor alike were to forgo elaborate dishes (which, given the rationing, was in itself an irony). Instead we were to eat a kind of pot-au-feu, mostly soup, made from lentils or dried peas. Louise considered this more 'Nazi nonsense'. We ate *Eintopf* on wash-day. The laundry was boiled in the basement in large cauldrons before being dried on the lawn – for this a special *Waschfrau* was engaged. Every Wednesday the Waldhaus was redolent of the smell of soft soap steam and lentils. This was the day for *Eintopf*, Louise had decided, not a Nazi Sunday.

Sometimes it was difficult for Louise to prevent me from doing what my friends did. I went once to look at the Führer – although when she found me out I nearly got a beating. Berlin was spared the big rallies of Nuremberg or Munich, but there were rallies nevertheless. Sometimes the school was asked to go. These mass meetings were Hitler's most powerful propaganda tool. We had all seen on film the gigantic spectacles with Hitler marching through a sea of flags and uniforms, a *via triumphalis*, as Goebbels described it. People formed groups and moved in unison. I had witnessed a parade in Berlin and seen the mindless ecstasy which overtook the spectators, as if moulded by an invisible will. I must admit I was impressed by the cavalcade of black shiny Mercedes driving along the streets of Berlin, but was embarrassed by the crowd going berserk at the sight of their Führer.

For a thirteen-year-old the sight of waving flags, the shouting of 'Heil!', the automatic raising of arms to the deafening sound of music, all seemed to be frightening yet fascinating, a sinister ballet which synchronised individuals, meticulously choreographed and calculated to numb the brain. Louise was right to want to prevent me participating in this; we just did not understand it then.

We had *Rassenkunde*, the history of race. It always struck me as odd that while blond healthy Aryans were constantly paraded before us, our leaders looked nothing like the muscular male sculptures of Arno Breker or Joseph Thorak. Goebbels was small and clubfooted, and neither the fat Göring nor Streicher looked like the beautiful Aryans Leni Riefenstahl displayed in her films.

Our instruction in literature was also guided by the regime. Being the French Lycée, we had access to Molière, Racine and Corneille, but not to the 'decadent' Rimbaud or Baudelaire. Of course Jewish writers or those who had turned their back on Germany were totally taboo. Stefan Zweig, Thomas Mann and Hermann Hesse were deprived of their German nationality.

There was so much we were not allowed to read, hear or see! And yet it is a mistake to think that we were entirely cut off. Not all foreign literature was banned. Publishing houses like Suhrkamp, Kiepenheuer and Rowohlt could still bring out even some 'undesirable' authors right up to 1944. Hemingway, Faulkner and Thomas Wolfe were published in big editions, as were Edgar Wallace, Joseph Conrad and Upton Sinclair.

Fortunately I also had the run of my father's library. I was quite intoxicated by the French Romantics, Lamartine, Musset, poems and novels in which the heroes always died on the battlefield and the heroines of consumption. There were also Frank Wedekind, the *Decameron* and Casanova's adventures as well as Balzac's *Contes Drolatiques* which opened my eyes to unknown and undreamed erotic possibilities. As soon as everybody was asleep I would turn on the lights and begin to read, sometimes until the early hours of the morning. The pallor that resulted from my vigils prompted me to invent a pain in my chest. Since this caused considerable concern, I was taken to the family doctor. Dr Fortner was an imposing old gentleman with a large beard, who had for years looked after the family and nursed us from our first inoculation through the whooping cough. Dr Fortner examined me from top to toe and then asked my mother if she might leave us alone. 'Klaus-Peter,' he said, 'since you have no father, I must ask you: do you sleep with your hands on top or under the blanket?' His voice stressed the words *on top* and *under* and he looked me straight in the eye. Oh dear, I thought, now comes the warning about going blind. 'On top, Dr Fortner.' 'Good boy,' he replied and stroked my innocent cheek. 'The boy has grown too fast, Madame,' he said to Louise. 'That's all.'

Most of our teachers were academics rather than pedagogues. Our art teacher was the exception. Dr Feist, a prim and rather prissy character, favoured tight-fitting suits. Despite his rosy complexion he always displayed a slightly hurt expression. He would explain to us the difference between Ionic, Corinthian and Doric columns and we would spent hours gazing at large reproductions of antique statues, the naked or half-naked figures of the Apollo of Belvedere, the *Laocoön* group and the Praxiteles *Discus-thrower*. Sometimes Dr Feist brought a projector and threw the images of Arno Breker on the wall. The muscle-flexing giants were called *The Army*, *Daring*, *The Party*. Gone were the fig leaves of the ancients. In their strong fists they held insignia of the Party: the sword and the torch. Some boys giggled while Feist expounded the virtues of comradeship and virile naturalness. 'To be naked means to be free,' he would pronounce. His voice rose very slightly, while his hand lingered longer than absolutely necessary on the shoulder of one of the pupils.

Under the shower after sports, while impersonating the artificial postures of Breker's statue *Comradeship*, we would imitate Dr Feist's voice: 'To be naked means to be free.'

There was little prudery. Unlike Anglo-Saxons we were brought up not to be ashamed of our bodies and were encouraged to be healthy and open about them. Germans have always been keen nudists and we had seen plenty of naked people at the sea fronts.

But sex talk, now common, was almost unthinkable. For all Louise's enlightenment she never discussed sex with us; few parents ever did in those days. I did not talk about sex with my sister either, for she felt far superior, and would not stoop to talk to a thirteen-year-old boy about those matters. But I did catch her once exchanging knowing glances with Anita when the latter described, in great detail, a love scene from a film which we were considered too young to go and see. Our neighbour's fourteen-year-old daughter once showed me her slightly bulging breast. I was not impressed, but recounted this to increase my status in school.

Sex education in school was all but taboo. A progressive teacher at Renate's school had called the parents to a meeting in order to explain that she was planning to give some sort of sex education to her pupils. When asked to expound on what she wanted to do she imitated the motion of sexual intercourse. Several parents stormed out in disgust but, strangely, Louise reported that the fathers had been extraordinarily attentive, as the teacher had been rather pretty.

Not that we needed any sex education – we were pretty up to date. Masturbation stood high on everybody's agenda. In class there were rivalries, pacts, friendships. Boys were very aware of their bodies and of the effect they produced on others. Jokes about wanking never ceased, nor for that matter did wanking. I soon picked up enough from my friends to know that I wasn't the only practitioner: most guys bragged about it. So with all the various emotional upheavals I had come to terms with in growing up, guilt was not one of them. We regarded sex as a kind of joke. I remember that one afternoon at a friend's house we played a terrible trick on one of the boys. We decided to turn off the lights and have a wank together to see who could come first. As soon as the lights had been turned off everybody started to moan and to groan, playing it up. When Karl announced that he was coming we turned the lights on again, and there we were all fully dressed – the only one with his fly open was Karl, red-faced and covered in shame.

Homosexuality was never spoken about or discussed in the newspapers, but a romantic attachment between children or young people of the same sex was not considered shocking. 'It's a phase. They will outgrow it,' was the usual reaction.

My school report now read: 'One must admit that Klaus-Peter has tried to become a little more discreet, but he has a long way to go to earn the approval of his teachers. Most of all, he must become more orderly' – orderliness being one of the great virtues of the day. I cannot say whether maturity was setting in or whether the discipline so liberally meted out at school was finally beginning to have an effect.

We were in what was known as the *Flegeljahre*, the rowdy years. Corporal punishment still existed but it had taken on more refined forms than being thrashed across the backside in front of the whole class, which had been the practice at my primary school. Corporal punishment at the Lycée fell to the headmaster, who, as you will recall, liked to parade in stormtrooper boots and uniform. At the end of the day he would summon a given offender to his office and then march him down to the school's cellar. A whole ritual would then begin: first the bolting of the door, then the lowering of the victim's trousers and pants. Dr Nix would unbuckle his belt with great gusto, and slide the belt from the loops. The generous beating, loudly counted, did hurt. Chastisement was meant to purify. The laceration of the flesh was supposed to lead to a higher spirituality, as the Church had taught us.

I cannot tell if Dr Nix was also hoping that my spirit would win the final victory over my body, but I suspect that the inflicted pain was more closely linked with something else and that it carried strong sexual undertones, which were not completely disagreeable. The ritual of these beatings and the circumstances produced a strange bondage between torturer and victim. I knew nothing of psychology at this time, but it must have something to do with my growing sexual awareness. I did not feel humiliated. It was more like something a man has to go through.

Every time I came home from school with a bad report Louise threw one of her great theatrical tantrums. 'This is the thanks I get for sending you to the best possible school, for doing everything to bring you up properly. I'm glad your father is no longer alive to witness the shame which you bring on our family. You'll end up as a street sweeper!' she would shout. Renate would stand in the corner and grin, for of course she had a good report. Once Louise got going she could not stop. She slipped into the role of the long-suffering widow with the ungrateful son. 'This is what comes of being too soft. My father used the whip on us, and we never had a chance to go to a decent school.' I was a good actor: I would feign repentance and vow to do better. I also vowed secretly to take a good swipe at my sister, that little rotten apple of my mother's eye, at the next best opportunity.

Renate had grown into a pretty girl with two long plaits. She looked dark and interesting. She had inherited the gypsy look of the Gurkes, and the exotic looks of Ida Adam had come down to her. I, by contrast, was tall and blond, the very image of an Aryan, the ideal Hitler youth. Not that this made any difference; in the eyes of the National Socialists, I was still Jewish.

We were now at war with America too. Hitler's Reich had never been larger. It stretched from Norway to Africa, from Brittany to the Balkans. And yet every night thousands of aircraft continued to bombard Berlin, Hamburg, Cologne, Dresden, Frankfurt and Munich. Hitler took it out on the remaining Jews.

The famous Nuremberg Laws 'for the protection of German blood and German honour', which forbade any Jew to marry a Gentile, also stipulated that 'no one of half-Jewish blood is entitled to any higher education, beyond the age of fourteen', which for Renate and me meant that we were only allowed two more years in high school. We were also banned from many things, such as the local tennis club most of our neighbours' children belonged to. We were lucky not to have to wear a star of David, or to be put away. The Nazis did not quite dare as yet to arrest Jews from mixed marriages. But for how long?

The Schillers – he a Christian, she a Jew – were under pressure to divorce. They refused. Not all made this decision. Some non-Aryans suddenly discovered an *Ariernachweis*, the pedigree which proved their Aryan ancestry. The three Jewish parents with sons in my class debated the possibility of turning one of the Jewish parents into a Christian. One-quarter Jewish was preferable to half. I am honoured to say that Louise, as did the others, decided against such manipulations. She wanted us to be proud of our family, for pride helped one to bear the many humiliations.

At one point Louise had tried to get us out of Germany by using some contacts in Switzerland. She wanted to send us there, with the Ruysdael painting as a surety. But no country would take two unaccompanied children, so we stayed, resigned.

There was very little organised resistance – at least we never knew of any – but there were many shades of behaviour. It was not as if the whole country was separated into Nazis and anti-Nazis. There were fanatics and hypocrites, opportunists and cowards. There were those who resisted and those who gave in. Hitler could bank on a huge silent majority, for as in any society almost everybody had good reasons to conform. Most Germans were preoccupied with getting hold of food, coming to terms with the nightly raids, the separation from husbands and sons. Almost everyone had lost someone or something. Survival was all that mattered, getting through intact. The Jewish question was secondary. It was not a time for great moral stances, for revolt, it was much easier to pay a little lip-service to the Nazis. Complicity through silence.

The silent, passive collaborators mattered more to Hitler than his party members, but we knew many brave people who made at least a small gesture, which in those circumstances could be called heroic. Not giving money to the Hitler Youth collection, sometimes using the excuse of having no change; never saying hello with 'Heil Hitler' (most people in private hardly ever used this form of greeting anyway, it was mostly used in officialdom). A few people would not sit down in the train when they saw someone with a star of David standing. Some brave decent people dared to speak out, although any opposition became increasingly dangerous. It was not unusual to hear people criticising some aspects of the regime or making political jokes among like-minded friends. I remember the one about the two Jewish emigrants sailing to New York. One of them had taken a Hitler portrait with him. 'Are you crazy? What do you want that for?' the other one asked. 'In case I get homesick.' In another, an s s officer offers a reprieve to a Jew condemned to death if he guesses which one of his eyes is glass. 'The left one,' says the Jew. 'How did you guess?' asks the officer. 'No one ever has.' 'It looks so kind,' replies the Jew.

One morning Anita, who had been out dancing all night, overslept, and I missed the bankers' train. In the next one a German officer with the *Rit-*

terkreuz (one of the highest decorations) sat at the window. He had lost both arms, and with the two pincers that had replaced his hands he attempted to light a cigarette. An old gentleman with the star of David in his shabby but still elegant suit watched him. He quietly approached the officer and struck a match. The officer looked up, smiled and thanked him. At that moment a young thug jumped on and pushed the old gentleman to the ground. 'How dare you, *Judenschwein*, offer a light to a German officer?' he shouted. I was appalled. The few other passengers, the officer among them, went to the rescue of the old Jew. The thug took off at the next stop. That whole scene had only taken seconds. Afterwards no one spoke, no eyes met. This too could happen in Germany under Hitler.

Another incident has stuck in my mind. In 1942 Jochen Klepper, author of the famous novel *Der Vater* (The Father), killed himself and his family when the Nazis threatened to take his Jewish wife away. Our small local church could not hold the congregation that flocked to pay their last respects to this brave family. This too was a show of resistance.

Louise had stored our most precious possessions, the large eighteenth-century tapestry and the Ruysdael, in a bomb-proof shelter at the Galerie Friedländer. One day Louise received a call informing her that our Gobelin had been taken by 'someone high up in the party', confiscated as 'Jewish goods'. Louise fought back. She was a Christian and so were her children. Friends advised her to lie low, but she would not give in. When she discovered the name of the taker, who turned out to be the industrialist Günther Quandt, the first husband of Goebbels's wife Magda, she wrote to him, and the tapestry was returned. We rolled it up and took it to our cousins in the country, together with some silver, and hid it in the barn under the hay.

The small Nazis were far more dangerous for us than the big ones. We never came in contact with the big shots, who merely made the rules, like banning us from school or the tennis club. But the small ones, with their petty vindictiveness, harmed us continuously. One day our neighbour Professor Stüwe decided to put up a notice in their garden: 'Die Juden sind unser Unglück.' Every time we looked out of our windows we saw it. We were accustomed to anonymous anti-Semitic graffiti but this kind of personal hostility was new, and most people in the neighbourhood were embarrassed by what had happened. 'The Adams are such nice people, how can they do such things to them?' was their response. The sign remained.

As there was less and less food, Anita made bread with flour from acorns, salads from nettles. So many of my childhood memories are linked with food. My *madeleines* are *Erdbeeren mit Milch* (strawberries with milk) and *Königsberger Klopse* (a kind of hamburger cooked in a caper sauce), but of course these were all things that one could only dream about then.

We also had very little coal, so we lived mostly in one room and took our meals in the kitchen. Only when we had guests did we eat in the dining-room. On these occasions, the good Meissen would be taken out of the baroque armoire. I used to gaze at its contents. It was like a big shop window display: vestiges from times past. Heavy silver trays with matching coffee and tea sets, rows and rows of sparkling crystal glasses. Two dinner services, one for daily use and one for festivities, 560 pieces for 72 people. Louise would point out stacks and stacks of blue and white plates in all shapes and sizes, for soup, meat, dessert, each separated from the next by a little lace doily, to protect them from chipping. The drawers were full of table linen: big white starched cotton-damask tablecloths with mono-grammed napkins the size of small sheets; a special set in dark pink 'for lobster dinners' and one for Christmas with hand-embroidered Tannen-baums, which was the only one we now seemed to use, for we hardly ever had guests. Yet once a month everything was taken out of the *Barock-schrank*, washed, polished, counted and put back. It was absurd perhaps, but also reassuring in a world where everything seemed to be crumbling.

Louise took great care to keep up appearances. However abysmal life might be, she always changed into a smart dress in the afternoon. What-ever the shortages, Anita continued to serve at table. Eventually she would eat with us, for she had become one of the family, much loved and much needed. But when there were guests, she had to wear the traditional black dress, a white apron and lace coiffe. 'Can't let standards drop into chaos,' Louise would insist. She also insisted on being addressed as *gnädige Frau*, Madam, a term still common today. But Louise also ensured that we did not get false ideas. She allowed no pretentiousness and we children were expected to do the washing-up on Sundays, when Anita had her afternoon off, nor was Anita ever allowed to polish our shoes.

The contents of the armoire also had another function. Louise went often to see her cousins who were farmers to 'organise' some of the things money couldn't buy – butter or the obligatory goose for Christmas. So the armoire began to empty. The cousins were celebrating their silver wed-ding. It was time to part with some silver lace Louise had been holding on to for an evening dress. The cousin had never had an evening dress, much less a silver lace one. There was food and drink in quantities we had not seen for years, and at the end of the evening old cousin Gerda went into the stable, lifted up her silver lace dress and sat down on the milking stool.

She returned with piping hot milk and the lace dress covered in cow dung. *Sic transit gloria mundi*, I thought, and laughed.

How much longer would this war last? We no longer believed in a German victory. By 1943, some doubts must also have crept into the Nazi circles, as the popular song 'Und wieder geht ein schöner Tag zu Ende'[1] disappeared from the radio repertoire, rather like the U-boat songs after the many heavy losses in the battle with Britain.

Louise tried to keep abreast of the news; the BBC broadcast daily in German from eight to ten o'clcock at night, the muffled sound of the opening chord of Beethoven's Fifth coming from underneath a duvet.

Sometimes you learned things from friends. Annemarie had married a fellow journalist, Gerd Hassenkamp, a tall attractive man who in the enthusiasm of his youth had joined the SS, a sad mistake which he was never able to shake off. 'Hass' knew things and hated the Nazis. When he could bear the guilt no longer he volunteered for the Front as a simple soldier. Louise had another friend, Katinka Graf, the wife of a doctor who served at the Front. Katinka was my mother's *Busenfreundin*, or bosom pal, an expression I found funny, because Katinka had no *Busen* to speak of. She too knew things and hated the Nazis.

Annemarie, Louise and Katinka used to go for drinks to Mampe, a bar in Berlin, as wives of men at the Front were entitled to cocktails. The sight of three women in a bar was nothing unusual, in a world without men. They would wear identical silver fox collars and Plexiglas shoes, which were all the rage. Like many soldiers, Katinka's husband sent her furs from Russia. Had they been bought or requisitioned? This was no time for great moral choices, and foxes were jolly warm and exceedingly chic.

We had a growing number of French prisoners of war working in our garden. 'Fraternisation with the enemy' was another of Louise's small efforts to beat the Nazis. The 1,000 square metres of land did not need much tending, partly because she enjoyed gardening herself. We were told that the presence of these prisoners was good for our French, but the real motive, we soon discovered, was somehow different. Louise had fallen in love with one of the officers in charge of the camp, Dr Fritz Walter, a handsome, diffident man twenty years her junior. We celebrated Christmas in the French prison camp. I impressed the prisoners tremendously by singing 'Sur le pont d'Avignon' and 'Parlez-moi d'amour'. I did not tell them that I also knew the Marseillaise, which my friend Pierre, who had a French mother, had taught me in the lavatory of the Lycée, while smoking.

1 'And once again a lovely day is ending.'

Then in 1943 came Stalingrad, the great turning-point of the Second World War. The official news that Hitler had lost the battle did not reach us immediately, but in the afternoon of 3 February the radio was playing Bach's third Brandenburg concerto, followed by Beethoven's *Egmont* overture and Liszt's tone poem *Mazeppa*. A sombre voice announced: 'The fight over Stalingrad is over. Faithful to their last breath, in accordance with their oath to the flag, the Sixth Army, under the exemplary leadership of Marshal Paulus, has been defeated by the enemy's overwhelming strength and the difficult circumstances.'[1]

The 'difficult circumstances' were the bitter Russian winter with temperatures never rising above minus 25 degrees. Two hundred thousand German soldiers perished, either killed or frozen to death, and 90,000 were taken prisoner, many never to return.

For four days cinemas and theatres closed as a sign of national mourning. After Stalingrad nothing in Germany would be the same. Hitler began increasingly to retreat from public life, and in school parallels were frequently drawn with Frederick the Great, 'the solitary king'. Goebbels assembled the masses in the Sportpalast and asked the chilling question: 'Wollt Ihr den Totalen Krieg?' (Do you want total war?) The crowd shouted back: 'Ja!' The yes of a blind and fanatical crowd blared from loudspeakers and in the headlines of the newspapers, but however hysterical, the messages seemed to be less and less convincing as increasing numbers of people began to ask themselves how this war would end. How could Germany win with the whole world ranged against it?

The propaganda machine shifted gear once more. No longer the Jews, but the barbaric Reds were out to destroy the German race, and the discovery of a mass grave containing the bodies of 4,400 Polish officers shot by the Russians petrified everybody. What would happen if the Russians advanced?

Hitler's opponents became more outspoken. One day Mrs Schiller phoned us to report that several thousand 'Aryan' wives of Jews had assembled in front of the police headquarters in the Rosenstrasse and shouted for hours demanding that their husbands be freed, as a result of which many were.

From the BBC we learned that Winston Churchill and Franklin D. Roosevelt had met in Casablanca and decided that only an unconditional surrender of Germany would be acceptable. The Allies obviously wanted

---

1 'Der Kampf um Stalingrad ist zu Ende. Ihrem Fahneneid bis zum letzten Atemzuge getreu ist die 6. Armee unter vorbildlicher Führung des General Feldmarschall Paulus der Übermacht des Feindes und den ungünstigen Verhältnissen erlegen.'

to ensure the total downfall of Germany, without negotiations or mercy. 'Hass' told Louise that many officers had been openly debating whether to revolt against Hitler, but that the news of the 'Allies' intransigence' was a terrible blow. Soldierly honour would not, under such circumstances, allow them to make a pact with the enemy. Revolt against Hitler, yes; but the destruction of their whole country, never.

On 11 July 1943 Louise heard that the Allies had landed in Sicily. Soon afterwards Mussolini was arrested and the disappearance of fascism, almost overnight, put the fear of God into many Nazis.

The bombs became increasingly lethal. Ordinary explosive bombs were replaced by firebombs setting whole streets alight. Rows and rows of buildings collapsed, burning for days. I remember those hopeless mornings, the sky still black with smoke. People in torn or burnt clothes, carrying a few bundles, searched for survivors, walking aimlessly among the ruins covered in dust and plaster, unable to grasp what had happened. The British now began to drop phosphorus bombs, and we were instructed to immerse our heads in a bucket of water when hit. But the most frightening were the air mines. Houses virtually collapsed and people's lungs burst from the pressure.

Berlin became the most bombarded city in Europe. In one air-raid alone 150,000 people lost their homes. The number of deaths was never announced. The cellars of individual houses were no longer considered safe. People took refuge from the bombs in underground stations. Opposite us was a hospital for the mentally ill, with a special air-raid shelter. Every night we would take our little bags, containing some papers and a few jewels, and run across the street to shelter with hundreds of patients and their nurses. It was a ghoulish experience. People lay on the floor or sat on the suitcases. In the dim light I saw someone sobbing silently. Occasionally someone cried out. Renate and I celebrated our thirteenth birthday there, at midnight on 2 August. Anita had baked a little cake and taken it with her.

Soon after the 'all clear' was sounded thousands of German soldiers arrived, and started clearing the debris that blocked whole streets, while others repaired telephone and electricity lines. Ambulances, fire brigades, even food supplies were organised with the renowned German efficiency. Within days, trains worked as normal and the city would resume its life, business as usual. Those who were bombed out were given a half bottle of cognac and 25 grammes of real coffee, very little to ease the pain of total loss of all one's belongings. I am still amazed how we managed to carry on. The next morning we were back at school and people returned to work in offices without doors or windows. Cinemas and theatres still played to full houses.

But the merciless attacks had a deeply demoralising general effect. All over Germany museums, cathedrals and monuments fell to ashes, and by the end of the war not only had half of all houses been destroyed but more than half a million civilians had died in air attacks alone. Many, even those who were opposed to Hitler, began to question the morality of such senseless destruction. People grew angry. They felt like innocent clay pigeons, and rage at times became the sole antidote to the desperation and fear of a civilian population which every night ran for cover from the lethal bombs. The bombs fell on everybody regardless of whether the victims were for or against Hitler. Some hoped that Hitler would fulfil his promise of revenge; others felt, deep inside, that Hitler had been wrong, that it had been a great lie, but they had so long believed in it that they could not even admit it to themselves. For more and more people the myth of Hitler the invincible began to wane.

All these terrible events brought our personal deliverance nearer, but faced with the loss of so many lives, how much could we really rejoice? We hated Hitler and many of the Germans, yet Germany was still our country, Berlin our home town. We loved its streets and churches, its buildings and squares, which fell to ashes before our eyes.

Non-essential people, mostly women and children, were encouraged to quit Berlin, and the Lycée's decision to evacuate the entire school came as a big relief to me. As the summer drew to a close, we boys were sent to Züllichau, a small town in Silesia. Meanwhile Louise, Renate and Anita left for Austria, where Louise had rented a farmhouse in Tressdorf, a village in a remote valley of Carinthia. There, she hoped, the Nazis would leave us in peace. Once again I was separated from my family. Louise wept and I, although at an age when it was considered unmanly, could barely control my tears. Yet, had we all fled to Austria, the Organisation Todt would undoubtedly have taken me off to their forced-labour camp. So the best thing was to let the three women leave Berlin, as if on a normal holiday; once they had gone, no one would ask after them. I boarded the train for Silesia together with about sixty other boys. Our parents stood on the platform, and when the train pulled out of the bombed station, there were more tears. Most of us were barely fourteen years old, and given the bombs and the hazards of war, how could any of us be certain of seeing each other again?

In Züllichau we all lived in a large school building with several classrooms and five dormitories. It was very Spartan, food was basic, but at least we were spared the nightly raids. In the morning we had lessons and in the afternoon we either played sports, loaded goods onto trains or helped in hospitals. I preferred the hospital, for sport was never my forte and the work on the station smacked of helping the war effort.

There were hundreds of wounded soldiers and the nurses could barely cope. I used to fetch food from the kitchen to the wards. One soldier had lost both his hands and I had to feed him and help him use the lavatory. I remember how he cursed 'the bloody Jews and Bolsheviks' and claimed that 'our Führer's new arms will kick the enemy out of our country'. It used to make me feel like throwing the soup in his face, but I didn't.

I also used to push soldiers in wheelchairs through the park. I became especially fond of a twenty-six-year-old officer who had light blond hair and resembled a Greek god. He had lost both his legs. His lungs were in pieces. He never smiled. On my third visit he asked me whether I was a Nazi. 'No,' I whispered, and then (I can't imagine what got into me) I added: 'I am Jewish.' The crippled officer gazed at me sadly. 'I'll tell you something, boy. For you the ordeal will soon be over. For us, this is only the beginning. We will pay for this for generations to come. I've already begun,' he said, pointing at his two stumps, 'but this is nothing compared to what is yet to come.'

Sometimes I sat by the soldiers' beds and read Rilke's *Cornet*: 'Riding, riding, riding. And courage has grown so tired and longing so great.'[1] I remember one soldier who had lost both eyes and wore dark glasses. While I was reading: 'Next springtime (it came sad and bitter cold) a messenger from Baron von Pirovano rode slowly into the estate of Langenau. There he saw an old woman weep',[2] he clutched my hand tightly. The soldier was only four years my senior. I even remember his name: Tobias.

I looked down the long row of beds. In each of them lay a shattered existence, a broken body, betrayed and sacrificed. These were my enemies: they had fought Hitler's war, not mine. What sense did all this make? I often cried at night, lost and confused, not unlike those soldiers.

Being parted from my mother, my sister and Anita brought a certain freedom. Perhaps from fear of rejection, I had established closer links with my fellow pupils. I had grown in confidence, became amusing and made the others laugh. I had become good company, *ein fideles Haus* (a jolly house), as the Berliners said.

Instead of sharing a room with homesick little boys, as was my previous holiday-camp experience, I now slept in a large dormitory with a bunch of rowdy boys, telling dirty jokes and discussing the world all night long. It

1 'Reiten, reiten, reiten. Und der Mut ist so müde geworden und die Sehnsucht so gross.'
2 'Im nächsten Frühjahr (es kam traurig and kalt) ritt ein Kurier des Freiherrn von Pirovano langsam in Langenau ein. Dort hat er eine alte Frau weinen gesehen.'

was fun. Not that any of the boys had actually experienced much with girls as yet, but they bragged. Boys of thirteen simply were not up to it, not in 1943. But they were up to having something with one another, about which of course nobody ever bragged.

The younger teachers had gone off to the war, and those who remained were too tired to impose the old discipline. Nevertheless Dr Nix continued to practise his disciplinary sessions in the cellar of the youth hostel, which had become both our home and our school. But now we had developed dirty minds and could at least snigger about Dr Nix's bizarre rituals.

Politically too we were more alert and we no longer accepted propaganda without scrutiny. The endless repetition of the same old clichés, about the strong and healthy *Volk*, the emphasis on clean living and the celebration of the family with countless children, no longer impressed us, despite Goebbels's skilfully crafted *Wochenschauen* (newsreels), in which cameramen trained in feature films and careful, selective editing produced a web of deceptions and lies.

One day we were informed that every boy between the age of fourteen and seventeen should volunteer to become a *Flackhelfer* (assistant to the anti-aircraft crew); 120,000 had already joined up, they told us. Total silence. Two of our 60 volunteered. The rest just sniggered in the dormitory. I as a *Mischling* was of course not even considered, for *Mischlinge* were *wehr-unwürdig* (not worthy to serve). Hitler wanted to ensure that, when victory finally came, he did not owe this success to one drop of Jewish blood.

By Christmas, the Allies were in northern Italy and the Russians were approaching Poland – a couple of hundred miles from where we were. The Christmas tree in the canteen sported a swastika at the top. We had combed the town for a bit of angel-hair and had even found a few candles and red balls. We secretly bent the swastika into a star, more a prank than a political gesture, but the upshot was that our Christmas dinner was cancelled. I enjoyed all this, I felt at home here and belonged. Everybody knew that I was half Jewish, but by now they no longer cared.

When the letters arrived bearing news from our families, boys often cried. I was relieved to know that Louise and Renate were safe in the countryside, but most of my friends had families in Berlin. One boy told us that the Zoo had been hit by a mine and that animals had to be shot, for fear of their escaping. We couldn't even laugh at the prospect of crocodiles swimming down the River Spree. As the end approached, I began to feel sorry for the bombed-out, starved and aggrieved German population. Some of my pals had lost their fathers and many had lost their homes. Were the Germans finally beginning to pay the price?

Then all pity suddenly evaporated and renewed hatred set in. On 11 March 1944 the time ran out for Kurz, the Felsensteins and Adam, the four *Mischlinge*. None of our classmates expressed any pity. I have often wondered what they talked about the next day, faced with the four empty benches. Dr Nix summoned us to tell us that we should never blame our parents for having married Jews. Then he handed me my final report, which simply stated: 'Klaus-Peter shows a lively interest in class. In the camp he has proved to be a good comrade.' At the bottom of the page was an addendum: 'This pupil leaves school, in accordance with a ministerial ruling, at the school-leaving age of fourteen.' Dr Nix turned out to be a man who simply performed his duty.

Louise came to collect me. We boarded the train and travelled, standing for several hours, until we reached Berlin. As our train pulled out of Züllichau station we had heard the rumble of the approaching Russian guns.

4

Pastoral Interlude
1944–1945

We stopped in Berlin for only one night. The sight of the pulverised city was terrible. The street where my grandparents' house stood was reduced to a pile of rubble. Even in the suburbs houses had been destroyed. In our Waldhaus many windows had been blown out of their frames and were boarded up. It was now occupied by the Dutch writer Rolf Italiaander, a friend Louise had met in the Elmau.

The Waldhaus was also the hiding place of another writer: Evelyn Clevé, author of the life of Helen Keller. Evelyn Clevé was Jewish, and when her apartment was bombed out, friends declared her missing. She lived in hiding in our house right until the end of the war.

That night brought a particularly severe air raid. I had almost forgotten how frightening this was. The Americans and the British now took turns, the u s Air Force attacking during the day and the r a f during the night.

There were many changes. Those who in the past had proudly displayed the party emblem on their lapels now left it at home, or wore it only to official functions. Fewer and fewer people would greet one with 'Heil Hitler!' People did not really have a change of heart, but many worried about the future. Some hoped that, if Germany could no longer *win* the war, it might at least not lose it. Many feared the approaching Russian troops more than the Nazis, after hearing horror stories of the cruelty, the looting and the raping that preceded their arrival. Over two million prisoners of war were supposed to have died in their camps. 'Enjoy the war, the peace will be terrible' was a popular saying. There was a sense of being doomed together.

After a week, Louise managed to get two seats on a train to Austria. We wondered if we would ever see our beloved Waldhaus again. We took a few more of our personal belongings, but there wasn't much one could carry. I went into the cellar and chose a large glass of cherry compote from the rows of Kilner jars filled with apricots, apples and pickled cucumbers from our garden.

The journey to Spittal took twenty-four hours in a train with no heating and many broken windows. From there we took a bus into the valley of the Möll, right up into the mountains. We were safe at last. It was the beginning of one of the happiest and most peaceful times of my life. It is very difficult to describe what I felt, seeing the village and the farmhouse which for the next three years was to become our home. The mountains rose on either side of the valley to 2,000 metres. Tressdorf was about 800 metres above sea-level – a typical Austrian village, before the arrival of tourism, ski lifts and cars. There were about thirty houses, nestling along the winding road that climbed towards the white church with its high steeple. Except for the main road, there was no paving.

It was only the end of March and snow still covered the mountain peaks, but the meadows were breaking out with buttercups and wild primroses, which fat brown cows devoured with a loud chomping. On the mountains, the snow was just melting, transforming the river which ran through the village into a clear, icy torrent. The first thing I heard was the tremendous rumbling of the River Möll, rushing underneath the wooden bridges. This and the mooing of cows was always with us, even in deepest sleep.

Man and animal shared the same house. Ours had a ground floor, rendered in white stucco, which contained the stables, and an upper floor, of wood, which held the living quarters. We kept no animals, but the whole house smelled of cows, straw and milk which had permeated the fabric of the building. It made you feel warm and protected. We had a large kitchen which was also our living-room. The walls were blackened with soot, for most families still cooked on an open fire. The smoke sometimes filled the whole room and, with streaming eyes, we had to escape outside. Louise had recently organised a more modern wood-burning stove with two big compartments for hot water, but as there was no paint available the soot still clung to the walls. The wooden floor was scrubbed to a light yellow colour. The furniture was simple: a large table surrounded by four benches.

There were also three bedrooms, one for each of us – Anita had found lodgings with a neighbour. The pine beds had soft mattresses filled with the husks of maize, which every day had to be fluffed up. Each bedroom contained a large brick stove, rendered in white plaster, on top of which was a platform large enough to take a mattress. In the cold of winter we slept there, the room suffused with the smell of apples baking in the warming compartment underneath. We had no running water and took turns to fetch the icy mountain water in large aluminium pails from a spring some eighty yards away from our house. Every Saturday an enormous wooden vat was brought up from the stable and filled with hot water, ladled out from big copper pots. It was large enough to accommodate three people, and Renate and I steamed in the water until it turned cold, after which Anita would rub us dry with large towels of rough, unbleached linen.

All inhabitants of the village were farmers, except for the priest, the innkeeper and the women who ran the two shops: a general store where everything from flour to thread could be had, and the *Trafik* which sold newspapers, stamps and tobacco. People were poor, most had only a couple of acres of land and a few cows. In the summer the animals were driven to pastures, high up in the mountains. There were only four horses in the village and one tractor.

We were the only *Zugereisten* or 'arrivals', as outsiders were called, but lived like everybody else. We fetched the milk, still warm from the cows, and made our own butter, churning it in wooden vats. We helped at calving and getting the hay in. We cut wood and thrashed the corn until our bodies ached. In the summer we gathered blueberries and cranberries in the mountains and basketfuls of chanterelles. This was not a quaint rusticated country-weekend existence in mountain chalets. It was a life without cars, running water, telephones, without theatres and concerts. It lacked everything that is considered essential to modern urban life. It was also a life without noise and fear, without bombs and deprivation. For Louise and Anita, who had grown up in the country, it was like going back to their childhood. They were among the most popular women in the village, Louise on account of her boundless energy and simple good humour, Anita because she was the only one with short hair at the weekly dances. She smelled of the city.

Most villagers had never ventured further than the next little town. They only knew the world from the cinema and the letters their menfolk wrote from the Front. Everybody wore traditional Austrian country dress, the women colourful dresses with aprons, and the men *Lederhosen* and knitted stockings. We too adopted these outfits. All the women wore their hair in braids wound around their heads. Many, especially the older ones, sniffed tobacco, which gave them brown noses. I watched them with fascination as they put a generous pinch of brown powder on the back of their hands and inhaled it with a loud noise. The corner of their apron was used for nose-wiping after a heavenly sneeze. The men smoked large pipes which had pretty porcelain bowls, or they rolled their own cigarettes from tobacco they grew themselves. The balconies were festooned with tobacco leaves drying a rich yellow in the sun.

People's taste in food was simple. Homemade bread and big slices of bacon for breakfast. Meat was a rarity, except in the winter when they killed a pig, or on Sundays when they sometimes had a chicken. The staple was polenta, a yellow porridge made from maize. They had always lived that way, there was no reason to change. I loved to eat with the farmers. The ritual was always the same: a large pan of steaming polenta, with a small pool of melted butter in the middle. There were no individual plates and everybody would dip their spoons (which when not in use hung behind the crucifix in the corner of the room) into the butter. A wooden container of milk would be passed round, and everybody drank from the same ladle. In our home, Louise would insist on individual plates, but there was of course no longer any question of Anita serving. She was one of us, though she still addressed Louise as 'Madam'. Forgotten was the Meissen porcelain, which was probably tinkling as the bombs fell on Berlin, and the silver, which remained hidden under the hay on our cousins' farm.

This life was paradise. No other word can describe it. It instilled in me a lifelong love of nature, mountains and animals. Yet, however peaceful, the war left its mark here too. From almost every house one, two or even three men were serving at the Front. The arrival of the postman was a daily event, eagerly awaited by almost every family. People would write letters almost daily, mothers to sons, wives to husbands, sons to girlfriends, sometimes waiting for weeks for a reply. The imagination and fear never stopped. What happened? Why are they not writing? Were they dead, crippled, maimed? Letters would arrive with 'prisoner of war' written on them, in black letters. At least the war was over for them, we thought.

Our neighbour's son came back from Russia for a short leave. He had left the village two years ago as a proud soldier, full of belief in victory. Now he was demoralised. He told us that most of his fellow soldiers felt betrayed. Gone was the Nazi ideology he so freely dispensed on his last leave. Now he spoke about the cold fear he had experienced. What did he care about the question of military honour? All he – and many of his friends – cared for now was the question of survival. 'Of course there are the "150 percenters", who still believe in the final victory,' he said, 'but we curse them.'

From time to time Louise went away to Lienz in the Tirol near the Italian border. She always came back with masses of scarce food: coffee, brandy, wine. Dr Walter, who had been looking after the French prisoners in Berlin, now looked after the provisions for the German army. Before leaving Berlin, Louise had arranged for him to be transferred to Austria. How she did this we never found out. But there he was, just 100 kilometres from us. We knew that he was Louise's lover, for she was not one to hide such a detail from anybody. Renate took it rather badly, but I thought it quite smashing, for she would always return from such trips more radiant and loaded with goods. She would also bring some political news of great interest to us, of the Allies' gradual advance. Hitler's days seemed to be numbered.

I too had the first pangs of love. The object of my lust, since this was the prime motive, was Anna (or Annerl as the Austrians pronounce it), the daughter of the owner of the general store. She was tall, cheerful and six-teen years old. I was only fifteen, but coming from the town compensated for the lack of years.

Annerl served behind the counter, and never was I more eager to volun-teer to do the shopping. It did not take long for Louise to discover why we suddenly had a super-abundance of baking powder, or why I always ap-peared to have forgotten something from the shopping list. On Saturdays Annerl and I went dancing at the local inn. The repertoire consisted exclu-sively of waltzes and polkas, played by a noisy brass band. In between dances we necked in the haystacks.

But there were other diversions, thanks to Goebbels's propaganda effort. Once every fortnight a man arrived with a horse-drawn cart. It car-ried a projector and cans of film. The dance floor was transformed into a cinema and as there were not enough chairs we had to bring our own. The entrance was one mark. The programmes consisted mainly of stories about earnest and Aryan German farmers, films like *Kohlliesls Töchter* (Cabbage Liesl's Daughters) or *Der Meineidbauer* (The Perjuring Farmer), the story of a villainous farmer who denounced a nice Aryan couple. He died under the debris of his house. The credits rolled over the image of his two fingers, sticking out of the rubble, the fingers with which he had sworn 'the truth'. The films came frequently to a halt because the reels had to be changed and rewound. In the pauses people drank, discussed the picture, and the younger people went for a bit more necking in the hay-stacks. The pauses were as important as the picture itself.

For more serious lovemaking, the young men had to sneak secretly into the girls' quarters through their windows. This was known as *Fensterln*, 'windowing'. At night you could see quite a few windows with big ladders. It was great fun to remove them and to incarcerate the lovers. The village priest, Father Franz, raged against the sinners from his baroque pulpit, and left it open whether he meant those who followed Hitler or those in-dulging in the passion of the flesh. Once he got so carried away that he threw the Bible into the congregation.

Annerl and I also climbed the mountains. Her father had cows grazing on the 'Alms', the mountain pastures, and we often stayed overnight in the wooden barns the shepherds used during the summer. We carried the milk down on our backs in large aluminium cans, and Annerl taught me

how to make cheese. In exchange I spoke to her about Hofmannsthal and
Rilke, and read her some of my own poems, in which 'love' always rhymed
with 'dove' (*Liebe* with *Diebe*).

Tressdorf was miles away from anywhere, but it was still in Austria and
Austria belonged to Germany, and Germany still meant Hitler. His laws
also applied here. About half of the villagers were Nazis, the others were
divided into those who were indifferent and those who thought Hitler was
the greatest gangster of all time. You always immediately recognised the
Nazis because they had a portrait of their Führer hanging next to the crucifix. Most people in the village had never seen a Jew. They were anti-
Semitic by tradition, clinging to the assertion that the Jews had crucified
their Saviour.

The woman who ran the little tobacco shop was a fervent Nazi. She had
once travelled to Vienna to catch sight of Hitler. A small woman, she never
succeeded: the many people lining the streets blocked her view. She cried
in frustration and the villagers laughed about her foolishness. Everybody's
political opinion was well known, and Louise had seen to it that ours was
too. Most villagers had grown up together, gone to the same school, married and intermarried until most of them belonged to the same family.
However different their political opinion, they all sat on the same bench at
the inn, and knelt together every Sunday in church, the women on the
right, the menfolk on the left. There was no question of denouncing anybody because they said that Hitler was an 'arsehole'.

Language, among the villagers, like sexual mores, was coarse, and Louise was only too aware that she had to do something to maintain a certain
decorum. Although nobody knew about our Jewish background, we did
not dare to break the Nuremberg Laws by attending the village school.

Fortunately there were two fairly well-educated men in the village, willing to give us some private lessons. One was the village priest, the other
his brother Alois. Alois had been a waiter in the Kulm Hotel in St Moritz,
the very hotel where my parents had spent their honeymoon.

Father Franz and his brother became our tutors, Franz to brush up our
Latin and Alois to help us with English and French. My French was far superior to that of Alois, but my English was non-existent. Renate, on the
other hand, had gone to a school where English was the first foreign language. We spent two hours every day with our teachers, except on Sundays
and on days of weddings or funerals, when Father Franz was otherwise
engaged.

On 20 July something extraordinary happened. Louise was called to the only phone in the village: a call from Berlin. This could only mean one thing – the loss of our house. She returned ten minutes later, pale but drunk with joy. 'Das Schwein ist tot!' I had never heard my mother using such language. 'Hitler is dead!' she shouted, crying and laughing at the same time. The news spread fast. There was numbness and joy. Nobody knew what was going on. The radio was only playing serious music, an ominous sign. People began to assemble in the church to pray, some for Hitler's salvation, others for his end. There was only one church for both groups and only one God.

That evening the radio announced a failed coup. There was some mention of an explosion at Hitler's headquarters. We burst into uncontrollable sobbing. Could he have escaped? Could the providence he had cited so often have saved him once more? Finally it was announced that 'the Führer would address the German people at midnight' over the radio. When he finally spoke, we could hardly bear to hear the hated voice, the waffling on about the 'miraculous rescue', the lies about 'a small clique of ambitious, wicked and stupid criminal officers' who had tried to assassinate him. Only one name was mentioned, that of Colonel Count Claus Schenk von Stauffenberg.

Since the late thirties there had been several plans to get rid of Hitler and his regime, but whereas they had been hushed up, this plot was widely publicised. The 'ridiculous small coterie of criminal elements' included the best of Germany's military elite. Most of them were aristocrats, brought up in the highest of Prussian tradition, names such as von Tresckow, von Seydlitz, von Lehndorff, Schwerin von Schwanenfeld, Yorck von Wartenburg, von Moltke, von Kleist, Leber, Oster, von der Schulenburg, von Haeften. Twenty-two officers, among them one field-marshal and eight generals. Many were patriotic but, faced with the moral decline of the regime, had become disenchanted with Hitler. Their upbringing made resistance, even rebellion, imperative.The old class antagonism again came to the fore. Many soldiers at the Front felt betrayed by their own officers at a time when morale was at a very low ebb. Also some people wondered why these officers had acted so late: what was their role before 1944? Had not many supported the regime beforehand?

We learned the details of the dramatic events of 20 July 1944 only after the war. Everybody told a different story and some information gradually seeped through. The original plan was to set off two bombs, which were to explode at Hitler's routine briefing of his staff. Von Stauffenberg was chosen to place the explosive devices under the table at the meeting, but as he had only one arm, he could trigger off only one bomb. After he left the room to take a pre-arranged telephone call, someone moved the attaché case containing the bomb away from Hitler, who was poring over maps spread on a trestle table. When the bomb exploded at 12.42, Hitler escaped with only slight burns and bruising. After the failed coup photographs of him smiling appeared again in all newspapers: Hitler in hospital visiting those wounded in the coup, Hitler with soldiers. The trick worked once more. His myth and the love he inspired were as hard to kill as the man himself.

One day Siegfried Pistorius, a young officer and war journalist, appeared on our doorstep. He too was on the run. He brought more terrible news: Hitler's hated Prussian Junkers were hounded out and, as he decreed, 'strung up like butchered cattle'. The population was shown film clips. Hitler stopped at nothing, not even at persecuting the culprits' families. Many were arrested and there were plans to kill their children. Martin Bormann's call for the ruthless destruction of all subversive elements had been heeded. Thousands of people in all walks of life were rounded up and nearly 6,000 anti-Nazis were executed.

Pistorius's visit also brought confusion into my personal life: sexual confusion. I had continued to experiment with the boys in the village. Fifteen-year-old boys in Tressdorf, I soon discovered, had similar desires and curiosities to those of the boys in Berlin. And girls were not willing to let us have our way. Certainly not Annerl. Most boys usually fantasised about sex, often two or three together, customs were basic and there was not much bashfulness about. There was always some bragging of having it off with a cow, but I never saw any evidence of that.

Siegfried was really the first homosexual I met. I had a vague idea of what they were up to, for there were enough jokes about them in school. Homosexuality was not only illegal but it was generally considered an affliction, a horrible disease. Louise had many homosexual friends, but their homosexuality was never mentioned. Looking back it seems extraordinary how ignorant we were in such matters. Films or books avoided the subject and there was no mention of it in newspapers. In school there were sometimes jokes about the *Schwulen*, the queer ones. Educated people referred to them as 'from the other faculty', and the vernacular word for them was 'Hundred-and-seventy-fivers', referring to Hitler's paragraph 175, which punished homosexuality with prison or even concentration camp.

Siegfried shared my room. He had suggested that when addressing him I should use the familiar *du* (you), at that time only used among members of the family and close friends. And we had sex, proper sex. I did not like it at all, but I was intrigued. I was glad when he left the next morning. Louise never found out.

We had been without mail for months, not knowing if the Waldhaus was still standing. But worse was the fear for friends and family. Were Aunt Emmy and Annemarie still working in Berlin? Aunt Friedl was living in Dresden, which had been practically wiped out by Allied bombing: 200,000 people died within a few days. Was she among them? The Russians were now only 100 kilometres from Berlin. We had almost forgotten about Aunt Alice and Uncle Job. Those who had left Germany seemed to live on another planet.

Even Goebbels spoke about the Germans now fighting up against the wall, and the *Völkischer Beobachter* admitted that Germany *might* no longer win the war. In October the Americans marched into Aachen. The taking of the old city had a specially significant effect on many Germans. This was the city where thirty-two German kings had been crowned, the city of Charlemagne, one of the figures Hitler had always talked about.

Hitler now lived constantly in a bunker surrounded by the models his architect Speer had made for him – models for a new Berlin, the capital of the world, emerging victoriously from the war as Germania.

We had been shown a documentary film, *The Word in Stone*, which spoke of a gigantic building programme with a triumphal arch, a vast National Assembly Hall, a city centre with wide avenues and squares: a scheme that was to outshine Luxor and Babylon. In the meantime more towns fell to ashes. We were asking ourselves if Hitler had gone mad. With the end drawing near, he was increasingly portrayed as a lonely hero and death as a glorification. Rumours about him grew more and more far-fetched.

The little film cart now brought us films like *Heimkehr* (Return Home), in which a tearful Paula Wessely mentioned the word 'Germany' thirty times in one monologue. Most films dealt with the great German past. Veit Harlan's *The Great King* was a big morale booster. It featured the blonde Kristina Söderbaum. She looked exactly like the prettiest girls in the village, her hair piled in braids. People could identify with her as she played a peasant. There were damp eyes in our little cinema when King Frederick, after losing a battle, rides into the village and is greeted by Kristina Söderbaum, carrying a child in her arms. 'Are you alone?' he asks. 'No,' she replies looking down at her child. 'I am,' he says. With music swelling to a crescendo the film cut to the king, played by Otto Gebühr, divine and solitary, sitting in the cathedral in Potsdam, contemplating the fate of his country. In his mind's eye he sees farmers ploughing fields, reaping corn, happy peasants and mothers with healthy children. This was a blatant piece of Nazi propaganda but Tressdorf's farmers were not so gullible. They might have enjoyed the story but they no longer swallowed its message.

The projectionist also promised to bring us Veit Harlan's *Kolberg*, one of the last films made in Germany, UFA's big blockbuster about a German town withstanding Napoleon, Goebbels's most expensive film, but before he could lay hands on it, Germany had disappeared. Many speeches in this film were based on those of Goebbels. 'Capitulation?' says Heinrich George, as an officer, in *Kolberg*. 'Never! We know every stone here, every corner, every house. We are not letting it go even if we have to claw into the ground with our bare hands. They will have to cut them off, to slay us one by one.' Then falling into the arms of Horst Caspar, who played another officer, he hears the soothing words: 'That's the spirit! Now we can die together.'

The call for sacrifice intensified. Someone in the village had spread the rumour that Hitler had a special gas which would put us all asleep. Those who would not face the fact that the war was almost lost found solace in the belief in Hitler's new arms. The V1 and the V2 employed against England would turn Germany's fate around, one heard and read.

In a last effort, women, especially young ones, were first asked and then forced to join the battle. Anita was one of the unfortunates who received the call to become a *Blitzmädel* (the equivalent of an English WAAF). We were heartbroken. Could we not hide her? She decided that it was better to go. In the last year the persecution of those who resisted orders was severe and quick and the fact that she was with a Jewish family would have weighed heavily.

On Christmas Eve 1944 we went to the little church on top of the mountain. From everywhere appeared small groups of farmers walking through the deep snow, carrying little lanterns. It was so cold that you could see people's breath; under their heavy head-scarves their brows or beards were white with frost. Above us a clear sky was lit by a thousand stars. What mercy there was in such a scene, while in the town there was only suffering. Everybody – mostly women, old men and children – assembled in the little church under the big tree with the wooden crèche and the hand-carved figures. For hundreds of years people have assembled thus, praying and singing and celebrating the birth of the Lord.

This year there was even less joy than in the previous years. While we had been preparing ourselves to go to midnight mass, Goebbels had announced over the radio: 'Forward over the graves! The army of the dead is stronger than the strongest army on land and on sea. When the bells of our victory ring out, the dead will return.'[1] Nobody in the little congregation believed any longer in what he had called 'das Fest der starken Her-

---

1 'Über die Gräber vorwärts. Die Toten sind stärkere Heere als wir auf dem Lande,

zen' (the feast of the strong hearts). The hearts of so many of us were broken by grief, despair and powerlessness.

On New Year's Eve we sat in our little kitchen with a bottle of illegally brewed apple *Schnapps*. But there was no real *Silversterstimmung*, no festive mood. We switched the radio on, which was now almost the only link with the rest of Germany. One was always listening, hoping that something extraordinary might happen. Instead we heard the voice of Heinrich George, reading the *Preussisches Bekenntnis* (Prussian Oath) by the nineteenth-century military writer Karl von Clausewitz. 'I will only be happy if I find a glorious death in the great fight for freedom and dignity of my fatherland.'[1] George's marvellous declamatory voice trailed off in the sound of violins playing the 'Deutschlandlied'. Then cathedral bells chimed twelve times. We all embraced, raising glasses to toast an early end to the war, while the radio played 'Oh Deutschland hoch in Ehren' (O Germany high in honour).

The next day, Hitler spoke in his New Year's Day speech about cities which would rise out of the ashes. 'A people that on the Front and at home does such extraordinary things and suffers so much cannot perish,' he shouted with trembling voice, 'but will rise out of the furnace of its ordeals stronger and firmer than ever before in its history.'[2] We listened to these mad and calculated utterances with an almost perverse pleasure.

Sometimes when letters did get through, they spoke about hundreds of thousands that had fled the eastern provinces of Silesia and East Prussia. The refugees arrived in waves of destitute human debris. Seventy years of German history were being wiped out by the plundering, raping and murdering Russian troops. Everybody hoped that the Western Allies would be fast enough to arrive before the Russians. In Berlin people began to buy cars and petrol on the black market in order to be ready to escape from the Russians, who had crossed the River Oder. Even Nazis bought stars of David on the black market.

On 30 January, exactly twelve years after his rise to power, we heard Hitler's voice for the last time over the radio. People had turned on the ra-

dem Meere. Beim Dröhnen der Glocken eines siegreichen Friedens werden sie zu uns zurückkehren.'

1 'Dass ich mich nur glücklich fühlen würde, einst in dem herrlichen Kampf um Freiheit und Würde des Vaterlandes einen glorreichen Untergang zu finden.'

2 'Ein Volk, das in Front und Heimat so Unermessliches leistet, so Furchtbares erduldet und erträgt, kann niemals untergehen. Im Gegenteil: Es wird aus seinem Glutofen von Prüfungen sich stärker und fester erheben als jemals zuvor in seiner Geschichte.'

dio from habit, nobody paid any attention any more. What did people in an Austrian village care about the 'Asian tidal wave' Hitler was warning against? All we wanted to know was when the war would be over.

In one of his last speeches, Goebbels in a brilliant display of theatrical rhetoric called for renewed faith in victory: 'Only yesterday,' he said, his voice trembling with emotion, 'the Führer told me: "We will overcome this crisis." ' Goebbels went on: 'If I ever believed in anything, then it is my belief that we will beat the enemy and I believe we will pin victory to our flag. Never in my life have I believed anything so firmly.' We were told that many who heard him found new hope even in this last death agony of the Third Reich. Bormann too called for faith: 'Reisst hoch die Herzen!' (Lift up your hearts!), he shouted. Four weeks later he disappeared in a flooded tunnel of the S-Bahn. Goebbels poisoned his six children, Holde, Heidi, Hedda, Helmut, Hildegard, and Helga, who had been my schoolmate, the only one who had bananas. When she died she was thirteen years old. The other children were even younger. Goebbels and his wife Magda took their own lives.

The last German newsreel showed the last pictures of the Führer, an aged and bent man, greeting a row of Hitler Youths in soldier's uniforms twice their size, all decorated with the Iron Cross. The youngest was twelve years old. Hitler touched his cheek, the boy smiled proudly. One of the first American-made newsreels also showed a twelve-year-old boy. He was sitting on a heap of rubble. While he took off his uniform, tears were streaming down his face. His head shook in disbelief.

At the beginning of April the countryside was crawling with retreating soldiers in torn uniforms, all Nazi insignia carefully removed – the sad remains of Germany's glorious army, bare of all hope. Unshaven, with feverish eyes, they looked exhausted and dirty. They had only one desire, to get home and to avoid being captured by the approaching Allies. The villagers took pity on them and let them sleep in their barns. We too offered shelter and food. Many of them were barely twenty years old. I filled the wooden vat in the kitchen with hot water and watched them as they sat in the bath, three at a time, half asleep with fatigue.

Sometimes there were civilians passing through the village, transporting their meagre belongings in baby prams, wagons, on bicycles or on their backs. Many radio stations were now in Allied hands. It could happen that a German broadcast was interrupted by the trailing in of a Russian or American voice. More than ever we were glued to the little box in the kitchen.

And then, on 18 April, the first Americans walked into our village. People stared at them in amazement. They were tired but they looked well fed and smelled of Lifebuoy soap. They had belts of green webbing instead of the leather belts of the Germans, and some had jeeps. The woman who ran the tobacco shop rushed into the garden to rake over the swastika she had sown with cress, but the villagers prevented her. When the Americans saw it, they took her away. Otherwise there were no hostilities. People hung white sheets from the windows and buried the portraits of their Führer under the steaming dung heaps in front of their stables, which I thought should have been done a long time ago. They were hastily burning the Nazi flags. We had never had one, but Louise rushed to the other houses rescuing them. After all, they were good cotton, and eventually Louise made shirts and underpants from them. For years I wore a swastika in my gusset.

For us the war was over. The deliverance turned into a kind of euphoria that lasted for days.

A few days later four soldiers walked into our house and one of them said to Louise: 'Hello, Fräulein.' They were courteous but cool. When we told them we were Jewish they laughed and said ironically: 'Oh yes?' One of them was called Rosenblum and was from Brooklyn. He told us that the Nazis had gassed all the Jews. But when we showed him some papers and the photograph of Moishe Adam, he fell around Louise's neck and called her mother. Fraternisation was forbidden to them, but we were Jews. His dream had come true: he had liberated us.

Once more I dragged the wooden vat into the middle of the kitchen. Seeing three naked American soldiers sitting there I smiled, thinking that only a few days earlier it had contained some German soldiers, but I kept my mouth shut.

The next morning they gave us very odd food, most of it powdered: powdered ice-cream, powdered coffee, powdered eggs and some Wrigley's Spearmint gum you chewed for hours. There was also butter made from peanuts, which we found quite revolting. Then they moved on.

Not all the Americans who drifted through the village were as nice as the first lot, but they were always nice to us kids. They were very keen on anything with a swastika on it, belt buckles or knives. In exchange for the 'Nazi-junk', a word we learned fast, they gave us chewing gum and sometimes oranges.

On the night of 1 May came the news we had been waiting for. The prayer of my boyhood had finally been heard. The usual broadcast was suddenly interrupted. Wagner's *Götterdämmerung* and Beethoven's *Eroica* followed. We were holding our breath. Then a voice: 'From the headquar-

ters of the Führer: this afternoon in the command cell of the Reichschan-
cellery, our Führer, Adolf Hitler, has found his death in his last battle
against Bolshevism. He died for Germany.'[1] We did not hear the rest. Louise cried with emotion. People ran into the street, all caution thrown to
the winds. Some rejoiced openly, others looked lost. What now? Many
could not believe and did not want to believe that it was all over.

All the vestiges of the twelve-year Reich had disappeared, except for the
swastika in cress. An American officer had ordered some barbed wire to
be put around it and forbade anybody to touch it, 'for evidence'. It became
the most photographed and laughed-at sight in the village. Suddenly nobody was a Nazi any longer. People began to feel like victims. The mourning for the dead took over from the mourning for the Third Reich. After
Hitler's death people woke up as if from hypnosis.

There was still some fighting going on in parts of the country. One day
we came upon a station with an English voice. 'This is Radio Hamburg, a
station of the Allied government,' a rather nasal voice announced, followed by what we knew was the English national anthem. Those who had
not listened to the B B C of course had not a clue what the anthem sounded
like. The next few days the remains of the German army surrendered. On
8 May the war was officially declared over.

This was such a momentous event, and yet it passed like any other day.
Bells should have rung out, people should have cheered and gone crazy. I
was longing for scenes like those I would later see on the newsreels, of
Paris being liberated or London celebrating. There was nothing but silence, numbness, desolation. So many had believed too long in the Third
Reich, sometimes against their own better judgement. How could they
give this up? A whole world seemed to have crumbled. People kept on repeating to themselves: 'It is over, it is over', as if the repeated litany could
bring home the reality of something many had never believed would
happen.

The men who returned from the Front had thrown their uniforms
away, and by walking only at night they had avoided capture. They
brought news of the total collapse of the country: city after city in ruins,
the soil scorched by flames, which had engulfed almost everything.

Hitler left behind a country in total disintegration. The German Reich
did not exist any more, the state had ceased to exist. There was no administration, no authority, no police, no legal institution, no finance ministry.

---

1 'Aus dem Führerhauptquartier wird gemeldet: Unser Führer Adolf Hitler ist heute
   nachmittag auf seinem Befehlsstand in der Reichskanzlei, bis zum letzten Atemzug
   gegen den Bolschewismus kämpfend, für Deutschland gefallen.'

For weeks we were cut off from most of the outside world. There was no mail, no telephone, no radio and no transport of any kind. 'What is going to happen? Who is going to take charge?' All those questions were drowned under the enormous relief everybody felt. People displayed a will to live but there was a total political apathy. The fight for food, clothes, even shelter pervaded everything. We were lucky to live in the country, where there was less hardship. In the towns there was a shortage of everything. The pictures of the deprivation which we saw in the gradually appearing newspapers were heart-rending: human beings like animals crawling out of the rubble of their houses, their emaciated, frightened faces staring aghast into the lens of the camera. Was that the end of the war for which we had so passionately waited and longed?

5

Aftermath and New Beginning
1945–1946

The war was over, for Europe at least, as the Japanese had not yet surrendered. I heard for the first time the term atom bomb. A group of American soldiers passing through the village had cheerfully talked about this new weapon, which could 'bring the Japs to their knees'. On 15 August the radio reported that two atom bombs had been dropped on Japan. The first one, with the name 'Little Boy', destroyed Hiroshima, the second, 'Fat Man', Nagasaki. Few people took any notice; it was just another bomb.

For the next twelve months we lived as best as we could. Gradually, normality was setting in, at least in Tressdorf: a kind of normality, for there was still no mail, no telephone lines from anywhere.

In the summer we at last received a letter from Aunt Emmy, brought to us by a soldier. It was several months old, written in the last days before the end of the war.

> My dear beloved,
>
> I do not know how or when this letter will reach you. I am well and alive, which is more than many of us. You know how you always teased me for being so fat? Now I have lost 15 pounds. I do not mind this, except that we are all so tired, we hardly get any sleep. My flat still stands up; most of our friends have lost everything so I should not complain. Berlin, our beautiful beloved Berlin, you will not recognise it. Yesterday I managed to get to town. The Kaiser Wilhelm Gedächtnis church is a mere skeleton, the clock is still there, it has stopped at 7.30. To the east and the north, as far as you can see, miles and miles of rubble. I walked down the Siegesallee and the entire Tiergarten is a sea of blackened stumps like black coal. Every other house seems to be destroyed, it is almost unbelievable that there are still people living in this desert and yet I saw people coming out of their holes buying newspapers. There are still some trains, but it can take up to two or three hours to get to work. Somehow we manage. There is even the odd movie house. During the last days there was a concert in the Berlin Philharmonie, but it was impossible to get a ticket at any price. Every-

body just seems to take refuge in a bit of art. They tell us to leave the city, but where can we go? Death seems to be everywhere.

I am worried about you too. Try at least to get some news through to me. Your loving Aunt Emmy, no longer die Dicke Emmy [Fat Emmy].

During the last days before the fall of Berlin 20,000 Russian guns had constantly fired on the few resisting German troops, and while the whole city was wrapped in a cloud of dust, obliterating the difference between day and night, the Americans and the French had made 350 attacks from the air.

Berlin's fate had been sealed at a conference in Potsdam. It was to be carved up into four zones between the four allies, Russia getting the biggest present. The other three would live to regret this.

Now that we were allowed to attend school again we enrolled in the high school in Spittal, twenty miles south of Tressdorf. We took lodgings with a local family and only went home on weekends.

In class my English created quite a stir. While the others were able to recite 'I wandered lonely as a cloud', my entire vocabulary consisted of hotel and restaurant jargon. I knew that a steak could be rare or medium rare, I knew the difference between chickpeas and peas and the word for asparagus, but almost nothing about prepositions. My Latin was almost entirely ecclesiastical.

There was an acute shortage of teachers, for most of them had been contaminated by their affiliation with the Nazis. Those who were allowed to teach did not know what to tell us. There were no guidelines and the existing schoolbooks were out of date and full of Nazi propaganda. The occupying forces, wishing to turn Germans into democrats and to teach them about history, did not know how to cope, faced with the almost total lack of everything, from pencils to paper, from books to new maps.

Our history teacher was Dr Huber. People said that until recently he had sported a little Hitler moustache, but he had shaved it off. He wore a tattered loden jacket with leather patches on the elbow. He tried to explain to us that it was all Prussia's fault, conveniently forgetting that Hitler was actually Austrian. 'Frederick of Prussia, look at him – the typical war king. Compare him with the Empress Theresa,' he expounded, and added: 'Our Empress Theresa, she, with her many children, was a *mater familias*.' Then he blew his nose loudly in a blue and red country handkerchief. 'The Germans are all yes-men,' he rattled on, and his eyes fixed on the many Germans in class. He again conveniently forgot that until a few months ago

Austrians had also been Germans and that, in their enthusiasm for the *Anschluss*, they had even worshipped Hitler's grandmother. When I stood up to ask him if the recent rumours that Hitler was not really called Hitler but Schicklgruber, and that he was the illegitimate child of a Jew, were correct, he looked rather angry and said: 'Adam, let's stick to the truth, *now* more than ever.' Someone behind me said: 'Heil Schicklgruber!' and the whole class broke up in laughter.

Dr Benesch was our biology teacher. His task was also to give us sexual instructions. He was young and progressive and used words like penis and vagina as if he were saying good morning. Girls and boys were no longer separated, and we looked with slight embarrassment at the revolting pictures of sexual organs eaten up by syphilis. Of course we now considered ourselves very sophisticated, and no one giggled any longer.

Part of the re-education programme was the obligatory viewing of films about concentration camps. Every German had to attend a film session, organised by the occupying forces. Nobody was excused, not even children or the very old. In some areas people were obliged to visit the camp and had to file past the mountains of human debris. The Germans, who for so long had ignored what the whole world knew, now had to face up to the camps.

I went with my class to the viewing. We saw the emaciated bodies of Dachau, Belsen, Oranienburg, the gas chambers, the mountains of human bones and teeth. We sat for an hour staring at picture after picture of utter horror: fields of human corpses. In the audience, some people sat with tears streaming down their faces. Others hid their faces in disgust or shame. Some were sick. I thought how many of those who watched them with me had only yesterday shouted 'Heil!' or marched proudly in the hated uniform of the Hitler Youth. I thought that none of these victims died of natural causes; they died because they were Jews, Poles, Russians. They also died because the many Germans now looking at these pictures in disbelief let it happen.

I waited for my tears to flow but they did not come. I tried to pray but the prayers died in my heart. This hour and the subsequent knowledge of more horrors to come changed me forever. I felt for a long time a deep shame about belonging to mankind where things like these were possible. I hated Germany with an unprecedented hate which took a long time to abate, and I have never been able to look at anything German other than through the lens of Auschwitz. For years I could never meet anybody without thinking: 'What was your role in Hitler's Germany?' The entire world became separated for me into those who were Nazis and those who were not.

Gradually many of the younger menfolk returned from the Front. Some had a large POW written on the back of their tattered uniform. Some found a home as 'uncles', 'cousins', lovers in the mostly female households. So there were again plenty of young people around. Every weekend, Renate and I took the bus up the Möll valley to Tressdorf. I spent most of it climbing mountains or making love in the hay. I was very much in love with Annerl, but where sex was concerned I never got far, her shapely body was a promise that never materialised. Thank God for Zenzi. She was much older than me – that is, three years older. She had done a stint as a chambermaid in Innsbruck, and was versed in the art of lovemaking. Zenzi was warm and cuddly and she always smelled of the cowshed. She would sometimes order me to lie on my back under her cows and squeeze the warm milk right from the udder into my mouth.

Lovemaking in the hay was problematic, not only because straw tended to get into every orifice, but also because I suffered from hayfever. As the pill was not yet invented, Zenzi insisted that we practise *coitus interruptus*, only she did not call it that. Sneezing, coming and interrupting, while Zenzi loudly evoked all the saints of the Bible, was a complicated and messy affair, but I liked it enough to return to her regularly. And I stopped going to confession.

On Saturday we went to country dances, sometimes walking an hour to other villages, or up the mountains, wherever a band was playing. I could only dance the waltz or the polka. The band did sometimes strike up a foxtrot, as a token gesture to modern life, but only the soldiers who had returned from the outside world managed these new dances properly.

Louise decided it was time to send us to dance school. All Germans of good society had always gone to dance class. In Spittal, as luck would have it, an enterprising couple had opened a new dance school in a hotel. We were registered in what must have been the first budding of a social life. The enterprising couple were from Czechoslovakia. He had brilliantined hair, dyed black, and wore a slightly greasy dinner jacket. His partner was dressed in a tight, lemon-coloured evening dress that matched the colour of her hair. Both smelled intensely of the same cheap scent. Miss Mila was a slightly dried-out exotic beauty with very hard breasts protruding under her low-cut satin dress. We all knew about the consistency of her breasts because she had the tendency to press us firmly against them, while demonstrating the quickstep.

In the corner of the large room stood an old gramophone, and with the help of His Master's Voice and a couple of old records, we learned the tango to a tune called 'So schön wie heut' so müsst es bleiben' (May it remain as beautiful as today) or 'O Mia Bella Napoli'. My dance partner went by the beautiful name of Herzeleide, meaning Heartache, a most appropriate name. She smelled of vanilla and had a sweet smile, but she was rather clumsy. Renate on the other hand had a dashing cavalier called Alfons Strammer, and as the Austrians invert first and last name he was equally appropriately called Strammer Alfons, 'strapping Alfons'.

I wore corduroy trousers and a jacket made from an American army blanket that Bud Rosenblum had left behind. The girls sat, neatly lined up in a row, on the opposite side of the room. All the girls were dressed in the same yellow nylon frocks. The reason for this uniformity was Miss Mila's discovery of a parachute that had come down in her garden during the last days of the war. She insisted that girls wore evening dress and sold the material to her prospective pupils before enrolling them. When the music started the boys rushed over, sliding across the parquet to fetch their partners. The dance was always preceded by a deep bow and the clicking of the heels, followed by the question: 'Mademoiselle, may I have the honour of the next one?'

The sight of those girls in their peepee-coloured nylon evening dresses of no particular shape or style, their faces distorted by newly discovered chewing gum, was not an enticing one. I decided that the gentle sex was maybe not so desirable as Annerl and Zenzi had made me believe. Out of boredom and curiosity I began to experiment with my landlady's son, a tall willowy fellow, loose-limbed and agile. This seemed to be less complicated than with Zenzi, not only on account of the lack of straw and the *interruptus* bit. It was straightforward and unemotional. Xaverl did not evoke the names of the saints but he finished nevertheless with a loud 'Jesus'. This proved to me that Catholics obviously needed some spiritual support when sinning.

As a result of the dance class there were also numerous parties given in the home of a girl called Laverne. Nobody was called Laverne in those days, but her mother had read a French novel when pregnant, and thought Laverne would give her girl a touch of class, especially as her last name was Kunke. Laverne Kunke was quite classy, for she wore a belt made of silver cigarette paper from American cigarettes. She was what Berliners call a *Früchtchen*, best translated as a 'hot caper', and her parties were a kind of *Ringelpietz mit Anfassen* as the Berliners call it, an untranslatable expression meaning 'a get together with feeling-up'. This was exactly what it was: a petting party. After an hour or so of trying out the newly learned dances, the lights were dimmed and people sank into corners, behind sofas or even under the table.

The girls always kissed with closed eyes, while the boys usually glanced over their shoulders, to see what the others were doing. When the atmosphere grew too steamy, the girls got up for some more dancing, and then the lights were dimmed once more. In this way the girls made the rounds. Those who knew how to 'French kiss' were the most popular. Laverne was an expert, so I was told, but alas, I never found out, as most of the time I ended up with Herzeleide, who couldn't get her lips apart.

By the middle of 1946 some trains began to run again, although there was no postal service, which meant that we were still cut off from everybody, including Louise's bank. We were running short of money, and eager to see the Waldhaus again. Repatriation became an obsession with millions of Germans scattered over the entire country. Of course one could not just simply pack up and take a train, one had to register for repatriation transport. We registered in the summer; four months later we were informed that a transport was going in the direction of Berlin, and we were to present ourselves at the Spittal railway station on 28 November.

It was sad to leave the village and the house which had been our home during the difficult years of the war, the evenings wrapped in the reassuring cosiness of *Gemütlichkeit*, with Louise pouring out some *Glühwein* or serving an *Apfeltorte* made with apples from our own tree. We had formed so many links with simple and resourceful people, with animals and plants and with the solitary beauty of the mountains. I strolled for days through the small lanes of the village, saying farewell to all the familiar things: the stables and the haystacks that smelled of hot summers, and the sleighs stuck under the roofs that reminded me of real winters, filled with snow, that clung to your eyelashes and froze your breath.

But in spite of the sadness of leaving, the closer the 28th drew the more excited we became. We knew that we belonged to a different world, a world of big cities, noisy streets, the stimulating chaos of urban life. But what to take? How much could we carry? It would be a difficult journey, and in the end all we took was food, a few personal belongings and blankets. We had been told to bring our own provisions and Louise had organised several hams and bread. She had bottled blueberries and mushrooms. The last night under our roof, which creaked in the cold, I lay in bed filled with the excitement of things to come and the sadness of things to leave behind. I always loved this hour between waking and sleeping, the strange state when the day gradually begins to recede inside one. I once more had the inkling that, for someone like me, living would not be easy. But before I could think this out properly, I fell asleep.

In Spittal we joined a group of about a hundred people, all laden with suitcases and bundles. We stood for hours on the icy platform in the perishing cold. It was the coldest winter for years. We waited all of the

28th and most of the 29th, not daring to leave the station for fear of missing the train. Then on the 29th, just as night was falling, a train pulled in – about twenty goods carriages, each marked with a big white number. We had been given an allocation for carriage 16. There were already twenty-odd people inside. The stench when the door was opened was terrible: the smell of unwashed people and of smoke billowing from an iron stove. That was the only source of heat and light. There were no benches; everybody lay on the floor.

We climbed on board and secured a corner where we spread our blankets. Four hours later we pulled out of the station. We spent fifteen days on this train, travelling the 600 miles from Spittal to Hanover, a journey which in normal times would take nine hours. Sometimes the train stopped for a whole day in the middle of nowhere, waiting for coal, for another locomotive, or because one of the tracks was up. There was no lavatory or water. Every time the train stopped everybody rushed out into the cold. We melted snow to get water. Many people were ill, most had run out of food. I sometimes thought of the goods train I had seen transporting Jews. We knew so much now about their sad destination. Our destination was home. Going home was our abiding thought. Louise was heroic. She looked after the ill and shared our food with the others. When we unpacked the dark loaves of bread that she had baked in Tressdorf, all eyes (and mouths) turned towards us. I asked myself again and again about the role they might have played during Hitler's twelve years. I thought about the difference between hate and contempt.

Sometimes in a station there was an improvised field kitchen with some hot soup. The journey seemed never to end. Days followed nights and nights days. Because of the cold we could not open the door, but through cracks in the wooden walls we saw everywhere the same pictures of torn-up roads, uprooted trees, burnt-out trucks, splintered telephone poles and scorched buildings reaching like ghosts into the clear sky. The paraphernalia of a defeated country.

To relieve the boredom of the journey, we made chalk marks on the wall. After the 170th burnt-out locomotive and the fiftieth destroyed station, we ran out of chalk. When the train slowed down we all huddled in the open door, trying to read the names of the flattened towns. Where were we? Except in the country, there seemed to be hardly any houses still standing. Then on 15 December the train came to a halt for the last time, in a big station without lights, loudspeakers, clocks or station-master. We could just make out 'Hannover'. We all had to alight; it was the last stop before the Russian border. Berlin lay beyond. From here people had to make their own way.

We spent the night in a bunker which had been turned into a refugee camp, sleeping in makeshift beds. We were deloused and we got a piece of soap. It was the first time for nearly three weeks that we washed properly.

The next morning, men came offering to smuggle us, for 50 marks, across the Russian border. The danger of such an expedition was described in lurid colours, including rape and frisking for watches and gold. We decided to have a go at it. Before leaving, Louise went to find a church and left her jewels with the local priest, except for one diamond ring, which she hid on her body. The women drew lines into their faces, to look as old as possible, and hid them under headscarves. The guide collected his 150 marks and we set out, walking along the railway tracks in the direction of the Russian Zone. Every five minutes we were instructed to throw ourselves to the ground.

After about two hours, we were once more lying with our faces buried in the snow. We heard voices approaching. I remember reaching for Louise's and Renate's hands. My heart was pounding. The voices came nearer, German voices, belonging to a group of people walking in the opposite direction, along the same railway line. When they spotted us, they began to laugh. 'What are you doing on the ground?' they asked, and when we told them they laughed even more. 'The Russians don't give a damn, everybody is crossing the border at night, just walk on.' We looked around for our guide. He had vanished into the night.

In the early morning hours we reached a little station. A rickety train was already packed with people, who had all made the same nightly border crossing. There were no windows, but a hand-painted sign said 'Destination Berlin' and that was all we cared about. Eventually the train began to move. Hours later we pulled into Magdeburg. We were exhausted, frozen and hungry. Louise decided to break the journey. In two days' time it would be Christmas. Her brother Fritz lived in Magdeburg and she knew that Emmy had taken refuge in his house, so we set off to find them.

Uncle Fritz was a 'Cucumber' whose earthy sense of humour bordered on vulgarity. He had owned Reuter's Winebar, a famous local establishment, frequented by those who liked drink and hearty talk – not a place you took your children to. I remembered the three large portraits that used to hang on the wall of the dark bar room, neatly lined up in a row: on the left Fritz Reuter, a local writer of humorous verses, on the right Adolf Hitler, and in the middle Fritz Gurke. Uncle Fritz hated the Nazis, but no public place was allowed to be without a portrait of the Führer. Over the door was the crest of the house, a cucumber and an apple – the apple on account of his wife Lene, née Appel.

Lene Appel, who weighed twenty stones, had fallen for the one-legged Fritz, who matched her weight and drinking capacity. My father had always found this part of Louise's family beyond the pale, but Louise was fond of her brother, and after my father's death we had sometimes visited them. I had been fascinated by the idea that these two jolly, fat people washing glasses behind the gleaming bar were also my aunt and my uncle, so different from Aunt Alice and Uncle Job, who only spoke French at table. But then I had always been partial to the Gurkes rather than the Adams.

Reuter's Winebar had been bombed out and someone told us that the owners had retired to the country, taking the remains of the wine cellar with them. We cadged a lift in somebody's ramshackle car and Emmy nearly fainted when she opened the door.

The house smelled of vanilla pudding. There was warmth, a Christmas tree, hot water and plenty of wine.

Aunt Lene looked older, her hair had turned white. The Russians had raped her behind the house while Uncle Fritz looked on helplessly. Her hands trembled while she told the story. Gentle cheerful Aunt Lene. She was over sixty. 'The pigs, the dirty pigs!' I muttered. These were our liberators. I also thought about the millions of Russians who had been tortured and had died under the Germans, and I found little consolation. Emmy too had turned white; she had spent the war with the bombs. I almost felt ashamed that the three of us looked so healthy and well-fed.

The Russians had taken a gruesome revenge on the Germans for all the evil the Germans had done to them. The looting and killing and raping had been horrible, so many stories that wrenched your heart and froze your blood. A neighbour had lost both her sons during the war; when the Russians saw photographs of the two German soldiers on her mantelpiece, they took the wife and husband out into the yard and shot the husband right under the woman's eyes. Many soldiers had walked around with twenty wristwatches on their arm. In another house they had taken everything, from the toaster to bed linen. Gone were the old lady's fur coat and the children's toy train. And what they could not take they simply threw out of the window. Five soldiers had transformed the living-room into a shooting alley, shooting the china off the shelves like clay pigeons.

Lene and Fritz had survived the worst just by sitting at the piano and playing endless music. The Russians were sentimental: 'Mutti play,' they would say. But then they got drunk and used the grand piano as a lavatory and washed themselves in the toilet bowl. Once the regular Russian army moved in it became a bit better; at least the indiscriminate shooting of people stopped, but people had to hand in typewriters and radios, just as the Nazis had ordered the Jews to do.

Christmas with our aunts and uncle was sparse, but suddenly Emmy entered with some little parcels wrapped in newspaper. Presents? Where did they come from? An apple and an orange for the children and some knitted gloves for the grown-ups. Emmy had undone a sweater of hers for this. How many times in later years, faced with the obscenity of Christmas shopping, have I thought about these presents, which meant so much to us. Later that night, in the icy church, the hungry and exhausted crowd sang 'Christ der Retter ist da' (Christ the Saviour is here).

Fritz and Lene had some drinking companions, and through one of them, a station-master, we managed to get on a train to Berlin. Sometime around New Year we found ourselves on the S-Bahn station in Nikolassee, whence four years earlier I had taken the *Bankierzug*, and three years earlier we had set off to Austria. It felt like a lifetime away.

We had heard so much about the terrible destruction of Berlin, but when we saw it with our own eyes the shock was heartrending. From the Zoo station, where we arrived, I saw that the Kurfürstendamm did not exist any more. Many houses showed their wounds, and as not all walls had fallen to the ground, one could look into kitchens on the third floor, the wallpaper still hanging; in one corner a couple of chairs, covered in snow; a high wall just holding up torn curtains moving in the wind. The remnants of human existence were a sadder sight than the mountains of rubble.

In Nikolassee many houses still stood, but the streets were dark and empty, for the streetlamps had no bulbs. Many of the gardens, once well-kept, were overgrown with weeds. Their owners were dead or had not yet returned. Behind some windows we saw candles burning on Christmas trees. We passed the church where Pastor Fichte had prayed for Pastor Niemöller, whom the Nazis had put in prison. The cypresses of the local cemetery were bent to the ground with heavy snow. So many memories! There was the grave of the Kleppers, who took refuge in suicide. Pastor Fichte had also prayed openly for them.

We knew from Emmy that our house was still standing, but in what condition? We practically ran the last five minutes to the corner from where we could see the Waldhaus. And there it stood, in total darkness, the windows all boarded up, most of them broken. When Louise unlocked the door she was moved to tears. The furniture, the books, were all covered in dust. There was some electricity, but it was freezing cold. The coal cellar was empty.

We opened the shutters and saw blazing light and music coming out of the house of Renatus Ziegenspeck, the director of Continental Rubber.

There was ice on their swimming pool. We rushed to their house and knocked at the door. Frau Ziegenspeck opened it. We hardly recognised her. She wore bright makeup and a black dress. Behind her we noticed some American officers dancing with elegant women to American music. It was like a film set. Everybody drank whisky and ate little sausages on sticks. We looked so out of place in our outfits. We were introduced as 'the Jewish neighbours we told you about' and the American said 'Hi' and called my sister 'sweety'.

'Welcome back,' they all shouted. 'We can get you coal, and food, anything you want.' Mr Ziegenspeck played the black market. He still had tyres to trade and he pointed at the diamond ring Louise had slipped back on her finger. Louise, always practical, bare of sentimentality, decided within minutes that diamonds on frostbite looked ridiculous. In exchange for the ring we got several cartons of Pall Mall cigarettes. These in return were traded for coal to heat our house, plus food and some army blankets that were transformed into winter coats for us.

We slept the first night fully dressed. Home, I thought, but the word had a sour taste. That night I dreamed of Tressdorf, the memories of something wholesome, of the smell of lodencloth drying on a stove, the taste of blueberries with milk.

If Ziegenspeck's joy at seeing us again was genuine, the reception from our other next-door neighbour, Frau Professor Stüwe, was scandalous and in character. A bunch of flowers was sent over, with a little card saying 'Welcome back to Germany', signed 'Stüwe'. Louise simply tore up the card and threw the pieces, together with the flowers, over the garden fence.

The next day Anita arrived to take up her post. We were complete again, and happy, and for the first time considered on a par with everybody else, or even a little bit better. Germans among Germans. Renate and I were seventeen years old, Louise was fifty-three and Anita twenty-three. The postwar years began.

6

A German among Germans
1946–1949

Eighteen million Germans were refugees driven from their homes, three million died in the flight. The news was hard to grasp yet I was shocked when someone showed me an English paper, the *Daily Mail*, writing: 'Why extinguish only the name? Extinguish the country!'

Cities had become cities of the dead. A report from the Evangelical Relief Organisation read: 'Men take their own life out of despair. Thousands of corpses float down the rivers Oder and Elbe into the sea. Thousands of corpses hang from the trees, no one cuts them down any more. Tens of thousands are on the road dying of hunger and exhaustion.' In the winter of 1946 the worst had passed but, even a year after the end, there were images that linger to this day in my mind: the simple wooden crosses that stuck out of the rubble, with the names of those still buried underneath; the desperate faces of the women at the railway station, holding up photographs of husbands, fathers and sons, always hoping that someone might arrive with news from the missing; people wandering like lost birds among the ruins of their houses, searching inconsolably for the remains of their belongings.

The *Schlüsselkinder*, the key children, left alone during the day, played among the rubble and the toppled statues in the park, a key to their home around their neck. Every third German child, we were told, had lost his father. Gradually the rain began to wash away the names of the missing people scrawled in white chalk on the toppled buildings. What remained was the empty silence and the terrible physical and spiritual exhaustion. Everywhere people looked hungry and poor, but it was not so much the shabbiness of their clothes which struck me as the defeat written in their faces. Many avoided looking at you, especially when you told them that you were Jewish.

Berlin had been divided into four sectors, the Russian, the French, the British and the American. All around Berlin lay the Russian Zone, linked to West Germany by a motorway and one or two rail lines. We lived in the American sector. It was easy to move between the three Western sectors, and until 1949 we could also freely enter the Russian sector, although there was a border post between what very quickly became the two worlds, of East and West.

In the meantime, Berlin began to rebuild itself. In the beginning most of the people in the street were women, as one and a half million prisoners of war had still not returned. One hundred thousand never would; they died in Russian camps. But soon the famous *Trümmerfrauen*, rubble women, who had formed large chains and passed brick after brick from hand to hand, were replaced by workmen. Everywhere people mended roofs and windows. It was as if the display of desperate energy and the constant work helped to erase the past. People were simply too tired to think.

For the first time I experienced what many Germans had experienced before: hunger. There were new ration cards. The average daily food amounted to 1,500 calories and in some areas it was only 1,000 (1,500 calories meant a slice of bread, some margarine, ⅛ of a litre of skimmed milk and sometimes a bit of meat). Renate and I were officially declared victims of fascism, and as such entitled occasionally to some special rations from the Americans: a bit of cocoa powder, a tin of condensed milk and some oranges – delicacies most people only dreamed of.

Almost more terrible than the hunger was the bitter cold of the winter of 1946, the coldest for thirty years. The temperature dropped to minus twenty degrees, and we had hardly any wood or coal. Living once more in one room, heated by a little iron stove, we cut down the trees in our garden and burned some of our furniture. People sat indoors with coats and gloves. Many literally froze to death. On many days we had only two hours of electricity and were forbidden to use gas or electricity for heating. Louise checked the meter every day, and when we had used up the permitted quantity panic would set in, as on the day we discovered that we were overdrawn. Some people tried to run so much electricity that the meter went back to zero, but with two hours a day this was not possible.

Mr Ziegenspeck, of course, had a remedy. He knew where one could get *den kleinen Otto*. Anybody caught with little Otto went straight to jail. Little Otto was a magnet which stopped the meter from running. For two packets of Camel cigarettes you could hire one for the day. This was expensive, but at least you did not risk the punishment most feared by all – having your electricity cut off. Six packets of Camels, also provided by Ziegenspeck, saved us from that.

Another way of getting some heat was *Kohlen klauen*, nicking coal. The police had given up trying to catch the reported 7,000 people who daily pilfered from the goods trains. At night I used to go with some friends to Wannsee station. On one of the dark platforms stood a goods train bringing coal from West Germany, waiting to be unloaded. Two lonely policemen made the rounds. The scenario was always the same. Someone climbed over the fence and made a noise; the policemen rushed to the spot where the noise came from and this was the signal for us. About thirty people ran forward with buckets, rucksacks and old bags. Within minutes we were back on the streets, hurrying home with our loot.

Hand in hand with *Kohlen klauen* came other activities and new expressions. All had to do with survival, none with morality. *Kippen sammeln*, cigarette butt collecting, was good business. The pavements in front of Ami bars, and at the special military bus-stops, were particularly good places for it. Ami was the nickname for American soldiers, the British were Tomis. Twenty Ami butts bought a loaf of bread on the black market.

Schnorren, scrounging, was another pastime. Children learned fast that American soldiers, especially blacks, were kind-hearted. By hanging around places where they gathered one usually ended up with some sweets or a couple of oranges. The children of Hitler's master race had lost all the pride which had been drilled into them.

Hamstern, hoarding, too was a common pursuit. Louise travelled to the country again to exchange a few bicycle tyres from Renatus Ziegenspeck for some butter and eggs. We sometimes went with her on the so-called *Hamsterzüge*, hoarders' trains, named after the hamster. To be sure to get on the train you had to spend the night on the station. In the early hours of the morning, when we heard the train approaching, pandemonium would break loose. Everybody grabbed their bags and jumped on the moving train. People travelled on the roofs or between the wagons. In the compartments they were virtually piled on top of each other. Gangways and entrances to lavatories were blocked by boxes and parcels. The windows had glass, but you could not open them because the leather straps which released the catch had been cut off. Someone always stole them to make leather soles.

The trains left Berlin carrying passengers loaded with carpets, china, irons, lamps, silver and clothes and returned carrying passengers loaded with sacks of potatoes, some flour, maybe even a chicken and dreadful sticky molasses. Hoarding was illegal and sometimes the police confiscated the lot, but most of the time they closed their eyes; people were hungry after all.

The black market boomed. It was near Alexanderplatz, the place of Dada's *Milljöh*, but it too had changed beyond recognition. The pretty *louche* girls with their pimps were long gone, and with them the warning notices which had amused us boys so much: 'Syphilis Walks the Street', 'Do You Actually Know Each Other?' and 'Hurry to See a Doctor'. Gone too was the Hermann Tietz department store, and with it the ominous inscription 'Kauft nicht bei Juden' (Don't buy from Jews). Instead a lively trade was going on among the ruins, even among the graves in the old cemetery attached to the bombed-out church of St Georg. Every day thousands of people would spread out their belongings on the ground – the good old Meissen next to ivory toilet sets and silver teapots, a pair of green satin shoes with one heel missing for a loaf of bread. Children and old women offered a threadbare pair of trousers, parts of an old lamp or three cups without saucers. No money was exchanged. The only acceptable currency was American cigarettes: 120 for a pair of shoes, 40 for some stockings. In those days, all over Berlin, cigarettes were the real currency. You could use them in restaurants or in antique shops. One packet of Luckies was worth 120 to 140 marks, a carton 1,300 marks. You could buy cigarettes from Russian soldiers for only 30 to 40 marks a pack; the Bulgarian tobacco they contained was considered inferior.

What surprised me most was the total silence in which all this bargaining went on. Only sometimes, when an ineffective policeman appeared on the horizon, would the tired crowd stir a little. But most of the time, he too would take something out of his pocket – say an old police belt, with the swastika on the buckle – and quickly exchange it with some American soldier.

The black market was the lifeblood of the city. It went on day and night. Some people just traded over the phone. People lacked everything. Louise and Renate shared one pair of high heels between them, and while Anita and I worked out who would take the bicycle on Saturday, they drew lots for the shoes. Those who had something to trade lived well; the butcher traded with the baker, the small industrialist with the chemist. The first capitalists began to emerge.

We had retrieved the silver and the tapestry from under the hay in Louise's cousins' barn. It had miraculously survived Hitler's war and the looting of the Russians, who had mistaken it for a piece of old carpet. It was time to dispense with these last vestiges of more feudal times. Louise and I took the Gobelin ('Diana at the Hunt, Brussels, seventeenth century, without border') and exchanged it for twelve cartons of cigarettes – no longer Camels but Lucky Strikes, an appropriate name I thought on seeing the two GIs carrying their loot off. I saw them disappearing behind the ruins, boarding a jeep. I thought of the entrance hall of our flat in Dahlem with the Récamier sofa, the last place big and grand enough for a tapestry of that size. Louise chased me out of my dreams. She had already opened one carton and was handing two packs to an old woman, in exchange for a pair of American army boots. I sometimes wonder where our Gobelin ended up. Probably in the lobby of a hotel or in one of those Californian bungalows I had seen in films.

Finally news arrived from Aunt Alice and Uncle Job. They lived in Sweden, their daughter had fled to England, where she ran a farm. Various cousins of my father, the Fontheims and the Neumanns, re-surfaced as Fontaines and Newmans in New York. Miraculously most had survived, only one aunt of my father had died in Theresienstadt.

Some of the people who had left Germany under Hitler returned. Many just came and left again. Klaus Mann had been one of the first; he was working for the US Army newspaper *Stars and Stripes*. Marlene Dietrich had come in 1945 to find her sister, whom the Nazis had put in a concentration camp in retaliation for Dietrich singing for the American troops. Lotte Lenya and the photographer Alfred Eisenstaedt came back and then left again. For many Berlin still held some good memories underneath all the pain. It was touching to hear Dietrich singing 'Ich hab' noch einen Koffer in Berlin' (I still have a suitcase in Berlin).

Not everyone could be persuaded to return. Einstein, for instance, turned down an invitation. Salka Viertel too refused to join her husband Berthold when he came to Berlin to direct again in the theatre.

Despite the much reduced scale, life seemed to cling on to normality. Our mood was often grim, but we always managed to find some joy. We formed friendships and love affairs and Louise did not hinder us. She loved her children and looked after our material welfare. As for our emotional or intellectual development, we had to make our own experiences and find our own way in a world of increasingly bewildering choices.

The new chapters of my life always seem to begin with a new school. Renate rejoined her old school, and I enrolled in a high school in Wannsee, as the Lycée had moved to the other end of the town. My new school, a five-minute bicycle ride from the Waldhaus, was a coeducational modern comprehensive school. Times had changed and the emphasis on modern languages and technical subjects was considered useful. Most of my new schoolmates came once more from the upper-middle-class families that lived in the suburbs of Wannsee or Nikolassee. Many were forced for a while to live in the annex of their houses, for the occupying forces had requisitioned the often grand villas for their officers' families. Some Germans resented having foreigners living among their own furniture while they had to look on through the windows, but the relationship with the occupier was on the whole good, even if occasionally people had to borrow a couple of their own glasses. The old white middle-class conspiracy worked here too. Few ever considered the Americans or the British as 'occupiers'. For us youngsters, it was almost a smart thing to have an American officer living in our houses.

We were determined to grasp life in all its aspects. I was only seventeen. We had experienced death more closely than other generations but, like most young people, possessed the human talent of discarding the bad and retaining the good. We lived entirely for the present. Every experience was fresh and powerful. We did not worry about the future, which in any case was a blur.

Germans who had been a member of the Party or in official positions had to fill in the famous *Fragebogen*, a questionnaire containing 131 questions about their past. Most claimed that they had been forced to enter the Party. One of the many misconceptions is that most Germans had to belong to the Party; membership was in fact low, as the Party always considered it an honour. Special de-Nazification committees had to decide into which of five categories former Party members fell: 1st, 'war criminals'; 2nd, 'wrongdoers' ('evildoers' would be a better translation); 3rd, 'minor wrongdoers'; 4th, 'collaborators'; and 5th, 'not incriminated'.

Many people tried to procure themselves a so-called *Persilschein* (Persil certificate), to clean up their past. They suddenly remembered a Jewish or half-Jewish family able to testify on their behalf to a good deed. It became almost embarrassing to mention one's anti-fascism, because so many were claiming the same thing. The Nazis seemed to have disappeared into thin air. For many the only guilty ones were those publicly condemned at the trials of Nuremberg. Stripped of their decorations and uniforms, they looked so ordinary, banal. The great collective forgetfulness began. People spoke about the hardships of the refugees from the East, about the terrible bombs and the Russian invasion. They turned into victims. Everybody had their own little story to tell, personal history replacing history. The Third Reich as a historical event was never discussed.

With the gradual realisation of what Germany had done to the world, we began to suspect our teachers, the generation of our parents and public authority in general. The majority of grown-ups refused to question the past, they wanted to move on to the next business as quickly as possible. All their energy was spent rebuilding. Imprisoned in their past by guilt and sometimes even remorse, it was convenient for many to regard the Hitler years as a kind of natural catastrophe people were unable to avoid. The past was never properly examined, and it clung to most Germans for the next fifty years, undigested, misunderstood, explained away. For us, on the other hand, eager to learn, to understand, the past stood behind us like a terrible curse we had brought upon ourselves. We searched in vain for the power to lift the curse. Teachers and parents, implicated by default, cowardice, opportunism or indifference, kept their silence.

It was difficult for us to find out anything about the past. Libraries had been purged, 'dry-cleaning' as it was called. Out went Hitler's *Mein Kampf* and Rosenberg's *Mythos des zwanzigsten Jahrhunderts* (Myth of the Twentieth Century), soon to be replaced by Churchill's and De Gaulle's writings. The swastikas on the remaining public buildings were chiselled off and the sculptor Arno Breker gave his figures a less fascistic hairstyle.

In school it was easier to open up our minds to the new world of Brecht, Kafka, Musil, Walter Benjamin and Thomas Mann than to examine why these people had been missing for so long from our curriculum. The art teacher enthused about the abstract shapes of Klee and Kandinsky, without referring to the fact that, only a short time ago, the choice between abstraction and realism was a political one.

There was so much to catch up with. Few of us had heard of Proust, Joyce or Faulkner. We did not know what Schoenberg's, Webern's or Berg's music sounded like. Braque and Picasso were as unknown as Count Basie or Charlie Chaplin. Never was a generation of young people kept more ignorant, in a supposedly educated part of the world. Never was a generation more eager to learn.

The war years had made us more serious, more reflective than previous generations. For us words like honour, fatherland, nation, courage had lost all meaning. Everywhere we looked for traditions which had not been tarnished by the twelve years of the Nazi regime. Conservatism was totally discredited and we viewed figures like Wagner and Nietzsche with suspicion.

The spiritual renewal also needed a new language. Out went the standard vocabulary of the Nazis – words like non-Aryan, master race and racial ignominy; in came supermarket, coexistence, teenager and jobs. Other words had changed in meaning. *Jude* had for so long been an insult that now we were incapable of giving it the right feel. I was not able to say simply 'I am Jewish' without being embarrassed.

The Americans opened reading-rooms, small libraries with magazines and American books: Hemingway, Faulkner, Melville. Steinbeck's *East of Eden* and soon Salinger's *The Catcher in the Rye* became cult books for us, and I discovered F. Scott Fitzgerald and Dorothy Parker. The British Council opened an Information Centre and the French, not to be outdone, began with a Centre des Etudes, the Maison de France, with a cinema and one of the best restaurants in Berlin.

All these cultural efforts coloured our outlook, and we became Americanised almost overnight, as if it were the most natural thing in the world and the most desirable too. For a youth who grew up in regimentation and deprivation, it was easy to love everything from America: jazz, the belief in progress, jeans, T-shirts, films. Women fell for the GIs, those handsome and clean-looking soldiers in their smart uniforms with their big chewing-gum smiles. In their casualness and their directness they looked as if they had stepped straight out of an operetta rather than like members of an army, and seemed to embody all the signs of the new freedom. They brought nylon stockings and lipsticks and the streets were littered with condoms. Many Germans dreamed of getting out of the misery and going straight to America.

I tried to have as many American friends as possible. I swam with them naked in their sports clubs, chewed gum, learned to appreciate peanut butter. I outdid others in looking and behaving as American as possible. I listened to the AFN, the BFN and to WQXR, the American broadcasting station for the troops, to Rosemary Clooney and Glenn Miller. I 'clubbed' at the Amerika Haus, danced the *Hokeekokee* and spoke with a very broad American accent. I also got hold of a pass for the buses strictly reserved for Americans and greeted the German driver with a loud 'Hi!'

Not all cultural activities came from the Allies. The Germans too looked for something spiritual as a way out of their misery. Everywhere there was a desire to have art. It was for many a sign of civilisation refound, a possibility for a contact with other human beings.

Rats and strange birds inhabited the ruins of many theatres. When you walked the streets you heard the cracking of broken glass under your feet. Yet there was, to our surprise, a sprinkling of theatre and concert life, which had begun almost immediately after the war. Actors, writers and directors formed little groups and played in cellars, schools and churches. One theatre even used a shoe shop. Three weeks after Berlin's fall the first play had opened in the little Renaissance Theatre, a comedy, *Der Raub der Sabinerinnen*. A few months later the famous Deutsches Theater opened its doors.

Louise, Renate and I had not been to a theatre for so long that we threw ourselves into theatre-going with great enthusiasm. It was not always easy to get tickets, but a bag of nails or a little pot of paint, badly needed for the set, sometimes did the trick, and Louise as always had connections.

The occupying forces helped a lot to get the theatre going. The choice of the repertoire depended largely on the taste or the briefing of the Allied theatre officer. Each of the occupying forces had one. The Americans insisted on American plays, like Thornton Wilder's *The Skin of Our Teeth*, the French brought Claudel's *Silk Slipper*, the British, Eliot's *Murder in the Cathedral* and the Russians, Gorky and more Gorky. There was much rivalry. The Russian theatre officer stopped the performance of Thornton Wilder's *Our Town* in the Deutsches Theater (in the Russian sector), because it was too American. He also sacked the first intendant, Karl Heinz Martin, and replaced him by a trusted communist, Gustav von Wangenheim.

The rest of the repertoire consisted mostly of 'safe' plays, the classics. In some, Germany tried to make good. Suddenly Lessing's *Nathan the Wise*, which the Nazis had banned because the main character is a Jew, was performed all over Germany. *The Merchant of Venice*, on the other hand, had been a favourite of the Nazis. It took years before the German theatre tackled Shylock, and then it made sure to have him played by a Jewish actor.

It was unlikely that the emigrants would return and Berlin needed players, but I was surprised to see that most names reappearing on the programmes, which at that time were mimeographed sheets of paper, were still the same as those who had made a career in Hitler's Germany.

Only some names were missing. Heinrich George, star of so many films in the Third Reich, had been arrested by the Russians and died in prison. Others kept a low profile. Werner Krauss, who had been in the infamous *Jud Süss*, stayed away from Berlin. 'If Krauss plays, the place of the critic is outside the theatre,' wrote Friedrich Luft, who was the most formidable Berlin theatre critic, witty and well-informed. His reviews appeared in *Die Neue Zeitung* and he spoke regularly on the RIAS radio, a broadcast no one interested in the arts wanted to miss. He became the voice of conscience of the theatrical world.

Germany's most famous actor/director, Gustaf Gründgens, who had a brilliant career under the Nazis, spent a year in Russian custody. Gründgens had been married to and divorced from Erika Mann (she later married W. H. Auden). He was the subject of Klaus Mann's novel *Mephisto*, and later Istvan Szabo's film of the same title, which castigated Gründgens's role in Nazi Germany. However, as he had helped many Jews, he was released. In 1946 he directed and played again in the Kammerspiele des Deutschen Theaters, in the Eastern sector.

The Allies saw in film not only an important element in détente, but also a great possibility for re-education and reorientation. Instead of Cabbage Liesl or her Aryan counterpart, we now had Doris Day and Rock Hudson, Mae West and Marlene Dietrich. There was also a showing of *Gone with the Wind*. I was not much moved by the suffering, having just come out of a war far more frightening than the one Margaret Mitchell described, but I thought Scarlett O'Hara and Rhett Butler the most stylish couple I had ever seen.

The German film industry began to re-emerge. In the autumn of 1946, in the DEFA studios in the Russian sector, the first German film, *Die Mörder sind unter uns* (The Murderers are Among Us), was shot under British licence. It had a very young Hildegard Knef in it. The director was Wolfgang Staudte. The German cinema seemed to be more willing than the theatre to tackle problems about our present life. Käutner's *In jenen Tagen* (In Those Days) was an attempt to paint a picture of the post-war years. One film even tackled the subject of anti-Semitism, Erich Engels's *L'Affaire Blum*. But the budding German cinema had little chance with the general public – the entertainment coming from America was a much bigger pull. After a while we grew a bit tired of all that glitter and perfection in the American movies, we were looking for a bit of reality, but for that we had to wait for the Italian neo-realists and the French *nouvelle vague*.

Painters who for ten years had been forbidden to exhibit took their canvases out of hiding and travelled sometimes hundreds of miles by bicycle and train to offer them to museums. There was a sprinkling of new galleries and the Berlin Academy of Fine Arts opened with an exhibition of the work of Karl Hofer.

People with a printing press or a duplicating machine had to register with the Allies. Everything needed a licence to be printed – not only books but also railway tickets or music sheets and of course most of all newspapers. The first German paper, *Die Neue Zeitung*, came out under American licence. It was basically an American newspaper in German, printed, ironically, on the same press that, a year before, had printed the *Völkischer Beobachter*, Hitler's most notorious newspaper. The first issue carried a leader by the military governor, Dwight D. Eisenhower, a name nobody knew. Other papers followed. The weekly liberal newspaper *Die Zeit* came out in 1946. It was not long before Axel Springer published *Die Welt* and Augstein brought out *Der Spiegel*, modelled on the American *Time* magazine.

Book publishing also revived. Peter Suhrkamp, ex-editor at Ullstein, who had looked after the publishing house S. Fischer during the war, applied for a licence to publish books again. But good paper was scarce and the books came out on coarse paper which began to disintegrate after a few months. The publisher Rowohlt brought out his novels on newspaper, the RORORO Zeitungsromane.

A handful of new German writers began to emerge, but they brought little work of substance, no new language or style. Few writers attempted to describe or to understand the horrors of the present. There was a numbing perplexity, as if so much lived reality had silenced a whole generation of poets and writers. The notion of a 'silent generation' was born; many had lost their voice in the war and the aftermath. 'Who can find a rhyme to the rattle of a lung shot to pieces, a rhyme to the scream of someone to be executed? Who knows the metre, the rhythm of a verse for rape, for the barking of the machine guns?'[1] wrote Wolfgang Borchert. Theodor Adorno had said that after Auschwitz art was no longer possible.[2]

The writer Wolfgang Borchert had come back from the front wounded and ill. His anti-war play, *Draussen vor der Tür* (*The Man Outside*), written in eight days, became the credo of a whole generation.

We are a generation without links, without depth. Our depth is the abyss. We are the generation without happiness, without home, without goodbyes. Our sun is small, our love cruel, and our youth is without youth. We are the generation without limits, without restrictions, without protection – thrown outside the pale of childhood, thrown into a world which they prepared for us and then despise us. But they gave us no God, to hold our heart when the winds of the world threaten it. Thus we are the generation without God, because we are the generation without links, without a past, without recognition.[3]

Draussen vor der Tür was first broadcast as a radio play. The day before its première in the theatre, Borchert died, aged twenty-six. The play became one of the great successes of the post-war years. But the biggest theatre success was Carl Zuckmayer's *The Devil's General*, the story of the air-force general Ernst Udet, who had sabotaged the war effort of Hermann Göring's *Luftwaffe*. It had been written in exile during the war. Many people were shocked to see so many actors in Nazi uniforms on the stage, so shortly after the war.

1 'Wer denn, ach, weiss einen Reim auf das Röcheln einer zerschossenen Lunge, einen Reim auf einen Hinrichtungsschrei, wer kennt das Versmass, das rythmische, für eine Vergewaltigung, wer weiss ein Versmass für das Gebell der Maschinengewehre?'

2 'Nach Auschwitz ist Kunst nicht mehr möglich.'

3 'Wir sind eine Generation ohne Bindung, ohne Tiefe. Unsere Tiefe ist der Abgrund. Wir sind die Generation ohne Glück, ohne Heimat und ohne Abschied. Unsere Sonne ist schmal, unsere Liebe grausam, und unsere Jugend ist ohne Jugend. Und wir sind die Generation ohne Grenze, ohne Hemmung und Behütung – ausgestossen aus dem Laufgitter des Kindseins in eine Welt, die sie uns bereitet, die uns darum verachte. Aber sie gaben uns keinen Gott mit der unser Herz hätte halten können, wenn die Winde dieser Welt es umwirbeln. So sind wir die Generation ohne Gott, denn wir sind die Generation ohne Bindung, ohne Vergangenheit, ohne Anerkennung.'

It was not easy for German intellectuals to find their own voice. Hitler was gone, but Germany was not yet entirely free. In the East the Russians kept putting their own stamp of communism on everything, and dissent was increasingly difficult. In the West it was of course much easier, but the Americans were not so keen either to allow political or cultural expressions which were not formed by their idea of capitalism. In 1947 the magazine *Der Ruf* (The Call), published under American licence by two writers, Alfred Andersch and Hans Werner Richter, was quickly banned because it proposed a more socialist vision for the new Germany. In the same year the Gruppe 47 was founded. It became the most important literary forum in post-war Germany, and included Heinrich Böll, Günter Grass, Ingeborg Bachmann, Ilse Aichinger and Martin Walser.

I followed the new writings with keen interest, but preferred the tested works of the classics, or the great writers who had stood up against Hitler. This gave them an aura of trustworthiness. The poetry of Rilke, Hölderlin and Hofmannsthal put me in a state akin to dream walking and I can still feel the 'holy shudder' I experienced when reading Thomas Mann's *Death in Venice*. I learned whole passages of *Tonio Kröger* by heart, identifying with its protagonist, whose deepest and most secret love was for 'the blond and blue-eyed, the fair and living, the happy and commonplace. . . this love. . . is good and fruitful. There is longing in it and a gentle envy, a touch of contempt and no little innocent bliss' – although I was not so sure about the innocent bliss bit.[1]

Everybody was busy making a new life, not just the intellectuals. Shops opened again, and once more people began to take care of their appearance. In 1947 Dior created the New Look, but we only knew it from magazines. Louise, Anita and Renate applied a brown colour to their legs, 'painted stockings' it was called, and I, being the only one with a steady hand, knelt behind them to draw on seams with an eyeliner.

I also fell head over heels in love with a pretty and calm girl, Nelly, so much more assured and poised than the rest of the young people I had met so far. Cornelia Henning was the daughter of the owner of a pharmaceutical factory. To us, coming from Tressdorf, the Hennings seemed

1 'Aber meine tiefste und verstohlenste Liebe gehört den Blonden und Blauäugigen, den hellen Lebendigen, den Glücklichen, Liebenswürdigen und Gewöhnlichen. Diese Liebe ist gut und fruchtbar. Sehnsucht ist darin und schwermütiger Neid und ein klein wenig Verachtung und eine ganze keusche Seligkeit.' English translation of German text by H.T. Lowe-Porter.

tremendously sophisticated. Their mother, a vivacious, elegant lady, had passed on her love for painting, poetry and music to her children. Nelly, her brother Robert and her sisters Heidi and Juliane were the centre of a small group of the most interesting and often precocious youngsters, among them Götz and Jan George, sons of the actor Heinrich George and his wife Berta Drews. Jan and I were in the same class. His brother Götz, known as Putzi, was a child star and played on the professional stage. Berta Drews, who was a famous actress on the post-war stage, did strike me as marvellously theatrical, in long flowering dresses. Sometimes we all went to George's house on Lake Wannsee. Photographs of Heinrich and Berta were displayed everywhere, which we found tremendously impressive. There were also a Picasso drawing and an Otto Dix painting. No one ever mentioned the father and his fate. Another member of the clan was Bautzi, a girl aptly named for her bounciness. Her father ran a restaurant on one of the lakes and hired out boats. We spent many afternoons just lazing around on the water. There was also a dark and interesting boy, Peter Block, whose father was a well-known architect and whose mother, Ernestine, appeared to me one of the most elegant women I had ever seen. We formed a close-knit circle, aware of the privileged class we belonged to – after all not everybody was invited to the Hennings'. It came as no surprise to me later on, to learn that Peter had married Heidi and Bautzi had married Robert.

My love became the source of much suffering, especially as Nelly was also interested in Reinhard Morgenstern, a rather pink and chubby young man. I liked Reinhard, despite his snobbish background, which he did not let anybody forget. I once overheard his mother spelling out her name M O R G E N S T E R N and adding: 'No, not Jewish', a remark I did not much care for. I would write heartfelt poems for Nelly, which did not impress her. This was not surprising, for 'love' was still rhyming with 'dove'. Shifting to more established poets, I copied Rainer Maria Rilke's and Hofmannsthal's most ardent verses into little books and put dried flowers between the pages, but Nelly thanked me coolly. I swore to give up smoking if she would kiss me once more, and stood for hours under her window, waiting until she turned the light off. I was very romantic. When she took my arm I was in heaven and when she looked away I was ready to die. Both states were blissful, tears or exhilaration alike. I have always wept easily. Falling in love, being in love and loving have always been deep affairs for me.

Nelly continued to vacillate between Reinhard and me, which caused the greatest pain to both of us. We spent hours discussing the situation, hoping she would choose. The three of us even went on a trip together, only to come back more wretched. Nelly made a choice, but only years later did she marry Reinhard. Before that she turned her back on both of us and walked away with a handsome older man.

I tried to find some solace in Nelly's sister Juliane, or to be honest in Juliane's love for music. Juliane was a great concert-goer. In 1946 the Berlin Philharmonic had began to play again. In 1947 Leopold Stokowski came to Germany, invited by the American Ministry of War, and toured the country. As in the theatre, in music forgiveness came easily. Conductors such as Hans Knappertsbusch and Wilhelm Furtwängler, who had not been allowed to conduct because of their association with the Nazis, took up the baton again. Furtwängler, who as it turned out had done quite a lot for Jewish musicians after all, conducted every week with the Berlin Philharmonic. The public rehearsal was on Sunday morning and the proper concert on Monday night. We went to both and sometimes even managed to sneak into the church in Dahlem where he rehearsed, hiding behind the organ. As the Philharmonie had been destroyed, all concerts took place in a cinema, the Titania Palast. It served as both a theatre and a concert hall. In the Titania Palast I heard the young Georg Solti and Sergiu Celibidache for the first time. Yehudi Menuhin came back to play with the same orchestra he had first performed with, aged thirteen, under Bruno Walter. I heard Elisabeth Bergner recite Schnitzler's *Fräulein Else*. All these experiences were unforgettable; the world had suddenly opened wide.

All radio stations were under Allied control and made sure that restitution was done. We listened to a lot of Mendelssohn and Mahler, but also to modern music. The German radio stations, in particular the Südwest Rundfunk, promoted modern music under the conductor Rossbaud and an enlightened French theatre officer, Pierre Ponelle. It would be an exaggeration to claim that we were converted overnight to modern music, but we probably heard more modern music than any young generation anywhere else in the world.

Listening to music, even with Juliane, was no solace for my unhappy unrequited love. I wanted to live more fully. I had looked up Siegfried Pistorius to find out if I liked better this time what he had to offer, and I did. I realised I was homosexual and I have never regretted it. Maybe thanks to a happy disposition, maybe because I had enlightened intelligent friends, I never had any of the customary feelings of guilt. Homosexuality or bisexuality seemed to me, right from the start, a true alternative to heterosexual life, neither better nor worse. It might give you trouble, but it also gave you options. I never considered myself a freak. 'Je ne crois pas comme ils croient, je ne vis pas comme ils vivent. Je mourrai comme ils meurent' (I don't believe as they do. I do not live as they do. I will die like they do), wrote Marguerite Yourcenar. All my life I have suffered for love in the same way as everybody else. I had a deep relationship with a man, which lasted twenty-one years. It was no less complex, difficult, enriching and overwhelming than most heterosexual relationships

I came out of the closet before ever going in. Louise was a great help of course. She had many homosexual friends, and once made the classical remark to some of my gay friends staying in our house: 'I don't mind your friends trying on my dresses, but I like them to put them back on the hanger.'

Having to live on the margin of a society still unable to fully accept me helped me to sharpen my sensibilities, my wits and my understanding of other people. It gave me a love for the arts and a compassion for those who suffer and are lonely. In later life, I often looked at some conventional couples with their craving for respectability, their often overwrought obsession with their children and their air of superiority, only to realise that homosexuality was the right road for me to take, as far as one can ever know this oneself, and that, if there was ever a crossroads, I would follow the same road again. I owe many of my closest and most wonderful friends – men and women, hetero- and homosexual – to my homosexuality. It makes me the person I am.

Friends have often asked me if I believe that people are born homosexual or if they are conditioned to be that way. I let psychoanalysts argue this question; they will point out that I am the archetypal case, growing up in a female household. I am certain that I was born that way, programmed by my maker, and it suits me fine.

Of course when I loved Annerl and Nelly, even when I experimented with Zenzi, I might have changed, but it would have been a betrayal of all that I am. Once I had began to discover the real me, I embraced it with all my capacities – my brain, my heart and my body – for homosexuality, contrary to popular belief, is not just a physical preference: it is also one of mind and feeling.

In the so-called Cold War, East and West drifted further apart. Berlin was the great pawn in the middle. Long before the wall, Berlin was basically cut in two. The East was much smaller and poorer than the West, but it was open to the hinterland, while the West was totally cut off by the Russian Zone. The Eastern sector was supposed to demonstrate the blessings of the great Communist Revolution, and the West was to be the shop window for the capitalist world. Both sides called themselves democratic, a word which was constantly pushed down our throats. It was supposed to be like a magic potion, able to heal all our illnesses. Early in 1948 the British, Russians, Americans and French met in London to decide what to do with Germany. The conference broke up because nobody had a solution.

More emigrants returned. The young novelist Stefan Heym settled in East Berlin. So did Arnold Zweig, Anna Seghers, Johannes R. Becher and Stefan Hermlin. Heinrich Mann died shortly before he could take up his residence in East Berlin. Bertolt Brecht, who had lived in Zürich, after having been thrown out of America for his communist leanings, also chose East Berlin. To many the East was the place of conscience, the West the place of wanting to forget the past.

Goethe's centenary came in 1949. Thomas Mann, whom the Nazis had stripped of citizenship and doctorate, came back to speak about Goethe, a gesture of reconciliation, but he got many people's back up because he spoke in both Germanies. A few years ago Weimar and Bonn had belonged to the same country; now they were worlds apart, and neither the writer of *Faust* nor of *Buddenbrooks* was able to heal the rift.

Many fled to West Berlin. The Russians tried to put a stop to that by blocking all access by road, rail or water between West Germany and Berlin. We could hardly believe what was happening. Many had friends and relatives in the other half of the city. Soviet soldiers now controlled the border between East and West. And then all traffic to West Germany was suddenly stopped. I went to the Potsdamer Platz and saw barbed wire being erected. The motorway bridge over the River Elbe, which linked the road from Berlin to the West, was blown up and Berlin was virtually cut off from the Western world. They tried to starve out the two million people living in the Western sectors. People could no longer write to each other, not even in the same city.

It was a warlike situation. The Americans wanted to get their tanks out and Churchill thought of using the atom bomb, but fortunately reason prevailed and the Allies opted for the famous airlift, which was organised by the Americans. Berlin was kept alive. Every three minutes a plane landed at Tempelhof Airfield to bring food and coal. The Berliners were baptised *Insulaner*, islanders, a name coined by Günter Neumann, who published a witty and aggressive magazine under the same name. A cabaret, *Der Insulaner*, was also founded. It was not easy in the beginning to do cabaret with the usual target gone – no one dared to criticise the occupying forces, for fear of losing the licence. But now the Berliners refound their habitual humour and instinct for survival, and there was plenty to criticise both in the East and the West.

Just as we were beginning to look up, another hard winter threw us into despair. Four thousand small factories were closed down, because there was no electricity. Once more we had hardly any food, and electricity was cut off for most of the day. People were allowed to spend an allotted time in heated public rooms to get warm. The Berliners cut down more of their beloved trees in the Grunewald and Louise burned some more of our furniture. The four of us slept and lived once more in one small room.

More and more planes landed with coal and food. Every sixty-two seconds a plane arrived at Tempelhof. Some seaplanes even landed on the Wannsee. They flew day and night, around the clock. The noise of the incoming planes never stopped, but it was a friendly noise. We got so used to the hum that we woke up if there was a lull.

I sometimes wondered what it would be like to live in peace and plenty. On New Year's Eve I went to a concert. Everybody brought some coals on stage for the big iron stoves that heated the icy hall. Everywhere people sat wrapped in blankets. Sergiu Celibidache conducted Beethoven's Ninth in the traditional New Year's Eve concert. When the choir started *Freude schöner Götterfunken*, people began to cry.

Despite the hardships we still had to go to school. We were still writing essays, but instead of the regimentation of the past the emphasis was now on imagination, as when our young German teacher put a bouquet of autumn branches on her desk. 'Das ist euer Thema für den Tag,' she announced: That's your subject for the day. I wrote the story of an old countess who dreamed about a ball of her youth. The leaves had turned into the colourful gowns and uniforms of the dancers. After a long time the countess woke up in a dark room. The sunlight, which had illuminated the leaves, had set. When her foot kicked the small *guéridon*, the leaves fell to the floor. The essay, 'Shattered Dreams', was read out aloud in front of the class, and I, always craving public attention, felt proud and elated.

I was preparing for the *Abitur*, the German final high-school exam, without which nobody could ever get a decent job. The *Abitur* is a most frightening exam. Pupils are examined in everything: nobody is given any preference or choices. We had spent months and months preparing for it. The written exams lasted several days and the final oral examination took a whole day.

I actually passed my *Abitur* not in Berlin but in Frankfurt, where, because of the blockade, the whole class had been evacuated in order to have some proper schooling. I had to live once more in a dormitory. For Anglo-Saxons brought up in schools and colleges this might not be unusual, but for a German it was rare. I decided once and for all that communal life was not for me.

The final day passed in agonising suspense. We stood for the last time in the makeshift classroom we had occupied for months, waiting for the results to be read out. Everybody wore a dark suit or a dark dress. It was June, the windows were open, everybody was nervous about whether they had passed or not. The names were called out in alphabetical order. Thank God, mine was the first one to be called out: 'Adam: passed.' I did not hear the other names. One girl who had failed wept loudly. Then came the name we had all been waiting for: Schuster. Arno Schuster had been a soldier in the war; he was older than the rest of us, a sensitive young man of great obstinacy. I liked Arno very much, but I was almost the only one. I could hear my heart beat very loudly.

Then came the damning judgement – 'failed'. Arno very quietly stepped over to the window and jumped to his death, five floors down. There was first a loud cry from the class, then numbness. We stood aghast. When the police arrived, we filed out in silence. I still see in my mind's eye the blanket which covered the body, surrounded by onlookers. The indecency of human curiosity. I know nothing about the rest of the day. I lay awake the whole night and the three following nights too. The hate which I carried in me, the hate for Germany, for anything to do with authority, came to the surface. 'Why could they not have let him pass?' I kept asking myself.

There were inquests and interviews. 'Grown-ups' with those awful kind and understanding voices were trying to coax the truth out of us. But the truth was so easy to grasp. Arno had died because of people not caring enough, because he was different, because of the self-righteousness of a system only able to force others into moulds and models dictated by society. Arno died because he failed in a competition some schoolteachers had set up for us.

My Certificate of Maturity testified that my knowledge in literature, music and the arts was good, so was my knowledge of biology. But while chemistry, geography, mathematics, physics, philosophy were considered adequate, Latin and English were not.

In May 1949 the blockade was over. It had lasted almost a year. The Berliners, who felt cheated out of the celebration at the end of the war, went into the streets and cheered and danced. They had withstood the Soviet plans to starve and freeze Berlin out to force it to its knees. The communists had lost their last chance to win friends in this city. Germany found itself closer than ever to the Western side, especially America.

In 1949 the Germans elected their first new parliament, the *Bundestag*.

It was a vote for democracy. A new kind of Germany was on the horizon, the *Bundesrepublik*, the German Federal Republic. It had a new constitution, and a provisional capital, Bonn, of which few people outside of Germany had ever heard. Germany also rearranged the national anthem. It had dropped the *Horst Wessel Lied*, which was a Nazi song, but kept 'Deutschland, Deutschland über alles', which stemmed from the time of the Kaiser. (Prussian militaristic, yes; Nazi, no.) It had after all words by Hoffmann von Fallersleben and music by Haydn, and nobody could accuse either of them of being a Nazi. The first verse was discredited and a bit embarrassing, 'Germany above all others', so it was discarded and we went straight into the third, which used words like *Einigkeit*. Unity, freedom and all that. Many hated this decision, I among them, and for many years refused to rise when it was played. The East at least had enough imagination and tact to find a new national anthem.

That year, 1949, the *Währungsreform*, currency reform was introduced, on which part of the German economic recovery is supposed to be based. Konrad Adenauer became associated with what the world called the German economic miracle. The date of the currency reform had been one of the best kept secrets. The money had been printed abroad and brought secretly to Germany; 900 tons of spanking new deutschmarks sat in the Bundesbank, guarded by American soldiers. Then on 18 June the news was out. We were told that, in two days' time, all our marks were going to be worthless. No exchange, no nothing. You could chuck them in the bin. I took 300 marks, queued one night at the opera for a ticket and saw *Carmen*.

On 20 June we had the new deutschmark. I am not an economist, but this change was so simple that it worked. It killed black-market profiteering and stopped inflation. Every German, doctor or milkman, actor or chimney sweep, was given 40 brand-new deutschmarks. Employers got a further DM60 for each employee. For one glorious week we were all equally rich or poor. Then by the end of the week the old injustice began again. Doctors were paid DM500 while the chimney sweeps went home with DM75.

The Russians did not want the East Germans to have a new mark, so they introduced their own currency by stamping it on the old notes, which earned them the nickname wallpaper money.

On the day after the currency reform, the shops filled with goods like tomatoes, cauliflowers, cakes and fresh bread. The reform had also killed rationing. Money was now the ordering principle and Jupp Schmitz, one of the popular singers, sang the latest hit, 'Wer soll das bezahlen, wer hat soviel Geld, wer hat soviel Pinke Pinke, wer hat das bestellt ?'[1]

We were not rich. The average pay per hour was only DM1 and the monthly income of a family of four was estimated at DM300, but it felt good to have some real money again. In order to supplement my pocket money I began to sell the *Abendzeitung* (Evening News) in the street – an interesting occupation, because it allowed me to enter restaurants and bars. I soon developed an interest in the nightlife of Berlin. The American clubs were off-limits for the Germans. One had to know an Ami. But there were quite a few German bars, such as the artists' club, Johnny's, on the Kurfürstendamm, and Resi, a huge bar with a dance floor. Each table displayed a large number and had a telephone. You just picked up the phone and chatted to somebody at another table. It was vulgar and popular.

Berlin was still the city of women and old men. The women would sit at Resi's and stare longingly at the telephone, for the light to come on, always hoping that someone from another table would phone to ask them for a dance. It did not take me long to discover that *Die Volle Pulle*, The Full Bottle, was chic, the Kleist Casino was for gentlemen who wanted to dance with gentlemen, and *Die Ewige Lampe* (The Eternal Lamp) for ladies only. In The Golden Horseshoe, tables were arranged around a circus ring. Its main attraction were the female guests riding in the middle, their skirts hitched up high over their thighs, cheered on by the crowd.

My favourite haunt was Elly's Beer Bar, not only because I usually received the biggest tips there for my newspapers. It was a rather friendly and sleazy working men's bar. The area was so rough that people took their bikes inside. It was the favourite meeting place for intellectuals, artists, prostitutes, workers and boxers. Behind the bar presided Elly, an old-fashioned Berliner transvestite. 'Your husband has to come himself,' the Nazis had told her when she reported for the Army. She had a heart of gold and a mouth which spewed dung. It was strictly off-limits for the occupying forces, but there were always plenty of American and British soldiers in civilian clothes, despite the routine checks by the military police who always travelled in groups of four, one for each of the occupying forces. 'Come on in boys,' Elly would shout to them, in perfect English, French and Russian. 'Have one on the house, we don't bite, we kiss.' Every Thursday the place was packed for a 'catch-as-catch-can' night. The tables had been pushed to the side, and the toyboys of Berlin, scantily clad in a leopard G-string, wrestled in the middle of the room, cheered on by Elly,

---

1 'Who can afford this, who has so much money, who has so much dough, who has ordered this?'

A nightclub in Berlin

Hiddensee

who went around with a large plate calling out: 'Money for my boys.' Elly was fun. It was the *Milljöh* and it offered opportunities for chance encounters I had only dared to dream of.

People began to travel again, and Germans were even allowed to go abroad, but this was for 'cultural and economic purposes only'. So I decided to visit Hiddensee again. Although it lay in the Eastern Zone one could still travel there. It seemed unbelievable that after our transport from Spittal to Berlin and the excursions with the Hamster trains, we should ever have wanted to board a train again. The trains were still packed, but at least they had windows. People stood like sardines in the corridors, even in the lavatories and in the shaky space between the carriages. There were no lightbulbs; for half the journey there was water in the lavatory, but every time you wanted to use it three people had to get out of the small compartment.

I got a great thrill out of travelling alone, getting out of town, away from the ruins to see meadows and cows. Hiddensee had not changed. There were still no cars and roads. It was again the favourite place of many artists. The playwright Gerhart Hauptmann, Hiddensee's most famous inhabitant, had died, but the actress Asta Nielsen sat once more in front of her little thatched cottage, clad in black and looking every inch the great star of the silent movies. The new stars now were Jürgen Fehling, the ebullient theatre director, and his companion, the striking actress Joana Maria Gorvin, the painter Erich Heckel and the Russian dancer Tatjana Gsovsky.

People came to swim naked in the sea, to walk in the heather, to dance in the only inn and to get drunk in the island's only bar. Life was free, crazy, promiscuous, and we felt very daring. I loved it all. The demonstration of so much naked hedonism was bliss for a twenty-year-old ready to have a good time. I became a regular, returning every year, until the border came finally down.

7

Alma Mater

1949–1951

In November 1949 I enrolled at the Free University, as a student of the Philosophical Faculty. The Free University had only been founded in the previous year. Berlin's old Humboldt University, dating from 1810, founded by Wilhelm von Humboldt, lay in Berlin's historical centre. Thus it had come under Russian occupation and had fallen more and more under communist influence. In 1948 the students and many of the teachers decided they had enough of communism and broke away from the old alma mater to open a new and truly free university in the Western sector of Berlin.

It was not easy to form a new university in a bombed-out city with almost everything missing. In the first few years it was very much a makeshift university, consisting of many small buildings in the suburb of Dahlem, mostly private villas, very like the one I was born in. The classrooms were churches, air-raid shelters and even a disused underground train shed. A cinema served as the auditorium maximum, the main lecture hall. The primitive accommodation gave a feeling of a new beginning, in line with the pioneer spirit of the students and teachers who wanted a place of study free of any political influence.

In a festive ceremony I and a hundred other new students walked up to the platform to shake hands with the Rector, Edwin Redslob, Professor of Visual Art and Cultural History. We swore 'to show ourselves, in character, mind and diligence, worthy of the high aims of a university dedicated to teaching, learning and searching for the truth, in total freedom', in accordance with the motto inscribed on the coat of arms of the Free University: *Veritas, Justitia, Libertas*.

I registered in German and French Literature and History of Art. Lectures drew from 100 to 500 students, according to the popularity of the professor. Some were standing-room only. Seminars were more private, usually attended by around twenty students, who were expected to join in the discussion and to write several papers.

Education was free or practically free. We were also spared a stifling exam system. You could spend all your study years without ever passing an intermediary exam. During the first years we were free to study and read whatever we felt like, and I attended lectures not only on philosophy, journalism and theatre, but also on criminal law and even on medicine.

At the end of their academic career, which lasted between six and seven years, students were expected to finish with a doctorate or the State Exam. Most students opted for the former. In Germany the title 'Doktor' has always been held in high esteem.

Quite a few of the students had returned from the war. Some were already married, some widowed. The university was for many an opportunity to build a new life. When I look at the cheerful casualness of today's students in their jeans and colourful outfits, I think about our dour and drab clothes and the seriousness of our demeanour. The relationship between professors and students was very formal. 'Ladies and Gentlemen,' the professors would start their lectures, and even among us students I was strictly *Mr* Adam. But what a glorious time of discovery and learning it was! I attended lectures on German literature of the twelfth and thirteenth centuries by the eminent Germanist Helmut de Boor, and students queued to hear him talking about Tristan and Iseult and the *Minnelieder*. I read French literature of the seventeenth and eighteenth centuries and followed a seminar on Cervantes. I studied Italian painting of the fifteenth century and at the same time painting in Germany in the nineteenth century. I also attended seminars on Renaissance architecture and Michelangelo. I took courses on the history of philosophy and on Flemish painting, and attended lectures on Expressionist drama.

I sat mesmerised in the underground shelter that was our lecture hall, as Hermann Kunisch, under the dripping pipes, opened up to us the world of the great German writers. Kunisch had been a pupil of the poet Stefan George, an elitist cult figure who, in the twenties, had surrounded himself with a group of aesthetes. Even Goebbels, as a student, was supposed to have been one of the George Circle. Kunisch not only looked like a magician, he was one; always dressed in black, he did not talk about poetry, he celebrated it with beautiful gestures and a delivery which would honour a great actor. Nobody could talk more eloquently about Goethe's last love for the young Ulrike von Levetzow. Reciting the first lines of the *Marienbader Elegie*, 'In the unopened blossom of this day, what hope have I of meeting once again?'[1] Kunisch evoked the image of the seventy-four-year-old Goethe sitting in the darkness of his coach, and made us feel the pain of the old poet as he poured out the words of one of Goethe's strongest and most passionate poems. We relived his kiss, the last one he gave

1 'Was soll ich nun vom Wiedersehen hoffen, von dieses Tages noch geschlossener Blüte.'

to the young girl, while the walls of our hall shook from the constantly passing trains. Kunisch's voice became almost inaudible when he uttered the words: 'He would never see her again.' The lecture ended with Goethe's quote from Tasso: 'And when man grew silent in his pain, God gave me a voice to tell about this suffering.'[1] Thunderous applause swelled up from the spellbound students, which Professor Kunisch acknowledged with a suppressed smile. He quickly put on his black coat, which reached almost to the floor, and a large black felt hat. Before any of the girls who rushed forward could reach him, he had escaped through the door.

With Kunisch we would study the work of Heinrich von Kleist and Adalbert Stifter. He gave us matchless insights into the fate of artists and the processes of creation, and a love for poetry that would never fade.

At last I was with people who shared my love for the arts and who spent their days on things which mattered to me. In an atmosphere of discovery I made friends, with many of whom I am still in contact. Links and friendships were formed with future writers, critics, theatre directors. We were the first generation after the war to occupy posts in universities, newspapers, theatre and television. We believed in a new society. We rejected the possibility of a world split into two halves, new war and more soldiers, and argued for the need to lead a life based on spiritual rather than on material values. We also believed at that time that the only truth and lasting beauty is that transmitted by artists.

The most exhilarating theatre went on in the Eastern sector, in Brecht's Berliner Ensemble. Every Brecht première was hotly debated not only in the press but also in the little bar, Die Möwe, where we met after the performances, often joined by the actors. Sometimes Brecht too would be part of our group, always dressed in an old grey jacket in a kind of military cut and a cloth cap. He often looked unshaven, smoking big cigars. Helene Weigel sometimes joined him, a small woman, her hair brushed back revealing a stern face. Brecht was the driving force in the German theatre at this time. The first Brecht production I saw was *Herr Puntila and His Servant Matti* and I was simply bowled over by the new style. Brought up on the lyrical qualities of German literature, the heightened language of Goethe, Schiller and Kleist, I was seduced by the simple magic of this theatre. Here was a new playwright, new for us, able to express artistically what we felt was happening in our lives. We shared his mistrust of the old and inherited values and his belief in the dialectic of all art.

---

1 'Und wenn der Mensch in seiner Qual verstummt / Gab mir ein Gott zu sagen was ich leide.'

The second Berliner Ensemble play I saw made even a stronger impression, thanks to a remarkable woman, Therese Giehse. This great actress had returned from exile and joined Brecht in Berlin to play in Gorky's *Vasya Shelesnova* in a production by Berthold Viertel. Giehse played the main character, spiteful, always on the lookout, full of hate and yet with a disarming charm. Her realistic gestures were again something new for us. The declamatory style on the German stage had made room for a pathos that came from her total naturalness. I can still picture her tasting a very hot cup of tea, her lips smacking, while she tried to cool the drink by blowing gently over the surface of the liquid.

Giehse was also a great Mother Courage. She had been the first to play it, during the war in the Züricher Schauspielhaus, the theatre that became the refuge of so many German actors during the Hitler regime. I saw Brecht's anti-war play with his wife Helene Weigel, a heart-rending performance. Weigel was cool and ironical, dragging the cart around and around the stage as though for the first time. At the end the song of the old woman returned, but with the piercing sound of war to prevent us from being too moved by the terrible sadness of Mother Courage's life. All the devices Brecht used, such as the interruptions by placards and songs, and the harsh lighting, to de-romanticise the play and to destroy its magic, only strengthened the poetry of these evenings.

With the communist system increasingly stifling any creativity not linked to their political credo, Brecht, Weigel and the director Walter Felsenstein had become the artistic conscience of East Germany. Brecht wanted to establish the link between politics, history and the aesthetics of the theatre: a now widely accepted method which at that time was much misunderstood on both sides. While the politicians in the East bemoaned the absence of social realism on stage, those in the West accused him of making communist propaganda.

Walter Felsenstein, who ran the Komische Oper and whose two sons had been in my class in the Lycée, also brought us a new kind of theatre, full of visual and dramatic inventions far removed from the seriousness of traditional German opera productions. We saw a *Carmen* with dialogue and ballet, interchanging singing and speech in a way we had never seen on an opera stage. He also staged a modern German opera, Carl Orff's *Die Kluge*, in a boxing ring.

Compared to the East the theatre on our side seemed to be less exciting, but there were exceptions, such as an expressionistic production of Sartre's *Les Mouches*, directed by Jürgen Fehling with Joana Maria Gorvin. My contacts from Hiddensee allowed me to attend some rehearsals, and I remember Jean-Paul Sartre and Simone de Beauvoir sitting in the stalls and telling us later about the Paris production. He also spoke about the necessity 'to look forward rather than back', a reconciliatory gesture which surprised me.

Tickets were often difficult to come by, and I often queued the whole night in line with other enthusiasts equipped with blankets and Thermos flasks. This too was a way to make friends. The most interesting ones were Maria and Thomas Harlan-Körber, the children of the actress Hilde Körber and the film director Veit Harlan, director of the infamous film *Jud Süss*. The children still suffered from the stigma attached to their father's name. Maria was a budding actress and we began to put on plays in her house.

Among us were several hopeful actors trying to make a career: Horst Buchholz, Hardy Krüger, and the daughter of a famous film couple, Wolf Albach Retty and Magda Schneider, whose name was Romy. So maybe it was not surprising that I too toyed with the idea of becoming an actor. I made my stage debut in Edna St Vincent Millay's *Aria da Capo*. We performed in a cinema, and in the audience sat Bertolt Brecht and Helene Weigel. They had come because their daughter Hanne Hiob was also part of our group. After the performance he generously congratulated us, but he also told me: 'Peter, never look at the audience.' I had and he had noticed it.

Despite the size of Berlin, everybody in the artistic world knew each other. There were not so many places one could go, and communication lines were short; one saw the same faces in the theatres, galleries, bars or even in private homes. Everybody was eager to meet other like-minded people; it was almost like a conspiracy. You did not need to be famous yourself; all that was required was to be bright and interested in the arts. Being young and attractive helped too. People sometimes told me I was, often with ulterior motives. At twenty-one I was vain and believed them. I had learned from Louise that to know writers, actors, painters is more rewarding than to know civil servants.

We had hardly any money to go out and usually met in people's houses. One place artists gathered was the house of Wolfgang Ebert. Wolfgang was the son of the composer Hans Ebert and a small Russian Jewess who spoke with a funny accent. She had miraculously survived the war. She was the very image of a Jewish mother, overprotective, loving and very funny. Before sitting down, she would count the amount of Jewish blood at her table: two half-Jews made a full one, two-quarter Jews a half one. When she was sure that the Jews outnumbered the goys she would bring out the cake. Wolfgang Ebert later set a monument to the memory of his mother in the book *The Porcelain Was So Nervous*, named after one of her sayings,

Playing Mac the Knife

referring to the clinking of the porcelain during a bomb attack. Wolfgang was hopelessly in love with my sister Renate, and in his house I met the children of many emigrants: Manni and Peter Kortner, the children of the great actor/director Fritz Kortner and Nina, the daughter of the painter Jankel Adler. All of them had spent the Nazi period abroad and their outlook was international, which instilled in me the idea that soon I must leave Germany and live elsewhere. I was eager to meet people from abroad.

Katja Marowski, another of Wolfgang's friends, gave a party one night for the Royal Ballet, which had come to Berlin with Moira Shearer, Margot Fonteyn and Michael Soames. This evening has stuck in my mind because it was the first time that I danced with a man. Berlin was famous for nightclubs where men could dance together. I had often looked on, amused and intrigued by those interlaced couples, sometimes bricklayers and soldiers, but I had never joined in. At Katja's party everybody danced, and suddenly a distinguished gentleman in a very tightly cut dark suit got up, bowed and asked me for a dance. I accepted, rather embarrassed; I must say he danced terribly well. His name was Freddy Ashton.

The war was only five years behind us but we lived already in a new world. Adenauer had persuaded the Germans that democracy was not only good for them but also lucrative. Soon industrial production would exceed that of 1936. Forty million people not only needed irons and tea kettles but now also wanted refrigerators, washing machines, radios, cars, and hair driers. Margarine had been replaced by butter but it lived on in a song: 'Ei ei Sanella, Sanella auf dem Teller' and Cornelia Froboes, a seven-year-old girl, filled the Titania Palast when she sang 'Pack die Badehose ein' (Pack the bathing suit).

In 1950 I travelled to Paris. My friend Klaus Geitel had gone there to study and I decided to visit him. Klaus was the first man I had a proper affair with, a good-looking aesthete with sad eyes. He had fallen in love with me and I was touched by his attentions, his interest and his willingness to share his considerable knowledge of the arts with me. After the pains of basically unrequited love with Annerl and Nelly, here was someone who was deeply committed, and so I let it happen, with all the cruelty of youth. I know I hurt him very much.

In Paris, Klaus waited at the Gare du Nord with two friends. I was so excited that I hardly listened to their names. One was a German composer, the other a French set designer. Their names were Hans Werner Henze and Jean-Pierre Ponelle. We took a taxi to the Hôtel Gît-le-Cœur, where they all lived, a modest hotel like thousands of others mostly used by artists and students on the Left Bank. My room was on the fourth floor, and when I leaned out of the window, I could see the Seine.

France, still smarting from the German occupation, was rediscovering its composure. Paris, exuding sophistication and energy, was the first big city untouched by war or deprivation I had seen. It had an air of unshakable stability and permanence; a picture-postcard dream with all the delicious clichés: the glittering lights, the cars, the elegant shops and women. Not much had been built in the last hundred years, and it looked as it did at the end of the nineteenth century. For those who only know Paris today, it is difficult to imagine its earlier charms: a city structured and chaotic at the same time; a city of little villages, filled with small shops handed down from father to son. One could wander for hours through little streets where men walked with sheets of glass strapped to their backs shouting: 'Vitrier.' Each *immeuble* had a *concierge*, who responded to the call 'Cordon' to let you in. It was just like the Paris of the films by Marcel Carné and the photographs of Kertész, Capa, Brassaï or Lartigue. Beggars slept on the air vents of the Métro, in the middle of the pavement, and old ladies in extravagant hats fed hordes of cats roaming the parks. One could sit and eat a sandwich on the little Place Fürstenberg without being disturbed by cars or tourists, or walk for hours along the banks of the river, where the *clochards* slept wrapped in newspaper, an empty bottle at their feet. The horrible motorways had not yet been built.

The buses had little open balconies in the back, and at the stop everybody took a number from a machine, waiting for the conductor to call it out. Les Halles, Zola's 'Belly of Paris', was smelly and noisy and no one worried much about hygiene or ecology. This was Paris before supermarkets, boutiques, drugstores, high-rises, and shopping alleys. The France of the 1950s owed still more to the past than to the future.

I had to pinch myself to know I was not dreaming, that a city of such visual and sensual pleasure did exist. I realised how much we, the Germans, were the losers. I spent hours watching the chatty crowd on the terrace of the Café Flore or the Deux Magots. At night I joined *le monde chic* for an after-theatre souper at the Bar des Théâtres and *le monde louche* to drink the night away in the Bœuf sur le Toit, looking for the ghost of Jean Cocteau and his acolytes, long departed from this scene.

I stayed for two months full of art, theatre, restaurants and nightclubs. Klaus loved the ballet and took me to see Roland Petit's *Carmen*, with a colourful set and costumes by Antoni Clavé – a brilliant ballet, combining the best of ballet with that of showbiz. The lead was a dynamic and sexy dancer, Zizi Jeanmaire. For someone like myself, used to approaching ballet with reverence, it was a riveting experience. I was even more surprised when, in another ballet, *La Croqueuse de Diamants*, Zizi Jeanmaire opened her mouth and sang: 'Chui une croqueuse de diamants.' The house came down. Here was a ballerina, brought up in the classical school of Petipa, rendering, with a croaky, penetrating voice, a French chanson.

Jean-Pierre had given up the study of law in order to paint. He was the son of Pierre Ponelle, the French military controlling officer in Baden-Baden, responsible for the Südwestdeutscher Rundfunk, the South West German Radio station, which had done so much for our knowledge of modern music. Jean-Pierre's family owned famous vineyards in France. He was much more urbane and much better dressed than we were. He was one of the victors of the war, delightful, always willing to help and also very handsome, with dark curly hair and a very sensual face which could have belonged to a bullfighter. He oozed physicality and everybody was crazy about him. Jean-Pierre decided that I should not only see culture but the Paris of naked ladies, delicious frivolity and popular art. He took me to the music hall, the Lido, the Folies Bergère and the Olympia. The extravagance of the sets and costumes, the luxurious and generous display of flesh, glitter and feathers, was liberating for someone who had just escaped a world where everything was still grey and full of seriousness.

Hans Werner became a lifelong friend. For over forty years we have kept in touch, although there was a time when he did not like me very much. 'Dear Peter,' he wrote, warning me not to be too frivolous: 'Watch out that they don't destroy you. Cynicism is more than just a wall to protect your vulnerability. It can turn against you and destroy you. All our sadness and desperation can be turned around, changed into a revolutionary potential. One day, in the middle of prosperity, when God is coming to Mahagonny, in the middle of the whisky, your eyes will open up and "decadence" will no longer be enough reason for our tiredness.' This was in 1969, when we had drifted apart, politically mostly. But then we rediscovered each other in a friendship which keeps on growing.

Hans's life so far could not have been more different from mine. I have met few people with such a loathing of their youth. He was born in the small town of Gütersloh, in Westphalia, the oldest son of five children. His father was a schoolmaster; there was no money and very little fun. Henze's father was a fervent Nazi. Summer and winter, the boys had to wear the Hitler Youth uniform and before going to bed they had to say good night with a 'Heil Hitler!' Hans was an outcast like myself, although for different reasons. In school he had sympathised with the Jewish pupils who disappeared overnight from his class. He had befriended French prisoners of war and had tried to help one of them to escape. Everything had to be done behind his father's back. Hans became an expert in concealment. The only consolation of his early years was his music. He began to compose in primary school. While in high school he joined a small chamber music group and made his début as conductor of Bach's Fifth Brandenburg Concerto.

In the Music Academy he studied the piano, musical theory and percussion. He was not allowed to perform his own works, because they were too modern. He secretly familiarised himself with the forbidden works of Hindemith and Stravinsky. In the autumn of 1943 his father was called to the Front. A few months later Hans too had to join the *Arbeitsfront*, the Nazi's labour service, three months of senseless exercises and parading with spades. His father wrote to him: 'I greet you, workman Henze, the straw mattress will become your comrade.' In May 1944 Hans was called to the army, and at the end of the war he was captured by the British. From captivity he wrote to his mother: 'I fear neither hunger nor other deprivation. I am young and I have one aim which I have never lost.' He was talking about his music.

Hans was handsome with sad eyes, his blond hair receding and revealing a high forehead. We talked about the Germany we both hated and he made me translate Jean Genet for him. He was tender and protective and had a refreshing down-to-earth sense of humour. He was also an incurable romantic, able to fall in love again and again. He confided in me that he had tried to kill himself the previous year, for someone we all knew.

When we met, Henze was already an established composer of the avant-garde, with three symphonies, a piano concerto, several chamber music works and a ballet to his credit. He was working on a ballet based on the story of Manon Lescaut, *Boulevard Solitude*, a title he had taken from a film he saw in Paris: Billy Wilder's *Sunset Boulevard*. *Boulevard* was premiered in Wiesbaden and was a great success. Jean-Pierre Ponelle designed the set and costumes.

Part of our little group was a very jolly young girl, Annette, the daughter of the publisher, Gottfried and Brigitte Bermann Fischer, always known as Goffi and Tutti. The Fischers were among the very first to return and to publish again in Germany, now in Frankfurt. Annette lived in the Cité Universitaire and appeared to us terribly sophisticated and international. She had grown up in America and she had dollars. Insanely generous, she was always writing cheques, a form of payment which was new to us. There is still a photo of her writing a cheque for us hungry young Germans.

One day a strange couple arrived and took lodgings at the Hôtel Gît-le-Cœur, Thomas Harlan and Klaus Kinski. Tom was studying to become a

Hans Werner Henze 1956

film director, like his father, and Klaus wanted to become an actor. The two young men were, I suppose, the first drop-outs I met. Even in my tolerant eyes, they were deliciously scandalous and outrageous. They looked like gypsies and smoked hash. Guilt-ridden by his father's role during the Nazi years, Tommy wanted as a kind of atonement to go to Israel and work in a kibbutz, and eventually to make a film there. They talked a lot about the project and borrowed some money. Then one day they were gone, leaving behind a suitcase with old clothes, an unpaid hotel bill and the memories of some crazy nights. Tommy and Klaus eventually reached Israel but the film was never made. Thomas Harlan became a film director and Klaus Kinski a famous actor, surrounded by the same kind of madness he already displayed then. In 1952 Kinski played Myshkin in a ballet based on Dostoevsky's *The Idiot*. The music was by Hans Werner Henze and the choreography by Tatjana Gsovsky, Berlin's grand old lady of ballet.

When I returned to Berlin, I was determined to go back to Paris as soon as possible, come what may. Paris had become a drug for me, I could never be without it for long. For the next forty years I would return there, sometimes for a short stay, sometimes for several years. Eventually I even made my home there.

After Paris, Berlin looked terribly scruffy and provincial. My relationship with Germany was still painful and ambiguous. I knew that it would take a long time to overcome my prejudices. Herbert Marcuse said that 'the rupture between the fatherland and the emigrants from Hitler will only heal the day the last refugee is dead'.

There were other things which filled me with gloom. Too many people with a shady past resurfaced. Alfred Krupp, condemned in 1948 to twelve months in prison and the confiscation of his entire fortune, was featured in *Life* magazine sitting in his baronial home, warning the world about a Marxist takeover. Two years later he would sign lucrative contracts with America, France and Great Britain. The Thyssens and the Flicks were back again. Everywhere the same names, not only in industry but in the government. One minister, Hans Globke, had helped to cement the Nuremberg racial laws, and Heinrich Lübke was rumoured to have been involved in designing concentration camps. In the gleaming foyer of the new Schiller Theater stood the busts of Fritz Kortner and Werner Krauss; Nazi and Jew peacefully united. It was not as if the Nazis were coming back, but the past just would not go away.

Then there was the question of a new German army. The fear of Russia increased the pressure of becoming part of the Western Alliance. Even

Churchill called upon the Germans to help to defend the West. For me the idea of once more fighting a war, of people willing to kill each other for an idea, was unthinkable.

Gradually everywhere conservatism crept back. Artists and the students moved where they had always been, into the opposition. Those who would not toe the line were criticised and writers like Günter Grass and Rolf Hochhuth were attacked for being too far on the left. The old puritanism and its ally, philistinism, also found its way back. A *Saubere Leinwand* (clean screen) action committee demonstrated against the showing of the film *Die Sünderin* (The Sinner), where for a few fleeting seconds the naked figure of Hildegard Knef had been seen rushing across the screen. It would not be long before the Catholic Church, supported by the Bavarian cultural minister, managed to ban Werner Egks's ballet *Abraxas* from the opera stage because it was considered lascivious.

I was still living at home with my mother. Anita had married and left us and Renate worked in Baden-Baden as an editor for a new women's magazine. She had grown into a spirited and poised young lady. This and an affectionate nature made her many friends. Louise was often out, and I was free to come and go as I pleased – a freedom I enjoyed. As we lived in the suburbs and hardly anybody had a car, I had to rely on public transport. If you missed the last train you had to shack up somewhere, which at that age never seemed to be a problem.

My favourite nightclub was *Die Hexenküche* (The Witches' Kitchen), a *louche* place, run by the actress Valeska Gert. It was painted black, and the little tables were scattered around a small stage. Valeska Gert had in the pre-Hitler years played in Pabst's *Freudlose Gasse* (Joyless Street), with a young Marlene Dietrich. She had also been Mrs Peachum in *The Threepenny Opera*. She had emigrated to New York, where she ran the Beggar's Bar. Now she had come back to open a small cabaret in the ruins of the city she still loved. There she performed nightly, a small muscular lady always dressed in a tight black dress. Her face was painted white with a big exaggerated red mouth – the face of a rascal. With her eyes tightly shut, as in a trance, she did impressions of anything from death to whores, pimps to Oscar Wilde. The waiters were prostitutes of both sexes, a rat catcher and some budding actors and actresses, all picked up practically from the street by the owner.

I met here at least twice a week with a small and rather unconventional group of friends. There was Barbara, a doctor in the Ministry of Health; Peter, who owned a flower-shop; Rainer, who was a leading dancer in the Berlin Ballet; Ruth, a fashion designer; and a constantly changing group of poets and painters. What we all shared was a fondness for that sort of decadent, semi-literary nightlife and a passion for Cordy. Cordy, a sexy young actress, performed on stage, served at the tables and drove everybody crazy, regardless of their sex, age, or status, moving between partners of different sexes with ease.

It is difficult to explain to people the pleasures, the high spirits, the life-enhancing qualities of a free and often randy life which I was discovering for the first time, the total breaking down of what D. H. Lawrence had called the distinction between the activities of the day and the activities of the night. Standing outside 'normal' judgement, I hoped that pleasure could just be clinging to my skin and tried to find happiness in unmitigated sensual indulgence for its own sake. We were fully aware that such a freedom flouted the given social order.

I owe much of the feeling of freedom to Barbara, a woman of the same age as my mother. I could talk with her about things I could not with Louise. Barbara helped me to accept the fact that an unconventional life could bring with it loneliness. She taught me much about tolerance and she knew about resilience and courage. Barbara had married a fellow doctor. They had one daughter. A few years later, her husband had another child with a nurse by the name of Lilo. When I met Barbara, she and Lilo lived together, bringing up their children in harmony.

Valeska was part of our life for quite a few years and then suddenly we had outgrown her. Barbara became a minister, Rainer a star, Peter still sells flowers on a grand scale and Cordy became a writer, married a composer and has two sons.

There were new friends, Vladimir Lindenberg and his wife Dolina. 'Valodja', a small man of about fifty-five of great charm and attraction, was said to have had several passionate love affairs with St Petersburg's leading aristocrats of both sexes. He had fled from Russia after the revolution and settled in Berlin as a doctor. He was also a writer and painter. His warm and deep understanding of human nature made him the confidant of many young writers, musicians, painters and actors, who would seek his advice or come to hear him read from his strange and mystical books about the positive forces of life, or about Russian poets who had died young.

Dolina, Countess Rödern, was a concert pianist of indefinite age and makeup of frank and undisguised artificiality, a tall and elegant figure who had known everybody in international society. The grand life was something of the past, but their small house, surrounded by the birch trees of a Chekhov play, was filled with the memorabilia of privileged times. Old icons, books and Valodja's paintings lined the walls, and on the grand piano stood silver-framed photographs of the Romanovs, whose surviving members were often among the guests. Every Sunday the drawing-room hummed with the voices of people reading from their latest novels or poems. The samovar was always bubbling and sometimes Dolina would play the piano. It was one of the happiest houses I have ever known, and for many years a source of joy and inspiration, a place of tolerance, generosity, intelligence and human warmth.

Jean Cocteau had come to Berlin for the opening of his film *Orphée*. His visit brought my plans to return to Paris one step nearer. I had devoured Cocteau's novels almost as quickly as those of André Gide. For a twenty-year-old adolescent, the shimmering hermetic world Cocteau evoked was full of temptations, a mixture of one's longing to die or to exhaust oneself in sensuality and physical pleasure. The beautiful black and white images of his early film *Le Sang d'un poète* had haunted me for a long time. I had also seen *Les Enfants terribles*, which he had made with Jean-Pierre Melville, based on his own strange and suffocating story of a brother and sister living mostly at night. The decadent stickiness of their relationship, their refusal to live in the outside world, had been deliciously disquieting. His latest film featured Jean Marais as Orpheus and Maria Casarès as Death, accompanied by black leather-clad motorcyclists, their faces hidden behind goggles.

Cocteau gave a lecture in the Maison de France and I sat in the first row, fascinated as much by his hawk-like face as by the brilliant manipulation of the French language. He was provocative and seductive. Afterwards I ventured backstage. I do not know how I had the guts, but there I was looking like someone straight out of a novel by André Gide, dresssed in a brown dufflecoat, the pockets stuffed with books, talking to him about writing and about his films. He listened patiently, and after ten minutes he fished a book out of my pocket. It was Thomas Mann's essays, *Bekenntnisse*. Cocteau opened the book at the page with the title 'Kosmopolitismus'. He paused for a moment. Then he drew a star and wrote: 'Si Thomas Mann le permet, à Peter Adam, Jean C.' He also asked me to look him up in Paris.

8

Vers un Intellectuel:
Paris 1951–1953

Dolina had written to two French ambassadors, André François-Poncet and Roland de Margerie, asking them to help me get a scholarship. As a result I embarked in the autumn of 1951 for my second trip to Paris. I had obtained a *bourse* from the French government, lasting one year, plus the right to study at the Sorbonne.

I received the princely sum of 20,000 francs per month. The deutschmark was low and the franc high: DM14 to F1. Twenty thousand francs was enough money to settle in one of the many small hotels in the Quartier, and I took a room on the top floor of the hotel at 50 rue du Bac, a stone's throw from the Boulevard St-Germain. From my window I could see the vast ocean of rooftops and chimneys.

I enrolled myself at the Sorbonne, following a *Cours de la Civilisation Française*, a foundation course mostly tailored for foreign students. They came from Africa and the United States, from South America and from every country in Europe. They were black, yellow, Jewish and Muslim. For a lot of them the war and Hitler were a thing of the past, or that had happened far away, and I was determined to feel the same, but the feeling against Germans was still strong among the French. In a country that considered itself invincible and supreme, there were those who had not forgotten the humiliation by the Germans. Like the Austrians, they had quickly erased the role many of them had played under the occupation. I was tired of explaining to everybody that I was Jewish, anyway most people did not believe me, so I decided to rid myself of any trace of an accent and enrolled in a special phonetic course run by a small and vivacious actress, Mademoiselle Roussel. She tried desperately, for hours, to make Americans, Argentinians and Japanese pronounce rows of *pain, pin, saint, vin*. Her heavily made-up mouth kept on miming the vowels, while her red fingernails pointed at the position of the tongue. 'Plus en avant, mes chéris,' she would shout. When she heard the class saying something that sounded like 'pang, vang and sang' her face took on a tragic expression. 'Mon Dieu, quelle horreur.'

The students at the Sorbonne were very different from the ones at the Free University. They were more affluent, many had jobs in bars or restau-

Paris

Le Bal de Quatz'Arts

rants, and some drove little cars. (The 'intelligent' tin box of the 2cv had just come in and was very fashionable.) Their manners too were much more casual; they addressed each other with the familiar *tu* and made fun of the '*profs*'. Everything was always *formidable, sensass* or *extra*. They spent as much time in the many surrounding cafés and small restaurants, discussing the pros and cons of existentialism, as in the lecture rooms of their ancient university. They were gay and lighthearted and out to have a good time, despite their natural tendency to discuss the most profound intellectual matters constantly and passionately. While we in Berlin had been trying to build a new world, the French played a kind of intellectual ping-pong game with inherited cultural ideas, tossing them back and forth just for the fun of it. I felt at home at once, for the Lycée in Berlin had prepared me well for their desire to theorise and to focus ideas.

The buildings of the Sorbonne reflected the same free and chaotic spirit. The old and dark corridors swarmed with noisy and rowdy students. The walls were covered with very crude graffiti shouting the most controversial political, cultural or sexual slogans, sometimes combining all three, like 'Fais-toi sucer en Russie, Simone!'

Many cafés were the meeting places for intellectuals. On the terrace of the Montana someone pointed out Louis Aragon and Elsa Triolet, and at the Flore one could sometimes see Jean-Paul Sartre and Simone de Beauvoir, who lived just around the corner in a flat above the Café Bonaparte. They looked rather like a pair of schoolteachers who had fallen on hard times, certainly not like two of France's most successful and influential writers. Sartre usually wore a run-down formal suit without a tie. From the corner of his mouth dangled a cigarette or a pencil, sometimes both, his eyes were hidden behind dark-rimmed glasses. Beauvoir usually wore a headscarf.

The cheapest places to eat were the *restaurants universitaires*. These canteens were also great meeting places. The best and the most amusing one was in the Ecole des Beaux-Arts, but to be allowed to lunch there one had to be a student of the Art faculty. Fortunately, I had found out that they were looking for life-class models, so I applied. A funny man with a moustache and a beret, the very cliché image of a French painter, asked me if I had modelled before and if I was able to stand still. I lied to both questions, and was engaged.

The atelier of the life class was even more filthy than the corridors of the Sorbonne. There was a smoky old iron stove in the middle. Paint scrapings from generations of French painters were all over the walls. The students were extravagantly dressed and very noisy. I was asked to take off my clothes, stand on an elevated platform and strike a pose which resembled the plaster cast of the antique figures lining the corridors. I was quite narcissistic by nature and certainly not a prude, but with the eyes of about thirty students, of both sexes, focusing on me, I felt rather strange. I quickly got used to it, and besides making some good pocket money I was also admitted into the Restaurant des Beaux-Arts.

It was a good moment to arrive. France under the Fourth Republic was beginning to renew itself. Not that France was really prosperous – the economic recovery would only begin years later – but it felt prosperous, despite its antiquated sanitary system and peeling façades. The inherited feeling for quality and style, together with a desire to compete with each other, made people look rich and worldly.

For people of my generation Sartre represented absolute moral authority. His play *Le Diable et le Bon Dieu* (The Devil and the Good Lord) at the Théâtre Antoine had been one of the major events of the season, and I rushed to see it. It was the last production of the great Louis Jouvet, who had just died. The cast was as famous and as splendid as the French theatre could muster: Pierre Brasseur, Jean Vilar and the grave face of Maria Casares. The set was by Labisse and the costumes by Schiaparelli.

Sartre's call to free oneself from any conventional morality struck a profound chord in someone like me, trying to carve out a new life. I saw myself as a kind of Lucien de Rubempré, exploring and discovering, while displaying an air of insouciance, quoting French poetry, most of all Baudelaire, whom I studied as a kind of alibi for a free and easy life. 'O Seigneur! Donnez-moi la force et le courage de contempler mon cœur et mon corps sans dégoût.' (O Lord! give me the strength and courage to contemplate my heart and body without disgust.) I was vain and self-important enough to regard both my heart and my body with a certain pleasure and I enjoyed, unabashed, the role of the prey. The moral tabs attached to our behaviour were simply not big enough for the complexity of the life I was leading. In Sartre I found the man who rejected the moral stances of society and declared that whatever we choose, good or bad, will lead to absurdity and the only moral stance man can take is to choose freely.

I met two young writers, Daniel Mauroc and Elliott Stein, who published a bilingual small review, *Janus*, devoted to poetry. Elliott was from Brooklyn and lived in the small Hôtel d'Alsace. His room was cluttered with ashtrays, books, dirty clothes, coffee cups and wine glasses growing beards. He claimed that Oscar Wilde had died in the same room fifty years earlier but I never believed him. He had a sophisticated, exhilarating mind, a topsy-turvy intelligence. We talked the nights away about the problems of the world and our own, sometimes falling asleep to wake up when the sun was rising above the roofs. He wrote:

> Music is in the night
> at two o two o two clock
> is like a sudden
> touch of hand
> upon the back of all your plans.
>
> It files away the nights
> at two o two o two clock,
> it speaks of HEARTS
> and all their plots
> and curtain speeches,
> it chats of pause and time to understand.

> To dear Peter simply Elliot and tenderly

Friendships among the young were easily moulded. Sometimes they lasted only a few days, sometimes longer. The links which I formed for a night and sometimes less were as strong as many others, just shorter. They could carry all the outside signs of love and yet they had nothing to do with love. It was all part of the new hedonism that filled our minds. Another friend, Claude Vigée, summed up the many relationships picked up and set down with perfect irresponsibility, no ties on either side. Their strength lay precisely in their total honesty.

> We passed each other a moment of the night
> But lost each other in the wind and rain.[1]

I finally looked up Jean Cocteau, who lived in a flat in the rue de Montpensier, the windows overlooking the gardens of the Palais-Royal. He received me sitting on a bed which was littered with books and papers. The curtains were half-drawn and the room was bathed in a reddish diffused light, just bright enough to make out a few of the many objects which cluttered the room. Somewhere stood a blackboard for drawing on, and some tables with more piles of books. There was a strong smell of musk in the room I could not quite recognise, but I wondered if it was

---

1 'Nous nous croisions l'un et l'autre un instant de la nuit / Mais nous nous reperdions dans le vent sous la pluie.'

opium, which Cocteau was famous for smoking.

Cocteau told me that he had just written a play whose main character was a German called Hans (Bacchus), and asked me about my youth in Berlin, a city which he considered full of dark forces and sexual temptations. The mixture of the healthy and the strong, the blond and the romantic, with the underlying trend towards decadence and even brutality, appealed to his homosexuality. I felt at ease. We talked about erotic fantasies in literature, and he told me that he had written a homosexual *récit* in the twenties, as a kind of answer to Gide's *Corydon*. It could not be published then under his own name and was only printed in a few copies. In 1957, when Girodias published it at the Olympia Press, it had a preface by Cocteau saying: 'Who wrote it? Did I? Perhaps.'

Sometimes he would get up and pace across the small room, watched by a Siamese cat. His voice rose high and became agitated. His vocabulary was scatological. He talked a lot about Rimbaud and his *vierge folle*, Paul Verlaine. 'Ton cœur bat dans ce ventre où dort le double sexe,'[1] Cocteau said, citing Rimbaud. He looked at me with piercing eyes, almost like a predatory bird, as if to test instantly my reaction. From time to time his veined hands would attempt to tame his frizzled hair, while his lean body straightened up.

His mind was very sharp, almost cynical, but he was also kind. He gave me the impression of being generous, but I suspected that he wanted generosity in return. He paid me a lot of compliments, and I could not help feeling that he wanted me to pay some back to him. 'Tu es faune et tu l'es de la tête au pied.' This time he was quoting Baudelaire.[2] I was of course flattered.

Cocteau took me to meet Colette, who also lived by the Palais Royal, in the rue de Beaujolais. I had mentioned that I would love to meet her, and he was somehow keen to show that he could open any doors. If Cocteau's place was all dark and den-like, Colette's flat was full of light. She too received us lying on a bed, reclining on a lawn of silk cushions. I immediately noticed her clear blue eyes under a theatrical makeup of several layers of powder. Her hair was immaculately dishevelled. She had a large shawl draped around her so that her figure was one large round lump. I thought she was still beautiful. Her hands were crippled by age, but she moved them with great elegance when she spoke. To say that she looked like a cat would be too much of a cliché: everybody had compared her to one, but she really had that look. We stayed only a few minutes, during

---

1 'Your heart beats in your guts, where sleeps the double sex.'
2 'You are a faun, from head to toe.'

which the two neighbours exchanged a lot of embraces and 'chéris'. A few polite questions were addressed to me: What I was doing in Paris? 'Jean m'a dit que vous travaillez sur Rilke.' Then the conversation died away in a barrage of niceties. I sat silently while the two talked. Suddenly Cocteau got up, kissed her hands and we were out as quickly as we had entered.

I never saw Cocteau or Colette again. For them, I was a small diversion, a German student who came to pay homage to two great people. 'Un si joli garçon,' Colette was supposed to have said about me. The memory of some weird and magic hours has remained.

I also began to look up Dolina Lindenberg's friends. Roland de Marge-rie lived in a *hôtel particulier* in St-Germain-des-Prés. What the Marais had been for society in the seventeenth century, St-Germain had for a long time been for the *beau monde*. The Margeries were like something out of Proust, whose name pervaded the conversation. Madame de Margerie's salon was famous for writers. She had known Rilke and many of the leading French poets; Paul Valéry and Mallarmé.

I was invited for 'un déjeuner tout à fait simple', Jenny de Margerie had said. I presented myself in my only suit clutching some flowers, to be shown in by a butler. The whole apartment smelled of luxury, ease and privilege. It was the natural habitat of a society that put a lot of emphasis on titles, status, culture and upbringing, not the place where one could sit on the floor or whistle. Coming from a world where society had totally broken down and where everybody had lived through the war's egalitarian effect, this was indeed unsettling. After a glass of champagne and the pre-sentation to half a dozen of *Madame telle et telle, Monsieur tel et tel*, we proceeded to the dining-room. All the footmen, the many different kinds of cutlery, the dignified presence of his excellency the ambassador and the animated chatter of Madame, in full regalia, made my head spin. I tried not to appear confused or impressed. Thank God I knew my Rilke and Dolina Countess Rödern, as she was referred to here. As so often in similar situations I said as little as possible and smiled a lot. I must have passed somehow, because I was asked to come back in a week's time.

I decided to read Proust. A week is not much to read Proust, but I did. A reading which began as snobbishness turned into an obsession which continued throughout my life. I plunged into the world of Odette and the Duchesse de Guermantes, the passion, the incest, the jealousies of Swann, the feeling of loss, the homosexual obsessions. I could not stop reading. It was like being struck down by a virus. I did not know that a book was able to do all that: move you, confuse you, console you, turn you inside out, maybe even change you. I felt the reaction of an over-sensitive and impressionable young man in a new world. But next Sunday I looked at the society I was invited into with different eyes, not because I now was familiar with *madeleines* and Vinteuil's Sonata, but because Proust had opened my eyes to the social milieu, which had not changed since *A la Recherche du temps perdu*.

I began to make the rounds of the salons. People still had *jours*, a fixed day they received: Wednesdays, Marie-Louise Bousquet; Thursdays, the Noailles.

Marie-Laure de Noailles had been hostess to the art world since the 1920s. Her salon in Paris, at the Place des Etats-Unis, and her house in Hyères had been frequented by virtually everybody from Buñuel to Cocteau, Chanel to Paul Eluard, Georges Auric to Igor Markevitch, Diaghilev's last love. She gave famous balls, and her salon was one of the places everybody wanted to be seen in. I was very curious, when I was finally invited. I never became a regular, for I was socially too shy and too unimportant, more a spectator than a guest in these circles, where the guests, the food and the wine seemed to be subtly blended and orchestrated in the pursuit of the beautiful in life and art. I noticed the mixture of the artistic and the fashionable, so special to French social life. Impressed and intimidated, I watched the celebrities that were pointed out to me: Darius Milhaud and an exotic-looking painter, Leonora Fini, Juliet and Man Ray, and Balthus mingling with total ease. I only managed to speak to a few people. One of them was a young composer from America, Ned Rorem – a favourite of Marie-Laure, I think she was even in love with him. He and Elliott Stein were working on an opera together. I liked him, despite the fact that he was quite vain and obviously hobnobbing with the rich and famous, but he was deliciously rude and wore a black polo-neck sweater or colourful shirts. He struck me as unconventional. He was also very good-looking, the all-American boy. I am afraid I did not make much of an impression on him, however hard I tried.

These evenings taught me at least the virtue, charm and interest of good conversation. The French were natural conversationalists, unafraid of showing off their knowledge. They talked because they liked the activity, no matter what the subject was; it could be the collection of Balenciaga, the latest song of Piaf, a political speech by André Malraux or the constant malaise of the French intellectuals, marked by 'dégoût' and lassitude. The Germans too were great debaters, but it was always in order to come to profound solutions to solve the problems of the world. In Paris one talked because one wanted to be entertained.

I realised that this glittering world which fed on the young and famous was entertaining for a while, but ultimately boring. All that clever talk about first-rate writers and second-rate yachts must be avoided. This was not the ground on which friendship could grow, not the kind of friendship I was after. I sometimes saw Ned all by himself, sitting in a café or on a cheerless and lonely excursion into a bar, looking drunk and lost, and it sort of consoled me to find that even he, who seemed to know everybody and be the American toast of the town, was profoundly alone.

On Sundays I felt the rising waters of despair. I imagined everybody having such a good time, while I sat in my bed, this fragile paradise, hunched under a blanket, more for protection than to keep warm. The noise from the street trailed through the window, making me feel shut out from the world.

For my first holiday, I went to a still undiscovered Ibiza. I hitchhiked, like most students, a time-consuming but delightful way to travel and to sample the flavours of the country. Some drivers took you just ten miles to the next village, others advanced you by several hundred miles. I travelled in 2CVs and on the back of trucks, on motorcycles and once even in a Rolls-Royce. Many people still took hitchhikers, for stories of gangsters disguised as nuns hardly troubled us. Young people usually stopped because they had hitchhiked themselves, middle-aged couples because they had children your age. Some drivers took you because they were curious, others because they were lonely. There were those who just wanted company, others who hoped for an easy adventure. Some invited you for lunch, others never stopped asking you questions.

After four days, I reached Barcelona, where one took the overnight boat to Mallorca and then onwards with another boat to Ibiza. Nobody went to Ibiza in 1951 except a few artists. Mass tourism did not exist, although Gerard Blitz, a young, blond athlete, had put an ad in the papers inviting people to join him in a holiday camp on Mallorca. He had bought some US army surplus tents. He had over 2,000 replies. This was the beginning of the Club Mediterranée.

I put up at San Antonio Abad's only hotel, a simple pension, run by six or seven sisters from Leipzig. It was July, but with the exception of a French lady, there were no guests. I still have a photograph of a very skinny young man wearing a large Spanish hat, smiling at a very skinny dark-haired woman on a deserted beach. After a few days I felt lonely. The beauty of the still untouched landscape, the heat of the sun which gave way to cool nights, filled me with a longing for someone to share it with. I felt overwhelmed by so many unanswered questions: my own inconsistencies and contradictions; the constant state of sexual tension, quite enjoyable, but also irritating with its all-invading force.

Then something unusual happened – the changing pattern of life, I thought. I met two incredibly handsome guys. Bill was American, Stig, Swedish. They too had left their countries and shared my thirst for life. A few days later I moved into their house. There are days when the world seems not to belong to one, days drenched with *le cafard*, and then suddenly the whole world unfolds under one's feet in full splendour. We drove around the island in a little M G, the most exciting car I had ever seen, and went out fishing in a boat. We slept under a flawless sky, exhausted by wine and physical pleasures. We had a sort of *ménage à trois*, a thrilling but foolish combination for which one of the three usually pays dearly. In this case it was Bill. I do not have an inbuilt feeling of guilt, although everything around one conspires to make one feel guilty. Of course I had a feeling of conscience, but that is not the same as guilt. For the time being, the high spirits and sensuality held the three of us together. Things like that cannot last. They are not meant to. After three weeks a lot of ugly scenes invaded the room, emerging from anywhere and going nowhere, so I thought it was time to move back to Paris. I do not know what has happened to Bill, but I visited Stig several times in Sweden. He now lives in America and sells teak furniture.

Around this time I fell in love. I guess it was the first time since Annerl and Nelly that I had felt that way, that feeling that hits you in the stomach and makes you behave without reason. His name was Daniel, a tall, willowy boy in sneakers from Oshkosh, Wisconsin. Defeat and even loss marked his face in repose, but when animated it was inundated by a large and liberating smile. Together with his childhood friend, Wayne Lawson, he had come to Paris to study art and architecture. Wayne had translated Montherlant's *La Ville dont le Prince est un Enfant*. His father was a janitor and the two boys had decided to break out of their provincial life and try their luck elsewhere. Princeton University had given them a scholarship to study in Europe. Theirs was a typical American story, which, for someone like myself, brought up in a system based on social privileges, impressed me greatly. The step from Oshkosh to Paris, via Princeton, was only a small one for two bright and determined young Americans. Wayne was sharply observant, killingly funny and did not suffer fools gladly. He could destroy someone with a few well-honed remarks. Danny on the other hand was very kind, and it was this which made me fall in love with him.

I was hopelessly romantic and I was not very good at it. My excess of love usually scared people off, for I have never learned to economise my feelings. I would wait hours for Danny to come home, I suffered pangs of jealousy and then lived through days of extreme happiness. I was over-emotional, over-possessive. One moment I wanted to die, the next I ran around embracing trees in the park. On the whole I suffered a great deal.

Part of our small group, *la bande américaine*, as we were known, were two American girls, Rusty and Marie Frances. Marie Frances was supposed to be very rich, but she despised any outward sign of wealth. She certainly did not look like someone from New York, more like a little girl who had just left a small village school. It was a sort of hippy look, only the word was not yet invented. She was very shy and very kind. Rusty on the other hand was very smart and very New York. Rusty was in love with Wayne and Wayne liked her. Danny liked Marie Frances, who was in love with him. Since Danny was supposed to be in love with me, neither of the girls liked me. It all had the ingredients of a very contrived play, although the combination, as I later found out, was quite common.

American students were much richer than European ones, so we went a lot to nightclubs, like the Lapin Agile, in Montmartre, where Lady Patachou cut off the ties of the guests to hang them on the wall. It was rumoured that she was in love with a singer who played the guitar and sang beautiful songs with a husky voice. His name was Brassens.

We also went to the many *caves*, which were all the vogue. The most famous was the Rose Rouge, where Sidney Bechet played and Juliette Gréco poured out her black-clad anguish. American tourists went there to experience a *soirée existentialiste*. We usually got in because, in our jeans and sandals, we looked the part. The owner used us as a kind of décor, and when the place filled up we had to leave.

Another haunt I liked was the Bal Nègre, a dance hall in the Montagne Ste-Geneviève for ladies who had a penchant for them. It was considered very *louche*. Single society ladies went there to dance to the steaming rhythm of the black band. At a certain time all lights were turned off and everybody danced in the dark.

Paris, at that time, was full of little *boîtes*, where people sang or played the guitar, but the proper way to hear the French *chanson* was to go to the music-hall theatres like the Olympia. Here Gilbert Bécaud, Yves Montand, Mouloudji, Charles Aznavour and, most of all, the celebrated Edith Piaf appeared. Now everybody knows about *la môme Piaf*, her records have been around the world, but in the early 1950s hers was new and powerful stuff. The tiny woman in her little black dress, almost dwarfed by the large stage, pushed pathos to the limit. 'Moi j'essuie les verres' she sang, making us believe that the story of the boy and the girl she had just seen killing themselves was an episode from a Greek drama.

It is hard to believe that so many of the things that have become part of the canon of French culture were new then. What a rich crop of plays in the theatre: Anouilh, Giraudoux, Sartre, Montherlant, Camus were all still writing plays. The Renaud-Barrault company was going strong at the Théâtre Marigny, with productions of the great plays by Claudel, like *Partage de midi* with Edwige Feuillère and Pierre Brasseur.

The most exciting place was the new Théâtre National Populaire, TNP, in the Palais de Chaillot. As the name indicates it was truly a popular theatre, a vast modern auditorium of nearly 3,000 seats. Highly subsidised, the tickets cost only two francs. The audience was young and casually dressed. They were enthusiastic and grateful. The great actor/director Jean Vilar, in his desire to bring theatre to a large number of people, not just the French classics, but also the many great European plays, broke with the tradition of the Comédie-Française, with its inherited service to the classics and its rather stilted style. In a few years he would put on Corneille's *Le Cid*, Kleist's *Prince of Homburg*, Büchner's *Danton's Death*, and plays by Musset, Pirandello, Brecht and Shakespeare. Vilar was a magician. He had grouped around him many young and talented actors, including Jeanne Moreau, Maria Casares and Gérard Philipe.

Gérard Philipe, with his sensitive and beautiful face, was the idol of all young people. He had been propelled to stardom almost overnight in 1945, when he appeared in Camus' *Caligula*. I was fortunate to see him in all his great Romantic roles – le Cid, Lorenzaccio, the Prince of Homburg and Danton.

Another theatre where I hardly ever missed a production was the Théâtre des Nations, the first international theatre festival on a large scale, presenting the best productions from all over the world, not unlike what Peter Daubeny did much later with his World Theatre Season in London. As this was a much grander affair, socially speaking, than the TNP, the tickets were much more expensive and I returned to the traditional student seats in the *poulailler*, the Gods. If one was determined enough to queue one almost always managed to get the much-coveted seats, high up under the ceiling. This was just as well for someone squeamish like myself, for the first play I saw there was *Titus Andronicus*, a bloody affair with ripped-out tongues. It was the first time I saw Laurence Olivier and Vivien Leigh.

With the help of the Margeries I managed to get a grant for a further year and moved into a small apartment at 44 rue Dauphine, a famous address, for it had been a well-known bordello, or as the French call it a *maison de tolérance*, although tolerance had run aground as many brothels had been closed down by a puritanical streak in the government (the same government that later got rid of the *tasses*, the traditional French *pissoirs*). The whorehouses were turned into student lodgings. My first apartment consisted of one room with a large mirror on the ceiling and a small bathroom with six bidets. I pinned a photograph of Kafka and a Picasso poster on the wall and put a lighted candle in the window, a signal to Danny that I was back. He sometimes came to stay with me, but often didn't.

Unfortunately soon afterwards Danny, Wayne, Marie Frances and Rusty left for the States, and for a while I missed them greatly. But then I began to forget even Danny. Danny eventually married Marie Frances. A private helicopter carried them away for their honeymoon. They lived for years in a small Indian village, designing stoves for the natives. Rusty married someone else and became an editor in a famous New York publishing house. I believe she still loves Wayne.

As for Wayne, he has remained a bachelor and one of my best friends. He has become a devoted Catholic and spends much of his time and money helping others. He is still as witty and as brilliant as ever, although no longer cynical. Because he knows what is really significant, he also has a love and understanding of the absurd. He did a stint at the Book Review of the *New York Times* and helped Gloria Swanson and Jerzy Kosinsky to write their books. It is hard to believe that this modest and unassuming man would end up working on one of the mauling papers. He became the literary editor for *Vanity Fair*. He is also the only saintly person I know, a quality which helps him to survive unscathed in a world which lives off trivia, frivolity and scandal.

For my second academic year, I enrolled at the famous Ecole des Sciences Politiques, to read Twentieth-Century History and International Relations. The *Science Po* was a very different affair from the Sorbonne. It was not quite as exclusive as the famous Grandes Ecoles, like the Ecole Polytechnique, which furnished France with its most brilliant politicians and industrialists, but here too the students looked more like future ambassadors than artists and revolutionaries, and talked about treaties and oil deals.

Still trying to understand my country's descent into barbarism, I enlisted in a special course on Germany, looking at it so to speak from the outside. Hannah Arendt's book *The Origins of Totalitarianism* had just appeared. She was trying to explain the many disparate circumstances which led to the plight of the Jewish refugees. Arendt helped me to question my attitude towards Germany and the Jews. Her scepticism, her intellectual vigour, was so much more to my liking than all the sentimentality which would soon surround the plight of the Jews in stories like that of the life of Anne Frank. Canonised by the Americans and applauded in the theatre, her story thus always seems to reduce the horror of Nazism to a sentimental tale.

Later Arendt's *Adolf Eichmann in Jerusalem* had a similar effect. She had been sent to Israel to cover the trial of Adolf Eichmann and had come back with a report with the subtitle 'On the Banality of Evil'. She disliked the growing Israeli nationalism and mistrusted the many conciliatory gestures from the new Germany towards the Jewish state.

Arendt's contradictory book made me question the roles of the Jews. Could some of the horrors of Nazi Germany have been avoided if they had been politically more aware, even politically organised? I thought of the Adam family with their old-fashioned values, and their lack of political astuteness. Then there was the question of the rich Jews who had been able to flee while the poor perished in the camps. Arendt had often pointed out how the Jews sacrificed their culture in order to be assimilated. This was certainly true of my family and many others of the same background. They had given up their Jewishness in order to succeed socially. I remember their anti-Semitism: 'Don't wave your hands when you speak,' my father used to say. 'It makes you look Jewish.' When, at the age of twenty-eight, I moved to New York and met my Jewish cousins, the first thing I heard was: 'Thank God you do not look at all Jewish.' The same superior feeling and arrogance they once manifested against the Eastern Jews was now directed against the Jews from Brooklyn or those holidaying in Miami. It was all right to be Jewish, but not too much.

Few countries had changed so much within a lifespan as Germany. I had witnessed, though not all consciously, four Germanies: the end of the Weimar Republic, Hitler's Germany, the post-war years and the Germany of prosperity. (I should now add a fifth: Germany reunited.) They had little in common with each other: each brought a change of society, geography, politics and cultural changes which reverberated almost throughout the world.

Eventually I would turn my back on all four and make my life elsewhere. Was that fate? I could not quite believe in Schiller's dictum that man's fate lies in his own heart, however beautiful. My fate was coloured by my reaction to outside forces in history, by a few irrefutable facts: the date and place of my birth and my homosexuality. These facts have determined my life and my reactions to events; all others are secondary.

To counterbalance the rather stiff atmosphere of the *Science Po*, I continued to eat at the Restaurant des Beaux-Arts and recruited most of my friends there. For us the sexual revolution, so often associated with the sixties, began then. I attended the infamous Bal des Quatz'Arts, the annual ball of the Académie, the high point of the carnival season, a bacchanal of French artists and arts students. It was the freest and most permissive event in Paris, and even by today's standards pretty outrageous. I had been to the Berlin Academy balls, which were very easygoing, but the display of nudity and open sexual activities at the Quatz'Arts was something else. Long before the beginning of the ball, people formed tableaux vivants, imitating famous paintings. They swarmed through the streets and invaded the restaurants of the quartier in the most fantastic dress and undress. Respectable families locked up their daughters for the night, others flocked into the restaurants and onto the terraces of the cafés to see the arrival of the various groups on carts and horses. I joined the students of the life class and we went as *The Raft of the Medusa* by Géricault. It gave us ample opportunity for exhibitionism.

Not that everything was so free as these goings on. Jean Genet's books were hard to come by. I had been invited for a screening of his *Chant d'amour* in the Henri Langlois Cinémathèque when the police cancelled the show. The hauntingly beautiful film had been shot in the Rose Rouge and we were all keen to see it. Fortunately the young film-maker François Reichenbach secured a copy and projected it on the walls of his living-room.

On stifling hot days I went to the Piscine Deligny, a small bathing place on a boat in the middle of the Seine. There the bathers lay, in such intimate proximity, body to body, as usually only lovers do. The smell of perspiration and Ambre Soleil was quite intoxicating.

Of course I couldn't possibly mention Jean Genet or the Piscine Deligny at the Margeries' table, nor that I had been to the Quatz'Arts ball, but my exam results, which oscillated between *bien*, and *très bien*, were a sure topic of conversation and gave rise to the hope that I would one day enter the diplomatic service.

After each of my relationships, with their doomed and desperate qualities, I emerged with the same pattern of longing for something indefinable, something magnificent, a way out of my troubled nature, and after Danny had left I entered a new circle of friends, mostly girls and boys from the francophile Moroccan-Jewish middle classes. I still suffered Tonio Kröger's pangs and was trying to escape the highly strung homosexual relationships with their morning *cafard* and their excessive nights looking for love. It was not that I consciously changed from one group to another; I drifted into a new pattern, propelled by an excess of energy, curiosity and a great fear of being alone or left out.

The little Moroccan group was very different from *la bande américaine*. They did not discuss existentialism or any other great intellectual problem, they were ordinary students, continually broke, enthusiastic about the theatre and cinema but mostly out to have a good time. Having a good time meant hanging around cafés and going to the movies. The centre of our clique was a vivacious girl, Marcelle. She was very pretty with her curly black hair and generous figure, and when she laughed the whole street turned around. Marcelle and I became friends, and for a while inseparable. Not that the life in this new group was free of drama. There were scenes of jealousy, couples breaking up and forming new links – there was even an abortion, a dangerous, highly illegal and very messy affair, per-formed in my apartment, which left me with feelings of confusion and even some guilt.

We went to see a film almost every night. The cinema was one of the cheapest ways of spending an evening. In France it is as intellectually respectable as the theatre. A *cinéaste* is on the same level as a writer or a painter. Many writers have transferred their ideas to celluloid: Cocteau, Resnais, Robbe-Grillet, Duras. The notion of the *cinéma d'auteur* emerged in the fifties. For me it was a whole new cinema world in which literature and pictures merged. I regularly joined the queue of French and foreign students in front of the little Cinéma St-Michel, one of the many art houses devoted to French film. The erotic charm of Simone Signoret, Arletty or Jeanne Moreau seems to me so much more real than that of their celluloid sisters from across the ocean. The quietness of the French films, even in the most dramatic moments, the elegance of the economy, the care for each detail had a greater attraction than the slickness of the American movies with their faked fights and bullets and their musical numbers with their improbable dancing routine every time an actor declared his feelings.

My love for the French cinema did not totally eclipse my interest in the theatre. With Danny and Wayne I had mostly explored the theatre of the established playwrights. I now became increasingly interested in the avant-garde. There were many small theatres in the quartier, trying out new plays which would change the theatrical landscape throughout the world. The two names people talked about most were those of Adamov and Ionesco, especially Ionesco. On my first visit to Paris I had seen *La Cantatrice chauve* (The Bald Primadonna) at the Théâtre aux Noctambules. I found it amusing in its grotesqueness and its absurdity of language but I could not really make head or tail of it.

But then one day Marcelle told me that Roger Blin would be putting on a play by a new playwright who for years had been trying to find a theatre. We went to the Théâtre de Babylon where some people were queuing outside. I remember it was very cold and we had to stand in line. Somebody fetched some chairs from the café next door, but the small theatre with its rickety benches never filled up completely. The curtain rose on a brown sand-hill and a tree to reveal two tramps, one of them with the beautiful name of Estragon. Then two more clown-like *clochards* entered, circling the stage like a circus ring. Nothing much happened. The characters stood around talking, obsessed with their boots. Nothing moved very much, it was a theatre of non-communication. Most people in the audience watched quietly, some were visibly bored, but I do not remember anybody leaving. Like the actors on stage we waited for something. Many were watching transfixed, as if the waiting was part of our condition. At one point one of the characters said: 'Let's go.' 'We can't,' replied the other. 'Why not?'

Waiting for Godot was Beckett's first play. After it the theatre would never quite be the same. I was not sure, at that time, if it was a great play, but I felt as if someone had pulled the switch at the junction and the train rushed off in a totally different direction. There was pain and solace, expressed in short sentences interrupted by long pauses that fell like musical cadences. I went to see the play four times. The theatre was never full and the reviews were very mixed, but the story of the little play spread like wildfire in the quartier. Soon *Waiting for Godot* became a sort of joky catch phrase – the futility of man's existence, the constant struggle with illusions. 'We've arrived,' said Vladimir. 'Who are you?' asked Pozzo. 'We are men.'

Despite the relatively orderly life with Marcelle and her group of friends, I was still drawn to the darker side of life. A chance encounter or a visit to the steam bath was intoxicating: the complicity of sensual nakedness, intimate and yet anonymous, a world for men.

While one side was drawn to debauchery, the other longed for salvation. Who was I? I constantly seemed to swing between the serious and the frivolous, between the snob and the one with a social conscience. I looked with envy upon those well-balanced determined people and asked myself whether I would ever find my identity. I was so easily swayed. The nihilism of Beckett and the existentialism of Sartre seemed to offer some solution for my disjointed life. Sartre's dictum that 'if God exists man does not exist, and if man exists then God does not exist' satisfied my longing for total choice but left unsatisfied my need for a kind of union with some metaphysical forces. However liberating, the movement of existentialism appeared to me a sad solution. The truth I was looking for could not only come from within myself. The seductive appeal of religious thought and ritual was never far away, and the ideas of Teilhard de Chardin, the great Catholic thinker, the heretical Jesuit whom the Church had embraced again, were also attractive.

Jenny de Margerie opened my eyes to a number of Catholic writers whom I began to study: Paul Claudel, with his great sweep of poetry, Georges Bernanos, Jacques Maritain and most of all Charles Péguy. Here was a man willing to accept the tragic and the profound in mankind. His noble and exalted poems and *pensées* presented us with a hope that man might be saved. I went on the pilgrimage for Péguy, an annual students' event. I walked from Paris to Chartres through the night with thousands of other students, reciting his verses, guided by 'l'espérance qui marchait devant nous', until in the early hours of the morning we saw the silhouette of the cathedral rising above the flat land.

Constantly short of money, impoverished by visits to the theatre, restaurants and nightclubs, I was always looking for jobs. I helped Jenny de Margerie to organise an exhibition of letters which Rainer Maria Rilke had written to numerous French personalities. I had to arrange the *vitrines* and translate some of the letters, and the idea began to ripen of writing my Ph.D. thesis on Rilke's translations.

When the composer Nicholas Nabokov, cousin of the writer, organised the Festival of Cultural Freedom, I worked as a general dogsbody and made myself useful by helping with Pierre-Jean Jouve's translation of Berg's *Wozzeck*. This grand old man opened my eyes to the works of many French poets. It was he who prompted me later to write my essay on Paul Valéry and Maurice de Guérin.

The darling of the festival was an American, Virgil Thomson. His opera *Four Saints in Three Acts*, with a libretto by Gertrude Stein, was given for the first time in Paris. I tried to stick around rehearsals as much as possible, always eager to learn something, and was introduced to a group of young and handsome musicians, who usually surrounded the composer: 'Lenny' Bernstein, 'Tommy' Schippers and Giancarlo Menotti, all names I had never heard of. I watched in amazement and slight admiration the mixture of sophistication, wit, bitchiness and camp banter, while they laughed about what Virgil Thomson called my 'naïveté'.

With the money I made I went on little trips into the French provinces. Malraux had not yet began his cultural decentralisation programme and the provinces truly were provincial: sleepy, lethargic towns with small streets and glorious cathedrals; places wonderful to visit, hell to live in.

But change was in the air. It was as if people began to wake up from a dream. Our pleasant existence was gradually being threatened from all sides. The split between the right and the left became deeper. The war in Indochina and the Rosenberg affair brought out much anti-Americanism. When the two were executed for spying we demonstrated on the Place de la Concorde.

The disenchantment with communism had also begun. Sartre's power and influence were on the wane and the existentialist movement, that had dominated French intellectual life since the war, began to wither. His political engagement with the communists, which he had fiercely defended in a series of articles in the magazine *Nouvelle Revue Française* under the title 'Le communisme et la Paix', had put many people off. Sartre and Camus had quarrelled over politics. Camus had attacked Stalin and compared his regime to Hitler's. Sartre was still defending communism in all its forms, and in his magazine *Les Temps modernes* had almost ignored Camus' *The Rebel*. Camus encountered with an attack on *Les Mains sales*. Not since the controversy between Aragon and Breton had the press and the public relished a debate between two writers. But somehow this was more than just an intellectual debate, it affected us more deeply. Someone like myself, who had experienced both Hitler and Stalin's soldiers, sided with Camus. There were rumours of Stalin's labour camps, soon to be confirmed at the twentieth congress of the Soviet Communist Party.

There was also the first inkling that the role France had played under the German occupation was not as innocent as most people believed. Somebody told me about the raid of the Vel d'Hiv, the Vélodrome d'Hiver, where the French had rounded up the Jews. It happened in July 1942, when 28,000 of them, French and German, were handed over to the occupying Germans, among them 4,000 children. The Paris police did the work for the Germans. Pétain's government and many Frenchmen looked on, even sanctioned it. It would take another forty years for the French to own up to this darkest hour of their history.

Students began passionately to debate the dubious role many countries had played during the war. Was there no difference between the evil of Nazism and communism? Both systems were evil, they both brutally suppressed liberty and enslaved the very people they pretended to serve. Hitler's concentration camps and Stalin's gulags must rank equal in the history of evil. Yet we still looked more leniently at one system than at the other. Communism had to do with ideas I heartily embraced, deeply humanitarian ideas. Hitler's ideas were mostly the ideas of murderers who decided who had a right to live and who must die. Communism as I knew it in East Berlin and later in Russia was perverted by the practitioners of the ideas; Nazism was perverted from its very roots.

In the middle of all that, my years in Paris came to an end. Looking back from where I stand now, I find that few years have been as fruitful in forming my mind as those Paris years, a time when I was as much formed by the encounter with persons and events as by metaphysics and thought. They were also years during which I experienced loneliness more acute and more painful than ever before. Despite all the diversions of my life I was aware of the illusory nature of it. The quicksand of relationships and the loneliness within. To the outside world I presented a picture of cheerfulness and irresponsible lightness. It was still the old desire to be popular and to be accepted which made me take on this pose. I kept on making gestures or taking stances in the hope that people would notice me, but underneath ran a river of sadness. I realised of course that much of my unhappiness came from the continuous pull towards introspection.

The time in Paris made me aware of the constant simmering of my emotional energy and the need for physical outlets. Neither of them would ever leave me. I had also begun to recognise that to be isolated, to be receptive to everything, to decline nothing, was necessary to the person I wanted to be.

I spent my twenty-fourth birthday on Ischia. I had gone there to visit Hans Werner Henze. *Boulevard Solitude* had been staged in several opera houses and his ballet-pantomine *The Idiot* had been a great success at the Festival in Berlin. Tatjana Gsovsky was the choreographer. The success had taken its toll. Hans was tired and agitated. Someone had suggested that he take a rest and he decided to spend some time in Italy. This was in 1953. He still lives there, although he hardly rests.

He had rented a small house in Forío, that consisted of two white-washed rooms, one with a large table to work and to eat on, the other with a large bed under a mosquito net. There was also a little terrace with a splendid view over the sea and the vineyards. The original owners had moved out and let Hans have the house, but Lucia Capuano, a local peasant woman, continued to look after him. After the noise and activities of Paris this was bliss. Hans worked on a new opera, while I swam in the sea or explored the island. He seemed happier than I had seen him for a long time. Some of this feeling spilled over in his *Ode an den Westwind,* dedicated to Lucia and Giovanni Capuano.

There were few guests. With tremendous discipline, the composer would rise early and work almost all day. It was not a time to disturb him. From time to time his neighbours, the painter Werner Gilles, or Enrico, Prince of Hesse, would drop in, and Hans would even cook. The writer Heinz von Cramer, who was working on the libretto for Henze's next opera *Il Re Cervo* or *König Hirsch*, came over from Procida for a work session. On the whole Hans kept a low profile.

This could not been said about another famous inhabitant of the island, who held court at the local Café Maria. W. H. Auden had also rented a house in Forío. It was much larger and much more untidy than Henze's. There was a large vegetable garden of which the poet was very proud. Auden was quite a celebrity on the island. Together with his lover Chester Kallman, he had written the libretto for Stravinsky's *The Rake's Progress*. It had opened in 1951 at La Fenice in Venice, with Elisabeth Schwarzkopf and Otakar Kraus. The success had put him into the limelight, although he led a modest existence compared with the third prominent inhabitant of the island, the composer William Walton, and his Argentinian wife Suzanna.

Auden shared the Spartan house with Kallman, a roughish American boy with a sensual mouth, beginning to put on weight. Auden usually wore a white linen suit, which had become the colour of bird droppings. His smooth sunburnt face had not yet cracked into the well ploughed field it later became. He loved Germany and Germans. It was strange for me to encounter somebody who was actually happy to meet someone from the country most people shunned. He was mostly interested in talking about Berlin and the boys.

Usually there was a stream of illustrious guests – Christopher Isherwood, Stephen Spender, Truman Capote, Golo Mann, Vladimir Nabokov. Fortunately the summer I was there Auden and Chester were alone with two cats called Lucinda and Pamina and a dog who went by the name of Moses. There was also a houseboy with the unlikely name of Giocondo. Hans would keep his distance, but I could not resist seeing Auden as much as possible. He too would work in the morning and then stop for lunch and drinks on the piazza. Auden did the talking; one could not interrupt or argue. He held us in his sway with a not-to-be-interrupted expression, while he spoke about literature or entertained American students with salacious gossip. 'Dante was a terrible prima donna,' he remarked. Sometimes we would meet in the house for some very strong dry Martinis. Auden loved his food and Chester was a very good cook. Then at 9.30 he would rise abruptly and retire to bed, Chester remaining behind.

One night Chester took me on a long ride in an old banger of a car that Auden had bought in Berlin. He had just learned to drive. We only returned to the house after midnight. Wystan was standing on the balcony. 'Chester, you are late,' he shouted. 'Oh dear,' is all Chester said.

Auden went two or three times a week to bathe in a hot spa. In order to reach it you had to take a small boat. I volunteered to row him there. This was fun. Auden sat in the hot tub and I had him to myself. Without a large audience he was a good listener. I told him about my life in Germany during the war and the exhilaration of my Paris years. I realised how little I knew about English literature and it was from Auden that I heard for the first time the names Isherwood, Spender and E. M. Forster. He also quoted to me from a pornographic (his word not mine) poem called 'The Platonic Blow' which he did not intend to publish. I remember a few lines:

> It was a spring day, a day for a lay, when the air smelled like
> a locker-room, a day to blow or get blown

I did not think it was nearly as funny as the one I always liked and which became so dreadfully true twenty years later with the arrival of AIDS. I heard it for the first time from Auden's mouth. We were both very drunk:

> As the poets have mournfully sung,
> Death takes the innocent young,
> The rolling in money
> The screamingly funny
> And those who are very well hung.

Hans was generous, but eventually he became rather irritated with me, and I could not blame him. The house was simply too small for a working composer and a chatting and laughing holidaymaker. As so often in life I decided to move on.

9

Small-Time Diplomat
1953–1955

In the early summer of 1953 I found myself once more on the train to Berlin. I thought of all the things that had happened to me during the last two years and my head was filled with fear. How could they all be accommodated?

But soon the gloom made room for the excitement of new things to come. Life would bring new sensations, experiences, friendships. The world was coming together, and Paris and Berlin were only a train journey apart. How easily we adapt, I thought, and I felt like a king.

After twenty hours, my chatty fellow travellers grew silent; we were approaching the Russian border. The smile of the West German passport official and his 'Have a nice trip' was the last friendly gesture of a familiar world. 'Don't take a Western newspaper,' they had warned us, and I threw *Le Monde* away. My papers were in order, I was not smuggling anything, and yet I was nervous. The train stopped at a no-man's-land station, guarded by barbed wire and soldiers and festooned with the familiar slogans of the workers' paradise. Loudspeakers ordered everybody off the train. It was like the old times most travellers had not forgotten: control, authority, intimidation. During the last hour they entertained each other with stories about arrested citizens. Old people began to lug heavy cases, and there were people with crying children in their arms. We were filtered through a barrack, one by one.

I have always resented passport controls, the representatives of the country, often behind glass, examining my papers, leafing through a book, trying to find my name, people standing behind me, at a distance, marked out by a line – always one by one so that no one could witness or overhear what was said, an isolating experience out of Kafka. Helmstedt in 1953 was something else, more sinister, more intimidating.

The inpenetrable *Volkspolizist* and I were of the same age. He examined my passport, filled not only with the exit and entrance permits from the Allies, but also with numerous transit visas for the countries I had passed through, and then waved me on without a smile. I wonder if he really believed in his regime or if he would rather come to West Berlin with me. As soon as we were back in our compartment, everybody started to talk again. The next stop would be Berlin, a different world, with neon lights inviting one to drive a Mercedes and to smoke Camels.

Once at home, I settled back into my familiar life. I got out my old bicycle and began the round of telephone calls. Most of my friends were where I had left them, at the same spot, which amazed me.

A few days later the reality of the cold war hit me with vigour when, on 18 June 1953, we heard on the radio that the workers in East Berlin had gone on strike and were assembling in the streets to demonstrate for a change in the government. After eight years of the communist regime they turned against the hated government of Otto Grotewohl and Walter Ulbricht, with its police methods. The workers, not the middle classes or the small shopkeepers, rebelled against what was known as their paradise. Everybody was stunned, even the East German government. Hundreds of thousands marched down the Stalin Allee, with its pompous architecture, resembling the 'Stalin Gothic' of Moscow.

News of demonstrations in other towns also began to filter through. We rushed to the East. One large building, the Columbushaus, was engulfed in flames and demonstrators tore posters with communist slogans from the walls. Four young men had climbed up the Brandenburg Gate and threw the red flag into the cheering crowd. It was burned to applause. I saw the hatred in their faces while the police on both sides, in the West and the East, looked on. This is the end, I thought, of yet another hateful regime. All the things which the Germans had not done under Hitler, they were doing now.

The rioting went on for twenty-four hours and then Russian tanks suddenly appeared. I saw a worker rushing towards them, begging them not to shoot. Then the first stones were thrown, and were answered at once by a barrage of bullets. I ran as fast as I could. I can't remember much except fear. I ran and ran until I reached the Western sector. All around me people were crying and running.

A few hours later came the news over the radio. People armed only with stones were an easy target. They were crushed, and with them all hope for change. Many of us wept that night.

The Russians cut off all telephone lines between the two sides. We were no longer able to phone family or friends in the same town, and the stream of refugees from the East reached the half million mark. We could still visit the East, but we felt less and less inclined to do so, except maybe for a Brecht performance.

In 1954 the Berliner Ensemble had moved into their new and final premises, in the Theater am Schiffbauerdamm. There Brecht, until his death in 1956, directed many of his plays: *Mother Courage, Puntila, The Mother* (after Gorky) and *The Caucasian Chalk Circle.*

Berlin was the poor relation of West Germany, economically always a step behind, but politically and even intellectually one step ahead. The old fighting spirit of the capital was hard to kill. But gradually we too became more prosperous. The university was still scattered all around the villas of Dahlem, but we now had a proper main lecture hall and a refectory, all spankingly modern and financed by American money. The number of cars on the students' car park had increased visibly – there were even some convertibles. Students wore sneakers and jeans and talked about Klaus Fuchs, who had passed on atomic secrets to the USSR. I was homesick for the Sorbonne with its untidiness and its preoccupations with sexual and intellectual activities, for suddenly everything was serious and significant again.

My old idol Professor Kunisch had consented to become my *Doktorvater*, my doctoral sponsor. I proposed to write a thesis on Rainer Maria Rilke as a translator. Rilke translated all his life. Naturally he only chose texts for which he felt a strong affinity. They included works by Paul Valéry, André Gide, Maurice de Guérin, the mystical letters of the nun Marianna Alcoforado and the sonnets of Louise Labbé. He had also translated the *Sonnets from the Portuguese* of Elizabeth Browning, although his English was shaky. There were some sonnets by Michelangelo as well. The writing of the thesis took two years, much of it spent in the library. I always found working in libraries very enjoyable, with their hushed atmosphere, the smell of dust, leather and brittle paper. The people sitting over the books, oblivious of their surroundings, each totally immersed in a world of their own. Libraries always have a sacred feeling for me, an air of privilege.

Renate too had returned to Berlin and, for a while at least, the family was reunited. I got on well with my sister, although I was not yet able to confide in her totally. We were simply too close and I was always slightly defensive around her. In the eyes of the outside world we were a closely knit couple, known as the Adam twins. Renate was very popular at parties; with her dark good looks and sense of humour, she had many admirers. She had the reputation of being less 'accessible' than her brother – girls were in those days. Many of her beaux, in desperation, confided in me, which in itself was not disagreeable. I considered myself an expert in the matters of the heart and body. There was a funny saying that if you wanted to get at Renate Adam you had at least to take a shower with her brother.

One of Renate's most desperate admirers was our old friend, the writer Wolfgang Ebert. He used to sneak into the garden at night to watch her through the window. He also threw his father's gold watch under an incoming train when Renate refused to marry him. More successful was a young and attractive publisher, Andreas Landshoff, who a little later managed to whisk her off to Amsterdam. Andreas was the son of the famous publisher Fritz Landshoff (who had emigrated to Holland, where he founded the division of German 'Emigrantenliteratur' – Querido Verlag) and the actress Ruth Hellberg. He became like a brother to me and eventually was to be my publisher.

Renate too had spent some time in Paris studying, and there were rumours of overtures by a young writer called Günter Grass. She also maintained a correspondence with a young composer, Luigi Nono.

I do not want to enter into the story of my sister's life. In any case she has been included in other people's memoirs. All I can say is that none of the above had a shower with me, although some of them became close friends and still are.

I still felt the same wild restlessness, and there were new bars and clubs to go to. How quickly Berlin had moved up and turned to normality could also be measured in its budding new social life and the sort of people who formed the new social set. They congregated in the Volle Pulle, a fashionable meeting place for actors, painters, writers and their hangers-on, of which, I am afraid, I was one. Everybody was beautiful, rich, famous or all three. It was the set which always had tickets for opening nights at the theatre and opera. They had read the latest books and seen the latest paintings. They knew about Paris, London and St Tropez. I became part of the Berlin set, drinking, discussing and sometimes dancing through the night. I wore the black coat with the sealskin lining my father had got married in, and sometimes an astrakhan fur hat. It was a world of social snobbery, vanity and artistic one-up-manship. I am embarrassed now to think how well I fitted in.

Going out was expensive, and I was still only a student in a crowd who, either by marriage or profession, earned a good living. Too proud to be always invited, I began to model. Tobias was a crazy fashion photographer, much in demand. He suggested taking a couple of photographs. Soon my picture decorated several mail-order catalogues. I was modelling sweaters, suits and raincoats. Once Tobias took a nude photograph of me, lying on the transparent ice of the frozen lake in Wannsee. It was supposed to be for an advertisement for vodka. The directors of the agency were rather shocked. Times were not as advanced as that and Smirnoff refused to use the picture.

Modelling

Germans travelled again, and not just to get brown or drunk; they travelled to broaden their horizons, to learn. The *Bildungsreise*, the Grand Tour, promoted by Goethe and Baedeker, was once more essential. Trips to Florence and Rome, educational trips to Paris, Madrid, Lisbon, Gibraltar and Palermo, stood high on the list. For 1,000 deutschmark one could spend three weeks in Greece or on the Côte d'Azur. Many Germans returned loaded down with photos and stories, somehow amazed and hurt by the fact that they were not popular abroad.

I decided to visit my first festival. There were quite a few choices. Bayreuth had opened its doors in 1951, but I had not yet discovered my love for Wagner, and it was tainted by Hitler's visits and the hysterical crowd scenes which greeted him everytime he had appeared at Wagner's shrine. I decided to go to Salzburg. I knew Wilhelm Furtwängler's secretary and I was sure that she would be able to sneak me into some of the performances. I also hoped to see Annette Fischer again, whose parents had rented a house on the Mondsee, near Salzburg.

Dr Gottfried Bermann Fischer and his wife Brigitte were the perfect hosts in a house where the interest in literature and music was paramount. Maybe it was their natural way of being, maybe it was the years they had spent in the United States, but one immediately felt at home. This was not easy, because I had dropped in on an illustrious crowd, among them Thomas and Katja Mann and the singer Ramon Vinay.

I had met Annette's mother, Tutti, in Paris. She struck me immediately as a remarkable personality, which was not surprising, since at the age of six she had sat on Gerhart Hauptmann's knee, and Hermann Hesse had written a poem for her when she was only nine years old.

Most of the happenings of that weekend have been totally eclipsed by one experience so unique that I knew that it would be without comparison in my life: Thomas Mann read from his new novel *Felix Krull*. Part of it had been published as a short story in 1922. After the war he had decided to extend this 'fragment' into a novel – the last picaresque work, summing up the experiences and thoughts of Germany's great man of letters.

During the afternoon we all went boating on the lake and Ramon Vinay sang some arias. Then in the evening we settled in the drawing-room and Thomas Mann began to read. His extraordinary voice, non-actorish and yet very finely tuned, filled the room. The harmony of the sound and the mastership of his prose were nourished by the same source, the sheer enjoyment of the word. He read from the encounter of Krull and Kuckuck on the train. From time to time he lifted his thin and expressive face as if to reassure himself that everybody was listening. His wife, a small woman who seemed to belong to another century, smiled as if to encourage him.

He savoured the laughter of the small audience, looking up with a coquettish grin. Then he readjusted his glasses and continued: 'Life on a star is limited. Life has not always existed nor will it always exist.'[1] The testament of an old man, whose life was nearing its end. We were all moved, honoured, spellbound.

The reading lasted twenty minutes. Afterwards over a glass of punch he spoke about the writer's link with the culture of the twentieth century. Mann did most of the talking, his hands with a golden signet ring underlining every word with sparse but expressive gestures. I never said a word throughout the evening, but I watched that imposing figure of a bygone age, dressed in a formal grey suit, with a bow tie and an impeccably starched white handkerchief in the breast pocket. At some point he grumpily remarked: '*Tonio Kröger* and *Buddenbrooks* are more popular than *Faustus*. In the States I am known as the author of *The Magic Mountain.*'

Russian tanks were moving once more, this time in Budapest. A sea of people protested in front of the town hall in Schöneberg and cheered Berlin's future mayor Willy Brandt. He more than most represented the spirit of the city: an anti-fascist, who had spent the Hitler years in exile in Norway – a step which some people had already begun to consider 'unpatriotic'.

It is strange to think that my growing up and maturing ran parallel with the growing up of the country I was living in. The war was slowly receding into history and things in Germany were moving so fast that it was sometimes difficult to adjust. In any case some of the changes went too fast for many of us. We wondered what happened to the slogan of the leading party, the Christian Democrats: 'Keine Experimente' (No experiments). In 1955 we had a new German flag – black, red and gold instead of the old black, white and red. Only ten years before I had worn the emblem of the last one in the gusset of my underpants. Adenauer had taken us into NATO. The young shouted: 'Ohne mich!' (Leave me out). We were still deeply mistrustful of too much patriotism, too much personality cult. It wasn't long before some politician began to talk about atomic weapons for Germany. The then Minister of Defence, Franz Josef Strauss, thought they were indispensable. Eighteen prominent physicists signed a famous manifesto warning of the consequences. Many agreed. Ten years after the war how could anybody even contemplate such a step?

---

1   'Die Bewohnbarkeit eines Sternes ist begrenzt. Es hat das Leben nicht immer gegeben und es wird es nicht immer geben.'

On 15 June 1955 I was awarded the doctorate of the Free University *cum laude*. The German Ph.D. exam is daunting. You have to defend the thesis in front of the faculty, and you are questioned on a number of selected subjects in the fields of your studies. I had chosen landscape painting of the seventeenth century, Middle High German, the plays of Corneille, Racine and Molière, and the work of the four giants of modern German literature: Thomas Mann, Franz Kafka, Robert Musil and Hermann Broch.

I was now allowed to call myself 'Herr Doktor'. In Germany that means one moves up in the world. Even today these two little words open many doors, and Louise was terribly proud; she pointed out that none of my cousins had even gone to university. She bought me my first car, a black Volkswagen convertible. No car ever gave me quite the same pleasure.

I drove down to St Tropez, a journey which from then on I would make almost every year, and still do. Every year the road became more congested, more horrible. But after Lyon the clouds usually disappeared. With the sun breaking through you could smell the South, and I began to feel happy.

St Tropez in the mid-1950s was a very different place from what it has become. It was already famous and crowded, but it was not yet afflicted with commercial vulgarity and the greed of the promoters and shopkeepers. Augustin and Félix had not yet made their considerable fortunes, and they cooked the fish they caught right on the beach for a few happy customers. St Tropez had only one bar at the harbour, L'Escale, and only a few boutiques, like Vachon, where one bought T-shirts and shorts. There was a shop called Au Paradis des Dames and a hotel Au Bout du Monde, where I stayed many times. The early summers in St Tropez are all jumbled up in my head, but in the first few years all I could afford was a room above an *épicerie*.

In the port Vadim filmed *Et Dieu créa la femme* with a young actress who would be partly responsible for the decline of this place through no fault of her own. But at that time Brigitte Bardot could still take her aperitif at the Bar des Pêcheurs without being troubled by too much curiosity. One day I was minding a little gallery belonging to Manja, a Russian woman, when a crazy and colourful man walked in. He was wearing working man's slacks and a striped T-shirt, his head was almost totally shaved and the colour of terra cotta. I nearly dropped one of Manja's tiles, I was so excited. It was Picasso. Later I saw him sipping a drink at the port and taking photographs; nobody seemed to bother. All seems to be almost unbelievable now.

I met a young writer who lived in a small house, right at the little beach at La Ponche, and I do not remember if it was that year or another one that I joined *la bande* around Françoise Sagan. She had made a name for herself and quite a lot of money when, not yet twenty years old, she wrote *Bonjour tristesse*. She had short dark hair, dressed like a boy and was prone to look like a small monk. When she spoke she looked straight into your eyes, which gave you confidence. She struck me as someone profoundly serious, even sad, two qualities I found very attractive, and at odds with the world which surrounded her and which she wrote about. She had a wonderful capacity to listen. We used to drive in her convertible Jaguar to a restaurant in the vineyards underneath Gassin and danced *la Java* at the Restaurant Palmyre to the sound of a barrel organ. The days were filled with sunshine and naked bronzed bodies and the nights with drinks and debauchery. Those early years in St Tropez were unbridled bliss.

Louise's greatest wish was that I would somehow follow in the footsteps of my father and join the diplomatic service. I could not really see myself in a career which consisted of representing Germany abroad. As a compromise I joined the Europa Union in Bonn, a semi-official organisation, whose main task was to prepare the German population for the future Common Market. In those years a formidable educational programme was launched to inform the six future Common Market countries about each other. I was engaged as the Director of the International Relations Department. The title sounded much grander than the job itself, but it was the first of many jobs which gave me a chance to travel and to make use of my languages. I had to organise international meetings and conferences between various professional groups, exchange visits between brewers, teachers, mayors, architects, actors, car manufacturers or people who worked in museums.

I was in my element. It was a job which brought me together with different nationalities and it had a certain glamour attached to it. We were received by the Mayor of Paris or Berlin. Once I danced with the Queen of the Netherlands, another time I shook hands with the Italian President.

It was also very educational. I had to spend two hours every morning reading the newspapers, not only the leading German ones but also *Le Monde, The Times* and the *Neue Zürcher Zeitung*.

I had a secretary called Fräulein Schmidt, a forester's daughter from a little village near Bonn. She would put a candle and flowers on my desk, and wore handknitted dresses. She had a face which she had borrowed from someone else and burst into tears at the slightest confrontation. She gave me my first ballpoint pen and hummed 'Tutti Frutti'. I hated both.

I was certainly unfair to this devoted and loyal person, but my sense of

Small-time diplomat

social justice was not engaged by her, a thing I now feel deeply ashamed of. I loved to dictate, and the poor girl spent the whole day on her typewriter writing thank-you letters to anybody who had received us on the last trip. This was before photocopying machines and other modern office equipment. Every evening before leaving she put a large file with 'Herr Doktor Adam your signature please' on my desk, staring at me while I signed about thirty letters. I think she hoped that I would take her for a drink. I never did, but once I took her to Paris.

Paris was still my favourite destination and I now travelled in style. Modern Trans-Europe-Express trains ran between Bonn and Paris with only first-class carriages, and as I was hopelessly snobbish and superficial I wallowed in this kind of treatment. For these trips, I dressed smartly in grey flannel suits or pinstripes. I bought expensive luggage and made sure that everybody noticed. At 7 a.m. I was mingling among the diplomats and businessmen, waiting for the train to arrive, when my eye caught an apparition: a lady in a black dress, wearing a pink hat with matching satin gloves, elbow length. It was my secretary.

Fräulein Schmidt's idea of a business trip to Paris was obviously not mine. I looked in horror at the figure waving at me, hoping that nobody would notice her. It was difficult not to notice a lady who looked as if she had just emerged from a nightclub standing on a railway platform at seven o'clock in the morning. We silently boarded the train and sat in silence for 200 kilometres. Fräulein Schmidt had not removed her pink satin gloves, not even to smoke a cigarette. 'Since when has Fräulein Schmidt smoked?' I thought.

At the Belgian frontier I showed my passport to the customs officer. Fräulein Schmidt looked out of the window. She was smoking again. 'And your wife's passport, Sir?' I heard the voice of the officer. I couldn't help it, I burst into laughter. It was the first and the last time that I took Fräulein Schmidt on a business trip.

Sometime around this period I had fallen in love with Dieter. He was a successful dress designer, who had started by modelling dresses on his brother, his mother and himself and selling them in the neighbouring villages. When I met him the business had grown into a thriving affair with twenty employees. Dieter was suave and very, very good-looking, with dark hair and long eyelashes. Everything about him was terribly well groomed – his figure, his face and his wardrobe. For our first holiday we decided to go to Capri, which was one of those dream destinations for the homosexual diaspora, the island of Tiberius, where August von Platen, Hans Christian Andersen, Tchaikovsky, Johann Joachim Winckelmann,

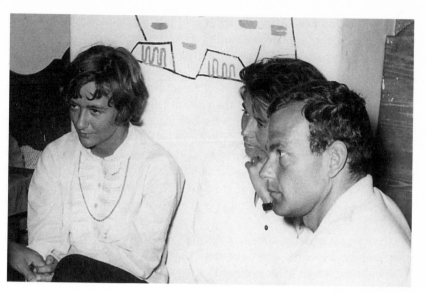

In Capri with Françoise Sagan

Dieter and Peter

Oscar Wilde with Lord Alfred Douglas, and finally Friedrich Alfred Krupp had found a sort of modern version of a Greek island, devoted to hedonism and beauty. It seemed to be the perfect place for two young Germans in love.

We departed, the suitcase full of silk trousers with matching shirts, all designed by Dieter, to conquer the rich and the beautiful of this year's season, and conquer we did. A rich fur merchant invited us to his incredible villa in Positano and offered us a pair of bikinis made out of real fur if we would divest ourselves of our very skimpy cotton ones. Later, the indomitable Peggy Guggenheim and a lady friend burst into our room while Dieter was ironing one of our silk outfits – Dieter was always ironing our outfits – and the two ladies literally went on their knees making dirty propositions.

We were an amazing couple. I blush when I look at the photographs now: two good-looking queens in matching silk suits.

After three weeks of showing off at the Canzone del Mare during the day and at the terrace of the Quisisana at night, Dieter was whisked off on a boat by an American. I wept for three nights. All that remained was a couple of silk outfits, the memories of an amusing, frivolous holiday, plus a set of photographs which I stuck into a green leather album labelled 'Dieter and Peter': Dieter and Peter with Gracie Fields, Dieter and Peter with Eve of Rome and Dieter and Peter dancing with Zsa Zsa Gabor and her sister Eva, all silver and gold and shaking like a lemon jelly. It was the era of ankle bracelets, Pucci scarves and many artificial bronzed smiles.

After this overdose of high life it was not easy to return to Fräulein Schmidt's fierce efficiency and the *Bundesdorf* where an army band played the *Radetzky March* or the *Thieving Magpie* overture in the park. There were few cultural events, and if you wanted to see a decent production you had to travel to the neighbouring cities of Cologne or Düsseldorf. There were of course some concerts – after all this was the town of Beethoven – but most of the social diversions consisted of ambassadorial receptions.

The only really interesting people were the foreign journalists. I made friends with the brilliant Alain Clément, correspondent from *Le Monde*, a shy man of great knowledge, experience, sensitivity and a superior mind. Another friend was Stéphane Roussel, a lively woman, who represented *France Soir*. Stéphane and I, being single, usually found ourselves sitting next to each other at official dinners. Alain and Stéphane had worked in political journalism for a long time, and I learned a great deal from them. They planted the first seeds which would one day germinate into my life as a journalist. They also taught me to look more objectively at my past. This was not always easy. Many books began to appear, life stories in which people tried to explain their positions, to justify their roles during the Hitler years. A host of artists reassured the public that they had no interest in politics – they were artists, nothing else. Fame and money was a better seducer than exile in a foreign land and culture, with little prospect for work. Traitors come in all forms, ideological and mercenary, some of them both.

There was the problem of restitution, *Wiedergutmachung*. As 'victims of the Nazi regime' we were entitled to some financial compensation. Was this a truly humble gesture of regret by the new government? A kind of mercy? An attempt to whitewash history? Many people recoiled when they were told that the loss of a father or mother in a concentration camp would be compensated by a sum of money. Many victims lived in difficult financial situations. It would have been worse for the government not to do anything, like the East German one. Renate and I were offered 10,000 deutschmark each for the loss of our school years and the indignity suffered. We debated a long time whether we should accept it. In the end, like most, we did.

It was at this time that I acquired what is known as a public profile. Not much of a profile, but my picture frequently appeared in the papers, mostly surrounded by groups of French truck-drivers or Belgian postmen. 'Dr Adam helps French brewers to acquaint themselves with the beer from Dortmund' or 'Dr Adam and twenty signalmen form the link between Bonn and Paris,' ran the headlines in the local papers.

On one of my many trips to Rome I had met Enrico Medioli. Enrico to me was perfection: blond, aristocratic in manner and dress, tall, elegant, worldly, sensitive, cultured and of caustic wit. He was the epitome of the dream Italian. He came from an old Parma family. He had suffered from tuberculosis, which added to my romantic image of him. His sense of style was impeccable. He drove smart cars, lived with exquisite antiques in a flat with a roof terrace which looked out on the roofs of the eternal city. He knew everyone worth knowing in Rome. Enrico possessed a momentum of life which was very catching. We raced down to the beach in Fregene, to lunch in restaurants only the Romans knew, or we dined in fashionable restaurants on the via Appia. He would refer to them as 'una piccola trattoria, molto semplice', and was waved at by half the other diners. We had drinks at Bricktop's and *granità de limone* at Rosati's.

How could I not fall in love? I fell in love easily. I had not learned how to economise myself and I loved either too much or too little; the good measure was still absent. What I did not know yet was that Enrico was very flighty, quickly bored with emotions. Once his goal was achieved, he was a typical Italian male who thrived more on seduction than on sustained relationships. And did he know how to seduce! At night we drove out along the via Appia Antiqua and walked between tombs and cypresses. It was so romantic, I felt like Katharine Hepburn in *Summer Madness*. I began trying to imitate his style. I bought silk shirts and linen suits, I wore dark blue socks, 'the only colour possible for a gentleman', and Vétiver cologne, only from Guerlain or from Mary Chess in London. I learned Italian, peppering it with French and English words, and addressed the waiters with the familiar 'tu'.

Whenever I could, I would fly to Rome. Rome, Paris, and later New York always produced a *frisson* not unlike the thrill of meeting a lover. I love cities as I love people, and sometimes with similar passion. Rome for a while replaced Paris in my affections. All my life I would return to it, much helped by the fact that Renate eventually made her home there. Germany's cities had lost almost all visible traces of history. In Rome I found a splendid past again. Everything seemed to be on the right scale, even the monuments – except of course the pompous one to Vittorio Emmanuele. The reddish-brown-coloured façades, bathed in the afternoon sun, the rooftops with hanging gardens, the terraces of the very rich, all seemed to express sensuality, graceful living, well-being. If Paris struck me as a place of international elegance and sophistication, Rome for me was the place of profound civilisation; even the poverty and the chaos in the streets took on a timeless dignity. So it was not surprising that in the battle for European unity, France was definitely losing out, for the trips to Italy in the name of the European union multiplied.

Around Enrico were a group of *jeunesse dorée*, most of them working in the cinema or the arts: Giuseppe Pattroni Griffi, Ruggiero Nuvolari, Mauro Bolognini, the actress Alida Valli, the writer Elsa Morante, and Philippo San Just, who gave a very funny imitation of Edith Evans in *The Importance of Being Earnest*. I was sort of handed around, introduced to most of them without making much impression. Enrico was also a close friend of Luchino Visconti, soon to become one of his most important collaborators. Together with Visconti, and sometimes with Suso Cecchi d'Amico, they wrote the script for *Rocco and His Brothers*, *Vaghe Stelle Dell'Orsa*, *The Damned*, *Ludwig*, *The Innnocent* and *Conversation Piece*.

To say that I was a fan of Visconti is an understatement. I admired him more than most directors, and much of my own work later was under the spell of this great stage magician. The first film of his I saw was *Bellissima* with the stupendous Anna Magnani. It begins with the choir singing Donizetti in a film studio, then a voice announces a competition for 'la più bella bambina di Roma'. Anna Magnani begins to dream. She has the vision of her plain and charmless child becoming a child prodigy. *Bellissima* was sarcastic, socially critical and with a strange and savage beauty, much helped by Anna Magnani's performance, dragging her awful child from audition to audition until both, defeated by the cynicism of the movie world, return to their poor settlement.

In *Senso*, I was struck again by the strength of Visconti's opening scenes. It was as if a curtain was drawn allowing you to enter a magical world. The title 'Venice, primavera 1866' dissolves into the stage of La Fenice, where the third act of *Il Trovatore* is in progress. The chorus sings 'All'armi, all'armi' and Visconti cuts to the audience breaking out into a pandemonium, revolting against the Austrian officers in the audience. It is the Risorgimento. Against this sumptuous background the personal tragedy of the characters is played: the love affair between Livia (Alida Valli) and the Austrian officer Franz, played by Farley Granger.

Visconti's stage work has somehow been unjustly eclipsed by his films. Together with Giorgio Strehler and Paolo Grassi, he was the most important theatre director of the post-war era in Italy. He introduced Tennessee Williams and Arthur Miller to the not very well-informed Roman audiences with *Streetcar*, *Death of a Salesman* and *The Crucible*. His Shakespeare productions were equally innovative. He had staged *Troilus and Cressida* in the Boboli Gardens in Florence, with an evocative set by a young set designer, Franco Zeffirelli – an event as legendary as his production of *As You Like It* with Vittorio Gassman and Rina Morelli. Marcello Mastroianni played the small part of a courtier. The designs were by Salvador Dali.

I had seen two of his early opera productions. The first was *La Sonnambula* with a dazzling Maria Callas. It was my first visit to La Scala, which was at its peak in the early 1950s. All the great singers appeared there: Renata Tebaldi, Mario del Monaco, Giuseppe di Stefano, Giulietta Simionato.

Callas and Visconti were the kind of combination one could only dream of. It was Visconti, to some extent, who made Callas, at least everything in her which made her the *prima donna assoluta*: her style, her movements, her presence. When they met in 1953, she was a fat young singer making her début at La Scala, in *La Vestale*, by Gasparo Spontini. She shed 75 pounds in order to play in his production of Cherubini's *Medea*.

The evening of Bellini's *Sonnambula* turned out to be as glorious an evening as I have ever spent in an opera house. Callas was dressed all in white by the young designer Piero Tosi, who also designed the set in soft romantic colours. The conductor was the young Leonard Bernstein. When Callas did the famous sleepwalking scene across the bridge she was silhouetted against the sky; the audience held their breath. At the end of the aria 'A, non giunge' (Oh, not to reach), when the lights came on in the house, I was in tears.

I also saw Callas in Visconti's *La Traviata*. Giulini was conducting and di Stefano was Alfredo. The set was by Lila di Nobili. It was of such refinement and elegance that it made reality look shoddy. At the end of the first act, when all the guests have left, Visconti had Callas take off her jewels and throw them onto the floor, then kick off her shoes as one would after a large party. The last act of *Traviata* was the antechamber of death. Di Nobili had designed a denuded stage, a ladder leaning against the wall, which still showed the traces of the picture once hung there. In this room Callas appeared really to die. She dragged herself once more to the mirror. At her 'Come sono mutata' (How changed I am) people in the audience wept. Incapable of dressing herself properly, she tried to put on the gloves. 'Ah, gran Dio, morir si giovane' (O God, to die so young), she sighed. It was unforgettable. I was so moved that I left immediately after the curtain fell, while the audience after an unusual silence went into thunderous applause.

When the moment came to meet Visconti, I was very nervous. The occasion was a small dinner at his house in the via Salaria. I had expected some splendour from Luchino Visconti, Duke of Modrone, but the house outdid all expectations. It had an aura of great flair and refinement, from the row of large porcelain dogs which flanked the terrace to the gold plates on the lace tablecloth. Visconti's taste in decoration reflected his sense of extravagance and came as a shock to my naïve notion that a communist should live in sack-cloth and ashes. The conversation about the Russian invasion of Hungary was depressing, and did not dispel my confusion. I kept on secretly glancing at the servants, who stood motionless behind the chairs, in white livery, their hands behind their backs.

Visconti's manners were courtly, but behind the delicate façade lay a dominating personality. He also, as I later discovered, could be kind and considerate. Among the dazzling talk, the discernment of wit, alas, I was a total flop. All these elegant guests lived in remote splendour, protected from the fray of life, and seemed to produce erudite works of art I knew little of. We exchanged a few niceties, but I felt terribly out of place. As so often before, and I am afraid many times after, I had been taken along as someone's *petit ami*; everybody knew everyone else and I was merely a pretty accessory. I was aware of the power I sometimes had over others, but the time when I would pay less attention when others spoke and people began to listen more attentively to what I have to say was still years away. With Visconti, it would take twenty years for the ice to break. Still I was grateful to Enrico for opening so many doors to different and new worlds, and I was always willing to listen and to learn.

After a while the novelty began to wear off on both sides. The Rome set was no longer so exciting, and neither was I for them. I drove eighteen hours in my little car from Naples to Cortina d'Ampezzo, where Enrico had a chalet, only to find out that he had time just for dinner. I got the message. I suffered terribly – still, it was good while it lasted. How easy one loses people in life. For a while you see them all the time, three times a week, you call each other up in the middle of the night; and then they are gone, lost. Enrico was the most seductive, most stylish, film-like lover I ever had. He sort of gave me the right polish, and he sharpened my taste.

I saw Enrico again a few years later in London, where he was staging his own production of *Sonnambula* at Covent Garden with Joan Sutherland, and a few times in Rome. He was as charming and witty as before. We were both a bit embarrassed. I asked myself what would have happened if we had *just* been friends. We would probably have seen each other more often, but would we know each other better?

Those two years after I finished university were silly years, often filled with the most facile pursuit of the easy, the famous and the frivolous. Nevertheless, it was all part of growing up, of finding out who I was and who I wanted to be. How everything in life seems to interlink. Anyway I was happy. Once more I had managed to organise myself an interesting and entertaining social life which suited my gregarious nature. I had a job which was stimulating and rewarding. But I was restless again. As always I wanted more and different things. It was time to move on.

10

America Here I Come!

1956–1957

For a long time America had held a great attraction for me. It was as much an intellectual as a sexual one. Antioch College in Ohio advertised a grant for European students, offering a special programme consisting of three months of academic studies followed by some practical work in an American firm. I applied immediately. To the horror of Louise, I was willing to give up my budding 'diplomatic' career and live for a year or two in the States. A few weeks later a questionnaire arrived with pages and pages of the most amazing questions. I filled in my hobbies ('jiving' and 'ping-pong') and my favourite books (*War and Peace* and *Pinocchio*), gave details of my race and faith and swore that I did not belong to a subversive (i.e. communist) organisation. Then I stumbled over a question: 'Do you have a speech defect?' After a short hesitation, I put down 'thertainly', sealed the envelope and sent it off.

A few weeks passed, then I received an invitation to travel to Frankfurt for an interview at the American consulate. A young consulate official, very Brooks Brothers, in a pale-blue button-down collar shirt and bow tie, was chuckling over my questionnaire. He was sitting under the American flag and a picture of Eisenhower, which gave him a sort of official gloss. After an informal lecture during which I was told that travel grants must not be used for immigration, he decided to support my application and finance my tuition at the college, including board, and give me a Fulbright travel grant.

In the summer of 1958 I sailed from Bremen. A tearful Louise stood among a large group of crying and waving people, gradually getting smaller and smaller. It was just like in the movies. I was travelling modestly, third class, but I had my most valued possession, stored away below deck: the little black Volkswagen convertible.

Five days later I was on my first American highway in a car with a Berlin licence plate, heading towards Ohio.

Antioch is a famous college, very liberal, very progressive, known for its Shakespeare festival and its academic standards. It looked like a typical American college with fraternity houses, a clubhouse, libraries and many small dormitory houses scattered around a very manicured garden. Everything looked expensive and, as I found out, it was. Only the brightest and most affluent kids could afford it, or those who had a scholarship.

As a foreigner I was quite a novelty. I was greeted by the president, who addressed me as 'Dr Adam' and mumbled something about pleasure and honour, and how Mrs Dickensen would be so glad to meet me in their home. A fellow student showed me to my room in a clapboard house known by the rather grand name of 'hall', which I shared with five other boys. There was an awful lot of 'Hi Pete' and curious glances, and in view of my age I was voted in to be the 'hall president'.

I went to bed rather tired, feeling a bit out of place among all those kids, many years younger than I was, but I was happy to be in America. For my first breakfast I stood in line for orange juice and pancakes with maple syrup, eggs 'sunny side up', and a bewildering choice of cereals. Everybody was chatty and asked a million questions. I decided there and then to drop the Klaus from the Klaus-Peter, although I refused to be known as 'Pete', and sat down for a hearty American breakfast, the first one without *Le Monde*, or *Die Welt*. I seemed to be on a totally different planet.

In class we had history, literature and French. For all its academic pretensions, for someone like myself Antioch was a bit of a joke. On that particular day, students were examined on Dickens; they had read to a predetermined page in *David Copperfield*. No one had progressed further. In French my new mates were declining: 'je parle, il parle' etc., leaving out the 'tu parles' because, as the teacher told me, 'Americans always mix up the *vous* and the *tu* and we don't want them to be rude.'

My academic training exceeded that of some of the teachers. A meeting of the staff was called and it was decided that, while continuing to live like a student, I should take over some tutorials in French and German Literature.

My three months in Yellow Springs were bewildering and amusing, to say the least. I did all the things American college kids do. I played baseball and toasted marshmallows and crackers on an open fire. I also went 'double dating' in a great big Buick. One of the sexier members of my hall had asked me, and, expecting something a little bit more in the line of a foursome, I agreed heartily. We set off, Bobby and Jackie in front, Ruthie and I in the back. Bob drove the car into a dark spot, turned the engine off, and the two in the front seat went immediately into a clinch, while my date looked at me, her mouth slightly open. I noticed her rather large gums. From the front came the sound of lots of panting and I felt obliged to kiss

Ruthie. I did it rather unenthusiastically, partly on account of her gums, partly because of the discomfort in the car. This went on for about ten minutes. Then the two in front separated and Ruthie, as if on cue, unglued her mouth from mine. Bob started the engine and we dropped the girls. I noticed a wet spot on Bob's jeans. 'Gee ! This was great,' he said, 'the girls are so free here.'

There was an awful lot of heavy petting going on, the girls insisting on keeping their 'cherry' for their husband. The boys were frustrated, and thought and talked a lot about sex, of which they were not getting enough.

I noticed a fair amount of gay sex going on too. The students who came from New York or other sophisticated towns carried on quite openly; those from smaller places pretended they were drunk.

This was America *profonde*, the real America, not Hollywood or New York, and Yellow Springs was a small town. It did not cater for a very glamorous social life. It had two barbers, a bar and a funeral parlour. It also had a Rotary club. News got around that a foreigner was 'teaching' in the college, and I was invited to my first Rotary meeting. Everybody sang 'R-O-T-A-R-Y, that's what spells Rotary', before the chairman called for the man who had travelled furthest to step forward to receive this week's present. 'Berlin,' I said. 'Berlin Germany?' I was asked and received, to thunderous applause, an enormous ball of string contributed by this week's chairman, a string manufacturer.

Once I was invited to speak at an association for college women. It was agreed that after the sales of cakes for a charity, I would give a talk about 'Rilke and Women'. I can't vouch for the success of my lecture but I am certain that it was the first time that the names of Lou Andreas Salomé or Paula Modersohn-Becker were mentioned in Yellow Springs, Ohio.

Sometimes on long weekends I left the confinement of Antioch and travelled. Being the owner of a car, I was a popular travelling companion, and on one of those trips I went with two students to Chicago. Chicago, with its skyscrapers, some dating back to the turn of the century, was for me the most beautiful modern city I had ever seen.

My travelling companions took me to a drag ball for Halloween. My Berlin experiences paled at the sight of thousands of men in the most flamboyant disguises, dancing to the steaming rhythm of an ear-splitting band, shaved and depilated creatures, stuffed out in some places and tucked in others, figures of artificial perfection in a pagan feast, an orgy of kitsch, a kind of lived-out fantasy of people all wanting to be stars. I counted at least ten Marilyn Monroes, twenty Mae Wests and as many Marlenes. It is a strange complex phenomena of the gay culture that it always seems to be obsessed with celebrities. Of course they were only stars for the night, and most, like Cinderellas, would assume next day their role behind a desk or a counter, wearing a grey suit.

I had escaped the sea of swaying hips into a box from where I could watch the crowning of the Queen of the Night, the prize for the best get-up. A large and muscular mixture of Carmen Miranda and Zsa Zsa Gabor, with large breasts that matched the circumference of her biceps, stepped onto the stage. The crowd went berserk. So did a little black lady in front of me. 'Isn't she fab, isn't she a beaut?' she screamed, turning to me, and when I agreed she sank into my arms. 'It's my son, darling!'

The three months in college passed rather too quickly. Most of my school-mates had found jobs as clerks or post boys in firms where they could get the 'practical work experience' which had been advertised as part of Antioch's training. I had stipulated New York or at least Chicago, because the idea of spending another six months in a provincial place in the Mid-West was not to my liking. The school failed to find me an employer. American firms, as it turned out, were exceedingly suspicious of a German Ph.D. who spoke several languages and had studied in Berlin and Paris. 'This is the stuff our vice-presidents are made of. We cannot employ Dr Adam as a clerk,' wrote one firm which in the past had always taken an Antioch student for the mail room.

The college offered me the chance to stay on for another term, but I was desperate to see New York, and as so often before, I decided to take fate into my own hands. I got hold of a manual of advertising agencies and wrote the following letter to the presidents of the five leading agencies in New York.

You are the president of a very big advertising agency. You employ skilled men with long backgrounds in agency and client organisation.

I have never worked for an advertising agency. I have never worked for a client organisation. In the short time I have been here, I've become acquainted with the fantastic role that advertising plays in American life. It's amazing! It's everywhere! It fills (and, I have learned, supports) your magazines, your newspapers, your radio and television programs. It teaches people how to dress better, to eat better food, to protect their families with insurance, to decorate their homes, to guard their health, to drive safely, to save money, to do all the things that people just want to forget! I want to work in this business.

I want to work for you and the (J. Walter Thomson Company). This is my background.

My cv followed. I do not know how I had the audacity or the cheek, but America being what it is, I got five answers and invitations for interviews.

I packed my bags and set off. I was desperately short of money, and too proud to cable to Louise. To be precise I had $35. By the time I reached the outskirts of New York City and had refilled my car with petrol, I was left with $9. I stopped at a giant Howard Johnson's ice-cream parlour, boasting '75 flavors'. A couple of dollars bought an awful lot of ice-cream and ice-cream is nourishing, I thought, and sat at the counter listening open-mouthed to a girl reeling off the specials: 'Coconut Twirl, Hawaii Wonder, Honolulu Surprise, Pineapple Kick.' I ordered 'two balls of vanilla'. 'That's rude. We call them scoops, sir,' her face taking on a sententious expression. Meanwhile, my eye caught sight of a smiling young black man who had been watching the scene. 'Hi, where you from then?' I had learned to reply: 'Berlin, Germany.' I had also learned to tell people my life story. It was not such a sob story: no work, no place to stay, hardly brings tears to the eyes of the young.

Luiz was a dancer on his way to Cuba 'for a couple of weeks, maybe even months'. We talked for two hours, and afterwards he travelled south and I drove north. In my pocket I had $7 and the key to his apartment, on West 63rd Street. As so often before and since, I was struck by the trust and generosity of the American people.

The Lincoln Center had not been built yet and West 63rd was a pleasant street of run-down brownstones, with people sitting on stairs leading up to what the Americans call the first floor. It was a lively and friendly black neighbourhood, where in the summer kids cooled themselves off under the fire hydrants. Not that I saw any of this when I arrived, first because it was winter and second because it was dark by the time I reached Manhattan. Luiz lived in a 'cold water' apartment, a suite of narrow rooms almost like a railroad carriage, with the kitchen with a bathtub in the middle. It was simple, cheap and cheerful. I fell asleep under colourful pictures of nude dancers, which I thought was a good omen.

The next morning, a Sunday, I ran a bath and sat in the tub that stood against a window blocked up by some brown packing paper, when I heard the beautiful chant of black voices coming from behind the paper. I stood up to peel a small corner of paper back, when the entire camouflage suddenly came down and I stood, separated only by a transparent sheet of glass, in a revival meeting. Loud shrieks of 'hallelujah' greeted the naked figure, who tried to pin the paper up again. This too, I thought, was a good omen.

Over the next few days I had my first interviews. Straight away I was taken by the refreshing informality and natural curiosity about anything foreign. I was somehow a novelty in the advertising world, and the interviews often led to drinks or even lunch, a most welcome help because I was totally broke, though I tried to disguise it by wearing my most conventional pin-stripes, which was considered 'terribly continental'.

My dossier at the distinguished J. Walter Thomson agency, considered the classiest in the advertising world, was getting longer. 'Dr Adam,' they told me, 'we are very interested in employing someone of your calibre and experience, but we do not quite know yet where to put you. Maybe you should see Bill Weaver, vice-president in charge of...' While I was handed from vice-president to vice-president I was getting desperate. I might have to sell my beloved car.

Then came the day of the interview with the Ted Bates agency. Ted Bates stood for the hard sell. 'Hi Pete' said the vice-president, his feet firmly planted on the desk during the fifteen-minute talk. 'We'd like you to work in our research department, we'll pay you $100 a week, you can start tomorrow.'

I had my first American job. I was part of Madison Avenue, I was in seventh heaven. My excitement was slightly dampened when I arrived the next day at 666 Fifth Avenue, one of the taller and more glitzy skyscrapers of that time, only to discover that my office was on the second floor. Every day I would watch with envy the people lining up at lifts marked 24th to 44th and even some with 45th to 60th floors, while I boarded an elevator marked 1 to 7 to step out at the first stop.

On my first day I was taken 'to do the rounds'. I had never seen an office like it, a vast space with some little cubicles, but no windows. Only vice- presidents, I was told, had those desirable offices with a view to the outside world. An ice-cold wind blew out of the air-conditioning system and machines everywhere dispensed iced water, Coke and coffee in all shades. Most people arrived carrying little brown paper bags which contained more coffee in plastic cups and lots and lots of paper napkins and plastic spoons, and little packets with mustard and ketchup, which people tore open with their teeth. I thought of Fräulein Schmidt's little tray, with the dainty blue and white porcelain cup, and the intimacy of my office.

I sat down at a desk looking just like any other desk, and felt rather miserable, but misery was soon dispelled by the friendliness of my colleagues. Everybody came to introduce themselves and I kept repeating my name, stressing 'Peter' loud and clearly, in order to discourage any 'Petes'. Only once, to a lady, did I introduce myself as Klaus-Peter. She was called Elinor, I would pronounce it Elinora. She looked elegant, sophisticated and well-travelled. Elinora took me for lunch, I told her my story and we became friends and allies. She also lent me $50, because my pay check was not due till the end of the week.

In 1957, $100 per week was not a lot of money but one could live quite well – at any rate I did. Elinora lunched in the members' dining-room of the Museum of Modern Art, M O M A, as the connoisseurs called it. It was practically next door to our office, and deciding that it would be fun to be a member too I wrote a letter asking if there were special rates for foreigners, former art students, etc. The letter was dated 6 December and signed Dr Klaus-Peter Adam. Three days later I received a free membership card with a little note: 'It is a pleasure to give a complimentary membership to someone called Klaus, on December 6.'

After three months Luiz returned and I moved into a one-room flat on Third Avenue & 69th Street. Third Avenue at that time was not at all what it is today. It was unfashionable, popular and cheerful. There were hardly any high-rise buildings; it was more residential than commercial. I lived above a handsome Englishman, Robert Walker, who had arrived in New York a few years earlier. He was kind and fun and different from the rest. He also had many friends in the gay community.

In 1958 American homosexuals had not yet 'come out', and in many states homosexuality was still illegal. Almost everywhere it was totally unacceptable socially, the biggest shame you could bring on your family. Many young men had gone to psychiatrists to be cured of this 'terrible affliction'. There were few sympathetic straights, for most straight men were so insecure about their own sexual identity that they would not broach the subject. Understanding sympathetic women, like Elinora, were a rarity in a world where to have a husband and many children was the desired norm.

American homosexuals moved mostly among homosexuals, and this is still true today despite the sexual revolution. The social discrimination forced many into a kind of ghetto existence. Even in New York, they would lead practically two lives. At work they were 'in the closet', many wearing wedding rings and having pictures of girlfriends on their desks or in their wallets. Their boyfriends were always called 'room-mates'. In the evenings and on weekends, the gays came out of the closet, at least among themselves. They went to clubs, bars and saunas and gave endless parties. In New York there were gay restaurants and gay movie houses. It was a life separated from the rest of society, which led to much unhappiness, solitude and a great deal of sexual promiscuity.

Of course at a time when homosexuals were still desperately fighting for their place in society, and the respect and understanding of their fellow men, in the face of bigotry, ignorance and fear, to be in a place where one did not have to pretend to be someone else was essential. This was only possible among one's own kind. And nowhere was this more evident than on weekends on Fire Island.

Fire Island was the magic word among homosexuals. It is a long narrow stretch of land, a hundred miles from New York. There were no cars, no roads. Boardwalks, made of sun-bleached planks, linked the houses of the small communities. You never mentioned Fire Island at work, you said: 'I'm going to Long Island', because Fire Island was synonymous with being gay. Although there were a few non-gay communities on Fire Island, the two communities, those at the Pines and most of all at Cherry Grove, were almost exclusively gay.

Anyone who could went there to spend the weekend, and people saved months and months in the winter to rent a house for the summer, usually with two or three friends. On weekends the little beach houses were full to the brim. People slept literally everywhere.

To own a house in Cherry Grove, or the slightly more posh Pines, was considered very smart. Robert's friend Valerian Rybar was a successful interior designer and of course the owner of a house. At that time 'the Island', as it was simply known, was not so commercialised as it is now. The sea had not eaten the dunes away and swallowed up many houses, and in Cherry Grove there was no electricity. We ate and danced under light from kerosene and candles. As almost everybody was gay, even the police and the much-needed firemen – a job much prized by lesbians – there was no embarrassment, no shame, no intimidation. Men danced openly, walked hand in hand, and even, if they wanted, openly made love. It was the most liberating, soul-strengthening and friendship-forming place I had known. But it could also be a place of sadness and solitude. Relationships were formed more easily than elsewhere and they also broke up more easily and more quickly. There were simply too many temptations. With the cruelty of the young and successful, this was a place where everyone wanted to score in a race for the most beautiful, the sexiest, the newest. With so much effort and energy devoted to hedonism and narcissism, it was no place for the elderly.

I have always found that places and circumstances have formed different parts of me. I took from each what was most on offer. Germany gave me my formal education and turned me into a more politically aware human being; it sharpened my feeling for social responsibilities. The years in France developed mostly my mind: I learned the thrill of conversation and debate. America gave me an unabashed affirmation of my sexuality.

A morality based on the denial of pleasure was not for me, and in the constant battle between the moralist and the seeker of pleasure the latter had obviously won the day. I would not want to have missed one iota of it. I was twenty-eight years old and quite set in my ways, I could well afford to experiment. My sexuality has never been a burden to me. Only when it was too distracting and threatening my mental landscape did I try to curb it. Lovemaking has been very important to me even with a stranger. It is good to make love to an old lover, not with ruthless passion but with the knowledge of tenderness that evokes all the tenderness exchanged before. It is also good to make love to a stranger, with the intoxicating power which comes with conquest – the joy of being wanted by a stranger with the freeing complicity in the very act, no cheating, no feigning of pleasure. Making love always confirmed to me that I was alive.

The work at the agency was not too demanding. As a member of the Research Department I had endlessly to evaluate questionnaires determining the motivation of the American housewife for using this or that washing-up liquid. We counted the people who found too much 'fluff' in one brand of cigarettes and those who disliked the shape of a package. We were supposed to be the brains trust of the organisation. Our findings helped copy-writers to find the unique selling proposition (USP), and enabled account supervisors to have expensive lunches in the smart restaurants. No one took me out. I did not care about Martinis 'shaken not stirred with one or two twists of lemon', as I heard my colleagues in their identikit Madison Avenue outfits order. I stuck to my lunches at the Museum of Modern Art, with its many wonderful exhibitions and films, to which I had free access. I was a cultural snob.

I moved up within the agency world, although I never got the key to the Executive Men's Room. Thanks to Elinora, I was given my own little work cubicle. I hung a Picasso print from MOMA on the wall and learned how to sit with my feet on the desk. I also got a $30 rise. From the first increment, I bought myself a Brooks Bros shirt and a bow tie; from the second, I took Elinora to see a new musical, *West Side Story*, by Leonard Bernstein. The Picasso print did not go down well. It was too arty, smacking of someone who went to Fire Island. Real men had a photo of their wife and kids on the wall, or a picture of someone holding up the winners' cup of a baseball team. I didn't give a damn.

I also saw Wayne Lawson again, who was editing books and teaching Shakespeare to poor black kids. He did not earn much money but he was remarkably 'finished' for his age. As in Paris, he always knew what was going on, off-Broadway and off-off-Broadway too.

With my usual gregariousness, I soon encountered interesting and amusing new friends. John Emery, actor and ex-husband of Tallulah Bankhead, had married Tamara Geva. The story goes that both had met in a famous male brothel and got immediately engaged: the loss for the establishment was a gain for them and their many friends. As Tamara Gevageva (Zhervecheyeva) she had been one of four young dancers who, in the 1920s, had joined Serge Diaghilev's Ballets Russes. The other were Alexandra Danilova, Nicolai Efimov and Tamara's husband, Georgi Balanchivadze. When the Russian Ballet folded, Tamara and George went to America, George Balanchine to become one of the world's greatest choreographers and Tamara an actress. Their first triumph was the musical *On Your Toes*, which propelled Tamara into stardom. Everything about her said 'star' – her stunning good looks, her bearing, her elegance and capriciousness. Underneath this gloss was a warm-hearted woman of sharp intelligence, who wrote and painted and who was a terrific hostess.

The elegant Emery house was a sort of Hollywood and Broadway rolled into one. Tamara and John enhanced my life and gave counsel in a bewildering city. Among the many writers I met in their house was John Steinbeck, who was writing speeches for Adlai Stevenson. There was a lot of talk about a young Cuban lawyer, Fidel Castro, who had fled Batista to Mexico, from where he and a handful of friends returned to Cuba on a boat. I heard for the first time the name of Che Guevara. The woman who pronounced it was a writer and teacher by the name of Mary McCarthy. She had just written *The Group*.

At Tamara's I also met Richard Barr, a prominent theatre producer, and a young playwright, Edward Albee. Edward immediately struck me as someone extraordinary and desirable. I had actually seen him for the first time leaning against a car in the village in front of a small theatre, an enchanting and handsome young man in jeans and a leather jacket. Albee had an air of brooding defiance about him, which was softened by immense charm. I was immediately taken by his sharp intelligence and subtle irony. He was a sort of rebel, which I believe had something to do with the posh upbringing and prep school background that he was trying to hide. He had a strange and not very happy relationship with his parents, who were actually his foster parents. All this gave him an air of someone quite mysterious and very private.

Richard Barr, a jolly, rumbustious and sometimes stormy man who had inherited a bit of money from his mother, spent it all on the theatre. He brought out new playwrights such as Arthur Kopit, Jack Gelber and Edward Albee. Until his death, he looked after Edward's career for almost thirty years. Neither ceased fighting for a decent and serious theatre in a

Edward Albee and Richard Barr, by Alix Jeffry

world increasingly swamped by commercialism. Dick's faint traces of pomposity were compensated by a generous spirit. His small flat was always crammed with budding writers, actors, painters, for he saw himself as a kind of protector of artists, and one of his great pleasures was to have a protégé. I was a suitable subject, and he opened the world of Broadway to me. He took me to some unforgettable performances, among them Tennessee Williams's *Sweet Bird of Youth* with a handsome Paul Newman and a fluttering Margaret Leighton, directed by Elia Kazan, and the musical *Gypsy*, directed by Stephen Sondheim with dance numbers by Jerome Robbins, and starring the dynamic Ethel Merman.

These evenings were followed by the customary dinner at Sardi's or the Russian Tea Room, where Richard had friends at every table. I was terribly impressed.

Of course I suffered once more the pangs of an unhappy love affair: short, passionate and ultimately painful. Roger Sammis was a young painter of unusual promise never quite fulfilled. He was complicated, complex and very beautiful, all ingredients for failure. He was at odds with himself, his family, with America and finally with me. For a while of course it was bliss. We went to sleep to the sound of the waves in a little shack without light or water right at the edge of the ocean in Nantucket. I tasted for the first time the immense beauty of these American shores with deserted sandy beaches. I read Rilke to him and he spoke to me about Marianne Moore. I introduced him to my friends, to Richard and Edward, and they all thought he was terrific. Then after about six months I reached over in the bed and the place was empty. I asked myself once more what went wrong or where I failed and I found no answer. Once more an excess of loving had scared a friend away. I was always hankering after those who were unattainable, or at least on my terms. I had not yet understood that relationships, if they were meant to survive, are based on compromise, adjustment and negotiation.

Roger, in a letter, had quoted Byron: 'The great object in life is sensation – to feel that we exist, though in pain.' Yet I was longing for a tranquil existence – not delirious happiness, but contentment.

I decided to stay in America. I was hooked on New York and its drive, lively informality, pioneer spirit, kindness and generosity, but also its danger, its open sexuality, even its brazen vulgarity. I had already obtained an extension of my visa and I was now applying for an immigration visa. It was refused, as the charming consular official in Frankfurt had told me it would be. I tried pulling strings but nothing could be done. I had to go back to Europe. I was crushed. I hated not to succeed.

Ted Bates decided to send me to England for two years, to help them open agencies in Europe and then to apply properly for a re-entry visa. At least it was not Germany. England was *terra incognita*. I hardly knew anything about it. My interests had so far been directed towards France and America. England, to a new German generation bent on excitement and new horizons, seemed like an old, backward-looking place. The British had won the war, but they had shared too many things we wanted to forget: the bombing, the rationing and the deprivations. America, with little tradition and a seemingly classless society, was nearer to our ideals than a country bent on class, patriotic traditions and love for the military. Also Hemingway, Steinbeck or Tennessee Williams seemed to be so much more exciting than Evelyn Waugh, Kingsley Amis or Terence Rattigan.

In 1958 I sailed once more, this time cabin class, a little surprise present some of my friends had arranged. I was almost in tears at the champagne send-off. There were Richard and Edward, Wayne, Tamara and John, and Elinora. It felt like a wake. I swore to return as soon as possible.

I have kept my promise. I have returned often and regularly, but little did I know then that in England I would finally find my home, my country and the love of my life, three things I had only dreamed of.

11

A New Life:
London 1958–1965

The crossing was uneventful. In Southampton I gathered my luggage and my car and drove towards London, trying to keep to the left side of the road. I had been given the name of a little guest house in South Kensington. I also had a job at Hobson Bates in Gower Street, the London branch of Ted Bates.

I had been thrown out of New York's whirlpool of sensations into a city where I knew hardly anybody. I thought of all the friends I had left behind in New York, Germany and Paris. How often had I started in a new place? Now I found myself pitched once more into a new territory, a new culture and, as I soon discovered, a new language. The wounds which my love for Roger had inflicted had not completely healed. The cruel failure of love, of communication or the absence of it, which I had experienced so often before, took pieces out of my heart – and yet the heart miraculously seemed to survive. I was still trying to understand the riddle of life, but however much I examined and questioned it, it seemed to become no clearer. Was it our destiny to start again and again where we failed?

It was once more a time of severance. If the change brought loneliness it was also an opportunity for new beginnings, for taking on new roles, the possibility to develop a new personality, to erase, to perfect or even to embellish. I was again a new and unknown person, without history, blemishes or qualities. Nothing and nobody told me that I should be the person I should be. The older I grew, the more I watched this person inventing himself, sometimes in amazement, sometimes in anger, sometimes even in admiration.

My first impression of London was of respectability and a certain dullness, a dignified city that lacked the multiple enthralling and maddening qualities of New York and the *joie de vivre* of Paris. I had arrived on Good Friday 1958 as people left town like lemmings to go to their cottages. So I followed and drove to Cornwall. I discovered a picture-book England, exactly the way I had always imagined it. I could almost see 'old maids bicycling to Holy Communion through the morning mist' as George Orwell made us believe. A landscape heavy with leaf. A cosy and genteel

In London

existence of little churches with toppled gravestones in overgrown church-yards and rows of toy-like cottages peeking out from immaculate and neatly fenced-in gardens. *The Sunday Times* and *The Observer* mustered on well-tended porches. Places that presented such an over-polished face must have a dark secret, I thought. This may have been 'the country' but it had nothing to do with the one I knew, the country of Tressdorf, where the farmers ate from the same large dish and the old women snuffed tobacco. This was the country, as I was soon to find out, where ladies in sensible shoes made water-colours, and 'resting' actors shared a rose garden, and where retired company directors showed off their collection of Chelsea pottery.

I stayed in a small hotel with a thatched roof and an excess of shiny copper. The discretion of the fellow guests in their slightly damp country clothes was comforting after the curiosity of Americans. Nobody cared where you came from or who you were; no enquiries, only a faint exchange of smiles over tea or coffee served in what was called the 'lounge'. Ultimately these were things I learned to love.

Back in London, I contacted the only people I knew, Hanna and Rudolf Strauss. Rudolf had once been engaged to my cousin Annemarie, but then decided to marry his own cousin, a painter. Hanna was brimming with vitality and was the source of much joy and trouble. She liked a good story and was quick on the repartee. Rudolf was a scientist and as such sometimes prone to think that most people were fools. They had lived most of their lives in England, but had never shed their European outlook. It manifested itself mostly in a healthy cultural appetite and an excessive love for anything Bavarian. The last to a Prussian like myself was most unhealthy. Both became like a family to me and they still are.

In 1958 London was only beginning to wake up to the modern world and to shed some of its insular image. At first sight it seemed to be a city very much like the one I had seen in the film *Brief Encounter*, slow, cumbersome, where school ties and knowing the right people were more important than the ability to speak a foreign language and a familiarity with the novels of Proust.

For me, the most endearing things in my new country were traditional. I was prepared for Buckingham Palace and the Changing of the Guard but not for the people in the City in bowler hats with rolled umbrellas, even on a fine day; this was reassuring in its quirkiness. People were polite and not too familiar. They stood in orderly queues and said 'please' even when paying the fare on the bus. London to me was like a bastion of the civilised world, for some of the liberalism of the nineteenth century had survived. However, I soon discovered that much of the tolerance was based on indifference and an inbred lack of curiosity.

There was also a kind of delusion of some mythical grandeur and a notion that England had a democracy superior to any. In the beginning I was taken in by all this, until I realised that they were talking about the past rather than the present, and that this belief in the uniqueness of the English had something to do with an astonishing ignorance of what went on in other countries. Most of the culture still seemed to be home-grown. It included stars like Vera Lynn and Gracie Fields, but also Noël Coward and institutions like the B B C, a kind of secular model church. War heroes were still glorified in feature films and few people seemed to question the institutions. England had come out of the Suez crisis and the young had begun to rebel against the 'Establishment', although when I arrived the 'angry young men' as represented by Jimmy Porter, the working-class hero of John Osborne's *Look Back in Anger*, had already become part of a new Establishment.

I exchanged my hotel room for a small apartment in Chelsea. Among the few addresses I had, none was more valuable and appreciated than that of Patrick Woodcock. Patrick was everybody's doctor: from Noël Coward to Marlene Dietrich, from Peggy Ashcroft to David Hockney. Writers, actors, painters, dancers, in short *le tout* artistic London passed through his surgery. He was the true *médecin malgré lui*. For Patrick, art always rivalled medecine, and his surgery was really the ante-chamber to his living-room.

Patrick was absolutely convinced that he could organise everything better than anybody else and decided to take me under his wing. He was a most gracious and generous host, able to show affection and sympathy. He regarded my romanticism with mounting suspicion, but I suspected that under his calm reasonable surface lay an immense suppressed vitality, a current of secret existence. He opened for me the door to London's cultural life, to a bewildering array of names and talents. Among the Woodcock regulars were Peter Shaffer, John Gielgud, Keith Vaughan and a very young David Hockney. Among his many stimulating and enlightening guests I met the writer David Hughes and his vivacious and outgoing wife, the film maker Mai Zetterling. 'This is Klaus-Peter,' Patrick would say to his guests, Joyce Carey, Alan Bates or Sheila Hancock. 'German and Jewish and Catholic, my God you are in trouble,' Miss Hancock said, in a funny accent, and went on to point at the hundreds of Christmas cards from the very famous that lined Woodcock's mantelpiece. 'You would think this is Patrick's birthday, not Jesus'.' Everybody was so dazzling, witty and epigrammatic, and seemed to know everybody. All his friends dabbled in art, reviewing each other's books, applauding each other on the stage or on the screen. Most names meant little to me. Of course I would not let my ignorance shine through. I assured Joyce Carey that I liked her books. 'I am the actress Joyce Carey', she said with zestful scorn. 'The writer Joyce Cary is a man, and he has been dead for two years.'

Patrick also decided to get rid of my dreadful American accent. Soon I was cooing 'tomaato' instead of 'tomaito' and 'Shall we daance' instead of 'daince', and had a thriving social life. I still had a boyish fascination with the famous, as long as they were people for whom things of the mind were paramount. I always disliked mean-spirited people and fell for strong characters, to whom it was impossible to be indifferent. I no longer cared if I provoked strong reactions, for I realised that those who find friends easily also accumulate some enemies.

In retrospect, most of my English friends seem to have come from Patrick's stable, and with most of them I kept up a friendship which would renew and enlarge itself in the years to come, a sign of their stamina and a certain consistency on my part. For someone living alone, friends are paramount. They helped me to overcome my feeling of being nowhere, of not belonging, for something of the loneliness of childhood, the enormous nostalgia of adolescence, was still with me. Not many people allow us to be what we truly are. Friends usually do (although one of the more painful experiences is to discover that friends sometimes mistrust us, just at the moment when we are nearest to the truth).

I again tried calling myself Klaus-Peter and stuck to it for three years. The English with their innate politeness seemed not to mind, and to this day, for many friends, especially those I made in that first year, I have remained Klaus hyphen Peter.

At one of Patrick's 'little dinners' I also met two ladies who seemed to epitomise England. The two could not have been more different and yet both struck me as the very image of English eccentricity. Hester Chapman wrote historical biographies; Prunella Clough is a distinguished painter. It was a most stimulating evening. Hester, a woman of indefinable age in a low-cut short evening dress and impeccable makeup with frizzy hair, spoke about great women of the past and pronounced firmly 'the menopause does not exist' while deboning her fish. Prunella, who looked like an English schoolmistress in trousers and a sweater, was not easily thrown and acknowledged such sweeping remarks with a wry smile.

Hester lived in Bloomsbury, in a small house of splendid antique clutter. There was a slight smell of musk that nested in curtains and sofa cushions. It was the effect of under-heating and billowing smoke from the many chimneys. I soon associated this particular smell with many English homes, so different from the one in the over-heated and under-cooled American homes, or in the homes of Germany, which were always obsessively and vigorously aired.

Hester Chapman was a beguiling storyteller, witty and terribly worldly. She presided over stimulating evenings of artists, historians, politicians and aristocrats. One dressed for Hester's dinner parties, and they were as scintillating as they were famous. Sometimes one might sit at table with the writers Enid Bagnold, Rosamond Lehmann, Margaret Lane and her pretty and spirited daughter Selina Hastings, plus an assorted group of learned and erudite gentlemen, like George Rylands, whom everybody called Dadie and who spoke quite intimately about a woman called Virginia. I naïvely assumed that she was his wife but she turned out to be Virginia Woolf. On another evening the arresting guests might include Peggy Ashcroft and John Gielgud.

For me it was a formidable introduction to London theatre and literary life. Playing the role of the scoundrel and the charmer I had quickly learned to participate in conversation and not to be impressed. Dinner was served in a small candle-lit dining-room. Everything had the look of faded elegance so typical of many English homes – none of the ostentatiousness that so often characterised the homes of the American rich. The chairs had been covered a hundred years ago, the oil paintings had not been cleaned for centuries. The china, the silver, everything felt right, an atmosphere not of money, but of culture and discerning taste, a society which felt no need to show off or to assert itself. For someone who came from a country where all tradition and rules had been broken, this was an amazingly secure world.

Hester almost always served tasty stews. After several hours of conversation and gossip on such various subjects as Anne Boleyn, the model for historical portraits in the Queen's collection, or a naughty dresser in the Royal Shakespeare Company, Hester would rise and collect the plates, scraping whatever was left on them back into the casserole, the ash from her cigarette falling from her lips into the dish. Everybody knew that the next evening would be as illustrious as this one and that there would be the same stew. This seemed to bother no one. After the pudding the ladies would 'repair' upstairs, leaving the gentlemen with the port.

Prunella also served stews. She lived in a small house in Fulham, before it became fashionable. In Prunella's house one ate in the kitchen on a solid scrubbed pine table. Everything was slightly disorganised, nothing seemed to match anything else. Again, this looked right, felt right. In the houses of Hester and Prunella I realised that I was in a country of continuity and of unbroken tradition. Prunella too had paintings on her wall, but she changed them regularly. One day it would be a Lowry or a Patrick Heron, the next a Chinese print and a Wyndham Lewis. Around her table gathered her painter friends like Keith Vaughan, Bridget Riley, Patrick Heron, the art critics Bryan Robertson and John Berger. The conversation moved effortlessly from politics to books and sometimes music.

Prunella is a painter's painter much loved and respected by her equals. When I met her she had just had a remarkable retrospective exhibition in the Whitechapel Gallery, but her inbuilt modesty would shrug off any compliments. She was more interested in talking about other people's work than about her own. Although it was rumoured that she too came from an old family, the subject was never mentioned. For Prunella's dinners one wore jeans or corduroys. There was certainly no question of the ladies withdrawing to the upper parts of the house and there was definitely no port.

I must dwell a bit longer on Prunella, because she became and still is my closest and most enduring friend. There is much gaiety in her, but, probably quite young, she had acquired a seriousness and a calm which give her an infinite compassion and interest in all things and people. Although quite self-contained, she has a profound adhesion to the world. She has that rare thing, an original mind in which imagination and intellect are always at even flow, enhancing each other. Of great generosity to others, she hardly has any material need for herself; her desire is for space, space to work in and space between herself and others. She is in fact the freest person I have ever known, free of material want, free of conventions. Prunella enhances the life of many people, a woman of complete integrity and total incorruptibility.

My other painter friend was Keith Vaughan, a stocky, slightly balding man of about fifty. Hailed in the 1950s as one of the great white hopes of British painting, his fame had been slightly eclipsed by the younger generation. We drove in an old and immaculate Morris Minor to the country or we spent the evening in his London home reading Rilke or Rimbaud, whose verses he had illustrated. He spoke very good French and German, having worked as an interpreter for German prisoners during the war.

Keith lived in a Victorian flat in Belsize Park that consisted of a light high-ceilinged living-room, which also served as a bedroom, a large studio, and a kitchen where he loved to entertain. Not that he was very sociable: he had no talent for small-talk and a tendency to brood. Despite his success he had little confidence in himself. He was very critical, often too critical for many: his wide knowledge of literature, music and the visual arts, as well as an acute sense of observation, often made him harsh in his judgement of others. Everything about Keith – his manners, his flat and his appearance – was orderly in an almost old-maidish way, but under-

Keith Vaughan in his studio

neath ran a dangerous self-destructive current. He was often full of bel-
ligerent grumbles about boring dinner parties, failed expectations and dis-
illusions. 'Life is so over-valued,' he once said to me, and he talked about
voluntary-extermination chambers for the old and the sick. 'Clinging to
the primitive existence at all cost is absurd.' He regularly complained
about his mother, who stifled him. The memory of his brother would not
leave him either. Dick, an RAF pilot, had died during the war. Keith had
taken some evocative photographs of him at Pagham pond, a nude figure
under a transparent cloth.

He was fascinated by the human body and by people's poses. His
numerous small sketchbooks that traced his life were filled with drawings
of fellow soldiers, many in the nude. Returning from a trip to Italy, he
talked about the naturalness of the Italians, of 'their relaxed physical
greetings, so different from the self-conscious poses the English strike'.

But Keith's own fear of spontaneity always came to the foreground. It
became my role to free him from some of his strictures and to make him
laugh. He also could be magnanimous and generous, especially with
younger people. People writing about Vaughan have always concentrated
on his darker side, but in over twenty years I saw much light and a great
capacity for friendship, even laughter. He could be very funny and he had
great wit.

Through Keith Vaughan I met David Hockney. He had bleached blond
hair and wore a golden lamé jacket he had bought for the award of the
Golden Medal of the Royal Academy. He invited me to his place, where he
was working on some beautiful and very accomplished etchings for *The
Rake's Progress*. He was living in a room in Earl's Court so small that he
had to paint at the College. It was rumoured that he also bleached his hair
there. At that time he was a vegetarian and distributed leaflets for a vegetarian society. David was very erudite and could talk for hours on almost
any subject: Walt Whitman, Gandhi, Duccio, Durrell or Cavafy. He struck
me as a strange mixture of modesty and self-assurance. He was so intensely alive that ideas just came toppling out, interlacing the most contradictory ideas in a logical pattern. Like Keith he was fascinated by the American
magazine *Physique Pictorial*, and we used to swap them.

The first Hockney painting I saw was in a student exhibition called 'The
Young Contemporaries'. It included works by Derek Boshier, Allen Jones,
Patrick Caulfield and others. Hockney's work was called *We Two Boys
Together Clinging*, a cartoon-like painting with graffiti all over it. It created
quite a stir on account of its subject. Its title was taken from a poem by
Walt Whitman I loved:

David Hockney, by Cecil Beaton

We two boys together clinging,
One the other never leaving,
Armed and fearless, eating, drinking, sleeping, loving.

I think it was soon afterwards that Hockney went for the first time to the
States, and he came back totally smitten. He never stopped talking about
American boys in white athletic socks, which he found incredibly sexy.

I spent a lot of time in the theatre. One of the most memorable evenings took place at the Old Vic: a new production of *Romeo and Juliet*.
The director was Franco Zeffirelli, who had made a name for himself as a
set designer. Judy Dench and John Stride were the two protagonists, both
extraordinarily natural and untheatrical. Judy Dench was almost like a
little doll, and John Stride as handsome a Romeo as they come. They
climbed trees to look at each other, and in a tempestuous scene made love
in a giant four-poster bed. It was the *Romeo and Juliet* of the sixties –
young, modern, emancipated.

I had met Franco Zeffirelli the previous year. We had so many friends in
common that we were surprised we had not met before. Everything about
him reminded me of my time in Rome with Enrico. His youthful high
spirits, charm and good looks intrigued me, but also put me slightly on
guard.

We became instant friends, although it was difficult to keep up with
him, and we eventually lost sight of each other, although never completely.
One day he would be off to Dallas to direct Joan Sutherland in *Alcina*, the
next away to put on a production of *Don Giovanni*, or he would phone
from Florence where he was doing *Euridice*.

He would sometimes take me to opening-night dinner parties, but I felt
very inept among the stylish but empty in-talk. Laurence Olivier was
always 'Larry' and John Gielgud 'John G'. There were always plenty of
people who dished up knowledge or gossip, and others, I suspected, only
went to the theatre because it made a good after-dinner topic and pushed
the evening along.

Zeffirelli returned to London to do *Othello*, with Dorothy Tutin as Des-
demona and Ian Bannen in the title role. John Gielgud played Iago and
amused everybody with the stories of Franco's agitated and very un-Eng-
lish way of directing. *Othello* was not a success. Franco was quite hurt,
especially as Luchino Visconti had come for the opening night, a disastrous evening during which John Gielgud lost half his beard.

For a while I saw a lot of John Gielgud. Jonathan Swift's dictum that
'Good manners is the art of making those people easy with whom we con-
verse' was also his. He was very kind and one of the most civilised people I

knew. I spent many evenings in his house in Cawley Street, a place filled with antiques and the memorabilia of a long theatrical life and tradition. He also invited me to visit him in Stratford, where he had rented a cottage right on the edge of the River Avon. It was a warm sunny day and Gielgud had spread blankets and a tablecloth on the ground, with some iced champagne and fresh bread and smoked ham. We sat on the lawn, blissfully content, and watched the small boats sliding by, white-clad punters steering their beloved behind the tall reeds that rose like bristles on either side of the river. It was like an Impressionist painting – *La Grande Jatte*, English style. In those peaceful and pampered surroundings Gielgud suddenly spoke of friendship in the theatre, about Peggy Ashcroft, Ralph Richardson, even his great rival Laurence Olivier. 'We might have sometimes had reservations about each other's performances but we are linked by a long and sustaining friendship.'

Gielgud had directed himself in quite a few plays, but I got the feeling that this gentle man did not get quite the pleasure out of it that he had hoped. 'It is a mistake to direct your colleagues, especially in plays you yourself have acted in, because you will always search for your own performance and those on stage feel that and resent it,' he told me. John is a conventional man and he made no bones about it. He hated realism in acting, what he called 'the Stanislavsky method'. 'It kills the poetry on stage.' Walking along the canal, he had put his arms protectively around my shoulders. I asked him about success and failure. 'One must not worry about either,' he said, and his earnest face broke into a broad smile. 'I have always learned so much from both.'

Later that night he read to me from his recital of Shakespeare's verses, his beautiful voice filling the room, and I thought that he was the greatest actor and the wisest man I ever met. At the end of the reading tears started streaming down his face. I got very embarrassed and John burst into laughter. 'I always cry, Klaus-Peter,' he said when he saw me so upset.

He gave me two photographs of himself: one as King Lear, a shrouded white figure with a white mane in a set by Isamu Nogushi, the picture of an ancient and timeless man broken by madness and mourning; the other a handsome young man in a dinner-jacket in a Noël Coward play. 'Where are the snows of yester years...?' he had written on it. 'Love, John.'

I often realised how little I knew about English literature. I had read Shakespeare, Dickens, James Joyce, T. S. Eliot, but the Brontës, Jane Austin, George Eliot, Trollope or Oliver Goldsmith were only names for me. It is difficult to describe the joy, almost halfway through life, of encountering Dorothea Brooke or Jane Eyre. In the twentieth century the 'great novel' had moved to France and Germany – there was no Proust, Thomas Mann or Musil – but Virginia Woolf and even the rather tiresome Bloomsbury set became an obsession for me. After the impact of reading *The Waves* came the discovery of E. M. Forster's *A Passage to India*, which led to Cavafy and to Lawrence Durrell. The sorting out of cultural references, knowing where the word Malapropism came from, was another bonus for the traveller in a new language, a pleasure unknown to people who have only lived in one. The joy was great in discovering another dimension, merely through language and the perception of the almost unlimited possibilities it encapsulates. It was once more a time of learning, another station of my intellectual Odyssey.

I had once more arrived in a country in the process of renewal. There was a whole new theatre to discover, with young playwrights such as John Osborne, N. F. Simpson, John Arden and Alan Sillitoe. In Chelsea the English Stage Company became a home for new writers. The small Royal Court Theatre brought out new plays, celebrating the new working-class ethos: Arnold Wesker's *Roots* and *Chicken Soup with Barley* were plays for which the expression 'kitchen-sink theatre' was coined. In the cinema too a horde of new young directors, many working also on stage: Tony Richardson, Lindsay Anderson, Peter Brook, Karel Reisz, Peter Hall, and most of all, Joan Littlewood, who ran the Theatre Workshop in the East End of London and produced plays such as Shelagh Delany's *A Taste of Honey* and Brendan Behan's *Hostage*. The straightforward writing, the natural way of acting was a revelation for me, brought up on the stilted theatre of Germany or the intellectualised one of France

In the spring of 1961 I went to see my first English cabaret. It was called 'Beyond the Fringe' and had come from Edinburgh. In a sort of downbeat English way, four young, rather serious-looking lads, Peter Cook, Alan Bennett, Jonathan Miller and Dudley Moore, debunked the holy cows of the Establishment – the Church, the royal family, the Tories – and the Establishment sat there and laughed. Satire became big business. Three journalists, Christopher Booker, Richard Ingram and William Rushton, began a satirical magazine called *Private Eye*.

A year later we rushed to a new club, the Establishment, to see a performer, Lenny Bruce. The house was packed with artists, students and members of the smart set. A rather pale-looking American with closely cropped hair said the most outrageous things for over an hour, without ever losing the smile on his face. He had certainly rehearsed some of his speech, but while the monologue went on he began to invent things, and his show was never the same. What was most surprising was his language. We had never heard such a barrage of obscenities. Four-letter words just came pouring out. Some people got up and left, shocked by his often sick humour. Nothing was sacred any more.

The Conservatives were still in power and Lenny Bruce was fiercely attacked. But protest was in the air, for some spoke up for him. I remember Kenneth Tynan and George Melly hailing Bruce as the new messiah. Bruce was not unlike some of the great moralists of the past. He pulled down mask after mask, revealing the obscene world we were all living in. It was shocking and liberating.

Seen from today it is hard to believe how much fuss there was about sex. England was to become the laughing stock of Europe when *Lady Chatterley's Lover* was put on trial. I could hardly believe that for months the leading papers could be occupied by this so-called obscenity trial. Scholars and intellectuals were trying to prove that the book, which was printed in many countries, was not obscene. When it was finally printed in England, 200,000 paperbacks sold almost immediately. The trial had been won because it was art; double standards still applied.

Society's hypocrisy about four-letter words always struck me as extremely churlish, and patronising to boot. Everybody knew them and probably thought them, but it was considered impolite to pronounce them. The censor saw to it that they were not used on stage or in books. Instead we had asterisks and dots. F*** was permissible, fuck not. You were allowed to print the word bastard but fucking bastard became f... bastard. On television four-letter words were bleeped out, and when in 1965 Kenneth Tynan was the first man to say fuck on television the switchboard of the BBC was jammed with protest calls. Four motions were passed in the House of Commons making sure that the screen remained clean of such excess. It brought out much bigotry and prejudice. Self-righteous busybodies like Mary Whitehouse could only flourish in a country where hypocrisy reigns supreme. This was more shocking to me than Lenny Bruce.

More out of protest than out of inclination I let myself be photographed in the nude for a German magazine by an old friend, the photographer Christa Peters, who had also come to London and was photographing businessmen in the buff. The more repressive and hypocritical society became, the more open I became. Not hampered by repression nor confused by guilt, I made no bones about my sexual orientation. Strangely enough, it paid off. People began to respect my openness. Once I had accepted that homosexuality was an irreversible part of my life it became the source of much happiness. The general notion that homosexuals are something akin to women is absurd. As I increasingly found my identity as a homosexual I became more of a man.

Another friend I met in my first year in London was Peter Shaffer. An indefatigable talker with a penchant for compelling gossip, he was basking in his early success. Funny and witty, he spoke in perfectly phrased and polished sentences and never missed a chance to make a pun. Peter and his twin brother Tony had began by writing thrillers together.

Thanks to Peter, I had found another flat. It was in Kensington, in a row of twenty-four beautiful terraced houses with generous back gardens, which formed a large park. Earls Terrace was on the north side of Edwardes Square, a jewel of town planning, one of London's loveliest squares. The terrace was the work of a French architect, built to house Napoleon's officers in 1785. The once grand houses now revealed the crumbling bricks under the peeling stucco and many of the iron balconies had crashed to the ground. The houses were linked by a kind of underground moat – a concession, I presume, to its military origin. The five-storey houses were set back from Kensington High Street and front and back overlooked masses of green trees. Forty years ago, each house, once the residence of an affluent middle class, had been split up into five flats. The large staircase with the peeling William Morris wallpaper still testified to past splendour.

My flat, located on the first floor, consisted of two well-proportioned large rooms, with marble fireplaces and wooden shutters. The French windows gave out over a terrace which overlooked three green acres of Edwardes Square. Louise had generously begun to distribute some of the Adam furniture. 'It is better to give with the warm hand,' she used to say, and with the antique furniture from Berlin my first proper apartment looked quite elegant. It cost only £10 a week to rent, rates and hot water included. As so often before, I had hit the jackpot. I lived in Earls Terrace for the next twenty-one years, eventually also taking the adjacent flat, knocking down the dividing walls.

Earls Terrace was unique in more than one sense. Most of the occupants were still splendid, although no longer affluent. The roll-call of inhabitants was formidable: an array of actors, film-makers and writers. Alan Bates and Peter Wyngarde lived in number 1, Jean Muir and her actor husband Harry Lockhardt in number 5. (Peter Shaffer had modelled the tutor in *Five Finger Exercise* on Harry and the play was dedicated to Jean.) In number 12 lived the actor Richard Easton, Fenella Fielding in 13, Peter Shaffer in 14. The conductor Raymond Leppard in 18 as well as the journalist James Mossman. The grand couple of the theatre, Googie Withers and John McCallum, always lived in number 24 when playing in London, otherwise it was the flat of their daughter, the talented actress Joanna McCallum. I lived in number 24, and in number 25 director Antony Besch had a flat. So did Ian McKellen.

People moved in and out of the terrace, sometimes because the flats became too small, sometimes because the inhabitants had married or became too famous. They were quickly replaced by yet another name from the artistic world. Flats in Earls Terrace were like gold and passed from friend to friend.

The reason for this plethora of artists was simply that all the houses belonged to the father of Peter Shaffer, who had gradually managed to house all his friends in one of the most desirable places in London at a derisory rent.

The moat was not the only link between the houses. There was another link: Mollie. To call her a housekeeper is not fair, for like her grand French counterpart, the *concierge*, she was the Cerberus who knew everything about us. As she had the key to most flats, she was familiar with the inhabitants' love life, their pay slips and the contents of their refrigerators. She knew what Peter Hall had said to Peter Shaffer, what Covent Garden was willing to pay for a production and why X had split up with Y. It was better to be her friend than her foe. I was her friend most of the time. Nobody was Mollie's friend all the time, except Peter Shaffer. I am sure he will one day raise a proper monument to this intelligent, tireless and tiresome woman who ran many people's lives, a kind of Mother Courage.

Despite its nickname, 'Traitor's gate', it was a wonderful place to live. Many ideas were born, exchanged and put into a film, play or book here, and I was allowed to eavesdrop. Over drinks Maggie Smith and Robert Stephens would discuss some scenes with a cynically disposed John Dexter or Peter Wood. The idea for *Equus* was born over a dinner table and David Hockney showed his drawings for *The Rake's Progress* for Glyndebourne while a raucous Moura Budberg, a Russian aristocrat with a great appetite for vodka and literature, who had been Gorky's and H.G. Wells's mistress, fought with us about her new Chekhov translations.

I also had a new job. To say I had entered the film world would be an exaggeration, but I was on the first step, the most important I have ever taken.

In 1961 I had met Elisabeth Montagu, a delightful Englishwoman, a friend of Therese Giehse and Erika Mann, who had formed a small film company, Television Advertising (TVA), with the witty Tony Shaffer, a Colonel Heal (who, at one time, was the personal assistant to Prince Philip), and Doreen Merriman, a producer and the only one with proper experience in the film business. TVA made a name for itself by using feature-film directors such as Dick Lester, Tony Richardson and John Schlesinger to make their commercials. Elisabeth was keen to enter the

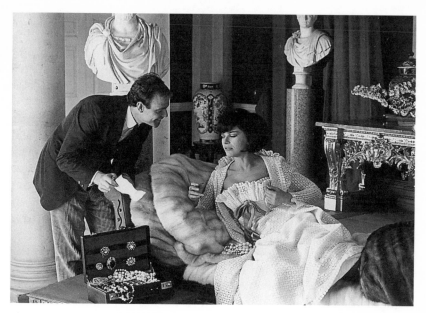

Filming a commerical with Fenella Fielding

lucrative German market and thought it was a good idea to engage me to look after this side.

I was travelling in style once again. The combination of an English lady, an English colonel with the Prince Philip connection, plus the Rolls-Royce borrowed from her brother Lord Montagu of Beaulieu, went down a treat with Germans, and we were soon in business.

I advanced quickly from a sales director to a producer for our star directors. I observed, copied and often bluffed. I was learning fast, and soon I tried my hand at directing. My début as a director was a Spanish margarine commercial shot in Portugal with a pop star singing 'La Margarina Serana màs fresca…' It was not terribly good. I shot forty-seven takes for the next one, Pepita chocolates – 'melt in your mouth not in your hands' – until the actress was sick on the floor, but it got third prize in Cannes, and when I engaged Fenella Fielding for a cigarette commercial, we won first prize in New York. Beginner's luck ? Chutzpah ? Self-confidence ? A bit of all three, but I was also keen to learn. I watched eagerly when John Schlesinger and Dick Lester directed, I persuaded the cutting editor to teach me how to cut and Tony Shaffer to instruct me in writing, and when Cleo Laine sang a jingle for a German commercial, I quickly engaged myself as a language coach. It was hard to get rid of me, and persistence paid off. I soon became a fully fledged director of commercials.

Much has been made of the sixties, but as it was the first of my English decades, it had a great impact on me. The magazines in New York and Paris assured everybody that London was where 'the action' was and I had arrived just in time. I thought how privileged I was to live once more in a time and a country that was rejecting established conventions. In Germany the new ideas had been imprinted onto a vacuum of a country that had totally lost its old values and beliefs, but in England any change had to fight old-established and tested concepts. This gave the 1960s an edge, an urgency.

There was quick and easy money, quick and easy success and quick and easy sex. French and Italian restaurants thrived, and the English took to Campari and scampi, adopting the new trends with amazing speed. Ladies who for years had dressed in Hardy Amies or Hartnell suddenly tried dresses at Biba or Mary Quant. Regional and working-class accents were in, as long as the speaker was energetic, articulate and daring. So on the surface at least, the class conspiracy forged in Eton, Oxford and Cambridge was pushed into the background.

For me, who had seen the many changes in Germany, France and the United States, all this talk about an English revolution seemed hardly revolutionary. The apparent 'swinging' and cheerful happenings were really only on the surface. Underneath lay much trouble and concern. It was a kind of schizophrenic existence. England had lost an empire but was still craving to hold on to world power. 'Damn you, England, you are rotting now, and quite soon you will disappear,' John Osborne had written in a vehement and damning public letter. Most newspapers were preoccupied with England's favourite game, spy-catching. The mixture of sex, society gossip and political intrigue filled the columns. Soon there would be the Profumo affair. While ministers in Britain were toppled, de Gaulle was supposed to have remarked that if behaviour like this were to worry the French he would have no ministers left. No wonder he once more blocked England's entry into the Common Market.

But there were also much deeper concerns. A picture shown on television haunted many of us for a long time: a Buddhist monk setting fire to himself in Vietnam, as a protest against the Diem regime. It was the first of many self-immolations staged as political gestures. (I often wondered why so many of the lasting images which have come on the screen all have to do with death: Jacqueline Kennedy throwing herself over her husband's body in a speeding car, the soldier blowing off the head of a young man, and the Chinese student stopping a tank on Tienanmen Square.)

I was against war, any war, and watched with horror the Americans and Russians indulging in the Cuban missile crisis, which threatened to throw the world into another world war, more lethal than any previous one.

I joined the crowds on Trafalgar Square, listening to Bertrand Russell castigating Khrushchev, Kennedy and Macmillan as 'the wickedest men in the history of man'. I thought of Hitler, and Stalin's soldiers 'liberating' us, and felt this wide of the mark, but judging by the applause of the crowd, which included Vanessa Redgrave, Doris Lessing, John Osborne, Philip Toynbee, Shelagh Delany and many others of the glittering set, other people seemed not to share my reservations. The eighty-nine-year-old philosopher, together with more than 1,300 people, was arrested – the biggest mass arrest in England's history. The right of free speech to me is not negotiable, not divisible, however uncomfortable to myself. I realised that all was not well with England. It was not the cradle of democracy and justice I had thought it was, a realisation which increased over the years with personal consequences I could not foresee in the waves of excitement and new beginnings.

In 1961 I flew to Berlin, armed with a grey tailcoat and a matching top hat hired from Moss Bros, to attend my sister's wedding. 'Welcome to the race course' was Louise's comment as she watched me unpack my suitcase.

Renate had given up the editorship of the women's magazine to study History of Art. She had fallen in love with one of the lecturers, an extraordinarily bright and very shy art historian. Some marriages they say are made in heaven, this one certainly was. Weddings, like funerals, always seem to have a surrealist and often comic element built into them, and so it was here. Renate and Mathias could not have been more different in temperament, upbringing and outlook. My impulsive sister and her quiet unobtrusive suitor. Mathias Winner was the son of a vicar and the clash of the families was tremendous. His family was upright, respectable and pious. The little church in Nikolassee was filled to the brim with friends and neighbours, among them Mathias's mother, brothers and sisters, and from our side the two aunts, Emmy and Friedl, Dada, Anita and Marcelle from Paris. Father Winner celebrated mass. Louise had refrained from donning too elaborate a hat, but Friedl wore a dramatic concoction of green feathers. The groom looked exceedingly panic-stricken and pale, and on the eve of the wedding had threatened to call the whole thing off. Renate looked radiant in a short dress and veil. There was much cheering when she threw the bouquet into the crowd. Unfortunately I caught it and tossed it, rather embarrassed, to Marcelle.

The reception was sumptuous. Mathias's family played a little piece of chamber music; each of the three children played a different musical instrument. Friedl recited a few verses. Everybody seemed to be quite happy and nobody asked me when I was going to get married.

I slept in my old room in the Waldhaus, which was still my home, and yet I felt alien, I had changed so much. It was almost as if I was a different person. I had cut all my roots except those of my affections. My love for my mother and my sister was undiminished, but Berlin was no longer my home, nor was German my only language. I had begun to think and dream in English, and London was the place I wanted to be. From now on I realised I would always be a visitor in the country of my birth.

I also realised that marriage would change my relationship with my sister, a relationship which in any case has always been tormented, despite our closeness or because of it. All our lives we have been very similar in many respects. I see in her many traits I want to correct in myself. Her often over-emotional response, her possessiveness, nourished by an excessive capacity for loving, regardless of the destruction it causes in others, are all things I recognised in myself and resented in her. From now on I realised she would lead a life surrounded by a family, while I would continue to live without closer ties. In the years to come we would increasingly live our predestined lives in opposite directions until they almost totally diverged. I often drew strength from the fact that there existed another person in this world absolutely sharing so much of my past. There were times when I loved her more than I liked her, but she has remained a loving and constant friend, sometimes too loving for my need for freedom.

There were other reasons for liking London. Friends were always passing through. Hans Werner Henze sometimes stayed with me in Earls Terrace. He was preparing his *Elegy for Young Lovers* in Glyndebourne. The libretto of the opera was by Auden and Kallman and was dedicated to Hugo von Hofmannsthal. Hans had a new friend, the actor Volker Bohnet, and they had rented a small cottage nearby. I spent some time with them and watched the work in progress. I especially admired Lila di Nobili's set designs. As so often before, this extraordinarily modest woman, who lived in two *chambres de bonne*, had produced magic. She had an almost masochistic humility and a closed nature at odds with all those inflated egos in the world of theatre and opera, like a strange bird who had fallen out of a nest. Eventually she gave up the theatre altogether, looking after her mother and a horde of stray cats.

Edward Albee had also come for the London première of his *American Dream* and *The Death of Bessie Smith*. They had so much of the America and the author I knew in them that I felt homesick for New York again. 'For Klaus-Peter, first and best friend in London,' Edward had written in my copy of the play. The days with Albee and his warm intelligence made me very proud and happy. Was I finally getting the recognition and affection I had been craving for so long? The fact that I was no longer the 'Jew boy', the outcast of the first part of my life, was exhilarating. He sometimes mocked my infatuation with America, where, as he never failed to point out, real values were constantly pushed out of the way by artificial ones. Albee's condemnation of complacency, cruelty and vacuity was, as he wrote, 'a stand against the fiction that everything in this slipping land of ours is peachy keen'.

Around this time I also bought a television set. It must be hard for people nowadays to imagine that I had spent nearly thirty-five years without television, but I was glad I had. I know I would never have been able to read as much as I did or devote so much time to the theatre or to films if I had had the box. I had resisted the temptation for a long time. I had sometimes watched it in the States, without much enthusiasm. It was not only the easy and passive distraction which put me off but also the excess of information, which I found worrying.

I was particularly interested in the news programmes *Panorama* and

Tonight. Many young, brilliant, erudite, university-educated journalists such as Richard Dimbleby, Robin Day, Ludovic Kennedy, John Freeman and James Mossman were reporting and making programmes. I also watched a new arts programme by Huw Wheldon: *Monitor.* Wheldon introduced a wide audience to the arts, like a benevolent father figure. *Monitor* was unique, but certainly not as intellectual as the reputation it later acquired. It too employed many young talents, Humphrey Burton and Melvyn Bragg among them.

I soon realised that television in England was different. It had grown from education rather than entertainment. When Malcolm Muggerridge interviewed the founding father, Lord Reith, saying that the BBC was regarded as the very image of a genteel and repectable society, the formidable Lord Reith replied: 'Anything wrong with that?'

Things were changing. The new director-general, Hugh Greene, a brother of the writer Graham Greene, had broadened the BBC's mandarin atmosphere of high culture, and, as a result, television began to take risks. The borderline between high and popular culture began to blur.

I never missed *The Avengers*, the story of a bowler-hatted Etonian turned secret agent, assisted by a leather-clad lady expert in ju-jitsu. The two sides of England, the respectable and the kinky, had finally joined forces, as someone remarked.

In the autumn of 1962 appeared a programme which collected instantly a sizeable audience: *That Was the Week That Was*, produced by Ned Sherrin. Ned lived in a small mews house in Chelsea, another of those invaluable meeting places for artists. He was very witty and clever and one of his great pleasures was to introduce people to each other. Like Patrick Woodcock, he sort of took me under his wing and handed me around. For his show he had surrounded himself with a brilliant team, many of them his friends: William Rushton, editor of *Private Eye*, Bernard Levin and David Frost, Peter Shaffer, John Mortimer and Kenneth Tynan. Looking back, this was another programme which has taken on a kind of glory. Probably not all the sketches were as clever and as good as we think now, but it was a breakthrough and a breath of fresh air. Millions of viewers were hooked the minute Millicent Martin sang the theme song.

In 1963 BBC2, a new television channel, was born and it is hard to believe that it was not a success.

My job at TVA kept me busy professionally and socially. The entire advertising business seemed to be conducted in the restaurants of Soho. For £5 a head you could have a terrific meal. I became a regular at the White Tower, La Capanina or Boulestin. Like the rest of the artistically inclined, I had my hair cut at Vidal Sassoon and wore flowered shirts to parties and wide candy-stripe shirts to the office – bought from Mr Fish. The people in the world of film and advertising lived well and played for high stakes. I went to the advertising film festival in Cannes, stayed in the Carlton Hotel and behaved like a star. TVA hired a yacht to entertain our clients, and we threw money out of the window. It was all part of the game.

Over many shared meals, I was forging new friendships or strengthening old ones. Some were quickly dropped, others maintained. I was always eager to encounter new people. So many things seemed to be happening all at once I decided to start a daily diary. In the beginning I only wrote down a few notes, mostly on outside events, people I met, plays I saw over the years. When the diary became a more intimate partner I used it for more thoughts and observations and it became quite an obsession. I kept a daily diary for the next thirty years. It was a considerable *aide-mémoire*. My diaries are full of people and names. Some recur and remain, others just drifted in and out of my life, sometimes only for a night or two. Now I cannot even remember what they looked like. Everything was fluid, always shifting. The diaries were also, I hoped, a way to escape the great confusion of a life that was often too full and sometimes broken. By writing I thought I could discover my mistakes and find an identity, maybe even the real me.

I saw quite a lot of David Hockney. He had quickly become famous, although he remained totally unaffected by it. He had moved into a much larger flat behind Notting Hill Gate in Powis Terrace. Basically it was a large room, where he slept and painted. Everything was always tidy and cheerful, on account of the many paintings just standing around. People would just drop in, like Mo McDermot and Ossie Clarke. I often wondered how he got any work done. He was very kind and could never say no. Later he would frequently change his telephone number, giving it only to 'his closest friends'. Within a few weeks everybody would have his new number. He sold a lot of work and made a lot of money, but often joked about the price people would pay. His paintings in 1963 cost about £300 I remember, and the sixteen etchings for *The Rake's Progress*, he told us, sold for £200 a set. We did not believe him. He had printed the set himself in College.

David loved to travel and he always came back with the most extraordinary stories about art and sex. He had been to Berlin, which he loved. I think it was in 1963 that the *Sunday Times* sent him to Egypt. They really wanted him to go to his native town, Bradford, but he preferred Cairo and Mark Boxer agreed. I remember he left wearing a white suit and looking very affluent. Soon afterwards he left to live in California. We all missed him greatly.

In 1962 Keith Vaughan had an important retrospective in the Whitechapel Gallery, and he proudly showed me a letter he received from E. M. Forster, who after he had seen the show wrote to him about the heroic nudes of Michelangelo. Forster was also the link to Christopher Isherwood. Isherwood did not think much of his native England. 'God must have been very tired when he made England,' he once said, but he came here every year to visit his friend E. M. Forster, always referred to as 'Morgan'. He and his friend the artist Don Bachardy had rented a small house in Hampstead, and we spent many stimulating evenings there, sometimes joined by the painter Patrick Procktor, a lanky, elastic and bird-like figure, who struck me as very English and very decadent in a sort of Aubrey Beardsley manner. He wore dandy-like and colourful clothes.

Christopher Isherwood was a small neat man with eyes the colour of periwinkle which seemed to scrutinise everything around him. I was much taken by Don Bachardy, who also had deep and beautiful eyes which, despite a broad smile, exuded a certain sadness. But there was also an alertness to the possibilities of life in him which was captivating. Christopher was a great storyteller and another writer who wanted to know everything about Berlin after the war. He usually sat on the floor in the lotus position, a habit, he claimed, he acquired while researching Hinduism with Aldous Huxley. Eventually he would get terribly drunk, but in a nice, non-aggressive way, while Don just sat there drawing.

I began to enjoy giving dinner parties myself. Before London I had mostly entertained in restaurants. Now that I had my own place, I took to this most civilised way of entertaining. In the beginning I was a terrible cook, and I am surprised that people put up with what could only be described as a student grub: spaghetti or German sausage with lots and lots of *Sauerkraut*. Gradually my skill and taste became a little bit more refined and I began to enjoy cooking. I experimented on the inner circle of my friends. I was not afraid of mixing people up, always hoping that the sparkle of the conversation would make up for the blandness of the food. Once I remember Bryan Robertson and Irene Worth getting in such a huff over the music of Aaron Copland that Bryan stormed out, leaving me alone with an actress I much admired but hardly knew, both covering up our embarrassment with unhealthy helpings of *Apfelstrudel*.

In 1964, Franco Zeffirelli had come back to London to stage *Tosca* in Covent Garden with Maria Callas. I sat in on many of his rehearsals,

Au Rènard avec tendresse
London Jan. '62
Franco (le Raisin)

Franco Zeffirelli, by Guy Gravett

watching Callas from close quarters. You could sense the strong complicity between singer and director. They had worked together before, in *Il
Turco* in Milan and *La Traviata* in Dallas. For Tosca he wanted her to be
very sexy and earthy, 'like Magnani' I heard him say, and she portrayed a
young and vibrant person in love. Franco is a compassionate actor. He
would jump on stage and mime the scene, singing and dancing with great
gusto. Callas was tremendously poised, very professional, hard-working
and interested in every detail. She would arrive, rehearse her scenes and
then sit quietly in the stalls.

In private she was easy and expansive with a display of feisty wit: the
prima donna was left behind. Callas stayed at the Savoy and Franco and I
often took her home. Sometimes we had dinner together in the little La
Capanina restaurant. Once we were so late the cook was gone and Callas
went into the kitchen to make omelettes for us.

During the dress rehearsal, Callas, in a black velvet dress, had to bend
down and put two candlesticks next to the corpse of Scarpia (sung by Tito
Gobbi). When she stood up and began to sing, smoke appeared behind
her head. Her wig had caught fire. Without losing a note, she quietly
removed the burning wig, stamped on it and continued the aria, undisturbed.

The opening night was a triumph for Callas and for Zeffirelli. Maria
Callas, whom many critics had begun to write off, blossomed once more. I
stood backstage and watched her getting on. I was surprised how nervous
she was, nearly demolishing a bunch of flowers Franco had bought at the
market that morning.

Through Franco I also met Rudolf Nureyev. I had actually been introduced to him before at Covent Garden, but that was such a disagreeable
meeting that I decided not to see him again. He was with Freddy Ashton,
and Nureyev's Tartar good looks, his charisma and his presence took my
breath away, but there was also something sharp, knife-like about him. I
had offered to fetch some drinks. When I came back with scotch Rudolf
very grandly said: 'No ice?' I went back to get some but I was taken aback
by his arrogant and thoroughly spoiled manner. Freddy apologised while
Nureyev took the new glass and just walked away to greet some other
people in the foyer. The dinner with Nureyev and Franco was a more
friendly affair, but I still felt ill at ease. It would take years before I could
have a better relationship with this great dancer. I made a film with him,
and even this episode ended in blows.

Another friend from those first London years is Bryan Robertson, who
had put on the Keith Vaughan show. He was cultivated and cosmopolitan

and began to mastermind exciting and pioneering art exhibitions at Whitechapel. With his open-mindedness and many-sided interests he had turned the Gallery into the most interesting place in London to see art and to meet people. He had already brought to London the American artists Jasper Johns, Willem de Kooning, Jackson Pollock and Mark Rothko. Bryan was also the most ingenious and generous host, although he never seemed to have any money, as people of his diverse talent are notoriously badly paid in a country where art is not a priority. In his house one would meet an array of different people. He had the wit and imagination to mix the film-maker Antonioni, Princess Margaret and new young painters such as Derek Jarman and Paul Huxley.

From 1964 to 1967 the Peter Stuyvesant corporation gave Bryan money for an annual show of contemporary British artists. The first New Generation Exhibition came as a great surprise. Here were a group of young talents, many only recently out of college. English art had finally woken up from its provincial sleep. David Hockney, Allen Jones, Derek Boshier, Patrick Caulfield, Brett Whiteley, Michael Vaughan, Bridget Riley, Patrick Procktor, Paul Huxley, Peter Phillips, John Hoyland and Anthony Donaldson – a formidable choice, in one single exhibition. Most of them would soon have an international reputation. The opening was a very jolly affair. They all knew each other and had invited friends and colleagues. All crowded into Whitechapel. Lord Snowdon had made the photograph for the cover of the catalogue. I made a note of the prices: for £65 you could buy a Patrick Caulfield, for £100 a Riley, a David Hockney oil was priced at £225.

I had thought that my silly years were behind me, but they were obviously not. So many things were happening. It was so easy to fall into temptation, and I had boundless energy and curiosity. So I let the world whirl around me, always hoping that I would not drown. I had accepted myself and I was neither particularly bothered by my faults nor by my virtues. I tried, as always, to be honest with myself. I always found more pleasure in discovering myself warts and all than in flattering myself, although I was very susceptible to the flattery of others.

It was probably during that time that my ego really started to inflate. I began to love success. I basked in it. At times I found this most unattractive. Gradually over the years I began to accept my ego and my love of recognition. It was a source of energy. In time I began to control my ego and to channel it, with varying success. I realised that an attempt at a more modest, self-effacing personality was alien to me and would certainly lead to falsehood.

On the whole, when I look back on those years I am astonished how orderly it all was, despite all these diversions and upheavals. How sensible and how lightly and how quickly life rearranged itself into a gentle and interesting pattern.

12

On the Dole: London and Elsewhere
1965–1968

In 1964 Edward Albee came back to London for the opening of *Who's Afraid of Virginia Woolf*, with Uta Hagen and Arthur Hill. The first night was a major event, and it was quite a shattering experience to sit next to Edward, watching the two protagonists tearing at each other like wild animals. Gentle, civilised, on guard, Edward had shown his savage side. I felt the tension mounting under his controlled exterior. My palms were getting moist while I caught a glance of his totally immobile face, but then rapturous applause broke the suspense and Edward smiled.

The play had been a huge success on Broadway. Albee was instantly hailed as the great new American playwright, inheriting the mantle of Eugene O'Neill and Tennessee Williams. Yet his success was short-lived. After his play *Tiny Alice* provoked a strong reaction from the critics (who could not quite forgive Albee for abandoning the commercially viable theatre for something more ambitious), he sent me a letter: 'The play has bewildered the critics and half of the audience, for reasons I can't understand. I am sure you will not be confused by it. It really is a very good play. I do say it myself, good for me at any rate.' He was right. I thought it a mysterious, provocative and beautiful play. It was a challenging attempt to write about the nature of faith. John Gielgud claimed that he was mystified by the text he had to speak but Irene Worth, who played Alice, was totally sold on it.

I gave a dinner for Edward. I wanted him to meet Peter Shaffer. The two playwrights were on opposite sides of the fence, and the conversation was a bit sticky. I guess Shaffer secretly accused Albee of obfuscation and Albee felt Shaffer had too light a touch. For Shaffer the theatre was about storytelling. The intellectual speculations of many of his contemporaries, 'with their twitchy and strained views of the world', as he put it, was not for him. In England, for a play to be labelled 'entertaining' was the worst crime, Peter had said.

I was not really surprised that the two playwrights did not see eye to eye. 'The Americans,' Peter said, 'always want goodies and baddies on their stage and in their cinema. Even Hamlet is limited by such judgement.' To think that someone in the audience sat there and judged the characters by their own moral standards made him quite angry. 'The characters on stage should be watched, listened to, observed, not judged.' This of course demands a high standard from the audience. In this Shaffer and Albee agreed.

At about that time Peter Shaffer too had a huge critical and public success with *The Royal Hunt of the Sun*, the play about Pizarro invading the Kingdom of the Sun, ruled by the thirty-year-old Inca King Atahualpa. He visualised a sort of *Gesamttheater*, with music, dance, mime, a grandiose historical spectacle against which the private drama of the two men could unfold in violent fury. Shaffer frequently spoke about the notion of great cultures being swallowed up by new ones, and he had given me the first version of the play to read. It was four or more hours long.

He was writing not so much a play about conquest but about how to survive it. 'It is a play about the quest for immortality, but immortality without the convention of a religion, a world in which man is free of all conventional loyalties, except that for love and friendship,' Peter explained. The play is basically a love story, beginning with the violent confrontation of the two men, the godlike figure and the earthy soldier, the old and the new order, ending in a healing relationship.

John Dexter had been chosen as director. The two had a great admiration for each other, although John was not the easiest of men to work with. He could be very impatient and sometimes quite aggressive, but his lively mind and inventive spirit were a joy to watch, dozens of ideas pouring out each minute.

As the Sun King they had cast Robert Stephens, but Peter was not sure who could play Pizarro. One night we saw Beckett's *Play*, with Billy Whitelaw and Robert Stephens. It was in a double bill with Sophocles's *Philoctetes*, with Colin Blakely. Peter was so impressed by his acting that he went backstage to ask him to take on the role.

Peter Shaffer has always liked to get involved in the production of his plays. Over the years I have been surprised that directors like John Dexter, Peter Hall and Peter Wood gave the writer so much leeway and accepted his often constructive interference. 'I am a servant of the theatre,' he often said, and that is true, for he knows exactly how to make an audience laugh, how to hold their attention and how to suspend their disbelief.

Shaffer likes to rewrite his dialogue, once he hears the words spoken, sometimes even removing characters or filling in empty passages. In his orderly workroom he would sit at an old typewriter, speaking the dialogue aloud, altering it, hearing it again and changing it once more until 'it sounded right'.

When the play was given in Chichester, it had been shortened, much to my chagrin, but the impact was still very powerful. Dexter had done a remarkable job. The doleful music of Marc Wilkinson which pervaded the whole play set the tone. It was a great epic evening, and I will never forget the moment when the darkened stage suddenly began to glow and shouts of 'Inca, Inca' could be heard. Robert Stephens, who had honed his body for this role, dressed in gold, wearing a mask and a crown, stood in a large golden circle. 'Atahualpa! God!' shouted the crowd. 'God hears,' came Stephens's voice. When the Indians were slaughtered, their screams echoed through the theatre, a scene of violent beauty. The play ended with the sun glaring, the audience and Pizarro mourning his dead friend. 'See, see the fate,' he sang. 'O little finch, Of robber birds, O little finch.'

The London theatre had not been better for years. There were powerful productions: *The Master Builder* with Laurence Olivier, Peggy Ashcroft and Wendy Hiller, and *Danton's Death* by Büchner, with Laurence Olivier and John Gielgud.

Peter Brook's *Marat/Sade* was another electrifying evening, filled with images of madness, cruelty and eroticism. To this day I remember Glenda Jackson as Charlotte Corday standing in the middle of the stage and whipping de Sade with her long hair, her head swaying from one side to the other. For the anniversary of Churchill's death, while almost the whole of England would celebrate him as a war hero, Brook put on Rolf Hochhuth's play *Soldiers,* which accused Churchill of the bombing of Dresden. Peter Brook also staged an anti-war play with the ambiguous title *US.* It was not only attacking the Vietnam war, but also the British attitude to war. A butterfly was burned on stage, and at the end the actors stood in a silent row defiantly facing the audience.

We also saw many productions from abroad thanks to the brilliant theatre producer Peter Daubeny, whose World Theatre season would become a standard meeting place in the Aldwych for all those interested in international theatre. In the next few years, Daubeny brought the best productions of Bertolt Brecht, Giorgio Strehler, Pepino de Filipo, Roger Planchon and Patrice Chéreau. London audiences saw productions from New York, Athens and the Eastern countries. There were three memorable Chekhov productions from the Moscow Arts Theatre. Looking back it seems almost unbelievable how much London theatre owed to one man; by comparison, theatre in London has now become provincial, cut off from the European mainstream.

Despite the influences from abroad, England was still repressive. Because of censorship, the Royal Court had to become a club to present Osborne's *A Patriot for Me*, dealing with two of the most discussed topics in England, treason and homosexuality. Bond's *Saved*, too, could only be given in a club performance. During the shocking and powerful scene of a baby being stoned in a pram, some people in the audience walked out. It was easy in those days to create a scandal. When Peter Hall put four strip-tease girls in Schoenberg's *Moses and Aaron* at the Royal Opera House the curtain nearly came down during the bacchanal.

There was much hypocrisy. In the Round House I heard Marcuse speaking about One-Dimensional Man and the need to free ourselves from the repressive society. In the same Round House we danced to launch the new *International Times*, while they screened Kenneth Anger's *Scorpio Rising*, a film celebrating the homosexual leather cult, and William Burroughs's *Towers Open Fire*. Yet Burroughs himself was only given a fortnight's visa to stay. Robert Fraser had a painted car driven into the vast arena, but his gallery was raided by the police, because he showed some Beardsley prints. The same thing happened to him a few months later when he exhibited some work by Jim Dine.

Intellectuals talked about all these happenings at dinner tables, but the felt injustice would not send them to the barricades, for they always ended up making a pact with the Establishment. Osborne's hero in *Inadmissible Evidence*, a much older Jimmy Porter, was pleading for the overdue need to adopt to different conditions: 'change, change, change, rapid change'. Sometimes it seemed to me that England would never change, or only superficially. This was its weakness and its strength.

The commercials we made at TVA became more and more glossy and more and more expensive. John Schlesinger went to Paris to shoot Black Magic chocolates and dropped a parachutist on Irene Handl for Typhoo Tea. I filmed egg commercials with Beryl Reid and rented parts of Woburn Abbey to take some shots with Fenella Fielding for a cigarette ad. To advertise tomato ketchup we used a baronial hall and had a cast of twenty exquisitely dressed actors pouring it on plates of eighteenth-century silver, while the music played *Pomp and Circumstance*. Everybody loved our commercials, especially the Americans. We continued to harvest prizes at festivals, but by the end of 1964 TVA was bankrupt. Top directors and feature cameramen produced brilliant commercials, and the expense-account lunches at the White Tower made for good client relationships, but neither helped the cash-flow.

I was luckier than many of the ninety other employees, for I was 'taken over' by A. B. Pathé in Wardour Street to look after their German commercial side. The trips to Germany continued, but somehow business never picked up again. The work with Pathé was far less stimulating than with TVA. Most of our directors had now made a successful career in feature films and were no longer available. Dick Lester was shooting the first Beatles film, *A Hard Day's Night*, with a brilliant script by Alun Owen. I continued to work with Nick Roeg, who was not a director yet but an outstanding cameraman, and there were new directors such as Hugh Hudson, a likeable man full of new and daring ideas, but the good old days seemed to be over, and I was becoming disenchanted with my work.

Hans Werner Henze sent me harsh letters, castigating my enthusiasm and need for new people. 'My saddened heart,' he wrote, 'listened to your conversation, resembling the music played in a French salon. I hope that your easy and naïve belief in others will not too often lead to disappointment.' He sent me a page of a score, 'as a recompense for your slightly ageing charm. Hang it on the wall in your room and remain in front of it daily for ten seconds.' But however stern, his letters were also full of consideration and caring. 'When I watched you from my hotel window, stepping out of the car, I thought for a moment, "pity that I know this one already." See you soon. Hans.'

Hans was right – it was time for a change in my profession, in myself, in my social habits. I realised that I must stop just accumulating people and knowledge and rather begin to consolidate. I was feeding on other people's talents. A spectator in the arts is not a practitioner.

Louise celebrated her seventy-third birthday on 3 May 1965 and we talked a long time on the phone. Three days later I wanted to speak to her again, but Mathias took the call. 'I think your mother has just left us,' he announced. There are moments in life so poignant that they cut like a knife into one's body. Renate and I were incapable of speaking, the words died in our throats. Louise had passed away that night in her sleep. I had rung the minute Renate had discovered her.

I packed in a daze and hurried to the airport. Emmy and Anita were at the Waldhaus. Renate's face was marked by pain and anguish. I could not bear to see Louise again. I wanted to remember her the way she had been.

That night I slept in the house, alone with Louise's body. Her love, her furies, her support were with me. I thought about our shifting relationship, her change from a mother to a friend and finally to a child. I thought of the time when I began to see her no longer as a mother but as a woman, when I understood her longings and her needs. The sense of loss began to worm its way into me. 'Irrational, loving, strong Louise. How will I go on living in a world without you?' The death of my mother was the most painful experience I had ever known, and the most real one. I was not only mourning a beloved person, but also a house and a childhood.

The next day Renate and I sat hand in hand on the wooden bench at the end of the garden under the birch tree, which had grown with us from a small plant into a large tree. We watched the men carrying the coffin out of the house and tried to pray, but prayer was not forthcoming. Silent numbness, only the pulsing hand of Renate.

On the day of the funeral it was pouring with rain. Renate, Mathias and I were the only ones without an umbrella in the large crowd that walked along the small road to the grave of my father. In the little church the organ began to play and I heard Friedl showing off her expertise: 'Bach!' So even this darkest of all days had its amusing moments.

Work forced me to return to London almost immediately. I felt lost and bereaved. In order to forget or kill the numbness I did the only thing I could at that time. I threw myself into distractions. Little did I know that real pain and loss cannot be shut out – it has to die down naturally. I dreamed almost every night of Louise and woke up shattered. For many years I did not stop dreaming about her. Someone said the dead die first in real life and eventually in our dreams. Gradually the wounds began to heal, and on 8 October 1965 Renate's second son Jonas was born.

In 1965 I shot my last commercial; I had produced or directed over a hundred. It was an extravagant ending to a colourful time. I flew nine hours from Paris to Rio to film Mr Tschibo, the coffee expert's visit to Brazil. We shipped out three Rolls-Royces and several alligator suitcases and hired an entire samba band. We filmed on a coffee plantation, a sort of *Gone with the Wind* setting, with peacocks strutting on the lawn and flocks of birds in white cages. When I showed it to the clients in Hamburg they did not like it – the usual fight between copy-writers, account executives and marketing experts. That was it. I packed up at Pathé and said goodbye to all that. I took my new Sunbeam Alpine and drove to St Tropez, where I met Raymond from Caracas.

I was looking for work, hoping for some sort of producer's job in feature films or the theatre – anything that had to do with the arts. This was easier said than done. I began by contacting a few people I knew. Tony Richardson promised some work. I spent a weekend with John Schlesinger in Dorset, where he was shooting *Far from the Madding Crowd*. He too had some ideas for me. For the next two months, I carted my show reels of prize-winning commercials from production company to production company. 'Don't phone us, we'll phone you,' they said. At some point Tony Richardson promised to let me direct the second unit on *The Charge of the Light Brigade*, then silence again.

Renate and Mathias Winner

Louise at 70

After five months without work I began to panic; a time of confusion and drift, of hectic and aimless loitering. I had left Pathé in 1965, and in 1967 I was still without work. It was the most miserable and humiliating time. Money was getting short and depression began to set in. Will I ever work again? I wondered. I would go to dinner parties but everybody I saw had a job, and I usually came home demoralised. Everybody was so successful. I heard myself flattering people, making myself interesting, in the hope that some work would emerge. Those who had solicited my company now moved away, invented excuses or looked for something else. Many friends were as nice as before, but I could feel their boredom creeping in. Nobody really likes a loser and I had, for too long, been a winner.

I began to loathe myself, living out fully the unending drama of self-doubt. I went to the movies in the afternoon or hung around the streets trying to pick someone up. I sat at home looking at the phone, waiting for it to ring, with news of some job application I had sent out. One day out of the blue an invitation and a ticket arrived from Raymond, and I decided I might as well be miserable in the sun. I wisely and meanly changed the first-class ticket he sent me for one in economy with a return trip via the States, and set off.

Raymond of Caracas was the leading hairdresser from Venezuela, and he lived in style. He had a penthouse apartment, and while he coiffed Caracas's *beau monde*, I was driven in a limousine to the city's exclusive sports club. I quickly got bored. His sister (or was it his mother?) was also sharing his flat and hoped that Raymond would one day marry. The nature of our relationship had to be kept secret, of course, an arrangement which at our combined age of eighty was totally ridiculous. The whole thing was a mistake. In St Tropez everything about him had been fun and light-hearted, but in Caracas all became terribly conventional. It was like meeting a gorgeous ski instructor in the summer on Hampstead Heath. After three weeks of this enforced play-acting and Venezuelan *dolce vita* I said goodbye to Raymond of Caracas and caught the next plane to Los Angeles. I didn't even bother to pack. All I took with me were two pairs of jeans and a couple of T-shirts.

It was the first time that I had been to the West Coast. I looked up Christopher Isherwood and Don Bachardy. They lived in Santa Monica, in a small house built into the steep wall of the canyon. The sea was gradually eating the land away and you practically had to slide down a narrow passage to reach their house. The living-room was spartanly furnished but had many books and modern paintings. Christopher was away, but Don made my stay memorable by showing me Los Angeles and making me love it, in all its glorious vulgarity and its manifestation of the American way of life. He took me to the cemetery of Forest Lawn and to Disneyland, or we lazed the day away on the beach, happy as two sandboys.

David Hockney was also in Los Angeles. The last time I had seen him was on his annual visit to his family in Bradford (his mother still thought that it was the sun that bleached his hair). On that occasion we drove in his new Morris Minor convertible to visit Keith Vaughan, who had bought a country house in Harrow Hill in Essex, with a little natural pool we splashed about in. David had brought a friend from the States, Bobby, the all-American boy, pretty, sexy and quite dim. They had come to Europe by boat, the revamped posh *France*, for David was now terribly successful. Something must have gone wrong, because a few weeks later he announced that Bobby was gone. All that remained of Robert Lee Earles was a drawing of a delicious bottom entitled *'France'*; it didn't even show Bobby's face. I believe he became a go-go dancer.

It was wonderful to see David again. He had totally set into Los Angeles. He stayed mostly in the house of his agent Nick Wilder. Around the pool were always hordes of naked boys. Most of them ended up in one of David's pool paintings. He also had a studio somewhere downtown. He had a new lover, Peter Schlesinger, who must have been all of nineteen years old (he was still in school). Soon there were drawings and paintings of him all over the place: Peter coming out of a pool, Peter stretched out on a table, Peter sitting in a chair. David never stopped drawing and painting. Whenever you looked up he was sketching you.

He took me on one of those tours along Hollywood Boulevard to look at the houses of the great stars. Tudor mansions, Rhine castles and Roman temples, all part of the dream factory. I watched the swooning eyes of my fellow tourists, scanning the façades in the hope that the figures of Gloria Swanson or Marlene Dietrich would peek out from the drawn curtains. Few realised that their dreams were as unsubstantial as the houses, concoctions of plaster, pretending to be wood or brick. All these things delighted David, and they too would eventually find their way into his paintings.

After a while I packed my bags again and hitchhiked to San Francisco. This was the era of flower-power. It was all about loving each other and about experimenting with life and drugs. I wore flowers in my hair, and danced all night around fires on the beach. One night someone just took me by the hand. He was on his way to Mexico and invited me along. His name was Oliver. We had very little money but we travelled in an old

Chevrolet and slept mostly on the road or in strange motels, which reminded me of the movies.

By the time we reached Mexico City the flowers had wilted and so had
my travelling companion. I was again alone and I didn't mind. Mexico
City was not yet polluted or infested by so many tourists. Life was incredibly cheap. I bought a guide book, *Mexico on $5 a Day*, but most of the
time I spent less than that. I stayed in little inns and ate *tacos de carne*
bought from the street vendors, all washed down with generous helpings
of tequila. I fell in love with Mexican food, architecture, the people and
their music. I visited the ruins of Teotihuacan and the old town of Tepozo-
lan. I sometimes hitchhiked on the back of a truck or shared a seat with
Indians and goats on a crowded bus. I had not felt so free for years.

In Puebla, with its seventeenth-century buildings and its churches
glowing in the dry white sun, I stayed in a small inn, sleeping in an open
patio. In San Cristobal I found a room in a guesthouse run by some Scandinavian archaeologists. One of them took me in his little twin-engine
plane to Palenque, the most remote place I had ever seen. No road led to it
and there was only one house. I was given a hammock to sleep in, which I
strung from two hooks. In the magnificent setting of the deep green semi-
tropical rain forest lay, hidden from sight, the mournful beauty of the
Mayan temples. In the morning, the forest was cool and dark, but then
with the sun rising a misty vapour began to emerge above the emerald sea
of the trees and hung there like a cloud.

After three days of this perfect solitude I was told that another small
plane was coming to fetch me. I waited for five hours in total silence,
interrupted only by the noise of the birds in the trees. A white sock hanging from the tree served to measure the wind. I wondered what would
happen if no one ever came. To step out of my life like this would be wonderful.

Suddenly I heard the roar of the engine of an old plane that turned out
to be carrying four people: the pilot and his son, an American journalist
and a very pregnant Indian woman on her way to hospital. I climbed into
the already overcrowded plane and ascended, while the overgrown ruins
of the temples began to disappear. We flew right above the tops of the
trees, a marvellous feeling of freedom and danger. All of a sudden the
Mexican woman began to howl as she went into labour. The contractions
were coming very fast and we had two hours yet to fly. The pilot was
trying to activate his radio which of course did not work. The American,
father of three children, looked very pale.

I tried to remember the scene from *Gone with the Wind* where Melanie
gave birth. I knew that something had to be cut. After half an hour, the

contractions came in great waves. I told the American, very coolly, to ster-
ilise some scissors in mouthwash, which I was certain he would be carrying. I spread the woman out on the floor, trying to remain calm. Then
suddenly we had some radio contact. The plane looked pretty messy by
now. Ten minutes later we touched the ground, and the woman gave birth
to a screaming little Indian right on the tarmac. An ambulance was standing by. I felt very proud when the pilot congratulated me. Two minutes
later I was sick. I blamed the tortillas and pulque, which an old Indian in
Palenque had given me.

When I returned to London in July, I had been away for five months. I was
thin, brown, totally broke and still out of work. I threw myself into a hectic social life. Many people who had been a novelty or fascination for me
suddenly looked hollow and unrecognisable. I resumed the now familiar
and depressing trawl for possible employers or contacts. I tried television.
I went to see Stephen Hearst from the BBC and Jeremy Isaacs. Everybody
was very friendly, very civilised and very interested in the things I had
done. I must have seen over a hundred people, among them Harry Saltzman, the producer of the James Bond movies. Saltzman seemed interested. He liked a treatment I wrote for him on the life of Colette, and there
were further meetings, each with new hopes and disappointments.

By the beginning of 1968 I was willing to take on any job. I did not dare
leave the house in case someone phoned. Every morning I skimmed the
papers to look through the employment ads. I suffered bouts of depression, a thing I have never known before, forever looking eye to eye at who
I was or who I might have become. Days of dark loneliness were followed
by a heightened appetite for new people, for new sexual encounters. I was
at my most promiscuous. Sex became like a drug.

One morning I saw an ad in the papers: BOAC was looking for a PR
man. The successful candidate had to speak at least two languages, know
how to deal with people and have a good dress sense. I put on a grey flannel suit and presented myself. I spoke to some personnel lady in German,
French and Italian and showed her my record at the Europa Union. I did
not get the job.

That night I dined at Peter Shaffer's. At the table sat a man who would
change the course of my life, the journalist James Mossman. Two weeks
later I was employed by the BBC.

13

To Be a Witness: Berlin, Biafra, Cuba
1968–1969

On 4 April 1968, I signed my first contract with the B B C to work for the
Current Affairs Department as a researcher for *Democracy on Trial*, a
series of three *Panorama* programmes examining democracy in Germany,
England and the United States. James Mossman, who was the maker of
this series, had simply decided that it was absurd that as he put it 'a man
of your qualifications can't even find a job with the airlines'.

I had known Jim for a number of years. He and Peter Shaffer had been
at university together. Jim was only three years older than I was, but he
struck me as someone much more mature. He seemed to be the very
image of the well-brought-up reserved Englishman, a throwback to the
Edwardian era, graceful of bearing and utterance. He was lanky and good-
looking, with slightly stooped shoulders. He had very beautiful hands,
which he used when talking, and an infectious smile. When I first met him
he gave the impression of someone very cool and detached, a debonair
personality somehow always on guard. He had a very sharp mind and a
superior intelligence, but he carried his cultural knowledge rather wearily,
like a suitcase with too many unnecessary things. He was also wonderful
company. His wit, his sense of humour and all-pervading humanity was a
source of joy for others.

Mossman was a famous television journalist, one of the breed of reporters of passionate integrity and journalistic brilliance. The story of his
life was fantastic: three years liaising between the Greek army and communist guerrillas after the war, a stint in the Foreign Service and then in
M I 5. He had been imprisoned in Egypt during the Suez crisis and spent a
year in Australia. As a journalist, he had worked all over Asia and set up a
newspaper in Singapore. In 1958 he had joined the famous *Panorama*
team, for which he filed reports from the Mekong River, Macao, the Andes
and from all over the world. His language was always full of compassion
and yet without theatricality. He destroyed the myth of those who promised cure and salvation through politics or religious doctrine. 'The war is
total, it has spread its wings over an entire people. No one is safe from its
arbitrary miseries,' he reported from Vietnam, and from Peru he wrote:
'Year after year, from the stink of the worst slum in the world, they raise

James Mossman

the Queen of Heaven with the patient desperation of the undelivered.'

To be allowed to work with such a man was a great challenge. Would I be up to it? Fortunately, the first programme I was engaged on was about Germany: at least I could be useful there.

The Current Affairs programmes were still transmitted from the BBC's most unglamorous building, in Lime Grove, a small and ordinary residential street in Shepherd's Bush. It was a cluster of rundown barrack-like film studios linked by tortuous corridors, bridges and underground passages with dripping pipes. Many years before, Alfred Hitchcock had shot *The Thirty-Nine Steps* and *The Man Who Knew Too Much* here, and in 1949 the BBC had moved in. Many famous programmes – *Panorama, Tonight, That Was the Week That Was, Monitor* and others – were broadcast from here. The canteen looked more like a third-class waiting-room in a provincial railway station than the place where the *crème de la crème* of British broadcasting was taking its lunch. The compassionate voyeurs at catastrophes, whose faces were instantly recognised by millions, sat crammed at tables with plastic tops or queued with a tray in their hands: Cliff Michelmore, David Frost, Alan Whicker, Fyfe Robertson, Richard Kee, Robin Day and Ludovic Kennedy.

At this time the reporters – at least the top ones – were in charge of their programmes. Producers arranged the technicalities of the production, but the stamp of the programme came from the person who wrote it and the cameraman who gave it visual shape. This led to much friction. When I joined the BBC, a horde of young producers had come to the fore. They were no longer content just to be subservient to the almighty reporter; they also wanted to shape the contents in a creative way.

In Jim's case, he was in charge. Not that he was particularly interested in the images: he left this to his trusted cameraman, Erik Dürschmied, originally from Vienna. Erik was one of the top cameramen in England, and eyed with suspicion a newcomer from Berlin whose only experience was making films on Persil. But as I was only hired as researcher, a position which ranked even lower than producer, he did not mind my presence. Eventually I would grow very fond of this grumpy, passionate and talented artist who could spot the essence of a scene in minutes and bring it to life in his pictures.

The three of us set off for Germany to examine the new democracy. It is difficult to describe my elation at working again, and in a medium I found instantly fascinating. Making commercials had given me the necessary technical background, and the mixture of journalism and film-making in this job suited my temperament.

The encounter with Germany was strange and often difficult. So much of what we filmed was part of a Germany I wanted to have nothing to do with. We filmed a reception for the new Bundeswehr in a small Bavarian village, with minister Franz-Josef Strauss strutting about in *Lederhosen*. We also covered a party rally of the new Neo-Nazi party, and Jim interviewed its leader von Thadden in his little semi-detached bungalow in Hanover. All this was painful and fascinating; everywhere one only had to scratch the surface to find some 'brown' residues. But I was now a journalist and I had to keep personal feelings at bay, as Jim told me.

I was glad to go to Berlin, which still had the old pioneer feeling and was not so ostentatiously rich as West Germany. The 1968 student uprising had erupted here, after a protest against the visit of the Shah of Iran during which a young student, Benno Ohnesorg, had been shot by the police. It was a key moment in Berlin's history. People, especially young ones, were motivated by the same dream as those in Paris or in America. They hoped that they could form a new, better and more just world than their parents and teachers.

Not only students, the intellectuals too had joined in this great collective dream. While the so-called revolution of 1968 shook Europe so profoundly – André Malraux had spoken about a crisis of civilisation – it hardly created a ripple in London. In Germany on the other hand everyone was discussing politics. The bookshops were full of the writings of the new gurus – Theodor Adorno, Max Horkheimer, Georg Lukács, Walter Benjamin and most of all of Wilhelm Reich and Herbert Marcuse, the two 'liberators' of my own student years. On the walls of my old university were slogans like 'Under the asphalt lies the beach' and Paul Valéry's 'Le vent se lève, il faut tenter à vivre'.[1]

There were new and younger heroes, their names were Rudi Dutschke and Daniel Cohn-Bendit, a twenty-three-year-old German student who lived in Paris. They had led the students onto the barricades.

I had arranged an interview with Rudi Dutschke, a pale and deeply *sympathique* young man of great earnestness. Jim and he liked and trusted each other immediately. After Jim's first question, Erik said 'cut' and announced that the film was jammed in the camera. We decided to postpone the interview for one hour and Dutschke left to do some errands. From the window I watched him leave the building and get on his bike, when I heard a shot and saw him fall to the ground. Jim went frantic. 'Where is Erik?' he shouted. It was a journalist's nightmare. I realised suddenly that personal shock had to come second for the sake of a good picture.

1 'The wind is rising, we must try to live.'

The man who shot Dutschke was a twenty-three-year-old worker, Joseph Bachmann, who read right-wing papers such as the *Deutsche Nationalzeitung*. He did not even know Dutschke. 'Are you Rudi Dutschke?' he had asked timidly before he fired, and then he added: 'You dirty communist pig!'

That night we followed the students' march to the hated right-wing press centre, Springer House. 'Dutschke lives, if Springer burns,' they shouted. There were police on horses everywhere, and when the students broke the great plate-glass window in the entrance hall, the police charged. There were 10,000 demonstrators against 20,000 policemen, tear gas, truncheons, water cannons against stones, bottles and sticks. 'Three bullets for Rudi Dutschke / A bloody assassination / Who is the one who fired / Oh Germany, your murderers,'[1] wrote the poet Wolf Biermann, still living in East Berlin, unable to leave. It was frightening. As Jim and I took cover under a car with glass and bullets flying, the Springer House went up in flames. Erik stood filming right in the middle of the menacing crowd, a mixture of bravery, stubbornness and the desire always to get the best picture. As for Rudi Dutschke, mortally wounded, he and his American wife went into exile in England, then Sweden. One could sometimes meet him at Hans Werner Henze's house in Marino. He died on Christmas Eve 1979 from the consequences of the attack. His murderer had committed suicide in prison.

Democracy on Trial: Germany was transmitted on 23 May, at nine o'clock. It was the first time my name appeared on a television screen. It gave me a strange *frisson* when I saw the credit, Research: Klaus-Peter Adam.

The *Observer* called it the best documentary of the year. Jim was generous and let the Head of the Department, the powerful David Webster, know about my contribution. A few days later I had an interview with him. I heard that Huw Wheldon had also put in a good word for me. Three months later I had another job, this time as a producer. Tony Smith, editor of *24 Hours*, had engaged me for this nightly political magazine programme. The story I had been asked to film was about Czech refugees in Vienna.

In August 1968 Russian tanks were once more rolling against civilians, this time in Prague. The journalist Linda Blandford, an attractive dark-haired young woman of determined disposition, fetched me in the morning from

1 'Drei Kugeln auf Rudi Dutschke / Ein blutiges Attentat / Wer hat da geschossen / Ach Deutschland, Deine Mörder.'

Earls Terrace. After a few words of introduction she looked at me and said: 'Are you German?' Linda was Jewish and did not think much of the Germans. At the airport in Vienna I met the BBC crew, a typical film crew: three experienced men, who had done it all, seen it all and let you know it. They did not believe much in the need for a director. I was determined not to let my inexperience show and I was the only one who spoke German.

Linda turned out to be warm, helpful and very professional, and she gladly took direction. I tried to use all the skills I had picked up in making commercials. While I lined up the shots, I sent her to the hairdresser, then I rehearsed them with her. The crew looked on in boredom. Reporters usually just did their piece and that was it. Nobody rehearsed takes, nobody cared about the looks of reporters. I kept cool, very cool. Luckily Linda thought that this was marvellous, it smelt of real cinema.

A few days later we were back in London. In the cutting-room I felt much safer, for I had learned how to cut at Pathé. My editor did not like it, but I told him exactly what I wanted and it did not take me long to gain the reputation of 'that bloody German who is very difficult'.

The Czech refugee story was a success. The management seemed to like it. Some of my new colleagues also did and it was noticed by the press. I breathed a sigh of relief.

Linda and I became friends. I think she was the only one who saw through the whole game, but she liked chutzpah.

The day on 24 Hours always started with the same routine. The twenty-odd reporters, producers and researchers assembled at 9.30 around a large table, littered with the daily papers. For about half an hour everybody was buried behind pages, trying to distil the newsworthy stories of the day. Then Tony Smith began to question everyone. The programme for the night was being formulated.

In times of political upheaval the priorities were quickly sorted out, on quieter days the choice of the items was hotly debated. Everybody scrambled to the phones to set up the stories. People spoke to the BBC offices in New Delhi, Paris or New York, or contacted 'stringers' in Rome or Beirut. A link line had to be fixed with the German finance minister, the British embassy in Cairo had to be contacted. Reporters were being dispatched to the trouble spots of the world. Producers began to arrange filming, researchers skimmed old newspaper files to prepare the interviews, and graphic artists drew up charts and maps. A filmed report from Washington became obsolete, pushed out by a more urgent one from Hongkong.

For me this was the most stimulating work I had ever done. Speed and flexibility were paramount in the race for actuality. The work on a daily magazine required an alert mind, an acute sense of priorities and very little *amour propre*. It was challenging, competitive, informative, and it suited my temperament.

Working for a magazine like *24 Hours* meant that you were called upon to do all sorts of stories. My next one was on the Farnborough Air Show. An air show is one of the least inspiring subjects for a young director. I shot it like a commercial, with no commentary and a pop song instead. Then came *Old People*, a story about the plight of the poor in London. I filmed an old people's home and meals on wheels arriving in a council flat. I shot it like a mini-feature with closeups of faces and details of their possessions. I had also asked permission to film a pauper's funeral. There was no speech, no music, no flowers, no relatives, no friends, just the crew and the vicar at the graveside, who seemed not to mind when I asked for a retake. Fyfe Robertson spoke the commentary. Fyfe was a lovely man, with a strong Scottish accent, a tweed jacket and hat. He gave me much encouragement. 'You're different, lad,' he said. 'Make the institution serve you, not the other way around.' Advice I tried to follow.

I did not realise then, but I know now, that these little filmlets were different from most other magazine items in Current Affairs. The filmic treatment and approach of an ambitious and eager newcomer made them stand out. Later, when I was well established, I would often notice young newcomers bringing the same kind of freshness to programmes that we, the old guard, had lost in the routine of our work.

I had reached the first step on the ladder to success and this pleased me greatly. I could now look my friends in the eye, and could invite them for dinner without ulterior motives.

'Dinner at K. P. A. with David Hockney and Peter [Shaffer],' Keith Vaughan wrote in his diaries:

> Good evening. The more I see of D. H. the more he impresses me. He has all the best qualities of his generation. Modest and self-confident, honest in speech, unconcerned with impressing, yet considerate and well-mannered, impatient with all fraudulent or compromised behaviour, ardent, curious, warm-hearted, uncorrupted (and probably incorruptible) by success – his generation have never known dire poverty I suppose. I feel so much better after such an evening.[1]

Keith admired the openness of the new generation, especially in sexual matters, although he could never quite be as open about himself. In 1967

1   Keith Vaughan, *Journals 1937–1977*, published 1989 by John Murray Ltd, London.

homosexuality had been made legal, and we rejoiced in the newly-won freedom. Ian McKellen, who lived in the flat below mine, had not publicly come out yet, but we talked a lot about politicising the whole homosexual issue. Keith on the other hand thought it was better to keep it secret. 'The whole thing seems to be in bad taste when it is flaunted in the face of the public,' he noted in his diaries. 'K P thought this point of view feeble and timid. Yet it seemed to me that deviant sexual behaviour, provided that it is not actually criminal, as opposed to merely illegal, can perfectly well be indulged provided a little tact is shown for the sensibilities of others.'

Keith felt no real guilt about his homosexuality, his whole work was an affirmation of it, but he belonged to the generation of people brought up with the idea that it had to be kept a secret. I remember how crushed John Gielgud was when he told me about his arrest. 'I saw all the journalists outside and I felt like dying. I had let everybody down, my friends, my colleagues.'

James Mossman had not only become my professional mentor, but our friendship had grown into something central to me. I noticed how my cheerful friend had become very introspective. Something strange had happened to him and I did not quite understand what. He began to talk about the uselessness of his work, even his life, and he sometimes wept. For all his intelligence and common sense, he was incapable of controlling the sadness and desperation that would suddenly well up in him. Jim had a new lover, Louis Hanssom; Louis was a very gifted potter, making large sculpture-like pots. He also wrote plays. He was erudite and very intense, and Jim was totally under his spell.

Most of Jim's friends did not like Louis, with his abrasive manner and eccentric behaviour, and his obsession with drugs. He was neither witty nor funny, he did not fit. These were the very qualities Jim liked about him. I liked Louis, but I also soon discovered that there was something destructive about him. He made Jim question the worth of his life and it was he also who made Jim weep. One evening, Louis spoke about wanting to kill himself, and he wanted us to film the act. 'A really courageous gesture from the three of us,' he taunted. Jim became very depressed and then Louis just walked out on us.

In September I left for Cairo. I had an assignment to film the oil tanker stuck by the blockade in the Suez Canal. I was a bit nervous on account of my Jewish background. At that time Jews simply could not travel to Egypt, and journalists always had two passports, one with a visa to Israel, one without. The first thing we were shown was the destruction of Somalia by

Israeli bombs. I tried to get an interview with Nasser, but only managed to get a minister. The rest of the filming was easy. We shot a day on the mostly American and British ships. The poor sailors were bored stiff. Everything was very casual, people ran around in shorts, it did not look like war at all. They had organised a sports competition between the many ships and issued a first-day cover. We were also allowed on board a Russian tanker. Everything was very serious, there was a lot of drill, and commands shouted in front of the British cameras. I thought it was perfectly ridiculous, those poor chaps in their big uniforms in the sweltering heat. Of course there was no sports competition and no stamps.

The *24 Hours* items had to be on the air as quickly as possible, and often there was no time to wait for the producer to be back in London. One was expected to ship them with a cutting order on the next plane. Someone in London would cut it in accordance with your written instructions. It had usually been broadcast by the time you came home.

I disliked this, for most of my films were 'made' in the cutting-room and in the original concept of the story. During the filming one has little influence, always relying on the weather, the circumstances, and on the mood of the people you film and those you are filming with. I discovered too that travel on assignment was not as exciting as people always assumed. Cooped up in the Hilton Hotel in Cairo, I had my first experience of the loneliness of the director.

The linkage of the crew with the director was very often them-and-us. Four men who hardly knew each other were thrown together for a few days for one job. I was still the outcast. I had no wife or girlfriend to talk about, I knew nothing about football or cricket, I wasn't even English. The crew was usually getting drunk in a bar while I rushed to the museums or tried to see a play. When I began to make longer documentaries, things changed, but on the whole the filming period was always my least favourite one. How many times I found myself in a distant part of the world, longing for the conversation of a few compatible friends.

One evening I received an urgent summons from the Controller of BBC1 and I rushed to Lime Grove. I had not met Paul Fox yet, but he had a big reputation in the corporation for toughness and corporate spirit. He was sitting behind a desk, an impressive man with a large frame which filled the small office easily. 'You still have a German passport, Peter?' he asked. When I confirmed that I did, he continued: 'The BBC has to send someone into Biafra and that someone can't be British. Think about it and phone me tomorrow morning. This is a dangerous job and a big one.'

Pictures of atrocities of the deadly and bloody civil war between the Ibos living in the province of Biafra and the Yorubas had filled the television screens for weeks. We were not yet anaesthetised by the media, the war was not yet the daily wallpaper it would soon become, and everybody was deeply moved by the suffering, especially of the children.

The political situation was complicated: old alliances and economic interest made strange bedfellows. The British were on the Nigerian side and so were the Egyptians, and through the Egyptians also the Russians. The French were on the side of the beleaguered Biafrans.

It was indeed a dangerous mission to infiltrate Biafra and to report for the BBC, the arch enemy. If found out, one could be shot. Paul Fox knew this, I am sure. I knew it too, but there was no doubt in my mind that I had to go, not because it would be a journalist's coup but because of the need to tell the story of hundreds of thousands of victims. Linda and Jim, whom I consulted, only strengthened my determination. Both were journalists at heart, for whom the role was, as Jim had put it, 'to tell the truth, untarnished by sentimentalism, unmodified by any hint of conformity'.

Paul Fox gave me a French reporter, Olivier Todd, and a French crew. He also arranged for a few hours of training with the BBC health unit. I learned about bandages and injections, and when they handed me a special Red Cross emergency kit, I realised how serious it all was.

In the meantime the office was busy arranging visas through a mysterious office in Geneva. On the last evening I once more went through my clothes to make sure that all the labels that could identify me as someone living in London had been removed. To my horror I discovered in my health certificate the incriminating stamp: 'Yellow fever inoculation, BBC Health Unit.' It was almost midnight. I phoned Paul Fox at home. 'I'll phone you back in a minute.' Twenty minutes later I was on my way to the Television Centre. The BBC doctor had been called out of bed and she changed the offensive stamp.

I did not sleep much that night. I phoned my closest friends and Renate, and then with the first plane I was off to Paris to meet the crew. This was 3 December 1968. Olivier Todd, tall and good-looking with impeccable English, was the typical French intellectual. Jean-Paul Sartre was godfather to his children. Before becoming a famous journalist and writer he had been a teacher. Our cameraman, Raymond Grosjean, was a small, vivacious, randy French version of Erik Dürschmied. He proudly showed me his clapperboard with the blood of the Vietnam war on it.

We were to leave the next day for Lisbon, from where planes took off to São Tomé. Unable to sleep, I went to a little bar and ran into Françoise Sagan. I had not seen her for years. She was with a group of witty Frenchmen. I joined them for a short time. Something bothered me and it sat like a piece of grit in my eyes. I suddenly could no longer cope and got up. Françoise followed me to the door. 'Forgive my friends,' she said. 'I wish you good luck.' The sad and sincere face of Françoise Sagan was the last I saw of a world I had once cherished. Once more, I was becoming someone else.

São Tomé was the last 'official' link with the outside world. From here only Red Cross planes would fly into Biafra. Planes could only take off at night for their highly dangerous missions. At the airport many people were waiting: politicians, arms dealers, journalists, missionaries and nuns. Everybody wanted to be involved in one way or another. We had to wait for two days, it seemed eternal. The unknown was unnerving, even for the others, who had been in Vietnam. Raymond followed his favourite pastime, chasing girls, while Olivier very calmly read a philosophical treatise. I, in my organised German *Hausfrau* way, bought a large parcel of emergency food: crackers, Nescafé, tinned condensed milk and corned beef.

In the middle of the second night Olivier woke me up. A plane was ready to leave. We hurried to the airport. In the far corner of the tarmac stood a small plane, marked with large red crosses, but we discovered that it was carrying ammunition. It was too late to turn back and we were eager to go. We climbed on board. The seats had all been removed and we had to crouch on the floor. Through the window I saw a priest blessing the plane. Then we were off. Silence descended upon everybody. In the almost total darkness, I could just make out Olivier's face, silhouetted against the sky. 'Will we ever come back?' I thought.

The flight took about two hours. Nobody spoke. I could hear the beating of my heart. Suddenly there was a terrible noise of gunfire. The plane was lit by red flares exploding all around us. The Nigerian anti-aircraft guns had spotted us. The tiniest hit would have blown us to smithereens. The lethal boxes shook. Then, for a second, the lights went on on the ground, just long enough for the pilot to see the airfield before all was dark again. From the bumping of the wheels I knew that we had touched ground. The firing had not stopped and someone shouted: 'Leave everything on board and run.' We fell out of the plane and ran into the bush. After twenty minutes the firing had stopped and people hurried towards the plane to unload the boxes. We too climbed on board and fetched our equipment and the few pieces of luggage.

We were escorted into a little hut. The country might have been in ruins, but the nation had to assert itself. We had to get in line. Even here, it was a world of tidy conformity. An officer sat behind a wooden table

and stamped our passports: 'Entrance permitted. Chief Immigration Officer.' It was by far the largest stamp in my passport, bigger than that of the
United States. Then we had to wait again, watched by the chilly politeness
of officialdom. In the dark room I could just make out the other passengers. Later I found out who they were: a young journalist from *Die Zeit*,
Haug von Kühnheim; a nun who turned out to be a member of the Spanish Royal Family; an arms dealer from Milan; and, to our horror, a British
delegation led by Lord Brockway. Olivier appeared regularly on *Panorama*.
What would happen if he recognised him? He looked at us with one of
those long inquisitive stares. I just managed to put my finger to my lips.
Lord Brockway understood instantly. Later that day, we learned that an
ITV film team was sitting in prison 'awaiting decisions'.

At dawn an army truck took us into Enugu, the provisional capital of
Biafra, a small place of ramshackle houses. Everywhere sunken-eyed and
half-starved people on the run, without homes or possessions. The once
lush and fertile fields were singed to brown dust. The sun was just coming
up, but it was already stifling hot. We were shown to our quarters, a
wooden house with two small rooms; on the floor, three bloodstained
mattresses. I took out the disinfectant and poured it over them. Olivier
shared a room with Jean, the sound man, I shared the remaining mattress
with Raymond. There was a little piece of paper informing us that lunch
was being served in the press club, another wooden shack. Two long tables
with benches. There were about twenty men all looking at empty metal
plates, journalists from all over the world. There was a sort of fraternity
feeling but we made sure that everybody understood that I was an independent German film-maker with a French crew. I spoke as little English
as possible and exaggerated my German accent, which made Olivier
laugh. Someone poured some rice and bits of meat on our plate. I looked
at it. 'What is it?' I asked my neighbour, a silent bearded fellow. 'Rat,' came
the cool answer. He was from a Midwest newspaper and had been there
for two weeks. I couldn't eat, neither could the others.

We stayed fourteen days. Every day I gave out a ration of cigarettes,
malaria pills, crackers, some sweetened milk and corned beef. Sometimes
we managed to buy bananas or some beans. Sometimes we even ate at the
press club or with the army. There was no bathroom in our house. Every
morning we poured buckets of water over each other, grateful to have
some soap. I knew that to survive we had to give our life some structure. I
insisted that everybody shave every day. As a result they nicknamed me
grand-mère. During the day we filmed mostly at the Front, in the camps or
in hospitals. Raymond was courageous: like a child he had no notion of
danger. During an air raid he stood up pointing his camera at a deadly

plane strafing a village. I often got angry with him. No piece of film is worth a life.

When we were not working we helped in hospital. One could not sit around waiting, or one would have gone mad. Four French doctors looked after hundreds and hundreds of wounded. Most of the time they had to operate without antiseptic or anaesthetic. I saw a man's leg being amputated while I held his head. Normally the slightest bit of blood, even on film, makes me feel faint, but here I could cope. I tried not to show emotion, but the suffering of the children was too much to bear, thousands of emaciated little brown bodies with large eyes, staring at you with incomprehension. Once a child died while we were filming. I shouted at Raymond to stop the camera – it has no place when someone dies, only prayers and tears. There were lots of both. At night we fell asleep out of sheer exhaustion and sadness akin to despair.

Every day, at lunchtime, the Nigerians attacked from the air, Russian planes piloted by Egyptian soldiers with British ammunition, killing people for oil. A nightmare tied up with global strategy and lived out by a poor people who knew little about politics nor the places where they are made. Their daily diet was death and hunger.

Once I was caught alone in a field. I could see the plane coming towards me, strafing the road. A man collapsed twenty yards from me. I lay there with only one thought: 'Oh God, let it not hit me.' I pulled my arms and my legs in like a child in a womb.

People behave so differently in extreme situations. I saw nuns' faces glowing with their mission and a general who quietly read Henry James in his tent. We ran into a girl in uniform, Ghislaine Morel, a Swiss photographer. She lived with one of the generals and loved war. She said: 'It makes us all the same, no difference of sex, class or colour.' After the war she wanted to live there. I was tempted to tell her who I was but it was not wise.

We filmed the few pockets of 'normality', surrealistic scenes: a black judge with a horsehair wig condemning, in the Queen's English, a thief to be hanged; a groom and bride in white chiffon dress hurrying into church, right in the middle of an air raid, the church bells almost drowned out by the shooting.

One evening we found a typewritten note on our door, inviting all journalists 'for an exchange of niceties in the palace'. The palace was a white wooden house, heavily guarded, where President Ojukwu held office. He greeted us heartily, thanking us for bringing the Biafran cause to the attention of the world. A few days later we were granted an interview – a wonderful-looking man who pleaded passionately for his country's independence from Nigeria. His voice rose like an actor's on stage. Olivier and I totally fell for it. A few months later he had fled the country, taking with him a couple of Rolls-Royces, leaving behind a brutalised, defeated population who had believed in him, just as we did.

After two weeks, when we ran out of film, I decided that it was time to go home. A few days later I managed to find another Red Cross plane. We took off again at night and landed in Libreville. We took a taxi to a hotel, a proper hotel.

Everybody had their own room, and their own bath. Outside my balcony was the sea, and I watched people go bathing. The next morning no one wanted to move: we were physically and morally exhausted. The idea of meeting people, friends, colleagues, family, all asking questions, waiting to be told how it was, was unthinkable. We were *der Welt abhanden gekommen*, lost to the world, a small unit, living under a spell which would be too painful to break. We stayed two more days, almost in silence. Simple things like water, a freshly made bed, food, the privacy of one's own room, took on new meaning. Gradually words came back, even jokes and laughter. On 22 December we arrived in Le Bourget, a city lit by Christmas trees, shop windows bursting with goods.

I flew to London. Prunella, soothing, intelligent, as so many times before and after, fetched me at the airport. She did not have to ask questions; she knew.

I went straight into the cutting-room and edited all over Christmas and New Year. I could only bear to see a few very close friends; Prunella, Keith, Hanna and Rudolf. Together we toasted in the New Year. From now on and for a long time, life would get better.

The programme went out on 9 January. Seven million people watched it. I think it is still one of the best programmes I ever made. I can say this without blushing, because it was not really me who gave it strength, it was the circumstances. Reality had imprinted itself on us all: the cameraman, the reporter, the director. It was as if the pictures dictated themselves, shouted out to be assembled. Each frame told such a powerful story that it would have been difficult to fail.

There was a note on my desk from Paul Fox: 'Congratulations for getting in and out of Biafra. The people involved deserve enormous credit for what they achieved. Altogether a great piece of work.'

I had set out to make a film which would shake up people's minds. Maybe I succeeded. 'There may have been more appalling sights on television, but nothing I had seen previously on Biafra had moved me to such dismay and compassion as this film, with its juxtaposition of horribly starving kids against scenes of Life Going On,' wrote *The Times*. The programme outraged the Nigerians and created a political row. 'Nigeria threatens to ban BBC,' ran the headline in the *Sunday Times*. The BBC upheld the fiction of the independent film company but was nevertheless banned from filming in Nigeria.

In Lime Grove, I had suddenly moved to the forefront. Jim was very proud. I now sat at the table of the top journalists.

A few days before the transmission, I had gone to Paris to record the commentary with Olivier Todd. I also began to prepare my next story, 'The House of Christian Dior'. It included interviews with the designer Marc Bohan, the writer Louise de Vilmorin and the socialite Jacqueline de Ribes – an ironical contrast, but such is the life of a journalist. 'It's a job,' Jim used to say. *24 Hours* had asked me to make a programme for budget day. I thought a profile of the firm which makes so much money by creating frivolity and luxury would be a suitable and diverting item to relieve the gloom. I had another reason to go to Paris: Prunella's aunt, the designer and architect Eileen Gray, was in hospital. I wanted to see her, perhaps for the last time.

I had met Eileen for the first time in 1960. She was eighty-two years old. The woman who is now regarded as a pioneer of modern design, and in the 1920s and 1930s was celebrated in architectural circles, had been totally forgotten. Prunella had sometimes mentioned her aunt, but with the modesty so characteristic of the two women, neither their success nor their careers were much discussed.

I had no idea who Eileen Gray was when I drove Prunella Clough from the station in St Raphaël to St Tropez. We drove to the little quartier of Ste Anne. Eileen lived in the middle of some vineyards in a small *cabanon*, a low country house like thousands all over Provence. I noticed immediately the unusual bold abstract design in blue glass in the front door. An upright lady in a blue trouser suit with a silk blouse opened the door. She was hard of hearing and one of her eyes was clouded behind a dark lens. We were asked into the large vaulted room of unobtrusive simplicity with some modern furniture which, as I discovered later, she had designed herself. A large blue vase with white flowers stood on the floor.

Eileen began immediately to shout for Louise, her housekeeper. 'Des cocktails s'il vous plaît!' Visitors were obviously an event. Honed down by age and illness Eileen led a solitary life. The only person sharing it was Louise, who had joined her in 1927 at the age of nineteen and remained with her for the rest of Eileen's life. Louise appeared, a lively peasant woman, carrying a little tray with small glasses also made of blue glass.

Eileen Gray 1926, by Berenice Abbott

It was the beginning of a long and exceptional friendship during which I learned much about the changing life of this great artist. I tried to capture part of it in my first book, *Eileen Gray, A Biography*, which I wrote twenty-five years later.

In 1968, when I visited her in the small hospital room, Eileen was still totally unknown. The faithful Louise had slept on the floor right next to her mistress's bed. Eileen had often spoken to me about her wish to die. She had at one time shown me a little ivory-inlaid pistol, holding this fatal object in her trembling hand as a child holds a toy. With the loss of her few friends, solitude was closing in. 'Death seems to have forgotten me, it is time that I was off.' The fear of becoming a burden to somebody was almost as terrible as the fear of losing her still formidable intellectual capacities. She had once quoted André Gide to me: 'Some putrefy, others ossify: all age. Only a strong intellectual flame triumphs over the fatigue and decline of the body.'[1] Having seen her body almost cave in from age and illness I had sometimes hoped that her wish would be granted, and yet that day seeing her lying there strapped by tubes to some horrible drip-feed, something strange happened to me. I wanted this woman to live. I loved her.

'Let's take her home,' I said to Prunella. 'If she stays here a day longer she will die.' I knew that despite all appearances there was still some of the fighting spirit left. The life of this woman was not finished yet.

I do not know what gave me this certainty, but I was right. She lived eight more years, and saw the beginning of her fame and recognition. Eileen was allowed home. There, as if by a miracle, she gathered her dwindling forces and, almost by sheer willpower, decided to live. In a few weeks she began to design again. She was ninety years old.

While filming the Christian Dior story, I sat at one of those snobbish dinner parties the French so love, opposite a young Argentinian actor with an extraordinary, slightly Indian appearance. As usual I talked a lot, trying very hard to impress. I had learned the art of self-defence and had added cynicism to my natural scepticism. Intrigued by the inquisitive eyes of this boy, I spoke about the sufferings in Biafra but also about the grand ball at the Paris Opéra, Le Bal des Petits Lits Blancs, which I had attended the previous night – another of the many contradictions that made up my life and my personality, inconsistencies I was not particularly proud of.

1 'Certains pourrissent, et d'autres s'ossifient: tous vieillissent. Seulement une grande ferveur intellectuelle triomphe de la fatigue et de la flétrissure du corps.'

Facundo, for that was the name of this awkward and handsome boy, never so much as uttered a word during the entire evening. At the end of the evening I gave him my London address. Three weeks later I received a letter: 'Dear Peter, please destroy this letter, I have never written to anyone like this, but for the last three weeks I have not stopped thinking of you and I wanted to let you know it. Please forgive me.' It was signed 'Facundo Bo'. Three hours later I was on the plane to Paris.

I do believe in love at first sight. During the next twenty years Facundo became the source of much happiness and much heartache. No one ever came closer to me and I believe no one ever will. Facundo became the absolute centre of my life. I longed for 'the pleasant rolling land' Albee had written of: 'I find that both joy and sorrow work their... wonders on me more... evenly, slowly, within, than most: a suntan rather than a scalding. There are no mountains in my life... no chasm. It is a rolling, pleasant land... verdant, my darling, thank you.'[1] Maybe Facundo would be able to provide it?

It is difficult to write about people one knows best. The knowledge of things to come is clouding the image of the person I knew ten, fifteen, twenty years ago. As Facundo is going to weave in and out of my life from now on, the pivot and the mover of the wheel of fortune, I must try to give him some coherent shape.

Facundo Bo was born in Buenos Aires. I never met his father, who had died in a mental hospital, but I had a very close relationship with his mother, Pepita, a proud and simple woman who came to stay with us frequently. Not much distinguishes Facundo's childhood from that of other middle-class families, except that the Bos were poor. Children were brought up with a longing for North American culture and a love or hate, as the case may be, for Eva Perón. In the case of Facundo it was hate, for his father had served some time in jail for anti-government activities. Facundo and his two sisters, Marucha and Lucia, were also brought up with the beliefs, legends, charms and superstitions of Latin America, among them those that the Jews were money-grabbing bastards and that some things bring bad luck. We were never short of photographs with pins stuck into them. My favourite story is that of a Fabergé egg which was believed to be the cause of a lot of misfortunes in the family. As a result it was buried in the garden, never to be found again. Both superstitions and prejudices survived long into our relationship and were the source of much laughter and ardent discussions.

Facundo had done a stint at university, while his beautiful sister

1 Agnes in *A Delicate Balance*.

Facundo Bo

Marucha worked as an air hostess and a model. Neither the university nor Aerolineas Argentinas were able to satisfy their dreams, and they soon joined a group of like-minded artists and began to make theatre.

While the theatre seemed to be a natural choice for a powerful and out-going personality like Marucha's, one could scarcely imagine the with-drawn Facundo entering the stage. But underneath his shyness lay a wild and abundant disposition, a love for danger and extreme situations.

When I met Facundo he was the leading actor in the Argentinian theatre company Groupe T S E, a group of talented actors, writers and painters under the directorship of Alfredo Arias. Together with a few friends – Facundo, Marucha and the painter Roberto Plate – Arias had formed this small theatre group in Buenos Aires. The audacity and visual power of their productions had caught the attention of many people, and after a visit to New York they had been invited by the Musée d'Art Moderne to perform in France.

Facundo, although still shy and withdrawn, had not lost his love for drama, and in fact he never would, a kind of feasting on disaster that tended to magnify rather than to heal wounds, his own and those he inflicted; a mercurial nature that raged through life. There were so many contradictions that cast a shadow over our lives that I cannot recount them all. Disorderly in his private life, he was fastidious in his professional one. He could never be on time for a private date, yet he never missed a performance. His energy could be invigorating, but misdirected could also be terribly destructive. He was, as E. M. Forster once wrote, always 'at a slight angle to the universe'. He could be warm and tender and then sud-denly chillingly remote. Maybe because of the love he received from the mostly female household, Facundo was thoroughly spoiled, an adolescence postponed until almost middle age. Our very different tempers and dispo-sitions led to an often doomed and desperate relationship, but at times also produced a luminous happiness, a sort of reassuring silky peace, for he was also insanely generous, with not the slightest streak of meanness or calculation.

The Argentinian playwright and cartoonist Copi had asked him to play the lead in his play *Eva Perón*. Both play and production would make the-atrical history, and some demonstrators tried to burn down the theatre. It was the first time I saw Facundo on stage and it came as a shock. My handsome lover had turned into a monster in a blond wig, wearing a yel-low evening dress, dripping with jewels. The role of Evita was the first of many monsters to come, for Facundo hated to play conventional good-looking men, he was only interested in character acting. I realised that on stage his shyness was pushed aside and he developed a rare passion and tension which became the basis of his performance.

The Cuban revolution was eleven years old. Everybody was interested in the Cuban experiment and I suggested making a film, *Cuba 11 Years After*. In May I was on my way to Havana.

Notes from a Voyage to Cuba

In 1969 ordinary tourists are not allowed to go to Cuba. We are only nineteen passengers on the plane which leaves Lisbon once a week. A Dutch salesman in sanitary equipment, a German on his fourth trip representing Bayer pharmaceuticals, some Spanish diplomats, an English student with long hair and a rucksack, and my crew of four. Upon our arrival in Havana, at four in the morning, the student is taken aside to have his hair cut, for the revolution shuns the hippy look. Officials in uniform rummage through our luggage, a pretty academic affair, because we have been thoroughly briefed about what not to take. Everything is finally removed and taken away 'to be sprayed against yellow fever'.

An old black Cadillac takes us to the Havana Hilton, now re-baptised the Havana Libre. It is reserved for official guests only, every room is heavily bugged. In the lobby I notice most of my fellow passengers, except for the student. I wonder how he is getting on. Someone has a mail bag marked 'Cambodian Embassy'. On the wall of the marbled lobby I notice faded signs, in English and Spanish, directing guests to the health club or the hairdresser. Through a broken glass I see gilded Louis XVI chairs collecting dust. The rooms still carry the Hilton stamp, but the plug in my basin is missing. The taps are rusty and the Formica top is broken. There are nevertheless two clean towels and the familiar little pieces of soap in a green wrapper without inscription, for advertising is ruled out as a capitalist disease.

A few minutes later an old bell captain in a tatty uniform brings my luggage. He calls me 'Sir', but refuses the tip and asks me to address him as 'comrade'. Everybody is now comrade here, the old 'Signor' is considered bourgeois. Another man in a white jacket comes to make up the bed.

We are handed a white card with a number on it, which allows us to eat in the restaurant. In the dark restaurant for foreigners, only one bulb in the chandelier is working. I overhear an American girl talking on the phone: 'I can't give you any details, but stay away from the hippy'; then she hangs up. A little later the young Englishman from the plane joins her. He actually looks much better with his hair cut short. It has all the ingredients of a Graham Greene story.

Our man in Havana, who never let us out of sight, takes us to the Ministry of Information. He turns out to have studied in the States and to have spent some time in Holland as a diplomat. He smokes Kent cigarettes and watches over everything we say or do.

In the Ministry, pictures of Che Guevara are everywhere. I also notice a photograph of Bertrand Russell on the desk of the official who interviews us. Everybody, even our assistant, already has a file with our names on it. A girl with an old typewriter takes down all our particulars once more: name, age, studies, people we want to see. Then we are shown to the basement for our photographs to be taken. The young photographer buttons up my shirt before he takes the picture. Puritanism reigns now in a place which was once the fleshpot of the States and where Americans came to see girls being fucked by donkeys. Even Bermuda shorts are not allowed around the pool of the hotel.

Havana is run down but clean, like the people. Many houses still have a middle-class appearance. Their rich façades once gave a false image of prosperity and culture in a country of barbaric poverty and a brutal political system under Batista. Castro wants to build up the countryside. Cities, according to him, are now a luxury, too expensive to run, an unnecessary liability for a country trying to survive with generous subsidies from the USSR. The constant blue sky and the flowering trees mellow the impression of sadness one feels looking at the decaying houses with their crumbling wrought-iron balconies. Private business has been forbidden and most shops are closed. Some display a few cheap dresses in large windows that once belonged to luxury boutiques. Hardship of course is nothing new for the Cubans. I notice people queuing everywhere for food, cinema, clothes. The queue has become the general meeting place. It is only 8.30 in the morning but queues are already forming at the ice-cream parlour. Cubans have a passion for ice-cream, which is cheap and, with so little food available, also filling.

I left my Spanish dictionary in London, so go to a bookshop. On the empty shelves, I see a few books on medicine or on Cuba's economy, but no dictionary. 'You won't find one in Cuba,' I am told.

Eleven years after the revolution, the heat has gone out of the speeches and the anti-imperialist slogans have been toned down, yet the words of Castro and Che Guevara are on everybody's lips and sometimes bring tears to people's eyes. I film some of the 100,000 schoolchildren now living in the once splendid villas of the smart suburb of Merida, whose inhabitants have fled the country. 'We have seen the light, we are not going to be thrown back into darkness,' says one girl quoting Bolívar.

It is difficult to find much sympathy with the Cuban middle classes who, as in so many Latin American countries, offered little to their country. Most of them were culturally illiterate and aped an American lifestyle. The traditional role of the European middle classes as the representatives of economic and cultural vigour was almost unknown to them, the reason they were so easily overthrown by the revolution and left in droves, finding a new life in what someone called the 'thin-minded civilisation of Miami'.

Edmundo Desnoes, the writer of *Inconsolable Memories*, a much-praised novel of Cuba today, comes to pick me up in an asthmatic old Volkswagen, which threatens to break down any minute. A man of about thirty-eight, with the looks of a well-brought-up Englishman, Desnoes has organised a small party for me. Among the guests are a secretary from the British embassy, an American correspondent of several US papers and a beautiful German girl from East Berlin. She is married to an Argentinian writer who teaches at the university. She has never been allowed to leave Germany before and is quite critical of the DDR. 'Communism, German style, has no vision and so much repression,' she declares. 'I want to live where the revolution has meaning.' I talk with a Cuban girl; her middle-class parents have just received permission to leave Cuba, but she has decided to stay on. She teaches English to waiters in a restaurant. She is proud of her sacrifice. 'I have almost no food, no clothes, but it is worth it.' 'The revolution is a very fast train,' says Desnoes. 'You must not miss it.'

The next day we film Desnoes in his large living-room. On the walls hang stunning modern posters; the bookshelves are lined with books by Kafka, Mao, Eldridge Cleaver and other black Muslim leaders and all the standard works of world literature. On the table is a copy of the *Sunday Times*, with an article by Edna O'Brien.

Desnoes is courteous, but I can feel that he is slightly bored with yet another journalist interviewing him – a weary man, who views outsiders from behind a solid wall of indifference. His frankness is remarkable as he warns me not to over-praise the revolution: 'The revolution is hard and cruel. It has little to do with the clichés which one hears everywhere else. You cannot read or talk about a revolution. That's what you do in the salons of Paris and London. The only way to experience it is to live it.' He tells us how isolated he felt before the revolution, with his Western middle-class background. 'I was more at home in Europe or in the States than in my own country.'

The next evening I am invited by some Americans, the Sterns. They had heard that I was in the hotel and had left a note on a little scrap of paper, 'Mr and Mrs Stern would be glad if you could join them for dinner in room 1705 on the 17th floor.' I can hardly believe my eyes when I enter their suite, filled with books and a real Matisse painting on the wall. I try to find out what they are doing here; they seem to be followers of the revolution. The Sterns, I am told, live most of the year in Havana, the rest in Czechoslovakia. The other guest is an American lawyer from New York who represents the Cuban government and the Sterns. This is again like something out of Graham Greene. There is also Lucia, a Cuban girl in a slinky black dress and a pair of crocodile shoes, which I realise the lawyer has brought her from New York. He calls her Lucy. The conversation is quite critical of Castro's politics, although all are devotees. 'If you want to do the right thing for so many,' says Lucia, 'you always have to do wrong to a few. It all depends which side you are on.'

The hostess apologises for the meal, which is perfectly adequate except that Lucia has failed to organise a turkey. She had only offered 100 pesos, but the farmers wanted a blanket and Mrs Stern did not have one. At the end of the evening I escort Lucia down the hall. 'I would like to have some clothes but they are not essential. The revolution is,' she says, while she kisses me goodnight. I see her stepping into a taxi, an almost impossible thing for lesser mortals to find.

The statutory meeting with the British ambassador turns out like a scene from an old-fashioned movie: club tie, Earl Grey tea, the picture of the Queen and the exchange of niceties included. I am surprised to find out that the British embassy maintains a weekly air link between Cuba and the Bahamas.

In the hotel, usually at the pool side, one meets the strangest assortment of people: an American urologist on a conference tour, some British agriculturists and a noisy group of Canadian and American revolutionaries getting cheap suntan oil on Karl Marx's *Kapital.*

Saul Gelin, a lively Jew with a strong American accent, runs the Cuban Film Institute, producing films that are winning prizes at international festivals. In his office he has abstract paintings and two Marcel Breuer chairs, and film magazines from all over the world. Gelin is up to date with the work of Helene Weigel and has read Olivier Todd's latest article in the *Nouvel Observateur.* Gelin too is frank, and speaks of the danger of the revolution falling into the hands of the bureaucrats, as in Russia or in the D D R. 'Even Castro warns about this. Capitalism too suffers from the same malaise,' he adds. Gelin also criticises the policy of letting cities die. 'Cities are the breeding ground of culture.'

The new Cuban cinema is a cinema of partisans, not of aesthetes, but it is remarkably free of the restrictions of the Russian or East German cinema with their obsessions with socialist realism. A film on coffee-growing used Godard-like techniques of text insertion and stop-motion pictures. 'We are trying to make aesthetics out of our difficulties,' remarks José Massip, a young film director who had joined us for drinks. Some films are even satirising the revolution. One pokes fun at the agrarian reform. Cows are listening to Castro's long speech on artificial insemination, which comes over loudspeakers in the stable. I also see a remarkable documentary on a village whose inhabitants had never been to the cinema. Asked what they thought a film was about they replied: 'Ballrooms and beautiful women.' Then they were shown a Chaplin film while the camera recorded their reaction. The joy and laughter expressed was one of the most beautiful and moving effects I have ever seen in a documentary.

Like all party bureaucracies, the Cuban system does not work. Everybody relies on orders and rules, so there is no initiative and no incentives. It takes days to get permission to film at one of the new farms. The inefficiency is indescribable. There is always someone above you who has to sign a paper, and then when you get to the top of the party suddenly everything is possible.

Like many revolutions, the Cuban one was also made by intellectuals. I assume a journalist arriving in Russia in the first two years of the revolution must have felt as I do. 'It is always the intellectual, the artist, who is being sacrificed in a revolution. This was the case in Russia and the same is true in Cuba,' says Roberto Blanco, a young theatre director who has spent one year in Berlin with the Berliner Ensemble. He is successful, but culturally isolated. 'We need contact with Paris, London and New York. How can I go on making theatre when I am not allowed to see or even read what other people are doing? Yet we are constantly told that the revolution needs artists.' 'Artists and intellectuals are too soft for a revolution, too vulnerable. The revolution is hard and cruel,' Desnoes had said. 'It so happens that we are responsible for the most honest crimes, the most beautiful lies,' are the lines of one of Cuba's famous revolutionary poets.

I finally meet my first anti-revolutionary, Julio Gomez, a talented theatre director now without work. He had twice been allowed to the West and had spent some time with the Living Theatre in New York and with Peter Brook's Open Space in London. Julio and I meet in the hotel lobby, as no one is allowed to receive guests in the rooms. He is shy and nervous as he tells me: 'There are spies in the hotel who can lip-read.' We go for a walk.

Julio had remained behind when his family left for the States, for he too wants to be part of the revolution. He has just spent several months making theatre for workers in the sugar fields and talks with enthusiasm about bringing art to the masses. But Julio is no dreamer, he fears that the revolution is failing. 'Privileges for the party bosses are everywhere. Even the artists are beginning to be corrupted by favours,' he tells me while sadness and anger mount in his solemn face. I have to think of Gelin's brand-new station wagon. Julio has no car; his father's Lamborghini and an old Jaguar Mark 5 still sit in the garage. They have given up life, a long time ago, silent relics of a time forever gone. He would give anything now for a bicycle, 'but I cannot play the political games.'

Julio invites me to his home. I have to go there late at night, for in every block live people whose only task is to spy on their neighbours and the visit of a foreigner would certainly be reported. Repressive systems always have their informers.

Julio hates material possessions. He has sold most of his furniture except for a beautiful Tiffany lamp, which he immediately wants to give to me. Sadness mounts in both of us. What is the meaning of this revolution that incarcerates a man slightly younger than myself, who is dreaming of travelling, of seeing plays and museums all over the world? 'I do not care for the material things you have in the West, but the choice of art, the freedom to see what you want.' Neither of us can believe in the sacrifice of a whole generation for an idea that might not even work, that might impoverish rather than enrich people's lives.

That night I cannot sleep. I think about the people who try to escape in little life-rafts drowning halfway between Havana and Miami, only a hundred miles away. Half a million Cubans have turned their back on the revolution. The next day I decide to film the Mexican consulate, where the exit visas for which people wait years are issued. I watch with mounting pity the long line of mostly elderly middle-class people queuing outside the elegant villa. *Gusanos* – worms – they are called. They are quiet, resigned, all hope blown away, no signs of emotion on their faces. They have no proper ration cards and have to work for months in the sugar fields. 'The revolution is not merciful.' Desnoes's words take on sinister meanings. Once you apply for a visa, your house and most of your possessions are taken away. I think of the Jewish immigrants of my youth and of the Berlin wall, which also keeps its citizens imprisoned. Why must a revolution have such an ugly face? Lucia's dictum, 'To do the right thing for many always means doing wrong to a few', has a hollow ring to it.

I manage to get a ticket to the most popular nightclub, Bolla di Nieve (Snowball). I go with Lucia. In Cuba, once the haven for American homosexuals, homosexuality is now punishable by prison. The audience roars with excitement at the performance of a very camp old-fashioned entertainer from the 1930s. Lucia takes me backstage. In his dressing-room two gentlemen straight out of Proust dish out bitchy remarks and exchange loud kisses with each other.

There are other contradictions, some less pleasant. There are special shops full of goods from the West. They are supposed to be for 'foreigners only', but people with political clout also make use of them. They are the same ones who can get tables in restaurants without queuing. The revolution for the people is not really for the people. It educates and feeds them, but it gives them no choice. It dictates what you read and how you behave. The few choices available are for the party bosses. The revolution creates as many inadequacies as any other system. It is naïve to believe that it would be different. Of course it works on some levels. In the countryside I find some dignity and some purpose. It has become the real battleground for the revolution while Havana is sentenced to rot; the less attractive it becomes to the people, the better.

I film in Camagüey on a vast cattle ranch which once belonged to one man. Now it is the 'property' of six hundred farmers. They are still 'employed', but they receive a salary all year around and even a paid holiday, $120 per month instead of the $80 they once had during the three months of harvesting. The village, built a few years ago, looks bright and friendly. With its freshly painted houses and well-kept gardens it is not depressing like Havana. The 'head man', a former bank clerk who had spent three years in America, shows us around. In the school for eighty-five children, the different parts of a flower are chalked up on the blackboard: *peduncùlo, raiz, capullo.* For lunch the farmers return from the fields and eat together. There is much laughter. One of them tells me about his three sons who are now at university in Havana. Maybe this is what Castro meant when he said that the cities must die so that the country can live. It feels like a happy enough place with clouds of flamingos in the shallow water. It all seems to make sense to me. 'I have what I have, / A place to work, / To earn / Something / To eat / Let's see. / I have what I had / To have,' wrote Cuba's great poet, Nicolas Guillen.

Everybody in Cuba works in the sugar fields to reach the almost mystical figure of ten million tons. Besides the economic importance, the psychological importance of this quota is enormous. One nation all working together towards one aim. 'Diez Milliones,' billboards and posters proclaim. Propaganda comes through the loudspeakers and fills the speeches of the politicians. Each day the newspaper lists pages and pages of the names of volunteers, among them lawyers, teachers and painters. At five o'clock the whole country is still wrapped in a silky mist, but everywhere people leave their houses to go to the fields.

Another communal effort is the Campaign for Literacy: 260,000 people of all professions have volunteered to teach their fellow men to read and write. In the past one person in four was illiterate, now the figure is down to 4 per cent. On the wall of the co-ordinating office hundreds of letters: 'Thank you, I can read now.'

I meet Doctor Marta Couri, an outspoken and brave woman of about fifty. She runs a hospital; her husband is a psychologist working for UNESCO. Both cannot hide their middle-class background. 'I have no grudge against those who left, but I feel sorry for them, because they have failed history,' she tells me. 'I wanted my children to grow up with the revolution in order that they can live their time.' Dr Couri too speaks openly about the faults of the revolution, but she adds: 'You must leave behind your preconceived notion about the importance of individual choices for the advantages to the whole community. Hospitals are working, most women have their children in a proper ward. We are hungry, but no one dies from lack of food as I remember from the past. So what does my own personal freedom matter?' I cannot argue with her. It is difficult to explain that my own personal freedom is also the freedom of all others.

I would not make a good politician, because I can always see the other side too. I learned early that the world is governed by men who make laws for themselves and expect others to abide by them. Almost daily I am caught between affirming and rejecting the revolution. The typical dilemma of the liberal middle classes. I rejoice at the sight of the many children in school, but have a horror of seeing them so orderly and demure marching up and down shouting Castro slogans, five-year-olds behaving like soldiers on a drill. It makes sense that everybody now has free access to what was once an exclusive club for the rich and the dollar-laden tourists, but it worries me that one is constantly reminded of the necessity for political obedience and respect for party authority. The man who has worked the lift of the Havana Hotel for twenty-five years tells me that he likes the Americans, 'but we wanted the revolution and that is good', while the old chambermaid hates the system: 'Everything is so drab now, we live without hope. I have always been poor, but I saw rich people and I was allowed to dream.'

After three weeks I left Cuba with regret. I had admired the many people struggling for a better world, but also I thought of those too frail to survive the ruthless machine of change. The young painter Raoul Oliva, who was responsible for some of the most stunning film posters; the painter Raoul Martinez. Roberto and Julio were trying to carve out a small slice of individuality and personal freedom in order to be able to function as artists. I decided to come back soon. The revolution had made me uneasy and made me rejoice. I had to find out more.

How trivial everything looked back home. The Swinging Sixties began to fade into memory. London became increasingly a tourist curiosity, a quaint watered-down version of its former self. It is not that I became disenchanted with England, but so many things began to turn into a non-event, and my travels had shown me that there was a whole new world which was changing fast.

I could even see it at work. There were hardly any foreigners working in the BBC except in the specialised services. Women were mostly employed as assistants, 'BBC trouts', as I called them, devoted to their work and their bosses' ruffled egos, women whose talents were running to waste. They usually sat in the canteen together, four or five at the same table, looking like creatures in constant mourning for their unlived lives.

In order to work permanently at the BBC, I had to become a British subject, although I nearly failed the test. I had given the name of three sponsors. A painter/teacher, a GP and a journalist seemed to be a good mixture: Prunella Clough, Patrick Woodcock and James Mossman.

One day Jim arrived at the office. 'I blew it,' he announced. He had been woken by a phone call asking him where he had met Peter Adam. 'At a drag ball in Berlin,' he replied jokingly. 'Thank you, Mr Mossman, this is the Home Office,' the voice said and hung up.

One morning, as I was doing my exercises, the bell rang. I rushed down and the first thing I saw was a pair of brown suede shoes. They belonged to a serious-looking man in a perfect, slightly worn suit. 'Mr Adam, I'm from the Home Office. May I come in?' The grey figure with the impenetrable face produced a yellow writing pad, a very sharp pencil and the *Daily Telegraph* and began to dictate. This was to test my proficiency in English. I was still only wearing a pair of white shorts, but having already written three lines, I felt it would be a bit prim and prudish to get up and to put on some clothes. While dictating he removed his spectacles, revealing a pair of moist and disagreeable eyes. I also noticed an unhealthy patch of white flesh protruding above his short socks. 'Life is not fair,' I thought, looking at my brown thighs. 'Thank you,' he said almost in mid-sentence. 'I can see you have a sufficient knowledge of *our* language.' He was obviously in the habit of dealing with little Polish ladies.

Trying to break the tension, he commented in a semi-friendly way upon my tan. It was not meant as a compliment but as a hidden question. I fell into the trap and replied: 'Thank you, I have just come from Cuba.' 'Cuba?' he said and his voice took on a sharp note: 'Castro's Cuba?' His pencil began to race across his little notebook. 'Is this a Francis Bacon, and if so how did you acquire it?' he asked, in his Civil Service nasal drone, pointing at Brett Whiteley's painting of Rita, the nurse murdered by John Christie. After I explained that it was actually a British murder story he asked if he could see the rest of the flat. Inspecting the bathroom, he remarked: 'An awful lot of scent bottles. I presume you live here alone.'

To my surprise, a week later I received a phone call to tell me to find a notary in order to swear my allegiance to the Queen. I was busy editing the programme on Cuba, but on the corner of Shepherd's Bush was a notary's office. A friendly black man received me. On his desk stood a photo of Her Majesty the Queen; I noticed the two corgis at her feet. I stood up. Reading from a white card I spoke solemnly: 'I swear allegiance to...' I had not finished the last word when the friendly lawyer with the thick Jamaican accent said: 'You arre English now, congrratulations, Misterr Adam, that will be £5.'

To become British was an important step in my life. Not that I had any special nationalistic feelings for my new country, but it cut the last ties with Germany. I was no longer obliged to admit that I was German – a small detail which only those who have turned their back on Germany can understand, but an important one. I could now simply say I was British. I kept my German passport, by special permission of Willy Brandt. The BBC had encouraged me to keep it, in case there was another story like Biafra.

As a direct result of my filming I met Alba Griñan, the Cuban ambassador to London. A former schoolteacher, she had been part of the small Cuban delegation at the United Nations in New York, which included Fidel Castro and Che Guevara. One day Fidel had said to her: 'Compañera Alba, I will send you to London as my ambassador.' No one ever refused Fidel. Anyway, it was a clever appointment – a young half-caste revolutionary with a middle-class image, and a woman.

Alba had already spent a couple of years in London, when we met. As she was single, her life was lonely, shared only by her old mother. From time to time it was interrupted by the tedium of endless receptions and cocktails at other embassies. Her every step was recorded by both sides, West and East. She hardly knew any English people and was not even allowed to go for a drive without a driver. I immediately liked this exotic woman of natural elegance. As it turned out she was a friend of Julio and Gelin. Alba and I became close friends. She was a refreshing mixture of intelligence and naïvety. The first time I invited her for dinner to my house she remarked: 'Oh Peter, how capitalistic, how wonderful.' I took her to meet all my friends and she began to see a different London. Everybody loved her. We drove with a driver and bodyguard to hear Hans Werner Henze conduct at Aldeburgh, where we lunched with Benjamin Britten and Peter Pears – three names Alba had never heard. We went to a ball and Alba danced with the Aga Khan and thought his name was Cohen. It was all a new world for her.

Once, at an official ceremony at Highgate Cemetery, we stood at Karl

With Alba Griñan

Marx's grave. After the third endless speech she said to me: 'I've had enough, let's go. Karl Marx, Karl Marx, I joined the revolution because children had no shoes. I had never heard of Karl Marx.' Alba was a true revolutionary, not a communist. She was a loyal representative of Fidel's Cuba but she would never talk about *gusanos*, nor would she wear the mink stole her government had supplied her with, the usual accoutrement of ambassadors' wives, especially from Eastern bloc countries. Facundo and I would frequently dine at her home, just the three of us with her mother, a zestful black woman, who always referred to her daughter as 'her Excellency'. Mother Griñan baked the most tasty cheesecakes, which the driver delivered regularly to Earls Terrace: a friendly gesture that later got me into trouble.

Louis Hanssom, James Mossman's lover, had committed suicide – an overdose of pills. He had passed out in a restaurant and was taken home. He never came around again. Jim was devastated. As a result we grew even closer, and I began to see him almost daily as he became more and more morose. He had been working for the BBC as an independent and had even contemplated retiring altogether from television. The many war reports he had filed were taking their toll; the deaths were piling up in his head, fuelling his depressive nature. One night we spoke about Flaubert, and Emma Bovary's life of suffocation. I quoted: 'Her life was as cold as a garret, whose window faced North, and boredom like a spider spun the web in the shadow, to all the corners of the heart.' 'That's it,' Jim replied. 'The spider.'

I invited him to my house to meet the writer Rosamond Lehmann. She and her brother John Lehmann were part of a distinguished literary clan. I was a frequent guest in Rosamond's flat on Eaton Square, a kind of green silk splendour, filled with books and learned people. The author of *The Echoing Grove* was of statuesque appearance; her still-beautiful face was framed by a theatrical hair style. Voluminous evening gowns usually hid her heavy frame. She was fluent in French and liked to enrich her English with French phrases. I knew that she had an obsessive side to her, but she was almost too agreeable, too equable, to harbour anything sinister. Rosamond had lost her daughter and we had often in the past talked about death and consolation.

Jim and Rosamond immediately took to each other. Rosamond spoke ardently about ways of communicating with the dead. She had even written a book about it. From that evening on she became a great influence on Jim's life. A few days later he told me that he had seen a medium who would put him in contact with Louis. He spoke half jokingly, but I knew instantly that he was caught up in something which frightened me. There were other strange things about Jim. I was as close as one could ever get to him, but there were always some corners of his life he would not reveal, such as that he had known Kim Philby and that he had worked for MI5.

One evening, at Peter Shaffer's, Jim told us the story of a boy blinding some horses. Elisabeth Cavendish, who was a magistrate, had been working on the case. John Dexter was also at the dinner and he and Peter were very intrigued. The seed for his next play, *Equus*, was sown.

Jim had been asked to take over the arts magazine *Review* on BBC2. It was the BBC's most distinguished arts magazine, successor to Huw Wheldon's *Monitor* and *Release*, run by the writer Lorna Pegram. Jim was reluctant; he was more a man of politics than of the arts, although he was writing his second novel, but he was ready for a change in his career. We talked a long time about the pros and cons of this offer. The British looked down on anybody who would talk about ideologies and most of all those linked with the arts. I often complained about the lack of broad cultural concepts, no one like Roland Barthès or Michel Foucault to influence cultural ideologies. The arts always seemed to be something a few people did in private – it was never central to the country. Here was a chance to make the arts available to the maximum number of people, an exhilarating but also a frightening task. Would we be able to break the mandarin hierarchy of taste which still dominated the arts coverage on the BBC? Or would we fall into the trap of vulgar popularisation and trite generalisations? Could we infuse some new elements into the arts coverage, still crippled by waves of nostalgia, without betraying our dedication to excellence?

Jim finally decided to take on the post of editor, provided I would come along. It was not an easy choice, I liked Current Affairs. Although *24 Hours* was meant to be a magazine with several shorter items, I had been allowed to do long programmes. Those on Biafra, Cuba, Berlin and De Gaulle had been specials, and took the whole of the *24 Hours* slot. I knew that this would not always be possible, I also knew that I was more at home in the arts. I applied for the new job and was accepted as one of the four producers responsible for the weekly arts programme. The others were Colin Nears, Christopher Martin and Tony Staveacre. Around us was a brilliant team of young directors such as Leslie Megahey and Gavin Millar. A new chapter had began. I was forty years old.

14

Review I: From Malraux to Visconti

1969–1970

In the autumn of 1969 I received a letter from Louise de Vilmorin, inviting me to spend a weekend at Verrières-le-Buisson, a grand and elegant house she shared with André Malraux. 'Malraux is bored and a bit depressed. Your presence would cheer him up,' she had written, enclosing a small drawing of a flower with the inscription: 'Je cherche l'inspiration, mais je ne trouve absolument rien. J'ai la tête vide.' Vilmorin was also hoping that he and I could work something out for a television programme. To begin my work on *Review* with a programme about the author of *The Metamorphosis of the Gods* and *The Voices of Silence*, that scrutinised the language of the arts and examined man's relationship to it, would be a formidable and challenging task.

Malraux was still married, but he had moved in with Louise de Vilmorin, a friend of long standing. Vilmorin, a poet and a novelist, was the author of *Madame de*, which Max Ophüls had adapted for film. Although slightly lame, she had been a celebrated beauty, known to her friends as 'Lulu'. She had had several husbands and had been engaged to Prince Esterhazy. Her past had been clouded by the fact that she was supposed to have had an affair with a German soldier during the occupation. She was a peculiarly fascinating woman, a friend of Cocteau, Coco Chanel, Magritte and many famous people, among them Diana and Duff Cooper. She often practically lived in the British embassy.

I was nervous about meeting Malraux. *La Condition humaine* and *L'Espoir* had completely bowled me over when I first read them. He had been France's most famous minister of culture, a formidable man of letters, *l'homme engagé* of French literature, a friend of De Gaulle. He had drunk with Pablo Picasso, André Gide and Paul Valéry.

The weekend at Verrières was easy, with mounting gaiety, exhilaration and delight. The two lovers were alone; I was the only guest. There were not even any servants. We cooked some delicious meals and sat and talked. They did most of the talking. 'Malraux and Vilmorin' was a performance perfected over years. I was mesmerised watching the two French intellectuals exchanging ideas just for the fun of it. Both seemed to live in a kind of permanent intellectual exaltation, both craving an audience for their different kinds of spectacle. They talked about Plato, Dante, Dickens, Shelley, Michelangelo as if they had been close friends.

Malraux's spellbinding personality and eloquence were touchingly well matched by the sparkle of his partner. Louise de Vilmorin was a superb conversationalist in the French tradition. In her mouth the most light-hearted matter could take the most profound meaning. She combined wit with great charm and evoked a world of flowers and love. Vilmorin had made an art of her affectations, her restless lips seemed to want to perfume every word, and I could see how this man who had such an acute sense of the genuine could, in a kind of romantic Byronic way, fall for someone whose charm was her artificiality.

Malraux was very rational in his arguments, able to go right to the heart of things, and was a brilliant talker, while Louise's interjections took us higher and higher into the world of fancy. Malraux spoke about one of his favourite subjects: man's relationship to images – the artist as conqueror of gods and idols, man's ceaseless struggle to impose art as something absolute, eternal, in line and in competition with God's creation. While he spoke, his face, like his mind, would never stand still. This was part of his hypnotic power. Despite the formality of the conversations, the weekend was filled with a natural ease and rare human warmth. We talked about and listened to a lot of music.

Vilmorin and Malraux were very much in love, and even the most erudite conversation was like a declaration of their feelings for each other, acted out in front of a much younger person they trusted. It was as if the very act of public manifestation of their love would give it more reality. I was moved and flattered. 'Thank you, dear Peter, André Malraux and I enjoyed your presence in Verrières,' wrote Louise de Vilmorin, 'and we both hope you will be back very soon. Lots of love from your friend, Louise de Vilmorin.'

A few months later Louise de Vilmorin was dead. I spoke to Malraux on the phone. He was devastated. Vilmorin had told me about the many tragedies in Malraux's life: the mother of his two sons had died in an accident and both boys were killed on the road in 1961. 'I am sometimes amazed that he is not choking in grief,' she had said. His grandfather's skull had been split open by his own axe when felling a tree, his father had committed suicide and two of his brothers had died during the war, one in Bergen Belsen. I sent him the little interview I had done with Vilmorin for the Dior film, and Malraux wrote, 'Je vous remercie de la part que vous prenez à mon chagrin...' We spoke a few times on the phone, but I never saw him again. I was left with the memory of a rare weekend of imaginative empathy.

Our film project never materialized. Insularity and philistinism prevented me from selling Malraux to the BBC. Instead I began my life at *Review* with two small stories, an item on naïve painters with John Berger and a film on Pisano with Henry Moore. John Berger, an ex-painter, was a friend of Prunella, which endeared me immediately to him. His lively mind and passionate delivery were very compelling. When he spoke everything moved with passion. His large expansive gestures and vivid eyes seemed to want to hypnotize the viewer.

The next item I made was a film with Nureyev and the Netherlands Ballet. He was working with Rudi van Dantzig on a new ballet, *Memory for a Dead Boy*. Nureyev was unshakably self-centred but he was never cold-spirited. This and his keen intelligence soon made one forget his arrogant manners. His physical presence, which he never ceased to use freely, gave him a sexual magnetism which was difficult to resist. Not for nothing did people compare his magic to Nijinsky's.

I engaged Ed van der Elsken as my cameraman, one of Holland's leading photographers, whose book *Love in St-Germain-des-Prés* was a great success. Ed was crazy – no other word will do – but he was an exceptional artist with an eye for the unusual, the awkward. His camera caught the reflection of the room in the eye of a dancer, as in a parabolic mirror. He shot a *pas de deux* lying on the floor, filming the dancers from below, making them appear to fly through the air. His pictures recorded the fatigue of the dancers, the sweat running down their bodies and feet exhausted, dirty and bruised. A formidable homage to an art form in which the body is asked to do something unnatural in order to achieve pure beauty.

Working with Nureyev was a pleasure. I quickly learned to respect and even to like him. His energy was boundless. He was totally devoted to his work, rehearsing for hours, consuming large cups of hot tea. Six hours practice in the morning, an hour in a sauna and then back to class. He could be very mischievous. Once in the sauna he had spotted two Englishmen, wrapped in their towels. Rudi got up, and strutted about naked, loudly talking about the rigid correctness of the English with their sexual indecisiveness. At night we consumed large amounts of vodka and got quite drunk, roaming through the nightlife of Amsterdam. We were friends then.

The next morning he was fresh and totally relaxed. He seemed to be tireless. His explosive energy was directed towards everything – work, sex and the acquiring of knowledge. He was always keen to talk about books, the theatre or art, and his retentive memory was astonishing.

Filming Rudolf Nureyev

Filming Roman Polanski

Ed's creative camera and the unusual view of the profession of the ballet dancer was something quite new. It was a very beautiful film, but Nureyev hated it. His luminous imagination and electrifying personality could suddenly vanish if he did not receive what he considered his due. The slightest constraint and his temper would explode. There was an untamable pride in him and a total lack of humility. One night at a dinner at Earls Terrace – Facundo had cooked him lentils – he became almost hysterical. 'No one has a right to show dancers like this. Dance is the art of illusion, there is no beauty in a sweaty body. You are not an artist, you are a butcher,' he screamed, tearing out a page from the book he had given me. His face became distorted by rage, then he stormed out. I was much hurt by this.

Later I sometimes visited him in his house in Richmond, a large place filled with art and antique furniture. Passion and energy still pulsed through him, but I was surprised to find him mostly alone among the books and pictures he so gregariously collected. Despite his many 'grand' friends, he disliked society, he once told me, and I believed him.

The last time I saw Nureyev was in Paris. I had gone to visit a friend in an AIDS hospital. He saw me and looked away. He was a man without manners, untamed to the last.

In my private life I had finally achieved what I had so long waited for: I was loved. I am not sure that I handled the beginning of our relationship very well. There was no real commitment on my side yet. I even spent a short time away from Facundo in New York and indulged in the sexual excess it always seems to offer. I did it without joy, more out of habit, and I rushed back to London to be with him. We spent Christmas together and the year ended with great hope for the future. From now on two things would fill my life – Facundo and my work. The rest became totally immaterial. I had finally understood that the only things that made life worthwhile were love and work.

Jim Mossman had bought a house in a small Norfolk village and we drove up there on weekends to work out the subjects for next week's programme. He was often depressed but tried to forget it in a hectic social life. Jim could be brilliant at conversation, and it was very difficult to find anybody who did not like him. He lunched with the Queen Mother at Diana Cooper's, who was devoted to him, or with Elisabeth Cavendish and John Betjeman. Many people were very fond of this noble and tortured man, but Jim could not love people in return. He liked some of them and admired quite a few, but also despised many. There was an emptiness in him and he suffered because of it. He often joked about my excess of emotion, which he found useless. 'The condition of man is his loneliness,' he had said. Once, driving to Norfolk, I babbled on about the beauty of an apple tree in blossom. 'This senseless renewal of nature, every year, for what?' is all Jim could say. It was the reaction of a man, displaced, living in a world increasingly devoid of a spiritual centre.

It was about that time that something strange began to happen with my phone, for every time I finished speaking, it went dead. Alba Griñan often mentioned that she was worried about me and my relationship with the BBC, but I laughed it off.

I embarked on another film about Cuba, *Art and the Revolution*. Thanks to Alba, Fidel Castro had seen and approved of my first programme. He realised that a film that did not fully back his revolution, but basically affirmed it, was more useful than a hagiography.

This time I was allowed to stay in a hotel usually reserved for friends and VIPs of the revolution. I was also given my own car and a driver. I engaged Julio Gomez as my assistant.

The mood in Cuba had changed since my last visit. The word 'freedom' was on everybody's lips, but there was very little of it. People were afraid. They did not speak so openly any longer, looking behind them when they criticised the regime. The hated Committee for the Defence of the Revolution (CDR) now had their spies in every house or block. Big brother was your neighbour. Julio was not the only one who had been in trouble because of his association with me. The brave Dr Couri, I was told, had been severely reprimanded after the BBC interview. The young composer and guitarist Leo Brower was forced to return to Cuba while he was staying in Henze's house in Italy. Among the intellectuals, doubt was replacing certainty. Personal truth did not always coincide with the official one.

Hans Werner Henze was in Cuba, invited by the Cuban government, preparing the première of his sixth symphony. He had also set Miguel Barnet's *El Cimarron* to music, the tales of the black slave Esteban Montejo, who was supposed to have lived to the age of one hundred and ten. Like many of his Italian friends (Luigi Nono among them), Hans had become a Marxist. Some of it was the result of his rejection of his father and, closely linked with it, his rejection of anything to do with fascism. 'The nation of soldiers, the nation of fathers,' he had called Germany. But much of it came from his changing attitude towards his art. Since the première of his opera *The Bassarids* in 1966, Hans had lived in what he called a 'crisis'. He complained that his music had became exceedingly private, music for the *cognoscenti.* 'I have been a bourgeois who served other bourgeois with music. The result was nostalgia and scepticism,' he wrote. Then in 1967 he had met Rudi Dutschke and became involved with the student movement. Cuba and the experience of the revolution was an opportunity for him to break out of his isolation.

My relationship with Hans began to suffer during those years. I envied him his strong convictions; mine were always full of doubts. He of course disapproved strongly of my 'liberal' attitude. My weariness with ideologies and mistrust of the priestly power of the problem-solvers had only increased over the years. I could not keep quiet when he told me that 'art had become unimportant'. It seemed to be a betrayal of everything that I believed in. 'Socialist music' was a concept I could not endorse. Hans's idea of freedom was to write music that could be understood or sung by the greatest number of people. 'Freedom is the right to be useful,' the Cuban freedom fighter José Martin had said.

Artists were still surprisingly free of party control, but tension was mounting and they were constantly reminded that they too had a role to play in the formation of the new man. With the writers the revolution felt most vulnerable. There were those who toed the line – Alejo Carpentier, Nicolas Guillen; and those who opposed the system – Virgilio Piñera, Lezama Lima, Luis Rogelio Nogueras, Reinaldo Arenas, Heberto Padilla.

Desnoes was still the most outstanding defender of the revolution, but he now admitted that it was full of mistakes. 'We have a right to make mistakes. At least they are ours, we create them,' he shouted when I told him about prison camps for homosexuals and special hospital wards for party members. 'You intellectuals in the West always think about the revolution as something cosy and nice and just. It is a heart-rending affair,' and he quoted Stalin's words to me: 'Freedom is a bourgeois myth.'

The leading poet Heberto Padilla was one of the most outspoken critics of the revolution. 'Cuban poets no longer dream, not even in their sleep,' he had written. He had travelled extensively to the West and was a foreign correspondent for the *Prensa Latina*. The officials wanted him to leave Cuba; they did not dare to arrest him – his work was very popular and had been translated into fourteen languages.

When I asked to interview him, hell broke loose. My car was cancelled and for a whole night two inscrutable men from the secret police offered other suitable interviewees. When I refused they began to threaten me. I stood my ground. I tried to explain to them that for me freedom is simply not negotiable. The interview took place. 'Do not judge the revolution by its bureaucrats; the question is not to discuss the notion of freedom,' Padilla said, 'but if you think freely and speak freely, then freedom will never leave you.'

My film *Cuba, Art and Revolution* ended with the following words:
No one who has been to Cuba can remain indifferent to the people who are making their fate out of history. The better the artist, the greater his struggle, which is true to his own creative vision as well as fulfilling the requirements of the revolution. For most of them, art is telling a collective truth, more important than their private one. Will these artists share the fate of Mayakovsky or Lissitzky of the Russian revolution? Will the party in the end not merely dictate the goal, but also define the means? Will power stifle originality or drive it underground? These are the questions which every honest artist asks every day. Most do not want to become merely critics of life, propounding moral and social ideas, but hope that their art will extend the quality of life. Whether this will survive depends mainly on Fidel Castro, whose own cryptic dictum has set the tone: 'Within the revolution everything, outside nothing!'

A few years later Edmundo Desnoes, Miguel Barnet and Leo Brower had turned their back on Cuba and left. Padilla after prison and beatings had officially confessed his guilt and finally left the country, a broken man. Nogueras, Lima and Piñera had died under strange circumstances, Arenas after years in jail had also fled, and Hans Werner Henze had become *persona non grata*. Most of my painter friends were no longer allowed to teach. Julio, after being put in jail, managed to leave for the States. These were only some of the many who had believed in the revolution and paid for it.

My 'revolutionary stances' brought me into contact with two delightful people, Ella Winter and Donald Ogden Stewart. Ella was a dynamic woman with an untamable rebellious spirit. She had been one of the first journalists to visit Russia in 1930, one of many visits to follow. Born in Australia, she grew up in England and finally became an American citizen. Her first marriage was to the famous journalist and fighter for social justice, Lincoln Steffens. After his death she married Donald Ogden Stewart, the Oscar-winning stage and screen writer.

Ella and Don knew everybody from Clare Boothe Luce to Gertrude Stein, from Malraux to John Steinbeck. As a girl Ella was exposed to the left-wing establishment, the Webbs, Wells, Bertrand Russell and the young Francis Meynell. She had met Freud in Vienna and Alfred Adler in Oxford. Through Don, who wrote the script of the film *Philadelphia Story*, she befriended many leading Hollywood writers and stars.

The Stewarts lived in a lovely old house in Hampstead, that stood in the middle of a large garden. Once more, as so often in my life, I was fortunate to enter a circle of people where things happened. Once Ella had adopted you there was no way of escaping. A refugee from the McCarthy persecution, she made her house in Hampstead the centre of many glittering parties, a haven for passing Americans. Ella Winter had described her eventful life in a book aptly called *And Not to Yield*, which carried on its cover a dedication by her friend Katharine Hepburn: 'Ella Winter is alive and vibrant and hopeful and has a green thumb for plants, people and politics.'

Ella did not go in for conventions, she liked to mix in décor as well as in people. She was an avid collector of friends and even more so of art. Her house was filled from top to bottom with paintings and objects. In the early years she had bought Kandinsky, Klee, Arp, Feininger and Miró. From Russia she had brought back several Lissitzkys. We were told she had bribed one of the cultural ministers with a dress from Neiman Marcus. When prices were so high that she could no longer afford great art, she concentrated on popular art, mostly from Latin America. The mixture was delightful – a ghastly stuffed rabbit sat peacefully under a Kurt Schwitters.

The centre of the Stewarts' social life was Sunday lunch. It was always informal, like a family gathering, and one never knew whom one would meet. The conversation was always at high pitch; Ella saw to this, Donald sometimes cutting her flow of words with a sharp and funny remark. After lunch, more people arrived for coffee and cakes. Ella reigned supreme, stimulating, flirting, driving the conversation along. There were the regulars: Patrick Woodcock, the Argentinian psychiatrist Estela Weldon, Eileen O'Casey and myself. Around the regulars were the occasional guests: Kenneth and Kathleen Tynan, Jules Feiffer, George Cukor, Katharine Hepburn, who might just drop in from jogging on the Heath or inquiring if the garden needed any weeding, the Chaplins and their children on a visit from Switzerland, often Ingrid Bergman. In Ella's house I met Salka Viertel, the wife of director Berthold Viertel. She was the centre of a famous immigrant salon in America and became the great friend and protector of Garbo. I listened to Arthur Miller and Edward Albee talking about a 'lost America' or Dr Spock lecturing about child-rearing on a lawn littered with parents and babies. Everybody loved Ella and Ella never stopped loving everybody.

Ella was what the Americans call a mover and shaker. If she did not like a programme on the television she would phone up the director general, mentioning that she was a friend of Peter Adam's. Ella liked the telephone and she could phone you up at seven o'clock in the morning without a qualm, engaging you in a conversation on the Black Panther movement or asking you to sign a petition for some Peruvian refugees. She could be totally manic and totally infuriating, but when Ella and Donald died almost in the same week we all realised the gaping hole they had left in our lives. For months I did not know where to go on Sundays.

In May 1970 I travelled to Venice to try to arrange a film on Luchino Visconti, who was filming *Death in Venice*. The combination of Visconti, Thomas Mann and Gustav Mahler was very seductive. Aschenbach was being played by Dirk Bogarde. In the winter Visconti and his team had undertaken a quest for the face of Tadzio, the boy who would unwittingly destroy Aschenbach. The search had taken them to Austria, Hungary, Finland and Sweden, where he had found his ideal: Bjørn Andresen, a young Swede.

Venice's old Grand Hôtel des Bains with its bustling beach life had been painstakingly reconstructed. The set was by Ferdinando Scarfiotti and the costumes by Piero Tosi, Italy's leading costume designer. There were carpets on the sand and old-fashioned beach huts. Every glass, lamp, piece of furniture had to be right. The reflection of a glass on a boy's face was as important to Visconti as the dialogue in a scene.

When I arrived Visconti was shooting the opening of the film: the arrival of the boat in the harbour in the early hours of the morning, the haunting scene of the ship slowly emerging from the black smoke which was eventually to cover the whole screen.

At first our meeting was not easy. He was not at all willing to let anybody film him working and was very strict about journalists on location. The only other one allowed was Kathleen Tynan, writing for an American magazine. I had asked for permission to watch him filming during the night, and we set out at three o'clock in the morning. It was bitter cold. We were standing on the old boat waiting for the sun to rise. When it finally rose, after three hours, it was not the shade the director wanted. I spent four more nights at Visconti's side, shivering, waiting. On the fifth day as the sun rose Visconti filmed his scene. Combined with Mahler's music it would be an unforgettable opening to his film: the boat arriving in the morning mist of Venice. In the icy morning hour, before going to his room Visconti looked at me and smiled: 'Reviens, Peter, fais ton film.' My tenacity and patience had paid of. I nearly jumped around his neck, but I knew better. Public familiarity was not for Visconti. Nobody called him Luchino in public, it was always 'Visconti'. Only in the evening, among friends, did we revert to the familiar first names.

One week later I was back. I hired the crew who had worked on *The Damned*, hoping this would make things easier.

Visconti arrived usually an hour before everybody else on location; he wanted to make sure that every detail was right. He alone decided if a day lasted eight, ten or twelve hours and if the lunch break was at 12, 2 or 4 o'clock. After the filming he would disappear to his room at the Gritti Palace Hotel, an hour later calling you on the phone: 'Viens dîner.' Dinner would always be at the same place, Harry's Bar, where he had a special table at the end of the room. There he held court, around him the main actors and his friends: Silvana Mangano, who played the mother, and Nora Ricci, who was the governess. Sometimes Nando Scarfiotti and Piero Tosi and other guests who had come to watch the filming: Marcello Mastroianni or Enrico Medioli.

To refuse Visconti's invitation could be fatal. One day, tired of long dinners with celebrities, Nando and I had decided to have a boys' evening in a trattoria. The next morning I found a little note on the board: 'Today no filming for the BBC.' I felt terrible. The next day we were allowed to film again. There was no mention of the incident. That night I sat again at Harry's Bar. After everybody had been served an *eau de vie*, Visconti turned to me and said with chilling politeness: 'Tu veux boire aussi?', then he smiled like a king who gave favours, but also took them away. Volatile, he could throw a terrible temper if he did not get his way. He demanded absolute loyalty, and when Kathleen Tynan wrote a less than flattering article in *Vogue* the roof fell in. Visconti wrote a ten-page handwritten letter to Bogarde accusing him of being a traitor, as it was he who had brought Tynan onto the set.

But Visconti could also be warm and generous, as when he took me to art galleries, sometimes reprimanding me when I talked too much. I was soon under his spell, like most people around him. It was not difficult to love him.

Bogarde was the only person who refused to be part of the Visconti court. The relationship between the two men was distant but full of respect and affection. Visconti had a great admiration for Bogarde the actor, but Bogarde the man he found too serious, too English, not outgoing enough, more an actor than a film star. Visconti was used to the glamour of Alain Delon, Romy Schneider or Maria Callas. Dirk Bogarde is a generous man without pretensions or false vanity. He would never indulge in the little games actors often play. He was totally genuine and slightly melancholic and laughed at what he called the 'Italian theatre' that most people on the film affected, 'the constant flatteries and the insincerity which seem to be their daily bread.' He preferred to be alone to read a good book. He had taken a house on the Giudecca and after the filming went straight home. I sometimes had lunch with him, joined by a cheerful Kathleen Tynan.

Bogarde usually arrived on the set at ten o'clock. It took several hours to put on his complicated makeup. He always brought Thomas Mann's novella, not the script, and consulted it. Visconti usually looked outwardly distant at this attempt to get to the text. His expression was impenetrable. He only communicated when he felt like it. Bogarde was a man of words, Visconti a man of images. Despite the fact that all his films, except for *Bellissima*, were based on literature, Visconti would always find words secondary to images. 'I don't know what to think,' Dirk wrote to me after the film was finished. 'I always hated the stuff that was not in the book, written by V, and nothing will make me change my mind.'

Visconti did not like to rehearse a lot, he preferred to go right into a take. He was not a director who went in for long speeches on motivation. 'I want the actor to be as natural as possible,' he told me, 'that is why I mix professionals with non-professionals. I do not like when the acting shows, not in film and not on stage.' I asked him once if he changed a scene a lot during filming. 'All the time. A scene on paper is nothing. I have to see it, then it comes alive,' he replied. 'He is a great improviser, I prepare the tracks for him,' Bogarde told me. 'To build his bridges, his level crossings on.' Before shooting the death scene he had told Bogarde: 'I want your face to express pity, pain, love, fear, indignation and ten other things – you must know what they are.'

One evening we filmed on a piazza. Visconti sat motionless on a chair. All the extras were hand-picked: a mixture of Spanish, German, Italian, French. Nobody ever worked on a Visconti film without his personal approval. The same applied to all the technicians, with most of whom Visconti had worked for years. The extras were waiting in the wings. Piero Tosi was always at hand, adjusting a button or a scarf, but every detail needed the approval of the maestro. Then Visconti whispered something to his assistant Albino Cocco, and the extras were brought on, one after the other, as in a ballet, and suddenly the scene came alive. It was intensely moving to watch.

The most wonderful moments were when we were alone; he was Luchino then. We spoke about loneliness and unrequited love. He had loved a great deal, always seduced by beauty, real physical beauty. Visconti, at sixty-three, was still handsome with his grand profile, his clear eyes and masculine bearing. As a young man he must have been stunning. I quoted von Platen's lines to him: 'Wer die Schönheit nur geschaut mit Augen ist dem Tode schon anheim gegeben' – Those who touch beauty only with their eyes belong already to death. He would eventually put these lines as a motto at the beginning of the film. We listened to records, mostly Mahler, selecting pieces for their dark sound of longing and readiness for death. Visconti had studied music and at one time wanted to become a cellist. He told me that Mann saw Mahler once in a train going to Vienna, which prompted Visconti to change Aschenbach from a writer into a composer.

When I accused him of reducing the essence of Mann's story to a homosexual parable, pointing out that it was Plato's Phaedo dialogue about the seduction of the mind that was the basis of the book, the Apollonian balance and the Dionysian freedom, he replied: 'This is a film, not a novel. I am trying to tell the human drama of an artist, his solitude and his desperation.'

I realised that this film was also the story of Visconti's own solitude and despair, a continuation of what he had been saying in *The Leopard*, Lampedusa's story of ageing and decaying. The transience of all beauty and the approach of death was a subject which increasingly preoccupied Visconti too.

For my programme, *Visconti at Work*, I had decided to concentrate on one scene and I had chosen the one of Aschenbach's hopeless walk in pursuit of Tadzio and his sisters, stealing along the infested streets. I spent ten days on the shoot, but the audience perceived it as a day in the life of this director.

For this particular scene Visconti was filming in the Jewish section of the town, bare of any tourist attractions. As in many scenes in the film, there was no dialogue. Visconti knew that he could rely on the suggestive power of his images.

He had ordered the rubbish that usually litters the streets to be burned, and the smoke was billowing in the air. The sky was laden with fine mist, like rain. The air was heavy and foul. The peeling walls were covered with public announcements about the plague. They were wet with carbolic acid. Visconti used real disinfectant and he had meat cut up to attract rats. The beautiful but slowly dying and sinking city, like the artificially painted face of Aschenbach, was the very image of advancing death.

Visconti had set up the camera in a kitchen window of a private flat. I was allowed to put mine right next to his. He directed by giving instructions through a megaphone. Bogarde's hat was not tilted at the right angle. Piero Tosi rushed on to the scene to adjust it. Visconti wanted a button on Tadzio's suit to be undone and was getting impatient. I could see the mood changing in his face, like a dark cloud. Then he was ready for the first take and his mood suddenly changed again, as he clowned around with a clothes peg on his nose. This was for the benefit of my

Visconti filming *Death in Venice*

camera. Visconti hardly ever looked through the camera, completely trusting his cameraman, Ruggero Mastroianni. He gave the minimum of instructions, but they were very clear. 'Crouch behind the lantern, Dirk, no, more to the left.' He shot six takes, none of them printed, then we broke for lunch. It was two o'clock in the afternoon.

Visconti invited me to share his lunch on the terrace of the restaurant La Fenice. He was meeting Nicole Stéphane, who acted in Jean Cocteau's film *Les Enfants terribles*. She had become a producer, and her greatest dream was to persuade Visconti to make a film of Proust's *Un Amour de Swann*. It was a magnificent and inspired idea, for Visconti loved Proust more than any other writer and knew many passages by heart. There were so many similarities in their worlds, it seemed an obvious choice. Unfortunately their project was never realised, although he had worked out a script in great detail, even including the costumes. He wanted to cast Brigitte Bardot as Odette. Silvana Mangano was to be the Duchesse de Guermantes. Delon was also to play a part.

After lunch at about four o'clock we were back for the filming. Take nine: this was the one Visconti would finally use, but by no means the last one he shot. We had come a long way from the first take. Bogarde's shambling walk conveyed accurately Aschenbach's moral and physical decay. This is what Visconti had been waiting for; the actor's movements looked completely natural.

At seven o'clock the day was over; it had yielded about four minutes of film. For eleven hours seventy people had been executing one man's will. They submitted to his autocracy because they had complete confidence that he, better than anybody, knew what he was trying to capture. It was my last evening. Visconti was tired and there was no dinner at Harry's Bar. I was glad we sat in his room and watched the World Cup football on television.

I had stuck to the idea of only covering the filming of one scene. Thomas Mann's words were read over the many stunning production stills Visconti had given me, making my programme more literary. I used Mahler's music and by strange coincidence had chosen the same pieces Visconti would later use in his feature film: Mahler 3 and 5. I nervously sent my documentary to Rome, where Visconti was still editing. I wanted his approval. I needed it.

Ten days passed, ten very long days. Then a little parcel was delivered to the BBC. It contained a beautiful book: *Vecchie Immagine di Venezia*, old photographs of Venice. It bore the following inscription: 'Avec Amitié, Luchino'. There was also a short note. 'Seulement un artiste peut voir un autre, merci', and an inscribed photograph of himself on location: 'Pour ta

Vie à Venise sur ma Mort à Venise'. No compliment in my entire career has given me greater satisfaction.

England must be the only country where the word intellectual is an insult rather than a compliment. I slowly gained the reputation of making elitist programmes. Making documentaries about Thomas Mann, André Malraux and Albert Camus was not helping to break down the barrier between high and popular culture, as fashion was demanding. The coherent traditional values I had been brought up with were challenged everywhere: from the left, from the feminists, from the populists. It was suddenly considered elitist to celebrate or to talk about the joy of being part of a general consensus. Kenneth Clark's mandarin *Civilisation* was dismissed by some because it took absolutely for granted its own assumptions of what constitutes civilisation. This trend began in the seventies and continued for the next two decades. The result was the total fragmentation of values and a loss of cultural confidence.

My old-fashioned liberal middle-class notion that all my endeavours have somehow to improve people's lives was frowned upon. But I refused to feel guilty. I clung to the notion that the making of arts programmes had more to do with education than with entertainment, but it was not always easy to convince people that the arts were joyful and life-enhancing because they were serious. I have always tried to capture the imagination of the largest number of people with my programmes, but I did not believe in buying their attention by lowering what is known as 'standards'.

The new thinking of the trendy opportunists began to shift these standards. Many programme-makers became culturally confused, trying to convince us that Bob Dylan was just as good as Keats or Rimbaud. I had nothing against Bob Dylan, he was a poet, but Rimbaud and Keats were on a diffent level.

In this climate many of the projects I proposed were rejected. I approached Hannah Arendt. 'The interview business, I never do anything of this sort,' she wrote, 'especially if it is on television.' I did not give up, the less so when I found out that the reason for her refusal was that she did not like 'to be recognised in the street'. She finally agreed: 'For England in principle it is o k, but what will your questions be? I shall have to know them beforehand.' Alas the idea of an interview with this profound and influential thinker was considered too elitist.

Not all lost opportunities were the fault of the b b c. Not surprisingly they accepted my idea of a film on Marlene Dietrich, but Dietrich wanted $5,000 for it (*Review* usually paid £150 for an interview). Such a sum was out of the question. I wrote to Ingmar Bergman, who had just finished *Cries and Whispers,* and received a refusal but with the possibility of 'doing it another time'. The Bergman interview, too, is among the many missed opportunities.

Of course one of the main tasks of *Review* was to reflect the arts of our time and to cover recent books, exhibitions and artistic events. It was an honourable effort to deal with the arts on television, and our programmes were by today's standards positively highbrow. We featured many writers: Kurt Vonnegut, Graham Greene, John Updike, Gore Vidal and a bird-like Muriel Spark.

Vladimir Nabokov, the refined and sharp observer of the world, gave an evasive interview, wanting to talk more about butterflies than about literature. 'Do you see yourself sometimes as Nabokov the writer, isolated from others, a flaming sword to scourge them, an entertainer, a drudge, a genius – which?' Jim insisted. On the last word Nabokov chuckled:

The word genius is passed around rather generously, isn't it? At least in English, because its Russian counterpart *renuu* is a term brimming with a sort of throaty awe and is used only in the case of a very small number of writers – Shakespeare, Milton, Pushkin, Tolstoy. To such deeply beloved authors as Turgenev and Chekhov, Russians assign the thinner term, *tareht.* Genius still means to me a unique, dazzling gift – the genius of James Joyce, not the talent of Henry James.

James Mossman was a brilliant interviewer, for he listened patiently and was never nervous. He hardly ever prepared questions. They grew naturally out of the answers. We did most interviews together, he as the interviewer, I as the director. There was never any competition, and I learned most of my craft from him.

Not all our interviews were done in the studio. Sometimes in order to be out of the limelight we filmed them in my flat in Earls Terrace. Edward Albee, Peter Shaffer, John Gielgud, Doris Lessing and even Mick Jagger were filmed there. Mick Jagger, conscious that he would appear on Britain's most prestigious arts magazine, wore a tweed suit and gave the impression of being frightfully respectable, although he complained about the tea which I poured out of grandmother Adam's silver tea service.

Filming so many different personalities in the same environment produced a letter from a viewer: 'I do understand, Mr Mossman,' a lady wrote from Leeds, 'that John Gielgud, Edward Albee and Mick Jagger live in the same flat, and I want to point out that this does not shock me, but may I ask what Doris Lessing is doing there?'

Sometimes *Review* would commission some small films of strong visual power, like one on Stubbs by Leslie Megahey and one on Pavese by Gavin Millar, two of the most talented film directors in the department. We would ask Eleanor Bron and Alan Bennett to do some sketches for *Review*. They were challenging people to work with, very cerebral and quite elusive, despite their fame. Many of Bennett's sketches were written for us, along the lines that he later took up in his *Talking Heads*. Among them was a brilliant one on Bernard Berenson in *I Tati*.

Jim and I also filmed John Berger. I had kept in contact with him since our first work together. Berger was always falling in love with ideas, which gave his writing such personal passion. 'The Woman as Object', 'The Rural Savage', 'The Man Free from Institutions' were only a few of the themes he would hammer out in his iconoclastic attacks on present-day life. Berger believed that, if we were able to understand the way the media changed our perception of the arts, we would also be able to understand better who we were. He had thought more than most about the relationship of art and television, all things he later exposed in a brilliant television essay, *The Art of Seeing*, directed by Mike Dibb.

The sharp and sometimes quirky mind of Berger appealed greatly to Jim. Here was a man without pretensions, who lived according to his vision. That was precisely what Jim had been trying to do himself. There was an instant empathy and a deep rapport between the two men, and it was moving to watch the liberal and the Marxist confronting each other, hammering some public truths out of their private worlds.

Jim did not believe that the role of art was to present an alternative reality to that which exists. 'Can you demand more from art than to receive an extraordinary sense of life?' he asked. 'Yes! The role of art is a kind of preface to that life when people can really determine their own lives: a preface to a life of freedom,' Berger replied.

Both shared a great pessimism. John Berger saw art as a tragic phenomenon, because he thought that the human situation is tragic. 'The result of self-consciousness. It is not the tragic that is intolerable. What is intolerable is that our tragedy is not given its due dignity.' 'The shit of this life and its beauty,' as Berger put it, which matched Jim's favourite saying from Tolstoy that 'life was a *tartine de merde* which one was obliged to eat slowly'. When Jim had cited Tolstoy's quote to Nabokov the Russian writer had replied: 'The old boy was sometimes rather disgusting. My own view of life is like a fresh slice of bread with country butter and Alpine honey.'

Jim's life was not butter and honey; alas too often he only saw the shit and failed to see the beauty, although his humour sometimes still shone through, as when he described a fat oriental ambassador slipping and bouncing down some steps at a carnival 'like a painted football'.

Another memorable interview and an important one for me was with the author Enid Bagnold. Bagnold, a friend of Hester Chapman, Diana Cooper and Rosamond Lehmann, entertained us at lunch with delightful and quite scandalous anecdotes about 'those truly liberated ladies'. Frank Harris had said to a young Bagnold: 'Love is the gateway to life.' 'I knew I had to go through the gateway of life,' she told us laughingly and added: 'In an upper room in the Café Royal.'

It was a lucid interview. She spoke about her attempt 'to catch life as it goes by. Writing is like pulling up windows, so that more and more landscape shows.' She described the landscape of her childhood in Jamaica. 'I gave this meadow life again by the power of my sensibility. That meadow had no life, it's gone, I brought it back in my writing.'

Many years later, when I began to write myself, I recalled Bagnold's desire to remember and record life out of her imagination and thus to explore the world inside herself. There was another lesson I learned: 'Writing is discipline,' she had said. 'You must leave a space in your day. Every day, I go down and sit at my desk and wait. One is always hoping that something extraordinary would happen, like a wet mermaid coming out of the water; of course it doesn't. But sometimes I feel it coming down my arm, and then I can write. Without that space it would not happen.'

There was one area where Jim and I would always fight. He did not care much for contemporary art. His love in the visual arts was rarely accorded to the pretty, never to the sensational. He liked Henry Moore and Keith Vaughan, but the newest trend in modern art was not for him; he considered it shallow or even rubbish.

When I would bring back from New York prints by Lichtenstein, Rauschenberg and Warhol, which at that time could be bought for $5 each, he laughed. I had bought Warhol's *Liz Taylor* and *Flowers* for $10 at Castelli's and an extra $3 to have them signed. In 1988 I sold both for $9000 at Sotheby's.

In 1956 when I was living in New York, Gene Moore, the king of window dressers, of Bonwitt Teller and Tiffany's, had taken me to a Crazy Golden Slipper Show, an exhibition of drawings of shoes. Each carried the name of a famous figure: Mae West, James Dean, Elvis Presley, Truman Capote. The artist was a young man who had recently changed his name from Andrew Warhola to Andy Warhol, a strange gaunt figure, surrounded by hustlers and junkies. He looked terrible, a pale mottled face crowned by a silver wig, always worn slightly askew. There was something unsavoury and creepy about him. Later I realised that this was something he cultivated.

I liked Andy. He could be kind and he was often very funny, especially when it came to gossiping about other people. When he laughed his weirdness suddenly disappeared. I think he liked me too, but he was never very communicative, though he sent me his catalogues, signed on almost every page – Warhol loved signing – giving me funny nicknames: 'For Dick', 'For Kraut' and so on.

Everything about Warhol was exaggerated: his camp bearing, his limp wrist, his artificial voice, even his frailty. It was as if he had decided to make a caricature of himself in order to prevent other people doing it. There was an almost masochistic pleasure in being surrounded by all those beautiful people who depended on him. He courted them without any sign of envy. He was always distant; that was his power.

Warhol was totally asexual, but he was a typical voyeur, who got great kicks out of talking about sex. He was always encouraging everybody to talk about sexual details and under the slightest pretext of either drawing, photographing or filming, he tried to persuade the boys to take their pants off.

He was already very famous, but London had to wait until 1971 for his first large show at the Tate Gallery. I wanted to film him for *Review*, and argued passionately with Jim. Here was an important artist, able to change the history of art by making us look at the world differently. After Warhol's and the other pop artists' simple and strong images, we saw pop paintings everywhere in real life. They enriched our vision of reality. I could not get this into Jim's head, however hard I tried. At least he agreed to let me make a film about Warhol.

Warhol and his entourage, Jane Forth and the handsome Joe Dallesandro, stayed at the Ritz Hotel. When I arrived, the clerk at the desk gave me a strange look, and after a few calls I was allowed upstairs.

We had all seen Joe in the buff, for he had generously shown his body in films by Warhol and Paul Morrissey like *Flesh* and *Trash,* and the very sexy photograph of a naked father with a child decorated many people's walls. He opened the door of the suite they all shared, stark naked and grinning, a very pleasant sight indeed. Jane was also naked, lying on the bed. The only one dressed was Andy. It was stifling hot in the room, but he was wearing a sweater and a leather jacket. I noticed his expressive hands which he waved about. He insisted on calling me Dick – 'Get undressed Dick,' he said, like it was the most natural thing in the world. 'It's hot in here.' We spent the rest of the day together working out what we could film. We agreed that Mossman would conduct the interview at the Tate.

In the afternoon I took them to David Hockney, who lived in a flat behind Notting Hill Gate. The two painters liked each other and shared a passion for photographs, especially Polaroids. Andy laughed a lot, which was rare, for he usually shrouded himself in a sort of mysterious silence which was slightly disconcerting. I thought how different the two painters were, despite their superficial similarities. Both came from working-class backgrounds, both had known spectacular popular success. They enjoyed their public image to the extreme of eccentricity. Both flaunted their homosexuality with abandon. But they were like the different faces of the same coin. Warhol craved fame and affection, and when he found them, he looked at them with ice-cold detachment. Hockney also enjoyed fame, but he savoured it with a childlike joy. Both were the centres of a large group of hangers-on, but Warhol governed his collection of debris with a demonic grip, leading them on in a kind of dance of death. Hockney was the benign centre of cheerful youngsters and friends.

The next day I filmed a whole sequence of images with Warhol: Coca-Cola bottles on a shelf, Brillo pads and soup cans in a supermarket. I also filmed the scene in the hotel, with the girl voluptuously curling up against Joe's naked body. It was very sensual and erotic. Andy clowned around fully dressed, but he once lifted up his shirt, which was not a pretty sight.

In the Tate, where they were still hanging the paintings, I filmed Warhol talking about his techniques and about what he was after. Unfortunately when Jim arrived Andy clammed up, I do not know why. Joe tried to speak for him and to reply to Jim's questions while Andy put on the act of non-communication I had seen so often. I thought that since this was typical of Warhol, it had a place in the film. It turned out to be a strange piece of work; disorderly, defiant, using popular images. When Jim saw it, especially his struggle to get some sense out of Warhol, he decided to scrap the whole subject. 'Gibberish,' he said. I was devastated. It was the first and – I am glad to say – the last time a film of mine was not broadcast.

I remained friends with Andy Warhol – friend is maybe too strong a word, but we kept in contact, seeing each other intermittently. He somehow blamed me for the lack of vision of the BBC, and the one thing he could not take was rejection. Twenty years later when Warhol died, the BBC looked frantically for some material on him. It had been destroyed.

I have often looked back at the strange and exhilarating time of the late sixties and the early seventies, of New York, Warhol and his Factory, a time of soaring high. Where have all those dreams led us to?

I saw Warhol for the last time at the Anthony d'Offey Gallery in London, where a series of portraits of the sixties were shown. On the walls the ravaged and demonic faces from the high time of the sniffing, shooting and smoking Factory. I wanted to embrace Andy, but knowing how much he hated any physical contact, I just shook his hand, which was cold and lifeless. 'Hi Dick,' he said and then moved away into the large crowd of aficionados. A few minutes later he was back. 'I am so bored, I have been for a very long time,' and he was off again before I could reply. I thought about his many friends, many no longer alive. Some had also been mine. Both Ted Carey, who introduced me to the Factory, and Mario Amaya, who was wounded when Valerie Solanas opened fire on Warhol, had died of AIDS. Herko had jumped out of a window. Edie Sedgwick died of an overdose. So many icons that Warhol had tried to immortalise in his films and paintings were no more.

In London too life was free and easy wheeling. Seen from today it is hard to understand how daring and exhilarating this new-found freedom was. Kenneth Tynan, who for years had written a regular and very entertaining column, 'Shouts and Murmurs', in the *Observer*, was one of the most brilliant theatre critics around. He became a sort of apostle of sexual freedom, openly spoke up for pornography and about the rights and pleasures of masturbation. Words that are now almost common usage were then totally taboo. Tynan put on an erotic entertainment, *O Calcutta*. The title was based on the pun 'O quel cul t'as'. The humour struck me as pretty collegiate, despite the distinguished writers who had collaborated: Edna O'Brien, Jules Feiffer, David Mercer. Samuel Beckett had written a sketch on my favourite Paris strip club, the Crazy Horse Saloon, and John Lennon on the Liverpool Wank, but most of it was not even witty or funny. It was certainly not shocking.

At the Royal Court a play by David Storey was set in the changing-room of a soccer club. For almost the entire evening a rather stuffy audience faced a group of naked actors. No play seemed to be complete without people stripping. We had seen nudity in *Hair*, and *Romeo and Juliet* in the buff. I filmed Hans van Maanen and his Netherlands Dance Theatre in a ballet danced entirely in the nude. The BBC had to be more careful and I received a note from Huw Wheldon saying: 'Peter Adam should refrain from using too much nudity in his programmes. I suggest that he limits them to three female and two male frontal nudes per year.'

Jim and I talked about making a film on Joe Orton (who had been murdered by his lover in 1967), but we realised that we could not do justice to this *enfant terrible* on television, so dropped the idea. I had met Joe Orton and his lover Kenneth Halliwell shortly before they died, through

Kenneth Williams. I liked Kenneth, he was not at all the camp actor most people saw, but a deeply serious person with strong religious convictions. He had been in Peter Shaffer's double bill *Private Eye* and *Public Ear* and in the first production of Orton's *Loot*. One day he suggested that I meet the two *enfants terribles*. My first impression of Orton stuck firmly in my head. He was out to shock and very eager to show off his sexual prowess. The old Priapus boast de Sade had already fallen for was his favourite. 'Dix-huit pouces de long sur seize de circumference, surmonté d'un champignon vermeil et large comme le cul d'un chapeau.'[1] 'The whole of London, I am told, has seen your dick,' were his first words. 'Why don't you let me see it too.' Kenneth was embarrassed, although he must have witnessed scenes like this before. When Orton realised that I could neither be shocked nor provoked he changed tack and became very charming, without dropping his brilliant and caustic wit. Halliwell never said a word, he was sort of sulking. I saw Orton only once more when I went to his flat in Islington, a very small and very untidy room. I later often thought that it was in this room that Halliwell battered him to death with a hammer. Orton was thirty-four years old.

Facundo and I dreamed of finding a small country house in France. We had spent some time in La Garde-Freinet, twenty kilometres from St Tropez, one of those small unspoiled hillside villages not yet overrun by tourists. Olivier Todd had bought a small house there and Tony Richardson owned a little run-down hamlet, Le Nid du Duc, right in the middle of nowhere. The first time I was invited to Le Nid du Duc, I immediately fell in love with the area.

Tony was a wonderful and generous host. It is difficult to describe the charm and the euphoria of this magic place. Everybody who was anybody would eventually be invited to Le Nid du Duc. Tony was a mixture of Mephisto and Prospero; he stage-managed everybody's stay, and given the chance, even their lives. He took a real pleasure mixing and matching people, regardless of background and sexual preferences, and many a couple was founded or split up in those blissful summers in his place. The houses were always filled with actors, painters and writers. In one house David Hockney made sketches for his painting *Portrait of the Artist's Pool with Two Figures*, in another John Gielgud was immersed in a book. The wonderful and lively assortment might include a racing driver, Eileen Atkins, or a beach boy one of the guests had brought home the previous

---

1 'Eighteen inches long and sixteen inches in circumference, crowned by a vermilion mushroom, and large as the ass of a hat.'

night. One day there could be Simone Signoret or Niki de Saint-Phalle, another time Vanessa Redgrave, Jack Nicholson or Helen Dawson.

Stars and the people who worked in the kitchen or on the land all joined in. Yolande, a lively woman from the village, cooked large casseroles of Provençal food and entertained everybody with her stories. Lunch was taken under a big tree, with peacocks and ducks strutting around. Tony organised games, picnics and theatre evenings; treasure hunts could last the whole day. He would always make sure that the most unsuitable couples or the most unconventional ones were teamed up together. One never knew what one would find: bottles of champagne hidden in a stream with glasses, or a book with pornographic photographs. There were also always plenty of children, as colourful as the grown-ups; all of them were allowed to sleep in a huge room. There were Tony's own children, Joely and Natasha from his marriage to Vanessa Redgrave, and Katherine, whose mother was a lovely young woman, Griselda Grimond. Joined to them were Gian Carlo, the son of Vanessa and her lover Franco Nero, the children of Penelope and John Mortimer or Roxana, the daughter of Kenneth and Kathleen Tynan. One day they all put on a show, *Gypsy, The Greatest Show on Earth*. Joely, aged five, did a strip-tease to a trumpet which brought the house down.

STARRING

Joely Richardson	*Gypsy*
Jemma Redgrave	*Baby June*
John Mortimer	*Mr Goldstone*
Natasha Richardson	*Rose*

And featuring

Jacky Rufus Isaacs,	
Penny Mortimer	
and Gian Carlo	*The Strippers*

The production was directed by Natasha and Penny and the script was by John Mortimer QC.

I kept the little programme, and when Tony died in 1992 I sent it to Natasha and Joely, by then both established actresses in their own right.

One morning Facundo and I stumbled upon a little hill with sheep grazing between olive trees. It was exactly what we had dreamed of – three acres of blissfully secluded land with a little *cabanon* on it. We bought it that very morning, and La Garde-Freinet would become our second home for the next twenty years.

15
Review II: From Borges to Man Ray
1971–1972

I lost my diary for 1971, a year of great gain and great loss, but many events are engraved in my memory.

With the advancing illness Keith dug himself in. He had become quite dependent on the few friends he still saw: Prunella, Patrick Woodcock and myself. 'Come back soon,' he wrote while I was abroad, 'the group is miserable without a leader.'

His studio was always in immaculate order with every painting catalogued in little files. Taking them one after the other from their neatly stacked racks, he listened attentively to what I said, gracious and full of modesty. 'I especially appreciated your observation last night on the later pictures. It was precisely the impression I longed to convey, but so many people erect barriers between the "figurative" and "abstract" and stay on one side or the other.' Extracts from his many diaries had been published and revealed how much he reflected on every aspect of painting and its relevance to life.

He had three shows in the Marlborough Gallery. None gave him much joy. He felt that the fashion and the time had passed him by, yet he continued to work in an almost unchanging routine which began at 9.30 in the morning and finshed at night, to be interrupted by two meals he cooked for himself. Sixty-one notebooks chart the daily happenings of this life. They talk about much dismay and personal anguish, and chronicle the slow decline.

A melancholic dignity surrounded everything he did with a trace of bitterness. Sometimes his gloom would shift, and he played the piano. 'I'd forgotten what it was like to laugh and feel happy,' he wrote after an evening we had spent making marmalade. 'Now I am going to work on die Marmelade.' After the opening of a show of Patrick Procktor with the usual mixed crowd of artists and art lovers, he wrote me a note saying: 'I believe the show ended in some bloodshed, which is what comes from letting anarchist poets loose among the visual arts.'

Keith taught me a lot about English culture, the poetry of Larkin, the writing of Ruskin, even the use of the English language. 'A lesson on English use,' he wrote in reply to a goodbye note from me, 'you leave FOR a place not TO, e.g. I am leaving FOR New York, but I leave TO Klaus P all my worldly goods. Love Herr Professor.' There was hardly a subject one could not discuss with him: the ballets of Diaghilev, Beethoven's correspondence with his nephew or the memoirs of the art dealer René Gimpel. His letters were always full of a kind of franglais: '*Manchmal lustig manchmal traurig*' (sometimes gay and sometimes sad), he replied, after I enquired about his mood. 'It was so good of you to listen to my *langweilige Klage* [boring complaints] last night, I am now full of hope and determination and anxiety about the *cordon sanitaire* against the onslaught of Mama and R [Ramsay McClure, his longtime lover]. I remember your advice, most of it wise and all warmly sensible and supportive. But time cannot be regained and as you have sown, or be sown, so must you reap. However, *lasset Beides mit einander wachsen* [let both grow together] and wait for *die Erntezeit* [harvest time]. I detect slight signs of what *Wonne* [pleasure] is. It is beginning to form.'

There were other dark clouds looming in my life. Jim continued to see new mediums, all promising to put him in contact with his deceased friend, Louis. Sometimes he laughed about it, shrugging it off as humbug, but more often than not he came back with a garment of Louis' in his hand, claiming that he felt some connection. Death began drawing him nearer and nearer. It was frightening to watch the pain heading our way. Sometimes in the morning I caught him sitting alone at Lyon's Corner House.

On 24 March we drove to Oxford to interview the philosopher Stuart Hampshire. Jim talked as so often before about the senseless renewal of nature. I tried as best as I could to cheer him up. In a few days' time his new novel, *Beggars on Horseback*, was coming out. The next day we interviewed Doris Lessing. Her noble humility struck a warm chord in Jim, and I could see how moved he was by the fierce and lucid integrity of the woman and the writer, which seemed to invade everything she said. It was an interview with dark foreboding, of things not yet possessed or even presumed. 'We are living in the middle of a whirlwind,' she had said, talking about the disgust, doubt and self-division which afflicts people everywhere. Afterwards Jim complained bitterly: 'These talks are all wrong for television, where they will be debased. Why am I doing this, it is all so pointless, trivial. Here is a real writer and we squeeze five minutes out of her beautiful mind to make an item on the box. It is obscene.'

The programme went out nevertheless and a courteous Doris Lessing sent me the first edition of *The Golden Notebook*. 'Thank you for a lovely programme,' she had written on the title page. These were the real compensations for our work.

Jim and I had made plans to drive to France to visit Elisabeth Frink and Dirk Bogarde over Easter. I had persuaded Bogarde to give an interview. 'My dear Peter,' Dirk had written in his inimitable style, 'I am a bit old hat, marketing, painting doors, cutting logs, digging the potager. Life fills up. I have no intention of showing the great unwashed, or answer Delon-like questions, but if you think O.K it is fine.' (He was referring to an interview I had done with Alain Delon.) I was looking forward to spending some time in Bogarde's welcoming house near Cannes and I knew it would cheer Jim up.

On 2 April I drove to Paris with Jim's suitcase in the boot. He was to join me later in Nice. A few days later Facundo and I ran into Jeremy Noble, the music critic of *The Times*. I had not seen him for a while and I, as usual, bubbled over with excitement about my life and my work with James Mossman. 'Not any longer,' Jeremy said. At such moments one is blown apart as if by a bomb. My heart stood still, while he pulled out *The Times* obituary. Jim had already passed into history.

I do not remember what happened then. Life can be so cutting, so painful, that you move as if in a haze. The B B C had been trying to find me for three days. The inquest had already taken place. Jim had taken sleeping pills in his house in Norfolk. There was only one letter, to his brother. The funeral was set for next day. I left the car in Paris and flew to London. That night I sat in the garden of Edwardes Square until I saw the day coming up. Jim and I had often walked here. It was like our garden. I could not stop crying. I sat almost motionless, except for the tears, trying to understand the meaning of this pain and the feeling of loss.

Next day, I took the train to Sheffield, where the funeral was to take place. Our small group wrapped our grief in silence. Only an old friend of Jim, an army colonel, could not stop talking, it was his way of trying to come to terms with the shock. I could not cry any longer, it was as if something had clammed up in me. I think it was anger. He had not even waited for the publication of his novel. Nothing seemed to have any hold on him, not his work, not his strong conviction, not the love and friendship he received from all sides. He just let go. I felt so cheated, so let down. He had it all planned, the trip, me leaving alone. He had not even left a letter. There was no room for sentimentality or gesture in Jim. I could almost hear him saying: 'What could words possibly mean? Faced with the finality of death, they are as meaningless as everything else.'

From time to time Anne James's hand groped for mine. Anne had been

Huw Wheldon's assistant and was now a producer of beautiful and highly sensitive films. She was one of the many people Jim had trusted. On the station we waited a long time for a taxi; finally one arrived. 'Butterfly Taxis' it said, on its roof a big colourful butterfly. Jim would have liked this, it was almost as if he had arranged it. We drove to the little chapel. There, like a big dark cloud, stood the entire B B C establishment, the black clump of controllers, heads of departments, colleagues. They advanced towards me. I suddenly realised that I was considered the 'official widow' by the sympathetic liberal establishment, who could only think of one thing. Two gay men must be lovers.

Then it was all over. I took the train back, for I could not face any of the offers of a lift. I went straight to the office. I passed Jim's little office. His secretary Sarah Miller sat there, like a lost child, staring out the window. A meeting was going on in Stephen Hearst's office, with Aubrey Singer and other executive producers. Everybody looked up in surprise and embarrassment when I entered. 'We have a programme to get on the air in three days' time,' I said, very calmly, and then added: 'You have all been very wonderful, but Jim and I were never lovers. There are as many shades of relationships between homosexuals as between heterosexuals. Ours was one of love and friendship.' I almost had to laugh when I saw their embarrassed faces, and Lorna Pegram, wonderful, warm, vulnerable Lorna, got up and embraced me and said: 'Thank you, it is a good lesson.' Then we drafted the next programme. It was decided that Tony Staveacre and I would run *Review* in a shared editorship.

There was a letter addressed to Jim which he had never received. 'Thank you for letting me read your book. What immediately struck me was what a good film it would make, quite apart from its literary merits, which are great. You also ought to be writing plays. I did so very much enjoy the novel. Doris Lessing.' There was another one from her, written a few days later, addressed to me. 'I heard tonight that James Mossman is dead. If there is anything I can do please let me know. I am so very sorry.'

Some deaths seem to strike people more strongly than others, even those who were not his close friends grieved deeply. People wandered in the corridors as if lost. Some of the younger people like Alan Yentob were profoundly changed and even older colleagues had tears in their eyes when they talked about Jim. It was as if everybody had lost a friend. 'Dear Peter, Our thoughts are continually returning to Jim,' wrote John Berger. 'I have tried not just to register but to receive his death – which is what his dignity and integrity demands I believe, for it is to continue the meaning he sought.' John was right. My first concern was to make a programme on this rare journalist and to raise some money for a James Mossman scholarship. I wanted to use the impetus of all the declarations of sympathy and put them to good use.

I began by viewing all of Jim's films. It was a painful task seeing his ghost on the screen in Vietnam, in the Congo, speaking to Haile Selassie, to Nyerere or Solzhenitsyn. What would he have thought of my vain attempts to conjure up some reality out of facts and shadows? Slowly during his short but intense career I saw his eyes shifting from the outer world to the inner. I called the programme *To Be a Witness*.

Peter Shaffer had come back from New York where he now lived, and I asked him to write the script about one of his oldest and closest friends. Only a writer could do Jim justice, I thought. The result was poignant. Choked by emotions, he began:

> This next hour belongs to James Mossman, born 10 September 1926; died 5 April 1971. A renowned journalist. A famous commentator. A passionate examiner of the world through himself – and of himself through the world. A man who left behind in the guts of many of us the feeling of a presence so authentic, so dazzling, so warm and so original that we know we will never encounter its like again.

So many people were asking, why? They could not understand the soul-sickness, the tragic mistake of the self-chosen death by this handsome, successful, esteemed person. Peter and I had decided that we owed an explanation to his friends, his viewers and also to ourselves.

> What killed him was a multiple grief. The wearing out of the possibility of personal private love, but also his sickening of making comment for the public. What killed him was the constant changing of instinctive past into plastic present; the turning of our need to adore into a passion for making false gods; the shout of sexual joy fading into the stillness of cemeteries. What killed him was the clamour – that clamour of follies – and behind it, always felt, and feared and finally wanted, the silence.

Jim's long-lasting love affair with death had been strengthened by his strange dabbling with the occult. The day of the funeral Rosamond Lehmann phoned me up, offering to put me in 'contact' with Jim. 'Our beloved Jim lives on,' she later wrote, 'after a time of the dark night of the soul, he will grow and function in an expanded consciousness. He needed so much help to get through the fog of inertia and despair, but the worst is over and he will recover his great stature. If you can't believe this then just let it sink into the basement of your mind. One day it will find its time. Love, Rosamond.'

I did let it sink into the basement of my mind. I had long understood that Jim's depression was no ordinary one. He suffered from manic depression, an illness just like any other illness, which needed medical attention and can be cured. In the last year of his life, Jim had seen much of Jonathan Miller. It was Jonathan who suggested to me starting a scholarship for research into mental illness. I founded the James Mossman Scholarship. Robin Day, Jeremy Isaacs, Huw Wheldon, Humphrey Burton and many more signed the petition. Everybody sent money. John Gielgud, Peggy Ashcroft, Elisabeth Frink, David Hockney, Christopher Hampton, Arnold Wesker, John Schlesinger, Peter Brook. Their letters spoke of the impact he made on their life.

Enid Bagnold wrote about the pain she felt. It seemed like yesterday when this optimistic woman made Jim laugh. 'Why should it all go down the drain?' she had said. 'Writing is like love – oh dear I shall be sounding so absurd if I say this, but I sort of tremble with excitement every morning as though something wonderful would happen. It hasn't. I am going to be eighty. But perhaps between eighty and ninety, I might be visited by God knows what and I will write something wonderful.' I wished Jim had had some of her optimism and her energy.

'James Mossman used to question the necessity of art at all,' wrote Peter Shaffer. 'Is it a refuge or a true way? Is it as dispensable as flesh, or finally as irrelevant as cloth?' Jim never knew the answer.

> A man sets himself the task of outlining the world. Through the years he peoples a space with images of provinces, kingdoms, mountains, bays, ships, islands, fishes, dwellings, instruments, stars, horses, and persons. A little before he dies, he discovers that the patient labyrinth of lines traces the images of his face.[1]

These were the words of Jorge Luis Borges, whose strange and compelling stories had fascinated me for a very long time. Although he was admired and discussed abroad, I felt that the English were suspicious of this 'metaphysical detective', and I was pleased that my first story as the new co-editor was about him. The baroque world of *El Aleph* and *El Zahir* was also Facundo's. I knew that Borges was reluctant to be filmed, as he was blind, and I asked V. S. Pritchett, who was a friend of his, to put in a word for me. To my delight Pritchett offered to conduct the interview himself.

I noticed immediately the frail old man of refined elegance and great naturalness in the hotel lobby, his suit hanging loosely from his slightly stooping shoulders. He was leaning on a stick, looking into the void.

---

1   *El Hacedor; Dream.*

Filming Jorge Luis Borges and V.S. Pritchett

When I introduced myself one of his hands began to explore the outline of my face, his eyes now firmly fixed on me although he could not see me.

Noticing my accent he changed immediately to German. Borges had been in charge of Argentina's National Library, but it might as well have been the Great Library of Babel, for this urban and cosmopolitan man spoke twenty or more languages. After a while he switched to Middle High German. Thanks to Professor Kunisch's excellent teaching I was able to reply. He asked me to take him for a walk, and wandering around Green Park we spoke about Gundolf's interpretations of Stefan George. His gestures were sparse and his almost inaudible voice seemed to come from someone else. Sometimes he laughed a sort of happy giggle. It was slightly disconcerting to listen to him while watching his unfocused eyes.

A little later Pritchett joined us, and we went to the room where the crew had set up the camera. The two old men of letters sat opposite each other, rather lost. Their conversation was halting. Pritchett, self-conscious and slightly embarrassed, was groping for questions. Neither man was used to exposing his thoughts and feelings in front of the camera. They shared a resistance to analysing their own work, and remained on safe and common ground like the role of the writer in society and general literary influences. 'If one thinks of other literature, one thinks of books,' Borges said. 'If I think of English literature, I think of men: Chaucer, Dickens, Shakespeare.' Borges's paternal grandmother was English and he had been brought up with a very fine library of English books. When Pritchett mentioned Chesterton, Borges's not quite dead eyes lit up. 'Marble like solid moonlight, gold like a frozen fire,' he immediately quoted from Chesterton's 'Ballad of a White Horse'.

Asked about his preference for short stories, Borges spoke about the panic which seized him whenever he had attempted to write a novel. 'It is too wide, I cannot see it from beginning to end. Intensity can only be in a word or in a sentence, not over four hundred pages.' While I listened to the two men talking, I thought how much humanity there was in both of them and how much modesty. 'I am not concerned with success, I write for five or six friends,' Borges said, 'that's all. Opinions are not important, but what is behind them, my forefathers, the history and landscape of my country.'

At the end of the interview, I asked Pritchett to read something by Borges and he chose a piece from the end of *El Aleph*. During the reading, I kept the camera on the writer as he was listening. I hoped that the image of his face would imprint itself on the viewer. For four and half minutes no other image filled the screen, only the blind man's face. Pritchett's dark voice was flawed; one could see that he too was deeply moved.

I saw the Aleph from every point and angle, and in the Aleph I saw the earth, and in the earth the Aleph. I saw my own face, and my bowels. I saw your face, and I felt dizzy and wept, for my eyes had seen that secret and conjectured object, whose name is common to all men, but that no man has looked upon; the unimaginable universe.

Borges listened with an intense pleasure to his words, haltingly read out to him by his friend. Borges's lips moved in silence, reciting the entire text. Sometimes his face lit up with delight, as at the words '...it is London.' At the end of the text his eyes slowly filled with tears.

I had almost fifty minutes of film but on the air it was shortened to twenty. It had to be tailored to the length of television: Borges was reduced to an 'item'. I was once more saddened and angry. In a world conditioned by instant news and quick consumption, there was little place for the modesty and reticence of a blind poet.

To work on a magazine was difficult, the choice was bewildering. Every week books and exhibition catalogues poured in, cluttering up my desk. Plays that wanted to be filmed, exhibitions that demanded a reaction. The excess of everything had also reached the arts, as if plenitude and many numbers were the same. The speed with which we constantly created new heroes on the box and toppled others allowed no rest, no time for reflection. Everything had to satisfy the nebulous dream of modern man's omnipotence. News, any kind of news, had become the junk food of the masses. I kept questioning myself about the nature of my profession. What kind of people were these producers? We made films but we were not film-makers. We wrote scripts, but were not writers. We were more often than not feeding on other people's talent, a kind of parasitical existence, packagers of culture. Twenty minutes of Borges, twenty minutes of Camus and thirty minutes of Dostoevsky: some interesting, life-enhancing thoughts, coated in breathtaking platitudes, high-sounding jargons, meaningless superlatives.

James Mossman's often-voiced doubts about television had also infected me. We were rarely allowed to contemplate things. We were constantly shortening, changing, editing, and what was worse, explaining. It had so little to do with the anguish and the tenacity, the drive, the doubts and the joy an artist feels. All that had to be made palatable for mass consumption, the dreaded word 'fun', and then on to other things. The generalisations, both moral and artistic, were always so inadequate.

I had only been with the BBC two and a half years but I had already made thirty-two programmes. I began to think it was time to slow down and to concentrate on a few subjects. Urged on by a garrulous crowd, the professional I wanted to be was constantly usurped by the one the media demanded.

I was toying with the idea of going back to Current Affairs. In Cuba and in Biafra I was at least feeling the sap of real life. I missed the urgency and the sense of reality, and at best the invitation to compassion that it offered. Is it more useful to report from the embattled world of Vietnam or about the famine in Ethiopia than to dabble in the arts? I wondered. People, watching night after night, took much of what they saw on the box for the truth. But what truth was I telling? Truth picked up from the television set, not lived, inherited, tested. Was I not merely expanding the collective lie? I loathed the voyeuristic side of my profession, catering for the ever-increasing greed of the viewer for more sensations. The viewers suffered only by proxy, at a safe distance. Even in Biafra or Cuba I was painfully aware that I was only really a visitor, I never belonged, for it was not my blood that was being shed. Even in grimmest Africa I was always the gentleman from Kensington, moved for a while by the horror and the dying, but always sure to return to his untroubled existence. I asked myself often if anybody ever learned from the stories I told them. Was I not just shifting emotions – and guilt – from one world stage to the next? 'We have tongues and we must use them, if only to speak partial truths, because silence is no better,' Peter Shaffer had said in *To Be a Witness*. So I remained in the Arts Department.

Visconti at Work had explored the working of the film-maker. My next choice fell on a composer. It was natural to choose Hans Werner Henze. Hans was enormously prolific, composing symphonies, concertos, operas with scores full of allusions and quotations from literature. Restlessly inventive, he had become without doubt one of the most gifted and original composers of the post-war generation, wielding great slabs of music with a distinct lyricism.

I flew to Rome and stayed for two weeks in his beautiful and welcoming house in Marino, ten miles outside Rome. We talked, planned and sometimes filmed. The good spirit of the house, Fausto Moroni, Hans's old and most caring friend, watched over everything. It was the first time for months that I was happy. Hans's wise and level-headed presence was able to shift the gloom. The house was filled with animals, books and music and the table always brimmed with food and wine from his own land. I tried to capture a bit of the charmed existence so necessary to this composer's life and work in my portrait of him.

With Hans Werner Henze

The morning was always reserved for composing. Nobody was allowed to disturb the master, who worked in a large studio, set apart from the bustle of the house. On the wall, photographs of friends or people he admired: Ingeborg Bachmann, Stravinsky, Che Guevara. Henze sometimes composed at the piano, filling many pages of large sheets of paper with notes. From time to time a few chords of music would emanate from his studio and fill the house.

> Composing is a state of mind, it is a process of self-confrontation, full of exhaustion, loneliness and sadness. You have to delve into yourself, into your childhood; you have to be calm, free of fear. It sometimes helps me to overcome my sadness and my loneliness. I can hide and find shelter in my work. It gives me the impression that life can be almost perfect.

Sometimes there were guests, mainly from Germany: Hans's 'revolutionary and committed' friends, Rudi Dutschke, the film-maker Volker Schlöndorff or the writer Hans Magnus Enzensberger. This was 1972, and political disillusion had not yet set in. I realised that the radical movement had given him, for the first time, some love and hope for Germany, the country he had turned his back on.

In the afternoon we would take long walks through the vineyards of the Campagna Romana, whippets running after their master.

I was determined to take time over the making of this programme. We did five interviews, hammering things out, going again over ground we had already covered. This was the way I wanted to work from now on. No more just dipping in and out of people's lives. Henze allowed us to set up our camera in the corner of his studio while he composed. I observed him playing a few bars then writing them down, playing again and revising.

> Composing needs a long gestation. Collecting the necessary material can take months, sometimes years. Routine can befall you, like an evil dream... One has to cancel things out that are in your mind, things you might have heard, what other people have written and that are not yours.

Composing and political engagement for him were closely linked. Music for Henze had always been something that had to be protected from authority, hidden. Ever since he had made music secretly during the Nazi years in the house of a neighbour 'who had a Jewish wife' he had felt that way. He believed, like Stravinsky, that music could improve morals. But we both knew about the ss-guards in concentration camps who listened to Beethoven while others went to the gas chambers.

Henze's music had often been attacked by the avant-garde and he had – not always successfully – to defend his position. For him music was the great communicator. 'If a mass movement asks me to compose their messages I will! I will write in C major so that a child can sing it!' It was Henze's refusal to be speechless, to be uncommunicative, to be as far away as possible from people's concern. He wanted to wrench the music from 'the hands of specialists to become playful again'. He could be very touchy. He had the memory of an elephant and once wounded, he would never forget it. One evening in Earls Terrace, Georg Solti, trying to be a peacemaker between Pierre Boulez and Henze, asked about the nature of their famous antagonism. Boulez had made in public some wounding and gratuitous remarks about Henze's music. Hans never forgave him.

When I was young I wrote without hesitation, I was full of certainties. I thought that music was something wild and beautiful. Now I am filled with fears and doubts and preoccupations, searching for the meaning of music. I want to express the mental sadness of our time. Increasing knowledge of myself and the world helps me to reflect in my music who I am. I, a German, forty-five years old, in this world.

With these words my film *Hans Werner Henze at Work* ended.

The Henze film strengthened my wish to quit *Review* and the magazine format and to make programmes with more depth and greater length, but before leaving *Review* I made a number of twenty- to thirty-minute films that gave me pleasure, including a programme on Käthe Kollwitz, with Flora Robson reading the letters of the painter of the German working classes. I also went to Paris to interview Pierre Boulez and Richard Rogers on the Centre Pompidou and the new modern music institute in the making.

One day, while I was staying with Facundo in the south of France, I received a telephone call from London, telling me that Maurice Chevalier had died. I was asked to interview the veteran film-director René Clair, who lived in St Tropez. René Clair, a charming gentleman of the old school, civilised and very modest, received me at his house. Suddenly, in the middle of the interview, the lights went out. The whole of St Tropez was without electricity. Clair picked up the phone and demanded to speak to the mayor. 'Donnez-moi quinze minutes, Monsieur le Maire,' I heard him saying. Three minutes later the lights came on again: art's sublime victory over bureaucracy.

The homage to Chevalier is not really worth mentioning, except for the fact that it marked Alan Yentob's directorial début. He was still only a production assistant. Alan had been sent to Paris to help me. When I arrived to talk to Zizi Jeanmaire in her dressing-room, the enterprising and determined Alan had already done it. He sat very proudly on the dressing table, obviously more impressed by her legs in black net stockings than by anything else. He had also filmed the funeral with a giant straw boater made from yellow daffodils bobbing up and down above the black crowd. It was the first of many occasions when I was unable to be cross with this difficult but lovable monster who eventually became my boss and even the controller of BBC2 and even of BBC1, the youngest ever reaching such a post.

The programme which gave me the greatest pleasure was a film with Man Ray. It took a long time to persuade Man Ray to grant me an interview and when I finally arrived at his studio behind the church of Saint-Sulpice, he would only let me in, not the cameraman nor the sound. I spent a further hour obtaining permission for the rest of the crew to be allowed in. Man Ray received us in a large studio, the room of an alchemist. The walls were covered with the most disparate objects, springs, pieces of cars. There was a large table also laden with strange objects, a chess game, a torso of a woman, a string of pearls. Man Ray was wearing a beret and a Texan check shirt, his countenance and manners were expansive. Somewhere in the background I noticed his beautiful wife Julie, who did not want to disturb us.

While he showed me around, he explained how he found the famous flat iron and stuck some drawing pins on its bottom. I fought my way through French *baguettes*, painted blue, 'pain peint', the maestro gaily chirped. There were mysteriously wrapped parcels and brooms dipped in paint. 'I am only interested in differences, not similarities, look how boring a *corps de ballet* is, they should not be on stage but in the army,' he explained. He also showed me some of his famous photographs. 'I photograph what I do not want to paint and I paint what I cannot photograph, a dream for instance. Photography is so quick, it is the same gesture whether you take a beautiful woman, a potato or a famous man,' he said, pointing at a photo of Schoenberg. 'Mind you, Schoenberg looked so dull when he arrived in his dark suit, so I draped a silk scarf around him. I should have tried that on a potato too,' he added with a giggle.

After a while we settled on a sofa, covered with a large piece of cloth. We talked about his early years. Man Ray had arrived in Paris in 1921. Marcel Duchamp was already there and took him under his wing. 'I felt like a new-born baby after the struggle in America.' There was no false modesty about him; on the contrary, he was very proud of himself. 'I met everybody in the art world and I was accepted. I gave as much as they gave me. I always wanted to be accepted,' he said, his face breaking into a mischievous grin, while he puffed away ostentatiously on a huge cigar. 'I have smoked everything in my life, pipe, cigarettes,' he mused with his broad guttural American accent. I noticed on each arm a large bracelet. It was not always easy to know when he was serious and when he was in jest, there was so much of the old surrealist left in him.

The camera had begun to roll. Man Ray pretended not to notice it. 'There is no such thing as progress in art, as there is no progress in lovemaking, only different ways of doing it, you have to make something different. I never think of art, for me creating is the pursuit of pleasure and the pursuit of liberty,' he suddenly said, looking straight into the camera. I asked him if those early days of Dada and Surrealism were as much fun as we always heard. 'Fun? no there was no fun, it was very tense and no humour, we all took ourselves very seriously. We wanted to clear the way for something new, not something funny. The tricks of today will be the truths of tomorrow.' Man Ray rejected the notion of hankering after posterity. 'I wish my things would disappear with me.' The old Dada feeling was still alive. I asked him what had satisfied him most in life. 'Women,' he replied, ending the interview abruptly.

I left his studio quite elated. I carried with me the image of a serious clown, who had put a *baguette* on his head and stuck his tongue out at the camera. In my pocket I had a little painted stone sculpture of a foot, made from a pebble he had picked up on the beach. It was a present from him and carried the inscription 'Cadaques 1965, Man Ray'.

I said goodbye to *Review* with a film called *Royal Dreams: Visconti and Ludwig of Bavaria*. Visconti was making a colourful extravaganza of pictures and music, an homage to two men he loved: Ludwig of Bavaria and Richard Wagner. He had invited me to join him, but as I did not want to make another film of Visconti at work I shifted the emphasis by trying to tell the story of Ludwig II of Bavaria through the eyes of Visconti. *Ludwig* was the third part of a German trilogy which had began with *The Damned*. Like *Death in Venice* it was another search for absolute beauty, which had to be paid for with death and madness.

It was Easter, and I ran into Albino Cocco and Piero Tosi at the airport. The assistant was flying to London to arrange for white horses to replace the brown ones, as suddenly snow had fallen; the designer was on his way to Rome to find more suitable horn buttons for Helmut Berger's suit.

The production had taken over an entire hotel in Neuschwanstein. There were many old acquaintances: Folker Bohnet, who played Kainz,

Silvana Mangano and Nora Ricci, Romy Schneider and Helmut Berger, John Moulder Brown and Hans Moog, and of course the usual Visconti court. As always on Visconti pictures it was a cacophony of different languages – German, French, Italian, even Russian. An American coach was trying to teach people to pronounce English, but eventually she too ended with a part in the film.

The filming had already begun in January and much had been shot. I spent two weeks on the haunting locations of Ludwig's castles. Neo-Gothic Neuschwanstein, rococo Linderhof and baroque Herrenchiemsee were all brought to new splendour through Visconti's set designers Mauro Chiari and Mario Scisci. The rooms and follies of the great artist king had been painstakingly refurbished to the smallest detail. Millions were spent to furnish the castles with authentic antiques, assembled from all over the country. Museums had lent jewels, royal coaches and sleighs. The costumes by Piero Tosi were sumptuous. The boat in which Ludwig cruised the lake during the night with his beloved Kainz had also been reconstructed.

Helmut Berger played Ludwig. He was charming but very irresponsible, a beautiful sexy object, hardly aware of the formidable present Visconti had once more given him. Visconti patiently directed him, repeating again and again the same scene, only getting angry when Helmut did not know the text.

Shooting happened mostly at night. It was an eerie experience to walk through the vast glittering halls of Ludwig's castles, many of which he had only lived in for a few days. At times the life we led was almost of the same extravagance. The snow had melted and Visconti opted again for the dark horses. But before that, as a goodbye present for Romy Schneider, who played Sissy, the Austrian empress in love with Ludwig, Visconti had laid on a sleigh ride to Füssen to watch the famous ice hockey team. The sleigh was taken from the set and drawn by four horses. We sat smothered with large blankets of silver fox Piero Tosi had provided.

Once Romy Schneider left, life for Visconti was lonely. Helmut Berger preferred to escape to Munich rather than stay with his director and friend. I sat many evenings alone with a sad and disillusioned man. It was as if he had some premonition about the many things which would befall the film and its maker. Like Ludwig he knew that the realisation of pure art was not possible in a modern world. 'We should have lived at the times of the Medicis,' he once remarked, 'then the realisation of our ideals would still be possible.'

Visconti had aged. He laughed less. He certainly suffered for Helmut Berger, but it was also something deeper. His preoccupation with subjects dealing with the schism between art and life, and the celebration of death as their central theme, began to take its toll. Was he not like the Dream King, constantly fleeing into greater and greater artistic excess, to fill his solitude in an alien political world? Maybe it was also the increasing awareness that absolute beauty is an illusion and that the search for it is always repaid by the destruction of its worshippers. This melancholy mood did not deceive us, although neither of us could have guessed that this was the last time we would meet. A short time after the filming he suffered a stroke. I received a letter from a clinic in Switzerland. By the size of the handwriting I could tell that he was not well. 'J'espère que tu peux venir me voir et me montrer ton film, je t'embrasse, à bientôt.' This was in September 1972.

Visconti, partly paralysed, made two more films, *Gruppo di Famiglia in un Interno* and finally *L'Innocente*, more sparse, more concentrated than the previous films but of no less artistic strength. He was still searching for the mystery of beauty. 'Civilisations seem to disappear, but beauty has been almost immovable,' he once said to me. We sometimes spoke on the phone. Three times I went to Rome to see him and he refused to see me, I never found out why. He died on 17 March 1976.

Ludwig too was doomed. Visconti had told me several times that he had installed an editing table in his hospital room and later in his sister's house at Lake Como where he stayed, to supervise the editing. The original version was three hours and nine minutes long. The producer not only cut out three-quarters of an hour, but destroyed the complex shape, the poised balance Visconti had intended. As with *The Leopard* it would take years for us to see the original version.

My second Visconti film was not as light and carefree as my first. Maybe I was changing too. I was forty-two years old. The search for a kind of perfection in my existence continued. 'Maybe we never attain it, maybe we will only know the truth the minute we die,' Visconti had said one evening.

At least I discovered the tranquil and soothing qualities of true love, although I also experienced the bitter and ugly quarrels which always seem to erupt when people are close to each other. In a world of shifting emotions my love for Facundo seemed to be the only certainty. Sometimes he joined me during filming. I did not want to 'own' him. In fact what I liked most in him was his freedom, his independence. The constant separation had its good and its bad side. It kept our relationship fresh, but living with a suitcase in sight also began to take its toll. Cracks were beginning to show. I often wondered how relationships survive misunderstandings, lies and tears. There were fights, beginning usually with a small dis-

Visconti directing Romy Schneider and Helmut Berger in *Ludwig*

agreement, but I could see the argument flaring up. We both tried to stop it, but we knew we could not stop ascribing the most appalling motives to each other, until we drew blood. It was a tumultuous relationship, yet I despised people whose lives were devoid of incident, with their constant bids for sympathy.

Groupe TSE was at the height of its success. They played now in Le Palace, an old theatre which they had rediscovered and put back on the theatrical map. One weekend they presented four of their plays non-stop, a marathon which began at three o'clock in the afternoon and ended twelve hours later. Soon after they opened with a stunning new play, *Comédie policière*, at the Palais de Chaillot. It became their greatest success so far. Facundo played seven different roles in it, four women, three men. The other lead was played by his sister Marucha.

Then one day he told me that he had met a younger boy, Jacques. I am not jealous by nature. Faithfulness had never been a physical issue between us; a matter of heart and mind, not of the body. One can be unfaithful by putting one's hand on the shoulder of someone else and perfectly faithful by going to bed. Most men, I believe, are not monogamous – I certainly was not. As with many homosexual couples there was a high degree of tolerance and understanding. I have known a great many homosexual couples with a deep mutual love and friendship, who openly and honestly accepted their partner's infidelities, and I have known many heterosexual couples who lived with lies and jealousies, regrets and guilt feelings. But when Facundo told me that he was actually in love with someone else, planning to share his flat in Paris, I was devastated. True to my principle that no man has a right to own the other, I withdrew.

16

Them and Us: The European Grand Tour

1972–1975

When I returned to London I left *Review* and embarked on programmes entirely of my own. For my first work I proposed to make a series of programmes on art and culture in the European Community, which we were finally about to join. Even the better-educated British knew little about the cultural life of their neighbours. Europe – the Continent – was the others; exotic, nice to visit, never quite trustworthy, always foreign. I called the series *Them and Us*.

The BBC liked series, but they were rather sticky about who would represent the sacred BBC to the public at large. The right image and the right spirit were essential. The line of distinguished presenters was indeed formidable: Kenneth Clark, Bronowski, J. K. Galbraith. Many spent only a few days on the shoot, just to film their pieces to camera. The realisation of their script was left to the director. The script, more often than not, had to be rewritten by him. We often joked about the plight of the poor director who, having conceived, shot and cut the film, totally disappeared behind the fame of the man whose face the audience saw. *Civilisation* became *Kenneth Clark's Civilisation* and few in the public knew the name of Michael Gill, who produced the series, or Ann Turner, who researched it and who knew more about art than many learned art historians.

I was determined to write my own script and present it, for I could not bring myself to become merely the printer of other people's ideas. Script and visualisation had to be one and the same process. Although not everybody agrees with me, this has been my view throughout my professional life, and I stuck to it.

There were many obstacles. I was totally unknown outside of BBC Kensington House, I was not a writer, and I had an accent, which was a serious handicap. I was a good battler, a sly diplomat and a puller of strings. One day someone, I think it was John Drummond, said: 'Why should not someone who speaks all those languages and has lived in many of these countries make a film about what he knows and present it?' The men in power in their offices on the sixth floor of Television Centre agreed. I was allowed to produce, write, direct and present the series.

On Saturday 30 December 1972, nearly two million viewers watched me standing in a grey flannel suit in front of a modern building. I said: 'The European Community will not only bring us economically closer together, it also forces us to learn more about the cultural life of our new partners.' I was presenting *Them and Us: Germany*, the first programme in a series which would occupy me for the next two years and bring me much joy, many good and some bad reviews and even some fame.

The basic formula of the six programmes was the same. They looked at the arts in three different towns; one large, one medium and one small, but the films were very different from each other, showing the marvellous diversity of Europe, which no common market will ever be able to destroy.

The series broke new ground for the BBC. Each part was ninety minutes long, made by a very small team and used foreign crews. I never believed in empire building. Programmes are not made by committees. I also like to be in control. The BBC was used to my erratic behaviour by now. Instead of the large group of executive producers, producers, directors, assistants, researchers, *Them and Us* was made by two people: Ann Hummel and myself.

Ann had many functions: researcher, secretary, librarian and accountant. She looked after the catering and even repaired torn jackets and suits. She smoothed over difficulties, explained my eccentricities to her countrymen and consoled those I had insulted or even hurt. In short she made herself indispensable. She was one of those many educated and devoted women the BBC seems to breed, and had worked her way up from a secretary in the building department to a production assistant in Music and Arts. She had been warned before she accepted the work with me that I was 'very demanding'. A friendly colleague had quickly mentioned that my last assistant had a nervous breakdown after two weeks with me. Ann joined me and remained for eight years, a time when she changed from a shy girl to a strong-willed troubleshooting lady who stands her ground. Things began mysteriously to move around her when she moved. Trays rattled, newspaper clippings avalanched or files crashed to the floor and sometimes she stepped into her own handbag. We laughed a lot and clashed a lot. When we separated it was like a divorce. The whole department suffered. After all I was from Berlin, Ann was from the Isle of Wight, as she never failed to point out, because she also had a sense of humour. She has remained a close friend. She is now a BBC producer, making films in her own right – much feared and loved.

It seemed logical that I should begin with Germany. It was a strange, unnerving experience to make a documentary about a country I knew so well and liked so little.

The Germany I returned to was even more prosperous than the one I had filmed in 1968, in *Democracy on Trial*. There seemed to be no end to its economic rise, but having satisfied their material needs, the Germans now sought something more spiritual. Dreams of growing prosperity had made room for the desire to join the civilised nations. Germany was eager to demonstrate to the world that she did not just produce beautiful cars and efficient machines, but also art.

We began filming in Bochum, a grey and anonymous modern town, typical of the Ruhrpot, the 'coal scuttle', an area half the size of London, with eight large cities gradually merging into one vast complex, that contained six repertory theatres the size of our National, several opera houses, five orchestras and at least fifteen museums. Until the 1960s most men had worked in the coal-mines. Then gradually one mine after the other began to close down. Soon hundreds of thousands were redundant, one worker in three. People were retrained and manufacturing industries moved in. Within a few years the average income greatly exceeded Britain's. Savings had grown in a way which even at that time was scarcely imaginable in Britain, still riddled by strikes. Class distinctions had almost disappeared. To make culture available to the workers was part of the retraining programme.

Bochum had built a thriving theatre. The German/English director, Peter Zadek, who had spent his childhood and most of his adolescence in London, had been engaged and was quickly making a reputation as one of the most inventive directors. His rise began in Bochum. I got on well with Zadek, a quirky, lively Jew with dark curly hair; our common background made working easy. He had a tremendous drive and knew how to transmit his energy to the stage. It was stimulating to watch him rehearsing in black polo shirt and jeans, freely mixing German, French and English. '*Los macht los*, off you go, *vite*.' He was rehearsing a musical version of Hans Fallada's *Kleiner Mann was nun* with Brigitte Mira, soon to become internationally famous through Fassbinder's film *Fear Eats the Soul*. Mira belted out: 'Ja das ist die Berliner Luft, Luft, Luft' and I felt for the first time something like homesickness.

From Bochum we travelled to Tübingen, a small town where Goethe once walked the streets and Hermann Hesse worked in a small bookshop. Hölderlin had been born here and shared digs with two philosophers, Hegel and Schelling. In the late 1950s I had worked here as a walk-on in the theatre. I was a peasant in *The White Horse Inn* and a devil in *Faust*. My acting career came to an abrupt end when, during a performance, I tripped over a cable, bringing down a spotlight and bathing the carefully lit *Walpurgisnacht* in a pretty but uncharacteristic pink light.

For the big town I had chosen Munich, the fastest-growing city in Germany. Most of the façades of the old churches and palaces had been restored and painted. It now boasted one million inhabitants, but still felt as provincial as ever. A third of all people living in Munich were not born here, much to the chagrin of the natives, for the old antagonism between Munich, the capital of Bavaria, and Berlin, the former capital of Prussia, dies hard.

Making a film in Germany was the beginning of a healing process for me. I saw a new Germany: open, international, tolerant and deeply committed to a free and democratic world. I was struck by how young and modern people looked, many born after the war. The traditional Gretchen type was fast disappearing and the young men looked slimmer than their fathers did. Among the many people who convinced me that the past would never return was a young writer and publisher, Michael Krüger, editor of the left-wing publishing house Hanser Verlag. Germany had once more become one of the leading book-publishing countries. 'After the student revolt in 1968 all the high priests of German literature had told the young that fiction was a sort of bourgeois thing, so they threw themselves into social history, sociology and politics, but now the pendulum has swung back. People look again to what the Germans call *belletristik* [fiction],' Krüger told us. 'The appetite for foreign literature is so great that not only most of English, American and French literature has been translated, but also that from Russia, Poland, Czechoslovakia and Latin America, including many non-fiction works.'

The many artists I met were the voices of the new democratic Germany, enjoying, without too much guilt, the advantages of an affluent country. They embodied what is best in the young. They were sensitive and tender in dealing with others, never lost their sense of social justice, never let their watchful eyes stray from politics. It was those Germans (and there were many others) who helped me to reconcile myself with the country which was no longer mine.

The Observer and *The Sunday Times* found my first programme on the Common Market 'stimulating', 'promising', and 'with plenty of liveliness which should break down our insularity'. The first battle was won.

In the autumn of 1972, for my second cultural *tour d'horizon,* I went to Holland. I always loved this flat, low land, with the immense sky and ubiquitous water, for it reminded me of the Nordic landscape of my youth: light and space.

In 1658 an English diplomat had written: 'The Dutch behave as if all men were created equal.' This was still true, and never more so than in the

1970s. Here too it was the young who had rebelled against the restrictive attitudes of the sober, puritanical and formalised society of their elders and had demanded a more open society.

For most people in England, Holland still meant tulips, windmills and clogs, but the Holland I hopefully brought back to England was a country that had heartily embraced the modern world. In the 1970s Amsterdam had begun to become the laboratory of experiments in the alternative society, a sort of Katmandu of Europe. As long as nobody cut too deeply into the flesh of the really vested interests – power and money – the Dutch accepted the most radical solutions. While England was still nannying its citizens, and continues to do so, Holland had stopped treating its subjects as children and accepted risks in order to achieve a more harmonious way of life.

Them and Us: The Netherlands was received with even more enthusiasm than the German programme. The Dutch temperament appealed more to the English than the Germans, so heavily bent on worthiness and their pronounced sense of duty.

Much of the success of the film belonged to the cameraman. I had worked once more with Ed van der Elsken, a strange and uncomfortable man. He was also an extraordinarily true artist, to his last breath. When I visited him for the last time in 1990, he was riddled with cancer, living in an old farmhouse packed with evocative objects: masks, old cameras, pin-ball machines. High up in a tree hung his old car, which he had driven into a wall. He was in a wheelchair and had just come out of hospital, an emaciated figure filled with the fire of what he was embarking on. He had put a large bed in a studio-like room, the floor had been especially painted to resemble a huge Dutch flag, and a special contraption held the camera he knew he would soon be too weak to operate.

I felt uncomfortable with all his morbid obsessions and yet, watching Ed's enthusiasm, my reservations vanished. Here was a man trying to come to terms with death, wanting, as an artist, to capture the last moment of his turbulent life. Without this obsession, he would merely have been a burnt-out, very sick man. Ed died in 1990, after finishing a film about his illness right up to his death watched by his little boy and his wife Anneke. The film was transmitted on Dutch television. This too shows what a radical and humane country Holland is.

The introduction for the Italian programme was filmed in the beautiful temple of Segesta in Sicily. 'Italy is a country of strong colours and dramatic effects, in landscape, temperament and art,' I said while the name Peter Adam appeared on the lower half of the screen. I had exchanged the formal grey suit and tie for an open-necked shirt, a sign of the increasing ease I felt. The crew was very Italian. The cameraman, Ennio Guarnieri, had worked with De Sica and had just finished a film with Elizabeth Taylor. He had flamboyant style: bottles of champagne were constantly produced and he drove a flashy Volvo, a present to him from his last producer. I had been surprised and honoured when he agreed to work with us on a meagre B B C salary.

We filmed with enthusiasm and humour. Everybody was lighthearted, free-wheeling and very professional. There was no *Angst*, no hysteria, none of the senseless boozy camaraderie of film crews I found so difficult to join in. Our local assistant was a young architect/designer, Adriano Magistretti, intelligent and full of invention. He not only found the most interesting locations, but also the best small hotels and the most memorable local restaurants, to which, on a day off, we once drove fifty miles. 'You will see, *la pasta e speciale, vaut le voyage,*' he enthusiastically exclaimed, while Ennio shouted to a passing policeman: 'Arrest me please.'

It is still unbelievable how we managed, on such a budget, to make a film like *Them and Us: Italy*. I think we had only £12,000. I interviewed Mario Soldati, Alberto Moravia, Luigi Barzini (author of *The Italians*), Vittorio de Sica, Franco Zeffirelli, Prince Lanzo Tomasi di Lampedusa, the designer Ettore Sottsass and the composer Luigi Dallapiccola. We filmed Giorgio de Chirico painting and Giorgio Strehler rehearsing. There were scenes from Goldoni's *Servant of Two Masters*; an operetta with the lovely name *Madame di Tebe* in the Teatro Massimo in Palermo; Sicilian puppet theatre; and a scene from Verdi's *Aïda*, a Folies-Bergère version of grand opera in the Termi di Caracalla, with 300 extras, 80 dancers and four horses accompanied by the clicking of American cameras in front of 10,000 spectators. They don't make programmes like that any more – for so little money.

The filming gave me a chance to meet up again with Franco Zeffirelli. We had not seen each other for a while and it was a pleasure to see how wonderfully he had arranged yet another house for himself. His villa, in the Campagna Romana, was like a sumptuous theatre set. A born set designer, he had always known how to combine splendour with comfort and all of his houses had this fantastic quality. His warmth and charm made us all instantly at home, despite the fact that he was in the middle of doing a screen test with Liza Minnelli for *The Lady of the Camellias*. He was in a very good mood. 'Just feel at home,' he said to the crew.

I watched him eagerly supervising Minnelli's makeup and then rehearsing her, taking on the part of Marguerite. I was amazed how good Liza

Minnelli was in the role of the consumptive French courtesan (not one that immediately springs to mind when you look at Judy Garland's daughter). She, Kay Thompson, author of the delightful Eloise books, Franco and I had lunch together, which was elaborate, like everything Franco does. The conversation was chiefly about what went on in London; both Minnelli and Franco were great *aficionados*. Franco spoke mostly about Italian theatre, or the absence of it. Two years before, he, Visconti and Strehler had proposed to the government to found an Italian National Theatre in Rome. Each of them wanted to devote three years to it. Nothing had come of it, he said bitterly. 'It sank, like so many things here, for political reasons.'

We sat in his beautiful garden. Zeffirelli, as always, was totally at ease. He had lost some of his good looks as a result of a terrible car accident driving with Gina Lollobrigida on a motorway, but he could still produce his youthful charm and he knew it. He spoke passionately about the difference between English and Italian actors. 'Here people are improvised actors,' he said, leaning decoratively back in the large wicker armchair. 'We pick them up in the street, because of their looks. We use them because they correspond to the part we need them for. This is what made the Italian *realismo* so great, picking up real people and making them just themselves; fresh, naïve, naked, with their own weakness and beauty.'

To find out about real acting I went to Milan to the Piccolo Teatro. Giorgio Strehler had invited me to a rehearsal of his famous Goldoni production, *The Servant of Two Masters*. He had first staged the play in 1947. Since then it had been seen in twenty-six countries. Strehler thought it was time to mount a new production, this one for a tour to Salzburg and Japan. I was told that the rehearsal would begin at eight o'clock. Strehler is a night bird and only rehearses at night.

I was there promptly. The stage was erected on a small, square, hand-painted set, beautifully lit with candles, the right background for the actors in their eighteenth-century *commedia dell'arte* costumes with leather masks. Strehler was nowhere to be seen. The rehearsal began and the actors were taken through their paces by an assistant.

It was bitter cold and the rehearsal dragged on. At midnight suddenly life came into the already tired cast. Strehler arrived in a camel-hair coat, which he threw decoratively over a bench. 'Andiamo, ragazzi,' he shouted, and the stage changed within seconds. He took over, acting, singing and miming, a man aware of his effect on others, good-looking, well-groomed, vain, exciting to watch. Everything about him was generous, expansive. The rehearsal stopped at four o'clock in the morning.

'For me the most important quality in an actor is his readiness, the capacity to give himself totally to what he is doing, to mould himself to the part,' he told me. 'The real personality of an actor is his lack of personality. The second quality is linked to the first. He should be aware of what he is doing. He must have intelligence and a critical sense of knowing what he wants to do. In other words, I want a human being, not just an actor, a person with his own ideas, his own world, even his own refusals. He must be a political, ideological and a philosophical personality. A modern actor is a conscious instrument, not a robot.' He spoke Italian: the only English word he used was 'self-conscious'.

I also had the fortune to meet and interview Luigi Dallapiccola, the last of the great avant-garde composers alive from the generation of Schoenberg, Webern and Alban Berg. Dallapiccola lived with his charming wife in a small flat in Florence. Everything about the flat was modern – the furniture, the paintings. After a few moments of chatting, the small man in the dark suit went to the piano lit by a large lamp and began to play one of his own short pieces. The noise from the street penetrated the room, but he was totally oblivious to it. 'I play badly, I haven't played it for a while,' he said with a shy smile. As soon as he began it was already over. Then he sat down. We talked about Italian musical life. 'We have first-rate orchestras who can't play a modern score. And the singers – when they have a voice and they are beautiful, a girl can become a star here for a few years,' he complained. 'In England or America I never saw a musician without wonderful preparation. Music is not an improvisation.'

I have made many films, and sometimes they contained magic moments, moments which make history. With Luigi Dallapiccola, one of these happened when he told me: 'My most important experience happened in Florence in 1924, 1 April. Schoenberg was the conductor of his masterpiece *Pierrot Lunaire*. It is superfluous to describe the reaction of the people, who had come totally unprepared. They laughed and jeered. Well, there were two people in the audience deeply impressed by this performance. Let me begin with the far less important.' He drew the 'far' out and gave a little chuckle. 'It was myself. The other one was Giacomo Puccini. He was very sick, but he had made this trip from Viareggio to Florence in order to hear this work. He was very interested in every new experiment. He sat there with the score. I had the impression he did not notice the scandal which went on all around him. After the performance he went to Casella and asked for the honour of being introduced to Schoenberg. That night I watched Puccini and Schoenberg talking to each other in the green room *a core aperto*.' The last line of his tale was lost, the camera had run out of film. But as always, Ann had written it down.

The other great man I filmed was Giorgio de Chirico. I went to see him in his studio on the Piazza di Spagna in Rome. His wife, who controlled everything he did, had agreed that we could film him, although he was not to be asked any questions. De Chirico sat in a pair of dark trousers and a white shirt in front of an easel. Next to it stood a plaster cast of a Roman bust and some fruit, which he was painting. When the camera started rolling, I heard the voice of his wife: 'Adesso, maestro!' De Chirico got up and began to paint, his brush resting on a stick. He had a huge head, with a fleshy face and large ears, but an almost perfect profile. He worked with complete concentration, totally oblivious of what went on around him. Ennio, the cameraman, zoomed slowly into his face – a strand of his straight white hair had fallen over one of his eyes, but it did not bother him. It was the face of an artist of another era. Than came the voice again: 'Basta, maestro!' and the session was over. It had lasted two minutes. But at least I had two minutes of Giorgio de Chirico painting.

The rest of the story about the making of the *Them and Us* series is quickly told. In the winter of 1973 I filmed Denmark, a snowbound country of great beauty where the temperature was never less than 30 degrees below freezing.

I spent several happy evenings with Erik Bruhn, one of the finest male dancers in the world. He had given up dancing and was embarking on a new career as an actor in a play based on the film *Rashomon*. He gave a dazzling performance, with incredible sword fights. Erik had been Nureyev's lover. He told me how much he liked the film I had made in Holland. 'Rudi can't take any adverse criticism,' he said, 'but he will grow up.'

A young actor, Peter Bonke, took me to Rungstedlund to see the house of a woman I always wanted to meet and never did – Karen Blixen. Ever since discovering Isak Dinesen's *Seven Gothic Tales*, I have read everything by and about the author. Her last 'friend', poet and publisher Ole Wivel, was there to receive us, as well as her long-time secretary and executor Clara Svendsen.

The low-slung house where Karen Blixen lived for the last twenty years of her life was whitewashed with a large roof, standing in a forty-acre estate. In the summer we were told there were cows grazing, as she had turned her land into pastures. The house faced the harbour. It was intensely moving to be in the place which still had so much of her spirit, the lion skins she had hunted in Africa and some of the guns she had used. The Masai swords and the Kikuyu heads bore witness to the deep love she felt for the native culture. Most of the simple but elegant furniture she had described in *Out of Africa* stood in the drawing-room, where she used to receive many visitors from all over the world. In her small study I noticed

Denys Finch Hatton's favourite chair and the old gramophone he had given her.

Cecil Beaton took the last picture of this much-photographed woman there, an elegant frail creature next to her own flower arrangement. A few days later, in September 1962, she died.

The room was still filled with flowers, although we were in the middle of the winter. 'Baroness Blixen could hardly walk any longer but she forced herself to go into the garden to chose the flowers herself,' Clara Svendsen told us. There were long curtains of transparent white lace and Biedermeier furniture. Ole, who had been her frequent companion, spoke vividly about her last years. He described her sitting at the small desk under the window, riddled by illness and marked by death, still writing, in what he called Ewald's room.

We walked out into the garden. Under the snow one could just make out her plain gravestone with the simple lettering. She was buried under a large beech tree, like the one in the holy places of the Kikuyu in the African highland. A Schubert Lied, 'Frühlingsglaube', whose last line was 'Now all, all things must change',[1] had concluded the simple ceremony of her funeral. Ole made me a small present, one of the most precious in my life: a private tape recording of her voice reading 'The King's Letter'.

Sometimes it was difficult to leave all those people who had made what was, after all, only a job so memorable. After a while, as in the theatre, the people you meet and work with disappear. You grow fond of each other very quickly, you vow to phone each other up, to meet again, and then they slide out of your life. Many years later you greet each other across a crowded room. But somehow all things interlink. Peter Bonke dropped out of my life to emerge again fifteen years later. He was living in Paris and acting with Jeanne Moreau in *Zerline*. One day when Jeanne Moreau was very sad I gave her a copy of the tape with Karen Blixen reading 'The King's Letter'.

France and Belgium concluded the series. France was a totally different country from the one I knew in the 1950s. Somehow it had become insular, intellectually speaking. It lacked the drive England and Germany had in the 1960s and clung to its old traditions. Most intellectuals were still living with the same myths of their superiority. Someone in a previous century had told them that they were the centre of the universe, and they still believed it. They considered themselves more intelligent and more cultured than everyone; they believed, largely due to Descartes, that their language was clearer, more precise.

1 'Nun muss sich alles, alles wenden.'

The last programme *Them and Us: Belgium* went out in March 1975. It featured such different characters as the painter Delvaux and Hergé, the creator of Tintin.

I had worked for almost three years on the *Them and Us* series: three years of many travels and encounters with people. The series caught the attention of many inside and outside the B B C, and as a result my professional life changed. It gave me a free hand to choose future subjects and the people I wanted to work with. As for myself, I have never had a feeling of complete achievement. All my work seems to be a preparation for something better, although I began to realise that I had received immeasurably more than I had ever expected and that I had undertaken more things than I had ever thought myself capable of.

Facundo was still living with Jacques on and off. He joined me sometimes in London or I flew to Paris where we had to stay in a hotel. Sometimes everything seemed to be as in the old days, or almost, but he always left again. Those were difficult times. We might not see each other for two to three months. But for the joy of making *Them and Us*, I do not know how I would have coped. I once drove through Paris, on my way to the South, and I did not even stop. I was building a house on our land and the walls were almost halfway up, but I could find little joy in it.

In 1973 Keith Vaughan's descent into sadness and old age had begun. He had been diagnosed with cancer. I would go to see him as often as possible, sometimes four or five times a week. Often Prunella came along. We would take a meal or something he liked. We even managed to laugh and to chat and to talk about other things than death, but it would become increasingly difficult.

Sadness kept on setting in, and not only around me. On 3 September 1973 Facundo phoned with the news that his sister had collapsed on stage. I took the first plane to Paris and rushed to the hospital. Facundo and I waited in front of the doctor's surgery in the old hospital of La Salpêtrière. Finally the doctor called us in; grave faces all round. 'I do not know if I can save her, she had an aneurysm, a rupture of an artery in the brain, but I will try.' The operation lasted nine hours, while she was immersed in ice. We saw the doctor coming out of the operating theatre, a pale and tired man. Marucha was alive, but paralysed.

Facundo looked at me in tears. 'What is happening to us?' She was more than a sister – she had been Facundo's partner. They had lived the agony and the glory of endless plays together, night after night. It seemed only yesterday I had seen her in *Luxe*, a visual and musical extravaganza on the theme of luxury, culminating in a sumptuous tableau with her walking naked down a giant staircase. Marucha Bo was the toast of the town, hailed as the most beautiful creature on the Parisian stage. Her picture was all over the papers. It was splendid.

A whole world collapsed for all of us, for the theatre, for her friends. Marucha was the life of the company. She had played all the leading parts. She drove the large van on tours, she was strength and energy and beauty, an actress of rare charisma. Her intelligence and animal sexuality were always in perfect balance. Now she was reduced to a mere vegetable, without speech, expression, movement.

We howled and cursed and cried. Marucha spent nine months chained to a bed. Facundo went to see her every day. At night he stood on stage with another actress, who spoke her text. If ever he deserved my love and help, it was then. I vowed never to leave him for the rest of my life, whatever he might do.

Gradually some of her speech came back. She could move part of her face, but she was broken. What would life be from now on? Facundo and I threw ourselves into work, just to silence the pain and the rage.

17
Spirit of Place: Durrell's Greece
1976

My next film was *Spirit of Place: Lawrence Durrell's Greece*. I had met Durrell in Paris, and fallen for this chubby and jolly man in battered tweed trousers and old suede shoes, looking more like a retired boxer than a poet. I had read with mounting pleasure his three island books, *Prospero's Cell* on Corfu, *Reflections on a Marine Venus* on Rhodes, and *Bitter Lemons* on Cyprus. I had not been to Greece, and the idea of seeing it through the eyes of a poet was a great temptation. I suggested skipping Cyprus, where war had been raging – hardly the time to make a poetical assessment.

Durrell had been born in India and really never settled in England, which he considered 'grey and damp'. He had travelled to Corfu when he was twenty-three years old, 'in search of sunshine'. He had cut off his roots and was trying to find some in a landscape marked not by geography but by writings and paintings: the landscape of the artist.

Durrell from the outset had been slightly worried about my plans. 'An invitation to reminisce is always rather terrifying,' he had written, but then he conceded:

> I feel perhaps there might be some point in trying to collect and perhaps to recreate a little bit of Greece, which is not finished now and gone for good, but which has changed very much and doesn't resemble the Greece I knew when I was a young and aggressive poet. It is good to see places where one has been happy in the past, to see them after many years and in different circumstances.

In September we were off to Corfu, to recall 'some part of those golden years whose ghost still rises up and afflicts him whenever he catches sight of a letter with a Greek stamp', as Durrell had told me. But he was lazy and not inclined to mull over his own writing, so had left it to Ann and me to work out the script and select the passages from his writing which we would use in the film.

> Entering Greece is like entering a dark crystal, the form of things becomes irregular, refracted. Mirages suddenly swallow islands and if you watch you can see the trembling curtain of the atmosphere.

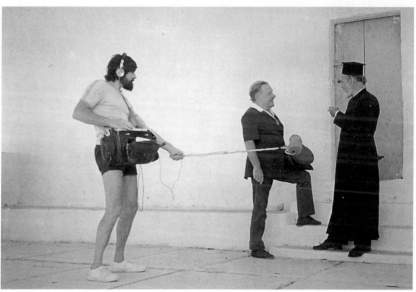

Filming Lawrence Durrell

The whole journey was one of those enchanted voyages one makes sometimes under the guidance of an evocative poet. Durrell opened up Greece for us in the most extraordinary way. Unhurriedly, sometimes almost still, he took us through the Greek landscape, his 'landscape of the heart', a personal landscape which our cameraman, Jacques Boumendil, reproduced so vividly in his pictures: a landscape which did not need applause or praise, it just had to be caught.

In Corfu, the ante-room to Aegean Greece, Durrell was in a very good mood as he cheerfully sat on the terrace of the house he and his family had lived in, 'eating well and drinking well'. He described the family life that his brother Gerald had captured in a very different way in his book *My Family and Other Animals*.

Lawrence Durrell's strength was the capacity to evoke a place and the spirit behind it. Even just talking one could feel, hear and taste the 'extended' life he had led. He conjured up the crackling of the wood fire in the primitive stove and the smell of warm bread, 'half-eaten before we could get it home'. 'The primitiveness had a kind of simplicity which was the real stuff of poetry. The notion of cool, cold water, water of any kind, became very important, because we were always dying of thirst in this wonderful heat.'

Sometimes in the morning we took a horse-drawn carriage and drove through the town, with its imprints from the Venetians, the British and the French. We visited the many churches of St Spiridion, the island's patron, and felt the solitude of the monks who worship him: '*monaxia* – loneliness'.

On other days we hired a small boat and sailed around the island, drunk from chilled retsina and the Greek songs which Larry and his old friend Dimitri sang with croaky voices:

> Sea, you youth swallower
> O poison bearing element, Sea
> Who makes our island folk
> Always wear black
> Have you not had enough yet,
> Sea, in all this long time?

I filmed the little house in the north of the island where Durrell and his wife Nancy had lived under the shrine of St Arsenius, 'his second birthplace' as he called it, and where he had written his first major novel, *The Black Book*, which made him discover his real voice, 'the result of an intense inner life'. Durrell spoke at length about the encouragement he received from T. S. Eliot and Henry Miller. 'Was writing easy then?' I asked him.

'No, it is never very easy. You have to give yourself a sort of artificial nervous breakdown and then you communicate the fear, the horror or the suspense to your reader. If you are flat your writing is flat, and the reader is flat too. It's a very mysterious thing, because you are passing a kind of current with your writing through the eyes of someone else and through his appreciating mind, his soul, if you like, a certain wavelength that someone else can grab.'

From Corfu we travelled to Hydra. Dimitri had hired a small private yacht, which turned out to be a disaster. The sea was already rough and nobody could sleep with the smell and the noise of the engine. I decided to sleep on deck, to be woken up by Larry at five o'clock in the morning, doing his yoga and having a large tumbler of whisky for breakfast. The happiness of the Corfu filming was gone. Larry, as so often before, was getting bored, and we abandoned the boat and flew to Crete.

Sometimes the good mood returned. Durrell would disappear into the kitchen of a taverna, to emerge with steaming hot plates. He made us taste the coarse brown peasant bread, dipped in olive oil, which he claimed gave the children their brown skin and dazzling white teeth.

> The whole Mediterranean – the sculptures, the palms, the gold beads, the bearded heroes, the wine, the ideas, the ships, the moonlight, the winged gorgon, the bronze man, the philosophers – all of it seemed to rise in the sour, pungent taste of these black olives between the teeth. A taste older than mead, older than wine, a taste as old as old water.

When I accused him of too much richness he cheerfully admitted: 'I know I tend to overwrite. Fundamentally I write the sort of things that I want to read, using the language on maximum spread.' Writing had almost become too easy for him and sometimes he worried that he could not put 'enough punch behind it', and 'this does show immediately'. Durrell's modesty was amazing. He wanted no fame or immortality for himself.

One night we set out with the fishermen in an old boat with great carbide lamps to attract the fish to their nets. We relived the hour when night falls.

> The colour washing out of the world, leaving room for the great copper-coloured moon which will rise over Epirus. It is the magic hour between two unrealised states of being.

Durrell had written the *Marine Venus* in Rhodes. He and his second wife Eve had lived right at the edge of the little Turkish cemetery, with its toppled gravestones in the form of turbans. The memories began to float to the surface, memories of the worn stone figures of the resident Goddess, the great Aphrodite of Rhodes, which gave the book its name: 'As long as we are in this place we shall not be free from her; it is as if our own thoughts must be for ever stained by some of her own illumination – the preoccupation of a stone woman inherited from the past whose greatest hope and ideal fell into ruins.'

Durrell conceded that the relationship between this torso and himself was rather a suspect one, 'because it was literary. But I liked her for her defects, which is the way you go about liking real women.' She had been buried in the sea until fishermen found her. I pointed out the dark mark on her breast. 'A love bite from Zeus,' Durrell suggested. 'O God, I hope that doesn't sound too much like Sir Kenneth Clark.'

Durrell, a shy man, recoiled from too many personal revelations, retreating often into clowning. 'Is it an act of self-defence?' I suggested. 'Oh no, life is too important to be taken seriously.' 'What about art then?' I retorted. 'Art is for arting, fart is for farting – it must be taken absolutely straight,' and then he recoiled again. 'Straight from the bottle, *une dive bouteille de Rabelais*,' and then he suddenly took on a serious expression, adding: 'Art is really loving, finally. If you can love right, everything comes right.'

The last picture of the film is that of the naked body of the drily funny and unpompous poet, floating in a lotus position on the transparent blue of the Aegean Sea: 'I swim for a moment or two and then turn on my back to watch the sky through wet eyelashes and lying there, arms behind my head on that resilient tideless meadow of water, I see in my mind's eye the whole panorama of our Greek life. Nothing is ever solved finally. In every age and from every angle we are facing the same set of natural phenomena, moonlight, death, religion, laughter, fear. We make idolatrous attempts to enclose them in a conceptual frame. And all the time they change under our very noses.'

Back home I found a copy of his book *Letters and Essays on Travel*. With a note: 'Dear Peter – Hope this will not bring back too many unhappy memories of a hellish *tournage* in Greece. Gratitude for your thoughtful work on my behalf. Larry.'

While I was editing, Durrell came to London, and spent a few hours in the cutting-room. There was respect and even love between us, but we were both nervous, drowning our feelings with meaningless compliments. 'You

Lawrence Durrell in Greece

are right to take so relaxed a rhythm (Visconti rather then Fellini),' he wrote a few days later. 'It will be good and ripe as a plum. Now that I have seen what you are after intellectually and visually, we can dispense with all that slapstick - a weak tendency which comes from timidity.' I was still not happy. I felt too many things were just glossed over and I wanted a chance for one more interview. 'Come down,' he wrote, ' I try to fill in the gaps. Many thanks for so capably ironing out all possible anfractuosities which might make us gnash our collective teeth.'

On 6 January I drove to visit Durrell, who lived in Sommières, the first of many visits. Larry had moved to France in 1957 with his last wife Claude and occupied a small farmhouse, 'Le Mazet'. Claude had died of cancer.

There was a fourth or fifth wife around – with Larry one stops counting – a former model, Ghislaine Boysson, but she was nowhere to be seen. He had moved into a large nineteenth-century house, 'ten rooms of junk', a sort of Grand Meaulnes mansion which went by the grand name Villa Louis. Only one room and the kitchen were properly heated. Larry was notoriously stingy, always afraid of dying in poverty and moaning about the fuel bills. Most shutters were closed. The garden was overgrown with weeds. At the end stood an old tower, inhabited by a flock of white owls. There was a black bathroom called 'Hollywood' with a photograph of the shrine of St Arsenius.

The house looked very tidy, despite the piles of books and letters which Larry didn't find time to answer. He led a reclusive life, but he appeared to be glad that I had come. A little meal had been prepared. He was warm and surprisingly personal, telling me about his life. 'I had many relationships, but what I really like is to be alone.' Then suddenly he rose and phoned Ghislaine in Paris. When he returned to the table he asked if I had started my diary.

Next morning I heard him getting up at five for one hour of his daily yoga. After breakfast we went for a walk and to meet an old herbalist who lived around the old abattoirs. It struck me again how simple his life was.

A few days later I received another letter with a beautiful drawing – Durrell painted under the name of Oscar Epfs: 'My dear Peter, cut me out more, that dreadful accent and I was awfully jellyfishish, playing for laughter. But don't be afraid of being too highbrow in what you write or show. This is lovely. I think you will have a ripping yawn followed by an OBE and a furnished suite in heaven. Every good thing and thanks. Larry.'

I did not get an OBE, but we were nominated for a British Academy Award 'for outstanding service to television'.

Spirit of Place: Lawrence Durrell's Greece was a turning-point in my career, even in my life. It made me discover the pleasure of writing – not as a poet does, but writing to satisfy the growing desire to know what life is all about. It was Durrell who taught me how to have a proper diary. 'Just write down everything that passes through your mind, it's like talking to a friend,' he had said. I bought myself a very large notebook, one of many to come, and began painstakingly and methodically writing down the many things which filled my days. Soon the fragments of my life were drifting in at great speed. I tried to join them like a jigsaw puzzle. Some would fit instantly, for others I had to look and look. There are still many pieces I could not place, however hard I tried, and maybe I never will.

On 1 January 1976 I wrote my first page in a proper diary – not just a few notes but a large page for each day. I began in our house which bore the name 'Le Mazet', a small *mas* – or farmhouse, in honour of Lawrence Durrell, whose first house in Provence had the same name. Marucha was with us in a wheelchair, her head shaved. She had began to walk a few steps every day and was able to speak again. Facundo could not reconcile himself to her fate. He drank quite heavily, crushed between the excessive love of his mother, who had come from Argentina, and the powerful feelings of Marucha, who could not stop blaming everybody for what had happened. Her energy had turned into aggression. A family Christmas full of worries, but also of hope.

How honest will I be with my diary and how tedious will it be on days when nothing happens, which must be most days? I thought. There was also the problem of language. I wrote in English, sometimes falling into French or German.

Shall I just record the outward passing of the days?

Thursday 1 January: Facundo makes a little book of coloured drawings for Marucha about their last play *Luxe.* I am restless and I potter about the house, cleaning, half out of a sense of order, half out of boredom. Is it not also the pointed finger at the others, who are disorganised and untidy?

Shall I just record my feelings, neuroses, fears?

Saturday: I am incapable of concentrating, the constant fear that something could have happened to Facundo, who went for a walk. The fragility of one's moods. Shortly before dinner I feel suddenly depressed, lonely, in need of tenderness and consolation, and then suddenly happy to watch Facundo and Pepita at dinner. Les deux se parlent d'une façon tendre, ce qui est rare. J'ai senti une vague de bonheur, de bien-être, de calme intérieure. Can we never trust our feelings at all?

Or shall I talk about the things I read?

Wednesday: Reading Ronald Hayman's biography of Gielgud. A boring account of external events, telling you little about making a person into a formidable actor. I would like to write to John, but that would probably not do. It's not easy for me to flatter when I mean it. To bed wie die Hühner at 9 o'clock. Facundo reads Simone de Beauvoir, I read Proust's letters to Mme Strauss. At first I thought the sweetness of Proust's style in these letters is unbearable, but then I am swept away by this strange passion which links two desperately lonely people together, and through their suffering one can feel the growing of *A la recherche du temps perdu*.

In the end my diaries became a mixture. Often I was too quick in my judgement and had to revise my opinions. In time, I hoped, the things I wrote down would sort themselves out. I sometimes reread what I had written, only to discover that not all memories were soothing. I found many that gripped me and some that threatened to cripple and blight my life. 'We all have doubts, do not worry, just write and write, it will coagulate to a form by itself,' Larry had told me.

'It is good to see places where one has been happy in the past,' Durrell had said, but the return to a place we love is always flawed, because what we loved was not only a place but also a time. I returned to Tressdorf, a place where I had been so wildly happy. It still had a strong existence in my memory. It was as if man and nature at its most basic had allowed me a glimpse of centuries past.

The nature was still there and so were the houses, but they were defaced by all the modern trappings. Our old house looked on the main road, its silences no longer interrupted by the gentle clop of hoofs but by the noise of cars. Streets that in the past were known only by the name of the farmers who lived there had proper names. I saw the corner where Annerl and I had first kissed, but the girl that served behind the counter of the little shop had short hair and sold all the familiar brand-names: Palmolive, Persil, Prill. This was the measure of twenty years of peace and progress. Everything that once pointed towards the past now pointed towards the future, a future I didn't much like and had little affinity to.

18
Handmaiden of the Arts: Arena Theatre
1976–1977

There were changes in the office too. Humphrey Burton had come back to the BBC from the ITV arts programme *Aquarius* to run the Music and Arts Department. I liked his enthusiasm and international outlook and felt that we would get on well. Soon afterwards he asked me to become the editor of *Arena Theatre*. The ebullient future editor of *Arena*, Alan Yentob, who made the series famous, has persuaded himself and the world that he was the inventor of this magazine, but I want to set the record straight. It had begun in 1977, four years before Alan took over.

At that time *Arena* consisted of three separate programmes: *Arena Art and Design*, *Arena Cinema* and *Arena Theatre*. Except for *Arena Cinema*, run by the talented film-maker and critic Gavin Millar, it was in bad shape and had become parochial and insular.

I did not much like the idea of becoming an editor, for it meant looking after other people's work, but then the challenge was simply too strong a pull. 'Do not panic, I will succeed,' I wrote brazenly in my diary.

I formed a small but unusual team of well-informed people, untainted by the BBC routine. Our laughter and fun abounded and quickly became the envy of the department. I discovered to my surprise that teamwork suited me. To be in charge was very gratifying.

As a researcher I engaged a tall and handsome girl, Rosemarie Wilton, pungent and funny, with a sharp mind and a heart of gold. She also knew everything about the London theatre. We were joined by a lively and widely educated girl of Polish extraction, Cris Mohr, who always referred to me as 'Mr Ziegfeld'.

I also asked Julian Jebb to be a producer. I was very fond of this highly intelligent, extravagant and decadent young man, who wore bow ties and chainsmoked Gauloises. He was funny, worldly, cultured and slightly camp, like a character straight out of *Brideshead Revisited*. Julian came from a literary family – his grandfather was Hilaire Belloc. He had written book reviews for *The Observer*, *The Sunday Times* and the *Paris Review*, made some very individual films on Jean Rhys, Virginia Woolf and Elizabeth Bowen, and had gone with John Betjeman to Australia.

Julian travelled by taxi 'to save energy' and rarely came to the office before 11 a.m. He also made a point of not making an appearance in the afternoon. His excuses were long, distinguished dinner parties and equally long and distinguished lunches, 'after which one has to think'.

I began to enjoy the attention and power which came with the job. There were many perks. I received press tickets for every opening night, which pleased my constant craving for privileges. I went on a crash course to plays which were opening in London and Paris.

I wanted *Arena* to be a programme about the nature of the theatre and of writing, not one which passed judgement. I did not want to set myself up as a critic. Fom time to time it would be a celebration of a great performance or a great play. I was also toying with the idea of engaging people to front the programme who had not often been seen on television, practitioners of the art rather than journalists – Glenda Jackson, Delphine Seyrig, Jeanne Moreau.

We kicked off on a high note. I had asked Kenneth Tynan to front the first programme and to discuss with Claire Bloom the notion of 'great' acting. The three of us went to see many plays to make our choice. The first outing was a disaster: *Treats* by Christopher Hampton. I enjoyed it, Claire loved it, Kenneth hated it. Not a good start for our new triumvirate. We fought over dinner and Kenneth won.

In the end the programme included extracts from Peggy Ashcroft's performance in Beckett's *Happy Days*, Judy Dench in Shaw's *Too True to Be Good*, and Irene Worth, who was playing on Broadway in Tennessee Williams's *A Streetcar Named Desire*.

Kenneth Tynan was dry, witty, elegant, urbane and often difficult but he was also a great help, enjoyable and instructive to work with, for he knew more about the theatre than anybody. His judgement was sometimes unusual but always daring. Claire Bloom was not quite sure what her role was; shy and self-effacing, she was nevertheless very supportive. Without her constant encouragement I do not know how I would have put on the first programme.

I realised that to make a weekly programme with big names on a shoestring budget would not be easy. Actors and actresses have lawyers and agents and secretaries and courts, all trying to get into the act. My old direct approach worked sometimes, but not always. Cris and Rosie were brilliant diplomats but Jeanne Moreau did not want to know anything about *Arena*. Neither did Shirley Maclaine, whom I went to see after a brilliant performance in London. Delphine Seyrig was suddenly difficult too.

The second programme was devoted entirely to France, a celebration of four great actresses: Madeleine Renaud, Delphine Seyrig, Jeanne Moreau and Simone Signoret. I fronted it myself.

Arena Theatre with Kenneth Tynan

Moreau was starring in Wedekind's *Lulu*, a play about a child seductress. Many great German actresses had played her in their early twenties. Moreau was forty-seven years old. The production was terrible, the translation even worse. The French audience laughed and made jokes, but Moreau triumphed over everything: at the end there were a few polite handclaps.

As I went backstage, no one seemed to go into her dressing-room. Moreau was wearing a red dressing-gown and was washing her feet in the basin. I introduced myself, explaining that I had not come to persuade her to let me film her for *Arena*, but to tell her that I thought that she had been superb. We were both slightly embarrassed. 'Only an Englishman has such manners, come and film me whenever you like,' she said, her face bursting into the famous Moreau smile.

The next day I filmed a clip from *Lulu*, reserving her offer for an interview for another time.

I filmed Renaud giving a moving performance in Duras's *Des Journées entières dans les arbres*. She and her husband Jean-Louis Barrault, looking like two old lizards, received me in their Théâtre d'Orsay.

I interviewed Seyrig in a large, very light room on the Place des Vosges. She lounged very casually, like a wild cat on a sofa, shimmering and constantly moving about, an actress sure of her looks and the impression she made, loving to perform, even for our camera. Easy and totally accessible, she talked about her work with Buñuel and how difficult it is for a film star in France to get serious roles on stage.

The same day I interviewed Simone Signoret. The two women could not have been more different. Everything about Signoret was dark – her words, her moods and even the cluttered flat she shared with Yves Montand on the Ile de la Cité. She hated to talk about herself or the theatre. I had the feeling she was asking herself why she had invited me to come. It pained me to see her, for she had just got out of hospital. Her wonderfully strong voice was still there, and her charisma, but she was self-conscious because of her looks.

I was so moved by this woman who sat opposite me, her wonderful face all bloated by alcohol and sadness, that I did one of the worst interviews of my life. What was I doing here, I asked myself, squeezing a few moments out of the life of someone I admired for the sake of a programme? I was recalling her performance in London as Lady Macbeth with Alec Guinness. I had sat in the front row on the second night, when she suddenly dried up and stopped, hiding her face in her hands, sobbing: 'I cannot do it.' Guinness rushed on stage to comfort her. She went on heroically. One of the great and tragic moments in the life of an actor, 'the worst in my life,' she said. I cut this passage out of the interview. I could not let myself make public the humiliation and the anguish of this great actress.

We were slowly turning *Arena Theatre* into a glamorous, international, even original and innovatory magazine. Many of the great names of European theatre appeared for the first time on British television.

We said 'Goodbye to the Old Vic' when the National Theatre moved to their new building with a fine film by Julian Jebb, a moving tribute which included Laurence Olivier, Barbara Jefford, Joan Plowright, Billie White-law and Kenneth Tynan. I rallied a formidable cast to celebrate the twentieth anniversary of the Royal Court, with a programme which included Christopher Hampton, Tony Richardson, Lindsay Anderson, Helen Mirren and Michael Hordern.

This was B B C at its best, and I was only one producer of many doing similar work. When I look back at this time I am amazed by how many people were willing to help us to achieve the best theatre magazine on television. Directors, actors, playwrights, all busy with their own work, took time off to make *Arena Theatre* a success. I am also amazed that we managed to do all this on a shoestring budget with a handful of collaborators bound together by friendship and mutual respect. There were no big offices, no superstructure of executive producers and executive-executive-producers, no efficiency experts and budget control, which would later make life so difficult. All we had was enthusiasm and the conviction that only the most challenging and the best would do.

From my Diaries
Wednesday 21 January 1976: A typical *Arena* day. Arrive in the studio, a nice sign on the door, 'Welcome Peter Adam'. Kenneth Tynan and Jonathan Miller talk cheerfully about their stutters and how to overcome it, a black-bearded Trevor Nunn looks on. Then rush to San Lorenzo to have lunch with Gloria Taylor, enterprising and delightful P R from the Royal Court Theatre, and the cultural attaché from the French Embassy, the writer Pierre Anremy [Pierre-Jean Remy]. A puckish Julian Jebb, more brightly scarfed than usually, has joined us. Very entertaining. Lunch £17 for four, quite good. Back to work. Recording a commentary with Humphrey Burton. Telephone does not stop ringing – twice from Irene Worth fussing from New York. A drink in the B B C bar with my collaborators to talk about future programmes. We decide for Peggy Ashcroft and Ian McKellen and against Fiona Richmond, for she appears mostly in the nude and this is not possible before

9 o'clock. The club is really like a third-class waiting room in a station. Then off to see Wim Wenders' *Alice in den Städten*. The documentary part shot in America is excellent, but wears off when the character returns to Germany. Vogler is a marvellous actor, reminds me a bit of Michael Krüger. Dead tired to bed. The luxury of a sleeping pill only to be woken up twice by two mad women. Once by Ella Winter who wants to complain to the BBC about an item on Angolan mercenaries and then an hour later by Irene. She wants more money.

Tuesday 9 March: Another typical *Arena* day. Filming at Royal Court: Alan [Bates] just like in the old days, direct and simple: 'You are still in Earls Terrace and I pissed off.' Albert Finney very nice, a bit actorish, forceful and aware of himself. Then Peter Gill, sensitive, nervous, neurotic, movingly honest. It is so nice to see someone modest in the theatre, like Jocelyn Herbert. Osborne phones up and cancels – he has the flu. But not ill enough not to blurt out some nice lines against England. Bond also does not show up. But Arnold Wesker does, he has aged which suits him as he is now more mellow, more civilised. Meeting with the minister of the Arts, Hugh Jenkins, who strikes me as a total bore. When I think of Malraux in France, it really shows how little the English value the arts. Opening of Keith's [Vaughan] show. Prunella is wearing the amber necklace of Keith's mother who died last night. Keith strangely unmoved, but pleased to see us. Just time to rush to the National Theatre to see a great production of *John Gabriel Borkmann* with Peggy Ashcroft, Wendy Hiller and Ralph Richardson.

Hans Werner Henze had written a new song cycle, *Voices*. Each song was dedicated to one of his friends, among them Edward Bond, Herbert Marcuse, Miguel Barnet, Heberto Padilla, Paul Dessau, Harrison Birtwhistle, Hans Magnus Enzensberger. One was written for me – a wicked and delightful choice: 'Gedanken eines Revuemädchens während des Entkleidungsaktes' – Thoughts of a revue girl while stripping – by Brecht. The first line said: 'My fate on this strange Earth is to serve the arts as one of the poorest servants', [1] and ended with the line: 'I won't show my behind today but wiggle it a bit I must.'[2] It was first performed in the Queen Eliza-

1 'Mein Los ist es auf dieser queren Erde, der Kunst zu dienen als die letzte Magd.'
2 'Den Hintern zeige ich heute nicht, ein bisschen schwenken muss ich ihn.'

beth Hall on 4 January 1974, to the chuckles of many of my friends and colleagues in the audience.

I was indeed the poorest servant of the arts. I do not think that I ever worked so hard in my life. Life was full of twists and turns, and made sure that I got my fair share of constantly changing emotions. There was no room for complacency.

After six months work was taking its toll. However much fun, making a fortnightly programme means a lot of effort, work, meetings, talking and scheming. Furthermore the magazine format with the strings of short items did not really satisfy me, and I wanted to go back to making things at a more leisurely pace, with less glitter and more depth.

I asked Humphrey to release me. There were a lot of fights, even some threats not to renew my contract, but in the end the friend in Humphrey won over the boss. He promised to release me at the end of the year, and he also let me direct and write some longer one-subject programmes: two programmes for *Omnibus*, b b c 1's most prestigious arts programme: *Signs of Vigorous Life*, a film on the new German Cinema, and a film on Jeanne Moreau. I also promised Hans Werner Henze to help him in his new Festival in Montepulciano, by making a programme on this unusual venture.

The German cinema of the last twenty years had been abysmal. The effort to come to terms with reality, which had fired the film-makers during the first ten years, had soon been stifled by a general indifference to social comment or self-examination. The drive for prosperity permitted little questioning. With the rubble disappearing, most Germans wanted to be spared the memory of those sombre years and preferred to be lulled by entertainment films.

Then in the mid-1960s a group of young directors and writers called for an end to these stereotyped pictures and demanded some which reflected the experience of a new generation. As a result, the German cinema saw a renaissance, not unlike that in France during the *nouvelle vague*.

Not that the majority of the German audience, brought up on manufactured dreams, cared much about the new trend. They shied away from these often sombre and difficult films, considering them too intellectual and too self-conscious.

Volker Schlöndorff had already made eight feature films, Wim Wenders seven, Werner Herzog nine, Hans Jürgen Syberberg five and Rainer Werner Fassbinder no fewer then twenty-three. Most of them had also directed on stage, made documentaries and written plays. A formidable record, yet they were totally unknown to the British audience except to a small group of film buffs.

I was keen to meet Werner Herzog. I had liked his Buñuel-like film *Even Dwarfs Started Small*, and most of all his *The Enigma of Kaspar Hauser*, a stark poetic view of an extreme human situation: innocence betrayed by a complacent society. He had gone to Africa, to Alaska, and to Peru in search of the landscapes for his films. Landscape was as important to him as people.

Herzog, an affable man with long curly hair, received me in his house. The soft voice and gentle way of speaking were in complete contrast to the man of action who had travelled by raft up the Amazon to make *Aguirre, Wrath of God*, the powerful tale of the mad, obsessed Spanish conquistador looking for an Eldorado. 'Film-making is a very physical activity, the cinema resists if you just approach it with your brains.'

A few days later I saw what he had meant. We were walking through a rain-soaked field, Herzog wearing a leather jacket over a sweatshirt with a star of David. Suddenly he lay on his back in the wet grass marking out some camera angles. 'My films are very personal. Somehow I feel like I am stark naked when I show my films. They show who I am.'

One of his favourite actors was Klaus Kinski, whose mad obsessions seemed to have accentuated since our student years in Paris. Herzog liked, even needed, extremes: 'If you are a scientist and want to find out about the inner structure of matter, you will put it under extreme pressure and under extreme circumstances like radiation, heat. People too, under extreme pressure, under extreme circumstances, give you much more insight about what we are.' Sitting on the floor he spread out some photographs from his last film *Heart of Glass*. He had filmed an actress under hypnosis. When I voiced some doubt about the validity of such an undertaking he said: 'This is not a gimmick. It is a way to come to greater reality, which often lies deep down in us.'

In the evening we walked through the town. 'I am sick of the images that surround us, look at magazines or shops, it is all a waste. On television nothing but worn-out images.' We had reached the park and he pointed at a tree. 'Look at this tree, maybe I can film it as never before, I just filmed a cornfield in the wind. It doesn't matter where you go, it's the way you see things with a new perspective.'

Wim Wenders's films were also marked by landscape – the German landscape. Like Herzog he belonged to the new generation; casual, open and at home with the cinema of the world. His is a *cinéma d'auteur*, pictures used as a writer uses text. His *Wrong Movement* was based on Goethe's *Wilhelm Meister*. 'Like the *Entwicklungsromane* my films talk about journeys.' Sitting in his garden under an apple tree we talked about nineteenth-century literature: Fontane, Brentano, Stifter.

Wenders's latest film, *Kings of the Road*, was a road movie; but it was also a film about cinema that refuses to perpetuate the dream of a better world. 'We must meet and accept the conditions we live in,' he said when I left him.

I met Volker Schlöndorff in his cutting-room. He was viewing the rushes of his latest film, *Strohfeuer*. Schlöndorff had worked with Louis Malle and Alain Resnais and was the most international of the new group. 'The new German generation are great movie buffs, but all they see is Paris, New York, Rome. Now it is time for us also to show something of our lives,' he said with a big smile. 'The British cinema has lost its individuality by looking to America as a potential market, just because you share the same language. We were about to make the same mistake.'

His recent film, *The Lost Honour of Katharina Blum*, a semi-documentary, took on the Germany of that time, a Germany troubled by the Baader-Meinhof trial – a democracy taking off its polite mask. Hans Werner Henze composed the film music.

At lunch with Schlöndorff's wife and collaborator Margaretha von Trotta, we continued to talk about the French and Italian cinema. Facundo had joined us and the conversation switched effortlessly from English to French. I was struck by how international this new generation of Germans was. They seemed to have seen and read everything and to be at home in Paris, New York and London.

Von Trotta had worked as an actress but she had also written scripts for many of Schlöndorff's pictures. She talked about her desire to direct herself. A few years later she made the remarkable and moving film about the Baader-Meinhof group, *Die bleierne Zeit*.

I dreaded the meeting with Fassbinder. I had filmed him once before for *Them and Us*, while he was making his most lyrical film, with his favourite actress, Hanna Schygulla, based on Fontane's *Effi Briest*. At that time I had felt very ill at ease with the scruffy-looking man in jeans and a leather jacket who looked down on the 'British' journalist in a pinstripe suit and bow tie. I could not blame him: he was working in a tiny flat, with hardly any room for his own crew, and our arrival was certainly an intrusion.

We met in the small pension Die deutsche Eiche where he sometimes stayed with his crew and his actors. I had left the pinstripes at home. The Fassbinder I now saw was very different from the one I had first met. We went out together and roamed through the leather bars, drinking and talking, both in large quantities. He struck me as a man in search of something to hold on to. 'Everything that I experience somehow has to end up in one of my films. Only then do I have the feeling of really having experienced it.'

Fassbinder, like most of his heroes, was an outsider. Crude, seemingly banal, often bordering on kitsch, his art had raised ordinary happenings to the level of tragedy. He was pleased when I told him that the self-imposed artificiality of his films seemed to underline a belief that tragedy is unavoidable. 'Yes,' he said, 'they look real, but they are not. Reality is much more sad, people wouldn't want to see it.'

There was a lot of talk about the pursuit of dreams and how dreams imprison us. A man living against conventions, Fassbinder dreamed about the revolution and realised it would not happen. He belonged to the generation not at home in their own country, searching for a national identity elsewhere. 'Our melancholia stems from the many unrealised and unrealisable dreams. It is dreams which give the world some sense,' he said, 'not intellectual speculation.'

The interview with Fassbinder had been fixed for the next day. When I arrived with my crew everybody seemed embarrassed. Fassbinder had apparently quarrelled with his lover and had vanished. In the afternoon, he phoned me and apologised. We made a date to film him in a café around the corner from where he lived. He stormed in. I could see he was ill-tempered, unshaven but with a big smile. He said: 'That fucker.' These were the only English words he used; he insisted that we conducted the rest of the interview in German. I decided that I liked Fassbinder very much.

A few days later I watched him filming with Anna Karina and Mascha Meril. He always worked with a small team, most of them his friends. He improvised a lot, the atmosphere was cordial and very casual. Chainsmoking, he fixed his camera positions on primitive tracks. He arranged the hair of his actresses himself and joked with the crew. At lunch we all ate in the kitchen, seated around a large wooden table like a family. Somebody was making soup, while someone else passed some *Tom of Finland* drawings around. Fassbinder told us the delightful story about Jean Genet who instead of saying '*un ange passe*', as was commonplace when suddenly silence falls, used to say: '*On encule un ange*' (an angel is being buggered).

Fassbinder exuded an enormous physicality, which he broadcast freely, a capacity I always liked in people. To watch him flaunting his sexuality reminded me of Joe Orton, the same liberating effect that cut down all conventional barriers. There is nothing wrong in the separation between love and sex. Once the shame and guilt are gone, sex for its own gratification can be a source of affirmation of life. Many people I knew were promiscuous, even those in long-standing relationships, but it needs a strong

character to survive this freedom, because there can also be a kind of desperation about it, a feeling that life is running out, as if sex and death are
the only ways out of a world of conflict.

I saw Fassbinder a few more times; then like so many people he drifted
out of my life. On our last meeting I had read him some lines from Henry
James's *The Ambassadors*: 'Live all you can; it's a mistake not to. It doesn't
make so much matter what you do in particular, so long as you have life. If
you haven't had that, what have you had?'

He died on the 10th of June 1982 of a heart attack brought on by drugs.
He was only thirty-seven years old. He had made forty-two films, the last
one after Genet's *Querelle*. I remembered that he had quoted Oscar Wilde
to me: 'How grey and old the world would soon grow without sins.'

Festa in Montepulciano was a programme about a small Tuscan town,
known until then mostly for its *vino nobile* and its Renaissance palaces. It
had no cultural life to speak of. There had once been a theatre but the
beautiful eighteenth-century building had been closed a long time ago, its
red plush seats flea-ridden and broken. There was no musical education in
school. It was a poor city. Many of the men had gone to Germany to work
in factories or hotels. In the hope of stimulating tourism, the mayor had
decided to open a music festival here and had asked Hans Werner Henze
to become its mentor.

Henze had often spoken about a composer's need to become more 'useful' to society. He was not interested in founding yet another festival, with
stars drifting in and out for a short time and then leaving the towns empty
and barren of culture and guests. He set out to create for the people of
Montepulciano something more permanent, without the snobbish cultural hype which usually goes with such an undertaking. In the winter he and
Peter Maxwell Davies had visited schools and talked to children. He had
brought a small chamber orchestra and had stood in a church analysing
one of Mozart's symphonies for an audience that consisted mostly of
locals.

Henze spent the next months contacting musicians all over Europe,
asking them to help him to get a musical life going. All he could offer was
a ticket to Italy, food and lodgings and the promise of making music for
two to three weeks in one of Italy's most beautiful towns. The festival had
no director, no publicity agents, no committee; it was organised by Henze,
his secretary, the formidable Helen Grob, and the indispensable Fausto
Moroni, with hardly any money. Many people thought it could not be
done.

On 26 July 1976 three grand pianos arrived from Germany, on loan

from the manufacturer. The same day saw the arrival of musicians, singers, conductors, and two television crews, one from Germany and one
from Britain. Among the many artists were Julian Bream, Peter Maxwell
Davies, Homero Francesc, Gerald English, Martha Agerich, Richard
Blackford, Jan Latham-Koenig and Ricardo Chailly.

Montepulciano had hardly any hotels. People slept in houses, tents and
caravans. I stayed with Hans and Fausto in a cramped flat with hardly any
water, pouring some mineral water over our heads. How many famous
composers would live this way? I often thought. There was a large tent
where twice a day six local women cooked the most delectable pastas.
Singers, conductors, actors went to the market and washed the dishes.
People doubled and tripled in their functions, singing in two to three operas, rewriting scores, making music in schools. When I was not filming I
worked as the assistant to Hans, who directed an opera by Paisiello on the
main square. He had given up his original idea of asking the local amateur
brass band to play the entire opera and had rescored the work for small
modern orchestra, the band just cheerfully butting in on the famous arias.

Peter Maxwell Davies had brought ten young modern composers and
gave a masterclass. Julian Bream did the same for ten guitarists. Max's ten
composers wrote ten new works for Julian's guitarists. They were performing in the streets to revive the old tradition of the competing *contradas*.
The judges were the people of Montepulciano.

In the re-opened theatre, the paint still fresh and the fleas still in residence, Volker Schlöndorff directed a children's opera, especially written
by Edward Bond to music by Thomas Jahn. He was assisted by Mathieu
Carrière. The set and costumes were made by the children of Montepulciano.

Every day brought new people and new problems. The three grand
pianos had to be shared by at least ten pianists fighting over the instruments. Someone arrived and had to sleep on the floor in our already overcrowded flat. Hans needed a couple of composers to rescore bits of his
work. For Rossini's *Il Turco in Italia*, Ricardo Chailly was short of singers
for the chorus. Anybody who had a voice or could read a score was invited. The opera was performed with a small choir of seven, including
Peter Maxwell Davies, Hans Werner Henze, Julian Bream, Jan Latham
Koenig and Richard Blackford. The first act was played in an old set for
Tosca we found backstage, the second in a set for *Rigoletto*.

Of course it was not all fun. There were also fights and chaos and
exhaustion. People used to international opera houses, to proper hotels
and rehearsal schedules found it difficult to cope with the absence of all of
that and still be expected to give a great performance. There was the threat

of one of the works being cancelled. Hans carried all this on his shoulders. More television stations and journalists arrived to see a 'communist' composer making a festival in a 'communist' city. Many were only waiting for him to fail. He was doing the impossible. Lying in the grass, listening to Julian Bream playing the guitar, Hans admitted that 'these are some of the most dramatic days of my life'. Once when we were alone, he burst into tears. He could not stand it when his enthusiasm was undermined by the undying egotism of some artists. But his dark moods never lasted.

His anxiety transmitted itself to me. I had filmed Gerald English singing Monteverdi, and Homero Francesc playing Mozart with the sun streaming through the open windows, but I had no light to film the opera. The crew were ill-tempered, as they often are. They too were used to a less chaotic schedule. They were late for the interview with Peter Maxwell Davies and so he walked out on us. It took me two hours and a bottle of *vino nobile* to pacify the normally cheerful and generous Max. I made deals with the crew from RAI for some of their lights and the Germans borrowed some film material from us.

The local contessa, to save the old Italian culture from what she considered 'communist infiltration', had invited all the smart people of the area to a concert of eighteenth-century music. Max and I were sent as spies and sat on little gilt chairs listening to the refined sound of the period instruments, when suddenly their melody was drowned by the most horrendous noise of the brass band under the window of the contessa's palazzo, intoning Paisiello's march. Max and I could hardly keep a straight face when the contessa's concert had to come to a halt.

We celebrated my forty-seventh birthday in high spirits. Max, Homero, Hans, Fausto, Julian, Helen and Ann gave a lovely party, but I missed Facundo. I thought, as so often before, how rich my life was yet how troubled. On the way home Hans and Julian were singing a Neapolitan song, when someone from a window emptied a bucket of water over their heads. At least I think it was a bucket of water.

Montepulciano is now an institution soon to reach its thirtieth year. For those who came here in 1976 to create no fewer than four works for the stage, ten chamber and orchestral concerts and a multitude of events all over the town, Montepulciano Numero Uno was an unforgettable experience, unique in the history of modern music because Hans's enthusiasm had made everybody feel that they had done something worthwhile.

After Montepulciano I travelled to the Edinburgh Festival. The *Arena* team came with me, and we set up office in a little flat. Rosie had simply poured the contents of our office into a huge washing basket. I can still picture her on the station platform, heavy-laden and slightly bow-legged, swaying from one side to the other.

Instead of the usual report I had asked Germaine Greer and Gian Carlo Menotti to give us their personal version of the Festival. I have always liked and even admired Germaine Greer. However challenging, she always makes me feel good. I had met her when working on *Review*. She had just published *The Female Eunuch*. Her public image was that of an aggressive feminist and fighter for sexual freedom. When I collected this tall, hand-some woman with the dark foghorn voice and infectious laughter at Lime Grove reception, she lectured me in a crowded lift about penis envy. Her mercurial side is complemented by a formidable intellect and a compul-sion to manipulate and to challenge. Espousing sometimes the most outrageous ideas just to provoke, Germaine is a natural trouble-shooter. She is also a woman of deep moral concern, and a committed friend. Under the brainy side lie many warm human qualities nurtured by a strong feminine instinct. Nobody could call Germaine humble – she is proud and knows her own worth – but one could trust her totally. We shared many things: a love of Italy and a love of poetry, a lack of sexual guilt feelings and the taste for exploration.

Germaine Greer took a hard look at the Fringe offerings. Her particular edge of humour, the tough-mindedness of her critical eye, were challeng-ing. She had the capacity of transforming duty into passion.

I do not remember much of the many Fringe shows we saw, except for an evening with Fenella Fielding, whose considerable talent as a serious artist was so often overlooked beneath her outrageously camp exterior. Germaine did a delightful interview with Quentin Crisp, both of them very amused by each other. I filmed them walking in a garden, Crisp wearing a deep purple hat, talking about style, fingering a string of pearls.

We also filmed a typical Fringe production which one of Edna O'Brien's sons had put on. 'My darlings,' wrote Edna to us, 'I am surrounded by youths in sleeping bags. All very exciting. Come along, you will love it. Signed, an actor's mother.' There was nothing very motherly about Edna O'Brien. Someone had said about her that 'she had come to London and drowned in a sea of men', but she exuded formidable warmth and when-ever we met over the years she would always be fun and widely enthusias-tic. She was very theatrical, very emotional and very nice. We sat until the morning, while the two women talked about her last book, which she wrote as if under dictation, 'a long burst of creative dictation, I tell you my darrlings'. Her strong, cultured, slightly affected Irish accent drifted through my half-sleep and it made me laugh, so she mocked my German one.

Gian Carlo Menotti, who lived much of the year in a house thirty miles west of Edinburgh, had chosen to make his film a homage to the art of the human voice. Menotti was the most wonderful raconteur, an easygoing jester and generous host. He knew everybody, and in his outgoing flamboyant Italian way enjoyed introducing people to each other. We rallied an impressive array of singers: Judith Bleggen, Frederica von Stade, Elisabeth Schwartzkopf, Teresa Berganza and Galina Vishnevskaya.

I began by filming a rehearsal of *The Marriage of Figaro*. The atmosphere was very tense and I was made to feel terribly like an intruder. Geraint Evans interrupted the rehearsal every three minutes and Fischer-Dieskau was obviously annoyed by the cameras. Everybody's nerves were on edge. Judith Bleggen was furious because they had forgotten to put her picture in the Festival programme, and did not want to hear anything about television. Only Teresa Berganza seemed to ignore it all and sang like an angel. Menotti watched all those goings-on with slight amusement. He arranged a 'small' lunch with von Stade and Bleggen in his house, a rather grand and beautiful manor situated in a park, 'to make up for the unhappiness during the rehearsal. It will make your filming much easier.'

He was right. The lunch was a very lighthearted affair, to my relief. The two stars turned out to be two American girls full of fun.

Filming Elisabeth Schwarzkopf was a nightmare of a different kind. Schwarzkopf is the most exacting and self-critical artist I have ever known. Close up she looked like a very attractive middle-aged matron, more a singing teacher than an opera star. She agreed to sing two *Lieder* for us and started practising. 'Oh God, I am flat, my voice is gone. Let's stop this.' Her husband Walter Legge, the famous record producer, reassured her and helped along. Then she went to change for the filming. The transformation was amazing. Here was the elegant woman we had all admired over the years. 'Maybe I should put on another dress, my arms look so old.' She tried to muster a smile, but she meant it. Twice more she wanted to call the whole thing off. I felt sad watching the torment of this great artist trying to produce a perfection which nature now denied her. She refused to delude herself. She sang again and again the same *Lieder*, listening and correcting until they were absolutely right. She had perfect pitch, frequently interrupting herself dismissively.

Two days later, she and Walter Legge came to listen to our sound recording and to look at the pictures. She was unhappy with both. I knew that the tape from the concert she had given the previous night had to be wiped on her instruction; she did not want it to remain even for the archive. She had also cancelled an engagement in Spain. I offered to erase my footage, seeing that it made her suffer so much. She was obviously touched by this gesture. 'Keep it. I wish you had filmed me twenty years earlier.'

Twenty years later I had the good fortune to film her once more, when I embarked on a series on *The Art of Conducting*. She was no longer singing. She told me that she was listening to all her past recordings, wanting to keep only the very best, destroying the others. She was still her sternest critic.

I was still working on *Arena*, I interviewed Peter Stein in Berlin, Patrice Chéreau in Paris and Roger Planchon in Lyon. Every programme was a struggle: the old fight for 'standards'. I was sometimes irritated, and the sinewy affable personality which I had cultivated for so long began to show its rough edges. I had rows with my colleagues, I even sacked one of the cutting editors. The graphics were awful, the commentary did not fit, the laboratories were two weeks late. The inefficiency was unbelievable, nobody seemed to care.

I do not like to cause pain, but I am never afraid of giving offence. I did not hide any longer my natural arrogance, my feeling of superiority. People in the office either hated or liked me. I had always been able to inspire strong loyalties and also strong antagonisms. I did not mind, I really quite liked a good row. The worst irritant was praise from people one does not esteem. My friends were angels of patience and generosity, listening to my egomaniac stances, although Prunella pointed out that generosity, of all kinds, was also a form of calculation.

Germaine came around with a large casserole and home-made bread, and in her rational way put my head right. We talked about the real problems of the world, which made my own problems small and self-indulgent, those concerned with work at least. Julian Jebb too talked about the injustice and death which was everywhere. Catastrophic news had become our daily bread on television, domesticating everything: Vietnam, Biafra. The dead were piling up around us and humanity reduced to its tribal behaviour was terrifying. Man is capable of committing almost any atrocity possible, out of hate, greed or thoughtlessness. This is the terrible lesson our century has taught us.

From my Diaries
Sunday 19 May 1976: One of those days when loneliness, restlessness, sadness, randiness all seem to have the upper hand. The worst days are when the tears come for no reason at all, when your eyes are blinded with sadness. Tears which are not coming for a lost love or a lost dream but just for everything, the sadness of just

being alive. I woke up in a hotel in Brighton with H P sauce, soggy cornflakes and greasy eggs and sausages on a tray. Last night Hans played with a percussion player the music to Griffiths's silent film *Greed* as part of the Brighton Festival. The hall was only half full.

I take a bus back to London and dine with Sabine Lietzmann, who is now the German correspondent for the *Frankfurter Allgemeine Zeitung*. She tells me how in 1945 during the last days of the war, she walked for three hours through the burning Berlin to reach her professor to present herself for her Ph.D. exam, which she passed covered in dust. We talk about the Prussian spirit and what is best in it. It must be the deeply humanistic tradition which has nothing to do with the military side. Later I switch on the television and hear that Ulrike Meinhof hanged herself in her cell. Only that morning Hans had spoken about her. How things always interlink!

I looked at the strangely split life I led. I guess most people live several lives all kept apart. On one hand was my work, which must have appeared so dazzling to many people. The life of an interviewer, meeting the 'great and the famous', constantly making new relationships which are impossible to keep up with. Talking to so many people, so many inflated vanities and ruffled egos, to be charming all the time and attentive, to make everybody feel important, these abilities did not always come naturally to me. A life like this was not only pleasure. Art for consumption, even the highest art, was no longer safe from our increasing appetite for it. People appeared on chat shows for instant fame and instant demise, artists promoting their image. One experience chased away the other, at such speed that sometimes they became undistinguishable, interchangeable. I was lucky, I could select and spend some time near the people I filmed, for a moment at least, especially when they were vulnerable, but many were so busy, preoccupied with themselves, that they did not even notice when I disappeared from their lives.

My personal life too was littered with friendships picked up and dropped. What happened to all those people for whom I would lay down my life, if they had asked me? Or those I tried so hard to forget and that kept on floating back, filling me with emptiness? Were my two lives, the public and the private, the condition of the other? Maybe one made me live the other, better, deeper. I tried to become 'a man of balance', in Thomas Mann's phrase. Not that I believed in the perfectibility of man, although most of us have a serious longing to perfect ourselves. I for my part always fall back into the same mistakes, dictated by my desire to please, to be liked. It was at the root of much of my behaviour, the silly as well as the compassionate.

From my Diaries
September 1976: Marucha is in a special home where they teach handicapped people to adapt to a normal life. The sad image of Marucha, standing in a large kitchen, trying to cut a potato which was stuck on a nail, is heart-rending. She has regained the control of one hand, but the doctor has confirmed that she will never be normal again. Facundo's pain almost breaks my heart, and I realised that she can no longer look after herself, she cannot wash herself and has to be fed. The reality of her life will be like a shadow over ours.

Keith is dying. I try to see him as often as I can. After his colostomy he has lost all desire to paint. He explains to me that with the loss of his libido his desire to paint is gone too. 'How can I endure it?' Last night he spoke to me about his desire to commit suicide while Prunella and I sat in the next room. I can't help crying and he is moved. I realise that from now on it will be a battle to keep him alive. Every time he seems to be sliding more into darkness, he stops shaving and looks scruffy. Sometimes he sits by the window and watches life going on outside. 'An existence like in a Beckett play,' he tells me. Prunella gives him a television set which he will never switch on.

From Keith's Diary, 8 September 1976
My ideal of death would be a ceremonial suicide in the presence of my friends, P. W., Pru, K. P., Bob, Veronica [Patrick Woodcock, Prunella Clough, K.P. Adam, Bob and Veronica Gosling]... we would have a meal here in Belsize Park. I would take the necessary pills, alcohol, change into my night attire and go to bed. The others would be drinking, laughing, perhaps playing some music by my bedside. As I get dozy I would take my leave of being, one by one, with sadness but not despair. And not lonely. It would be a ritualised affair, civilised and well conducted.

On 31 October Eileen Gray died. She was ninety-eight years old. For the last fifteen years she had been a constant feature in my life. I never went to Paris without seeing her and she visited Prunella and me in London. I would see her in the South of France, and when we did not see each other we wrote letters. I tried to give her a little bit of the affection and care I could no longer give my mother.

Eileen's outer life had drastically changed during the last few years. In 1972, one of the screens she had made sixty years earlier, belonging to the dress designer and art collector Jacques Doucet, was sold at the famous auction house of the Hôtel Drouot. As the lacquer screen fetched the tremendous sum of £12,000, newspapers and collectors took notice. Her name appeared, for the first time in thirty-five years, in *Le Figaro*, *Le Monde*, *The Times* and the *Herald Tribune*.

The search for the mysterious Eileen Gray had begun. She was suddenly fashionable. Not that it made any difference to her. 'C'est absurde,' she used to say. She continued to take her meals alone as she had done for the last thirty years. Her only contacts with the outside world were Louise, Prunella and myself. As with Keith, we formed a kind of lifeline, people to whom she could unburden herself of the daily problems of a life made increasingly difficult by illness and old age.

In the last six years of her life there were exhibitions of her work in Paris, London, Los Angeles, Brussels and Vienna. Eileen would not attend any of the official openings. She came to London to see her furniture at the RIBA after the crowds had disappeared. When she was awarded honorary titles in London she would send Prunella and me to collect them for her. The other winners were Jean Muir and the television designer Tony Abbot, fifty years younger. The belated accolades she now received gave her small pleasure. More and more the world took notice of her, much to her surprise and not always to her liking. She complained about the constant flow of requests from journalists, students and scholars, but she was often too shy or too polite to decline. 'Letters have always been a nightmare to me' or 'The damp has made my machine I write on almost unusable' were only some common complaints. Some of the people she saw helped to break the tedium and loneliness.

Bruce Chatwin was sent from *The Sunday Times* to do an article. Alarmed, she phoned me up and when I reassured her that he was a very nice and easygoing young man, she consented, writing to warn him that there was nothing to photograph in her flat. Bruce, that dangerously charismatic man who had seduced us all, had the same effect on Eileen. He later told the story how he and the ninety-three-year-old woman spoke about their desire to travel to faraway places. He had not been to Patagonia yet, but he dreamed about it . 'Me too,' she said, pointing at an old map of the very same place on the wall of her flat. 'Allez-y pour moi, go on my behalf' – this map would later hang in Chatwin's home.

I saw Eileen for the last time on 14 October 1976. Prunella, Eileen and I had gone to the exhibition '1925' at the Musée des Arts Décoratifs. The exhibition contained several pieces of hers. She stood in the queue, like everybody else, paid her entrance fee and walked among the considerable crowd. As always, despite her ninety-eight years, her posture was impeccable; while her body was in ruins, her inner strength held the frail body upright. That day Eileen was awkward and nervous. Since she was deaf, her voice carried above the others. She was in her most censorious mood. Suddenly she called out: 'Over there is my screen.' But her joy was soon tempered by the observation that 'The cupboard would have looked better if they had opened the door.' Then she saw the lamp – 'It surely must have been redone!' That night over a meal in her workroom, sitting on her beautiful dining chairs still covered in green plastic from the war, she made me a present of a set, but the seats on mine were recovered by her in brown suede and had a little rosewood finish. We had a few laughs about the 'monstrosities' of the Art Deco period.

Once she had threatened to cut the tassels from her famous lacquer table, when she saw it in a catalogue. When it was time to part, as we embraced, I thought how sad and arduous her life and art had been, how frail her body and how strong her spirit.

Prunella and I went to Paris to arrange Eileen's funeral, one of those dreadful early-morning flights. At the funeral parlour, a rather greasy gentleman in a dark tail suit entered the room just at the moment when Prunella took a large gulp of brandy from a hip flask. Later Facundo, Prunella and I took Eileen's old governess, Louise, to a restaurant – she had not been in one for years. For fifty-five years she had worked for Eileen, watched over her. I tried to understand how she must feel, but could not. Men are islands after all.

At the simple funeral at Père Lachaise only three people were at her graveside. She was buried in a ceremony without music or speech. It would have suited her fine. 'There is a road which leads upwards and one that leads downwards. Both are one and the same,' she had written to me once.

I spent Christmas in Berlin, in the Waldhaus. It is a strange feeling to retrace one's steps, after so many years, the first Christmas in the house where I grew up. Christmas is for families. I had long learned to dislike it. Renate, Mathias and their two boys, the same ritual of churchgoing and roast goose, made me feel lonely.

The year ended in Paris. Marucha and Facundo lived together now, an intense life, full of misunderstandings, torture and deep love – just like my relationship with him. Peace is obviously the most difficult thing on earth to achieve, and yet peace and contentment is what I really wanted.

I know that the heart
Doubting every real thing else
Does not doubt the voice that tells
Us that we suffer. The hard part
At the dead centre of the soul
Is an age of frozen grief
No vernal Equinox of relief can mitigate, and no love console.[1]

I look back at the year 1976 and wonder if it was a richer or a fuller year than others before. Did it only appear so because I had begun to note things down, day by day, things which would have disappeared otherwise into the darkest corner of my memory, never to surface again? Recording one's daily life, the outer and the inner one, is a disconcerting affair, no chance to escape from oneself. My diary began to talk more often about defeats than about conquests. Weapons and arms one relied on were no longer so easily available. The terrific buoyancy of my youth had made room for a certain melancholia, even a certain disappointment. I felt the beginning of a fear of spiritual void, the fear of being dead inside. In my relationship with people I felt a kind of drift, as if relationships did not really happen, but were self-invented. I became more aware of the passing of time, the unrepeatability of each gesture. Death was no longer that far-away adventure.

Was I beginning to confront the phenomenon called age? Looking in the mirror no longer gave one the pleasing reflection which in the past satisfied my strong narcissistic streak. At the bottom, one knew, lay other more cruel images, gradually coming to the surface, relentlessly, inescapably.

My decision to leave *Arena Theatre* was now irreversible. For my last programme, I chose to take a look at the hopes, aspirations and concerns of the playwrights of the 1970s. Political theatre always had a rough ride in England, it was something continentals indulged in. With the gradual advance of Conservatism, the British theatre began to speak with a different voice.

I had asked the writer Albert Hunt to help me. We were a strange pair. 'A continental aesthete,' he was supposed to have said, after having met me. 'A stuffy English don,' had been my verdict. I thoroughly enjoyed working with this sharp and slightly sardonic man, who was a brilliant analyst of the socio-political context.

1   George Barker. 'The True Confession, Book One.'

We took a look at five writers: Howard Brenton, Trevor Griffiths, John McGrath, Barry Keeffe and David Hare. Most of them had produced plays for television and at the National Theatre, but they lacked the popular success of the playwrights of the 1960s. The grievances they expressed in their plays were too subjective and the changes they demanded too political to attract a wider audience. Barry Keeffe, the attractive, elegant and rather cool author of *Gotcha* and *Mad World My Masters*, was amused by my Germanic effort to understand the British through their theatre. He saw the future in building a better world for children, and warned us not to ignore the violence among the young, a strangely prophetic view.

Howard Brenton, a big bear-like scruffy figure, expressed his fear of a 'fascist England' in such an intense way that I had to force myself not to smile, thinking about the fascism I had known. David Edgar's play *Destiny* had raised the same spectre.

Trevor Griffiths talked a lot about 'fun', but humour was not much in evidence when we met, and his play *Comedians* was rather an earnest affair. Humour, as Albert remarked in his typical downbeat way, was obviously not the best way for these writers to look at the state of their nation.

It was difficult not to sympathise with many of the causes of these writers, nor to be touched by their ardent arguments. But in the end it did not add up to much. Their left-wing and often pessimistic views contained few constructive elements. There was much rebellion, but few recipes for change. 'Their inability to show how change might come about leads to a particular greyness,' as Albert Hunt had put it.

We showed scenes from several of their plays of contrasting styles and shared interests, packaged between extracts from Osborne's *Look Back in Anger* and Brecht's *Arturo Ui*; the first as an example of socially committed theatre which can have a truly popular success, the latter as an example of taking up politics with comedy and sarcasm.

The taut and incisive programme created quite a stir, and we were all stunned by the attention it received in the press. There were many intelligent and analytical write-ups. Not all agreed with Trevor Griffiths's belief that we were living in a violent age, and Brenton's warning of fascism in the guise of Churchill worship drew rebuke from David Wheeler in *The Listener*, as 'too blinkered' a view.

The most interesting attack came from the playwright Dennis Potter, in *The Sunday Times:*.

> Struggling against the pain and degradation of my illness and the reclusiveness thrust upon me during the past decade have left me either armed against or indifferent to certain established proprie-

ties. Thus the loathing I felt when listening to Howard Brenton, Trevor Griffiths and Barry Keeffe may well have more to do with my actual reason than my too easily presumed rivalry. These new reactionaries cannot see change unless everything changes. They glimpse Fascism around the corner because they refuse to look at what is capable of repair in the road directly in front of them. Violence and corruption take centre stage and there is nothing else in the wings. Their wilful pessimism and occasional overblown rant is shameful to contemplate alongside the Czech writers shown in last week's *Panorama* struggling so bravely against real tyranny.

Potter was right. However real the grievances of those writers were, they were like much of the political problems of Great Britain – luxury ones, and mostly concerned with little England, while the same generation of writers in Europe already saw the world in a much larger context.

Free from Arena Theatre I went for a few weeks to Paris, where the Group TSE had its greatest triumph in *Les Peines de cœur d'une chatte anglaise*, an adaptation of Balzac's story about animal life. It had been Lila de Nobili's idea to dress the actors in costumes based on Grandville's famous animal drawings. They were executed by Claudie Gastine and the set was by Emilio Carcano, both from Lila's stable. But the most stunning features of the production were the extraordinary lifelike masks by Rostislav Doboujinsky, a splendid old Russian known by everybody as Tonton. The fusion of these elements with the flawless movements of the actors is unforgettable to the many people who have seen this play. The production would eventually tour the world. Hans Werner Henze was so enthralled that he turned it into an opera, *The English Cat*, with a libretto by Edward Bond.

The opening night of *La Chatte* was like all the opening nights of the TSE – a social and intellectual event, with *le tout* Paris crowding into the theatre. Facundo played Brisquet the romantic cat who had to die for falling in love with the white cat 'Beauty', played by Marilu Marini. Afterwards, in Facundo's dressing-room, I saw Jean Genet (who wanted to make a film with him). I was proud and delighted for him.

A visit to a dressing-room is a strange convention in the theatre. Most actors like it and expect it. I usually avoided them with their hysterical atmosphere of kisses and exalted compliments. Facundo's was special to me. It had the look and the smell of all dressing-rooms, the smell of makeup and perspiration, too many flowers, and stale sandwiches lying around half-eaten. The mirror was almost totally plastered with messages and telegrams and underneath stood the disarray of creams, paint and

357

wigs; the many secrets of an actor's face. The costumes lay tired and crumpled like servants in the evening, on the floor or hanging on racks to be taken away by the wardrobe mistress and resuscitated for their next performance.

In Facundo's dressing-room I felt at home – I belonged. I was always the first one in, I did not have to knock at the door. That night I looked at Marucha, standing in the corner, still beautiful, a bit forlorn, leaning on her walking stick. How must she feel? The TSE had looked for a long time to find someone to replace Marucha's unique talent. For a while, Delphine Seyrig was keen to play in the company, but then the choice fell on the vivacious Argentinian actress Marilu Marini, who would be Facundo's partner for the next ten years.

I have a deep love for the theatre. Not the one the audience perceives from the stalls, but the theatre of the actors with their toils and fears. Many of my memories of actors are linked to dressing-rooms. Some were glamorous, impeccable, smothered in flowers like tombs, like Callas's when she sang *Tosca* or Uta Hagen's for *Virginia Woolf*. Sometimes I had to wait outside in a queue, at other times there was nobody. Others were sad and lonely, like the one Jeanne Moreau inhabited after *Lulu*, or the one I fetched Irene Worth from in Greenwich, when she was too poorly paid and too poor to afford a taxi. I remember the night when Facundo and I went to fetch Ingrid Bergman after a performance, for a quick meal, and found her alone in a vast dressing-room, too tired and already too ill to come along. I saw Hildegard Behrens in triumph; I could not get through her dressing-room door for all the well-wishers. I saw the same woman after a concert in Aix, sad and defeated and totally alone, taking off her makeup behind a makeshift curtain, knowing that it was not her finest hour, and remembered what Jeanne Moreau once said to me: 'It is marvellous to be an actress. It is a useless profession, but an essential one. Actors are always giving something; their curiosity, their fear, their interest, sometimes their guts. I wish there would be more of this giving in the world, and it is very moving to work together.'

I finally had time to realise my plans of making a film on Jeanne Moreau and I filmed her in her beautiful old farmhouse in La Garde-Freinet. It stood in acres and acres of olive groves and wild land. She had chosen these lonely and poetic surroundings for her directorial debut in *Lumière*, the story of four actresses – one of them herself – a moving and intelligent homage to women and to her profession and inadvertently to this house she loved.

By 1977 Moreau had acted in sixty-seven films. She had also had a distinguished stage career. Now she had become a director. She had often been compared with the great movie queens of the past, but to me she is the truly modern woman, with an extraordinary range of emotions. Her rich personality allows her to slip easily from tragedy to comedy. It was Louis Malle in *Lift to the Scaffold* who encouraged her to explore her own personality by not disguising the irregularities of her face and making her act without makeup. Audiences discovered for the first time her extraordinary gift for transmitting ideas by apparently doing nothing.

It is difficult for me to write about Jeanne Moreau. However hard I try, Moreau always touches something in me which I can only call love.

On a hot summer's day in 1977 I discovered many things which later struck me so intensely about her and which seem not to alter, despite the many changes in her outer life. Her quintessential quality has always been her savour for life. It is her prime source of energy, paired with her total refusal to submit.

Sitting in her garden, Jeanne Moreau, smoking heavily, spoke in impeccable English about her work. 'It is a way of life, it opens me to other people, it gives me greater insight into others, men and women.'

Moreau had worked with many of the greatest directors, but she refused to discuss them, except Truffaut, for whom she had a special feeling. 'We lived such a marvellous life together. They all have marked me in a different way,' she said. 'How can I talk about these directors or compare them? If you take Orson Welles, Buñuel, if you take Kazan, Louis Malle, Antonioni, I could not tell you what was good in one or in the other. They all have marked me.'

When I asked her if she had marked them, she replied without hesitation: 'I think I have.' And a large smile invaded her articulate face. 'When an experience is good there is always an exchange.' There has never been any false modesty about her, no conceit either. Jeanne Moreau knows who she is.

In Russia many years later, when I observed her over weeks at work, I could see what she meant when she told me that the most important thing for her is 'to be open'. Unlike so many actors I have known, who have such preconceived ideas about their roles, she is totally at the disposal of the director: 'In earlier years I studied the script, looked for motivation, I plotted; now I just let it happen. I trust my instinct. The body is full of surprises and it does its work without thinking.'

At the end of our interview I quoted to her what I once read: 'In life nothing ever changes and everything is an extension of what went on before.'

'I do not think that is right,' she told me. 'Life changes all the time. But it is like a tree. You have the same trunk, you have the same branches, but as time passes the tree grows. A human true to himself changes in the same way, but it belongs to the same roots.'

After my Moreau film, I hardly saw her again, despite the fact that we often lived in the same village. Shyness on my part and her intense sense of privacy must be the main reason. She has erected an elegant floating distance between herself and the world, like the trembling needle of a compass between the two poles.

Our friendship was a long time coming. In 1990 I was sent to the USSR to write a profile of her for a German magazine. She was making her first feature film with a Russian director, Rustam Khamadov. A few weeks later I was back to make a film on the new Russian cinema for *Arena*. It was then that our friendship began, a friendship that gave me a lot of joy and much strength. For three weeks we were cooped up in a hotel, short of almost everything: food, luxuries, distractions and all the amenities usually associated with the life of a star. She did not mind.

I filmed her many days and nights at work, a woman totally dedicated to her art. 'You have to dig deep down in your character. You are your own material and sometimes you discover things you had never thought of before.'

I often watched her face, which still reflected the underlying presence of her unusual, unique beauty. Then, when you could see it disappearing under the fatigue, it suddenly blossomed afresh, giving a glimpse of how ravishing she had been. Jeanne does not worry about age. She sees it almost as a privilege, giving her the freedom to be honest and direct. 'I have now learned,' she once told me, 'that time is never lost. I am happier now than when I was thirty, then I was full of anxiety. Now I know who I am, nobody has to tell me. That's why flattery embarrasses me. I am lucid, I know my faults. I do not try to please, not in life and not on stage. People who are not nice can still be fascinating.'

The actress and the woman complement each other in an extraordinary way. Unlike so many theatre people, who can never leave the actress at home, Moreau is almost always the woman first. She is very self-contained. After filming she stays alone, reading or playing patience. She carries her own world with her, wherever she goes. In Russia in a simple hotel room, we unpacked a huge trunk with her own china, a kettle for boiling water and what she calls her 'own personal altar': little objects her mother or some friends gave her. Despite her inbred poise and distinction, there is something of a small girl in her. She is a marvellous cook and even in Russia, like a magician, created wholesome meals for us. Extremely pri-

Jeanne Moreau in her hotel room in Leningrad

Setting out for the filming

vate about her own life, she is interested in the life of other people, and will listen and counsel without ever being nosy. She knows about the many dark forces that lie buried in human nature, often only held at bay by a thin veneer of respectability. Sometimes, almost as a gift, she will talk about her own life, the love she had for her mother or the concern about her son. Impatient by nature, anger can suddenly well up and then disappear again. She is usually sorry if she hurts someone but is never afraid of confrontation and never minces her words. Her uncompromising stances have cost her the affection of many friends, but she seems to be a person who refuses to live in detours. She can look like a queen and swear like a truck-driver. However consistent at work, in private she often changes. She can be warm like a mother or a lover, funny and mischievous like a schoolboy. She can also be demanding and difficult. She is never cruel or unreasonable and she is always herself. When she is at work most of her moods seem to have vanished; they make room for great concentration and tranquillity.

My first portrait of her had included many extracts from her films. I had sent her a copy of the programme, but I was never sure if she had seen it. Moreau refuses to look at her own pictures. Maybe much later she will view a film she made years ago. 'I sometimes see a new woman and that is very exciting,' she told me once when we looked at one of her films together. Still now she refuses to look at rushes, except of course if she is the director. 'I am not a viewer, I am an actress.' She rarely even goes to the theatre, unless a friend is playing, or out of professional curiosity, as when we went to see Joan Collins in *Private Lives*.

I had brought the film I had made twelve years earlier to Russia. She had arranged a screening. It was attended by a captive Russian audience. Jeanne Moreau never showed up.

19

Alexandria Revisited:
Durrell's Egypt

In October 1977 Lawrence Durrell, Ann Hummel, cameraman Colin Waldek, his crew and I were on our way to Egypt. The account of this extraordinary trip was published in America in a Festschrift to celebrate Lawrence Durrell's seventy-fifth birthday. 'Alexandria Revisited' was taken from my diary, kept during the filming of *Spirit of Place: Egypt*.[1]

ALEXANDRIA REVISITED
Written and Presented by Peter Adam

From Lawrence Durrell's notes
In 1975 the BBC took me back to Greece to make a film called *Spirit of Place*, based on my island books and the memories of the years when I lived there. In between these happy Greek years lay darker ones, marked by war, which I had spent in Cairo and Alexandria. In 1977 the director Peter Adam suggested we travel again together, this time to Egypt, to the scenes of *The Alexandria Quartet*, and try to touch all the points which, either from a literary or personal point of view, meant something to me, marked me or moved me.

Filming is a sort of composite art – one is always manufacturing the work of two or three people and trying to assemble it into a coherent image. The writer is a solitary animal sitting in a garret, and when the stuff comes off his typewriter nobody else interferes with it. So to try and make a film about a subject which was precious and probably, from a general point of view, out of date was a trepidation added to traditional neuroses.

The idea filled me with unease. After 30 years or so, the country must have changed. And I myself? Had I changed also, as Egypt must have?

---

1 First published in *Twentieth Century Literature*, Hofstra University, Hempstead, New York, Winter 1987.

Lawrence Durrell in Luxor

From Peter Adam's Diary
Cairo, 17 October 1977: Our plane is 3 hours late. All through the flight Larry has been grumpy, cursing himself. He had seen the film I made about his Greek island books only the night before our departure, and felt that 'he had given too much of his personal feelings away'. 'My god, what a lot of drivel,' he pronounced, hiding his anger behind some gauche compliments. While the plane hovers and sinks over Cairo in a colourful sunset, he begins to marvel about the constancy of nature. Once earth-bound we are invited to the VIP lounge, a sort of old-fashioned hotel lobby filled with Saudi sheikhs, Japanese businessmen and a sprinkling of distinguished British embassy employees with their assorted wives. Larry moans, so we decide it would be better to supervise the unloading of our luggage in the official arrival hall. Larry sits patiently on his rather tacky-looking suitcase enjoying the huge pandemonium, admiring the 'now uncovered' faces of the Egyptian women, a sight he was not prepared for. In the meantime I count the pieces of our luggage – 29, 32, 23, 26, cameras, tripods, suitcases and all. We arrive in the middle of the night at the Cecil Hotel in Alexandria. He rejoices; the old place seemed to be as it was when Justine met Nessim. But our joy is clouded over when we discover that our rooms have been given away. I have to spell out Durrell's name 4 times to the receptionist. We finally manage to get one room for him where he sleeps surrounded by our 27 pieces of luggage. Not a very glamorous return after 32 years of absence.

Alexandria, 18 October 1977: At breakfast in the old dining-room served by splendid Nubian waiters in snow-white turbans, Larry talks about the extravagant colourful life in wartime Alexandria at the old Cecil Hotel. It was then the centre of everything that happened in the press corps. The long line of visitors included André Gide, the Greek poet Seferis and Patrick Leigh Fermor... munching a croissant he describes laughingly the dancer Diana Gould (now Mrs Menuhin) doing an entrechat on the roof.

'It was a good writing period, in a sense, though, of course, the war was an exhausting moment to think about writing because there was no future attached to anything one did. But perhaps it was a good thing, in a way, because it compressed up life, and forced one to do what one should always do: namely, not think about tomorrow. Live entirely for today.'

After breakfast we set out, following E. M. Forster's advice, 'the best way to see Alexandria is to walk aimlessly', in search of locations for filming, and most of all to find the house Lawrence Durrell lived in. There are moments of discovery, of delight and recognition. 'The trees... the Greek bookshop which saved me...' and then we stumble upon the house, an enchanting place with a garden littered with broken columns and statues. He climbs up the stairs to the tower where he wrote *Prospero's Cell* and some poems for *Personal Landscape*. 'Here we sat for dinner,' he shouts. 'There is the studio of the woman who owned the place, the studio where Clea worked.' The memories come tumbling out, like in the old days when he kept scrapbooks full of cinema tickets or leaves, 'an old garbage-heap of stuff, a bus ticket or an entry to the Alexandria Museum stuck in a book is full of radium and even years afterwards flipping through it you suddenly remember whole sections of things which come in useful in writing.' Grivas, the old bookshop, is no more, but Eve's father's café is still there, less elegant and rather run down. Then Larry rushes again through the streets. We can hardly keep up with him. First into some bookshops where he laments the poor stock. 'They used to be full of La Pléiade editions.' Then to an old Greek tavern Larry used to love; a healthy dose of ouzo puts Larry in the right mood for a siesta. The rumour that the famous Lawrence Durrell is in town has spread. The lady who owns the house has invited a few local celebrities to meet him. Larry doesn't want to go, but is too polite and too much of a social coward to refuse. 'Please save me from social do's,' he says to me, and then wanders off, grumpy and totally bored.

Alexandria, 19 October 1977: Larry is up as usual at 6 o'clock doing his yoga. The noise of cars and fleabites have kept him awake, so it's not surprising that he is ill-tempered. Also I suspect the thought of doing our first interview annoys him tremendously. Although a brilliant interviewee, Larry hates doing it. As usual he is reluctant to speak about himself or his work. It is difficult to keep him on a serious track. But once he gets going his language, even in speech, is polished. He piles image upon image of Alexandria, and he catches for us the true spirit of the place.

'Here you smell the desert and you smell the heart of Africa being poured down that funnel the Nile, like smoke, and arriving in silt in this big delta. Whatever the Greeks have done to Hellen-ise this town it does smell of desert, and it does have its kham-seens – desert winds. And it gives the air a prattling, lustful sort of quality which, mingled with the sea, is very bracing and rather disorienting. You could easily go mad here.'

Durrell's hostess from last night, a stunningly beautiful woman, a mix of Anaïs Nin and Isak Dinesen, lets us into a drawing-room filled with her own paintings. She knew 'Clea', who has since died. She wears a brown tunic and her beautiful face is framed by a headscarf. Two long turquoise earrings and a long necklace of different coloured pieces of amber complete the picture.

I ask Durrell if there are any real people in the *Quartet*. 'No, they're all tremendously composite, in that rather evanescent form. The number, the ratio, the amount of people one meets in a lifetime really isn't all that numerous – people who mark you, I mean. So you're forced to use the narrow range that you have in-side yourself, of meetings and situations and places. That's why I'm so grateful to have travelled so widely, and have been mixed up in all kinds of different situations, because I really have got, I think, a fairly large ragbag full of possibilities.'

Alexandria, 20 October 1977: We film in the reconstructed living-room of the Alexandrian poet Cavafy. The little museum is filled with oriental furniture. It is very moving to see Larry sitting at the desk Cavafy wrote at. Larry studies the books which fill the shelves linking the room, mostly French – a lot of Corneille, Racine, Mus-set. Few English books except for the Oxford dictionary. A row of the History of Costume, some German book on Byzantium. Larry talks touchingly about the great Alexandrian poet and reads for us from 'The City' in Durrell's own translation. He refuses the idea that Cavafy is Balthazar but concedes that he has 'been tarnished' by him. 'Cavafy is more like Tiresias,' he says, 'who moves through the minds of the characters of the *Quartet*.' After the interview we play a fleeting visit to Cavafy's old house, which is now a pension above a brothel.

After lunch we film the streets of Alexandria. 'Alexandria. Prin-cess and whore, the royal city and the anus mundi,' as Larry described it in *Clea*. Or, as he now says, 'Alexandria, teetering like the house in the Chaplin film on the edge of the precipice always in despair.'

For the dinner at a rich Alexandrian house Larry has put on a tie and looks delightfully scruffy. Larry is very flirtatious, and much taken by the voluptuous and elegant ladies of French, Greek and Jewish origins, real products of Alexandria, the sort of people which inhabit the *Quartet*. Everybody of course wants to know who is who in the *Quartet*. Although totally bored, Larry accepts the questions gracefully. Beautiful women can get away with anything. If I had put such silly questions, I would have had my head bitten off. Later, in his room, before he goes to sleep, I ask him why his characters are so wounded by sex.

'It's obviously the weak point. It's not only Alexandria, it's the whole of Europe. It's also a critique of our twentieth-century notions. I was using, as best I could, the available psychology of our epoch. The double-sexed thing – which is an ancient gnostic thing – was a very important weapon that I tried to use. You make love with the opposite side of yourself, so to speak. The male has to mobilise the male in himself, otherwise you don't get a love affair four square. You get it stunted in some way. And that, by the grace of Freud and God combined, seemed to me suggestive and quite possible to achieve. At least it would be a sort of ideal worth expressing. So I tried to pass my characters a bit through the wringer of sex, so to speak, in the hope that the dice will fall out of their pockets and assume that sort of fortunate configuration.'

Alexandria, 21 October 1977: Larry very funny about last night. 'The beauty of these women is their low IQ. It's like making love to crème Chantilly.' It is a day for joking. Two enormous tarts in leather mini-skirts pass our table. According to Larry, they have just been laid by an English sailor. Larry breaks out into ecstatic cries: 'Thank you, thank you, Egypt! What magnetism, what magical wobble!' He has a terrible cold and tries to cure it with massive doses of scotch. He reads to me from the *Egyptian Gazette* a report about an English lady who had a child by a gorilla. 'The child is living off nuts,' he adds. The childlike joy, the grumpiness, the feeling of being bored all lie only skin-deep under the surface and can break out at any moment. Later he tells me that he read Isak Dinesen here in Alexandria and that he wrote her a fan letter. He tells me that when she was very old she used to go upstairs touching, like the blind, the vast map of Africa on the wall. He also tells me about meeting Borges when he lived in Argentina. In the evening, in the hotel bar, a few Egyptian beauties, one looking like Justine – but Larry has gone to bed.

Alexandria, 22 October 1977: Last day. We film a beautiful scene – the beach at Chatby. The little tin tram which bore Melissa and Darley with the clicking of its wheels is still there, and so are the mansions where Nessim and Justine gave their parties.

'Here and there the remains of properties abandoned by owners too poor or too lazy. Their gates, half-smothered in bougainvillaea, opened rustily into gardens of wild and unkempt beauty where marble fountains and rotted statuary still testified to a glory since departed.'

The girl we baptise 'Justine' comes to the hotel with a copy of the book *Justine,* and Larry signs it cheerfully. He asks Dimitri, his old photographer friend who has come with us, to take a photograph of him, and while clowning around at the table, he baptises the photograph 'Elephant slicing Feta'.

Cairo, 23 October 1977: We stay at the Mena House Hotel. Larry and I talk about the German theatre and the famous actor Gustaf Gründgens. I am surprised to hear that Gründgens produced Durrell's play *Sappho,* with Maximilian Schell and Elisabeth Flickenschild. While he walks around in his bathroom in his red nylon bathroom slippers which he pinched from his hostess Mrs Thomas in London, he apologises for his constant change of mood: 'I had a bad year. The divorce, and all that.' Together we watch the great Egyptian cliché, the sun setting behind the pyramids from the terrace of my room. Suddenly Larry says: 'Too much talk in the world. When two people love each other, silence sets in.'

But soon he changes again to joking and talks about mosquitoes looking innocent but having snouts of fire. He talks also about old times, about the cookery writer Elizabeth David. 'The Jane Austen of the cuisine,' as he calls her. But then comes some magic moment such as only Larry can produce. Forgetting the camera (or does he ever?) he suddenly recites a few lines of a poem:

Palms and tombs
Tombs and palms
A river flowing like smoke
Under a sky weighing a ton.

The poet Durrell, as so often, had saved the interview.

Cairo, 25 October 1977: Larry much elated to find that a shop he phoned up to describe a special most effective incense burner against mosquitoes has delivered what turns out to be a Nose Vick. I am less cheerful because Larry's early morning call for his yoga at 4.30 has come to my room. I feel that Larry is longing to go back home. He is bored with the whole undertaking. The constant presence of all these people is difficult for him. His bad mood affects us all. Also he drinks quite heavily. As a result his breathing is difficult, and his interviews not what I hoped they would be. We have eighteen more days to go and I am rather worried.

Cairo, 26 October 1977: We drive into the desert to the Coptic monastery of Wadi Natroun. Larry is totally changed again, enthusiastic and co-operative. After a few hours' drive we reach a small monastery, the colour of the desert under a burning sky, only a few palms give some relief. We begin by filming a church service. Larry, like all of us, is much moved by the beauty of the singing, the place and its peacefulness. Outside you could hear the noises of the desert, inside only the grumble of the word. The black-hooded monks receive us with enormous kindness, and we share their meal consisting of a simple but strong lentil soup, homemade bread, water and sardines. The monks giggle like little girls while Larry keeps a solemn and serious face, but he looks happy. I try to do an interview on religion, but Larry brushes away any suggestion of religion putting up shield after shield when I get too personal.

Adam: Are you yourself a religious person?

Durrell: No, no. I don't think so. Do I look like it?

Adam: You say you're not a religious person, but you have a great affinity to mystic qualities.

Durrell: Well, I'm simply trying to find out where I fit in the universe you know.

Adam: Where do you think you fit?

Durrell: Well, I'm trying not to show!

Adam: Were you ever tempted by any monastic life?

Durrell: I think everyone is, don't you? I don't know any exceptions. Because the bleakness has a great appeal, I think. Also one has the hint that one might get closer to an understanding of oneself if one resisted the enormous current of worldly noise which is going on about one, which prevents one from really thinking.

Adam: This search for truth, is that something which came to you through age or have you always had it?

Durrell: No, everybody's got it. Don't talk as though I'm a leper! Everybody's got it. I'm simply representative, slightly more articulate than most people of the same malady.

Cairo, 27 October 1977: This time it is my turn to be ill. Larry gives me a sort of opium-based remedy which makes me dizzy. I think we have reached the point where we have got used to each other, and our fourth interview is splendid.

'It is very strange to come back to it now, after such a lapse of time, and to find this country relatively unchanged, because the emanations of the ground (and one verifies them by going from one sacred site to another, in the course of making this film) seem to me on the same frequency, the same vibrations, and the changes are simply superficial. In fact, from time to time you hear the winter cuckoo instead of the spring cuckoo of Greece. There is a particular kind of emanation, a context, a signature of any given country, which is expressed through its wild flowers, through its trees, its plants, its flora and its fauna and its human beings who form part of that. And that is the basic kernel, it cannot be altered. You have Augustus and Caligulas, and you have dictatorships, and democracies and so on, and they all follow one another. But they are purely waves that flow along the surface of the country's history, and underneath there is something very stable and that will need a new Ice Age to change. Well, that is, of course, what we mean by the "spirit of place".'

Cairo, 28 October 1977: We dine with an Egyptian journalist. When I attack him about the way educated Egyptians let the country run down, Larry defends Egypt and attacks England in return. 'Civilisation there is measured by courtesies,' he exclaims angrily.

Cairo, 29 October 1977: Day off. Larry and I go to meet the great Egyptian architect Hassan Fathy who wrote *Architecture for the Poor* and who built the village of Gourna. We sit this great old man on the roof of his house, and while Fathy explains to us the shape of the minarets, Larry listens carefully. Fathy tells us that trees are wiser than man and talks about organic shapes. It occurs to me that Larry, living alone in Sommières, has lost almost all taste for intelligent conversation. Living alone has made him crawl more and more into himself; the only conversation he has is with books. Looking at the vivacious and enthusiastic eighty-five-year-old Fathy, I think how outwardly burnt-out Durrell appears at only sixty-five.

Cairo, 30 October 1977: Filming in the oasis of Faiyum, one of the most beautiful scenes of country life we have yet seen. Everywhere the creaking of the water wheels and mud-brick houses nestling in palm groves, donkeys sleeping under mango trees. The country-side is in constant rhythmic move; people riding on donkeys borne down by their weight, camels carrying huge jars, crossing little bridges over canals. Larry is in his worst mood, totally bored with it all; he doesn't even bother to get out of the car; only once when we reach a pottery village of indescribably black dirt and dust – one can hardly breathe – does he step out. I feel hurt by his indifference, more sorry for him than myself, and I have to remind myself that it was I who dragged this reticent man away from the peacefulness of his home and desk, and made him clown around in front of cameras. I feel rather ashamed by impatience. The day is not saved by an evening given by a French newspaper owner, who had invited Larry and myself for a lavish dinner. As always, Larry is furious that he has been used for some social occasion and as usual is too polite or too cowardly to decline the invitation.

Cairo, 31 October 1977: Larry surprised me at breakfast with a copy of *Monsieur*. He has put a beautiful drawing inside and has written: 'Peter, thank you for such patient and careful work, burnishing my image with your pious filming.' I feel ashamed about yesterday, and there are more surprises. In the interview which we film the same morning, he describes beautifully and astutely the scenes he had watched yesterday stubbornly from the car.

Cairo, 1 November 1977: Larry has promised to give up drinking and he sticks to it. News comes from London that our rushes are beautiful. Everybody is happy.

Cairo, 2 November 1977: Getting up early at 3.30 to catch the plane to Aswan. Only Larry can stand up cheerfully to such an ordeal.

Once in Aswan, Larry is delighted that the old Cataract Hotel is still there. We film him sitting in the old wicker chairs shaded by carpet hangings while beautifully dressed Nubian waiters serve him tea. It looks like time has stood still. Larry remembers:

'There was a very pleasant night train, a sort of Edinburgh express, which jogged up here, comfortably. And you arrived in the morning. And the place had an endearing mixture of Darjeeling and Bournemouth. I can't swear that there were bath chairs with a line of liveried attendants, but there were practically. There were certainly some old nannies on this terrace, brooding over their knitting. And somewhere inside was what looked like the remains of some Edwardian gun room, full of books, which you had to get the key to a cupboard to examine. And they were all Tauchnitz editions of early novels, Victorian novels – nanny novels, in fact, *Mill on the Floss* and Charles Reade, and that sort of stuff. Ideal reading if you were a little nervous or upset – stomach upset or nervous upset. And here, of course, one was sent for a rest cure if one had been ill, because in Cairo one traditionally got ill. The breakfast on that train was particularly memorable, and I have been spending all night trying to remember – what one was served at dawn was marvellous coffee with Bath Oliver biscuits and mango juice, followed by a traditional English breakfast.'

Aswan, 3 November 1977: This time it's Colin Waldek, our wonderful and patient cameraman, who has been struck by Montezuma's revenge. He is so ill we cannot film, so we have the day off. The beauty of the Nile inspires Larry to the most beautiful passag-es in our whole film. While sliding along the water in one of the feluccas I suggest to him that he should write Piers's lost diary in *Monsieur* as a diary of the trip on the Nile. I am surprised to find out that he had totally forgotten that he had left himself this loophole in the book. With his usual modesty he thanks me for reminding him.

We buy a horrible-looking pair of plastic earrings, Larry bargaining fiercely; he wants to have them set in Sommières ('for a female') and talks about them as if they were real diamonds. He has no feeling for any material goods and can live in the most modest of circumstances.

Aswan, 4 November 1977: Wake up at six o'clock and spot Larry on his balcony next to mine. The sun is just tinting the island opposite. Small white houses, a few groups of palm trees, the first feluccas mark the mirrored surface of the water, but their sails are still closed. The river has hardly begun to stir. We both look on silently, each of us from our separate balconies. Then he calls over: 'Peter, we must catch that feeling in our film.' In the afternoon, floating along this great river, Larry gives a memorable interview. He is a changed person. He had kept his promise and not touched a drop of alcohol.

'The life-blood of Egypt, to mix an accurate metaphor, is really the water: the long steady ribbon of water flowing down from the heart of Africa towards the sea. It carries not only the rich Nilotic silt but also the whole trade of Egypt with the outside world. It is as precious as it is protean, and everywhere one hears the characteristic squalling and shrieking or whispering and thudding of the ubiquitous *sakkia* of Egypt – the water wheels. If you sleep in the country, they have to be got used to. The sound can be maddening at night. But it is eternally there, eternally flowing out of the darkness of Africa, so various in its tones and speeds that it is always different even in its sameness. Sometimes it runs like steel. Sometimes it slows down to the pace of smoke. Sometimes, in blocked canals, it turns green with slime and has to be purged. But water is always there, water prime. It is the bloodstream of the Egyptian soul and the nervous system of the country's life.'

Abu Simbel, 5 November 1977: Flying to Abu Simbel we spot the 'salvaged monuments' from the air. Once land-bound, we quickly escape the herds of tourists to find a quiet spot to film. Larry gives a complicated interview about prime symbols which needs pruning. A marvellous moment occurs when Larry, sitting in front of those venerable monuments, claims that by shifting them we only shifted stones. The magic remains in the sacred ground of the original setting and can never be transplanted. At the edge of the monument they are shooting the feature film, *Death on the Nile*, using large wind machines to blow up the sand. Our small film crew looks ridiculous next to the feature film get-up. News got around that the famous Lawrence Durrell is here. In the meal break Mia Farrow and Lois Chiles come up and join us to share our picnic. Larry, always pleased with any female company, is especially excited being photographed with the stars.

Aswan, 6 November 1977: I am filming the interview which I hope

Lawrence Durrell with Mia Farrow, Lois Chiles, PA at Abu Simbel

to use for the opening and the ending of the film. Just as well that I kept it for now. Larry is totally changed, lucid and interesting. He looks marvellous in a pale blue fisherman's smock:

Durrell: I have to confess that I am terribly incurious. It sounds silly, but I am extremely incurious, and my real life seems to pass either in books or in dreams. And if I weren't pushed, I don't think I would have moved from A to B. Had the Germans not pushed me, I would never have moved from Greece. Pity, because look what I would have missed.

Adam: Does the passage of time alter your attitude towards a place?

Durrell: It's a convention – look how we use it. 'Time stood still', 'it went by in a flash', 'it's the same time.' Here we feel the time's Nile time, Nile time rising in the bloodstream and sinking again with the rising and sinking of the Nile tide.

At night we sit on the terrace talking a long time about his books. He plans to write a book about Provence. When I suggest that he publish four novels, as he did with the *Quartet*, he says: 'You can't repeat that. This sort of thing only happens once.' Then he pronounces the words I have been waiting for all those weeks: 'I am glad I came along. I need this kick in the pants to get me out of myself and sort myself out. Now I can return, I gave up smoking, I am off drink.' And this evening he believed it.

Luxor, 7 November 1977: We travel by bus to Luxor. The trip takes the whole day, only interrupted from time to time by getting out and filming. We listen to strains of Sibelius's Third Symphony. We film the sunset on the Nile, which is so beautiful that one is almost afraid to capture it on film. It is too much of a postcard setting, a dilemma we have encountered so often during the last two weeks.

Luxor, 8 November 1977: We stay at the Winter Palace. Larry clowns around with our assistant, Ann Hummel. They have become really good friends. When we all go to visit the monuments, Larry is marvellously irreverential.

'This is only one of the instances where Rameses has gone to town. His inordinate self-love and the way he peppered this whole area with monuments to himself and his exploits suggests somebody who is over-compensating. It is possible that he was excessively timid. Or perhaps the whole thing is a fraud. At any rate, the monumental type of architecture is awe-inspiring in its heaviness. But it's depressing also in its lack of variety, in its lack of give. And in some of these institutional-type buildings one feels they're really just about good enough to cash a traveller's cheque in. And also, I think, in the sculpture, which is so institutional, so heavy, it's not entirely due to the use of material, but that these people were much more interested in finding the ideal state than they were in finding an ideal arrangement between the ego and the heavens. They were not really metaphysicians, they were lawgivers.'

Larry proudly bargains two necklaces from ten pounds down to three. We are all beginning to look forward to going home now. Travelling in groups and the constant presence of other people, even in the best of times, takes its toll.

Luxor, 9 November 1977: The telegram arrives from London announcing the death of Keith Vaughan. Larry's reaction is warm. None of the conventional consolation business. We talk about death and about suicide in particular. I am again struck by the enormous discrepancy in his nature. Could this man who now so soothingly speaks to me be the same who behaved often like a spoiled child? We are friends now, I think, if this is not too presumptuous. At night he embraces me and thanks me once more for this 'useful and wonderful time'. He looks marvellous. He has lost weight and is alert and cheerful. We seem to be years away from the lonely, sad figure, slumped over the bar in Alexandria.

Cairo, 10 November 1977: Last day of filming. We film a poor peasant house standing on a little river. The friendly owners have put all their belongings – a rug and a bench – outside in order that we be comfortable. Without one word of common language between them, Larry chats and laughs with the Arab family. It is good to take this last picture with us.

Adam:	All your characters have a central experience. Have you a central experience in your life?
Durrell:	Ideally all experience is central. The problem is how

to centralise it, and that is the problem of life itself.

Adam: None of your novels deal with the present time, why is that?

Durrell: There is no such thing.

Adam: What do you mean?

Durrell: Well, I mean that the present in which we live and act is an absolute illusion. We are phantoms really. And perhaps it's only when we're asleep or in our dreams that we realise the fact. But it's terribly insubstantial, and the way you put the question suggests to me that you took the books to be a report on quotidian reality, which is what they were trying to undermine. They were trying to create precariousness, insecurity, precisely about that. Because underneath the whole problem there was another question which was agitating me very much: how to undo the hooks and eyes of that ego. Are we really the stable ego, as we think we are, or do we exist like old bits of cinema film – flap, flap, flap, twenty-eight frames per second? And that also creates the precariousness which is part of the message – if you can use such an ugly word for such a pretty book!

Adam: Do you think that ultimately history and politics are of no great consequence?

Durrell: It is of no importance whatsoever, because it's continuously going on. History is the endless repetition of the wrong way of living, and it'll start again tomorrow. If it's moved from here today. So it's a total waste of time for anybody who is seriously engaged in the notion that life is terribly brief and that one should try and catch every scrap of wind in order to form oneself, so that death means something – that you're really used up when you die.

From Lawrence Durrell's notes

I was relieved to have my feelings reassured by this visit. The terrifying thing about film-making is that one has to work against Egypt, because it is so damned beautiful, so extravagant, that everywhere one puts up a camera one is in danger of the picture postcard. But a film can catch that wonderful feeling of stillness that Egypt always conveys: the slow, green blood-time of the Nile.

We have such an album of pictures, and I realise that the still image is not comparable with the moving one, because the camera is actually photographing time passing. All this, of course, constitutes distress which directors must feel, as opposed to what writers feel.

Keith was dead. By the time I returned he had already been buried. The last entrance in his diary was on 4 November, the day when in Aswan the tide of my relationship with Larry had changed, a happy day. Sitting at his desk, fully dressed, Keith wrote calmly:

> 9.30 a.m. The capsules have been taken with some whisky. What is striking is the unreality of the situation. I feel no different. R [Ramsay] returned to H. H. [Harrow Hill] yesterday. But suddenly the decision came that it must be done. I cannot drag on another few years in this state. It's a bright sunny morning. Full of life. Such a morning as many people have died on. I am ready for death though I fear it. Of course the whole thing may not work and I shall wake up. I don't mind really either way. Once the decision seemed inevitable the courage needed was less than I thought. I don't quite believe that anything has happened though the bottle is empty. At the moment I feel very much alive. I cannot believe I have committed suicide since nothing has happened: no big bang, no cut wrists. Sixty-five was long enough for me. It wasn't a complete failure. I did some...

At that point the writing became illegible and stopped. A dignified exit of a dignified man.

20
Les Formidables: Lillian Hellman and Lotte Lenya
1978–1979

I was longing to visit America once more. It had been years since I had gone there. I also was looking for subjects to film.

New York had lost none of the fascination it once held for me. The danger and the rampant sexuality added to its attraction. Temptation or sinfulness can come in many guises. It can come as the devil or as Orpheus, it can also be a faun. The temptations of New York came in the disguise of Pan – they made me feel young again. I slipped effortlessly back into a more frivolous personality. I was no longer vulnerable, in danger of corruption or fall, and I plunged.

This was 1978. 'New York,' according to Truman Capote, 'was like living inside a light bulb.' Much of America seemed hooked on drugs and sex. The mouthwatering, handsome, narcissistic people were chasing one sensation after the other, living in a permanent adolescence. It was no longer just pot, now people sniffed cocaine. They carried little pills with them taken in groups or alone. 'Would you like an upper or downer?' was a frequent question. They shot up, drank orange juice spiked with LSD or swallowed amphetamines. It was a dance on a volcano, spinning out of control.

The sex life too was one of total fantasy. In the past most of my friends had not been exactly angels, but now there was something else going on. The total sexual freedom, which at first was so exciting, began to take on a frightening aspect. Everybody seemed to be hooked on something. Fred was into leather and went to bars where he was tied up in a sling. John was what they called a clone and went to discothèques where everybody was dressed in jeans with check shirts and sporting moustaches. People made love with their own images. I met Jake, who made a fortune as a porno star and spoke of his difficulties having an ordinary sex life. My old friend Howard, who had been a schoolteacher, had become a hustler. He didn't do it for the money, he assured me, but for kicks.

Bars, converted warehouses, private lofts catered for every possible sexual taste. Porno movies were big business, cinemas had sprouted everywhere. They were packed. Films changed twice a day, but people did not even look at the screen, celluloid had lost its power. There was sex every-

where, in the seats, in the aisles, in the lavatory, behind the screen, anonymous, wild sex. I was told that some people went there every day. It was
not only the homosexual community that had gone crazy, drunk with a
desire to live wildly. The tragic mistake of the Vietnam war had almost
been forgotten. It was smart to attend screenings of Andy Warhol's films:
Hand-job or *Blow-job*. There were steam baths like Plato's Retreat, where
everybody copulated in public.

It was like an enormous comedy of manners being acted out in public,
and I wondered if the Marquis de Sade's princes had felt the same. Much
of it was exciting in its chaotic abundance and often more honest in its
unconcealed despair and ferocious appetite than much of the suppressed
sexuality of a society made of bigots, unable to see beyond their prejudices. Above their own darker sides, respectability only forms a thin crust.
Most of us know about the strong sexual undercurrent which runs in our
lives. Only convention and lack of opportunity prevent many from taking
the plunge. But people's increasing dependency on kicks frightened me. It
was as if something had snapped.

Watching the anonymous coupling that went on quite openly in the
back rooms of the bars, in places like the Mineshaft or the Gloryhole, I
wondered whether we had reached the 'glorious' moment when we finally
had freed ourselves from the guilt which two thousand years of Christian-
ity had stowed upon us. Or was George Steiner right when he said that
pornography leads to monotony, because it limits the sexual act to technicalities?

The smartest thing in New York was to dance with a tambourine under
the flickering light show in Studio 54. It had opened in 1977 under a fan-
fare of high glitz. It quickly became the watering hole for the beautiful
people, who came from all over the world to dance the night away, to
drink, to sniff poppers or cocaine. The glitter and the superficial was paramount. The term 'beautiful' was only a euphemism: the very ugly could
buy their way into the ranks, and it was often associated with expensive
dress, jetlag, loutish bodyguards and disintegrating septums as much as
the really beautiful bodies and faces displayed on the rack.

Studio 54 was another ghetto: just to get in was a sign of status. Every
night hundreds of people queued at the door. Elegant ladies slid like
lizards out of big stretched limousines and joined the lines. The bouncers,
like casting directors, decided who had the right look, the right gear, and
picked out of the desperate crowd those who they saw fit to make up the
set.

Equality was restored inside in the sea of frantically twitching bodies to the savage noise. The pretty boys, drugged to their eyeballs, and the desperate beautiful girls could here for a moment fulfil their dreams to dance for a second with Liza Minnelli, Lee Radziwill and her sister Jackie Onassis, Rudolf Nureyev, Liz Taylor, Truman Capote, Mick or Bianca Jagger. Andy Warhol and his hangers-on were of course regulars, and so were several Guinnesses and the cream of New York's hustlers. Everybody was part of the 'famous for one-night' generation.

The very rich and the very smart sometimes rented the Studio for their parties. Films were launched there and some nights had a special theme. I was invited to the birthday party of a wealthy Indian prince. At the entrance stood a huge table made from ice with a large dent, filled with caviar. Next to it was a silver tray with white powder. At midnight, with everybody high on drugs, champagne, noise and sexual desire, the presents for the Indian prince arrived: ten New York police officers, actors probably, naked from the waist down, carried a giant cake, decorated on the top with a naked eighteen-year-old girl and her blond twin brother flown in specially from Berlin.

The chic of Paris and the money of the States joined forces to make New York the most glamorous and most lively city in the world. New York was in, New York was 'where the action is'. People came from Europe to buy flats, open boutiques, to shop or just to let their hair down. Much of it was 'Eurotrash', a sort of café society with phoney titles and dubious money. What London was in the 1960s New York was now in the 1970s. It was a constant party lasting two years, when the owner of the Studio 54 was arrested and convicted of cheating the tax authorities. The man on the moon on the ceiling of the club, inhaling the little stars up his nostrils, went dark, but the disco and party craze went on. The speed freaks and acid-droppers simply moved on.

Régine had opened a new nightclub. One night a dinner for Paloma Picasso and her new husband Rafael Sanchez, the author of *Comédie policière*, Facundo's and Marucha's triumph in the Groupe TSE; the next night a reception for the photographer Helmut Newton and his wife June. Frédéric Castet from Christian Dior in Paris gave a dinner at the Hotel Pierre to launch his new fur collection. On each plate a tail of a mink to take home as a souvenir.

I went to a party: 'Put flowers on your handcuffs,' read the invitation. In the entrance two guys were chained to the wall. Next to it a girl had taken her dress off and had her body painted by two well-known artists. Somewhere in the corner was a large screen which continuously showed the outrageous films of Divine. A thousand people danced under five gleaming motorcycles, strung up on the ceiling. There were men in dinner jackets dancing with men dressed in leather, a beautiful black model in a skintight silver lamé dress danced with a girl wearing only black garters. Everybody danced with everybody, all barriers had come down and yet nobody seemed to be dancing with anybody, everybody was lost in a kind of lonely trip. It was impossible not to be infected by the buoyant energy, this feeling of passion, and I threw myself into the swaying crowd with their hungry eyes and wondered where it all would end.

Everything was moving up in New York. Even most of my old friends were now successful. Wayne Lawson was a literary editor at the *New York Times*. Peter Shaffer was famous and rich enough to live in a large penthouse overlooking the river. Half of Earls Terrace seemed to have moved to New York. Raymond Leppard was constantly conducting and Ian McKellen, Irene Worth and Brian Bedford played on Broadway.

I spent six glorious, stimulating, silly and delightfully frivolous weeks in New York. It was like a big refreshing gulp of champagne on a thirsty morning. However exhilarating, I knew that New York was no longer a city I could live in. I was no longer able to subscribe to those who used their existential Angst to justify the constant floating out of a life they considered pointless or absurd, denying all responsibility and commitment, except for their own selfish indulgence. I was longing for the saner, quieter life in London, however dowdy and grey it was on the outside. I went home with the hope of returning to the Big Apple soon, for I had the promise for four new programmes in my pocket: Lillian Hellman, Lotte Lenya, Edward Albee, plus a film on Diaghilev with Tamara Geva.

I met Lotte Lenya for the first time in a lift, shooting up to the twenty-first floor of an apartment building on Central Park South. 'Please God, let her go to the same party,' I thought.

I had actually seen her two nights before at Sardi's. I was dining with Richard Barr when the sound of a peculiar accent hit my ear, a mixture of Berlin and Vienna. It came from a woman with carrot-red hair sitting at a table in the corner of this theatre restaurant. I watched her expressive but economical gestures, then again I heard her voice, which sounded like sandpaper. Could it be Lotte Lenya? I decided that night that my next film would be about Kurt Weill's widow.

She did go to the same party, a small dinner given by a German television producer for the brilliant German actor and director Boy Gobert. 'New York too is only a village, an old German saying,' joked Boy, as he introduced me to Lenya. As we talked about old friends, the theatre in Berlin, Lenya listened politely. She was reticent, but she wanted to know everything, who was playing what, who were the new playwrights. After dinner, I timidly asked her about doing an interview with her. I met with an icy reaction. 'I no longer give interviews, Mr Adam. Everything is always distorted and nobody really wants to know.' Boy intervened and at least achieved an invitation to visit her.

The next day I was again in a lift, this time in a 1930s apartment building. I rang the bell on a small door at the end of a dark corridor and waited three minutes. No answer. I rang again. After a further three minutes, Lenya opened the door, dressed in a coat wearing white gloves. 'I have very little time, Mr Adam, I have to go out.'

I entered the living-room and found myself in Berlin: books, a piano with scores by Kurt Weill, a poster of *Die Dreigroschenoper*, somewhere a photo of Marlene Dietrich and one of Joan Crawford. Three hours later I was still in the flat.

It was hard to believe that this poised, slim lady would soon celebrate her eightieth birthday. Lenya was born Blamauer in Vienna. Her father was a coachman and her mother a laundress. She became a singer and a dancer. Then in 1920 she moved to Berlin, where she met her future husband Kurt Weill. Lenya was a unique theatrical phenomenon. Her fame was based on a handful of records, some films and a handful of stage productions few people around could have seen. And yet she was a legend and she knew it, enjoyed it and basked in it. 'Better a legend than a scrapheap,' she said. But there was no pretension in her behaviour.

In 1933 the Weills had to leave Germany and eventually settled in New York. Despite her reservations about Germany, it was Berlin she still loved with a kind of unsentimental affection, and it was Berlin which had opened her up to me. We were drinking coffee and eating a cake she had baked. Her coat lay on the floor. Lenya was refreshingly simple and direct. She could be subtle and allusive and then again earthy. Servility and compliments were totally ignored. We gossiped and laughed like schoolchildren, while Lenya dispensed a few theatrical indiscretions, not malicious, but full of irony. She did not spare anybody – Brecht, Hindemith, Helene Weigel, Schoenberg – and certainly not herself. She loved gossip, and I told her the story about Weigel's visit to London. Asked what she would like to do on her day off she had mumbled something about 'seeing Marx'. Two hours later, with most of the actors of the Berliner Ensemble gathered at Karl Marx's grave in Highgate, Weigel turned around and said: 'I didn't mean that Marx, I meant Marks and Spencer.'

She soon dispensed with the formal 'Mr' Adam. I was now Peter or, in the theatrical convention, more often 'darling' or 'peaches'. She of course was and always remained 'Lenya'. Nobody called her Lotte, a name which did not seem to fit the face, which someone once described as that of a clock that had lost the small hand.

The interview was never mentioned, but she was interested in my work, and I arranged a screening of *Durrell's Egypt* and *Jeanne Moreau* in the BBC New York office for a few of my friends: Wayne Lawson, Tamara Geva, Edward Albee. I am always very nervous when I have to look at my own programmes with an audience, especially with friends. This time it was even worse. Edward sat very quietly, his beautiful face showed not the slightest reaction. Lenya was the total opposite – she registered everything with little giggles or sounds of approval.

'Darrling you can do me any time you want, excuse the expression,' she burst out enthusiastically, throwing one of her sunny mischievous smiles. Edward laughed, but never said a word about the programmes. That night he phoned me and said, imitating Lenya's voice: 'You can do me too any time.' I still did not know what he thought of the programmes, I probably never will, for Edward has never been very communicative, and despite our warm and long friendship I have never lost my shyness with him either.

The 'formidable Lillian Hellman', I was told, was also a very difficult lady to woo. The number of journalists and theatre critics and writers who came in contact with her or her work and who found themselves insulted or even in court are numerous. The mere mention of her name usually provoked strong reactions. Many feared her spiky, irritable nature, even hated her. Others were full of admiration and affection. Her lawsuits were as legendary as the lady herself. Some thought that she was the symbol of courage and integrity, others mistrusted her political motives.

I was not to be put off by all I heard and decided to make a film on this pillar of controversy, this 'unfinished woman', as she had called her recently published biographical account. There was much less disagreement about her status as a writer. Her plays *The Little Foxes*, *The Children's Hour* and *Toys in the Attic* had brought her a great deal of publicity, fame and money. They had been turned into films. *Julia*, in which Jane Fonda played the role of the author and Jason Robards was Dashiell Hammett, Hellman's life-long companion 'on and off for thirty years', had recently been released.

We had one friend in common, the photographer Richard de Combray, who had known Hellman for years. Referring to Richard I had sent her a letter, asking for an interview, and to be allowed to make a 'film profile' of her.

I was surprised when she phoned me back personally. Her deep husky voice was rather intimidating, but she was polite in an old-fashioned way and very direct: 'Mr Adam, I do not like television interviews, but I like the BBC. How much will they pay me?' The BBC at the best of times never paid much. Most of my interviews were done without payment or for a token fee. All my professional life I have driven the Artist Contracts Department to despair with my unorthodox payment methods: 'a hand-made Venini egg in lieu of payment for an interview with Luchino Visconti', 'a pot of homemade jam and flowers for Jeanne Moreau' read my accounts. BBC producers are of course never allowed to discuss fees; they had to be above commercial considerations.

When I told Miss Hellman this she harped back: 'Oh for Christ's sake' – I think she used a stronger word – 'don't be so British, ask your people what they are willing to pay and then we'll talk.' It was the first inkling of her proverbial anger.

A couple of telegrams and phone calls later we did talk. Hellman lived in a large comfortable apartment on Park Avenue, with elegant furniture most of which, she pointed out, came from her stage productions. She was used to living on a grand scale. There was a doorman with white gloves and a personal secretary. Hellman was elegantly dressed in a formal suit, a small woman with large spectacles with thick lenses. She must have been what the French call *une belle laide* and was, at seventy-two, still aware of the impression she made on the visitor. She displayed slightly unapproachable manners and never stopped telling me how difficult she was and how she dealt with this or that 'asshole' of a journalist. She used strong words in contrast to her polite and cultured manner. I liked that.

There was a lot I liked about Lillian Hellman. I had been told so many awful stories that I was determined not to be intimidated. The old fighter instinct was awake and we both knew that we enjoyed a good fight.

Hellman wanted to be seen as writer rather than a woman who wrote plays. She told me that she had enjoyed great benefits from the theatre, had felt pleasure in success and excitement and pain in failure. 'I had liked and enjoyed many people, counted a few of them as my friends, but I wandered through them like a kind of stranger, so I gave the theatre up or it gave me up.' Theatre had only been one part of her life anyway. There had been journalism, film scripts, political activities. An outspoken left-winger, Hellman had been to Russia, she had interviewed Tito and had occupied the press for months during the McCarthy era, when she refused to testify against her friends in front of the committee.

Our first encounter lasted exactly one hour. 'Tell your people to get in touch with my lawyer. Nice meeting you, Mr Adam. Is Claridge's still OK?' and without waiting for an answer she rang for Rita, her secretary, who escorted me to the door.

Two months later I was back in the States for the filming. We had decided, or rather she did, to interview her in her country house on Martha's Vineyard, the house she built after the death of Dashiell Hammett. It stood next to the Mill House they both inhabited. She had offered to put me up, but as I preferred not to get too close to the people I interviewed beforehand in order to keep the tension going, I refused. Once you have talked about everything, the interview tends to go rather flat.

As a present I had brought her a toy Rolls-Royce and Elsa Morante's *Historia*. She loved both, but what impressed her most was a compendium of her writing Ann Hummel had prepared. 'That's what I like about you Europeans, you work your asses off,' she said. 'Here, journalists just skip through an author's last book, fire a few questions at them and print something else.'

You are sometimes forced to bluff yourself through an interview, but I always hated the result, which is usually of little value. For me the preparation for an interview, at least a substantial one which stretches over several days, was always elaborate. I not only read all of the author's work, but also any major work about them. I never liked to write down any questions, as that often forces you to glance at your notes instead of listening. I like to have it all in my head. Interviews should be like a conversation, not just a question and answer game.

Hellman was warm and hospitable, I was gradually losing my fear. Over tea she was eager to talk about my childhood in Germany. She was born in New Orleans, her Jewish grandparents had come from Germany, but after a while I managed to shift the conversation to her life.

Hellman was amazingly open about herself. Her conversation was even tender. She never stopped smoking while we talked. With no embarrassment she told me that she had cancer and had lost twenty pounds within seven months. Her eyesight was also gone. She could hardly see any more, but a kind of inner strength was holding her frail body up. I thought about Eileen, as I started to feel very warmly towards her.

The waves of sympathy subsided fast when she took me for a walk around the little town. She had taken my arm. We rested for a moment on the bench looking out on the sea. She was talking vividly about the fishing trips she used to make with Dashiell Hammett and about her love for water, when suddenly two old ladies walked up to her. They had been watching us for a while and she pretended not to see them.

'Excuse us, aren't you Miss Hellman?' they asked rather timidly. 'We so much admire you.' Hellman lifted herself up, as if bitten by a snake. All her shutters came down. 'I certainly am not,' she said. Her voice took on such an icy tone that the two hurried away, probably still hearing the rest of Hellman's rising anger. 'Fuck off, one never has a minute's peace from the crowd.'

How could she be so cruel? The same woman who only a few minutes before spoke so warmly about the love she had felt for her black nanny, had turned within seconds into a mean and angry creature, despising two old ladies. This was the first time I witnessed the changing mood of this contradictory lady.

Hellman had always been a rebel. An only child, she had rebelled against her mother's aristocratic Alabama family and taken up the side of the blacks. She had rebelled against the film studios in Hollywood and against the people in the theatre. Her often over-proud, over-sensitive, over-daring attitudes were covering up for a frightened and often shy human being. 'My stubborn, relentless, driving desire to be alone has never left me,' she admitted, books often being the only refuge for her frightened nature. Beneath the swagger lay a more generous and sensitive reality.

I escorted her back to the handsome weatherboard house. 'When Hammett died the Mill House up there was far too big for me, so I bought an acre of land and a stretch of beach and decided to build a smaller house.' We stood for a moment in her garden, looking at the flowers she had planted only that morning. 'Come for dinner, Peter, I'll make gumbo for you,' she said. It was the first time she had used my first name, her anger had totally disappeared.

It was a very civilised evening. There was only one other person, Peter Feibleman, a writer from Los Angeles and one of her closest friends. The conversation was lively. Lillian at seventy-two still took much visible delight in the company of handsome young men, but they also had to be bright. One could tell that she was a woman used to entertain and to seduce. Lillian and Peter argued a lot in a sort of cheerful way. We talked about the forgetfulness of the Americans. 'We forgot about McCarthy and we are forgetting about Nixon and in a few years' time we will see him paraded down Fifth Avenue.' When I pointed out that Americans are also great compromisers, she rebuked me. 'No, Peter, you Europeans are the great compromisers. We just forget, we go on to something else, we have no national memory, like Europeans have.' The conversation moved easily from one topic to another, we talked about American writers. Many had shared a typical American fate. Rapid fame that had stultified creativity, drink that had led to physical ruin. Faulkner, Hemingway, Hammett, Parker, they had all been friends.

Hellman had refused to write her autobiography. She had also vehemently discouraged others from doing so. She admired people who refused to speak until they are ready. But recently in her unremitting effort to be objective about herself she had set out some facts about her own life in two autobiographical books, *An Unfinished Woman* and *Pentimento*. There had been a lot of speculation as to how honest these accounts were, and the next day I asked why she disguised herself so often behind fictional characters. 'I do not want to become the bookkeeper of my life. I belong to the generation that broke all the rules, that fought for sexual liberation, and my own life was certainly not sexually pure. But I have always shied away from personal revelations.'

Hellman thought the vulgar candour about sexual matters which seems to fire so many writers nowadays rather boring, but her reticence was surprising for a woman who, at twenty-seven, scandalised many with her play *The Children's Hour*, which dealt with the subject of lesbianism. 'Recalled passion is a very doubtful business. It was Dorothy Parker who pointed out to me that I have never written a single love scene.'

Listening to Hellman, I realised that the intelligence, the anger, the warmth, the humour and the aggressiveness are all nourished by the same source: a vulnerable nature. This strong woman, at the threshold of death, no longer wanted to live in detours.

In the evening we would drink a lot, Hellman telling funny and often bitchy anecdotes about her many friends. She had mingled with the rich and the famous: William Faulkner, Nathanael West, Tallulah Bankhead, Scott Fitzgerald, Hemingway, or her best friend Dorothy Parker. 'Dotty was a remarkable character, a very complex one. Her wit had a rare bubbly quality, everybody always quotes her withering remarks, but there were so many remarks that were not just withering, they were so deeply rooted.' When I pointed out that it was amazing for two so very different people and writers to become such close friends, she laughed. 'Yes, I have asked myself why so often and at first I did not like her at all, but then came the fast and loose years. Parker was a famous attacker and I liked that.'

After dinner she showed us an album that Sergei Eisenstein had given her with photos of her Russian trip. Lillian told me he had asked her to see the first part of *Ivan the Terrible*. Hellman and Eisenstein were devoted to each other. Shortly before he died he had asked her to send him thirteen mystery stories, because he was very superstitious and he wanted something with a thirteen in it. Later in her book on Russia Lillian Hellman revealed Eisenstein's homosexuality and it caused a great scandal. The Russian cultural minister shouted: 'We do not have any homosexuals in our country!' Lillian calmly pointed out that the previous night she had seen Horowitz, a close friend of the minister's, 'flying across the stage to the piano, like a female impersonator'. Lillian still couldn't help laughing at the trouble she had caused. 'A friend of Dorothy's if ever there was one.'

On the third morning, Lillian phoned me early at my hotel. 'Get up. I am going to take you on a boat trip.' She wouldn't hear about my decision not to see too much of her before the filming. 'Nonsense, I have been in the theatre all my life, I still know how to act. Be here in twenty minutes.' Lillian had organised the whole day: a boat trip, a lunch at her friends the Bruces', the American ambassador to London, a lobster dinner with the theatre writer Robert Brustein. He had once fallen out with Hellman, but was now again one of the few theatre people she admitted to her inner circle. Almost everybody one met around Lillian had at one time or another fallen out with her.

Our first filming day began in a disaster. When I arrived with the crew at her house at nine o'clock I heard her saying: 'Where is the fucking hairdresser? I thought we agreed, Mr Adam, that I have a hairdresser.' The cameraman who had promised 'the perfect hairdresser' he knew rushed to the phone. Two minutes later I heard a terrible crash. He had knocked one of those blue Chinese vase lamps to the floor. Lillian looked at me. I wanted to sink into the floor. I detected a tiny smile in the corner of her eye: 'We are insured, Mr Adam, aren't we?' I hastily confirmed. Lillian pretended not to care about the lamp, but it came up several times in the conversation during the day.

Finally after three hours waiting the hairdresser showed up. From the row that ensued between him and the cameraman, I realised that the two were linked by more than professional bonds. Lillian had also caught on and hissed at me, without lowering her voice: 'If the fucker is as careful with my hair as his lover was with my lamp, we are in fine shape.' I understood the terror she had spread in the past among colleagues and friends.

A little later she steamed into the room: 'Who is that dumb blonde in the kitchen?' The dumb blonde turned out to be the girlfriend of the sound man who had, unknown to me, come along because she was a 'great admirer of Miss Hellman'. By now I was fuming, and as a result Lillian became all protective.

After lunch we were finally set up and I filmed her on the boat. Hellman was in top form, witty and charming. I suddenly had found an ally. I asked the crew to leave their lovers of whatever sex at home and spent another delightful evening with Lillian and Peter.

After five days we had not done a single interview and I could feel how tired Lillian was. She coughed profusely and never stopped smoking; at one point she was so weak that I had to help her into her bedroom. I felt I had already spent a lifetime talking to her. How could I possibly make it fresh and spontaneous?

Lillian Hellman

The next day everybody was on time. Lillian Hellman looked very elegant in a pale beige silk dress, her face beautifully made up. She sat in a large armchair. By her side was a small table with a large tumbler of iced whisky plus a large ashtray.

We talked for about three hours. Then I sent the crew away while the two of us had lunch. We both felt that things were going well. Sitting on the large sofa from her play *The Little Foxes*, I asked her if she had a dream. 'Oh yes,' she said, 'to live as long as possible, to live as comfortably as possible, and with as much work as possible. I don't think I expected very much, in that sense. I don't think I was a dreamer. It's one of the reasons success has surprised me. It still does. If I had dreams, they were other kinds of dreams. I dreamed of a farm, and I had a farm. And I dream of another farm, but I'll never have another farm. As a little girl I dreamed of being a beauty, but I wasn't a beauty. So what was there to do about it? I dreamed of being dazzlingly brilliant at college, and I was very undazzling, I gave up and decided not to compete. Every American born in the world is dreaming of some vague thing called "happiness". We are told it's our due, we'll have it. But I never knew what it meant, and I still don't.'

The woman who had said these honest words had suddenly fallen asleep on my shoulder. I looked at her, intensely moved. I prayed that the first dream would be granted.

In the afternoon we resumed our filming. Throughout the interview, Hellman was very candid about herself and her shortcomings. Like many of her characters, she had the tendency to cling to the bad times and block out the good ones. There was a lot of talk about the fiasco when she got involved with Leonard Bernstein's *Candide*, for which she wrote the libretto. 'When I first started in the theatre nobody could move me from what I thought. Then about the time of *Candide*, I began to think I don't like this business any longer. Too many collaborators, too much talk about money and success.'

When I asked her: 'How important had success been for you?' she snapped back: 'Oh, that's a loaded question. I am not that big a sucker. It's important for everybody, and it is not as important as everybody makes it. It's fine in dealing with head waiters. I don't mean to make fun of it. It is just fine. But it shouldn't govern life and I hope to God it hasn't governed mine.'

'How about failure?' I asked. Hellman took a deep drag out of her cigarette, her eyes turned hard as she was stalling for the answer. 'You did not ask me what failure is like, you asked me about success. Failure can be very cruel, and awful and crippling.'

Failure had come in many guises into Hellman's life, not just in the theatre. When she was young she thought that she was very much in control of her life and I suspected she still believed it. 'But it depends if one has been given a fair shake in life, the place and the circumstances one is born in for instance.' 'Have you had a fair shake?' I ventured. 'I had quite a fair shake, not a brilliant one I think. It has been an enormously interesting time to live in, but everything should have been much better, it had a great deal of ugliness in it.' Would she, if she could, change the pattern of her life? The answer was no. 'It's a waste of time to think about things like that. Of course I would have done less time-wasting things... And perhaps some less foolish things. But if one is willing to accept punishment that life, or someone else, or society will give you, you are halfway through the battle.'

I could see she was getting tired and I decided to break off the interview for today with one last question: 'In growing old, so much leaves us: strength, anger. What is one left with?' 'You have got *me*,' she said with a laugh, and then taking a large gulp of whisky, she added: 'The hope for the best, I guess. The hope that not all anger is gone, not all strength. You know perfectly well a great deal has and you say a long prayer. Some people come out fine and some come out not only physically crippled, but beaten up. I have asked myself this question almost every day for quite a while now, and I have no answer for it.'

That night I thought about what hope there is for our last hour. Maybe the simple, healing phrase: *It has worked out all right.* Maybe few of us have been as happy or as miserable as we thought. And then to slide into oblivion with a smile or even a grin.

I sent the crew back to New York. Lillian and I decided to do a further interview at a later date, in New York or maybe in her old house in Pleasantville. I left the next day, happy, enriched, and with a broken lamp in my hand.

In October I was back in New York. Hellman could not bear to come with me to Pleasantville, the thirty-acre farm which she had bought from the proceeds of *The Little Foxes*. She and Dashiell Hammett spent thirteen years – the happiest years of her life – there. She had raised poultry, farmed, fished, cooked, filled the house with guests and had written five plays. Walking around the beautiful autumn garden I thought how sad she must have felt when she lost it all, for the McCarthy witch hunt of 1951 had brought a cruel ending to this life. Although already an old and ill man, Dashiell Hammett, a member of the Communist party, was tried and sent to jail. Soon after he died. 'He seemed to me a great man,' Hellman had said at his funeral. She was cut off from her professional earnings and was forced to sell the farm. When Lillian had told me the first time about it, she had tears in her eyes. When I brought her a large bouquet of autumn foliage, picked at the pond she had fished in, she wept again.

Hellman was pleased with the film I had made, although her first words at the screening were: 'I could kill that hairdresser.' From 1978 until her death in 1984, I saw Lillian regularly. Whenever I was in New York, I spent some time with her. Once she came to London, where she stayed at the residence of the American ambassador. She never failed to mention the broken lamp, even though the BBC had found a replacement at great expense. Still I could not help loving her. I saw much of her anger and hatred of the world, which she considered unjust and cruel. But I also saw a lot of her pain and vulnerability. When I hadn't written for a while, she reminded me, lovingly: 'Have you forgotten me? Fickle, fickle blows the wind. Do write, Peter, I need it.'

Ours was a strange relationship. Whenever I saw her too often or too long, she was bound to do something unpleasant, awful, and I was afraid that my great affection could disappear. I sometimes thought that she could only function after she had put terror into someone. 'That stupid coloured maid,' I heard her saying and cringed. Once we were looking for a certain passage in one of her plays. 'I will ask Rita,' I suggested. 'Rita has never read any of my plays,' Hellman snapped. She was wrong, Rita had not only read all of her plays but she knew instantly where the passage was. I wanted Lillian to apologise to Rita. She would not, but she wanted to come out well in my eyes, so when I left she handed me a book. 'For Peter, in memory of somebody else finding the needed passage and I thank him for a good time', she had written on the first page.

She was often ill and her eyesight was getting worse. Every time an envelope arrived with those magnified letters, I feared the worst. 'Come and see me soon, I need two more operations and I am already a bit jumpy and nervous, grab me while I still make sense. Affectionately, Lillian', and a few months later: 'I am writing to you shortly before another eye operation. It finally had to come and since I am a great coward, these are of course bad days and I am going in with little faith. And then there might be the second eye to worry about, rather dreadful of nature not to have given us only one eye, isn't it? Say a prayer for me to whomever you say a prayer.'

I have thought much about this strange and uncomfortable woman who spoke so much about truth, who had set herself up as a pillar of rectitude and was nevertheless so often accused of lying. I have always been mistrustful of the *Julia* story and wondered if it really happened that way. For years she was suing Mary McCarthy for saying that 'even the commas in Hellman's writing are a lie'. I think Lillian Hellman wanted to be truthful. Truthfulness was the one quality she had admired above all in Hammett. 'He taught me, in a sense, to write. And beyond that he took chances that very few people will ever take, particularly people they love. He told the truth! When I did something that he didn't like, he said it very bluntly and very sharply and he really didn't give a damn if I liked it or didn't. And that is the greatest gift anybody can make to anybody.' I believe that Hellman had always been searching for this 'greatest gift', but she probably no longer knew what the truth was.

And when she was gone, after a painful death, it suddenly did not matter any longer to me. She spoke her truth and she had made me another gift as precious and as fragile, the gift of her friendship.

My relationship with Lenya was much less complicated, with a tenderness of a different kind. Our filming was also marred by illness and age. Lenya had the idea of doing the interview on 18 October, the day of her eightieth birthday. 'What a wonderful way to celebrate my birthday in that way, darling,' she had written. Most people thought that she was born in 1900, her official birthday, but she had once confided that she had managed to drop two years 'when it didn't matter so much'. A few days later she had sent me a book with the following inscription: 'To Peter, who I hope will be my friend as long as I live, affectionately Lotte Lenya geb. [born] 18. 10. 1898.'

With Lenya too I had totally failed in my principle of keeping my interviewee at bay prior to the filming. She had invited me to visit her in the country house she and Kurt Weill had bought in New Town, an hour's drive up the Hudson River. Lenya spent much of the week there, driving back and forth from the city in an old car. It was a weatherboard house at the edge of a stream with a little wooden bridge. There was also an apple orchard and a fat cat sunning itself in the meadow. It was a wonderful place, not at all like anything I had ever seen in America, reminiscent of Europe: the furniture, the knick-knacks and the atmosphere of unhurried warmth.

Lenya seemed to enjoy having guests and had baked an old-fashioned apple pie, *Wiener Art*. She had put on an old record of 'September'. Her haunting voice filled the room, while she talked about Weill. 'Kurt wanted to be an American, a man of the world of musicals.' It was only eleven o'clock when I arrived, but Lenya insisted that we have a large whisky. She was very keen to know how I was getting on with Hellman and smiled: 'Has she seduced you yet?' But she admitted that she admired her work.

She never stopped talking and was full of more stories about Brecht, how he once had told her 'for me you are epic enough', after she had asked him about his 'alienation this and alienation that', and how he had unfolded the red flag in her house when he had come to see the Weills in America. She was bubbling over with childlike mischief. Helene Weigel forced Brecht to marry her with the words: 'Damit der Buoa an Vater hat wenn sie in der Schule deine Gedichte lesen.'[1] Brecht was at that time in love with the actress Carola Neher, whom he assured 'dass die Heirat nichts zu sagen hat'.[2] She was full of wicked gossip while she piled *Schlag* on the cake. 'One day I watched Stravinsky filling a very old bottle of brandy with some cheap stuff and then presenting it to Isherwood.'

Three days later Lenya phoned me; she had fallen and broken her arm. I rushed to her house. She was already in plaster. She told me how much it hurt but that she never cried. 'I have never even fainted.' Of course there was no question any longer of filming her on her birthday.

I flew back to London. We often spoke on the phone and she sounded very depressed. I tried to get her to come to London, hoping that this would cheer her up. 'Dearest Peter, I can't tell you how much I love to come to see you but physically I am not able. I still go 3 x a week to the hospital, I am so bored of not being able to move my arm properly, but let's wait for better times. Saw *Sweeney Todd*. Grand Guignol (I do not know the correct spelling) par excellence (Don't know how to spell this either). After show no taxi landed up 7th and 6th Avenue. Nothing but Schwarze, pimps, whores, Dschungel [jungle], well no more Big Apple for me for a while.'

When we finally got around to the filming, a few months later, she looked well again, even stunning. There was no question of a special hair-dresser and make-up. 'Darrling that old face I paint myself,' she said, and a little later coming out of her bedroom she mused: 'How do you like the living legend, can she stand up to the others, Greta and Marlene?' It was meant as a joke, but there was some vanity in it too.

She offered some champagne to the crew and we sat in the small living-room in front of a blazing fire. She was wearing the same red evening dress I had admired a few days earlier. We had been to a concert at Lincoln Center in honour of Kurt Weill. 'Twelve dollars at Corvette, don't give the secret away,' she had said laughingly.

The minute the cameras were set up she began to talk, and she did not stop until we ran out of film.

1 'So that the boy has a father when they read your poems in school.'
2 'Marriage means nothing.'

Lotte Lenya

'Lotte Lenya matches her legend' was the headline in the *Telegraph*, when the film went out. 'Like art, personality defies definition. It is either recognisable or absent. *Omnibus* was made memorable by the personality of a figure from the past with enough vitality to captivate viewers for whom she is only a legend.'

The rave reviews of 'the great Lenya', as the headline ran in *The Observer*, did not exaggerate. Lenya had been captivating. She told the stories, told many times before, as if she had just remembered them. How she had met Kurt Weill in Berlin and how he had proposed to her in a rowboat. She evoked the opening night of the *Little Mahagonny* in Baden-Baden, 'that highfalutin' festival with Hindemith and Schoenberg. Brecht in his foresight had said "listen they will whistle", and he gave us little whistles to whistle back.' She blamed Weigel for the flop of *Happy End* because in the middle of the third act Weigel had come out with a communist pamphlet in which she insulted the audience. 'Until then it went so well. It contained the most beautiful songs Kurt has ever written.'

She moved from English to German, and imitated Brecht's Augsburg accent: 'Derrrr Haifisch derrr hat Zähne.' Anecdote succeeded anecdote. 'Mister Brecht wasn't always so angelical. He was very jealous of Kurt. Where would *Threepenny Opera* be without Kurt's music? I ask you. Brecht got more political by the minute, but Kurt was not interested in composing Karl Marx and that was the reason why they split up.'

For the composer emigration meant the break with his musical past, for Lenya the actress the end of her career. They arrived one morning on a ship. 'Kurt had said come up quickly and there was this unforgettable thing, my heart stood almost still, the Statue of Liberty, I knew then that we were in America and once on land we rushed to the movies. We saw *Dark Angel* with Ronald Colman and Vilma Banky.' Lenya and Weill's gratitude and love for America was deep and lasting. They did not want to be immigrants, they gave up speaking German.

'Kurt wanted to absorb America. One of our best friends was George Gershwin and we went to the dress rehearsal of *Porgy and Bess* and I could see in Kurt's face how sad he was, because he wanted to write an opera too. That he ever made a career in this country, with his utter modesty, I had to push him. "Please Kurt throw your weight around just once." People always said that he was arrogant, that he was stupid, he was just terribly shy. Really nobody knew Kurt Weill. I was married to him for twenty-four years and we lived two years without being married so that makes twenty-six years and when he died, I looked and I wasn't sure that I really knew him. Does anyone really know another person that well? I doubt it.'

The interview did not have the same depth as the one with Hellman;

this was showbiz and Lenya knew it. 'Don't expect anything like that from me,' she had said very modestly when I told her about the Hellman interview. 'I am only an actress, not one of those highfalutin' intellectuals.' 'When you are blessed with a certain charisma, that is almost more important than the knowledge of your craft, to come on the stage and to know instantly that you have the audience in your hands, which happens to me all the time. I am sorry to say that, but it's true. I asked myself was everything in my career memorable? I do not say that, but people say that, they remember every gesture. I make very few, only when it's necessary, like in life when you talk, when we have to make it we make it.'

The BBC broadcast the Lotte Lenya profile together with *A Homage to Kurt Weill and Bert Brecht*. Lenya had lent me photographs and Weill's personal notes and I had staged the *Little Mahagonny* songspiel in a boxing ring, exactly as in the first production in Baden-Baden in 1927. As a companion piece, I devised a songspiel based on *Happy End*, for which I had concocted a simple story line, using some of the most popular songs. There was a brilliant cast including Sarah Walker, Meriel Dickinson, Yvonne Kenny, Peter Knapp, Philip Langridge and Neil Jenkins. I had asked Patrick Procktor to design the set and he gave us a most imaginative and painterly backdrop. The London Sinfonietta was conducted by David Atherton.

I can hardly describe the joy I felt directing singers and actors. There were few pleasures equal to that in my entire professional life. The use of opera singers was both a loss and a gain, but Lenya had often told me that Weill always hoped to do the same one day.

'The production of the songspiels is exactly right, one could almost believe that the pieces were written for television.' The reviews were good, except one claimed that the production evoked rather 'the poisonous atmosphere of old Bournemouth than that of Berlin'. It came from the Australian Clive James, who knows a lot about Bournemouth.

The *Homage to Weill and Brecht* was chosen for the coveted Prix Italia, but the greatest satisfaction came from a letter Lenya had sent me. 'Dearest Peter, This is just a short note to tell you how happy I am with our interview and even more happy, if this is possible, with the two productions: *Happy End*, which you brought to life again, and the *Little Mahagonny*, which I found flawless.' I was very proud, because she would not have minced her words if she had thought otherwise.

Like Hellman, Lenya became a central point of my New York visits. We would sometimes go to the theatre or to the opera together, to 'Stiletto

Alley', as she called the Metropolitan Opera. We saw Weill's *Street Scene*, Lenya looking stunning in a black trouser suit, with a large red cape and a beaded bag. Often we just had dinner together, Lenya always tender and wonderfully bitchy. She had once mentioned to me that she would like someone like myself to write her life story. I introduced Wayne Lawson to Lenya, hoping that she could be persuaded to let him write her biography, but then she could never make up her mind.

I believed in keeping my personal and my professional life separate, but sometimes the two overlapped, and I often thought how privileged I was to have struck up some special relationships with strong and unusual women. My friendships with Hellman, Lenya, and later with Hildegard Behrens and Jeanne Moreau, had all begun with work and had spilled over into my private life. With the exception of Durrell, this has not happened with the men I interviewed, except of course for Albee, Henze, Hockney, Shaffer and Visconti. They were friends before I filmed them.

21
Clouds

The work with Lenya also brought me another friend, the photographer Bill King. Bill was one of the most coveted photographers in the international world of fashion. His pictures figured on the covers of *Vogue* and *Harper's Bazaar* and he had photographed film stars and top models all over the world. I have been for a number of years the London correspondent for German *Vogue*, writing a monthly Letter from London. As I wanted a really good photograph of Lenya, their Art director had suggested Bill King. I soon gave up the idea, as I found out that magazines paid several thousand dollars for a Bill King photograph. Robert Mapplethorpe was also a friend of Bill's, and one day said to me: 'I'd gladly take the picture of Lenya, but why don't you call on Bill. You'll like each other.'

So I phoned for an appointment, and a few minutes later I was on my way to his studio. I was let into one of those large lofts in which photographers, fashion designers, famous editors, surrounded by models, makeup and hairdressers, produce very expensive and very desirable fashion images. Everything spelled money, glamour and instant fame: the racks with the *haute couture* dresses, a tray with priceless jewels attended by a uniformed guard, even the *de luxe* sandwiches and champagne which were delivered from a nearby restaurant. I was asked to wait while a photo session was coming to an end. Through the open door I saw a few assistants, moving about ceremoniously.

I could not see the photographer nor his model, but anybody expecting to hear a lot of 'That's it, baby', 'Great', 'Look over here', 'Great stuff' – the jargon made familiar by Antonioni's *Blow-Up* – would be disappointed. All I heard was the clicking of the camera. After everybody had cleared out of the room I was asked to enter. A lanky young man in college clothes was sitting on the floor, munching a sandwich and surrounded by fifty-odd photos of a model. 'Hi,' he said pushing a sandwich in my direction, 'what do you think of this one?' pointing at a picture of Isabella Rossellini. We both crouched on the floor. After about ten minutes his choice was made.

Something very nice and open about Bill King encouraged me to come straight out with my request. 'I can do that.' I mumbled something about the B B C and so on and asked what it would cost. 'I love Lenya and you can take me for a meal,' was his answer. He took an extraordinary picture of Lenya. She had arrived wearing a wig and Bill just removed it and ruffled up her hair. She looked very glamorous, although when the picture appeared in German *Vogue* with an article I had written, she hated the picture. 'Darrling glamorous maybe, but not me.'

Bill and I became close friends, a friendship which brought joy, anger and finally pain. Bill was one of the most civilised people I knew. He was very much a New Yorker, but he loved Europe and its fading values. Europe for him meant Paris, where he lived as a young man; Italy, where he studied art; London, which instilled in him the love for eighteenth-century furniture and gentleman's dress.

He was constantly on the move, mostly by Concorde. When I met him, he must have taken thousands of photographs, thousands of magazines carried his pictures. Bill moved in the big fashion world, which used up tons of money, talent and professionalism on inessentials. It was a high-powered business, glamour sold to a gullible public. The days with Bill were always very exciting. We flew in private planes, and whenever we met he had arranged dinners with the cream of the magazine world, brazen, stylish, sometimes vulgar, mostly held at the latest and most expensive restaurants. New York, Paris or London with Bill was like a constant party. He liked to be the centre of the shakers and movers and their hangers-on, and one never knew who would join us. One day it would be Baryshnikov, Isabella Rossellini and Eve Arnold, who were working on a film in London; the next time the Chows or Anna Wintour or any of the other powerful editors of the fashion empires, like Alexander Liberman, the king of art directors from Condé Nast. Bill basically despised this world of insubstantial and shifting characters, jetsam and flotsam of a trendy tide, but he was fascinated by it.

I spent many days watching him in his studio. Models, art directors, fashion editors walked in and out of rooms, while Bill checked the dresses and the accessories. The phone never stopped ringing; Paris, Tokyo, Munich. Assistants booked flights and tables in restaurants, cancelling others. There was never a lull or a pause.

Despite his success he was a modest man, too intelligent not to know his limitations, too wise ever to show off. He shrugged off any suggestion that he was an artist, always considering himself a commercial photographer. In a world eaten up by commercialism he had kept for himself a private space shared only with a few friends. Almost secretly, he had made many portraits of them and a series of photographs of nude dancers, pictures of rare strength and singular vision. He always hoped to publish these one day. We looked at them often, mulling over them, choosing, rejecting, planning and plotting, for his greatest dream was to make a book which would include his own choice of photographs and the story of his life. But his increasingly tight work schedule would always take priority over this dream. Sometimes we went out of town for two days, locking ourselves away in a hotel to work on 'our book', but he was usually called away after twenty-four hours.

Bill's favourite model was Isabella Rossellini, and Bill was Isabella Rossellini's favourite photographer. 'I owe my life to my parents, but I owe my face to Bill King,' Isabella said one day. Few people seeing Isabella arriving in the studio, sometimes by bus, would have guessed that this shy, very private young woman with no makeup in a simple grey outfit could be transformed into the beautiful girl of the Lancôme ads. It is not that she was not beautiful in real life, but somehow her modesty did not allow her beauty to be immediately apparent, it was like something slumbering underneath. Isabella Rossellini looked very much like her mother. I had noticed their likeness for the first time when Ingrid Bergman and her daughter had sat in my office in London several years earlier. Isabella was then working as a journalist with Italian television, and she hoped that she could find a job at the BBC.

Bill was a constant, but not always comfortable friend. Over the next nine years I saw a lot of him, as he drifted in and out of my life. He relied increasingly on my judgement and help in the conduct of his life. His fortune and success were often overshadowed by melancholia and doubts, which he drowned in an excess of temptations. Underneath the unassuming exterior lay many passions and curiosities. Bill loved danger and used to say: 'I work hard and I play hard.' He was the entrance to a darker life, to evenings with Robert Mapplethorpe, visits to apartments filled with strange characters selling drugs and sex. If I know much about the horrors of drugs and the destruction they do, I know it through him, watching him 'crashing' at my doorstep.

During the last years the joyfulness and freewheeling which marked our earlier meetings gave way to darker tones. While his career went from strength to strength and magazines were queuing up to get one of his photos, his private life went through many dark episodes. The world began to crumble for Bill, first slowly and then with accelerating speed. We watched together the painful death of his lover, slowly sinking into speechlessness and non-communication. The wounds from the love and death of his friend would not heal. And then it was his turn in this mad dance of death in the New York of the 1980s, and I had to watch Bill fighting illness and decay.

On 23 November 1987 Isabella Rossellini and I stood at the side of a brown coffin in one of those plastic, soulless funeral parlours in New York to say goodbye to Bill. We both delivered eulogies. Isabella, dressed in black, looked like a little girl. Dwarfed by the pain and the monstrosity of the place, she spoke movingly about her debt to the photographer and the man. In the congregation were the many friends who shared so many of his darker passions and the family who knew nothing of them.

The irony of our lives was such that later the same day, Isabella and I met once more, this time holding a glass of champagne. It was also the day when my book on Eileen Gray was launched in New York, and the art dealers Robin Symes and Christo Nicolaides had generously opened their New York house for this event. It was filled with Eileen Gray furniture and with paintings by Prunella Clough. Renate had come from Rome wearing Eileen Gray's own shoes from the twenties and Prunella had also made the journey from London. I stood there in a sea of names and people, chatting away, but the fact that a few hours before Isabella and I had been beside the coffin of a friend gave us a complicity I will never forget.

In the summer of 1978 life in New York was still rosy. I looked up my old friend Tamara Geva. After John Emery's death she had taken a smaller flat, but still lived on a grand scale. She had begun to write the story of her life. She had lost nothing of her stunning good looks, despite her advanced age, which nobody was supposed to know, but since she had come to Europe in 1925, guessing was not difficult. Tamara had suggested to me that I make a film on Diaghilev. A handful of people who had worked with him were still alive, although Karsavina and Massine had recently died. She promised to be the link with the surviving members of Diaghilev's circle.

The coming year 1979 would be 'Diaghilev year', the fiftieth anniversary of his death, and I immediately agreed. I also agreed to hand over the script to her and with it, reluctantly, the role of the interviewer. Little did I know what I let myself in for. This was to be the reckoning of the dancer Zhervecheyeva with the great impresario. 'Serge was arrogant, cruel and egoistical,' she had told me once. 'He was generous with the stars, but we had to live in third-rate hotels and never got paid.'

I should have been forewarned of troubles to come by the first meeting Tamara had arranged with the dancer Felia Doubrovska, Diaghilev's un-forgettable firebird. Felia sailed into Tamara's flat, dressed to the eyeballs. She must have been over eighty, but she did not let it show. 'Thank God for makeup,' she said, kissing Tamara profusely, leaving it open as to whether she referred to Tamara's or her own. Tamara invited her to sit

down and pointed at a very low armchair, facing a glamorous oil painting
of Geva. Doubrovska ignored her and sat very upright on a hard bench, a
bird of prey if ever there was one. Tamara, using her sweetest smile, suggested that we film Felia in Tamara's apartment or walking the dog in the
park. 'You do walk in the park, don't you, Felitschia darling?' she added.
Felia smiled an acid smile. When Tamara was out of the room, Felia whispered with the sound of a viper: 'I am *not* going to be filmed in this awful
flat of hers nor in the park, little old lady walking her dog or so. I will be
filmed in my dance class.'

'This is Monte Carlo, a place closely identified with the Ballets Russes de
Diaghilev – and rightly so, for it became his permanent home.' Tamara
spoke her first introduction piece in front of the Casino. 'On the stage of
the theatre inside the Casino, there appeared such legendary dancers as
Nijinsky, Pavlova, Karsavina and Fokine. Every year, from January until
late spring, the company came here to work. In the middle of the 1920s
four youngsters from the Soviet Union joined the company. They were
Alexandra Danilova, Nicolai Efimov, George Balanchine and myself,
Tamara Geva. It is through their eyes and voices that we will attempt to
show the personal image, the character, of that fabulous man Sergei Pavlovitch Diaghilev.'

We flew to New York, where Tamara had arranged an invitation for tea
at Vera Stravinsky's flat. Mme Stravinsky received us in an elegant apartment, overlooking Central Park. It was filled with photographs and
memorabilia of the maestro and Vera Stravinsky's paintings. A butler in
white gloves served tea and cakes. Mme Stravinsky looked sixty at the
most, although her real age as she told us was ninety. As Vera Sudeikina,
she had danced with the Russian Ballet and designed costumes. One day
in Paris Diaghilev had asked her to join him for dinner. 'There will be a
young Russian composer. Be nice to him,' he had said. 'It was Igor. I was
nice to him for fifty years, although I have only been Mme Stravinsky for
thirty-eight years,' she told us.

She was still a beautiful and jolly woman with the quintessential Russian look. She wore a green silk tent-like cocktail dress, hiding a big frame.
Her shoes were of matching material. Her impeccably made-up face was
framed by a large blond coiffure. From time to time she would break into
a winning smile or a girlish giggle. I let the two women talk. It had all the
aspects of a polite tea party. Vera Stravinsky dispensed the address of 'a
little man in Venice who has made my shoes for forty years'.

Tamara was on her best behaviour, she had promised me to leave all
competitiveness at home. She did not contradict our hostess when she

Vera Stravinsky and Tamara Geva

Alexandra Danilova

told her where to buy the best Russian bread and *piroshkis*. The conversation would switch from English to Russian, from French to German. Vera Stravinsky was full of funny anecdotes; how Diaghilev admired Lifar's *derrière*, and how his tailcoat was 'full of *trous*'.

The friendly atmosphere took on a slight chill when Tamara intervened and said Diaghilev had discovered Stravinsky. 'How can you say discovered? If you suddenly find a book on a shelf and say "*Tiens, c'est intéressant*", do you discover the book?'

Before we left she showed us a photograph which Inge Morath had recently taken of her. She was asking me what I thought of it. 'Inge Morath is now Mrs Arthur Miller,' Vera Stravinsky bubbled away, 'and she has done it for *Vogue*.' 'How nice for you,' I heard Tamara saying.

For the filming, Mme Stravinsky was floating in a pink chiffon dress, again with matching shoes. Tamara had opted for black. As I sat her on the sofa, Vera Stravinsky whispered in my ear: 'Can I sit on an upright chair? *Cela fait moins comme un sac de pommes de terre*.' Tamara was doing the talking. She was nervous, interrupting all the time. She was used to being in front of the camera, not behind, but in the end it was all right.

For the next three days we set up our cameras in the Central School of the American City Ballet. Three members of the Russian Ballet were still teaching there: Alexandra Danilova, Diaghilev's last great ballerina, Doubrowska and Balanchine. Danilova, a graceful seventy-five-year-old with a colourful chiffon scarf over her tights, had just finished a feature film with Baryshnikov, *The Turning Point*. Tamara and Danilova – Shura, to her friends – were at school together at the Maryinsky Theatre Ballet School in St Petersburg. Danilova remembered every word the 'master' had ever said to her. When she had joined Diaghilev's company, he had asked for her measurements. 'Are you buying a horse or engaging a dancer? Maybe you want to see my teeth,' and she still shuddered at her freshness. She turned to her pupils: 'I do not want to see too much *derrière*. Nobody wants it... and more smiles... No that's cheap. I do not want to see any cheap dancers. *Un, deux, trois, référence*, that's it,' and with an eye to the camera she added: 'The great Diaghilev always said with style and taste everything is possible, without it nothing.' Her dancers applauded their revered teacher.

Felia Doubrovska was demonstrating to three girls the perfect *porte de bras*: 'Heads high, *mesdemoiselles, la tête très élevée*.' Doubrovska did not walk, she moved like a gazelle. Later she explained: 'Mr Diaghilev did not like it when we showed too much emotion on stage. He liked pure dance, not too much feeling. One day I made a grand gesture, like this,' and she got up to wave her arms about, 'and Mr Diaghilev came after the performance. "What do you suppose our theatre is. Music hall?"'

To get an interview with the third teacher was very difficult. 'Mr Balanchine does not give interviews, never!' we were told, and certainly not in front of cameras. We ran into him after class, a small tired-looking man, visibly embarrassed by our request. Tamara would never take no for an answer and a few days later she announced: 'George will do it.'

Balanchine was refined, elegant and of great simplicity. He spoke a very natural English with a slight accent. He could be very animated and witty and suddenly become taciturn and withdrawn, but on that day he was full of humour. His famous guarded look had made room for great cheerfulness. 'One day I invited Diaghilev for dinner. I wanted to make *fond d'artichaut*, with mushrooms. God made them. You could really not fail, but I did. Then I did some cutlets, Russian cutlets, they too fell apart. Porridge he called it. Then I served baked apples with strawberries. "What's that?" Sergei Pavlovitch asked: "Porridge again?"' and Balanchine and Tamara fell over laughing.

It was strangely moving to see the former Mr and Mrs Balanchivadze sitting opposite each other. Tamara Zhervecheyeva had married the young Georgian dancer Georgi Balanchivadze when she was fifteen years old. It turned out Tamara's best interview. The words 'Do you remember?' were the magic key.

Balanchine turned out to be a sharp observer, but always kind, even in his criticism. Imitating Diaghilev's voice, he painted the picture of a great but often angry man. But he also admitted that he really did not know him, despite their close and long collaboration. 'In private he had little time for his dancers, all his time was spent with the rich and the famous: Coco Chanel, Picasso, Derain, Stravinsky.'

The two English dames, Ninette de Valois, a sort of English schoolmistress in a no-nonsense blazer, and Alica Markova, beehived and girlish, spoke about his triumph and his famous scandals. 'When Nijinsky danced *L'Après-midi d'un faune*, the reception was so cold that he had the entire ballet repeat it again,' Tamara prompted. 'But that happened to us in Paris too,' Ninette de Valois interrupted, totally forgetting the camera. 'Don't you remember with Nijinska's *Romeo and Juliet*?' 'Oh, of course I remember, we were both on stage, it was a riot.' 'We had to start the ballet again, he loved the scandal and I thoroughly enjoyed the evening.'

It was to Tamara's credit that the people participating in this programme took us through the frequent trials and tribulations of Diaghilev's life. They recalled his terrible temper and shrieking voice. They spoke about his many sides, the snobbish one and the kind one, 'the man who could charm stones and diamonds and pearls from a woman to finance his increasingly expensive ballets'. Money to Diaghilev was nothing but an asset to be spent. He had refurbished an entire theatre, the Théâtre du Châtelet in Paris, to match the opulence of his productions and placed the most beautiful bejewelled actresses in the front row.

Vera Stravinsky had shown us a photograph of the two maestros together in Venice. 'Always Venice,' she said. 'Stravinsky loved Venice and so did Diaghilev,' pointing at a large screen made of a photograph of the Accademia Bridge with a tiny figure of Stravinsky. 'Oh, I remember, one day in the Grand Hotel – it does not exist anymore – Stravinsky played a part of *Sacre* to Diaghilev on the piano. I am not a musician but it goes: "ta ta ta um ta",' and she hummed the famous repetition of the same chord. ' "How long will this go on?" said the impatient Diaghilev. "As long as it is necessary." '

In Venice we were joined by an impeccably camp Anton Dolin – Pat to his friends – in a salmon-coloured shirt with matching tie under a white vicuna coat, calling all the waiters 'baby'.

Vera Stravinsky had recalled the terrible time when Diaghilev received the telegram that Nijinsky had married Romola de Pulska in Buenos Aires. Superstitious in the extreme, he had refused to cross water and remained behind. 'Diaghilev's reaction was volcanic, he cursed and raged. But hurt as he was, his ego would not allow him to be destroyed by one man.' Nijinsky was dismissed. Massine took his place, only to leave him too – a departure which rendered him suicidal, never to recover the same verve. By 1928 the company was celebrating its twentieth season. Diaghilev went on stage to stop the celebration. 'I am not ready for it. I wish to continue working.' He paused for a moment and then added: 'I wish to remain young.' But time did not spare him, he was visibly slowing down. He was a creator of creators and his personal passions were irrevocably entangled with his achievement.

Anton Dolin stood on the balcony of a small palazzo in Venice and told the story of the revival of *Le Sacre du printemps* choreographed by Massine, paid for by Chanel. ' "You know," he said to me, "I was very disappointed with the arrival. There was no more excitement. The audience had heard German guns so the explosion of Stravinsky's music means little to them. This was the end of an era." He had become tired, he needed something fresh in his life and he did, as you know, when he met Igor Markevitch.' 'Oh yes, this was when I saw him for the last time,' Vera Stravinsky remembered. 'It was at a concert and I ran into Diaghilev. He had a big fur coat on, it was almost summer. My goodness, he had lost so much weight I thought he probably had a new lover. Shortly afterwards he died.'

I filmed a silent funeral gondola gliding through the canals on Diaghilev's

George Balanchine

Tamara Geva and Anton Dolin at Diaghilev's tomb

last journey to the little cemetery of San Michele. The old tyrant's tomb was only a few paces away from Stravinsky's. I had hired four splendid-looking gondoliers in funeral attire and a black gondola. On it stood a black coffin with gold ornaments, exactly modelled on the original one, crowned by gigantic bouquets of white lilies. It was a beautiful and strangely moving sequence, the dark reflection of the boat in the water reaching the open water. The wind had been still. Suddenly a large gust came up, whipping up big waves. While the small gondola was fighting its way to San Michele, Tamara spoke the last words of the film. 'Alone and hurting with the thought that his role of a creator was over, he went to Venice. For a while he showed improvement, only to fall into relapse, with pain and fever. Then he dropped into a coma. His friends Kochno, Lifar and Misia Sert watched over him all night. They say there was a storm, the water rising high in the canals. By morning his breathing stopped, and the prediction was fulfilled. He died on the water, 19 August 1929, in his favourite place – Venice.'

Tamara also added the codicil to his death – a day none of the participants in this programme had forgotten. 'Ironically,' she added, 'a few years later, Markevitch, his last love, married Kira, Nijinsky's daughter. The circle was complete.'

Diaghilev: A Personal View, my last programme in 1979, finished off a very rich decade of my professional life, but there were many clouds too.

Hans Werner Henze had had a small heart attack, which frightened me, and I went to see him in Marino. Our political antagonism had disappeared and we could talk about Cuba without having a row. 'The truth is so important for me now, I want to know the truth, even if it hurts.' He too was writing a daily diary and we read our thoughts to each other. Hans, better than most, understood my tortured relationship with Facundo. He knew too well from his own life about the lies, the silences which can build up between two lovers. When I told him that sometimes I was happier without Facundo than with him, he said: 'There are people that drag you down, so you must leave them.' But I could not. The emptiness would have been too frightening. Despite all the suffering Facundo made me want to live and nobody had done that for me.

From my Diary
Thursday 9 August 1979: Facundo fetches me at Nice airport, we drive to our house. He has been here for a few days, Pepita [Facundo's mother] is also here from Buenos Aires with Marucha. All the difficulties of the last few months seem to be forgotten. He

does not stop telling me how much he loves me. The shepherd has been grazing his flock on the land and the grass is short. There are lemons on the trees and the lavender is a hive of butterflies. We dine on the terrace in this blissfully beautiful land under the immense sky. The darkness wraps us up like a black soft velvet cape. Everything has such healing power.

Friday: In the afternoon the fire started. The first Canadairs[1] arrive, their bellies full of water, but they can do little, the wind is simply too strong and the forest burns like tinder. Every time the wind lifts up the flames shoot into the sky. The fire is still ten miles away, but the smell of burning resin fills our nostrils. We were expecting people for dinner, but nobody wants to leave their houses. The night falls and the fire is lighting the hills. The howling wind whips up the flames which creep up with an incredible speed. The news of the smouldering destruction is on the television and radio and people do not stop phoning. We sit in front of the house, hugging each other, praying and crying. I am afraid, not so much for our lives but to lose this house and the land I love more than anything else.

Saturday: The waves of fire advance with the noise of horses' hoofs, leaving behind the cindered ground of ash. Above the fire line the mountain is one black stump. The phone is off and so is the electricity. We drive to the village to get some petrol, in case we have to drive away. We are told that the roads are blocked and that people must stay in their houses. The village is crawling with soldiers and tired firemen, their faces black with smoke. Suddenly out of nowhere a fire starts only 500 yards away from our house, a burning tree had come flying through the air to ignite another site. I drive the car away from the house, it is full of petrol. I hose down all the wooden shutters and we close the doors and windows, hanging up wet sheets in front of them. I am surprised how calm I am. Then a Canadair arrives and the fire is out. The noise of the splashing water on the flame is terrific.

Sunday: The wind has died down and so have the flames. I hear that Tony Richardson's house has burned. I take the car and drive over to Le Nid du Duc through a blackened landscape. It is like driving through ash, the smell of the burnt-out earth is terrible. I have taken one pot of geraniums. I can't help crying. Thank God the houses are safe but all around the land is totally turned into

1   Sea-planes.

ashes. Two cars have exploded and the peacocks and ducks have perished in the fire. All the plants Tony has lovingly planted for years have turned to ash. My geranium pot is the only plant alive for miles and miles of desolation.

I had celebrated my fiftieth birthday, 'our birthday', in La Garde-Freinet with my twin sister Renate and Facundo. Round figures are always strange stock-taking events. Much had occurred in those fifty years. Countries and nations had lived through unprecedented trials, upheavals and transformations. Some had risen, others existed no more, erased from the maps of the world. Renate had given me an old print of the ages of man. Man climbing up some steps, one step for each ten years of his life. Fifty was the top. From then on the descent began. I sometimes look at photographs of myself at an earlier age and wonder how little I have in common with the person I see; me at five, twenty or even thirty. The only certainty I have is that I am the same person. I sometimes wondered if I was not my own most successful forgery, a self-invented person. Not that I was proud of many aspects of myself. My character had not improved much, despite the ripe age.

I had become less gregarious about new friends, consolidating my relationship with the old ones, but promiscuity and social curiosity still loomed large in my life. Out of one or the other or the combination of both, sometimes new and even lasting friendships emerged.

I had become very fond of Bruce Chatwin. After the visit to Eileen Gray we had seen each other only sporadically. Our friendship dated from the time he finished *In Patagonia*, around 1978. He no longer worked at *The Sunday Times*. Like many, I was soon captivated by this blond, nervous and vibrant young man with tousled hair and piercing blue eyes.

Bruce shared an innate restlessness with many of his characters, the feeling of being an exile, a man without roots and with few possessions. He had been to Russia and interviewed Nadezhda Mandelstam, a visit he never stopped talking about. But he was no less proud of his interview with Madeleine Vionnet. He had travelled widely to Afghanistan, to the Sudan on camel and on foot. He still looked like an undergraduate in T-shirts and jeans, but he talked like a man who had already lived several hundred lives.

Sometimes we saw each other every day for a week or two and then he would disappear for several months, never to give any news at all. Then suddenly a barrage of postcards in his almost illegible handwriting:
Your card eventually caught up with me in upstate New York

where I'm battling with a novel – suicidally – at least today! I suppose I'll be back in the summer sometime, but am greatly tempted to take a year out of the country. Love as always, Bruce.

After months of silence he was back again, filling my flat with tales about a rare cave painting or a buried scroll, while stuffing himself with lashings from my *Rumtopf*, his favourite desert – fresh fruit macerated in rum. Sitting in my small kitchen, Bruce would pull out names from his cultural luggage that contained Kierkegaard, Büchner, Goethe, Benjamin, Lacan, Croce, Leibnitz, Heidegger and other formidable authorities, to lend support to any thesis he was developing.

He knew he had a captivated audience in me. I guess he saw a kindred spirit for we shared many things, most of all the love for everything French: the literature, the language, the food and the *joie de vivre*. We showed off to each other by quoting Nerval and Rimbaud, '*l'homme aux semelles de vent*', a most apt description for Bruce, 'the man with soles of wind'.

Bruce had a brilliantly inquisitive mind and his interests were refreshingly wide. He often spoke mockingly about the narrow range of the English novel. 'Go on reading Robert Musil, Hermann Broch, Thomas Mann, Herr Doctor Adam,' he used to say, 'there are more ideas in the *Magic Mountain* than in the whole of the contemporary English novel.'

His knowledge of literature was prodigious, his curiosity without bounds. Sometimes in the early hours of the morning, with my eyes only half open, I watched him standing in front of my bookshelves pulling out Fontane, Schnitzler, Koestler, opening pages at random and sometimes quoting from them.

He often spoke of faraway places I had never heard of, or was not even sure if they existed other than in the landscapes of his mind. He also knew people nobody had ever seen, others I was never quite certain if he had really met. Jumping from country to country and from century to century, I never knew if the delicious young man he so vividly described to me was a dark prince in medieval times or an art student he had met in a pub.

There was a childlike obsession with himself and with the characters he invented. Had he invented himself? Ronald, one of his closest friends, once wrote to me from Australia, where they travelled together, describing Bruce's journey 'as the wanderings in search of some meditation on the desert. Another figure of his own invention'.

It was not easy to be a friend of Bruce's. I once accused him of not showing his heart in his writings. He shrugged it off with a big smile. 'The heart is there, come on look for it, it is not with the best sentiments we write the best literature.'

Bruce Chatwin, by Jerry Bauer

Where was his heart? Bruce led many lives and they were not allowed to mix or interfere with each other. I knew some of his most intimate friends and lovers, but I never met his wife Elizabeth, although he talked to me often about her. There was a kind of guilt feeling about his homosexuality, as if he had not quite come to terms with it. I had the feeling that he lived so much in an invented world that he could never quite let go in reality. 'My life isn't as it should be,' he once said, a remark he later repeated in an interview. He was describing how he, as a small boy, had watched, with envy, a gypsy boy on a horse. It was Tonio Kröger's longing for the *Wonnen der Gewöhnlichkeit* – the pleasure of ordinariness.

If you wanted to get a glimpse of Bruce's landscape of the heart you had to be alone with him. Exhausted by his intellectual excursions he could be very passionate, even tender and funnily camp. La Chatwina was his favourite nickname. I think it was Bruce who first told me the story about Michel Foucault having slept with Roland Barthes, a deliciously wicked bit of gossip and most unlikely. The victory of mind over body, or is it the other way around?

Much has been made of Chatwin's nomadic existence. There were certainly many intellectual reasons for his constant travels, but there were also practical ones. Chatwin was, like so many of us, drawn to the darker sexual possibilities of foreign places, and for a man of his uptight nature, travelling was almost the only way to catch a bit of living.

There were so many contradictions. At one point he had a small one-room flat in the exclusive Albany; I never found out how he got it. It was very spartanly furnished, with exquisite taste, just a bed, a table and a few chairs. On the wall Eileen Gray's map of South America which Prunella had given him. He often raged against the mindless materialism of the Western world, but he also enjoyed staying in the houses of the rich and the famous. He could be generous and caring, he could also be forgetful and elusive. He always sent me his books, sometimes in manuscript form. 'For Peter with all my love and apologies that the real copies have not yet appeared.'

One evening Bruce asked me to come to a lecture he and Paul Theroux were giving at the Geographical Society in Kensington. It was called 'Patagonia – An Entertainment'. Taking turns, like a musical duet, the two travellers told the story of their journeys to the same destination. Bruce began: 'Paul Theroux and I went to Patagonia for very different reasons. But if we are travellers at all – in the sense that members of this society understand the word – we are literary travellers.'

After about five minutes, Paul Theroux took over, much more controlled, suave, less urgent but no less compelling: 'Patagonia was the promise of an unknown landscape, the experience of freedom.'

For nearly two hours the two writers entertained a captive audience with the tales of a faraway country, seen and experienced through the mind and eyes of two very different temperaments, an experience that led to two very different books about the same place. With Theroux one always knew what the traveller felt, read or experienced; with Chatwin one only felt the people and the spirit of the place – about the author one learned very little.

He was reticent in company about any personal matters, and little could be gathered about his true feelings. 'Do not ask me who I am,' Foucault said in *Archéologie du Savoir*, a writer much cited by Bruce. Even in moments when I felt closest to him he carried an impenetrable aura of concealment. When I was furious I called him 'cagey', in more charitable moments 'mysterious'.

The Patagonia 'Entertainment' was one of the most exhilarating travel accounts I had ever heard, and when I told Bruce about it he said: 'You should have this' and thrust the entire manuscript into my hand, a sheaf of white and yellow pieces of paper covered with scribbles.

I was never in doubt that he was a very good writer with the possibility of becoming a great one, but as time went on I sometimes worried lest the cult which was building up around him, often fuelled by his own capacity for self-promotion, should water down his real vocation.

I saw Bruce for the last time in 1987. He had come to the launch party for the English edition of my biography of Eileen Gray. Afterwards he, Prunella, Facundo and myself escaped to have dinner. He was already very ill, he had been in and out of hospital, and I was surprised when he showed up at Zeev Aram's Gallery, where the book was being launched. It was like everything he did, surprising and totally unexpected.

At dinner Bruce was charming, but also manic. He never stopped talking. His irrepressible, unreasonable inventiveness always floated to the surface, he still manifested his ebullient appetite for culture. We knew about the nature of his disease and he had lost a lot of weight, but he spoke all the time about a mysterious illness he had caught, a 'fungus infection' he had picked up from 'eating a thousand-year-old egg'. AIDS was never mentioned.

He was told he had only a few months to live, but he believed that he would live forever. In the next few weeks, we sometimes spoke to each other on the phone. He had given me an article in *Esquire* about the filming he had done with Werner Herzog of *The Viceroy of Ouidah*, and we made plans to make a programme together, a kind of *Spirit of Place*. Bruce was very excited, but when I proposed it to the BBC, nobody was interested.

When he sent me *Utz* I was struck by a passage: 'I believe that in reviewing my life during these final months, he regretted having always played the trickster.' I thought about Bruce lying in the infirmary and I could not help crying. I suddenly remembered the dazzling man who had come to the Hayward Gallery, while I was filming some architectural models for a programme called *Russia, Art and Revolution*. Seeing the model of Konstantin Melnikov's house, he told me how he visited the real house in Moscow, and how he had tea with Rodchenko's daughter, sitting in Mayakovsky's chair.

I wrote him a letter. He was very ill by then, sitting mostly in a wheelchair. A few days later he phoned to thank me and tell me that he was really German – 'like you, Klaus-Peter', and laughed.

I made several attempts to see him, and we made plans and dates, but whenever we tried to meet, he had moved away to another place.

Almost at the end of his life, the BBC suddenly wanted a film on him, and asked me to contact him. I refused, bitter and full of anger, as so often the media had woken up to a 'story' far too late for all of us. Somebody else interviewed a broken man marked by death. I am proud not to be the maker of those harrowing images.

Looking back, I am almost glad that I never saw Bruce again. The memory of this crazy, radiant, unique young man, the citizen of the world and of all times, is still with me and enriches my dreams. I can still picture him sitting on a busy Saturday, in jeans and a T-shirt, on the railing on the King's Road, watching the world go by. I was spared the sight of Bruce in a wheelchair, and sometimes I look at my mail, half-hoping to find a card from him saying: 'With some luck I shall be in London in 10 days' time, love B.C.'

Bruce died on 18 January 1989. He died in Nice, staying once more in somebody else's house, that of Shirley Conran. 'Few people's deaths shrink the world. But Bruce Chatwin is one,' wrote Colin Thubron in an obituary. It certainly has shrunk mine.

In the Christmas edition of *The Listener* several writers were asked to sum up the 'smashing 70s'. Sheridan Morley looked at the arts coverage on television during the last ten years:

'Arts programming had entered the 1970s with considerable and understandable doubts about its own role and function. Throughout the 1960s the old didactic barriers have been swept away, Huw Wheldon's schoolmasterly approach of *Monitor* had been replaced by a kind of free-for-all in which it was assumed, and rightly, that the arts were there to be illustrated and celebrated and illuminated, but not necessarily taught, since the viewer was no longer regarded as a child. But for a variety of different and unconnected reasons, the very people who in 1969 might have been expected to lead the B B C television arts programming into the 1970s and to consolidate the quirky and vivid successes of the 1960s all began to fall away. James Mossman, a superlative and thoughtful presenter of *Review,* took his own life. Jonathan Miller went off to the National Theatre, David Jones to the Royal Shakespeare Company, Melvyn Bragg spent much of the decade on novels. By the end of the 1970s it was clear in retrospect that the great B B C T V arts successes of the decade had in fact been the work of names still less familiar in the world outside of Kensington House, whence cometh all Corporation tele-culture: names like Colin Nears, Tristram Powell, Peter Adam and perhaps above all the late and much lamented Robert Vas. It is not difficult to compile a catalogue of superb B B C arts programmes in the 1970s. Mine, pared down for reasons of space, would have to conclude Robert Vas on Solzhenitsyn, Bruno Walter, Hiroshima and the General Strike; Peter Adam on Lotte Lenya, Brecht-Weill and Lawrence Durrell's Egypt; Tristam Powell on Jean Rhys, Hardy and Susan Sontag.

Other programmes in his list included Alistair Cook's *Letter from America* and Kenneth Clark's *Civilisation.*

I looked back at the decade with great pleasure. I seemed to have begun to discover who I was and what I really wanted to do. I have always been afraid of routine. I began to know beforehand what kind of film I would make: the field was surveyed out. There were few surprises. The making of a programme was still absorbing and full of challenge, but the result seemed to pale behind all that. How much surprise can life hold? 'Life is pleasant and nice, but all is lived already,' I heard Jim's voice saying.

I hankered for more work with actors, thinking about the exhilaration I felt when I was doing the Brecht-Weill pieces. Then living as if in a trance, I discovered that I could direct people, fire them on, even inspire them. There was still no modesty in me. Would directing actors be my future dream?

22

Artists at Work: Edward Albee and David Hockney
1980–1981

My dream of working with actors came true when I directed a scene from Edward Albee's *Who's Afraid of Virginia Woolf* with Miriam Karlin, as part of a programme on Albee, *The Playwright versus the Theatre*. We both had reservations about embarking on such a programme; he on account of his mistrust of the media, and I on account of our friendship. It is always difficult to make films about friends. I prefer to film people I know less well, for love and admiration can overshadow one's critical capacities.

We had both decided to devote as much of the programme as possible to his work and to include extracts from his plays. I filmed him directing a scene from *Counting the Ways* in his kitchen and one from *Zoo Story* on a park bench in Central Park, the real setting of the play, and he generously let me direct a scene from *Virginia Woolf*.

Albee likes to direct himself. His experience with other directors had often been painful.

'I see a play when I write it. I know pretty well how it's going to look, sound, feel, and smell. When I am directing a play of mine I will be more strict with me, the author, than I will allow any other director to be. I will not necessarily make my plays as effective or flashy as other people will, but I will certainly, as my aim is clarity, make them clearer.'

Albee was not easy to interview. He was very much on guard, hiding himself behind self-mockery, an emotional reserve which can be sometimes mistaken for arrogance or conceit. Open in private, in public he was reticent: he absolutely loathed to analyse his work. Nor did he warm to any biographical interpretation of his plays. But he spoke illuminatingly about the genesis of his work.

'I think a person is born a playwright, or a painter or whatever, because it's a way of responding to reality, outside stimuli, and translating them into something else. I trust my subconscious a lot, it's far more intelligent and organised than the consciousness of my brain. I write for a very long time in my head without putting anything down on paper. When I actually write it down on paper it is fairly concentrated. It has irrevocably moved into the conscious.'

We began filming in his country house on Long Island, where he spent

With Edward Albee

the weekends and part of the summer with his friend, the painter Jonathan Thomas. I had often been in this welcoming, slightly Japanese-looking house, hovering over the ocean. It is filled with books, animals and music. Life was easy and carefree. Edward is a gracious and conscientious host, and there were always delicious, drawn-out meals. The playwright at his most cheerful and also at his most domestic, washing up, cooking and fussing about, while Jonathan teased him. Sometimes he would walk along the beach, a lean, lanky figure in corduroy trousers, two large dogs running after him. His tidy and orderly studio was set apart from the bustle of the house, reached through a secret door from the kitchen. He liked to listen to music there, looking at the always changing sameness of seascape just outside; as a young man, he wanted to become a composer.

Edward and I had often talked about wasted lives, lives closing too early, things dreamed of but not lived. These were the subjects of all his plays. His own life was certainly not a wasted one. One look at his engagement calendar showed a full schedule of university lectures, a demonstration for a fellow writer imprisoned in South Korea, a request for permission to stage *Zoo Story* in a university, a meeting with artists of the Foundation which he had instigated, a place for them to create in peace. Not the life of a man who views the world behind a solid wall of indifference.

I have often wondered about the decline in Albee's success and reputation. A few years ago he had been hailed as the most exciting American dramatist, and his picture had been on the cover of *Time* magazine. Now his plays were mostly produced abroad or in colleges. Norman Mailer said: 'America is a cruel world for the talented. It stunts them, blights them, or overheats them with cheap fertiliser.' Albee might have lost some of the rage of his youth when characters were hacking and slashing at each other in order to prove that they were alive. The reason for his popular decline in a country that expected easy answers from their playwrights was that he had turned to what is ambiguous and ambivalent in our lives. In an atmosphere of complacency it was difficult to see audiences warming to plays which are largely about failure or 'people missing the boat', as Edward had put it.

Albee has always spoken up against the laziness of the American audiences and the stupidity of the critics. It has been a running battle, which unfortunately the playwright has lost, at least as far as his Broadway career is concerned.

There was a brooding defiance about him. He had been hurt so often, he just coped and got on with writing. 'Maybe there is no place for my kind of plays on Broadway.' I filmed him on the empty stage of the closed Beaumont Theatre in New York. 'A theatre should not be empty,' he said, angrily. 'This week if I wanted to see a play on Broadway I could not see plays by Shakespeare, Sophocles, Racine, Wilde, Shaw, Ibsen, Strindberg or Chekhov. I could also not see plays by Beckett, Ionesco, Pirandello, Brecht, O'Neill, Pinter, Tennessee Williams or for that matter by me.' A terrible indictment of the state of the theatre in America and an indication of the company in which Albee wanted to see himself. This was not an arrogant statement of someone overestimating himself, but the plea of a writer who refused to sell out his integrity or to let what the public wants become the standard of judgement. 'Most people are unwilling to suffer the experience of great joy or great sadness, they prefer that barren mid-dle-ground of nothing.'

Edward had not changed much from his earlier years. He had always manifested an assurance which had little to do with self-satisfaction and a lot with an abiding sense of balance. He still had that studied gravity which at first had fascinated me so much, his deep brown eyes could suddenly take on a saddened look.

Everything about Edward was elegant, almost patrician – a life marked by comfort and money. His last town house had fourteen rooms – but it was warm and welcoming through its natural American casualness. 'Dear K.P., I moved to 27 W 10th Street, I suppose you say "chic",' he wrote after he had bought a house in the Village, 'but just think about me living there for a moment and you'll realise the incongruity and you won't worry about all this.'

He now lived in an old warehouse in lower Manhattan, a vast loft, filled with the objects of his other passion: modern art. Edward always surrounded himself with painters and sculptors. He appeared to be more at ease with the practitioners of the visual arts than with writers. He had just written the introduction to a catalogue for his friend Louise Nevelson, who showed us the little chapel she had decorated. She wore a long dress with a dramatic fur collar and looked like a large strange bird – 'I hope you like it. Cecil Beaton photographed me in it,' she said.

The reviews of *The Playwright versus the Theatre* were disastrous. It made me sick. Albee's known resentment of the critics came down on both of us. I should have known as much when I heard the questions fired at me at the press conference. 'Why does he come over as so arrogant? Has he got a girlfriend? Does he own two houses?'

'Disastrous,' was Sheridan Morley's verdict. 'It is a fact that most if not all the best things to have emerged in recent months from the troubled

BBC television arts programming have been the work of Peter Adam, but the delightful news that Mr Adam was giving us an hour-long documentary on Edward Albee turned midway through the show to groans of disappointment.' Sean Day-Lewis wrote: 'Of all the selfless beings who go about the world interrogating artists only the gently anxious Peter Adam would put a question like "Why are you so fascinated by the ambiguity of life's situation?"' The same question had also offended Julian Barnes. 'That's not a proper question. You might as well ask "Why is it three o'clock?"'

I have never refrained from putting simple questions, it is the answer that counts: 'If I confined myself to questions that I had the answer to I would be a very limited and dull playwright,' Albee had replied to this very question. 'I am more interested in examining things I do not have the answer to. And I do not find many things cut and dried. I find that most things are ambiguous and ambivalent, and I find great fascination in that.'

The Times was the only one that stood out in a barrage of insults and imbecilities. 'Peter Adam's admirable documentary about the multifaceted Edward Albee probably gets as close as anybody ever will to cracking the code by which this complex man lives.'

With the advent of my public image came vulnerability as a public person and the realisation that most people, artists especially, are hurt by criticism. The only public feedback a person working for television receives is from the critics and from friends and colleagues – there is no other audience reaction. I had been quite spoiled by the critics, which had partly to do with the subjects I had chosen. I was never quite able to take adverse criticism, pretend to laugh it off, yet it is like a very fine poison which penetrates you and remains there forever. I remembered how deeply Peter Shaffer was wounded by the adverse criticism *The Battle of Shrivings* received, and that *The Sunday Times* every week under the listing printed that the play was awful. Twenty years later Peter would still talk about it. Henze never reads any criticism. 'I can't afford to. No artist can be so arrogant as to say that it does not affect him. Unless the critic is at the height of what I do or what my friends do, at the height of their involvement, care and talent, it's not worth bothering. It is only one man's opinion and we know most of the time this person's capacity to judge. He is like a person who has only taken a glimpse of a person as opposed to those who actually live with the same person.'

I had been deeply hurt by the reception given to the Hellman programme, which I had considered one of my best. I was criticised for being 'too reverential'. The critics, mistrusting Hellman, wanted confrontation not clarification, exposure not understanding. They did not care about a sick woman at the edge of death, offering a few important thoughts about what her life and her art had been. I was accused of not probing 'into her excursions into lesbianism', 'into her communism'. Reviewers, that predatory tribe, that does not know the difference between frankness and cruelty, wanted to catch her out, unmask her. I had refused to play their game.

My relationships with the people I interviewed were built on trust, although I could be accused of a tendency to be too sincere in my interviews, a kind of Teutonic worthiness. Why bother to interview artists if you do not admire and respect what they are doing? My best and most honest critics were my friends, my colleagues and the real practitioners of the art.

The next programme under the heading *Artist at Work* was a film profile of David Hockney. We had worked a few months earlier on a ten-minute film in the series *100 Great Paintings*. Hockney had chosen Van Gogh's *Café in Arles* which hangs in the Kröller-Müller Museum, and David, Prunella Clough and I had travelled to Holland.

We had the museum to ourselves, a treat for the three of us. David, in sneakers and baggy trousers, spoke about 'Vincent': in the controversy about the pronunciation, 'the Dutch say Van Chgoch, the Americans call him Van Go; I will call him Vincent', he had said, a painter talking about a painter. With effortless insight he pointed out the thickness of the brushstrokes and speculated on the speed of painting. He paid a moving homage to a man 'in whose life every minute is accounted for. After a day's work he would wash his brushes. He painted thousands of oils and made thousands of drawings and then he wrote all those wonderful letters.'

On our last evening, in the hotel, he gave me a parcel. It contained a drawing he made of me at breakfast reading the morning papers. It was signed: 'Peter reading the *Herald Tribune* at the Hotel Ambassade. Oct 4 1979.'

Six months later I again sat opposite him in his studio in London to embark on an hour-long programme, *David Hockney at Work*. It showed him working in different media: photography, printing, drawing, and painting.

We began by filming the exhibition 'Travels with Pen, Pencil and Ink' in the Tate Gallery, which charted the path of his life during the previous twenty years: drawings and prints of places he visited, India, Egypt, France; objects that had caught his eye; a chair, a swimming pool in Le Nid du Duc, a vase of flowers. David walked through the rooms, pausing here and there, commenting, discovering, delighting. 'I keep drawing flowers. I like flowers. Everybody likes flowers and they are very difficult to draw. In the old hierarchy of skills, faces are the most difficult, hands are next, feet, the human body and after that flowers were thought the most difficult.'

He took a long hard look at the portraits of Celia or Henry Geldzahler.

'I think the line drawings are the most difficult to do because a tension is building up inside you as you go on looking for things and you have to go on doing it, to be able to draw well, to reduce everything to a line. It is not just an outline, it's different textures, different surfaces.'

An amiable clown in funny baggy trousers and a colourful cap, David thrived in front of a camera. A natural teacher and communicator, he was never disturbed by someone watching him painting or drawing; it was almost as if the public justification spurred him on to question his own motives. No one could better analyse his own work in simple comprehensible terms. He made the viewer part of his own process, he drew him in. Referring to his painting *A Bigger Splash*, he said: 'What I like doing is to paint something which in reality lasts only for one second, but takes seven days to paint. If you look carefully, it's painted in single lines with a small brush. Later I could make the water look very fluid and wet by putting very diluted acrylic paint on and when you put detergent in the canvas soaks it up.'

Living in California made him rediscover colour. 'Everything gets greyer when I am in England. In the past my paintings were always blue or green. In California you see bright yellow and orange. Colour draws you in, suddenly discovering all its possibilities. I suddenly realised that you could make things clearer with colour, not just line.' California has made him very prolific. 'In Paris I only did four paintings in five months, now I do a lot. That's what happiness does for you.'

We had decided to do some filming in America but he was difficult to nail down for a date. Finally in October I flew to Los Angeles to discover that David was nowhere to be found. I had learned to be patient: Albee, Lenya, Moreau, Hellman, all had me waiting around sometimes for days: the life of a television journalist was not always as easy as it looked.

I should not complain. I loved Los Angeles; the brazen vulgarity, its showbiz glitziness, its belief in progress and a better world appealed to me. This was the heart of America, much more exciting than the quaintness of San Francisco, a watered-down imitation of Europe. I loved the meals in the restaurants, under-cooled and over-lit with pretentious names like Bistro Garden. The women always looked exactly like the furniture, over-decorated and over-designed. Everything was terribly 'Hollywood'. A friend of mine had lent me his flat in West Hollywood, 'boys' town' as it was called. The flat was right above that of Bette Davis, whom I watched daily watering the plants on her terrace. She was terribly proprietary about the building and had sent her secretary down to inquire about the stranger swimming in the pool. There was a manager who never stopped boasting about the filmstars he 'made'. He ended up showing me what one can do on a waterbed, 'which a few days earlier was graced by the body of Sylvia Kristel, of *Emmanuelle* fame,' he bragged. She was also living in the same house. Everything was so deliciously unreal and tacky.

The days went by, with still no news from David. I was getting very anxious. I decided to start filming without him. The little colourful houses with the palm trees, the glass curtain of the skyscrapers, the sprinklers on the manicured lawns, were all images which David had elevated to icons of this town. 'Los Angeles is almost the first place I have ever painted. In London I was put off by the ghost of Sickert, it was too haunting. In Los Angeles there were no ghosts, there were no paintings of Los Angeles, people didn't know what Los Angeles looked like, and I suddenly thought, my God, this place needs a Piranesi, so here I am.'

I also got hold of a couple of his friends, Sam and Mark. They had all figured in David's paintings and I re-created a couple of his pool paintings. The willingness with which these Californian boys stripped for the camera was refreshing. Finally I got a call from New York. David was on his way. I went to fetch him from the airport. He and his lover Gregory were loaded down with books and paintings. He was very apologetic, and we drove up to his house on Montcalm Avenue, nestling on the hills over Los Angeles which spread like a twinkling carpet underneath. It was a lovely unpretentious house, in a garden with a swimming pool, a warm, welcoming place humming with attractive and ineffectual creatures, eloquent and charming. The large living-room gave out on a wooden terrace. On the wall among Hockney's own drawings was a painting of Laurel and Hardy by his father.

Mark brought in a huge pile of mail, which David shoved into a drawer already full of unopened letters. In the evening Don Bachardy and Christopher Isherwood joined us for dinner. Don was still very good-looking, as delightful as ever. The age difference between Christopher and him was now very apparent and Christopher talked about the burden he is on Don and his fear of being put in an old people's home. Christopher had been mugged a few days ago in his own home. Everybody teased him and Don did his best to reassure him.

The next day we got up early and Mark, David and I went location-hunting. David drove us in his open sports car around town, the radio blazing Mozart. David loved to drive. 'When I got here, within one week I got a driving licence. I had never driven before, everything is so easy-going.'

We drove to the sea and on to Little Venice. The Bohemian section was full of people on roller skates and a steel band played on the lawn. 'It's a bit like Europe in a sense,' David rambled on enthusiastically, 'a sunny naked version of Portobello Road.' He really loved California. 'The minute I got here I thought it is so sexy, all these incredible boys, everybody wore little white socks. It is always sunny. It's got the energy of the United States with the Mediterranean thrown in, which I think is a wonderful combination.'

As if to prove it to me he had invited some of those 'incredible boys' for a swim in his pool. I filmed them diving in and out of the pool, while David clicked away with his camera. The diffused shapes of the naked bodies under water turned David on.

'Water, I can't describe it with words, it's so elusive. It's a subject that has a lot of richness in it. Strange changing surfaces I find fascinating. When you look at a floor your eyes stop on the floor. With water you can look at the reflection, or you can look through it.' He directed two of the swimmers floating on a mattress. 'Move out there, boys,' and then he turned to me. 'Look at the shadow, the interesting thing about water is something you can't quite define, it's unclear yet clear.'

David was only at the beginning of his preoccupation with photographs. 'I have about a hundred albums full of photographs of my life. It's a pictorial record, most people who come into my life end up in it some way or other. Sometimes later, maybe I draw them. It's like a diary, there are lots and lots of pages of paintings in progress.' But he was also suspicious of photographs. 'I am only a snapper. I think it's a small medium, it's small in what you can do with it,' and to prove this he pointed at a painting of someone diving into the water. 'This oil painting is more real than the photograph of the same scene. The painting has layers of time in it, the photograph is the frozen moment. It means you are not editing. In real life, like in a painting, people edit. Look around in this room, your eye is editing all the time, depending what you think and how you feel. A painting is much closer to that experience and therefore more real and more valid. But, alas,' he added, 'the Home office would not allow me to put a painting in my passport.'

The next day I wanted to film him drawing a portrait of Gregory, but David looked pale and felt tired, so I decided to postpone. We sat on the sun-flooded veranda. David brought two large cups of tea and drawing paper. He talked about his disappointment with the Met, for which he was doing some sets, and how badly they had treated him. Gradually his good mood surfaced again and he began cracking jokes, speaking in funny accents, mixing Scottish, Irish and French, reading Kenneth Williams

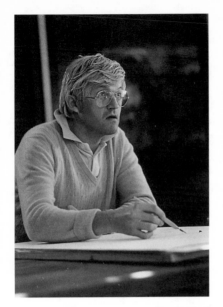

David Hockney drawing PA

asides to me. Then he turned serious again, saying: 'I do not understand anything about money. A print of mine sold a few weeks ago for $2,300 and now it sold again for $4,000. The world is mad.' He kept most of his paintings. 'I am not interested in selling, money means nothing to me now.'

While we were talking he had started a large drawing of me. With rapid fluent strokes he achieved a great likeness, his eye constantly moving from page to sitter, like a bird picking some grains.

'I never think that I am technically accomplished at all. In fact some people have said: "You must be able to do things easily." I have never found it easy. For every drawing that looks as though it was done easily there are probably eight drawings in a drawer where you just got it wrong. You know the great line artists, Matisse or Picasso, in that sort of Ingres style, spent a day groping around with their charcoal to be able to reduce it to two or three lines. I notice that every time I have spent a month drawing like that I draw quicker. It is much more accurate about your feelings.'

He had finished my portrait and looked at it, closing his eyes to a pencil line. 'It's fine, sometimes it works.' I mentioned that it really looked like me. 'Well if you are making a portrait, it should have a likeness, not necessarily just of the surface. You also want to look into somebody and find things about their personality and character.'

Gregory took up his position. 'I like to draw the same people over and over again. I do not want to have to struggle for a likeness and if you are drawing people you know well you do not have to do that, the likeness just seems to come.' He did four drawings of Gregory in quick succession, working with great calm and precision. His degree of concentration was astonishing.

We spent Thanksgiving together and David presented me with a wonderful head he had cut out of a pumpkin. There were many people. At night when the house had reverted back to silence David and I swam in the pool. I thought how fortunate I was in my job, to combine all those pleasures of friendship with my profession. I thought about the many grey people who have to spend their entire life in grey offices and wondered what I had done to be so lucky.

We sat on the edge of the pool in the still warm Californian night and spoke about the relativity of success. 'There is a superficial success that people might be taken in by,' said David with his usual modesty, 'but in a way I do not consider myself a successful artist. I mean one struggles to do something better. There is a kind of temporary popularity. People come and people go.' He got up and put on a record by Mozart. 'These are the real popular artists, Mozart and Beethoven, because in another hundred years people will still be listening to their music.'

The next day David took me to the studio he had wisely taken on Santa Monica Boulevard, away from the constant interruptions which were part of his life. He was working on large canvases of a rich and evocative freshness which gave out a sense of vibrant energy. There was colour everywhere. On the wall a very large painting of the boulevard just outside, full of hustlers, boys in jeans and sneakers hitching a lift, rent boys totally undisturbed by the old ladies with shopping bags. 'I like the idea that this is just going on outside, while I catch it inside.' The painting was a kind of collage of all these scenes. He suggested we film some of them, and it being Hollywood and everybody wanting to be in the movies, the hustlers did not mind a bit. Later David invited them into the studio for a cup of what he called 'charladies' tea'. He showed them large paintings he had done of the drag queen, Divine, and one of Christopher Isherwood and Don Bachardy, which they loved. 'The large painting is a bit of a mess but I don't mind spending two or three years on it really, the longer I work on it the more I alter it. Sometimes the more I work the worse they get, you can kill a painting or it just dies off. But you can bring them back to life again.'

I spent my last day in Los Angeles with him alone – Gregory and his friends had gone to the beach. We sat on the veranda and I took a couple of photographs of David, while we were talking about the past and about our friends in London, about Prunella Clough, Patrick Procktor and Mario Dubsky, but mostly about Keith Vaughan. Like most of us David was much saddened by his death. We contemplated a while about the future, his and mine. 'I don't plan too much ahead, I assume as you go through life that certain things take care of themselves. As disillusion sets in obviously it will occur in the work. And I suppose over the years I withdraw a bit more because you think it is all a bit too mad or fussy and I have always felt a bit out of step with the world in a way. I never quite understood its desire for destructiveness.'

Suddenly David got up and fished a drawing out of a drawer marked 'finished works'. 'I want you to have this as a souvenir of a few blissful days.' He had already signed it, 'For Peter from David, Hollywood October 1980'.

23

Soldier's Tale

1981

In 1981, I was again working with actors. Michael Vyner, the director of the London Sinfonietta, had asked me to stage *The Soldier's Tale* in the Festival Hall for the centenary of Stravinsky's birth. It was to be given on a concert platform, so it had to be very simple and cost as little as possible. *The Soldier's Tale* was written for a strolling theatre company. I decided therefore that the audience should watch the actors setting up the small stage and changing into their costumes in front of their eyes. The orchestra should also be in costumes and in full view during the performance.

As I wanted to place the action in Russia at the turn of the century, I contacted Covent Garden and the English National Opera in the hope of borrowing costumes from existing productions. I combed through the costume vaults and settled for Napoleonic uniforms for the orchestra from the ENO production of *War and Peace*; I also borrowed their cart from *Cavalleria Rusticana*. I did not care much for the existing English translation of the Ramuz text, and I wrote my own version.

Peter Gill put me in touch with two enthusiastic young men, who were beginning to make theatre, Declan Donellan and his friend Nick Ormerod. I engaged Declan as my assistant and Nick to do the sets. I wanted it to resemble the drawings in a Russian children's book. A photograph of Jean Babilée in a tattered uniform in the same role hung in my office, and I modelled my soldier on him. I cast the dancer Wayne Sleep. He had the right charisma and was eager to broaden his acting experience. For the narrator I wanted to use Alan Bates, but alas as so often before, he was not free, so I chose Alec McCowen. For the devil I engaged Murray Melvin, an actor I had long admired.

For the first read-through we met in my house in Earls Terrace. I had made no bones about my lack of experience with actors. Wayne was very eager to accept direction, but Murray's performance was already all there, and not in a way I wanted it. McCowen took an instant dislike to me. The next day his agent phoned me to say that his client would only read the text but not learn it. This was out of the question. I had one of my famous rows. I knew that I had to stand my ground. Rehearsal time was very short

Murray Melvin and Wayne Sleep in *The Soldier's Tale* (TV version)

and the idea of recasting at such short notice was daunting. The information that the performance had been sold out for weeks did not help to calm my nerves.

McCowen did not show up for the first rehearsal at the Old Vic. I tried to remain calm. I rehearsed alone with Wayne and Murray. Declan was very supportive and suggested Gordon Jackson. Jackson had just finished *Upstairs Downstairs* and was willing to do it. It was an inspired decision for all of us. He was charming, very professional and easy to work with. Wayne proposed Jennifer Jackson as the ballerina, a choice I gladly accepted, and Wayne also choreographed the dance sequence. We had exactly seven days and everybody worked flat out, doing several things at once.

One day before the opening we were finally able to rehearse on the stage of the Queen Elizabeth Hall. Nothing seemed to work and the set was still a shambles, but I was pleased with the actors. Murray Melvin played a lanky, sardonic devil with great flourish, while Wayne had found the right balance between ebullience and vulnerability. When we watched Wayne and Jennifer dancing in the empty rehearsal room with just the sun filtering through the windows, Murray muttered: 'Look at these children of God.'

Then came the day of the performance. In the morning we were still rehearsing. At lunch I dismissed the actors and the musicians. Declan and I tried to sleep for half an hour, lying on the stage.

By six o'clock the actors were coming back. Everybody's nerves were on edge. I took my seat between Bruce Chatwin and Facundo. I nervously looked around the hall, and saw the faces of many friends and colleagues. 'O God,' I thought, 'what have I let myself in for?' More than anybody else I did not want to let them down. There were my friends, Prunella, Hanna and Rudolf, Patrick Woodcock, and Elisabeth Bergner – 'Merde Darling,' she had written on a little note – and Valerie and Georg Solti with their daughters. I spotted Humphrey and Christina Burton, Gloria and Michael Birkett, Tony Richardson, Desmond and Jenny Page.

As the stage has no back doors all the entrances had to be done through the auditorium. The stage was totally empty. Suddenly the doors flung open and David Atherton in a fetching cossack's uniform marched in, followed by the seven noisy players in bottle-green coats and cocked hats, acting drunk. They carried their instruments and music stands. Their entrance provoked a first round of applause. The arrival of the cart, drawn by the actors in large army coats, brought more applause. I knew that the success of the opening depended on the actors, the curiosity they were able to evoke and the surprise each unpacked prop produced. For the next ten minutes the audience watched like children, the actors setting up the little stage, stringing up the curtain and putting on their makeup. From time to time the little band struck up a few notes. The lack of preparation time and the necessity to improvise gave the whole undertaking an edge. It worked. I could see the general cheerfulness on the stage transmitting itself to the audience.

Then David Atherton stood up, the orchestra struck the famous first chord and Wayne was off. 'Down a dusty country road walks the soldier with his load.'

During the entire performance I sat very stiff, my palms getting moist clutching Facundo's hand. Outwardly I remained calm, even when one of the tables came crashing down, or when the voice of the wardrobe mistress could be heard up to the tenth row, whispering: 'Where are the fucking beads?'

Suddenly it was all over. Shouts of bravo and thunderous applause. I stumbled to the stage. It was the first time that I took a bow. It was like a dream.

The evening ended with all the paraphernalia of an opening night. After the many friends who had lent me pieces for my décor had collected them again from the stage – Hanna her beads, Joseph Rykwert his lectern – we gathered for an after-theatre dinner. I was elated. It seemed to be so much more real and rewarding than any television programme I had ever made. Maybe because it had real sweat.

The next day the reviews were full of praise. 'The most convincing production of the *Tale* that I have yet seen,' wrote the music critic of the *Telegraph*. 'It was just out of this world,' wrote the *Guardian*. Every single paper gave it the thumbs-up. There were many telegrams and letters. None pleased me more than Elisabeth Bergner's 'Bravo, I am very proud of you.'

Like all Berliners I was crazy for *Die Bergner*, one of the truly great German actresses. Totally incorruptible and a stern critic, she always spoke her mind, so a compliment from her was precious to me. Her praise came sparingly and was always to the point.

Forty years earlier I had sent her a fan letter. She had come back to Berlin, the place of her greatest triumph, to read from Schnitzler's *Fräulein Else* in the Titania Palast. In London in the late 1970s we had become friends.

Her official age was eighty-one – like Lenya she had lost a few years somewhere. A small and still incredibly young-looking woman with the figure of a young girl, Elisabeth was fascinating in every aspect. She was what the Germans call *klug*, a strange mixture of wisdom and innocence. She also possessed the rare quality of lending some sense to the life of others.

Wayne Sleep, Jennifer Jackson, PA, Ben Kingsley, David Atherton, Murray Melvin

With Ben Kingsley

She saw everything, read everything and knew most things. She often spent the whole night reading when she could not sleep in her ice-cold room. She was all star and yet totally modest, she would never show off. Sometimes she would casually mention that Marianne Hoppe, Marlene Dietrich or Klaus Maria Brandauer had spent some time in her flat in Eaton Square. I too spent many instructive and rich hours there.

She was still acting, mostly now on German television, but each performance still carried her unique stamp. We shared many things, first of all Berlin and then a love for Rilke and the German Romantic poets. She sometimes read to me from Rilke's *Malte*, from Schnitzler or from Stefan Zweig's *Die Welt von Gestern*, the plight of the modern Jew:

> They were chased from their own country, but no one gave them a new one. They did not tell them where to live. They blamed them for everything and denied them the means of vengeance. And they began their flight with burning eyes. Why me? Why you? Why all of us? And nobody had the answer.

Her Austrian accent had now taken on a British tone. But the tremor in her voice was unmistakably Bergner's.

She liked to read from the Bible, which was one of her main sources of strength. She had a mystical streak, without any of the sentimental pretensions which sometimes go with it, as she was also totally worldly.

Nothing in my entire career had given me greater satisfaction than the staging of *The Soldier's Tale*. It was not its success – to achieve success and to know failure seemed to be, like so many things in life, straightforward – but directing actors was so life-enhancing. I began to regret that I had not done any of this before.

The following year I was asked to re-create the production for television. As Gordon Jackson was not free, I asked Ben Kingsley to take the role of the narrator. Kingsley had just finished the Gandhi film and his hair was shorn, which suited the part very well. I had more money and more time at my disposal. It was a more elaborate affair, and as so often with a larger production came larger problems. Somehow the amicable and close co-operation that had marked the stage production was replaced by artistic tantrums.

Hans Werner Henze had come to London to present his new piece *Autumnio*. It was dedicated to me. 'From one autumn-leaf sweeper to another'[1] he had written in my score.

---

1   'Von einem Herbstlaubfeger zu dem anderen.'

But there was not much time to rest on my laurels. The BBC had accepted my proposal to make a series on great photographers.

24
Master Photographers
1982–1983

The next year was mostly occupied with the making of the *Master Photographers* series, happy months during which I immersed myself in the history of photography. I have always been interested in photography and counted a few professional photographers among my friends – Bill King, Robert Mapplethorpe, Helmut Newton and his wife June.

Unlike the great painters, most great photographers had been protected from the attention of the media. Photography as a collectors' item and as the subject for popular books or large exhibitions was still in its infancy, although some of the more fashionable photographers such as Richard Avedon or Irving Penn were more widely known.

The Newtons also had a small farmhouse in the middle of the vineyards near St Tropez. It was a happy house furnished irreverential with furniture made of cardboard. Despite a stream of glamorous guests, their life was simple, filled with music, laughter and delicious dinners, which Helmut prepared on a barbecue.

Like so many refugees from Germany, Helmut was interned in Australia where he met June, who was an actress. In 1956 they had come to London to work for *Vogue*. He soon became internationally famous, but London was not to his liking and they settled in Paris. I often watched him photographing his models on the beach of the Club 55 in St Tropez, a superior meat market where the smart and beautiful people display the latest fashion and their tanned bodies. He was like a hunter with his camera and one could see that he enjoyed with an almost perverse voyeuristic pleasure the effects he was achieving. To this day he carries in his luggage two accessories: a monocle and a garter to lend any scene a touch of decadence.

The highly charged erotic settings of his pictures, so akin to film, have for a long time had a strange fascination for me, although the violence they sometimes express frightens me. But in his compulsive and often cruel homage to women is much beauty, surprise and honesty. Helmut loves women and he loves them rich and nude. 'It is a world I know well and I feel at home in,' he once told me, 'so why bother to search any further?' Most of his sitters belong to the world of fashion, society and the cinema. He makes them play a role which unmasks their own cynicism.

Helmut and June are a most unusual couple, whose marriage survives a bewildering palette of differences; Helmut, always out to shock, is provocative and very funny, June is wise, intelligent and peace-making. They are devoted to each other, although Helmut will say the most horrible things about her just to tease. It is easy to mistake his ruthless honesty for rudeness. Helmut Newton is not the cynical male his pictures suggest, although he likes to appear that way. Underneath is a very funny Berliner, deliciously vulgar, earthy and elegant.

When I met the Newtons, June was not yet the evocative and sensitive portraitist she would become under the name Alice Springs. 'One photographer is enough in the family,' she used to say. But she had begun to experiment on her friends, and I was one of them.

I would have liked to make a film on Helmut Newton, but as he was still young I thought this could wait for a later date, and I chose first six photographers all in their seventies or eighties.

The choice of the six was not easy. The first approach to people is often cumbersome, time-consuming and filled with embarrassment. I wanted Brassaï. Mme Brassaï was very protective of him and I never got anywhere. The whole saga dragged on for months, then he had a stroke and his face was deformed. I could no longer get myself to ask him to appear in front of a camera just for the sake of a television programme.

Cartier-Bresson, despite our various amicable meetings, only offered his voice. 'I have never allowed anybody to film me, it would finish the anonymity that I need for my work. I am sure you will understand.' I had an animated conversation with Berenice Abbott. I had phoned her several time in Maine, where she lived. She had photographed Eileen Gray in 1926, but was horrified at the idea of facing the camera. She finally wrote me a letter: 'I throw indeed my hands up in horror, the answer unequivocally is no, but thank you.' Irving Penn wrote: ' I cannot imagine myself in a film.' Richard Avedon was too busy. It was disappointing, but I also thought how nice it was to see people actually resisting the media.

I finally aimed at Jacques-Henri Lartigue, Bill Brandt, André Kertész, Alfred Eisenstaedt. For the last two programmes I kept my options open and decided to visit Horst, Yusuf Karsh, Ansel Adams and Andreas Feininger before making a choice.

In October I flew to the States to meet Horst, who had invited me to visit him on Long Island. I always liked his work, especially from the 1930s when he lived in Paris and New York. He had gone to Paris to study archi-

PA, by Alice Springs

tecture with Le Corbusier and was soon taken under the wing of the Russian Baron George Hoyningen-Huene, a friend of Cecil Beaton's and the principal photographer of *Vogue*. Huene photographed the delectably handsome young German in the nude, riding a marble horse on the roof of the *Vogue* studio, and opened the doors to the *beau monde* for him. Horst gave up his career as an architect and soon photographed everybody: Gertrude Stein, Colette, Dali, Marie-Laure de Noailles, Janet Flanner, Louise de Vilmorin and Gertrude Lawrence.

He moved to New York, producing stylish fashion photographs in theatrical settings making women look like Greek statues in white draperies by Balenciaga or Lucien Lelong. One of his most famous photographs was an advertisement for a corset with the back of a beautiful woman. A print of this hung in Bill King's apartment.

Horst always meant style, glamour, exclusivity; much of it was still evident in the small, handsome man who received me in an Austrian outfit that looked exotic in his Long Island surroundings. The house was filled with the paraphernalia of a charmed and rich life; a collection of antique silver boxes, 'a present from Coco Chanel', drawings by Cocteau, 'from dear Jean', and photographs in silver frames with personal dedications bearing the signatures of the rich, the famous and the beautiful from Noël Coward to Paloma Picasso.

The interview, when we got around to filming, yielded many stunning photographs and many anecdotes. He showed us photographs of a sensuous and aristocratic-looking twenty-eight-year-old Luchino Visconti. 'We led separate lives but our relationship was very mysterious, the ties between us were very deep,' he proudly confided. There were many stories about his friends Coco Chanel and Joan Crawford, who wanted to be photographed 'with a lighting à la Dietrich', and about Dietrich, who 'wanted to have a "Sternberg" lighting'.

Undisturbed by the camera, Horst vividly recalled the dinner parties he gave for Marlene Dietrich, 'who was eyeing Jean Gabin through the mirror of her compact, pretending to powder her nose, while Garbo walked down the lawn to look for frogs'. Edith Sitwell had talked about Noël Coward as the 'dreadful Noël Coward' because he had considered her poetry-reading boring. It was all delicious gossip, but it was no more than that. I was disappointed. I had very little insight into the nature of his art. The decision about what to do with it was taken out of my hands. The publisher Alfred Knopf phoned to tell me that I was not allowed to broadcast the programme before the publication of Valentine Lawford's book, *Horst, His Work and His World*. So my film died on the cutting-room floor, a decision I now regret, because however light, it was a record of a time forever gone.

I did not fare much better with Yousuf Karsh, one of the great classic portrait photographers. I had flown to Ottawa to meet the man who had made portraits of practically everybody from Churchill to Eisenhower, from Picasso to Hemingway, and of course of Castro, Prince Charles and Mohammed Ali. A portrait by Karsh of Ottawa was the *ne plus ultra* for every famous man or woman in public life. Karsh photographed the 'men who make the world. To be "Karshed",' said a publicity handout, 'has been a sign of personal accomplishment for a third of the century.'

It was not difficult to warm to this animated Armenian, who picked me up at the station wearing an old-fashioned coat with a Persian lamb collar. Karsh lived in a grand hotel. Except for Nabokov, Virgil Thomson and an old uncle of mine, I had never known anybody who lived in a hotel. He occupied a proper flat with dining-room, living-room and several bedrooms. He and his vivacious wife Estrellita, a doctor from New York, received me warmly and with great enthusiasm. After dinner we settled down to look at his work. Karsh called out the names of his sitters.

Shelf after shelf on wheels was pulled out by a willing assistant for my perusal. The faces of the famous, all dramatically and stunningly lit, photographs which revealed the obsession of a man with the perfection of printing. A formidable roll call: Chagall, with a wistful smile in front of a screen painted by himself; Albert Einstein, his beautiful hands folded as if in a prayer; the poet Robert Frost, one leg draped over a chair, his hand absently caressing a dog; Giacometti, melancholic, looking through his elongated sculpture, ignoring the butt of a cigarette that threatened to burn his fingers; Martha Graham, like a ghost or a vengeful angel. There were almost too many and too much of the same, and after a while all those staring eyes began to haunt me. They were pictures you wanted to look at one or two at a time, not hundreds. I feared the viewer too would soon tire of this barrage.

I did not film Karsh either. His publisher too did not allow us to do so. But I have never forgotten the uncanny file-past of the famous before me in a hotel in Ottawa.

There could be no bigger difference than between the world of Yousuf Karsh and that of André Kertész, the great Hungarian photographer, then eighty-eight years old. 'We all owe something to Kertész,' Cartier-Bresson had said and had called him his 'poetic wellspring'.

I met this gentle and softly-spoken man of steely energy in the flat he had lived in for the last thirty years. Had it not been for the New York skyline, visible through the vast windows, one could have been anywhere in Europe. One only had to step out onto the balcony from which Kertész still took his pictures to notice the rows of diminutive houses which reminded him of Montmartre. Paris was never far from his mind, a city he loved and that loved him in return. Overlooking a snowbound Washington Square, a view Kertész had photographed many times, the room was filled with memorabilia dating back to his childhood in Hungary and the happy years spent in Paris. Many little objects lined the shelves: a toy letterbox from the Austro-Hungarian monarchy rubbed shoulders with a porcelain owl picked up at the Marché aux Puces in Paris. On the wall a few photographs: Kertész as a soldier in the Great War, his portrait with his beloved wife Elizabeth, the half-face of a dark woman and a man's hand on her shoulder. There were also several colour Polaroid shots, Kertész's latest discovery.

The man who inhabited this world of almost childlike wonder received us visitors with great dignity and generosity. He was pleased to be the subject of a B B C film. 'The French government have offered me a flat and the British government is giving me a film. I am a happy man, what has the American government ever done for me?' he said. I did not contradict.

We spent much time browsing through his photographs and selecting the ones he wanted to speak about. Going through hundreds of boxes gave him much pleasure, like seeing old friends after a long separation. 'The blind musician, oh yes! I took it in 1921, there were many peasants who loved music in the Hungary of my childhood. Look at the expression on his face. If he were born in Paris, London or Berlin he might have become a first-rate musician. The Dôme in Montparnasse – it became my living quarters, I only went home to sleep.' Kertész had captured everyday life unfolding in sober and tender images. Brassaï said: 'André Kertész has two qualities that are essential for a great photographer: an insatiable curiosity about the world, about people and about life, and a precise sense of form.'

'I am self-taught, why I take a picture this way I do not know, it just offered itself to me. Look, the eye is only a mechanical instrument like the lens, you don't see, you feel things,' he said while we were looking at the famous pictures of a white horse trotting along the Paris streets between two cars, or of a clochard washing his feet in the Seine, both taken in 1929. 'These are dreams, my dreams.'

Our conversation was interrupted by a Hungarian visitor who brought some Hungarian dish. Kertész was obviously delighted, then we continued. 'Ah la voilà Kiki, Kiki the model of Man Ray. She came to my show in the Gallery Le Sacre du Printemps. All the surrealists came too, and Paul Dermée wrote a poem for my catalogue I liked very much.

'Kertész
Eyes of a child whose every look is the finest,
Who sees the emperor naked when he is clothed in lies,
No setting up or tidying, no gimmickry or fakery,
Your technique is as genuine and incorruptible as your vision.'

Kertész spoke with fire and intensity, freely mixing French, English and German, all with a wonderful guttural Hungarian accent. But the softness of his voice and the occasional chuckle were deceptive. Underneath the modesty of the man lay the self-assurance of the artist who always knew, despite the world's indifference, the merit of his work.

He was persuaded in 1936 to go to America. This was the beginning of an unhappy and not very successful life. Caught by the war, he tried to make a living. He felt trapped and cheated. Kertész did not fit, and nowhere was that more obvious than when he took us for lunch to a small Hungarian restaurant, enthusiastically dashing in and out of the kitchen to produce some food. He had battled against America and still did. America had to take the blame for his rejection, his poverty, his loss of hearing. He was a proud man, who did not like to owe anything to anybody. Underneath the warm and polite exterior, I saw a man whose wounds would not heal. They lay only skin-deep and bitterness welled up frequently in unceasing, swirling tirades of reproaches. 'My sort of photography was not understood here. Here they only want technical perfection, anything done with feeling is rejected.'

When Edward Steichen mounted his important mammoth exhibition 'The Family of Man' in 1956, which toured the world and included the work of 273 photographers, there were none by Kertész. Helmut Gernsheim's standard work on creative photography, published in 1961, did not mention his name. He had simply been forgotten. Only in 1964, when he was seventy, after having lived and worked in New York for thirty years, did the Museum of Modern Art give him a show.

Much of Kertész's insatiable curiosity was still in evidence during the three days of filming and the many times afterwards when we met to discuss the making of the book *Kertész on Kertész*, which I wrote with him afterwards at the suggestion of Andreas Landshoff. I saw him for the last time in 1985. The book had just been published, and he was very pleased with the quality of his prints: 'almost as good as the originals,' he said, a great compliment from someone who still supervised his own printing.

Kertész was determined to take up the apartment the French government had offered him. He had prepared a small parcel of his early Paris prints as a present for me. We sat and looked at the little glass bust which stood in the window, reflecting the Manhattan skyline in the sinking sun. The little torso had a special place in his life. It reminded him of the shoulders and the neck of his wife Elizabeth. He just sat in his room and photographed the little bust catching the changing light and shadows. 'Everything that surrounds you can give you something,' he had said to me once. But he had also said: 'The best photographs are the ones I never took.'

'Eisie' was the nickname of Alfred Eisenstaedt, the irrepressible bantam-size photographer also known as the father of photojournalism, the man who invented the candid camera. At eighty-five he was still taking photographs for *Life*, working from a tiny office on the 24th floor of the Time-Life building in New York. No fewer than 92 covers of this famous magazine have carried one of his photographs and he has toured the world in over 2,500 assignments, a formidable testimony of events and people who have shaped the contemporary world.

The cold statistics say little about this man who began in Berlin before Hitler came to power, working for Associated Press. Whenever something important happened Eisenstaedt was there. He had photographed Thomas Mann receiving the Nobel Prize in 1929 and Gerhart Hauptmann walking on the beach in Hiddensee in 1931. He photographed Lion Feuchtwanger, Heinrich Mann and Carl Zuckmayer, sitting in the wings of a theatre, and Sergei Rachmaninov with Bruno Walter before a concert in Berlin in 1932. 'Very famous pictures, never repeated,' he said proudly.

Photojournalism was just starting and Eisenstaedt often developed the pictures in his hotel room in a little tank he travelled with. He pointed at the little object still sitting under a table. 'And we did not get much money either, not like today, when every second word is "how much?"'

'Eisie is as strong as an ox and as agile as a mountain goat,' Henry Luce, the chief editor of Time Inc. had said, and he was still living up to this statement. Only a little over five feet tall, his energy and determination were boundless. He led me into his small office with just room enough for the two of us. The crew had to remain outside and film us through the door.

All around us were hundreds of stacked yellow cardboard boxes, containing unique historical records. They were labelled in bold handwriting – 'Germany', 'Great Americans', 'Children', 'Musicians'. Undisturbed by our television cameras or the natural chaos of hundreds of thousands of pictures, he fished out at great speed about fifty photographs and without prompting began to talk. 'Nathan Milstein, Vladimir Horowitz and Gregor Piatigorski, relaxing in the interval of a concert in Berlin of 1932. You name it, I photographed them all, but I never was conceited. This was a work of love. This is the fifty-year-old Stravinsky, conducting in Berlin's Philharmonic Hall.'

Eisenstaedt had made a name for himself by sitting hidden among the musicians on the concert podium, the pockets of his tails reinforced to hold the heavy glass plates. 'Many people have asked me how it was possible to take so many pictures of famous players and conductors. The answer is quite simple. In those days there was no other photographer doing that sort of thing.' The open immodesty was refreshing and disarming.

'People told me that Bernard Shaw was very difficult and inaccessible, I was also told that he was a vegetarian so I bought him a bunch of bananas. He was very friendly and did everything I wanted, he even played the spinet or the piano. He typed on an old Smith Corona. I remember everything about him like yesterday, I even remember the house number – it was number 4.'

Remembering every name and date, every circumstance in the taking of photographs, his eyes lit up and his hands gesticulated. Jumping effortlessly from a ball in Berlin to some events during the last war, from the elegance of St Moritz to the poverty of Ethiopia, he painted a panorama of encounters and experiences. A natural actor and a cheerful clown, he relished his anecdotes, some of them hilarious, others grave. Two photographs of Goebbels, one smiling and one menacing: 'these are the eyes of hate, he had spotted me.' Marlene Dietrich in top hat and tails: 'I asked her to pose for me in the Hotel Adlon in 1929 a year after she had finished *The Blue Angel.* She had to stand very still because the exposure was always between half a second and a second. If someone moved I had to take the picture again.'

After three hours of filming with no sign of fatigue, we decided to get some air. Eisenstaedt took his camera along and shot a couple of pictures of people eating their lunch on the streets, a funny little tourist in town. 'I like to be unobtrusive. I am also shy. If you say you are from a magazine you are dead. I am motionless like a stone and click away, like I do with you now,' and as he looked at me, his camera at the height of his belt, he had taken a picture of me. After lunch he took out some of the best-known Eisenstaedt photographs, the ones which made his name. Millions knew the images but few knew the man who took them, like the skating waiter in St Moritz: 'My great prize picture. I just put a chair on the ice and asked him to skate by, focusing on the chair, one leg in the air, holding a drinks tray.' The v e Day in Times Square, a sailor kissing a girl. 'People tell me that when I am in heaven they will still remember this picture.' During the hours of our filming and later when we worked on the book

Eisenstaedt by Eisenstaedt, he proved to be one of the liveliest witnesses of our times I have ever encountered.

From the proud boasting and the ebullient talk of Eisenstaedt to the gaunt, non-committal modest integrity of Bill Brandt. Bill Brandt had never been filmed, the idea struck him as absurd. 'Nobody for a long time was interested in photographers. Now everybody is,' he said with an embarrassed smile. 'I never look at my own, I don't dislike them, I just never do.' He listened with great interest to my stories about the other photographers I had filmed so far, but was adamantly against facing the camera. He had written almost nothing about his own work and his re-fusal to talk about it was legendary. Still I would not give up. I never do.

Brandt was born in England, but both of his parents were of Russian descent and he had lived many years in Germany and Paris. The conversa-tion, joined by his wife Mona, was mostly in French. I thought how strange it was that almost all the great photographers had come from my part of the world. I was pleased, it made the contact easier.

I visited the Brandts three times, always for tea, which was taken in the warm and comfortable flat, a fire usually blazing in the Victorian fireplace. Brandt would speak little, he rather listened. Lawrence Durrell had said that 'Brandt uses the camera as an extension of the eye – the eye of a poet.' But Brandt would shake off all accolades with a nervous chuckle. Finally, aided by his persuasive wife and a *Stollen* that I had baked for him, the ice would slowly melt as he told me how he had photographed Magritte. 'When I arrived in his studio, Magritte was impatient and in a great hurry. I am very shy and on the floor was an apple. I thought this apple must be very important; he probably was painting it so I never went near the apple, I was so frightened to disturb it, and then in the end Margritte said: "What is this damn apple doing there?" and kicked it out of the way.' Raucous chuckling finished the story.

When I finally arrived with a crew he trembled with nervousness and his frailty was even more visible than on our previous meetings. It was a non-conversation. He patiently showed his work to the camera but said only a few words, his voice hardly audible. 'This was Halifax... absolutely extraordinary... a real dream town... I'd never seen anything like it...'

I tried to prompt, to coax him out of his reserve. 'Mr Brandt, this is a very composed photograph.' 'Yes, I was lucky to have such a good compo-sition. I did not change anything. It was like this.'

I pointed out that in most of his portraits the sitter is placed at the edge of the picture. 'Oh yes, it is true. Never in the centre.' 'You never noticed it?' 'No, funny.'

When I looked at my rushes, I was shocked at first. I had the feeling that I could never make a film out of this material. But then in the cutting room the miracle happened. I kept all the silences, the hesitations, the flickers of recognition in the eye and the film came to life, more direct, more moving than any of the others, even that of Kertész, the other poet in the series. Brandt just sat there, almost detached, outwardly calm, looking at the photographs I spread out. His hawk-like face, his frail frame, the trembling of his hands were accentuated by the lights. He would scrutinise every picture very slowly, adding a few words, almost inaudibly, as if not to banish the magic of a dream: 'The Maids running a bath. Oh yes yes yes, the way the maids were dressed then. These funny caps. It's again one of those photographs I didn't really take. Anybody could have taken this picture, it was all there.'

The film ended with his voice almost dying away. Brandt was holding up the last photographs, a picture of great simplicity and great sureness: 'This is Avebury. It was in November and suddenly the sheep came over the hill. I took one picture. There is luck sometimes, one has to have luck to be able to take such a picture in the twilight on the Moors.'

I flew once more to the States to film Andreas Feininger and Ansel Adams. Bill King had suggested both. Feininger, the son of the painter Lyonel Feininger and his Swedish wife Wysse, lived an hour's drive from New York in a modern country house on top of a beautiful lake. Everything was in spartan order, two of his father's paintings hung on the wall and a basket of fresh apples stood on the scrubbed table. The interior was the reflection of the friendly but very earnest photographer, who had made a name through his experimental photography. He was one of the first photographers to work with telescopic lenses and was at present working on extreme closeup of very small objects.

After a very Scandinavian meal with delicious and very healthy food we walked through the dark forest. Feininger talked about his unshakable belief in the capacity of the camera to enrich people's way of seeing. He bent down to pick up a small stone, which his camera would later scrutinise in order to achieve new perspectives and new visual pattern.

The Feininger programme turned out to be a stimulating and fascinating lecture on nature and the camera's ability to reveal patterns in a way the eye can never do. 'The camera can show you more than what you see with the naked eye.' He is holding up a skull and then the enlarged picture of it. 'The photo shows you the structure of the skull, the braces that reinforce the joints. You see the way nature has constructed the skull and we can only see it now, but the idea of the skull has been around for a million years.'

The interview with the last subject, America's most revered photographer, Ansel Adams, was a very American affair. Unlike the other master photographers, Adams maintained a large staff with assistants, a secretary and a PR lady. I had travelled from San Francisco to Carmel where Adams lived in a house right at the edge of the ocean. An assistant picked out thirty photographs Adams had chosen for me, from large specially made black boxes with tidy labels. Another assistant wrote down each title and date. They were in mint condition, so totally different from the battered ones Eisenstaedt had shown me.

Ansel Adams cheerfully accepted my request to film him while taking a photograph. He arrived on the beach with a large straw hat and watched his assistants setting up the camera, every inch a master photographer. The assistants also took several shots with a Polaroid camera, showing the result to the master. The camera was re-positioned several times without Adams looking through it. Then one of the Polaroids met with his approval and he looked through the big camera. An assistant pressed the button. An Ansel Adams picture had been taken.

Adams had also arranged a 'typical American beach party' for me with toasted marshmallows roasted over an open fire. He was determined to please us in a straightforward unpretentious American way, a mixture of genuine joviality and cunning. The interview was done the next day, Adams proudly wearing some medals. 'They will like that sort of thing in England,' he said. He turned out to be a modest and astute talker. 'I have not taken the perfect picture yet,' he said; 'the best picture is around the corner – like prosperity.'

I had met Lartigue for the first time in 1981 and spent a day in his pretty house in Opio, in the South of France. The man Richard Avedon had called 'the most deceptively simple and most penetrating photographer in the art of photography' was a youthful eighty-eight-year-old, upright, of proud bearing and of timeless elegance. His sparkling eyes were those of a wicked schoolboy, enjoying someone slipping on a banana skin. He bubbled over with enthusiasm for everything; the garden, the light on the windowsill and the colourful socks I had brought as a present. There was also a great amount of gentleness and modesty about him. 'I never set out to be a photographer, I simply photographed the things I saw around me, the things that I loved, that excited me – beautiful elegant women, cars, airplanes.'

We were sitting on the terrace in the still warm autumn sun, talking about the many people he had known: Sacha Guitry and Kiki de Montparnasse, Cocteau spoon-fed by Picasso. I asked him about Picasso. 'Picasso was easy to photograph. He took no notice of me, a natural clown. He was a *copain* all right, but nobody really counted. I do not think he thought that I was an artist,' he replied without bitterness.

After the copious meal, prepared by his wife Florette, we climbed to the attic, for Lartigue was more interested in showing me his paintings than his photographs. We spent the rest of the day in his studio, looking at his large and colourful paintings. 'I paint the things I cannot photograph. Painting is a far more profound game than photographing, it comes from within me; photography comes from the outside.' He had seated me like an art collector in a large and comfortable chair, while Mme Lartigue took painting after painting from neat racks.

Two months later, we met again in Paris. He was photographing the dancer Ghislaine Tesmar for French *Vogue*. Lartigue sat on the floor, wearing jeans and espadrilles. In a little basket he carried his only camera. The dancer turned in front of a white background, an old-fashioned fan blowing her dress in the air. There was only one assistant, no special lights. In ten minutes it was all over.

The next day we filmed Lartigue in his flat. He was wearing a colourful sweater, every hair in place. He had seated himself underneath a large canvas of one of his flower paintings; it filled the entire background. From the museum at the Grand Palais, where his work is now kept, I had obtained his famous albums, large green folios in which for almost eighty years he had stuck his photographs, every single one labelled and dated as in an ordinary family album. 'Me and Picasso', 'My first car', 'Auteuil', 'First woman in trousers'.

All the famous photographs were there, the girl dancing down the stairs, the man in a striped bathing suit diving into the river, the ladies of the Bois de Boulogne, the women with their cigarettes, his first wife photographed sitting on the lavatory. Turning the pages he recognised them as old friends. 'All I did was to record my passions, to catch the fleeting time, to make it stand still for a moment.' A record of a century, of a time gone forever, preserved by a man whose sole aim was to capture the most enchanting moments of his life. 'I am like a good housewife, who gathers the fruit of the season and preserves it in a jar, but then I never look at it again. I rather go to the market to buy fresh fruit. I must have had a good fairy at my cradle, but I looked after her gifts like a gardener looks after his plants.' There was very little nostalgia in Lartigue. 'The elegance of the past is gone, two wars and the jealousy of people has seen to that, the world was much smaller then and there were less people, but when I can go to New York in six hours that is exciting too. Every time and every place has its merits as long as you know how to profit from it.'

Jacques-Henri Lartigue

Lartigue took his first photograph when he was six years old; at eighty-eight he was still photographing. 'I no longer photograph cars and airplanes; they have become vulgar, but I would not mind photographing those things that fly to the moon.' I had also brought some of his early cameras from the museum. Shrieks of delight greeted the old Blocknote camera Lartigue had last used in 1904, and the more sophisticated Kodak. There was even an unopened pack of glass negatives. As a sign of appreciation for this surprise, he pulled a minuscule album off a shelf. 'Les essais photographiques de Jacques' it said on it, in old-fashioned handwriting. 'This is something very rare and very special: *le cahier de maman*. I was five or six years old, and mother stuck all my early photographs in an album. You noticed we did not call them photographs, but "photographic try-outs".' Lartigue's first photograph was a group picture of his family, the portrait of a bourgeois French family, as one can find in many family albums. There was also his second photograph, taken at age six, a loving portrait of his father holding his mother in a protective gesture. The picture has faded but its poignancy, character and charm were undeniable. 'Where is your eye,' I asked him, 'in your head, in your soul?' '*Dans mon ventre et dans mon cœur*,' came the proud answer.

25
Taking Stock

The last three years have been good years, with *Hockney, Soldier's Tale, Albee* and *Master Photographers*. Reading through the daily diaries, I realise how much the landscape of my life had begun to change: so much quest, ambition and fulfilment. Nobody could have guessed twenty years before, least of all myself, that I would one day be making programmes, directing on stage, trying to become a writer, and yet my professional development seemed to have followed a logical, inevitable pattern, as if traced by someone else. It was based on my belief in people's capacity to do the most unusual things if they wanted to, a belief that came from my roots and my background. Each artist has inside himself a source which nourishes his life, everything he does and is. My source, I know, is in my childhood and adolescence. My education, my sensibilities, my marginality, all came from the place and circumstances of my youth, times when the roads were traced, and they pointed at the things I would do later. Destiny is maybe too big a word for it, but it sometimes felt like it. I seemed to be unable to interrupt the flow of events, as if life's design were made by others.

As always when things were going too smoothly, I thought it was time to take stock. The discrepancy between my inner and outer lives was still as strong as ever. I often looked with amazement at the smooth operator, the amusing and popular guest at smart dinner tables. Could this be the same person who so often felt alone with a strong longing for tranquillity or even death, the person capable of intense feelings, even passion and outrage?

A life marked by exciting adventures through travel and new encounters included also many arrivals, partings and leave-takings. There were new acquaintances and new constellations of friendship, but making friends became more difficult. My circle was simply too wide. My ever-changing lifestyle and job did not make for stability. With some, it did not matter if I saw them continuously or not, one quickly picked up dropped threads. But to sustain friendship is hard work and a serious business, like attending to a lovely garden. 'Friends drop in and out of your life,' Facundo accused me when I had neglected Ingrid Bergman. The next day I found out that she had died during that night.

There were people I wanted to be closer to but never dared to, like Peter Gill for instance, one of the most inventive and sensitive people working on the English stage, or my trusting and indispensable friend, the writer Mary Blume, who worked for the *Herald Tribune* in Paris, too far away to see her often. As usual I was attracted by the shy and withdrawn, so opposite to my own temperament: vulnerability is one of the most attractive qualities.

My love for Facundo ran like a red thread through it all – always present, miraculously surviving the constant fights and misunderstandings, a relationship from which I was never able to free myself, in which I could never steer my feelings into quieter waters. Our relationship was constantly changing. There was a time when we were lovers, then a time when we became a couple or a family, but the time of fewer outbursts or peaks was still far away. I thought of that love that had germinated in me for all those years and I tried to understand this feeling that had grown until it became almost the only thing that mattered beside my work. 'The year is over,' I wrote in my diary. 'It is terrible to belong so deeply to one person.'

In 1982, I experienced illness for the first time. I had caught hepatitis and was at home for nearly two months. The ensuing weakness and the helplessness made me weep. I had no reason to feel alone or starved of affection. I was spoiled as usual. I was surrounded by loving, protective, sometimes over-protective friends, and they were always welcome. There were many visitors. I realised, almost embarrassed, how many people had been waiting in the wings for me to be ill to show their feelings. I felt less lonely in their company, but also more doomed. I had never been ill before and the dependency on other people was disconcerting. Yet I was sometimes afraid of being alone, and the crumpled sheets of my bed seemed like a haven in the yet unformulated future.

I was still battling with passing time. The sadness of watching people growing old alone, of seeing them in the shops buying one steak, was an image that frightened me. I had not yet reached the point when ageing meant stronger definition of one's goals, that happy resignation to the larger issue, death – 'A life so flat that one could see the tombstone at the other end,' I read in a Victorian novel.

The fear of ageing has always been patronisingly attributed to women as a sign of immaturity and misplaced vanity, as if men never look in the mirror and see their sagging eyes and bulging shapes. The mirror I had for so long considered a friend had become an enemy. What happened to that smug image of myself, that self-satisfied look, which, however silly, was a loyal ally? It might have been repulsive to others, it was not to me. These

 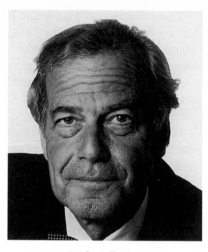

PA, by Tobias   PA, by Bill King

were experiences most people live through, and the preoccupation with art should have prepared us better for it. No Rembrandt self-portrait or the reading of *Lear* will steel us, when it begins to knock at our door. Some shrug them off, some cope, I found it hard. I was too honest with myself. I might pretend to others, not to myself. Ageing for me still meant mostly a reduction with little gain. I had often told myself that age would not make much difference, that it was silly to worry about something so superficial. But then when so many doors began to close on a whole life of physical prowess and conquest I was not prepared for the shock.

I thought about the image I presented to the world, the dancing clown, the amiable charmer, and wondered how many people knew or even suspected that I could cry. I was still promiscuous, always seeking 'the good orgasm' as Norman Mailer called it. But it was harder to score. The act of lovemaking had for so long been central to my life. It had been the access to so many minds and hearts and opened up many venues. It was the source of so much affirmation of the life force. Conquest was second nature to me, and when it began to slip it was a most shattering experience. It had partly to do with vanity and the fact that I was living with a much younger partner, but also with something much deeper, the loss of control. It was the increasing awareness of losing power and energy, of people averting their eyes, no longer to be able to command attention at will. I had always been sensitive to compliments and praise. I had been used to success, I knew about the gift of physical beauty, the exhilarating eye contact which did not necessarily lead to a conquest, but at least inspired some form of desire. I liked the power I had over people, the power to inspire desire, even love.

The search for the truth, however uncomfortable for myself, was always with me. 'Who am I?' There are always more layers to discover, to chisel away to come nearer to the kernel. Will I ever reach the last one that is my true self? Or are we condemned forever to descend, never to reach the truth?

Simone de Beauvoir's *La Force des choses*, a remorseless look at her life and the forlorn sense of lost time, struck a deep chord in me. So many moments gone beyond recall. 'Tournant un regard incrédule vers cette crédule adolescente, je mesure avec stupeur à quel point j'ai été flouée,'[1] she wrote. 'So much on the descending side of life,' I noted in my diary, 'almost everybody I meet now is younger. Still... still.' In that 'Still... still' lay the knowledge that neither our happiness nor our unhappiness is infinite, although they sometimes seem to be.

1 'As I turn an incredulous eye on that credulous girl, it stuns me to realise how much I have been cheated.'

Simone de Beauvoir's 'plus jamais' began to take on a menacing reality. I looked around my room and saw books I would no longer read, leafed through the pages of my address book and thought about the people I would no longer call, places I would no longer visit.

Solace came, as so often, not from friends, but from discovering oneself. Sadness loses its horror if one examines the circumstances that produce it. Sometimes I discovered things about myself through the writings of others. I read Karen Blixen's wise letters, written in the loneliness of her African existence. They spoke about a deep love for a person and for a country. Blixen, who prized her deep need for freedom above everything else and was willing to pay for it, made me understand that the need for greater freedom for oneself was also linked with the greater freedom I was willing to give to other people, especially to the one I loved.

I had almost forgotten the pleasure of reading without the purpose of making a television programme, wandering through my study, picking up books I never had time to read or books that just came my way, such as Doris Lessing's *The Golden Notebook*, which she had given to me after Jim's death. I plundered my library and read a strange assortment of books: the autobiography of Claud Cockburn, a new biography of Gertrude Stein and the story of Nancy Cunard's life. Musil's *Diaries and Essays* made me again plunge into his *Mann ohne Eigenschaften*, a book so dense with meaning that it made your mind spin. I discovered Janet Flanner's essays on Paris, a biography of Kipling, an author I hardly knew, and P. N. Furbank's masterly biography of E. M. Forster.

Lawrence Durrell, hearing that I was ill, sent me *Livia* and *Constance*, the second and third volumes of the series he called *Quincunx*. I found them a bit of a struggle, despite his note saying 'I hope the pattern is now starting to clarify the issue'. The elusive but faithful Bruce Chatwin appeared from somewhere and brought his novel *On the Black Hill*, the funny and often very moving account of a dependency of two brothers on each other and the land.

While I was lying in bed I thought for the first time that I should write down my early life, the story of a German boy with Jewish blood, who lived through the Nazi years, and survived. What I wanted to tell was not so much my own personal story, as the story of a whole generation, a generation on the move.

There were many accounts of butchers and of victims, but very little about the daily life of ordinary people, caught in the maelstrom of history. I wanted to talk about the horrors of normality and the ordinariness of evil, and show happiness can survive in adversity.

The presentation of the Nazi period in film and on television was a caricature of what really happened. Italo Calvino had pointed out that modern films are unable to evoke the historical density of this period because the experience that was once common property has gone from most people's minds. Maybe a television programme and a book from someone who lived it could help to redress this.

Alas, when in 1992 I published a book on the Art of the Third Reich, and made two films about it, I encountered the same prejudices. Book and films received a phenomenal amount of attention, even praise, but very little understanding. The view of Germany was still of black and white. I realised that no one who had not lived there during those twelve years of National Socialism will ever fully understand what happened and how.

What is my country? I do not like it when people take me for German, and yet I like German music, food, landscape, literature. I am glad to be English, without belonging. I guess my country is the country of the mind, an imaginary homeland made up of memories and friends. The word *Deutschland* will never be cleared of the sour taste it acquired for me during those twelve years. The English language has no word for *Heimat*; 'fatherland' or 'motherland' is not the same as *Heimat*, an all-embracing word which includes the landscape, the smell, the taste, the language and the customs.

I never really understand people with a strong national identity, although I always loved the story of how Eric Satie, when asked if he was French, replied: 'How can a man of my age not be French?' I like living in a foreign country; many of my closest friends do. Hans Werner Henze and my sister Renate live in Italy; Facundo is an immigrant from Argentina; Hanna and Rudolf have come to England from Germany. Most of my English friends, on the other hand, have never left their own country, they speak the same language, follow the same traditions, were born in the same city where they probably will one day die. They seem to have had only one life. I have lived in Germany, France, America, England. It sometimes feels as if I have lived several lives, inhabited many cultures, dreamed in and spoken several languages, and yet still belong nowhere and am a stranger everywhere. This suits me fine.

The loss of one's mother tongue is a strange phenomenon. I speak three languages, fairly fluently. I do enjoy what George Steiner called the 'riotous unabashed delight in languages as a global playground' and once one has been an exile one can always do it again. I know much of Shakespeare, I can recite Paul Valéry in French, but it will never be the same miraculous shiver of pleasure as when I stumble upon a line by Hölderlin or Goethe.

I miss the German language with its uninhibited power to express feelings (so suspect to the English), and I do admire the French capacity to exchange ideas, to receive impulses and to transform them, making them their own.

I sometimes ask myself why I live in England. There are other places which I find more stimulating, more open-minded, but I love the English with their inbuilt respect for each other, often the result of indifference or lack of curiosity rather than anything else. I like their capacity to mock and to deflate, their lack of ostentation in dress and manners. I feel well here, I like the way my friends live. Life in England has a certain texture, a mixture of comfort and shabbiness.

In the eighties my love affair with England began to wilt. Nostalgia and obsession with class was still the official ideology. But behind the theme park for tourists with the changing of the guard and a nobility with country houses set in Arcadian England lay the corridors of power clogged with public-school boys and drugged-up aristocrats. It became increasingly a country caught in a restless and insatiable desire for riches.

I was fully aware of the privilege of having been brought up in comfortable middle-class surroundings, however hard the circumstances of war and the ensuing deprivations, but we were brought up with a sense of responsibility towards our fellow men, with the belief that the strong must look after the weak, the rich after the poor. Now the great respect and passion the English had for their fellow men began to be replaced by something which soon would be identified as 'greed'. Real education was becoming less important than drive; getting on, smartness and acquisitiveness were considered higher assets. The mounting inequality, the soft cruelty of those with money in their richly upholstered lives, the complacency of those in power, the corrupting grabbing, became a way of life.

Not all of this was immediately apparent. The Yuppies had not yet arrived with their loud striped shirts and their red braces, with their pretensions and their wives with little handbags hanging from gold chains, all as interchangeable as their B M Ws or their coats with padded shoulders. Mrs Thatcher had not yet taken her most absurd stances, but the new mood was gradually seeping in, eroding many things I had loved about this country. It was only the beginning of a profound change.

I have always followed English politics with detachment. None of the causes here seemed to have the same urgency as those which had changed history: Hitler's Germany, the communism of postwar years and the 1968 'revolutions' in Germany and France. Then came the Falklands war, and I was pushed out of my cosy liberalism. Facundo of course was born in Argentina, but even without him I would have been against it. I was against war of any kind. I foolishly believed that after the last war civilised nations would be able to solve disputes without killing. To see such jingoism was quite disgusting. People had lost all reason. Pictures on television of cheering crowds sending the troops off to war was bad enough, the rows which I had with many friends were even more saddening. Some people tried to explain to me that Thatcher was doing what Chamberlain failed to do when he went to Munich. At a smart dinner party an ageing princess said: 'I wish I were young enough to go to war', and a famous actor, whom I had considered a friend, said: 'Peter will never understand, he is not even English.' Only a journalist from the *Evening Standard* voiced some objection to the senseless war. I got up and left, halfway through the meal.

Even the report of casualties did not temper the feeling of national pride. Quite reasonable people suddenly talked about a British holy war, a war to defend civilised values, and anybody who doubted it was looked upon as a traitor.

In some quarters Mrs Thatcher was seen as a saint, in others she was simply anathema. Everywhere people were fighting about the rights and wrongs of the Falklands war. The polarisation of Britain had begun. Thatcher had divided the nation. Not that the blame for everything which happened could be put at her feet. The nation was ready for it and many collaborated. The most amazing thing was to see how little time it took to change the fabric of a nation. People looked aghast when I told them that the time would come when they would hate her, and took me for a madman.

At work the decline of the B B C as the safeguard of culture continued. The grey men had also infiltrated here. Editors, organisers, management were driven by different motives. Everywhere we saw people propelled into responsible positions without the experience, creative strength, intellectual qualification, critical discernment and most of all the wisdom to lead. The top of the B B C was no longer driven by the same priorities as the bottom. When I joined, many of the top management – Huw Wheldon, Aubrey Singer, Stephen Hearst – had come from the Music and Arts Department. Now, more often than not, they came from Current Affairs, Light Entertainment and Sport, and that was where the money was spent.

I had a good and independent position and could practically do what I wanted, but all around me people became increasingly unhappy. A new management saw many of us as uncontrollable prima donnas whose freedom, in a world of increasing accountability, had to be curbed, supervised, controlled.

Bill Cotton, the new managing director, came to sort out the producers.

'Stop whingeing,' he shouted at a reputable producer after she had complained about falling standards. Many of the producers had become a nuisance to the management. 'The producer is king,' Humphrey Burton had announced when he had taken over the Music and Arts Department, for he knew that the BBC's reputation rested on their judgement, talent and taste. The weight of the corporation began to stifle our decisions. The informal meeting in small offices or the canteen was no longer the fertile ground for ideas and criticism; everything became increasingly organised from the top. People were boxed in, divided, left out. And when Una, the tea lady who twice a day for twenty years had knocked on everybody's door and who knew everybody by name, was replaced by a vending machine on the third floor, more than a quaint and much loved British custom was sold down the commercial road.

We suddenly saw the arrival of a new species: *the executive producer.* Their ponderous silliness and craving for position made creative life impossible. Our working lives became increasingly controlled, formalised and codified. The result was programmes without true authorship, without handwriting. Formula-ridden films made by committee.

It was no longer enough to make good programmes; they also had to bring in money. Popularity became more important than quality. Ratings dictated choice. The hunt for viewership had begun. In the search for trivia and high ratings, presentation triumphed over substance. Serious discussion or analysis was taken over by overvalued trash. Originality and innovation were pushed aside for the tried and tested.

Arena was now run by Alan Yentob. Alan was unpredictable and lively, and ideas had the tendency to run away with him, but his enthusiasm, entrepreneurial skill – combined with a craving for fame – pushed many projects along. *Arena* produced new talented film-makers: the dazzling Nigel Finch and the demure tease Antony Wall. Striking out boldly for new forms, they brought a formal inventiveness, lightness of touch and an uninhibited freshness to the Music and Arts programmes which was much needed. But the desire to make successful, popular, easy-to-digest programmes brought also new young people to the fore with instant formulae. The department was awash with hopeful new directors, rich in expectation, drunk on 'new ideas' and short on experience and sound knowledge of the arts. Many of them lacked the historical perspective and broad education of their elders. Flair was a more desirable commodity than knowledge. I looked at the new generation, their rapacious appetite of gain, their ruthlessness, their egoism, and wondered what had happened to the commitment of my generation with its dream of a better world. We were the children of suffering, genocide and terrible changes, but somehow we had been spared the information explosion. When I was young we lived in smaller circles, blissfully unaware of many happenings in the world. Now everybody's life was forever bound up with the destiny of the entire world, brought to them by television. There was a lot of talk about the need for change, but change for what? The new change, when it came, had more to do with fashion than with a profound shifting of ideas.

In an increasingly vituperative atmosphere, successful producers were sacked because their programmes were no longer fashionable. Serious and original documentary directors like the gentle Tristram Powell and Leslie Megahey were no longer in the ascendant and the rebellious Nigel Williams now spent more time writing plays than making programmes. The scoundrel and charmer Julian Jebb wrote book and opera reviews, to keep himself occupied. Others had left. Gavin Millar was now a full-time film critic and began to make his own films. Lorna Pegram decided to devote her life to writing. Producers moving on were not unusual – John Schlesinger, Ken Russell and others had all begun by making arts documentaries – but they were not pushed out, made obsolete.

When I began making programmes, I had free access to the Visnews film library and to one of the great picture libraries in this world, the Hulton. When I left, the BBC had sold both. It was more than two libraries that were lost to British television. It was the wantonly and callously dismantling of a living organisation we were once proud of. Why did we let it happen? We were not so disorganised, so inefficient, so wasteful as the perpetrators of this crime made the world believe.

The watering-down of substance did not happen all at once, but it began then and it has not stopped. What happened in the BBC only reflected a general trend. The politicians were full of reassuring platitudes and tired certainties and soon it affected newspapers, publishing and the arts in general. The barbarians were no longer just at the gate, they had invaded the town.

Italo Calvino's pessimism affected many of us. 'The end of the world has begun with us and shows no sign of ending.' From the 1980s things became intolerably bleak, annihilating all aspiration. Much that once was part of our life went, lost for ever, and we, in the constant changing of our civilisation, were trying desperately and forlorn to restore some meaning through our preoccupation with the arts.

I knew that the best way to get myself out of my black moods was to work, not just to do something I had done before but something new. My friend Andreas Landshoff had encouraged me to write down the life of Eileen Gray. Could I do this to Prunella, the most private person I knew? In writing about her aunt would I not automatically invade her life too? Prunella consented and sat patiently on my bed, telling me what she knew about her aunt. Eileen would not have approved of a book about her life. She was never tempted to write her own biography, and shied away from personal revelation. She did not like to look into the past, least of all into her own. Shortly before she died she burned almost all letters and notes that covered her personal life. The discretion she had manifested all her life prevented her from leaving any traces, except in her work. Only there did she want her passions and preoccupations to be read. She demanded no posthumous renown. She might have accepted a few words about her work, although she would have thought them 'unnecessary'.

My decision to write about her was not meant to betray a trust and a very special friendship but to dispel the rumours, numerous errors and speculation which had grown up around her name. The absence of almost any information about her personal life had made her into a kind of cult figure – a role she would have heartily rejected. She would have scolded me for writing the book, but she would not have prevented me from doing so.

To try to recount Eileen Gray's life was not an easy task. The span of it can be measured by the enormous changes that forged the century. When she was born Queen Victoria was on the throne and when she died man had flown to the moon. She had outlived most people's memories. Most of the protagonists had disappeared and could no longer be questioned. All I had to reanimate a life which was in the truest sense extraordinary were some notes, some letters, and the memories of our many conversations, most of them not meant for publication. A friend, not a public person, our conversations dealt with the banal happenings of daily life, such as replacing a blown fuse, rather than her thoughts about the Bauhaus. Questions that I realised now I should have asked were never put; in any case, being more interested in other people's lives she was not easily questioned. She was a reluctant and not always reliable witness. Faced with the frailty of recollection. I had to reinvent her past.

There were other more pressing worries. I had never written a book – scripts or articles were not the same thing – but I soon discovered the joy of writing. Nothing in my professional life had the same thrill as the intimate relationship between the writer and the page, when things suddenly emerged from somewhere and formed themselves into words and sentences. 'To gather up the scarlet threads of life and weave them into a pattern,' Bruce once said, quoting Dorian Gray.

Sometimes I could not wait to get to my typewriter, often writing in my head in the night, walking or just thinking. Of course I could not spend

Eileen Gray

much time on it; I still had a very time-consuming job to do. I longed for solitude, but at least my life took on another aspect.

I decided to buy a house. After spending a long time looking I bought Prunella's (she had found a large studio nearby) and I soon forgot the amenities of Earls Terrace in the euphoria of owning a place with my own front door and an old apple tree with a riot of white blossoms. The house was in Fulham, regarded as 'up-and-coming'. Prunella had bought it fifteen years before. Now the snobs had moved in and the local pub suddenly served Campari and the butcher offered braces of pheasants. No wonder she was eager to move away. I of course had no such qualms.

I love making houses and when it was all finished – the walls taken out, the ceiling lifted – I looked with pleasure and some pride at the result. I had become an architect by instinct. All good places are the extensions of the personality of their inhabitants. The two rooms which reflected most of mine were the study and the kitchen; it was there that my passions could be read. The walls of my library were almost entirely covered with books, but there was just enough room for some of my favourite paintings: *The Return of the Prodigal Son* by Keith Vaughan and the *Factory Girl* by Prunella Clough. I sat at a large respectable bureau plat with ormolu handles as faded as the brown leather that covered its top. There were ink spots everywhere, the colour of deep purple. I sometimes wondered if they were the accidents of my grandfather's quill or my father's mighty fountain pen. There was also a large and comfortable armchair, its tapestry cover braving the passing of time. It too dated from my grandparents' home. The room gave me the feeling of continuity, so essential for people without roots. I would sit in that pampered seclusion looking at the objects that summoned up my past, conjuring up glimpses of my childhood.

The cheerfulness of my kitchen was the exact opposite of the earnest character of my study. Not that it was less serious, but its seriousness was expressed in large Kilner jars, filled with olives, fruit in alcohol and fresh goat cheeses, macerating in olive oil from Le Mazet. Everywhere the vestiges of my mother's house: a battery of blue and white Meissen jars with *Reis, Kaffee, Zucker, Gries, Sago* in Gothic letters. It was an old-fashioned country kitchen, heated by an iron stove.

The gregarious collector of people and the loner still jostled and warred with each other, but my houses have also been places of solitude. I say that without bitterness or sense of loss. On the contrary, solitude has been something which has sustained me. I have often craved it with ferocity. It is something I have created myself, a comforting feeling, not a menacing one. Of course this is not easily obtained; it takes long practice. I am never alone during the day or when I am sitting at my desk. I am never alone in my houses. I am alone outside, in the streets, especially in restaurants.

In a life of shifting domiciles I had finally found the great good place – home – in the two countries I love best. My house in London is basically a house for myself – except for evening guests – while that in France is for my friends. There was always a stream of visitors contributing to the lofty-minded spirit of the place: Prunella, incapable of being idle, painted some shutters. In the ineffable tranquillity of the old stone walls of the guest-house, that once housed sheep, an amorous Hans Werner Henze composed a new work while wooing an enchanting and beautiful youth. A rollicking Peter Shaffer plotted a new play, and a springy Germaine Greer filled the house with poetry and scented geraniums, brought all the way from London. Sometimes Humphrey Burton and his wife Christina or Alan Yentob with his friend Philippa Walker tried – not always success-fully – to forget the strains of the BBC. The days were lit up by long meals and spirited conversations. Under the spell of the landscape, laid upon us, everybody seemed at once to relax and to expand.

There were also some changes in Facundo's life. Facundo had always been drawing, large colourful surrealist pencil drawings, and many friends had encouraged him to have an exhibition. He finally overcame his natural reluctance and agreed to show his work in public. His first show at the Caroline Corre Gallery in Paris and another one in Aix-en-Provence were a big success. He had also acted in a few more films, a film by Jean-Paul Rappenau, and Jacques Rivette asked him to appear in his *L'Amour par terre* with Geraldine Chaplin and Jane Birkin.

Facundo had become a formidably inventive actor of great depth and versatility. He liked the attention and the success, but remained totally unaffected by it. He had played very successfully the double title role in *The Venetian Twins* by Goldoni; I thought it his best performance so far. The director Jorge Lavelli, another Argentinian, had engaged him in one of Copi's disconcerting plays, *Madame Lucienne*. Facundo played the lead with Maria Casarès and Françoise Brion.

Copi had been a long-standing friend of the TSE. A fellow Argentinian, he also made a name for himself with his biting cartoons in the *Nouvel Observateur* and his bizarre and witty plays had caught the attention of the French theatre world. Like Alfredo Arias he became a cult figure, often performing in his own plays. A Copi performance was an event not to be missed. They were mostly monologues, often in drag. One was never quite sure if the evening would last three hours or one – an ad hoc decision by

Le Mazet

Facundo Bo in *Sortilèges*

the author after having finished a bottle of wine and his careful makeup.

As often as time permitted I went to Paris to watch Facundo rehearse or play, and sometimes the entire company came to live at Le Mazet while preparing a new production. The TSE had really become my family, which made me very happy.

From my Diary 1983
4 April: The first sharp warning of something dreadful to happen. Facundo is in love again, the person this time is called Silvain. 'You must not get too attached to people you love,' Hans tells me. How can I not? It is the best part of myself. Proust: 'C'est fini. Je renonce à jamais la voir. De l'état d'âme qui cette lointaine année là, n'avait pour moi, qu'une longue torture, rien ne subsistait. Car il y a dans ce monde où tout s'use, où tout périt, une chose qui tombe en ruine, qui se détruit encore plus complètement en laissant encore moins de vestiges que la beauté: c'est le chagrin.'[1]

27 May: I find a little note from Facundo under my pillow: 'Merci beaucoup pour des jours qui atteignent sinon la perfection, au moins des hauteurs que nous avons perdues ou négligées ou simplement oubliées.'[2]

16 June: Le Mazet. La nature, le calme, tout est parfait. Quel bonheur: la mer. Je nage des heures. Je suis seul mais content, au moins personne ne me fait mal, c'est déjà quelque chose. Le couple s'inscrit dans la durée. Un vrai couple sait mériter la joie de se voir l'un dans l'autre.[3]

Everywhere and over everything the impression of timelessness and space, the absence of hurry or constraint. An existence marked by the breathing of nature. When Facundo and I are in Le

---

1 'It's over. I will never see her again. Nothing remains of my feelings, which this past year have been in torment. In a world where everything wears out, everything dies, one thing that falls in ruins, which destroys itself even more completely and leaving behind even fewer vestiges than beauty, is pain.'

2 'Thank you for days which reached if not perfection, at least heights we have lost, neglected or simply forgotten.'

3 'Le Mazet, nature, silence, everything is perfect. What happiness: the sea. I swim for hours. I am alone but content, at least there is no one here to hurt me, which is something in itself. A couple proves itself in durability. A real couple knows how to deserve the joy of seeing themselves in each other.'

Mazet time does not exist. We go to bed when we feel like it and rise in the same way, usually in the early hours of the morning. The most beautiful thing to own is a piece of land.

26
Richard Strauss Remembered
1984

I always loved the evenings in Valerie and Georg Solti's house, especially when there were few guests. Holding his small daughters on his knee, the maestro would explain to them the plot of *Arabella* like the story of a fairy-tale. He spoke often about his youth and the time in Germany after the war. The Allied Forces had given him his first car, a clapped-out vehicle that allowed the young pianist to travel from Salzburg to Munich where he was making his name as a conductor. One night he told us about Strauss's funeral in 1949: 'I conducted, and it was the most moving experience of my life, not what I did, but because of how it happened.' One of Strauss's wishes was that his *Rosenkavalier Terzett* should be sung. Rummaging in some drawers Solti produced a small tape of the funeral rites. It was extraordinary to listen to the music and hear Solti making us live the scene again: 'One by one the singers broke down, not at the same time, but they began to cry and I went on playing with the orchestra without singing and then slowly they came back and we finished together. And Pauline was there, the famous Pauline, who was until that point strength itself, now crying and broken, and I think a few months later she was dead also. Couldn't live without Richard.'

That night, after dinner, I decided to embark on a project which excited me a lot: a film on Richard Strauss. I wanted the programme to be a journey into the world of the great composer. By speaking to people who had first-hand knowledge, people who had actually worked with him, I hoped to bring some of the composer back to life.

I travelled to Munich to meet the family and to search the archives for film material. The Strauss family had been profoundly wounded by Ken Russell's camp treatment of Strauss and the equation of Strauss and the Nazis. They broke with the B B C, vowing never to let them enter the house. I was surprised when they allowed me to come and see them in the Strauss villa in Garmisch.

He had been very much a family man, and he lived here most of his life with his wife, the singer Pauline de Ahna, and their only son Franz. It was still the family home, occupied by Strauss's daughter-in-law, Alice.

Alice Strauss was the daughter of a Jewish merchant from Vienna. A dignified, slightly shy woman of subdued elegance, she was the un-crowned head of a family which now consisted of the two sons Richard and Christian, their wives and numerous grandchildren. She acted for twenty-five years as the maestro's secretary and looked after the consider-able archive of photos and letters.

We took tea in front of the large window with the magnificent back-drop of the Bavarian Alps that Strauss so loved. 'The life of my father-in-law followed a regular pattern. At nine he came down to write – lunch at one, a short nap – and back at the desk until ten or eleven. He often said when he got stuck: "I will go to bed and the melody will be there."'

Alice Strauss spoke about the life in the Strauss household, but with the tone of a respectful, even fearful, daughter. The formidable and not always comfortable spirit of the master was very much present in the house she called 'the golden cage, in which my husband had sacrificed his life for his father'. There was still some bitterness in her voice. Strauss's biographer, the music critic Willi Schuh, had told me how Alice, during the Nazi time, had to make herself scarce at her father-in-law's public appearances, and how he once at an opening night found her hiding in the wings. 'They mustn't see me,' she had said. Maschatt, Clemens Krauss's secretary, told me too how 'Alice, the Jewess, always had to hide herself and was never allowed to be shown'.

It was a house of old-fashioned discipline. There was much talk about 'sternness of the world of men', and 'there were some family rows, stormy days, door slamming that brought the plaster down. There was always a pointed finger. "Learn more Greek, practise the piano",' remembered Christian. 'To us he was simply a grandfather. Perhaps he lacked humour, but he always had time for us,' said Richard.

I walked around the house, which Pauline had filled with antiques and paintings, the very image of a South German middle-class home with pewter and silver objects, old porcelain beer mugs and Bavarian glass paintings – a comfortable bourgeois home of rather heavy but pleasant taste.

With rising emotion I entered his studio. The room had not been touched except for the daily fresh bouquet of flowers. I pictured him work-ing at the large desk, which looked just like any other desk, sometimes twelve hours a day, dressed in a smoking jacket or in an English tweed suit.

To make a film on Strauss was not easy for me, much as I loved and admired his music. The film was the first of a series of programmes with which I was trying to come to a more dispassionate understanding of my own past. Much has been written and said about his role in Hitler's Germany. Much has been misreported and misunderstood. The part he played was very ambiguous. He had accepted the post of President of the *Reichskulturkammer*, the cultural chamber for music, and accepted it gladly. He had taken over when Toscanini refused to conduct in Bayreuth. He had also stepped in for Bruno Walter. But he had also fought for his Jewish librettist Stefan Zweig and refused to take Zweig's name off the score of the *Schweigsame Frau*. He stayed in contact with many Jews, and resigned from the Cultural Chamber. The Nazis accused him of not using the Hitler salute, but I had seen a letter to a Gauleiter which Strauss signed off with *Heil Hitler!* I had also found film footage of Strauss sheepishly giving the Hitler salute. He also composed and conducted the Olympic hymn in a ceremony presided by Hitler. His relationship with the regime was distant, but he never openly broke with it, a step which for a man of his stature would not have endangered his life, but would certainly have led to a ban on his music.

When Hitler came to power Strauss was seventy. One can impute to him the egotism and vanity of an artist whose main interest was to continue to write music. One can accuse him of political blindness and of a certain cowardice in accepting things in order to protect his Jewish daughter-in-law and her half-Jewish children. Although acquiescent, he was no Nazi.

A letter he wrote sums up better than anything the political and moral views of Richard Strauss.

Dear Herr Zweig,
Do you think I have ever let myself be guided, in any sort of action, by the thought that I am German? Do you think that Mozart deliberately composed in an Aryan manner? For me there are only two categories of human beings: the talented and the untalented. Who told you that I have involved myself so deeply in politics? Is it because I conducted a concert in place of Bruno Walter? I did it as a favour to the orchestra. Or because I stepped in for Toscanini? I did that as a favour to Bayreuth. It has nothing to do with politics. I hold office as president of the State Music Chamber to bring about good and prevent greater misfortune. Simply because I know my artistic duty.

This was the voice of a Germany that I knew well.

For the last thirteen years of his life Strauss lived surrounded by friends and family; his music continued to be performed. Stefan Zweig had to leave Germany. His novels, plays and poems were banned. In 1942 he committed suicide in Brazil at the age of sixty-one.

I engaged my old friend the cameraman Juergen Martin, with whom I had made so many films before. Our first stop was Switzerland to talk to Strauss's biographer, the eminent music critic, Professor Willi Schuh. Schuh in his eighties was frail and weary; his beautiful hands were trembling while he spoke passionately but not uncritically about Strauss, his disastrous relationship with his wife Pauline and how much the family suffered through his dominating nature. But he talked lovingly about his relationship with his librettist, Hugo von Hofmannsthal. 'Strauss valued Hofmannsthal enormously as a guide to cultural refinement, which he himself sometimes lacked. He once said: "I am not always sure of my taste, but Hofmannsthal taught me."'

Strauss particularly loved *Ariadne*. He once told Schuh: 'What I wrote casually has turned out best. I always want too much and sometimes I spoil it.'

Schuh had published the first part of his important biography several years before. It only dealt with the composer's earlier years. The whole music world was waiting for the next volume, but, as he told me, he would not publish while Alice Strauss was still alive. 'For nothing in the world would I want to hurt this great lady and I am afraid there would be things in my book which might. His son Franz was the real Nazi, not Richard.'

Schuh also confirmed my suspicion that the whole family was politically naïve. Alice showed me letters by Baldur von Schirach, Hitler's infamous Minister of Youth, that she could easily have destroyed. She also told me that her husband Franz had left the Church, a gesture much favoured by the Nazis and much frowned upon by others.

His biographer had also run up against the barrier that Strauss had erected between himself and the world. 'He was incapable of expressing what went on inside him. In his letters he wrote about his work, about concerts – but about his inner world, why he composed *Salome*, or *Rosenkavalier*, he remained silent.' Alice Strauss too had mentioned how withdrawn her father-in-law had been: 'He totally separated music and life and he did not tolerate any interference.' While she spoke one could still feel the formidable authority, even fear, which reigned in the house. 'Music was his own private world, he never talked with us about it. "You are lay people, you know nothing about it."'

Willy Schuh died before Alice Strauss, and the second volume of the biography has still not been published.

We drove to Salzburg to talk to Herbert von Karajan. Our instructions were to be there at 8.45 sharp. His secretary, Mrs Salzburger, who was like a fortress around the maestro, told us where to put the camera and from which side he could be filmed.

The maestro arrived at eleven o'clock. I could hardly believe that this was the same man I had sometimes seen in St Tropez, a dashing bronzed matinée idol who flew planes and steered yachts. Karajan was crippled, he could hardly walk, but once seated at the piano the old magic took over. With expressive gestures and great theatricality he evoked for us the day when Strauss came to a rehearsal of *Tannhäuser*. Karajan had just started the bacchanal and he had asked Strauss to conduct so that he could check the acoustics. 'Strauss gracefully accepted the invitation. From that moment the orchestra was changed. Not for better or worse, but it was in his stature. He had an impeccable sense of rhythm, there was always something going on, it was a most wonderful way of conducting, especially Mozart.'

Gradually the picture of Strauss began to emerge. In a snowbound Tyrolese village we found Viorica Ursuleac, Strauss's great Arabella. She was the widow of the conductor Clemens Krauss, who had written the libretto for *Capriccio*.

Ursuleac lived in a small house filled with bird cages and photographs of Richard Strauss. She remembered how the maestro conducted the scene with the glass of water so fast that she could hardly follow. 'Herr Doktor, how can you conduct this beautiful music in such a tempo?' she had said angrily, and he had brushed it aside: '"Ugh, these 6/4 chords." He was simply embarrassed by the sentiments this beautiful music expressed.'

Ursuleac at eighty-nine remembered most things as if they had happened the day before. We were talking about the war years: 'We totally ignored the war. Rushing in and out of air-raid shelters we rehearsed *Capriccio*. The stage hands were French prisoners of war. They asked permission to attend the rehearsal. It made them feel at home. One of them translated the libretto as a present for my husband. After the war we tried in vain to find him and the translation we lost in the bombs.'

I was moved and shocked by that story, which happened less than a hundred miles from where I was at that time: shocked by the fact that artists so often thought that if they just went on being artists they had a right to ignore politics, and moved by the memories of those last war years when a whole world had colapsed. 'With *Capriccio* my life's work has come to an end,' Strauss had written. 'What I write now has very little significance in the history of music. I don't enjoy writing operas any longer, I would rather write a dramatic thesis, a theatrical fugue like Verdi at the end of *Falstaff* or think of Beethoven's fugue. These are the conversations of old men.' I was thinking of these words returning to London, after this extraordinary trip into my own past. It brought back the images of Germany in 1945. The concert halls and opera houses where Strauss's music had been performed were in ruins. More than anything else this had made Strauss cry. 'I remember how in Argentina I conducted *Salome* at four o'clock in the afternoon, and *Elektra* at nine,' he wrote. 'Now I sit as a sad invalid among the ruins of Berlin, Dresden, Munich, Vienna. It is terrible. The Munich theatre where my father played the first horn in *Siegfried*, and where I conducted my first opera in 1886, was totally destroyed.' No word of regret for the dying, no mentioning of Coventry or Hiroshima. Strauss cried only for his Germany.

I had asked Christian Strauss to read to us the letter his grandfather had sent him thirty years ago. I caught the eyes of Alice Strauss and I had diffi-culties controlling my tears. Christian's voice was shaking with emotion.

> My dear good Christian, may Mozart's blessing from heaven accompany you throughout a happy life, and may the love of your grandfather remain as guiding star a long time after he has gone. Your twelfth birthday coincides with the terrible event of the almost total destruction of our beautiful old city... On your birthday you will always remember the barbarism and its cruel deeds which reduced our beautiful Germany to rubble and ashes. When after thirty years, you once more read this melancholy let-ter, I hope you will also remember your grandfather, who for almost seventy years worked for a German culture and the honour and glory of his fatherland. I send you blessings. I wish you health and the strength to work in a way worthy of our family tradition. Your loving grandfather, Richard Strauss.

In 1947 Strauss came to London on his first airplane trip, invited by Thomas Beecham, to attend a Strauss Festival. He conducted two con-certs. When he entered the Albert Hall the entire audience rose to its feet.

When I accompanied Alice Strauss to Strauss's grave, a large marble slab, she lit a candle and told me that shortly before dying he had opened his eyes and asked: 'Am I already dead?' and then added: 'If I only could set to music what I feel at this moment.' These were his last words.

Richard Strauss Remembered was allowed the exceptional length of two hours. The script was largely based on Strauss's own writing. Frank Finlay spoke Strauss's voice and John Gielgud read the commentary. I had tried to be as early as possible in the recording studio, but when I arrived John was already sitting patiently in Lime Grove reception. His professionalism, his utter modesty, made working with him a pleasure. 'Please tell me if you do not like what I do' or 'I am afraid my German accent is terribly bad, please correct me.' I saw tears in his eyes when at the end of the film the frail old Strauss walked through the garden of his house. The voice of Kirsten Flagstad sang one of the four last songs. 'Wir sind durch Nacht und Nebel ausgegangen Hand in Hand/... Wie sind wir wanderns müde/ Ist das vielleicht der Tod?'[1]

I had embarked on the Strauss film in the hope of understanding my country better, and I came back to London with the reconfirmation that greatness and morality have little to do with each other. I had put more of myself into this film than into many of my previous ones, for this subject was part of my life, it dealt with my roots. I watched it nervously in a packed theatre at the sneak preview at the BAFTA cinema. Many people in the audience were also immigrants from Germany. It was also their history: the glory of the early years of this century, the rise of Hitler and finally the total destruction and death of entire cities and their culture. I could tell many were intensely moved. It was Prunella who cut through all the emotions. 'What a bore Strauss was,' she said. 'He didn't even keep bees.'

Richard Strauss won the Golden Star for the best full-length documentary at the Houston Film Festival and another award for the best use of archive footage. But there was no time to rest on my laurels. Since the end of 1980, I had been trying to put a series on architecture on the air, but the money I needed could not be found. Five years later I could finally begin.

---

1 'Hand in hand we have walked through night and fog... how tired we are. Might this be death?'

27

Architecture at the Crossroads

1983–1986

The ultimate accolade of the BBC is to be asked to write and produce a series. *Them and Us* and *Master Photographers* were not really series, as they went out over a long period of time. A proper series was something like Kenneth Clark's *Civilisation* or J.M. Roberts's *History of the World*, and when Alan Yentob asked me to put forward some ideas for a series I was very excited. I proposed three: Great Rivers, Great Places of Pilgrimage, and Modern Architecture. The BBC opted for the last.

Architecture, more than any other art form, influences the way people live. It was rarely treated on television and called for a treatment which was both instructive and popular. I only had a general knowledge of the subject and I decided to study it. For the next three years, much of my reading was architectural books.

I made two important decisions: first to dispense with a presenter and to write the script myself; second to engage Roger Last as my associate producer. Roger was the best 'partner' I could have, as he had all the things I lacked: a fierce sense of duty, a love of detail and accuracy. He was also very stubborn, although not as stubborn as I. I was sad to see my assistant Sally Hunt leave, but she wanted to work somewhere else. She was replaced by Jane Bywater, a lovely and zany girl with a peachy surface. Her life was full of strange and slightly comical mishaps. One day her giant wisteria had split the front wall of her house into two. At work things were mysteriously 'mislaid'. Letters complaining about a colleague found their way into an envelope addressed to the very same person, or instead of an acceptance letter for an important ambassadorial lunch, His Excellency received a curt note saying: 'Kindly no longer bother us, as we have paid the bill,' a letter I had intended to go to a printer.

For the next two years the three of us tackled modern architecture worldwide. We shared an office with six phones often ringing at the same time from Tokyo to New York. The office was so small that sometimes we could not see each other for the amount of films, files, photos, and giant plants that Jane brought in from her garden. We had two cutting-rooms going and five hundred cans of film. There were fights and panics but most of all laughter which became the envy of the department, and we

Richard Rogers

I.M. Pei

Richard Meier

remained friends, which I am proud to say is also a record in a business where jealousy and yielding of power had become daily routine.

Professionally speaking, it was one of the most exciting periods of my life. I had always been interested in architecture and thought it the most fascinating profession in the world. If I had not become a film-maker, architecture would have been my choice.

Before embarking on the filming, Roger and I travelled to America, Mexico, India, Japan, Singapore, Bangkok and the Middle East. We saw thousands of buildings and met hundreds of architects, including two of my heroes: Luis Barragán and Doshi. Once more my work allowed me a rich crop of encounters; too many to name them all, but a few stood out. I remember with great pleasure meeting Frank Gehry, who wanted to talk about Lillian Hellman rather than about architecture. I helped him set up large buckets to catch the water pouring through the roof of his house. One of the seminal buildings of contemporary architecture was leaking! I. M. Pei, the elegant and urbane Chinese-American architect, offered me an apple while he spoke passionately about 'architecture as life. A civilised society must produce beautiful buildings – it's as simple as that.' He firmly believed in the dual role of the architect as both an artist and a social scientist. I met Richard Meier and Richard Rogers, two of the most accessible architects. Despite their success they were free of postures, still fired by a genuine concern for people. Philip Johnson took me for lunch to the Four Seasons, the smart New York restaurant where he had a regular table. It is in the Seagram building, one of the great examples of modern architecture he helped to build. 'All architects are whores,' he had said, 'the whores of society.'

It was a very good moment to make films about architecture. During the last few years more positive thinking had been taking place, giving hope for change and reorientation. People everywhere were concerned with better housing and a better environment. To look at modern architecture in ten forty-minute films was a daunting task. The subject was far too wide, it had to be narrowed down and made universally comprehensible. For every building or architect I dealt with, I knew I had to leave several others out. Almost everybody I met had some idea about modern architecture, had some favourite building or architect.

If in the beginning I was not quite sure what I wanted to do, I knew I did not want to prolong the useless polemic raging in the architectural press. Architects were, as I soon discovered, a strange tribe, blinded by prejudices, guilt feelings and preconceived ideas, few ever tested in the world of normal human beings. Many were more interested in polemic about styles than in creating buildings. Worse were the theoreticians and critics, aggressively verbal, staking a claim for their craft rather than producing it. They seemed not to know that the general public cared little about their philosophy and that what people like is not necessarily what the profession likes.

The series was to be a *tour d'horizon* of contemporary architecture, an introduction for a large audience to the themes and worries that were buzzing around. In the end, for practical reasons, I had to film where most modern building was happening – the States, Japan, the Middle East, Germany and France.

For the title sequence Hans Werner Henze had composed a signature tune for me as a Christmas present.

Ten years earlier, we had made a small film for *Review* about Peter Shaffer's home town, London. Shaffer had spoken angrily and with passion about 'the severed limbs, the pulped torso of a great city'. It was a programme about murder, architectural murder, a subject he later would take up in his play *Lettuce and Lovage*. 'Lifeless. Faceless. Hopeless. Meanspirited. Damning the sky with its load of untrying. Ruining everything around it. The people who designed this are the heirs of Wren and Nash. To me they are criminals. Worse are the people who commissioned it, who approved it, probably insisted on its mediocrity, and worse are the people who indifferently let it happen. You. Us.'

Most people hate modern buildings. They are synonymous with the many featureless horrors that surround all of us. I had seen entire cities in Germany destroyed and badly rebuilt with rows of streets that no longer belonged to a particular town or country, the endless images of uniformity. All over the world life-despising cities crammed with huge objects, bumper to bumper, a total waste of human and material resources. But while I shared the reservations many felt about modern architecture, I still loved it and hoped to be able to transmit some of my enthusiasm to a wide audience. I wanted to show that modern architecture, in the hands of the best, can still be life-enhancing.

The first two programmes, *Doubts and Re-assessment* and *Columns and Gables*, dealt with the two main philosophies in architecture: modernism and the then new postmodernism. They introduced a whole new generation of architects which grew up with radically different attitudes to those of their predecessors. It featured James Stirling, I. M. Pei, Richard Rogers, Norman Foster, Richard Meier and a whole group of newcomers.

Ada Louise Huxtable, the knowledgeable, level-headed and wise architectural writer, kept the right balance through all ten programmes. Not bogged down by prejudices, she reminded us constantly that the architect is building for society, not for himself or for the sake of a building. We were both 'modernists', and loved the denigrated modern glass skyscrapers of America. 'The greatest vernacular architecture since the eighteenth century,' she called it. 'The magnificent cityscape of New York and Chicago. Those glass boxes have just enough anonymity, just enough understatement, just enough similarity, to handle the enormity of the scale of modern life.'

The third programme, *Islam: The Search for Identity,* asked the question, how could Third World countries gain a collective identity in the course of modernisation. We filmed in Kuwait, Jeddah and Doha, the capital of the small but immensely rich emirate of Qatar. They had seen great changes. In one generation, people had moved from traditional courtyard houses into high-rise apartment buildings. An increasingly wealthy population wanted modern buildings and they wanted them fast. The traditional Arab quarters had almost totally disappeared, replaced by new housing, an airport, museums, mosques, TV stations and parliament buildings, all broadcasting to the world that these countries had arrived socially and economically. When this boom happened the Arabs knew almost nothing about town planning and modern architecture, so they looked to the West for help at a time when architecture here had reached its lowest point.

The evidence of this shoddy export was visible everywhere. It was humiliating to see how we in the West had thrown all integrity to the wind. So many architects had come to make a fast buck with trash no better than the gilded furniture and horrible chandeliers which flooded the market. We had turned these countries into the garbage dump of our culture by selling them the worst and not the best, arrogantly accusing them of lack of taste.

Kuwait, on its road to the twentieth century, had lost almost all traces of its old life. Impersonal spaces such as supermarkets and motorways had replaced the complexity and variety of the old quarters. Yet not all of Kuwait's new buildings were bad. The grand old man of Japanese architecture, Kenzo Tange, had built the airport, a giant white bird of a building ready to take off. Inside the cool, gleaming white marble hall, a circular mosque stood under a roof which looked like a star-spangled firmament. Kuwait also had one of my favourite buildings, the new Parliament, the work of the Danish architect Jorn Utzon (also responsible for the Sydney Opera House). The magnificent presence of the Parliament's two sweeping roofs, like giant sails on the waterfront, made it one of the most important buildings in the Arab world.

The three Arab states were very much governed by men for men. We hardly ever met or saw a woman, except on the streets. With the usual Arab hospitality we were dined and entertained by music and dances entirely in the company of men. Even in the private homes of famous architects or politicians who had travelled throughout the world we hardly ever met women. The exception was Sheika Hussa, whom I had met in England. She and her husband, Sheikh Nasser, had asked Hassan Fathy to build their house, a laudable effort to re-create and preserve the Arab tradition in a country where the rich lived in ostentatious villas copying anything from Palladio to Versailles. The size of those houses complete with television relay stations and their own mosques was incredible by Western standards: instant symbols of wealth and arrival. Sheika Hussa, dressed in a black dress, her face unveiled, did not only receive us in great style. She showed us the last few remaining houses of old Kuwait, an ensemble of intricate courts; each had its own special function, some for the men to gather, other for women to look after the children.

There was little charm left in those modern houses, or the hotel where Westerners drank and met women in bikinis. Life was governed by strict rules. One night I dined with a young American executive who was making a lot of money here, at a price. He showed me a copy of *House and Garden* with a page 'officially' ripped out because it contained a picture of a sauna. A friend of his had just been heavily fined because he kissed his wife at the airport when she arrived from New York.

The impression of a man's world, where women lived the existence of second-class citizens, was strengthened by our stay in Jeddah, where even Western women had to wear a black cloak on the streets. No Arab woman, even in the international hotel we stayed in, was allowed to ride in the lift with a man, except for her husband. Women were not allowed to drive a car or sit with the men in the front of the bus.

It was not always easy to cope with the very strong presence of religion, which governed everything – family life, the order of the day, even the making of spaces and houses – and to reconcile this with the ostentatiousness, the wealth and the fearful cruelty of the laws. One day we were invited to join a Sunday outing for the stoning of an adulterous woman, the tilting of a truckload of stones on to a defenceless human being. Of course we declined. Roger left his case with all his money in a taxi and it was promptly returned. Theft was punished by amputation. They cut off your right hand, so you could never eat in public or shake hands with another human being.

Our cultural background made it difficult to understand. Many women seem not to be unhappy in a society which determines their role and gives them their goals and limits. 'This leads to much greater happiness and ful-filment than in the freewheeling Western society with its bewildering choices,' a woman journalist told me. Not all women agreed. 'It is insult-ing for me to have to sit fully dressed and veiled with my children on the beach and watch the men coming out of the water in underpants that have become totally transparent.' The lady who said this was an American, married to an Arab oil executive.

Despite the constant feeling of repression, and the overpowering evi-dence of nepotism, I had come a small step nearer to understanding other people's behaviour, cultural differences and practical needs. The best ex-amples of modern Islamic architecture were the most visible cultural manifestations left and were helping the new societies to regain a personal and collective identity they so desperately needed and for which so many Third World countries were striving.

The biggest culture shock for me did not come from Islam, but from Japan. The first encounter was disconcerting but the second trip produced a fascination which has not yet abated. I tried right from the start to immerse myself in everything Japanese. I sat on wooden benches along-side stern businessmen, being served large bowls of noodles. There was total silence in the little popular restaurant. No one spoke; the only noise was that of the loud slurping. I crouched on the floor in front of a beauti-ful lacquer table in one of the most expensive restaurants in the world and was served food so exquisitely presented by a geisha that I forgot my aver-sion to fish and the cramp in my legs. I sat in boiling-hot water in the middle of Buddha-like figures in public baths, until my skin had taken on the colour of a lobster and I thought I was turning into a soprano. I had of course first copiously soaped myself; only dirty Europeans soap them-selves in the water they then lie in, we were told.

I had, with Roger and a young English architect, Benjamin Warner, booked lodgings in a traditional Japanese hotel that turned out to be very pretty and very uncomfortable. We had to share a room and looked ri-diculous in our happi coats which barely covered our essentials while tea was being served by a polite lady in a kimono. After two days I decided to check out in order to stretch out in a cosy Swiss chalet at £250 a night. I even visited a Japanese brothel, a so-called love hotel, a building in the shape of the Moulin Rouge in Paris. I had drinks in an exclusive club run by a man who was an expert in flower arranging. The place was filled with transvestites in kimonos and gentlemen with green carnations. I dined at the Key West Club, a dream of Art Deco in black and white. The mostly young clientele had dressed accordingly in black and white outfits by top fashion designers. All around the walls television screens broadcast video clips of Boy George. This was the haunt of the young, chic and affluent who came to see and be seen, to drink exotic cocktails and eat chocolate mousse in vol-au-vent cases or colourful water ices on plates shaped like the bullet train.

I joined the enormous and more popular crowds on Sunday in the department stores in search of yet another designer label or its poor relation. I did Kabuki, Noh and Bunraku and had *rösti* in the Mövenpick, which looked exactly like the one in Hamburg. I queued with giggling Japanese in front of McDonalds and played one of the 700,000 gambling machines.

In short I did everything I had been told to do in order to understand something of this multi-stranded, contradictory and ambivalent country. Still I felt totally out of place. The anarchic impact of the chaos of Tokyo was quite overwhelming and frightening: twelve million people in one of the most densely populated places in the world, all jammed in with cars and houses and motorways, sometimes one above the other. A visual cacophony of overhead cables, glaring neon signs, television aerials and millions of little houses, like a huge toy box that has been accidentally tipped over. This sort of chaotic and stressful life made a system of rituals and duties necessary in order to survive. 'If a nail sticks out,' says a famous Japanese saying, 'hammer it flat.'

In the making of *Building the Zen Way*, I met one of the gurus of modern Japanese architecture, Kazuo Shinohara. The influence of his brutal and ascetic designs on a whole generation of younger architects has been enormous. He had invited us to his house, a typical modern Japanese house, stark and inward-looking. Many architects have realised that the city cannot be saved and have turned their backs on it. They have given up the dialogue with the environment and created a private vision in their home. They look for silence, a pause, a pure gesture. We left our shoes at the entrance as Shinohara introduced us to his wife, who disappeared immediately, not to be seen again except through a glass door, where I saw her polishing our shoes. I had brought a cake. I was told that this is what the Japanese like best. It had been wrapped so beautifully that it looked like a jewel from Van Cleef. Mrs Shinohara never unwrapped it: it stood on the sideboard totally untouched. I was told that it would have been considered impolite to unwrap it in front of me. We had the last glimpse of Mrs Shinohara when we left the house: she stood outside, bowing. She was still bowing until we turned the corner of the street. I had to remind myself that this was 1986 and one of the most modern states in the world.

One day Roger and I visited another architect, Hiroshi Hara, in the country. Not that there is much countryside left in Japan, where 100 million people have to share the narrow corridor between Tokyo and Hiroshima. The country is still there, the traditional vision of a beautiful bucolic landscape, a patchwork of rice fields and wooden roofs, an image imprinted on my mind through screens and woodcuts. But it is only a backdrop to an increasingly urban society.

Hara had been one of the lucky few to own a plot of land. It was almost embarrassing to tell people about the size of one's houses in London or the South of France. Here even the very well-off had to do with a few square metres. Unlike Shinohara's house, Hara's was open to the landscape; nature was completing the design. There was hardly any furniture except one chair by Marcel Breuer and another by Le Corbusier. I realised that chairs, too, were something that had only recently come to Japan and that they were often used more for decorative than for functional purposes. Hara's wife was also an architect, but she sat aside, listening demurely, not interfering with our conversation.

Arata Isozaki, who flies regularly between New York, Barcelona, Los Angeles and Tokyo, received us in offices of elegant lacquer furniture. He was dressed, like many top designers and architects, in Issey Miyake. Through the door I heard the noise of fax machines and computers. While we sipped tea from little cups an elderly lady in an elegant suit entered with a letter. She first bowed to the man behind the desk, then to the young secretary, and finally handed over the letter with a stamp from America. When Isozaki spotted my slightly amused look, he explained that nothing ever goes away in Japan, the past and the present coexist everywhere. But it is not the sort of nostalgia we have in the West; it is an acknowledgement that history is always present, a view which allows them to be vigorously modern without fear of losing the past.

In Osaka we saw Tadeo Ando, an ex-boxer who presided over a small group of young architects. He was said to beat up his co-workers if they did not work properly. It was hard to believe this rumour when I met this friendly, small and incredibly vivacious man of tremendous energy. He told me proudly that when he visited France he never saw Versailles or Fontainebleau, but he made a pilgrimage to Lyon to see Le Corbusier's monastery of La Tourette. He and his wife, who spoke a bit of English, received us lavishly. We sat at a table in his crammed office laden with food, including sweets made from soya beans in the most garish colours. Ando never stopped talking, his chic and very Western-looking wife translating. She was one of the few women I saw totally at ease in the company of men. The assistants demurely looked on; the word slaves would be too harsh, they were more like faithful, bowing disciples. I wondered if the story about them being beaten up was true after all. They were allowed to eat what we had left.

We were shown his houses: concrete cubes, some of them only 35 square metres large, an architecture of denial. I rather shuddered looking at the three tiny rooms, all linked by an outside staircase. People had to go outside in order to reach the bathroom. Ando told us how our senses in the West have become soft through heating in the winter and cooling in the summer. 'You have lost contact with nature, and are no longer aware of our physical environment and therefore of life.' (I later recalled this remark when the Andos came one day to London and sat in my over-heated and overfurnished Fulham house.) Most of his houses were an empty space filled only with the changing light, the changing climate, that enters through small slits in the wall. What could be purer?

I was often shocked by the amount of ugliness which seemed to coexist right next to the most exquisite objects. Our sense of beauty always seemed to demand that one object relate to the other; in Japan a beautiful object exists by itself. My aesthetic notions were constantly forced to change.

As from my trip to the Middle East, I returned with many of my con-ceptions about the way we live in the West questioned and even revised. The clutter of my house, filled with antique furniture and the debris of an acquisitive and gregarious life, was only one possibility. The contemplative empty spaces of the imperial palaces and the small houses made me see that an empty room is not the absence of what we call décor, but on the contrary, plenitude, the richness of infinite possibilities. I also learned that nature is not just trees and rivers, but that all nature can be gathered in a tiny fragment; in one plant, a glimpse of the sky, the blowing of the wind or the coldness of a room. Many of the houses I had seen seemed incon-venient, irrational, even absurd, but the sculptural energy of many of the buildings I filmed had excited me, and when I finally managed to cast my preconceived ideas aside I was left with the memory of undeniable visual power.

The rest of the architecture series dealt with less exotic subjects. The pro-gramme *Houses Fit for People* was devoted to public housing; *Stop the Bulldozer* raised the question of what to preserve and what to destroy. It also dealt with our increasing nostalgia for Italian piazzas and cobblestone streets, with the love for pastiche, history dry-cleaned, brought up to date; how restoration of a few architectural details and the salvation of a few historical props could help us to regain a world which had totally changed economically, socially and spiritually.

487

One programme I was particularly keen on was called *New Market-places*. It dealt with shopping malls, large hotel lobbies, museums, all the places where people now gathered. Like the marketplaces of the past, they were meant to satisfy people's need to gather and their love for spectacle.

In the past, public spaces, like public buildings, had grown out of a communal effort and faith, not a desire for buying and selling; now everywhere commercialism replaced wider vision. The materialistic nightmare of our times could be read in the atrium of the Trump Tower on Fifth Avenue. It is a designer paradise featuring some of New York's most exclusive shops: an overblown, ostentatious, marble and gilt candy box. This was no longer a place for the people to gather, not a place just to wander in and to look. The visitor is expected to honour the amenities of lights and fountains and plants by buying or eating something; controlled privilege – the poor and the untidy are asked to refrain from entering.

The new markets like Covent Garden or the Fulton Fish Market in New York are more democratic. They are very popular, born out of a mixture of shrewd commercialism and nostalgia. They pretend to be the real thing, but a few clowns and cobblestones do not make a street. They are stage sets with food and boutiques as spontaneous as a military parade. As Ada Louise Huxtable remarked: 'They manage to make even the real look unreal.'

Some of the best new marketplaces were the new museums, among my favourite buildings. The lofty and bold extension of the Washington National Gallery by I. M. Pei, Richard Meier's High Museum in Atlanta or his Museum in Frankfurt were the last outposts of the modern movement. While the space devoted to the exhibition of art diminishes, space open to the public is expanding. But sometimes I asked myself if the pendulum has swung too far. Some museums, some exhibitions, are becoming like fairgrounds. Too much entertainment will ultimately distract from art's real purpose. Why should the visit to the *Mona Lisa* be automatically rewarded with an ice-cream?

I devoted the last programme, *Architecture Quo Vadis*, almost entirely to the voices of the architects themselves. Richard Rogers, Norman Foster, Richard Meier, I. M. Pei, Philip Johnson, all argued for a multitude of styles and saw in this diversity the salvation of modern architecture. I chose a number of recent buildings which in my opinion had expanded the architectural language of this century: Foster's Hong Kong Bank, Meier's Atlanta Museum, Rogers's Lloyd's Building in London, Isosaki's Museum of Decorative Arts in Los Angeles. Yet I had to agree with Ada Louise Huxtable that the perfect building does not exist. 'I do not know of any building that works perfectly well,' she had said. 'I think that the complexity of buildings and of cities and the complexity of the architectural task itself almost preordains that they are going to be imperfect, but there is excitement when you see a great building and you know it instantly.'

I had not lost faith in modern architecture, but after having seen more buildings and met more architects than most students of architecture ever would, in the end I had few answers. I envied the architectural critics with their slogans and solutions, so sure in their prejudices. The only thing I was sure of was that the seminal years of modern architecture were still the first thirty years of this century. That was when the basic syntax was put together. 'There is just no historical comparison to the brilliance, the magnificence, of the modernist revolution, right through all the arts,' Ada Louise Huxtable said. 'There has never been anything like it, and what was done with technology, aesthetically and practically, is thoroughly magnificent. And to lose all of this in the interest of something called postmodernism, just because it did not achieve all the high ideals it set for itself, is a tragic misinterpretation of art in history.'

Ada Louise, with her level-headedness, her immense knowledge and her warm friendship, had been a great ally during the two years it took to make this series. She was always there to give advice and support, even when much of the architectural press kept on closing in on me, the outsider who had dared to prick the balloon. 'Bravo, bravo, bravo,' she wrote when the series was finished, 'the intelligent innocent eye that sees more! All the things I have always tried to say.'

Right after the second programme, not even waiting for the end of the whole series, the architectural profession retaliated which such vindictiveness that it took many people by surprise. I had learned how to take adverse criticism and I liked a good controversy. I certainly got one. 'Peter Adam is, to me at least, a quite unknown character, who is presenting ten BBC television programmes on modern architecture on which he seems extraordinarily ignorant,' wrote the distinguished *Architectural Journal* about what they called 'Architecture's latest TV flop', or 'this sickly Architecture at the Crossroads'. For the first time a review of my programmes carried my picture to show what the villain looked like. 'Peter Adam, wrong turn at the crossroads' read the caption in the *Guardian*. Its architectural critic, Martin Pawley, under the sprawling headline 'Building a world in the image of Adam', devoted no fewer than seven columns to it, arrogantly claiming that 'no one on television knows how to deal with architecture'. A layman had dared to look at the sacrosanct field of architecture, and on top of it in such a 'vulgar medium as television' (as one architect told me at an IBA dinner). Pawley had only seen two of the ten programmes when he jumped to print, assuming that the audience must be 'a dedicated audience in the low hundreds'. *Sic tacuisses philosophus mansisses.* For ten weeks up to two million watched it every week.

To my surprise the television critics rallied to my defence. 'BBC takes long look at architectural Hubris' was the *Herald Tribune* headline. The 'TV Flop' of the *Architectural Journal* became 'Towering Success' in the *Telegraph*. And if Martin Pawley had urged his viewers to switch off, Richard Last called it 'required viewing'. 'Narrowminded' wrote one side, 'openminded almost to a fault' the other. What some considered 'ignorant' others called 'challenging'. Both sides excelled in critical catchwords: 'bland and boring', 'excellent and erudite'. Even journalists working at the same paper began to contradict each other. I had provoked a slanging match between the critics. Colin Amery, architectural critic of the *Financial Times,* found *Architecture on Television* 'bland and uninformed'; his colleague on the arts page, Christopher Dunkley, called it a 'thorough and engrossing series'.

The postscript to the *Architecture* series came in the Christmas edition of the *Listener*. In its annual Television Awards for 1986, John Naughton picked out as a hoax the winners of 'The Andreas Whittam-Smith Medal for Most Argumentative Series'. The five finalists for the 'most hotly contested series this year' were *The New Enlightenment* (a look at the Welfare State); *Questions of Defence* (about NATO); *Open the Box* (a look at television); *Lovelaw* (about man's behaviour); and *Architecture at the Crossroads,* 'Peter Adam's persuasive effort to get us to take modern architecture seriously'.

We came first. The prize was a signed photograph of Frank Lloyd Wright.

28
Memento Mori

It really felt as if the last three years had been entirely occupied with the making of the series, but of course this was not the case. Reading through my diaries I am amazed how much else did happen, some of it pleasurable, some marked by loss and pain.

I always liked to work on several projects at once. I often started new films before the old ones were on the air. It was a kind of self-defensive mechanism and it kept my mind fresh and sharp. While working on a film my mood shifted constantly. There were moments of feverish excitement, especially when I began to cut the film, assembling as in a jigsaw puzzle all the bits and pieces I had filmed. Then, usually halfway through the editing, doubts and anxiety set in. Sometimes, usually towards the end, all these fears made room for a kind of glow of happiness and pride, a moment of euphoria when all came together: the picture, the commentary, the selected music. It never lasted very long. Doubts always seem to gain the upper hand.

From time to time, just to get away from architecture, I agreed to make a small item or the odd interview like the one with Peter Stein, who was working in Cardiff on a stunning production of Verdi's *Otello*. He had rehearsed for several months, one of his conditions for directing another opera after his disastrous experience with the *Ring* in Paris. I was intrigued by the great intensity and the wide range of emotional responses which he coaxed out of the singers. Stein was still as awkward and evasive, but I felt that he was now more at ease with the press than before.

Writing too was a refuge from the intensive filming and editing schedule. In writing I found a new identity, joining all the other roles I had played. In January 1986 I finished the manuscript of my Eileen Gray biography. This came as a relief – I had been working on it since 1982.

I watched the friends I loved growing old, talking increasingly about the past, as old people do – their character etching its traces into their faces, looking out on a diminished world through stronger glasses. Some of them accepted it with panache, others reacted with resentment and sometimes envy. They took on a resigned and frozen attitude, as if they were running out of steam.

Death kept on mapping the drift of time. Pepita, Facundo's mother, had died in Buenos Aires, a woman for whom I felt affection and love. The boy who looked after Tony Richardson's place in La Garde-Freinet, Jean-Pierre, shot first his girlfriend and then himself. Drink and the loneliness during the long winter months in Le Nid du Duc had driven him to it, they said.

Lawrence Durrell's daughter Sappho hanged herself. Larry phoned me. He was shocked and deeply wounded, with a great sense of failure. I had once taken Sappho to Le Nid du Duc, which she was keen to see. She was happy and cheerful, wearing a new dress Larry had bought her. At that time I had no idea that this visit would be so important to her. Several years later, after her death, when her journals were published, I found the following passage:

> The film which had such an effect on me – probably out of proportion with its true merit – [was] A Bigger Splash. The pool in the final picture haunted me. It was like looking down on my myth – the tiny slip of blue – the very scene which held so much imaginative meaning for me. Le point du départ. The pool belongs to Tony Richardson and I can visit it tomorrow to pay my pilgrimage. Something that Peter Adam had said earlier in the day came back to me like a perfume: 'Nothing is real outside the head; all is illusory except what is in the mind.' When one's world is polluted to the soles of ones shoes – then the mind must recreate a liveable world. Hockney for me was one of those starting points for imagining a world one can taste again.

Durrell was later accused of having had an incestuous relationship with his daughter, an accusation I find absurd and unbelievable, and yet no one ever will lift the veil of uncomprehension that hangs about all our lives.

The world grew somber. At work too, death was a reminder of the only reality that did not reside in the mind. Julian Jebb, funny, bright, melancholic Julian, killed himself only a few months after we had all celebrated his fiftieth birthday. His buoyant and often unguarded spirits could not halt his ferocious drive for self-destruction. He was working on a programme on Rosamond Lehmann – a coincidence too strange to overlook.

Julian Jebb was the last of a long line of suicides in the department: James Mossman, Robert Vas, Bill Morton, Ken Sheppard. Once more the members of the Music and Arts Department huddled in a church; 'the little village of producers', as Melvyn Bragg has lovingly called it, shocked and bereaved and unable to understand. Julian's brother, Dom Philip, the

Abbot of Downside, celebrated the mass. Germaine Greer wrote an open letter to Julian in the *Literary Review,* accusing him posthumously of egoism :

> You are the product of generations of privilege; healthy, handsome, cultured, heir to a tradition the way other people are heirs to land and goods. You were fastidious and you were sometimes over-enthusiastic, silly sometimes... You were capable of pleasure that other people have never been able to dream of because you were as a receptor of a special kind. Your penalty was anguish and anxiety of an equal special kind but, if you cared for the tradition you were bred to serve, you would have borne them.

At the BBC the bureaucrats had further proliferated, because that is all they know how to do, and threatened to take over the position of Head of Music and Arts which had become vacant. Humphrey Burton had long been pushed out, replaced by a string of administrators, managers – the tough boys approved by the top. Germaine's letter was a call for many of us to fight back. I was urged from all sides to apply for it. I was touched by the admiration, even affection, expressed by the people I worked with, and for a brief moment I was tempted. The job of editor for *Omnibus* was also going. In the end I resisted both. I had no appetite for that sort of power. I wanted to use the remaining three or four years within the BBC to make programmes, not politics. It is by programmes that we are remembered; we do not leave our marks by shuffling people's talents and emotions around.

But I am a natural dissident at heart and I had decided I would fight for the right person to take up this job. For weeks my little office became the meeting place of the discontented. As I had made it known that I would speak my mind at the next departmental meeting, the conference room was packed to the last seat. In the chair the man who was to become the new 'head', a 'manager' – much favoured by the management. I stood up and spoke. I accused the management of selling out the quality for which we were once famous and envied. I accused them of stifling creativity by making the producer accountable to people with little understanding of the arts. I accused them of having turned an organisation people were once proud and happy to work for into a place of mistrust, fear and deep unhappiness. I remember that I was actually trembling while I spoke, both from rage and from nerves. I spoke for twenty minutes. I 'unpacked', I think is the word. I had nothing to fear. I was due for retirement in three years. I was also one of the senior members of the department. I spoke about the philistinism of our management, the heartlessness and insensitivity of the leadership, the lack of standards and the cowardice faced with political pressure. Then I sat down. Suddenly other people spoke up too and then the meeting was over. To this day colleagues tell me that they remember every minute of it. I had rocked the boat. A few weeks later a board for the new head was convened and an unconventional and unusual choice, a film-maker, not an administrator, was appointed head of the department: Alan Yentob. He asked Nigel Finch and Antony Wall to take over *Arena*, and Leslie Megahey to look after *Omnibus*. A new era began in the Music and Arts Department.

This was not the only struggle I had with my employers. The other one was more serious and certainly more sinister. Sometime in the summer of 1985 *The Observer* leaked a story which made the headlines: some of the leading people in the BBC had been hindered in their advancement because of secret security vetting. Inside Broadcasting House sat an MI5 man scrutinising BBC employees. The people so ostracised had a little design on the cover of their personal file: a Christmas tree. Every employee had a personal file which contained everything anybody had ever written about them in an official capacity, the annual report (another of those quaint BBC practices). We all wrote reports about the people we worked with. I wrote about my assistants, my boss wrote about me. Every year these reports written by a superior were read out to one by his superior. Then the report went on your file. It had always amazed me that these files were top-secret.

One day at a lunch at Hans Werner Henze's, Stephen Hearst, my ex-boss and in the meantime Controller of Radio Three, came out with the following remark: 'Now that it is all over the papers I can tell you that you have a Christmas tree on your file. They say that you are an ex-communist from East Berlin. I could therefore never offer you a proper established job.' I could not believe my ears. It was so absurd as to defy belief. I had never ever been near a communist party, and East Germany did not exist when I was born. So much for the accuracy of MI5's research.

The saga goes back many years. For some obscure reason which nobody understood, I had always failed to get on to the BBC staff. The first time I had asked for a pensionable staff job was in 1969. To my surprise Stephen Hearst told me then that I should wait for a further year. Two years later I was still waiting. I wrote many letters and received many promises, with no result. I was never told why. In the meantime younger, less experienced people became staff producers. Nobody seemed to notice that the two people who were prevented from joining the staff were foreigners by birth, Robert Vas and myself.

In March 1976, eight years after my first application, I wrote again, this time to the new Director of Programmes, Alastair Milne:

> Every Head of Arts Features – Stephen Hearst, Norman Swallow and Humphrey Burton – has recommended Establishment. There are minuted records by Robin Scott and Aubrey Singer [two controllers] to the same effect. With the utmost deference in the world I ask you as the head of the programme establishment to let me know if there is anything in my performance that makes me to be singled out in this unjust way.

I included a list of forty-seven programmes I had made, among them a nomination for a British Academy Award. The letter was never answered nor acknowledged.

It was on the personal initiative of Humphrey Burton that in 1977 Robert Vas and myself became members of the BBC staff. Humphrey simply thought it a disgrace that the only members of his department who were not part of the staff were the two foreigners.

The long battles were over, and I never thought much about it until that day when Stephen Hearst spilled the beans. Robert Vas was dead by then. I wondered why none of my old bosses had ever mentioned the 'flaw' in my file. They all had access to it and must have known about it. It was such a betrayal. They were also colleagues and friends, they had dined with their wives in my house. Were they all such good citizens, brought up in the acceptance of secrecy?

I demanded a meeting with the head of personnel, Glyn Price, a man I knew well from my time in Current Affairs. My file on his desk was the size of two telephone books. 'I am not in a position to deny nor to confirm what you are saying, and I cannot let you see the file, but I can tell you that there are indeed strange things in it.' I became suspicious. Were there other episodes in my life which pointed at some sinister dealings? Why had I had to wait six weeks to have my stolen passport replaced when Jane Bywater got a new one immediately? Why had the telephone always gone blank after I spoke to my Cuban friend Alba Griñan? What about Jim's connection with the secret service?

I decided that I must have access to my file, or at least get someone to inspect it. I could trust Alan Yentob (by then head of the department). He belonged to the new generation less in awe of authority and with a sense of loyalty to friends. He wrote a furious letter to the managing director about 'the injustice that has been done', asking not only to get to the bottom of it but also to get me financial compensation for the lost pensionable years. But silence fell from all sides. The BBC, cornered by the revelation that MI5 actually had an office in Broadcasting House, closed it down and announced the cessation of the odious vetting system. I was told that 'some of my file had been shredded and that there was no longer anything incriminating in it'. I still had no access to my file. England was one of the most secretive countries, and the BBC simply confirmed this.

Everybody in and outside the office was shocked by the fact that someone could simply be blacklisted without knowing it and, on top of it, with false accusations which could easily have been refuted. Grey Gowry introduced me to his lawyer, hopefully to be able to get at my file. After an exchange of a few letters I ran out of money and out of steam. One reply of the BBC lawyer is worth quoting as a sign of total hypocrisy and obfuscation:

> Unfortunately, the files in question have not yielded any information which might help us to identify the reason your client was not placed on a pensionable contract. I can assure you however that in arriving at a conclusion in this matter the management at the time would have taken into account a whole range of issues, although I am unable to say whether or not security was one of these as any sensitive information relating to such matters which may have existed would have been destroyed in accordance with current BBC policy.

It was signed David Williams, Assistant Legal Adviser.

The BBC had pulled rank. Were they afraid that other people would want access to their files? Would the admission lead to an avalanche of claims? I was no longer the trusted and respected member of the organisation. Had I become the adversary? It was disgusting. The Union and many people within the BBC urged me to go public. The press would have had a field day. The other option was to sue. I could not bring myself to do either. Whatever the outcome, it could only bring much pain and little benefit to all concerned. I had no wish to spend my three remaining years with the BBC feeling a victim of an organisation I was still devoted to.

The BBC has never reconsidered its position. My blood still boils when I think that now, when the Stasi files are open to everybody, the BBC files are not. From then on I liked the BBC a bit less, and alas, also the country it belonged to. It was not as civilised as I had naïvely believed after all. I never found out what I was accused of and I probably never will. The sour taste remains.

It became all too apparent that society was not as tolerant as many of us had thought, lulled by a period of liberalism and the honest desire for a deeper understanding of mankind. There was now a new kind of intolerance. The word freedom began to have a hollow sound. Censorship came from all sides, not necessarily openly: it sometimes came in more subtle forms. Oppression does not have to take the form of prison or exile; censorship has always been the dark shadow of the world. Freedom of expression might not be overtly stopped, but merely controlled, curtailed.

The BBC decided not to show a film on Northern Ireland after the government had put pressure on the Board of Governors. Many people were outraged, but not everyone was. I joined the many journalists on strike and wrote an open letter to the managing director, Bill Cotton, reminding him that the BBC stood for values which the management was at present flouting. I accused them of diminishing the BBC's reputation as the honest broker it was still held out to be all over the world. Any form of caving in to an oppressive government would only invalidate our claim to civilisation. The letter was posted in many corridors, but it was never answered.

Eventually the film went out. Few people understood what the fuss had been about, but the damage had been done. The moral majority, the politicians, the mullahs and the priests stood up, sometimes disguised as liberals or democrats, and tried to silence those who said things they did not want to hear.

I always thought that the measure of civilisation was how it treats its minorities, and on that account too Britain fared badly. AIDS not only bred fear and pain, but also a new morality. Homosexuality began once more to be viewed with contempt. Society that had been shamed into silencing its prejudices for a while saw in AIDS an opportunity that was gladly taken. The government too joined those who judged what is good for people and who set themselves up as apostles of a spurious morality. Soon Clause 28 of the Local Government Act was introduced, preventing libraries, theatres, television and schools from presenting 'too positive' an image of homosexuality. The idea that sex could be a source of pleasure was again questioned. The talk went from the disruptive power of sexual desire to its being a curse from God. AIDS was seen as a punishment for a wicked life – a convenient cover for the moral majority.

With the imposition of a public morality came the decline of personal responsibility. Gradually I noticed a lack of responsibility towards ourselves, towards the country, towards the world. A new complacency in the way people treated each other was the result of an increasing impersonalisation of our life.

With AIDS came also the big lie. It became a secret disease. Sons would not tell their mothers, husbands protected their wives from the truth. The list of people who died became longer, people one had known, loved, shared a bed or a drink with. The world of the arts lost some of its most brilliant practitioners. Soon no week would be without a visit to the hospital or the news that another friend was gone: Peter Bateman, Mario Dubski, Nicky Eden, Robert Fraser, Mario Amaya, Michael Vyner, Bruce Chatwin. When would it stop? The personal tragedies reached almost everybody I knew. Gentle and vivacious Jean-Luc shot himself in the head after his lover had died of AIDS. David, who seemed to be life itself, threw himself off the roof. Over the next few years the list of friends with the death warrant on their heads grew: David Hartman, Bill King, Robert Mapplethorpe, Michel Guy, Alain Salomon, Rudolf Nureyev among them. I lost count. It was usually the most brilliant, the most shining, the most hopeful who left us – people aged thirty, thirty-five, forty or younger.

I tried to help, to counsel; we all did. It somehow united people in anger and in love. The pleasure-loving, free-wheeling homosexual community discovered compassion, stoicism, responsibility. They discovered that they were marginal and alone. It was the single most devastating event in every homosexual's existence. I spent much time visiting friends in hospital. I saw parents who stood lost at the bedside of their children, not understanding what had happened, some not even knowing that their son was homosexual.

The promise of a special cure brought those who could afford it to the French hospitals in droves. Every day a new pill seemed to be found, some costing a fortune, or not available on the market. I received letters and phone calls from New York: 'Can you help? I hear there is a cure in Paris or London, a medication in Switzerland or Germany.' Everybody clung on to some cure, healer, special diet, exercises – all of them false hopes and illusions. Everywhere in New York you saw the desperation and sadness on the faces of the many you knew who had not long to live. The health studios where they made their bodies more desirable and the saunas where they showed them off were closed. The American stud, so cocksure and invincible, the very image of life and physical pleasure, had become an anachronism. Once in New York I saw a fairly young woman throwing sacks of clothes into the incinerator, all vestiges of a happier time: jeans and sports jackets, baseball caps, white T-shirts and tracksuits, the icons of healthy living, the garments of the all-American boy, the American Dream of Albee's play, who had died of AIDS.

When the disease was first discovered, people with AIDS did not live as long as they do now. The heterosexual world was hardly concerned. Unlike in France, in England the homosexual world had little support from the public. Only when it was discovered that we all were in danger did the public take notice. In the beginning there was more talk about the rights and wrongs than about the real cause of the tragedy.

In France people came out more openly. When Copi died, *Libération* and the *Nouvel Observateur*, where he had for years published his cartoons, brought out a special edition. His last play, situated in an AIDS ward, was performed. Famous people such as the philosopher Michel Foucault and the writer Jean-Paul Aron (*Mon sida à moi*) came out publicly and made memorable appearances on television, challenging once more our reasons and civility. The writer Hervé Guibert discussed his illness on Bernard Pivot's book programme, *Apostrophes*. When they died the press would speak at length about the inroads AIDS was making into the artistic and intellectual life of the country.

How will I ever forget the long row of funerals in New York, Paris or London? Facundo and I sitting in the icy and impersonal chapel of the Père Lachaise at Copi's funeral, holding hands, grabbed by raw grief. Across the aisle among the many friends whose life was linked with his: Patrice Chéreau, Paloma Picasso, Annemarie Muñoz, Pierre Bergé, Marucha, Alfredo Arias. Only two weeks before, we had sat with almost the same people at another funeral. Death had united us all: the famous, the rich, the beautiful and the anonymous. I sat facing a wall of hopelessness. We were finally all the same, linked by grief and loss. So many things that dislocated and disturbed me passed through my mind; the awareness of one's own helplessness, the grotesque endings of so many relationships. While the horrid and disquieting noise of the flames travelled up to us, the gramophone played one of Argentina's famous tangos, 'La vida es una porquería'.

I began to question why so many of my friends were dying. Had they lived more dangerously than others? In the desire to soar, many homosexuals, especially in America, had pushed life to its utmost. In the pursuit of more and more sexual thrills the stakes became higher, even violent, and increasingly removed from reality. They took on bizarre forms. People copulated with images rather than with human beings. But by pushing back the limits, homosexuals had also experienced an exhilaration, a joy few people know. They had nearly arrived at a point where society would have been free of the hypocrisy of sexual guilt it had carried for centuries. In the climate of new intolerance, those of us who had experienced it looked back with nostalgia at this time of innocence, and it seemed incredible that it had once been within reach.

Then AIDS hit Facundo and me more directly. Facundo's ex-lover Jacques had been diagnosed HIV-positive. The news was like being blown apart by a bomb. Jacques had become like a brother to Facundo, probably the most important person in his life. Jacques went into hospital, and as he had with Marucha, Facundo would sit daily at his bed, as the truth was gradually sinking in, living the drama to the fullest.

Then came the fear about Facundo's health, and sometimes about my own. Some people advised testing, others against it. What was the point of knowing if there is no cure? I began to suffer from depression and exhaustion. I sometimes had to hide my hands at work, they were trembling so much. I began to take sleeping pills: first one, then two, and sometimes in the middle of the night there was the temptation to take the whole lot. Facundo was playing in a sumptuous production of Marivaux's *Le Jeu de l'amour et du hasard*. I watched him standing on stage, pouring his heart out to Marilu Marini, his partner, his face streaming with tears. He was crying for Jacques, who was too ill to even come to the theatre. When Facundo wept, my heart always went to pieces. His whole being transmitted a helpless sadness, he was living the illness with such intensity. The words death and illness were hardly ever mentioned. I realised that most of Jacques's friends were actors who had grown up with make-believe: reality had always been kept at bay. But death was hanging over everything. It was no longer a metaphysical problem, it was a very real physical one.

For Christmas we took Jacques to Le Mazet. His cups and plates had to be washed separately, and everybody coyly tried to avoid too much physical contact for fear of contamination. We prayed a lot or buried ourselves in work. I was frantically planting some new trees, 'for the future', but what future? Everybody clumsily showered Jacques with presents, things he would never be able to wear. We cooked elaborate meals he was incapable of eating. We watched his daily deterioration, a process we could not halt and which would alter our view of the world and our values. We knew that we would never be the same again.

The entry in my diary for 1 January makes sad reading:

> What will the new year bring? Facundo is sad to the core. There have been so many changes in both our lives, too hard even to contemplate. All other New Year resolutions have vanished into thin air. I pray for our love to survive, that is all that matters now.

I had to go back to London to film and Facundo had to go back on stage in Paris. This was probably just as well, but we dearly wanted to stay. There was still some healing power in nature. I wrote in my diary:

> Facundo and I sit on the terrace and look up at the spectacle I have seen a thousand times. The stars, some white, some pink, some yellow. How insignificant we are faced with this immensity. And yet we are part of what is known as the universe and we try to find some comfort in the dark velvet coat of the night that envelops us. Suddenly inside the house Jacques breaks up in an uncontrollable fit of coughing and the dream is shattered.

It was then that Facundo asked me to come and live with him. Yes, I replied, I would do it in three years' time when I finished at the BBC. It would be difficult but it had to be done. For the next five months I flew to Paris every weekend. The extraordinary thing about the illness was that there was always some reprieve, weeks when people recovered and took strength. One evening for the opening night of a Schnitzler play which Alfredo had staged at the Comédie-Française, Jacques made an effort to get up. A mixture of bravura and provocation, for he knew that everyone in Paris would be there. Many people did not even recognise him any more, others approached him, shy, embarrassed. Then he was back in bed again, the nurses taking turns and the garbage and soiled cloths being collected every day in special bags to be burned. A few weeks later he was better again. The counting of the white blood cells became a daily conversation.

Jacques decided that he wanted to see Egypt, so he went. I watched him crossing the street to get into a taxi, walking upright to go to the airport, a proud old man walking on a stick, elegantly dressed. I thought of a picture of Cavafy I had once seen, but Jacques was only thirty-three years old.

By March Jacques was back in hospital. The bleak despair that choked one when one entered the ward is still on my mind: rows of rooms with the emaciated bodies of the young with faces of the old. The smell of hospitals was more horrific here, the smell of stale urine, vomit and disinfectant, a world of rubber gloves and protective garments. People were coughing and spitting with lung cancer, brown blotches. Karposi's sarcoma invaded their faces and bodies. They vomited, had diarrhoea. Why, I asked myself, has this illness so much reduced the dignity of people who loved life so much, to whom beauty was so central? Sometimes a door would be closed with plastic sheeting. We knew what that meant.

The devotion of the doctors and nurses, some even younger than the patients, was like a shining light, washing, spoon-feeding, consoling. In the corridors huddled groups of people, sisters, friends and parents, so that the patients would not see their tears. I will never forget images like the ritual washing of hands with disinfectant.

Facundo went twice every day, spending hours at Jacques's bedside. At night he was still playing Dorante. How did he do it? In the two beds next to Jacques's were two young men, too weak to say much. They looked with enormous eyes at the visitors who came to Jacques's bed. He spoke about wanting to die, then proudly announced that he was 'going to get better'. Jacques's eyesight was now affected. Many people with AIDS were going blind, in others the brain just collapsed. He announced that he wanted to die in Le Mazet. I knew then that we must take him there, but I was afraid.

We went by sleeper. The two cars were loaded on the train, Jacques's car too, although he could no longer drive; appearances had to be kept up, death must not be acknowledged.

Our local doctor had been advised by his colleagues in Paris. Jacques was his first A I D S patient. The first time he arrived we had to laugh. Facundo and I had long ago given up wearing rubber gloves all the time when we came in contact with the ill. The doctor arrived in a rubber suit as if for a trip to the moon.

We looked after Jacques for the next three months. Our beautiful house, the place of so much laughter and *joie de vivre*, became a hospital. Several times a day Facundo sat and counted out the endless pills Jacques had to take. The local nurses took turns giving those injections Facundo could not give. Twice a week the ambulance came to take us to Nice for a checkup in hospital. Then we gave this up too. We took turns during the night to sit at Jacques's bedside. Sometimes friends flew in from Paris to bring relief. Sometimes there was peace, but more often anger and the aggression of the dying against the living ruled the day. The anger was almost easier to cope with than the resignation.

One night Jacques took my hand and asked me to forgive him. He told me of his unending love for Facundo. Were they still lovers? The thought had crossed my mind many times. But then what did it matter now, in the face of death? Could I possibly begrudge Jacques's feelings?

I was the survivor. I had always rejected conventions – why would I claim them now? I was sure of one thing: Facundo's love for me.

From my Diary
Sunday 24 May: I have gone to the village and spoken to the priest. As someone who lives here, I have the right to purchase a grave in the village cemetery. I complete the sordid task. Jacques is now so weak he cannot stop vomiting and coughing. We turn him around every hour to relieve the pain from the bed sores. How long can this go on? I massage his poor body, I have given up wearing rubber gloves. Facundo and I sit at the table like the old days, but the words die in our mouths. The terrible silence is only interrupted by the coughing of Jacques. I catch myself wishing that it would be all over and that Facundo and I could start living again. But how will it end, what will the last hour be? People say they just suffocate. The phone never stops, people's curiosity for the dying is as baffling to me as the compassion. The doctor comes and gives Jacques some morphine to alleviate the pain.

Tuesday 28th: Suddenly J is better again, he even gets up and we drive him to the village. I feel ashamed about what I thought yesterday. J talks about the future and what he wants to plant around the pool. Everything is so unreal suddenly, even life seems to have no colour any longer. Whatever I do it is not acting but reacting. Mido and Jean-Pierre have come from Paris to be with us. J sits at the table. He has made a meal for us, but we know we must not eat it, he had thrown all precautions to the winds and touched the food. We do not know what to do. Then Mido begins to eat and we follow. Suddenly J speaks up, one sentence only: 'It is unjust, I wanted to live a bit longer.' This is not the place for lies so we sit in silence.

Sunday 13 June: J has been coughing and vomiting the whole night. Last night he begged us to help him die. Outside is the most beautiful summer day. J is in such pain that he begs us for another injection of morphine. We were warned that this would happen. The pain is now so bad that I call the doctor. Is this the end? The doctor goes into the room. Facundo and I sit outside the house holding each other. It is all happening so fast. There are moments in life so intense that you feel like living a thousand lives in a second. It's almost like before a car crash – you know it is happening and yet you cannot stop it. Then the doctor comes out. He does not have to speak. We know. I look at Facundo's face distorted by pain. 'God let me be strong.' I have never asked anything important from Facundo but now I do. 'Please let me go in alone.' The nurse arrives and takes Facundo away. I do not want to write about the face of death as I promised myself never to speak about it to Facundo.

I close his eyes and the doctor and I pray. Then I dress J. All I can find is a pair of boxer shorts with The Big Apple written on them. I feel the doctor does not approve. 'Where he goes I think there will be many already in boxer shorts with apples on them,' I say, and strangely enough inside I smile. That night Facundo and I sleep in a nearby hotel. Jean-Pierre, Mido and Richard have offered to stay with Jacques in the house shrouded in mourning. The next day he is already in a coffin which looks so large in the bedroom. He now looks peaceful.

Monday 14 June: The Family has arrived, his sister and brothers and the many friends from the Groupe T S E, the company Jacques has been looking after as their director for the last seven years. Many actors have flown down, others phone, just to express their feelings. The incredible loyalty of the theatre world. The little chapel is filled to the last seat. I hold on to Facundo when the coffin is brought in. He sits dry-eyed in pain. Then it is all over. The villagers carried the coffin as in the old days through the village in the blazing summer heat and put it to rest on the little cemetery right under the mountain.

That night it was Mido again who made her bed up in the room where, a few hours earlier, Jacques's coffin was standing. Now that someone had even died in it, our house took on a deeper meaning. Nothing I thought could now separate Facundo and me except death. Despite all that pain there was a feeling of profound happiness.

29

Harvesting

1987–1989

The last three years at the BBC were golden years of public recognition, of personal and professional achievement. *Architecture at the Crossroads* was televised in America, Germany and France. *Eileen Gray* was translated into Japanese, German and French. I never felt happier, lighter, better. I believed those who told me that they would miss me and those in France who said they were looking forward to my arrival. My relationship with Facundo too had reached an intensity of feeling which made me anticipate our living together in great happiness. Our ship was finally coming in. We travelled together to Argentina, and his deep and uncontained grief made gradually room for the pleasure of showing me his country. I fell in love with Buenos Aires. Its parks, colonnaded galleries, grandiose avenues were filled with people in clothes that had been cleaned and ironed many times but still testified to richer and more elegant times. In the Art Nouveau cafés black-tailed waiters poured hot chocolate out of tarnished silver pots. The ghost of Borges was never far away. In the Teatro Colon, where Strauss had conducted and Pavlova danced, the gold boxes overflowed with ripe, well-powdered and bejewelled ladies in hermine stoles which had turned yellow and exhuded a faint smell of camphor. They eyed each other through gleaming opera glasses or whispered in loud voices behind black fans, ignoring the tenor's efforts to sing 'Celeste Aida'. It was almost like a European city before the arrival of American culture.

My programme *George Gershwin Remembered* went out in the summer of 1987, both on the BBC and in America, as part of the series *Great American Masters*. After my initial reservations the search for the son of Moishe Gerzowitz was great fun. I met people I never thought I would, relics of a glamorous past – a pailletted Ginger Rogers and Fred Astaire, Ruby Keeler in flowing pink chiffon – living in their air-conditioned residences in Beverly Hills or Palm Springs. Glamorous Kitty Carlisle Hart, the widow of Moss Hart, all hostess gown, surrounded by photographs of the Reagans and other Hollywood stars, recalled: 'George had a little waltz that he played for every young lady. It had a blank space in it for the name of the young lady. I considered it his mating call.'

I saw Virgil Thomson again; he now lived in two rooms in the old Chelsea Hotel. Little was left from the old place, where Warhol had shot *Chelsea Girls* and William Burroughs wrote some of *The Naked Lunch*. The hotel looked shabby; most rooms leading off a dark corridor had special locks. People had been murdered and robbed here, I was told. Thomson was a grumpy old man who sat among the paraphernalia of his past charmed life in Paris: paintings by Bébé Bérard, a cushion embroidered with the notes from a tune in his opera *Four Saints in Three Acts* and a row of expensive hand-made shoes neatly lined up under the bed. He only reluctantly let the crew in, but then began slowly to melt. A young acolyte served cocktails in long-stem glasses. While we settled in the two huge armchairs, covered in flowery print, the maestro in his high-pitched voice was still dishing out the dirt: 'Gershwin's works are fine works, solid works and everybody loves them. And it's nice to imagine that's the way life is,' he said disparagingly. He had not changed much in his opinion from the time when, as a music critic, he gave *Rhapsody in Blue* a bad write-up.

I filmed Paul Duncan. Fifty years earlier Gershwin had asked the black *Lieder* singer to be his Porgy. When Gershwin played the music to him on the piano, Duncan was hooked forever. 'I thought that I was in heaven. It was so beautiful that I will never forget it until I die. It was an idiom, an American idiom I didn't hear in Schubert or Schumann or Wolf. It was in my skin, in my blood, in my soul, in my very heart. My solar plexus told me that is it.' The big black man got up and went to the piano and sang 'Bess you is my woman now', and there was not the slightest bit of a tremble in his voice despite his eighty years.

In Oslo I found Ann Brown. She was Gershwin's original Bess after having auditioned for his brother Ira, their mother and Ira's wife. A warm-hearted and attractive woman speaking with a slight Norwegian accent received me in a flat with the obligatory signed photographs of the American composer.

I went to listen to Ella Fitzgerald and later to meet her in the green room. On stage she looked large and powerful in a glittering gown; backstage I saw a frail old lady in a simple green dress, exhausted from the performance. I noticed how thin her hands were. She had great warmth and astonishing modesty, thanking me profusely for the flowers and the book I had sent her, as if I were the star, not her.

Gershwin's sympathetic sister Frances told me: 'George was a pretty wild boy. People used to say: "Mrs Gershwin has nice children, but that son of hers, she going to have trouble."' Frances Gershwin was full of anecdotes and still extraordinarily protective of her brother and her family. The idea of Gershwin the ladies' man, the man who stole all the hearts, the centre of brilliant parties, had to be protected at all cost. 'George was good at anything – if he played tennis he played a good game, if he played golf he was brilliant. He played the piano so wonderfully, with a wonderful sense of harmony, when he played songs they hardly ever sounded the same twice.' But she also spoke of a man over-protective and puritanical towards her, a man greatly concerned with appearances. What was he covering up? I began to wonder. Ann Brown told me that she 'always had the feeling that something was worrying him in the back of his head, and that there was a great and deep-down conflict in his behaviour'. Gershwin never married, despite a widely publicised row of girlfriends. So many of the American composers had homosexual relationships, Samuel Barber, Virgil Thomson, Ned Rorem, Cole Porter, Leonard Bernstein, but the image of George the successful son of immigrants, the all-American boy, had to be protected against such insinuations.

Ira's widow, the formidable Alice Gershwin, also would not allow a dent in the image of America's great composer. People told me that she had really been in love with George and then ended up marrying Ira. In a large Hollywood house a butler in an oriental outfit served me a glass of water. 'Mr Adam, we always drink water at this time,' she had said, letting me know that she would not appear in the film. We talked about Hellman and Lenya. 'Ira liked the men, Hammett and Weill, the trouble with the ladies was that they were such liars, but I can see they seduced you,' she said, making me exceedingly uncomfortable, a strong stubborn woman. When George died she prevented Ira from crying in public. 'I sat him in the sun. You cannot cry in the sun.' But she admitted that later at home he cried for two days, while Fred Astaire put on Gershwin records without interruption.

There was his musical friend the lyricist Irving Caesar. I met Caesar in his small and cluttered office. This eighty-five-year-old composer sang 'Swannee' for us in a husky but still strong voice. 'We walked down Broadway, and there was a song that was a very big hit, "Hindustan", a one-step. So I said George, why don't we write an American one-step? And we wrote "Swannee" in ten minutes. I started out and we were off to the races.' Al Jolson introduced 'Swannee' at the Winter Palace, and when sixty girls with lightbulbs in their shoes sang the chorus, the house came down.

Mabel Schirmer was another lady rumoured to have loved George. She sat reading his letters aloud to us, sad letters to a friend talking about loneliness and illness, about doubts and failure, about an incapacity to be alone. 'I do not know of any attachment he had except for Kay,' she told me. This was probably true.

I was keen to meet the composer Kay Swift, the only girl Gershwin was really thought to have had an affair with, although I never found out if that was true. Kay Swift, the writer of 'Fine and Dandy' and 'Can't We Be Friends', a vivacious old lady with a voluble tongue and engaging manners, sat at the piano and played Gershwin's piano piece, 'Meadow Serenade' for us, 'the way Gershwin played it to me often. The little running bit at the end – I remember him doing it.' Kay Swift was married when she met Gershwin. The two saw each other a lot. Then they decided to part 'for a year to see how it went. It went miserably.' Kay Swift's eyes took on a veil of sadness. 'I'm coming back for both of us,' he had said, but he never did. He died, thirty-nine years old. Kay Swift remembered sitting in a concert when she suddenly got up. Her daughter was with her and said: 'What's the matter?' 'We are going home. George is gone.' When the coffin went down she took off the ring he had given her, bought from his first earnings, and threw it in the grave.

George Gershwin Remembered was nominated for an Emmy Award and for a British Academy Award. It did not win either, but the film has been shown and repeated in many countries and is still selling on tape or on video disc throughout the world. New technology has finally made it possible to give our efforts a bit of a shelf-life, and that for me was the greatest reward.

There were many other enjoyable encounters, mostly to do with work: I interviewed a pungent Carlos Fuentes in Mexico City for a programme on Buñuel and I surprised Lenny Bernstein with a birthday tribute called 'Breast of Peacock Applepie' for which I interviewed Harold Prince, Stephen Sondheim, and the many people involved in Bernstein's first production of *Candide*.

Almost the last film I made for the BBC was a portrait of Hildegard Behrens. It was also one of the happiest. Behrens for me is not only a remarkable artist, but also a wise and deeply humane person. Neither of us was too keen on this project – I had never been very interested in making film profiles of stars (Moreau and Lenya were exceptions) – but I agreed to go and see her in New York. A strikingly handsome woman in a baggy sweater and jeans, a can of beer in her hand, pulled back the iron gates of the goods lift on the top floor of a warehouse. 'Hi,' she said, 'come on in.' In my dark suit, clutching a large bunch of flowers, I looked totally out of place. I had after all come to woo one of the leading opera stars. I accepted a beer and took care not to ask for a glass. On the floor her young daughter made tremendous noise.

'I have turned down several offers of films, Mr Adam,' she said firmly. The predatory side in myself was instantly aroused. 'There are things in my life, private things, I am simply not interested in telling.'

Behrens shunned too much public exposure and was happiest with her circle of friends, including Olga, a healer, or in the presence of her children. She fought hard and successfully to preserve the privacy of this sane inner circle in an increasingly public life.

We were on our fourth can of beer when we drew up a list of performances or rehearsals she was going to do in the next twelve months. It was a formidable list and by then we were sitting on the floor: *Tosca* under George Levine in New York, *Elektra* under Seiji Ozawa in Paris, *Wozzeck* under Claudio Abbado in Vienna, and for good measure, the entire *Ring* under Wolfgang Sawalisch in Munich.

Working with Hildegard Behrens was bliss. But to be with her was also fun. A woman of earthy and nourishing humour, as time went on she became a loving friend. Drinking gallons of beer, we talked about love and death, about jealousy, fear and pleasure, all the stuff opera is made of. Her ability to listen came from genuine curiosity, without ever being indiscreet. She was keenly intuitive and understood people quickly. She knew about human emotions and gave me endless signs of compassionate sympathy.

Her application and professionalism were astonishing. It was almost frightening to see her physical stamina and energy, dancing like a raving fury or a wild horse on the stage and then immediately bursting into song. 'She forgets about the danger to her voice, about the danger of missing a note. She just feels it in her guts and jumps in. She is like an instrumentalist – a violinist or a cellist like Rostropovich – they just do it,' said Ozawa, who shared his admiration for Behrens with many conductors.

Behrens had come to the opera stage late in life after having been a barrister. Herbert von Karajan picked her practically from nowhere and put her into Salzburg.

In the space of the months I watched her jumping from Brünnhilde to Tosca to Marie: great figures of heightened emotions. If ever the cliché 'becoming the part' rang true it was with Behrens. As a performance approached she physically changed. Gradually she not only began to wear clothes akin to her costumes but in feeling and gesture too she became Elektra or the working-class woman in *Wozzeck*. A deeply psychic person, Hildegard had mystical experiences which for her were not strange. 'People tell me that in certain roles I look small or slim. When I did *Tristan* in Munich for me the image of Isolde was a *pietà* with very long hands. All my friends know that I do not have long hands.' She pulls out a photo of the production and there was a woman holding Tristan's head with elongated fingers. 'For me these almost transcendental experiences are not astonishing at all. They enrich me. I am not frightened by them. I think I am like a person frightened to death who has enough adrenalin to jump over a high fence. Nobody later knows how they did it but they did.'

I too was no longer amazed by all the things which constantly happened around her. Her rich artistic and personal life spilled over into everything she touched. She had such strong and good influence that we all profited. *Hildegard Behrens* was durable, like *Lenya* and *Hellman*, another programme that began as a job and ended in a sustained friendship.

The last programmes I did for the BBC were *Art of the Third Reich*. I thought it was appropriate to round off my career with a subject at the centre of my life, to close the circle which had began in Germany sixty years earlier.

Art was considered one of the most important elements in the creation of the Third Reich. Its aim was to impose a National Socialist philosophy of life in which political and artistic expression became one. Not much was known about the official art produced between 1933 and 1945 not just in England but also in Germany, where the subject was shunned under the pretext of being unworthy of historical consideration. Few people had actually seen the works, which were still hidden away out of sight. They tended to be a great embarrassment to many. I was aware that this secrecy had created legends. Some feared that they had an accumulated power, able to rekindle National Socialist thought; others quite rightly feared that these works could once more appeal to the masses.

The series *Art of the Third Reich* was, like the one about modern architecture, made by a small team. Robert McNab, a lively spirited fellow, whose grandfather had been the Hungarian ambassador to Hitler's Germany, took Roger's role, and we had a new assistant, Judy Shears. Judy would never have stepped into her own handbag or misplaced letters in the wrong envelopes. She really wanted to go on stage, but ended up many years ago in the BBC after one of the producers had proposed to her on the ski slopes. A giggle surrounded everything she did. Childless, she had strong maternal instincts, and Robert and I basked in her affection and fierce efficiency.

Most people I saw were embarrassed by the subject – the question of guilt lives on in Germany. The number of paintings we were allowed to film was restricted to ten. They lined the shelves of the customs depot in Munich, many still in their original frames, with the little label 'purchased by the Führer' intact. A civil servant from the Ministry of Finance, not an art historian, watched over our filming, obviously uneasy. He certainly was not a Nazi but he nevertheless pointed out that the amount of restitution money 'was all right for some, but there were also quite a lot of criminal elements among the people in Hitler's concentration camps, Dr Adam'. The officer in charge of the Ordensburg Sonthoven, the site of Hitler's elite schools, which now belonged to the Bundeswehr, was also not a Nazi. That did not prevent him from keenly collecting photos of Hitler and the others who went there. Asked what the rooms looked like in those days, he replied: 'Very elegant, with beautiful furniture, I must say only the best for those boys.' There was not the slightest hint of irony in his voice.

The mostly young television producers in Baden-Baden who did not like my opening line and thought it 'a bit strong' were no Nazis either.[1] Could the eye of the art historian possibly be adequate to look at the art of this period? But Baden-Baden was not Berlin, where the equally young producer thought it a most important document to be shown on the air.

I was allowed to look at the requisitioned military war paintings that were held in Washington, and no one thought it odd. An American curator talked openly about them and I was allowed to film what I wanted. The Army Museum in Ingolstadt had strict instructions not to let anybody even see the war paintings that America had returned to Germany and the director took great pains to explain to me that they were out of sight 'for inventory'.

The differences between those still concerned and those who really had 'digested the past' were often subtle but they were always telling. I had spent ten days looking at newsreels, feature films of the period which in their images and language were much more powerful and more reliable witnesses of a time than any human being could possibly be. So in the end the two programmes consisted only of old contemporary material, and they showed a Germany that made one shudder.

What was so frightening about all the filmclips which featured those nude clean bodies, those wholesome families and faultless landscapes, was not what was fascist about them but what was so normal – a normality which pleased so many. Hitler and the other ringleaders not only shared the same taste as the masses but they were also the projection of popular desire. Looking at the mediocrity of the art on offer, skilfully packaged with banal music and trite commentary, I could only wonder if the popularity of the regime might not partly be based on the fact that it provided

---

1 The line they objected to was: 'The art produced in Germany in those years cannot be considered in the same way as the art of other periods. It must be seen as the artistic expression of a barbaric ideology. One can only look at the art in the Third Reich through the lens of Auschwitz.'

an art which corresponded to what most people liked, a pleasant reassurance free of anything esoteric or disturbing – art that gave answers and asked no questions.

The Nazis skilfully orchestrated their act of seducing the masses with the help of all art forms: painting, sculpture, film, design and architecture. The first programme, 'The Orchestration of Power', dealt not only with the famous big art exhibitions, but also with the party rallies and the many 'artistic' programmes which set out to form the new man. Part Two was called 'The Propaganda Machine' and looked at the media.

A philistine but powerful world is bound to reject aesthetic innovation in favour of anything that services popular opinions and convention and discourages moral ambiguity, something for the man in the street. Writing in the 1980s I realised that art that affirms a better brighter world will always have its supporters, whereas the new art that abandons certainty and questions the *status quo* will always be suspect. Most see conventional beauty as a kind of truth, a shield behind which they can shelter.

The work made me also question the role I played as a political human being. It was Hannah Arendt who had said: 'We are not saved by good works, but by good fortune.' Who would I have been if my father had not been a Jew? I discovered compassion for the suffering of the Germans. Both *Richard Strauss* and *Art of the Third Reich* ended on a reconciliatory note. Both finished with pictures of human suffering and the destruction of entire cities. People crawling out of rubble, barefoot, uncomprehending.

I wondered where in history does the suffering of those millions of people who so blindly followed their leader belong? Was their suffering in the cities and on the front less valuable, more in vain, than the sacrifice of those who died for a better cause? Is there a death more meaningful than others? Are not most people victims of something? Death as a result of war always seems to be meaningless and wasteful.

Art of the Third Reich was nominated for a British Academy Award for the best documentary of the year. Once more I sat with illustrious colleagues from the television and film world, who had selected four programmes from the cornucopia of offerings. I had long given up hoping to win; too often I had been the runner-up and I had not even prepared a speech. The ceremony dragged on and on. Finally the Huw Wheldon Award was called. The cameras were wheeled into position, creeping as close as possible so as not to lose the slightest emotional reaction on the faces of the four hopefuls. Four short extracts from the nominated programmes were projected. I thought how odd Goebbels and Hitler looked on a screen in

Winning a British Academy Award

the Dorchester Hotel. The actor David Suchet opened his envelope: 'The winner is Peter Adam for *Art of the Third Reich*.'

There are moments in life that are so exhilarating that your heart almost stands still. This was one of them. Walking up to the podium through the cheering crowd I thought about how to be witty and wanted to mention the sculptor of the statuette I was to receive, but as her name was Mitzi Cunliffe I thought of my accent and the Royal Highness bit and My Lords, Ladies and Gentlemen and gave up the idea as fast as it had occurred. What I finally said was: 'I would like to thank Huw Wheldon. Not only because he was among the first to give me a job at the BBC but also because his name guarantees that the endangered species of the arts documentary has a chance to survive in a world of increasing trivia.' The audience shrieked with delights of approval. Then I sat down. Someone put a little note into my hand: Her Royal Highness would like to meet the winners afterwards.

I do not remember much about the rest. The ceremony finished two hours later. I skipped the reception with Princess Anne. I went outside and looked at the rows of indistinguishable limousines and those trying to catch a taxi. Miraculously a night bus came. I jumped on it and happily rode home.

Together with my work on the film I had been preparing a book on the same subject. Writing would be a good way of bridging the lull which would logically come with the day I stopped making films. ·

The preoccupation with Germany of that period prompted me also to consider something else: to write down my childhood. It was again my friend and publisher Andreas Landshoff who suggested it. I am a story-teller and an observer of life – at the lunch table, in the canteen or with friends. Sometimes the tales came straight from my life, sometimes I would invent, embellish, anything to liven up a dull lunch. For years many people had urged me to write it all down. The years spent in Germany under Hitler never failed to fascinate. Meeting such formidable relics as Colette or Jean Cocteau, however fleetingly, wove a spell on my younger listeners. But how could I expect the world, beyond a small circle of friends, to be interested in my life?

The world I was born in had long gone and the one I had spent most of my professional career in was fast disappearing. Maybe there would be something in this chequered life and career that was worth preserving.

With my work in the BBC, I had been able to focus my diverging artistic talents. In the past I had only dabbled; I painted a little, wrote a few poems and acted a bit. Nothing came of any of these activities, because of a lack of focus, a lack of purpose and concentration. I discovered that my real talent lay in putting things together, as an *assembleur*. With my job I had also finally found the style of life I needed in order to be halfway content. The notion that I wanted to become a writer after the BBC was ambitious, but serious. The first thirty-five years of my professional life were like a vessel for so many artistic experiences – plays, books, films, paintings. I felt that soon I might enter a phase of trying to transform all these experiences, all this accumulated information, into something of my own.

Gradually the idea ripened to write down the story of my life, not out of the desire to present my life in an enduring form, nor out of vanity, but to make order, to discover, to understand. Sometimes in the morning I could not wait to get to my desk to write. Ideas began to pour out – the act of writing things down was too slow a process. I was afraid that I would forget things I wanted to say, making mental notes all the time while walking, in the middle of the night or during my daily swim. The rich murmurs of the past came constantly floating to the surface. It was as if someone else was dictating. It was an exhilarating experience. A line heard on the radio or something I read could be a seed for a new thought.

At times I thought it was ridiculous and presumptuous to write one's biography at the age of sixty. But in order to keep things fresh I knew that I must have at least something left of that energy, that lust for life, that had dominated much of my life. Not all must be resolved in wise old resignation. Then there is always the danger of self-importance. I know too well my Germanic need for high thoughts and abstract nouns. And in writing about the people I know how could I avoid a touch of social cowardliness and desire to be loved that tends to tilt the scale towards the charitable? I know I had good looks and never resisted exercising charm. Both were often used to disarm potential critics and to gloss over intellectual deficiencies.

I began to re-read my diaries and the scores of letters I had kept. I looked up my old school reports, found dedications from writers in books I had not opened for thirty years, notes written in the margins. I plundered my life trying to commit some of the re-visited events to memory, and the more I read the more the paradoxes mounted and the fascination. Who was this person, half hustler, half Herr Doktor with little talent for unhappiness, I was writing about?

I am afraid I have disappointed a great many people. When I began this book I wanted to conceal nothing, disguise nothing, and simply talk about the things that were closest to my suffering and my happiness. I tried to put into my memoirs all the tears, all the laughter, the feel of my blood circulating, but I realised immediately that I could never find the innocence of the person I once was, buried under the accumulation of perception, knowledge and experience. The search for oneself was jeopardised by the passing of time. Everything I wrote about was coloured by the person I had become. When I was young I was not only the person I was but also the person I would be one day. Now I am almost only the person I am. Memories only have a certain innocence until you add the knowledge you accumulate. For instance, not all my childhood memories are terrible, but if you add to them the knowledge of the political reality they tend to lose much of their charm.

In the telling I discovered a different perspective of the world which often challenged the way I had perceived things at the time. Where did my perceptions come from? Could there be a parallel universe in which we exist as fictional characters? People might ask me: 'But where is the truth?' My answer is I do not know. In most lives the boundaries between the invented and the real are blurred. Facts sometimes arrange and re-arrange themselves imperceptibly. The desire to chisel away some of the defences and evasions with which I surrounded my life has not got me near enough to the truth I set out to search for; I have merely scratched the surface.

I felt my limitations all the time. So many things always seemed to evade description, and for so many things I still had no answers. Verbalisation impoverishes the real experience, except in the writing of the truly great.

Curiosity has led me further into my life than I had originally planned. There were many days when I profoundly disliked the person I was writing about. There were also days when I loved him. Most meetings in my life were by chance. What I made of them by desire, scheming, determination, seems to me far more interesting than the actual meeting itself. Of course there are central experiences, but one is usually only aware of them afterwards. 'Tout sert' (everything serves), Claudel said. The discovery of love, the sunsets of one's childhood, are as useful as the discovery of a line in Proust. Cultural opinions are not as important as what lies behind them, Borges had reminded us.

All things are interconnected – this is probably the most amazing discovery I made in writing about my life. People I wrote about in the morning and whom I had not seen for years suddenly phoned up. Others reappeared in my dreams with such vividness that it was almost frightening. Maybe it is not good to look too deeply into oneself and yet I am unable to silence the never-ending monologue that goes on in my head.

I had reached the age of sixty when people have to retire, a custom I personally delighted in but found totally absurd. It was at this stage when I thought I had most to give. My life at the BBC was filled with affection for my work and my colleagues. Maybe the things I had been trying to do all those years with such stubborn tenacity were not totally in vain, and the multifaceted middle-European egghead with an old-fashioned respect for culture was appreciated. I, the foreigner, had been for a brief moment allowed to be part of a television which was such a glory of British life. I finally belonged.

The judgement of one's peers is the highest accolade an artist can receive, and I am not ashamed to record it here. Their opinion meant more to me than any public acclaim, because we shared the desire to make television an educational experience, and to keep alive as many links as possible between yesterday and tomorrow. 'With gratitude to you for having done so much to help to establish the character and distinction of BBC2' (David Attenborough). 'Your contribution to the art of television and, through that, to the arts of the civilised world, is outstanding. For your judgement, sympathy and exquisite taste my thanks' (Joan Bakewell). 'Here goes the prince of the European Artistic Community and bringer of light to the benighted barbarians of Britain' (David Jones). 'France's gain, England's loss!' (Melvyn Bragg).

The diary of 1989 had many sad entries after all. Many had to do with the doubts I had about doing the right thing. I was moving to Paris to live with Facundo, leaving a life I adored for something not yet traced, unknown. Most friends thought it was madness. Only Prunella, the one person with most to lose by my absence, told me that I must go. I was willing to take the risk of failure, but I was afraid of being hurt. I knew from the past about the wounds Facundo was able to inflict and they all carried the sting of death. Was it not madness at sixty to give up work, friends, house, the country I felt totally at home in, even the language which had become my own? It was a big step and all at once. And yet when I was asked at a dinner party by a lady who did not know me: 'Mr Adam, why are you leaving?' I simply said: 'For love', and in this word lay the whole truth.

Many entries in the diary also had to do with leaving, packing and parting. It was almost the same as it always had been, but all those happy events now carried the little bitter adjective *last:*

'The last dinner party at Moore Park Road' (a surprise birthday party for Hanna Weil).

'Rosie [Wilton] gives a last goodbye dinner for me with Alan [Yentob], Philippa [Walker], Peter [Gill], Penelope [Wilton] and Ian [Holm].'

'Last dinner at Nitie and Grey [Gowrie] with Selina [Hastings].'
'Elsbeth [Juda] makes a last meal for me, Antonio [Carluccio] had
picked a whole basket full of mushrooms which he cooked for us.
We all vow to see each other again soon. But will we?'
'Today I packed up my office. The last lunch at the canteen, the
place of so many discussions, arguments; the source of so many
ideas, suggestions and honest and much-valued criticism.'

The closer my leaving date came, the more I was sorry to part, except that
at the end of my B B C career stood a most wonderful future. The prospect
of living in Paris not only meant living with the person I loved more than
life, to use an old but true cliché, but re-entering a different language, a
different culture – things I knew I needed to get over the shock of retirement. Everything seemed to fall into place. The sadness of having to part
with Moore Park Road, a house I had totally transformed and loved, was
sweetened by the drawings and plans I was already making for a new
place. Facundo had found two flats, one above the other, and we were
busily putting in an inner staircase. The idea of exchanging the view of a
row of pretty Victorian houses for the view of the top of the Eiffel Tower
was not so agonising after all.

From my Diary
Sunday 11 June: The house has been sold, the removal people have
been ordered. I rush to the office for the last time. I can hardly get
to my desk for all the packing cases – boxes of scripts, photographs and papers from over 100 programmes. Someone had put
a T-shirt on my desk with a drawing by David Hockney printed
on it: 'A Hundred Great Paintings', the series I had helped to set
up. I sit for a while at my desk in front of the big charts which
traced the stations of my working weeks. Shooting, editing, recording, dubbing, press view. All these words seem like magic to
me. I feel like weeping. In an hour's time I have to go to the airport to fetch Facundo. I am so scared that my hands are ice cold.
What is happening? In twenty years I have never felt like this. It is
as if my love is suddenly turning into something totally different,
something menacing, something I do not want. Am I standing at
the threshold of the greatest mistake of my life?

Monday 12 June: The day of the good-bye party. Pru, Facundo and
I drive there together. In the car Facundo begins to cry.

Tuesday 13: Removal day. Sad sad sad. Payom, the great lady from Bangkok, who has looked after my houses for over ten years, cries and says to Facundo 'Look after him.'

The whole day the removal people had worked, sustained by Facundo's energy and Prunella's coffee. I had booked a hotel near the coast. Facundo and I were to drive to France to meet the removal van on the other side, but Facundo had decided to spend the night at the empty house. Prunella brought us a sheet and a blanket and we slept on the floor. Then Facundo announced, choking with tears, that he had fallen in love two months before. 'All will be all right, you will see, Don Pedro.' I was too tired even to answer, but it was as if a knife had been pushed into me. It was on that day two years before that Jacques had died.

Epilogue
Not Drowning but Waving

My relationship with Facundo was always located between sadness and exhilaration with very little middle ground. Both of us had worked to find the right balance between independence and commitment. Thomas Mann's *Wonnen der Gewöhnlichkeit* which I had always dreamed of was still as distant as ever, but when our relationship fell apart, little during the last twenty years had prepared us for failure. Deep down I always knew that Facundo would walk out of my life, without turning back, a person who does not hear your voice any longer. I also somehow knew that it would happen at a moment when I would be the most vurnerable.

Once we got to Paris, the furniture and packing cases still untouched, Facundo walked out to share a life with someone he had only known for three months. This was not the slow erosion of a relationship, not the gradual walkout which marks most divorces. He simply stepped out of our life, not taking anything except a few personal things.

In the months to come we talked and argued, we accused and fought, trying to understand what neither of us understood. Why? And why at that moment? Was it from fear of being caught in a situation he had so much helped to bring about, the fear of being trapped? He had always been obsessed with freedom. It was this very quality I had so much loved in him. How could I hate him now that he followed it to its ultimate end? Was his leaving part of the process of healing from the death of Jacques? Was he burying all those who had sapped his strength by their illness and dependency? Was he in the process of burying Jacques and his crippled sister, Marucha, also trying to bury me, before I would become another liability? After all, I was fourteen years his senior.

I stayed in Paris, waiting, praying, hoping. I spent some of it alone in our house in the South of France. The gradual realisation of loss began to choke me. It was a terrible betrayal. So many things that were stored up between us had suddenly vanished, drifted away, drowned as in a big torrent, irretrievably. Without Facundo I was only half a person; half of me simply closed down. The whole year faded into a black hole of tears and senseless pain that would not subside. Facundo kept on phoning or dropping in for lunch. He wanted 'to save something', but what was there to save? He babbled all the clichés about 'friendship' and 'still the most important person in my life'. All I wanted to save was the past, not to allow hate to emerge, hate which could even take our past away.

I did not sleep for weeks. What was my life now? I searched all the people I had been: the boy who had with such curiosity looked upon life; the young man who had so frivously embraced all the pleasures it had to offer; the man who had so fervently worked to distil a bit of truth from an encounter with art. What did it all amount to? I would gladly trade it all for the love of one person.

The love of my friends, especially that of Renate and Prunella, stood in the wings, waiting. I had no use for it. I hoped for my heart to break, but that was the stuff of operas and fairy tales. Twice I came close to suicide, and then something pulled me back. It was not the fear of dying. There was still some life-force left.

I had to understand. I stopped writing in my diary. I did not want it to be the vessel of this senseless suffering, the reception of the constant *Klage*, but I wanted to go back into my past to find the clues. Work might be the only way to come to terms with life and the passing of time. I went to Russia to make the documentary with Jeanne Moreau. I hoped that there reality would help me to drown the personal pain.

I joined a long line of people standing in the bitter cold night of Moscow to pay their last respects to Andrei Sakharov and I knew that some extraordinary changes were about to happen. In Russia I saw hardship, deprivation and political destiny in the making. I also was faced with the strong presence of someone who had been through hell. I heard the news that the Berlin Wall came down and I could not help crying, because so many lives would be altered forever. What could the personal pain possibly matter? It was Jeanne who told me: 'You will come out of it and you will be so different that you will be amazed.' And she said it with such conviction that I believed her.

We have but a few choices. Most of the time we do not make a choice but merely react to a given situation. But I made a decision that night: to get out of the role of the hopeless victim and break the crushing sense of loneliness. If fulfilment was not possible maybe I could find equilibrium. It was like cutting off a limb.

> For this is guilt, if anything be guilt.
> Not to enlarge the freedom of a love
> With all the freedom in one's own possession.
> All we can offer where we love is this:
> To lose each other: for to hold each other
> Comes easy to us and requires no learning.[1]

The wounds from this act are not healed; they probably never will be. But I have banished that terrible numbness and that longing for death. I went back to Paris and packed my house up once more and moved back to London.

When I was unpacking my books I stumbled upon a volume of Stevie Smith's poems.

> I was far too much out all my life
> And not waving but drowning.

And since my heart was not ready yet to 'give away', I decided to call this book

Not Drowning but Waving

1 Rilke, 'Requiem für eine Freundin':
Denn DAS ist Schuld, wenn irgendeines Schuld ist:
die Freiheit eines Lieben nicht vermehren
um alle Freiheit, die man in sich aufbringt.
Wir haben, wo wir lieben, ja nur dies:
einander lassen; denn dass wir uns halten,
das fällt uns leicht und ist nicht erst zu lernen.
(English translation by L.B. Leishman)

Index